IMITATING AUTHORS

IMITATING AUTHORS

PLATO TO FUTURITY

COLIN BURROW

OXFORD
UNIVERSITY PRESS

OXFORD

UNIVERSITY PRESS

Great Clarendon Street, Oxford, OX2 6DP,
United Kingdom

Oxford University Press is a department of the University of Oxford.
It furthers the University's objective of excellence in research, scholarship,
and education by publishing worldwide. Oxford is a registered trade mark of
Oxford University Press in the UK and in certain other countries

Published in the United States of America by Oxford University Press
198 Madison Avenue, New York, NY 10016, United States of America

British Library Cataloguing in Publication Data
Data available

Library of Congress Control Number: 2018966641

ISBN 978–0–19–883808–1

Printed and bound in Great Britain by
Clays Ltd, Elcograf S.p.A.

In memoriam J. A. Burrow, 1932–2017
With apologies that it was too late.

Preface

O ne of the great pleasures in writing this book has been that so many people whom I met while I was at work on it had something to say about the broad subject of imitation. Experimental psychologists, psychologists, comedians, anthropologists, experts in copyright law, biologists, classicists, art historians, poets, musicians, painters, philosophers would all say 'ah yes, that reminds me of...'. Even people without much to say about the topic in the abstract could put on a decent imitation of a colleague or a political figure. I am sorry that I have not been able to explore all the avenues which were suggested to me, or to acknowledge here everyone with whom I had a conversation which has borne fruit in this book. It originated as the Bristol Blackwell Lectures on Greece, Rome, and the Classical Tradition. At Bristol I had a wonderfully responsive and thoughtful audience, and comments from Charles Martindale, David Hopkins, Danny Karlin, Bob Fowler, Ellen O'Gorman, Ad Putter, as well as some bracing and thought-provoking responses from Duncan Kennedy, Paul Hammond, and others, have invisibly or visibly sustained and boosted the argument. Since then I have incurred additional debts to seminar audiences at Princeton, St Andrews, Cambridge, Oxford, and the Sorbonne. A version of Chapter 8 was delivered at the Canada Milton Seminar, and I am particularly grateful to my hosts at Toronto, Paul Stevens and Lynne Magnusson. Adam Phillips gave excellent advice on reading in the psychoanalytic tradition without suggesting that I needed my head examined. Tom Keymer gave some valuable leads on literary property. Members of the Montaigne reading group at Oxford (including Richard Scholar, Wes Williams, Neil Kenny, John O'Brien, Katie Murphy, Ian Maclean, Rowan Tomlinson, and Terence Cave—to whose work I am particularly indebted, and who, if anyone, is the *exemplum* to which this book fails to live up) have in various ways informed its thinking, not least by convincing me that other people were better qualified than I to consider this topic in relation to France. Sheldon

Brammall gave valuable pointers on translation theory. A conversation a long time ago with Alessandro Barchiesi about *eidōla* in Euripides was particularly fruitful, as were several more recent ones with Michael Hetherington and Micha Lazarus about early modern poetics. I have benefited greatly from both the published work of and conversations with Kathy Eden, in whose footsteps I tread at several points *non passibus aequis*. Stephen Harrison cast expert eyes over Chapter 3, and Martin McLaughlin offered very helpful advice on Chapter 4. Philip Hardie made valuable suggestions on an early draft. Early versions of the Milton chapter were kindly read by Nigel Smith and Stephen Greenblatt. Cecilia Heyes offered invaluable guidance on experimental psychology. Clare Bucknell provided very helpful feedback on later chapters. Charles Martindale and David Hopkins heroically read a near final version of the whole, and I am grateful to them for their extensive and searching comments. John Kerrigan has been the ideal reader, and has enabled me to unpick evasions and elisions of thought from nearly every page. Where such evasions and elisions remain, of course, they are the consequences of my own stubbornness or ignorance. Two anonymous readers for OUP provided reports which were themselves an education, and Jacqueline Norton at OUP has helped the project into print with a level of care and enthusiasm that is every author's dream. Library staff at the Bodleian, the Cambridge University Library, and in particular Gaye Morgan, Norma Aubertin-Potter, Catherine Mower, and Gabrielle Matthews at the Codrington Library at All Souls have been unfailingly helpful, even with my most tiresome requests. I could not have undertaken a book of such wide scope or developed the argument in such detail without the benefit of a Senior Research Fellowship at All Souls College, Oxford, and I am profoundly grateful to the Warden and Fellows of the College for their support and wide-ranging conversations.

Contents

Abbreviations and a Note on the Texts

In quotations from early modern sources other than Spenser i/j and u/v are modernized. Quotations from modernized editions are used where they are available and modernization makes no substantive difference. For ease of reference quotations from classical texts are usually keyed to the relevant volumes in the *Loeb Classical Library*, although I have sometimes modified the texts where they include emendations which were not available to early readers, and have where appropriate used alternative editions. Translations from Latin and Greek are generally from the Loeb editions, although I have frequently modified those translations where they obscure a crucial sense, and have indicated occasions on which other translations have been followed. The following abbreviations have been used:

Aen.	Virgil, *Aeneid*
CPW	John Milton, *Complete Prose Works*, ed. Don M. Wolfe et al., 8 vols. (New Haven, 1953–82)
DRN	Lucretius, *De Rerum Natura*
FQ	Edmund Spenser, *The Faerie Queene*, ed. A. C. Hamilton, H. Yamashita, and T. Suzuki (Harlow, 2001)
Fam.	Francesco Petrarca, *Letters on Familiar Matters: Rerum familiarium libri*, trans. A. S. Bernardo, 3 vols. (Baltimore and London, 1975–85)
GL	Torquato Tasso, *Gerusalemme liberata*, ed. Lanfranco Caretti (Torino, 1980)
Institutio	Quintilian, *Institutio Oratoria*
Met.	Ovid, *Metamorphoses*
OED	*The Oxford English Dictionary Online*
OLD	*The Oxford Latin Dictionary*, ed. P. Glare (Oxford, 1968)
PL	John Milton, *Paradise Lost*, ed. Alastair Fowler, 2nd edn (London, 1998)
PR	John Milton, *Paradise Regained*, in *The Complete Shorter Poems*, ed. John Carey, 2nd edn (London, 1997)

Introduction

'If a man should prosecute as much as could be said of everything, his work would find no end.'[1] So said Ben Jonson when he discussed imitation and learning in his *Discoveries*. This book is about imitation, but it does not seek to say as much as could be said about everything. So it is not about how authors have imitated reality, but the (slightly) more bounded subject of the ways in which authors imitate each other.

The reason this topic matters is that every language user is in some sense an imitator, although in different periods people have imitated in different ways and have thought differently about how it should be done. The core question which underlies the book is simple to state but more or less impossible to answer: how do human beings learn sophisticated usage of language from others, and yet end up sounding like themselves (or believing that they do)? Answers to this question vary through time and space, and I explore them chiefly in relation to the period and place in which imitation was unarguably central to literary practice—Britain and Europe in the sixteenth and seventeenth centuries—but *Imitating Authors* as a whole aims to show why this topic and its longer history matter today.

Contemporary Westerners stand at the receiving end of a very long, and in many respects very confused, history of thinking about how speakers and writers imitate each other. Throughout the ages poets, dramatists, and novelists have (largely) benefited from that confusion. As I suggest in the final chapter, that history has stayed with us, and its after-effects are visible in surprising places. It shapes many of the ways in which literary influence is thought about today, but it also colours the language we habitually use to think and write about other kinds of replication with a difference, from the

1. Ben Jonson, *The Cambridge Edition of the Works of Ben Jonson*, ed. David M. Bevington, Martin Butler, and Ian Donaldson, 7 vols. (Cambridge, 2012), 7.561.

way in which clones are represented in popular fiction, through arguments about artificial intelligence and other attempts to imitate human language-use by artificial and mechanical means.

Today being an imitator is generally regarded as less good than being whatever else it is that we are supposed to be—'original' or 'ourselves' or 'creative' or 'whacky' or 'unusual' or 'generative' or 'productive' or 'inspiring'. This book offers a partial genealogy of present attitudes in order to give some reasons why we have ended up being so uneasy about imitation. It also sets out a view of the topic that puts it close to the heart of what it is to be a language user and a human being. The book is in part a defence of imitation as a practice that enables people to learn from each other and to write. *Imitating Authors* discusses both authors who imitate other authors and the theory of this activity. To distinguish this practice from other forms of imitation I generally, unless the context is clear, use its Latin name of *imitatio*. I chiefly consider this strange and various process in relation to the reception of the classical tradition, broadly considered, and epic poetry is a recurrent though by no means exclusive focus of my attention.

Imitating Authors is partly a work of intellectual history, which unpicks how different people and periods have thought about and practised *imitatio*. But it does not offer a simple analysis of what imitation could and did mean in different periods. Rather I aim to show that the power and influence of this concept derives from two key features. It has wide human significance, since from infancy all human beings learn by imitating, and, in different ways in different spheres of activity, we continue to do so until we die. It also is an inherently complex concept, which is associated with a vocabulary of wide and frequently unstable sense. Its tendency to mutate into other kinds of activity is part of what makes it significant. An imitation of a parent by a child can be seen as part of a process of learning. But an imitation by an adult of another adult can be an act of homage or it can be an act of rivalry, or it can be a parodic tribute or a satirical attack, or it can be several of these things at once. And, as any parent knows, children can also sometimes mock or play with those whose solemn actions they imitate.

When one author imitates another there is a similar range of possibilities, to which others are added. Imitating authors are also readers, who are observing features of the texts they read, which are passed on through their texts to their own readers. So *imitatio* can blend outwards into the history of reading.[2] Since writers have often imitated authors in different languages from the one in which they are writing, *imitatio* can often become barely distinguishable from other practices such as paraphrase or translation. And since writers can either consciously or unconsciously signal the fact that they are imitating another author or text, *imitatio* can often be marked by allusions or verbal echoes, which might shade off into faint intertextual minglings, or generate texts which are tesserae of other texts. It has as its rebellious doubles acts of parody, forgery, and mimicry. All of those diffusive fringes of the act of imitating make it at once powerful and complex, and its complexity is often the main source of its power.

By the same token *imitatio* is not easy to pin down. Indeed attempting to pin it down too firmly can take some of the life out of it, since the elasticity of the concept is part of its appeal to authors and to critics alike. But there are ways in which the core of the topic can be distinguished from its periphery, even if there are no firm boundaries between its centre and edges. The act of imitating an earlier author entails constructing an imagined view of what is distinctive about that author. That could take a relatively systematic form, and entail extracting from a body of prior writing a set of attributes which the imitator believes are common features of those texts—a certain kind of subject-matter, perhaps, or favoured words and a preference for particular rhetorical or poetic forms, or even a particular way of presenting a text on the page. Each author might believe that different aspects of a given body of texts are what make it a distinctive object of imitation, and each age might encourage a different view of past writing. The imitation of authors therefore raises questions about how different readers analyse and remember the texts that they read, about how shared practices of writing and interpretation grow and mutate, and about how different writers in different periods have had different concepts not just of what authorship is, but of what the central characteristics of individual authors might be.[3] That historically transformative aspect of imitation is a further reason why the

2. On reading, see, inter alia, James Raven, Helen Small, and Naomi Tadmor, eds., *The Practice and Representation of Reading in England* (Cambridge, 1996), Heidi Brayman Hackel, *Reading Material in Early Modern England: Print, Gender, and Literacy* (Cambridge, 2005), William H. Sherman, *Used Books: Marking Readers in Renaissance England* (Philadelphia, 2008), and Stephen Orgel, *The Reader in the Book: A Study of Spaces and Traces* (Oxford, 2015).
3. On the history and theory of authorship, the classic though much contested essay is 'What is an Author?' in Michel Foucault, *Language, Counter-Memory, Practice: Selected Essays and Interviews*, trans. D. F. Bouchard and S. Simon (Ithaca, NY, 1977), 113–38.

subject is so rich. It is an agent of historical change and transformation which itself keeps on changing.

The rich fusion of concepts which gather around *imitatio* has made it central to literary activity—as well as close to the centre of educational relationships between human beings, between cultures, and between generations—for millennia. This conceptual richness begins very early indeed: as Chapter 1 suggests, it had started well before Plato attacked the fictional arts for merely imitating the world as it is perceived rather than the forms which underlie those perceptions. But, as Chapter 1 also argues, Plato's critique of literary *mimēsis* gave a powerful negative charge to many subsequent discussions of how authors imitate each other. If an artist is inferior as a result of imitating an imitation of a Platonic Form, how much more inferior must an artist be who imitates another artist?

Imitatio was given a particular vitality by writers in the rhetorical tradition, for whom it was a central element in the way in which the art of rhetoric was taught and acquired. The rhetoricians, however, did not simply provide a clear theory of imitation which poets could follow. As Chapter 2 shows, writers on rhetoric regarded imitation as one of the main ways in which a young orator learnt to become a skilled practitioner, but they tended to offer a series of suggestive but conceptually fuzzy definitions of what *imitatio* actually entailed.

This was not just because it is extremely hard to describe in the abstract how one person successfully imitates another in order to learn from them. Roman writers about rhetoric also wished to preserve the myth that the final stages of a rhetorical education were dependent on personal contact and an imitative relationship between a pupil and an expert speaker. It was the skill of an expert exemplar, manifested in practice rather than codifiable in the form of rules, which the young orator was supposed to acquire by imitating. Learning from an example of this kind went beyond the process of learning rules from a *grammaticus* or a teacher of rhetoric. It meant learning a practice, a habit of speaking that enabled the young orator to speak on any occasion. That necessarily made *imitatio* mysterious: it was the process by which an art became second nature, and by which the indefinable and practical skill of an earlier practitioner transmitted itself to a pupil.

Latin was not as well equipped with technical and abstract vocabulary as the Greek sources on which Roman rhetoricians (themselves imitators) chiefly drew. This is evident in one key sentence from Quintilian's *Institutes of Oratory* to which I return more than once, since it is both crucial and obscure. At the very start of Book 10, which includes a discussion of reading and of *imitatio*, Quintilian declares that mastering the art of rhetoric requires more than simply grasping a set of rules. It requires the rhetorician to acquire the kind of habituated practical skill which Aristotle described as a *hexis*. Here Quintilian (as he often does when he encounters a term of art) has to drop into Greek:

> But these rules of style, while part of the student's theoretical knowledge, are not in themselves sufficient to give him oratorical power (*vim*). In addition he will require that assured facility which the Greeks call *hexis*.
>
> Sed haec eloquendi praecepta, sicut cogitationi sunt necessaria, ita non satis ad vim dicendi valent, nisi illis firma quaedam facilitas, quae apud Graecos ἕξις nomitatur, accesserit. (*Institutio*, 10.1.1)

The Latin word *habitus* might have provided Quintilian with a rough equivalent for the Greek *hexis*, but it does not quite cover the full range of senses implied by the Greek word, or, indeed, convey the mystique which Quintilian elicits by using the Greek term. The successful imitator does not simply learn rules or vocabulary from his master, but acquires through imitation the ability to speak with an instinctive appropriateness.[4] This arises from practice (in the sense of exercise and rehearsal) and in turn enables practice (in the sense of an ability to do). That is a crude paraphrase of what Quintilian probably meant when he used the Greek work *hexis* in this passage. And it is a *hexis* that an imitator acquires from the imitated *exemplum* (which is the word Roman writers tend to use for the imitated text: it is preferable to the word 'model', by which it now often translated, because, as I show in Chapter 8, 'model' has its own distinctive and potentially distracting history).

Because Roman authors struggled to find abstract terminology to describe 'learning to be like and acquiring a similar skill to' a predecessor, their discussions of *imitatio* relied heavily on metaphors. Quintilian suggests that learning to become a practitioner is a matter of acquiring bodily force

---

4. On Aristotle's conception of *hexis* as 'an entrenched psychic condition or state which develops through experience rather than congenitally', see Thornton C. Lockwood, 'Habituation, Habit, and Character in Aristotle's *Nicomachean Ethics*', in Tom Sparrow and Adam Hutchinson, eds., *A History of Habit: From Aristotle to Bourdieu* (Plymouth, 2013), 19–36, p. 23, and on the role of habituation in Aristotle, see M. F. Burnyeat, 'Aristotle on Learning to be Good', in Amélie Oksenberg Rorty, ed., *Essays on Aristotle's Ethics* (Los Angeles, 1980), 69–92. *Nicomachean Ethics*, 1140a–b, states that 'architectural skill, for instance, is an art, and it is also a rational quality [*hexis*] concerned with making', and defines practical wisdom as a 'truth-attaining rational quality [*hexis*], concerned with action in relation to things that are good and bad for human beings'. Translations from Aristotle, *The Nicomachean Ethics*, trans. H. Rackham (London and New York, 1926).

(*vis*); he compares the skill of the imitator implicitly and explicitly to processes of biological replication; and he and other Roman writers— including, most influentially, Seneca in his 84th Epistle—urge readers to 'digest' their reading, and produce from it a new text which resembles the *exemplum* as a child resembles its parent. A rich store of metaphors—following the path of earlier authors rather than treading slavishly in their footsteps, gathering nectar like a bee and combining many savours into one, and sometimes necromantic metaphors of rebirth and revival—emerges from discussions of imitation in the Roman rhetorical tradition.

That storehouse was supplemented by further metaphors which imitating authors used to describe their relationships to their predecessors. In what is probably the most influential lost passage of writing from antiquity, the Roman epic poet Ennius suggested that he was a reincarnation of Homer. Later poets and critics were to use the idea of metempsychosis to describe genealogical relationships between authors. Francis Meres famously said in 1598 that 'as the soul of *Euphorbus* was thought to live in *Pythagoras*, so the sweet witty soul of Ovid lives in mellifluous and honey-tongued Shakespeare',[5] and Dryden declared that Spenser 'more than once insinuates that the Soul of Chaucer was transfus'd into his Body; and that he was begotten by him Two hundred years after his Decease'.[6] Other metaphors for *imitatio* might evoke the conflict that can be implied by the Greek word *zēlōsis*, which can mean both 'imitation', 'zealous affection', and 'rivalrous emulation': an imitator might seek to outrun an earlier writer, or master not just an art but also an earlier master or an earlier culture. That is one reason why the successful imitator could sometimes be represented as not just an independent being who had internalized earlier writing, but as a free and independent citizen, a 'master' himself. That could in turn give (as I argue particularly in Chapter 6) political overtones to successful performances of *imitatio*.

Discussions of *imitatio* in the rhetorical tradition consequently combined conceptual obscurity with metaphorical vividness. The gap between abstract commands ('learn a *hexis* from your *exemplum*') and metaphorical injunctions ('resemble your original as a child does a father rather than as a picture

5. Francis Meres, *Palladis Tamia* (London, 1598), fol. 281v.
6. John Dryden, *The Works*, ed. Edward Niles Hooker, H. T. Swedenberg, and Vinton A. Dearing, 20 vols. (Berkeley, 1956–2000), 7.25. See Stuart Gillespie, 'Literary Afterlives: Metempsychosis from Ennius to Jorge Luis Borges', in Philip Hardie and Helen Moore, eds., *Classical Literary Careers and Their Reception* (Cambridge, 2010), 209–25, and for Spenser's relationship to Chaucer, see Jeff Espie, 'Literary Paternity and Narrative Revival: Chaucer's Soul(s) from Spenser to Dryden', *Modern Philology* 114 (2016), 39–58.

resembles a sitter', 'digest your reading into your own substance', 'become a reincarnation of Chaucer', 'become free of your masters') was an immensely fertile space, in which both conceptual argument and poetic exploration could grow.

The combination of mystique and metaphor with which *imitatio* was presented in the rhetorical tradition had three major consequences. Firstly, writing on imitation in that tradition had what might appear today to be a surprising tendency to stress the inimitable talent or *ingenium* of the text or person imitated. The power or the force or the talent of Cicero were supposedly the ultimate objects of imitation, but those qualities Quintilian himself confessed were not imitable because they were innate (*Institutio*, 10.2.12). This, in later centuries, fed into the notion that great writers have an indefinable genius that was intrinsically beyond imitation.

Secondly and relatedly, strange things happened when the vocabulary developed in the rhetorical tradition to describe the imitation by a pupil of an exemplary practitioner migrated into the fields of poetry and poetics. A language rooted in personal contact between pupil and master was transferred to a relationship between a reader and a writer or writers who might be dead, or, indeed, belong to a distant historical period or an entirely different culture. This transfer was already occurring within the rhetorical tradition: Quintilian presents Cicero as the principal object for imitation, although Cicero himself was long dead by the time Quintilian wrote in the first century AD. It had long-term effects of immense significance. Rhetorical writing about *imitatio* encouraged writers to think about the texts they imitated as exemplary in the way that a personal instructor is exemplary; but although texts were in this respect regarded as akin to people, they were people who were only present through their textual traces or through memory, and whose practice had to be retro-engineered from their surviving writings. This meant that a poetics of renaissance and retrieval was already implicit within the tradition of classical writing on rhetoric.

The third major consequence of the way *imitatio* was discussed in the rhetorical tradition was that the comparisons and metaphors used to describe imitation became a vital part of both the theory and also the practice of *imitatio*. The living assimilation of one's reading—digesting it, or resembling it as a child resembles a parent, or seeking to reincarnate an earlier author—was frequently opposed to painting a mere copy of an original, or, in Quintilian's extremely influential terminology, creating a mere *simulacrum*, a superficial likeness, of an earlier text or author.

This metaphorical opposition—which connects the start of this history to its conclusion in the world of clones and replicants—became common because it provided a vivid means of marking a distinction which is more or less impossible to make in any other way. It is extremely difficult to differentiate in principle rather than in practice between a text which imitates a previous work competently (whose author appears to have mastered a literary system, and has learnt a practice from an earlier writer), and one which replicates the features of an earlier text but which does not display the same competence as the imitated text.

The opposition between 'living' revival and simulacral replication, which, as the first three chapters show, can be traced to literary and philosophical arguments in the fifth century BC and on through Lucretius's *De Rerum Natura* and into Virgil's *Aeneid*, ran through both the rhetorical and literary traditions. Imitating authors repeatedly revive and revise these metaphors, which often feed into the textures of imitative and allusive writing. They continued to do so right through into the nineteenth century and beyond. The spectral presences of Dante and other familiar compound ghosts that haunt the footsteps of T. S. Eliot are late offshoots of this long tradition ('I caught the sudden look of some dead master | Whom I had known, forgotten, half recalled | Both one and many; in the brown baked features | The eyes of a familiar compound ghost | Both intimate and unidentifiable'), and the way that Dante himself follows the footprints of his *maestro* Virgil's spirit through the inferno is an influential earlier instance.[7] The metaphors used to describe *imitatio* have a depth and richness that explain their durability. They allow or encourage authors to ask whether they are haunted by the ghost of the past, whether they are culling words from an earlier text or making honey with a new savour, and whether they are free, or are simply following in the footsteps of Homer, or Virgil, or Milton.

They also encourage imitating authors (in ways which can go significantly beyond the often aggressively masculine and highly patrilinear vocabulary of the rhetorical tradition) to think of themselves as more than simply male conquerors of an earlier body of material. The notion that an imitator brought about a live rebirth of the past was to make the language of imitation exceptionally fertile: it made a feminine ability to give birth a key

---

7. 'Little Gidding', 38–42. Quotations from T. S. Eliot, *The Poems*, ed. Christopher Ricks and Jim McCue, 2 vols. (London, 2015). Ricks and McCue list as 'spectrally present' in these lines Dante, Yeats, Swift, Arnaut Daniel, Milton, and Joyce, pp. 1012–13. See further Sarah Annes Brown, *A Familiar Compound Ghost: Allusion and the Uncanny* (Manchester, 2012).

component in the conception of what an author should do.[8] Imitators were supposed to be able to bear new children from the writing of the past. Milton's Eve, as Chapter 8 shows, owes much of her power to this aspect of *imitatio*, and she in turn played a part in enabling Mary Shelley (as I argue in Chapter 10) to create a new version of imitated life in *Frankenstein*. The opposition between a good imitation as a live birth on the one hand, and an ineffective (and sometimes also a morally bad) imitation as a shadow or *simulacrum* or image of an original on the other, was to become a constitutive element of the poetics of the European Renaissance. The literature of that period in turn had a deep and shaping impact on the imaginations and the vocabularies of later writers.

The question 'how do I bring about a living recreation of a past author?' is one with many possible answers. In Chapters 5 and 6 I concentrate chiefly on two main kinds of answer to that question which were proposed in the debates about the nature of *imitatio* in the fifteenth and sixteenth centuries. One, which I have termed 'adaptive imitation', was that an author might seek to adapt the vocabulary and conventions of ancient texts to new times and customs. This had consequences for the ways in which writers in the period thought about authorship. It encouraged the view that earlier texts embodied transhistorical principles which could be adapted to new circumstances and new vocabularies. Cicero or Virgil consequently could be thought of not as a specific body of texts or as a particular set of words, but as a set of principles for composition which could be adapted to new circumstances.

Imitating Cicero therefore did not simply mean reusing fragments of his vocabulary, or regarding him as a finite corpus of texts to be replicated. The aim of the imitating author was rather to treat Cicero as a subjunctive principle, and to write 'as Cicero would write' in a new set of circumstances and vocabularies. That mode of adaptive imitation later developed into one in which, in the words of Samuel Johnson, 'the ancients are familiarised by adapting their sentiments to modern topicks, by making Horace say of Shakespeare what he originally said of Ennius'.[9] Chapter 6 shows that arguments about adaptive imitation were immensely productive both of

---

8. See Katherine Eisaman Maus, 'A Womb of His Own: Male Renaissance Poets in the Female Body', in J. G. Turner (ed.), *Sexuality and Gender in Early Modern Europe: Institutions, Texts, Images* (Cambridge, 1993), 266–88.

9. Samuel Johnson, *The Lives of the Most Eminent English Poets; With Critical Observations on their Works*, ed. Roger Lonsdale, 4 vols. (Oxford, 2006), 4.45.

concepts and literary fictions. It argues that central features of two of the most popular and original works to emerge from sixteenth- and seventeenth-century Europe—Castiglione's *Book of the Courtier* and Cervantes's *Don Quixote*—arose from the debates and continuing uncertainties surrounding the nature of *imitatio*.

In English poetry of the sixteenth and seventeenth centuries adaptive imitation was often combined with what I term in Chapters 6 and 7 'formal imitation'. No aspect of imitation is simple, and formal imitation is no exception to that rule. The word 'form', like the word 'imitation', has a bewilderingly rich array of senses, and theorists and practitioners of formal imitation were correspondingly diverse. 'Formal' imitation in its sixteenth- and seventeenth-century manifestations was not simply a matter (say) of author B recognizing that a particular figure of speech or metrical form was favoured by an earlier author A. The 'form' of an author might be akin to a Platonic Form, which a subsequent author might seek to imitate. It might be a supra-sensible 'idea' of that author which might inspire later writers with admiration and a desire to emulate it. 'Formal' imitation which started from that sense of the word 'form' had much in common with adaptive imitation, since a quasi-Platonic Form of an author might be imitated in new words which were suitable for new times.

But other senses of the word 'form' were also extremely influential in the history of *imitatio*. The 'forma' of an earlier author might also be something more akin to the features which are now generally described as the 'form' of a text—its structure of argument, the shaping of its sentences, a pattern of preferred rhetorical figuration, or a general method of combining and ordering materials that is peculiar to a particular author. As I argue in Chapters 6 and 7, the arguments surrounding formal imitation (particularly among German rhetoricians) influenced the ways in which English authors from the late sixteenth century onwards attempted to create distinctive stylistic registers of their own, and hence become themselves objects of imitation.

Ben Jonson sought not just to imitate specific texts by Martial and Horace, but to write in a way that was analogous to the style of those writers. Hence a *style* rather than an individual author might be imitated, and style could encompass a wide range of features—a characteristic vocabulary or a taste for certain types of rhetorical figure or poetic struc-tures.[10] Ben Jonson brought to the adaptive mode of imitation—turning the

---

10. For stimulating analogous arguments about Spenser, see David Scott Wilson-Okamura, *Spenser's International Style* (Cambridge, 2013).

manners and customs of Roman authors into vernacular equivalents—an acute awareness of the syntactic and rhetorical structures of his originals, and he imitated those structures. That combination of adaptive and formal imitation proved immensely influential among Jonson's imitators, and indeed those who imitated his imitators, right through to the mid-eighteenth century. Jonson was therefore in every sense an imitating author: he imitated authors in such a way as to establish himself as an imitable author.

The reason I concentrate on these two aspects of early modern imitation in particular is that they were the aspects which mattered most for later writers, particularly in England. By the 1730s it had become common to use the word 'imitation' in the titles of poems in two quite distinct senses. An adaptive translation of a classical text, which embedded a satire of Horace in English customs, might be called an 'Imitation of Horace'.[11] But an exercise in stylistic pastiche of a past or present English author could at the same date be called 'An Imitation of Milton'. The emergence of these distinct kinds of poem at the same time and under the same name enabled Alexander Pope to work his characteristic kind of mischievous magic with imitation, and imitate Horace in the style of his friend Swift, and indeed to publish anonymously an imitation of Horace said to be 'Imitated in the Manner of Mr Pope'.

That, like so much of Pope's writing, illustrates the creative riches which could arise from the conceptual richness of the word 'imitation'. But it also testifies to the way that adaptive imitation of classical texts evolved in tandem with a set of conventions for analysing and imitating the style or 'manner' of other vernacular authors. The co-dependent emergence of these two quite distinct senses of 'imitation' derives from the history related in this book. Thinking of an earlier text as a 'form' allows that form to be re-embodied in the manners of new ages. It also encourages the generation of new forms of style, or 'manners' in the stylistic sense, which can then subsequently be imitated.

To put 'formal' imitation near the centre of the story of *imitatio*, as I do, might seem counter-intuitive. It is easy to assume that there cannot be an imitation which does not also include some kind of direct verbal allusion or linguistic debt. Gian Biagio Conte has recently declared that 'to allege an imitation without being able to point to convincing traces and proofs would

---

11. See Harold F. Brooks, 'The "Imitation" in English Poetry, Especially in Formal Satire, before the Age of Pope', *The Review of English Studies* OS 25 (1949), 124–40.

be a serious betrayal of the intertextual method'.[12] 'Allege' and 'proof' in this sentence, however, should sound warning notes: they imply that imitation is a kind of crime for which the only evidence that can be upheld in a court of law is a direct verbal debt. The examples from Ben Jonson, explored in Chapter 7, show that 'traces and proofs' need not be restricted to verbal allusions. Indeed the assumption that a verbal debt is the only criterion of an imitation has a history which ought to lead us to be circumspect in seeking to universalize it. Verbal allusions by one poet to another have come in commentaries to classical and vernacular editions to be called 'imitations'— and as Chapter 9 shows, the identification of such 'imitations' had by the eighteenth century become one of the pleasures of reading and a foundational skill in the emergent practice of literary criticism. It was by no means what 'imitation' has always meant.

That very narrow usage of the noun has to a significant degree occluded the strand in the theory and practice of *imitatio* which would allow that an 'imitation' might have no direct verbal connection with the prior texts on which the new text is based. It might instead display deep analogies to its form, in a variety of senses ranging from the 'idea' of the author imitated, through syntactic and rhetorical structures, right down to the appearance of a poem on the page. Gérard Genette made the striking claim '*it is impossible to imitate a text*, or—which comes to the same—*that one can imitate only a style: that is to say, a genre*'.[13] That statement might seem intuitively false if it is assumed that 'an imitation' can refer only to a work which contains a series of direct verbal parallels with an earlier work. But that assumption is itself historically contingent.

The act of imitating a text can be akin to what experimental psychologists now call 'emulation', or 'observing and attempting to reproduce results of another's actions without paying attention to the details of the other's behaviour'.[14] 'Emulation' in this sense is now generally distinguished from

---

12. Gian Biagio Conte, *Stealing the Club from Hercules: On Imitation in Latin Poetry* (Berlin and Boston, 2017), p. 2.

13. Gérard Genette, *Palimpsests: Literature in the Second Degree*, trans. Channa Newman and Claude Doubinsky (Lincoln, Neb., 1997), p. 83; cf. Gian Biagio Conte, *The Rhetoric of Imitation: Genre and Poetic Memory in Virgil and Other Latin Poets*, trans. Charles Segal (Ithaca, NY, and London, 1986), p. 31, where Segal contrasts the 'Exemplary Model, the single word to be precisely imitated' and 'the Model as Code.'

14. Michael A. Arbib, *How the Brain got Language: The Mirror System Hypothesis* (Oxford, 2012), p. 185. 'Emulation' or *zēlōsis* could in the rhetorical tradition describe either *imitatio* or a desire to excel an original, as in Longinus, *On the Sublime*, 13.2. The usage by experimental psychologists is distinct from that sense.

what experimental psychologists term 'imitation', in which the mannerisms or gestures of the person imitated are replicated (so a child imitating an adult who is opening a box might 'emulate' the opening of the box, but also 'imitate' incidental aspects of the task he is imitating, such as the adult scratching her nose). *Imitatio* can encompass either or both of these relationships. It can entail grasping the principles which underpin a particular text and extrapolating from them a set of practices for generating a new text. Those principles might be a large scale-set of relations between the different elements of an earlier text, or a rhythmic pattern, or a rhetorical structure, or any of the innumerable features of a text that constitute a 'style'. They *might* include verbal correspondences, but need not do so.

Hence an author might be regarded by an imitator as akin to a genre, or as a series of texts to which it might be possible to add a new contribution without making any direct verbal reference to any earlier instance of the series. The imitator might follow an earlier author's preference for stanzas of particular lengths or numbers of syllables, or that author's use of a particular rhetorical figure. That is one kind of *imitatio*.

Accepting that imitating an author entails reading in such a way as to learn from that author's practices rather than simply alluding to the words of that author has implications for thinking about both *imitatio* and authorship. It would be an exaggeration to claim that imitators invent authors, or that imitating authors always write so that they can become themselves objects of imitation; but those exaggerations point in the direction of truths. An imitator observes the features of an author which are distinctive to the body of texts ascribed to a single name, and draws those to the attention of later readers—either in a spirit of mischief (in what we now call a parody) or in a spirit of admiration, or (sometimes) a mixture of the two.[15] And imitators, particularly when they are working across languages, can imitate in such a way as to foreground rhetorical and lexical features of their own work which are analogous to those of the earlier text, and which themselves can become objects of imitation within the new language. It is partly as a result of authors imitating in this way that national literatures grow and mutate.

But *imitatio* is not simply a matter of individuals imitating other individuals. Thinking about a text as having a 'form' which is imitable, and thinking

15. Linda Hutcheon, *A Theory of Parody: The Teachings of Twentieth Century Art Forms* (New York and London, 1985), p. 12 suggests that 'Ironic "transcontexualization" is what distinguishes parody from pastiche or imitation.'

about an author as akin to a 'genre' or series of poems with shared features and genealogical relationships to each other can have a contrary tendency. It can depersonalize the process of imitation. An imitator of an 'author-as-genre' will imitate not just features common to the poems of Martial, but might at the same time imitate features of Catullus or of Ben Jonson or any other author who had written epigrams. And by the same token an imitator might also imitate texts which have imitated or been imitated by the author whom he or she is principally imitating. Or an imitator might seek to replicate not just the finished poems ascribed to a particular author, but to imitate the earlier author's modes of imitating. As the sixteenth-century humanist educator Roger Ascham put it 'the one who intelligently observes how Cicero followed others will most successfully see how Cicero himself is to be followed'.[16]

That form of meta-imitation follows from regarding an author as a transposable principle rather than a body of text: imitating Virgil without imitating the way in which Virgil imitated Homer would be to imitate Virgil's texts rather than his practices. The result of thinking about authorship in this way can be that imitating authors often imitate more than one earlier writer. It is possible to imitate Milton in the way that Milton imitated Virgil, or to imitate the way Milton imitated Virgil imitating Homer, or to imitate Statius imitating Virgil imitating Homer. This form of layered imitation can lead on to what have been termed 'window references', in which an imitated text alludes simultaneously to a source text and to the text which it is imitating.[17] Indeed imitating authors can explore such a wide range of interconnections between earlier authors that the notion of an 'author' might disperse into a web of textual connections, and lead outwards from a one-to-one relation between imitator and imitated into the necessary interconnections between texts which are now generally called intertextuality.

I have in the following pages made relatively little reference to this topic, or to the large volume of recent work on the reciprocal relationships between methods of recording one's reading and the processes of writing in the early modern period.[18] While it is certainly the case that reading and

16. Roger Ascham, *Letters of Roger Ascham*, ed. Alvin Vos (New York, 1989), p. 271.
17. See Richard F. Thomas, 'Virgil's Georgics and the Art of Reference', *Harvard Studies in Classical Philology* 90 (1986), 171–98 and the forthcoming collection, Colin Burrow, Stephen Harrison, Martin McLaughlin, and Elisabetta Tarantino, eds., *Literary Windows: Imitative Series and Clusters from Classical to Early Modern Literature*.
18. See, e.g., Peter Beal, 'Notions in Garrison: The Seventeenth-Century Commonplace Book', in W. Speed Hill, ed., *New Ways of Looking at Old Texts* (Binghampton, NY, 1993), 131–47, Mary

writing were (and remain) mutually enforcing activities, I have tended to emphasize the intellective processes which enable writers to imitate other writers rather than processes of collection and assimilation and selective quotation which in different periods and in different ways fuel textual production. This is partly a consequence of the kinds of writing with which I am principally concerned. Writers of discursive prose and of history were more prone to cull and recombine fragments of text from other authors than the majority of poets. Prose writers from Montaigne to Burton and beyond would frequently imitate the flight of Seneca's eclectic bees, taking a phrase from Seneca himself and juxtaposing that with an anecdote from Plutarch or a recondite fact from Pliny. The movement between such passages would very often be rooted in a systematic or unsystematic prior gathering of textual materials in a commonplace book.[19]

Poets could sometimes proceed in similarly eclectic fashion: Gordon Braden has shown how Ben Jonson appears to have produced 'Drink to me, only, with thine eyes' (*Forest* 9) from the prose of Philostratos 'as though he had opened his book, transcribed a few letters, flipped a couple of pages, transcribed two more, and strung his notes together to make a "poem"'.[20] Jonson's eye could also move through Seneca's *De Beneficiis* and mine it for phrases and themes in order to construct from it a poem thanking a patron for his generosity, as he did when writing *Underwood* 13 to Sir Edward Sackville. Playwrights might also assemble materials, or piece and patch together sections of text from a range of different works, as well as responding to lateral connections within and the scenic structures of earlier texts.[21]

Thomas Crane, *Framing Authority: Sayings, Self, and Society in Sixteenth Century England* (Princeton, 1993), Anne Moss, *Printed Commonplace-Books and the Structuring of Renaissance Thought* (Oxford, 1996), Ann Blair, 'Textbooks and Methods of Note-Taking in Early Modern Europe', in Emidio Campi, Simone De Angelis, Anja-Silvia Goeing, and Anthony Grafton, eds., *Scholarly Knowledge: Textbooks in Early Modern Europe* (Geneva, 2008), 39–73, the special issue of *Intellectual History Review* 20 no. 3 (2010) on 'Note-Taking in Early Modern Europe', Colin Burrow and Richard Beadle, eds., *English Manuscript Studies 1100–1700 16: Manuscript Miscellanies 1450–1700* (London, 2011).

19. For exemplary studies, see Terence Cave, *The Cornucopian Text: Problems of Writing in the French Renaissance* (Oxford, 1979), pp. 271–321, Angus Vine, 'Commercial Commonplacing: Francis Bacon, the Waste-Book, and the Ledger', *English Manuscript Studies 16* (2011), 197–218, and Jason Scott-Warren, 'Commonplacing and Originality: Reading Francis Meres', *The Review of English Studies* 68 (2017), 902–23.

20. Gordon Braden, *The Classics and English Renaissance Poetry: Three Case Studies* (New Haven, 1978), p. 168.

21. For recent work in this area, see John Kerrigan, *Shakespeare's Originality* (Oxford, 2018), Janet Clare, *Shakespeare's Stage Traffic: Imitation, Borrowing and Competition in Renaissance Theatre* (Cambridge, 2014), Colin Burrow, 'Shakespeare's Authorities', in Katie Halsey and Angus Vine, eds., *Shakespeare and Authority: Citations, Conceptions and Constructions* (London, 2018), 31–53, Colin

But even acts of culling and reassemblage were often combined with analysis of how earlier authors put material together—or what Philipp Melanchthon, following Cicero, was to call 'collocatio', the putting together of words and the structuring of arguments. The use of a particular word might trigger a memory of a quotation, which in turn may trigger an attempt to imitate the structure of thought of the text in which it occurs; or the same process might occur in reverse: an attempt to imitate the larger structures of thought in an earlier text might trigger a recollection of a fragment of text, either from the same author, or from the same page of the imitating author's commonplace book, or from some idiosyncratic conjuncture in the pages of the book of memory.[22]

For these reasons from a very early stage *imitatio* has been closely linked with textual appropriation, or what we now term 'plagiarism'. The fear that there might be something inherently dishonest about taking the words of another writer and incorporating them into a new text is a very ancient one. It has its own complex history, but that history is intimately tied in with the story of *imitatio*.[23] I begin my discussion of post-classical literature with Petrarch not because I believe him to have revived lost classical learning (I emphasize in Chapter 4 how deeply he was indebted to medieval scribal culture and to the scholarship of later antiquity) but because Petrarch developed his thinking about *imitatio* in close and uneasy relationship to concerns that an imitator might be accused of stealing the words of an earlier author.

It is for this reason, I argue, that Petrarch's Latin epic *Africa* was particularly drawn towards episodes from classical epic which Petrarch knew had existed, but of which no textual traces remained—of which the most notable instance is the meeting between Ennius and the ghost of Homer, which Petrarch recreates. Such episodes enabled the imitator to recreate the missing text on the basis of inferences from its surviving portions, but they also necessarily freed the act of imitation from any suggestion of plagiarism,

Burrow, *Shakespeare and Classical Antiquity* (Oxford, 2013), Laurie E. Maguire and Emma Smith, 'What is a Source? Or, How Shakespeare Read his Marlowe', *Shakespeare Survey* 68 (2015), 15–31.

22. See Raphael Lyne, *Memory and Intertextuality in Renaissance Literature* (Cambridge, 2016).

23. Studies of its history and prehistory include Scott McGill, *Plagiarism in Latin Literature* (Cambridge, 2012), Stephen Orgel, 'The Renaissance Artist as Plagiarist', *ELH* 48 (1981), 476–95, Hall Björnstad and Kathy Eden, eds., *Borrowed Feathers: Plagiarism and the Limits of Imitation in Early Modern Europe* (Oslo, 2008), Paulina Kewes, ed., *Plagiarism in Early Modern England* (Basingstoke, 2003), Joseph Loewenstein, *Ben Jonson and Possessive Authorship* (Cambridge, 2002), and Tilar J. Mazzeo, *Plagiarism and Literary Property in the Romantic Period* (Philadelphia, 2007).

since the words of the imitated text were lost. Imitating an episode which was known to have existed but where the text itself had disappeared—what I term 'the lost imitand'—gives both authority and freedom to an imitating author, and it was towards *imitatio* of this kind that Petrarch was particularly drawn.

'Imitating' or imaginatively recreating texts which are lost is one extreme way of separating the act of imitation from that of textual appropriation. It does not of course preclude other forms of appropriation, or indeed overt acts of dishonesty: the ability to create a plausible imitation of an author's style while reconstructing a supposedly 'lost' work was, of course, the key skill of forgers. William Henry Ireland's 'discovery' of *Vortigern and Rowena*, a play supposedly by Shakespeare, set the literary London of the mid-1790s in a roar.[24] Imitators who want their work to be recognized as imitations have this much in common with forgers: they are dependent on the ability or willingness of a particular group of readers to associate a particular style or turn of phrase with a given earlier author.

But doing as Petrarch did, and imitating a text that is not there, marks in a particularly sharp way the theoretical distinction between learning a practice from another writer on the one hand and direct verbal citation on the other. This theoretical distinction is often difficult to sustain in practice, and that is partly because throughout the history of *imitatio* imitators have often wished to *show* that they are imitating. As a result literary imitators have from the very earliest phases of the Western tradition tended to display the fact that they are imitating by providing what we now call 'allusions' (although some would prefer the less sportive term 'references') to an earlier text.[25] They might do so either to pay tribute to or gain credit from presenting themselves as analogous to a famous predecessor. But either way, 'imitations' in this sense are intended to be noticed by specific communities of readers, and stand as invitations to make comparison between the new text and the earlier one, or to remember a text related to the new one from which it might partially derive.

Even in earlier Latin writing questions were raised about the propriety of borrowing from earlier authors in this overt way. Terence in the second

---

24. See Paul Baines, *The House of Forgery in Eighteenth-Century Britain* (Aldershot, 1999), Nick Groom, *The Forger's Shadow: How Forgery Changed the Course of Literature* (London, 2002), and Jack Lynch, 'William Henry Ireland's Authentic Forgeries', *The Princeton University Library Chronicle* 66 (2004), 79–96.

25. On the rhetoric of such allusions, see Stephen Hinds, *Allusion and Intertext: Dynamics of Appropriation in Roman Poetry* (Cambridge, 1998) and Conte, *Rhetoric of Imitation*. On 'references', see Thomas, 'Virgil's Georgics and the Art of Reference'.

century BC can worry about whether he is a 'thief' when he imitates plays by Menander which have already been imitated by his Roman contemporaries. Macrobius in the fifth century AD discussed Virgil's borrowings from Homer, and seems to have been responding to an early tradition that criticized the Roman poet for his thefts.[26] If one adds in the involuntary traces of an earlier text which necessarily slide into the work of one poet who writes in the same language as another, the entanglement between *imitatio* and plagiarism becomes almost a necessary by-product of imitating authors.

This was one reason why it was so alluring to regard *imitatio* as a matter of adapting the formal or generic characteristics of past writing to new times: doing so avoided the stigma that might be attached to a direct verbal debt. And in the period just before concepts of intellectual property (or 'literary property' as it was originally called) acquired the force of law it became particularly useful to think about the object of imitation as a 'form' in a wide range of senses.[27] In particular—as Chapter 8 shows in detail—it enabled an imitator to think of a prior author or text not as a series of words, but as something akin to an architectural 'model' for later works. This 'model' could provide a template for the proportions or structure of a text which followed that 'model'.

The word 'model' is cognate with mould, so a text used as a 'model' might give rise to a later text of similar proportions and style, but which consisted of different matter. But if a prior text was regarded as akin to an architectural or scalar 'model' further possibilities opened up. The proportions of an earlier text might be reproduced on either a smaller or larger scale by an imitator, who would still be following the 'model' whether it was minimized or maximized, since a 'model' stipulates a specific set of ratios or proportions between parts or elements rather than a specific size. Hence an ancient act of heroism, viewed as a set of ratios between elements, could be imitated on either a larger or a smaller scale. The technique of upscaling or downsizing an earlier text is at least as old as the (probably) fifth century BC *Batrachomyomachia*, in which frogs and mice do battle in Homerical language; but the use of the word 'model' to describe the imitated text gave giddy new dimensions to that technique.[28]

26. See McGill, *Plagiarism in Latin Literature*.

27. On the ways in which women writers could imitate the forms of other writers, see Elizabeth Scott-Baumann, *Forms of Engagement: Women, Poetry, and Culture 1640–1680* (Oxford, 2013).

28. See Ritchie Robertson, *Mock-Epic Poetry from Pope to Heine* (Oxford, 2009), pp. 50–1, and John S. Coolidge, 'Great Things and Small: The Virgilian Progression', *Comparative Literature* 17 (1965), 1–23.

Milton played a key role in the emergent tendency to treat prior texts as 'models' in this scalar sense, and this is one reason he is positioned if not physically then intellectually at the centre of this book. With Milton, I argue in Chapter 8, we see *imitatio* being aggressively associated with the production of such scalar replicas of earlier texts. His angels can re-enact the wars of Homer on a cosmic scale, which can simultaneously inflate and deflate their heroism by making it at once sublimely, or, to mortal eyes, comically vast. Or his devils can shrink to the size of bees in order to imitate a Homeric council scene. These scalar effects were a significant aspect of the changes which Milton wrought in the practice of *imitatio*, and show the potential force of regarding a classical text as a 'model'. It could be the great template of an imitating author's own text, or it could be tiny anticipation of the massive divine archetype which came to supersede the tiny 'models' of the ancients.

This in turn gave the act of imitating an earlier poem a powerful double force. On the one hand an imitation of a 'model' might be no more than a miniaturized replica of an earlier archetype. But on the other hand by the act of imitating an imitator turned the prior text *into* a 'model', and therefore might reduce it in scale to a mere miniaturized anticipation of its later and greater realization. Like the plan of a temple, a 'model' was at once an archetype of potential vastness *and* a tiny unrealized source of potential greatness.

Many apparently contradictory elements in Milton—his own highly imitable and indeed eminently parodiable style, his wary treatment of human 'imitations' of divinity, his emphasis on inspiration—situated *Paradise Lost* within the long slow shift towards a poetics which valued originality and the development of a personal manner or style. But his simultaneous amplification and diminution of his classical models also had a significant effect on how later writers imitated. He displayed a method by which past writing could seem simultaneously big and small. The mock heroic and the mock epic as developed by Alexander Pope, in which tiny events—the theft of a lock of hair, the plagiaristic practices of bad eighteenth-century poets— become imitations of great originals which simultaneously amplify and diminish those originals, and which skew and unsettle the relative proportions and significance of the present and antiquity, is massively indebted to Milton's scalar poetics.[29]

29. See Robertson, *Mock-Epic Poetry*, pp. 49–99 and, for parodies of the War in Heaven, pp. 288–99.

In the chapters after Milton I turn to vernacular texts, and in particular to the imitation of Milton. I do so because by the mid-eighteenth century the category of 'the classics' was frequently expanded to include canonical English authors such as Shakespeare and Milton. But I also do so because Milton figured prominently in a series of legal and literary arguments about textual ownership which had a profound effect on the way in which imitation was thought about and practised in the later eighteenth century and beyond. Britain was the first nation in the world to introduce legislation about what is now called copyright. This legislation was preceded and followed by extensive philosophical and legal discussion of what was termed 'literary property'. British copyright legislation was, as many scholars have shown, driven not by a desire to protect the interests of authors but by an influential group of London stationers, who wanted to protect their right to print the 'copy' of early authors from their competitors.[30] These included the rights to publish the works of Milton, for which there remained a constant demand.

Milton was not just a piece of intellectual property, however. He was also something which resembled a common resource. He had imitated the style of classical epic to generate a style that was so readily identifiable as his own that he had himself become the object of deliberate stylistic imitation by 1700. That style was so widely imitated that it came to shape the nature of what Wordsworth, in the extended 1802 Preface to *The Lyrical Ballads*, was to describe with some hostility as 'poetic diction'. Milton by the end of the eighteenth century was part of the literary landscape and an element in the air that later poets breathed.

Those metaphors are not simply hyperbolical. The arguments that led to vernacular authors such as Milton being regarded as 'classics' or as common goods which could be imitated freely were full of comparisons of earlier writing to landscapes or water or the common goods of life. And that went along with some subtle but profound changes in the metaphorical language used by literary critics and legal theorists to describe the activities of an imitating author. As Chapter 9 shows, the 'classics'—both ancient writing and earlier English texts—were sometimes presented in legal and critical discourse as a kind of common property akin to a piece of publicly owned

---

30. John Feather, *Publishing, Piracy and Politics: An Historical Study of Copyright in Britain* (London, 1994) offers a reliable account. For wider implications, see Adrian Johns, *Piracy: The Intellectual Property Wars from Gutenberg to Gates* (Chicago, Ill., and London, 2009) and William St. Clair, *The Reading Nation in the Romantic Period* (Cambridge, 2004).

land, on which anyone could freely graze. The imitator might pluck the odd flower of fancy from this common store, but could not claim to own its full riches. An author might establish something akin to an estate within this terrain, across which others might pass, enjoying a right of way over it but no wider rights of ownership.

Classical literature was unequivocally part of that 'common store' from which all could draw. But earlier vernacular literature was not quite so straightforwardly a common resource. Like the work of contemporary vernacular authors it could simultaneously be regarded as a species of personal property, trespassing on which was potentially fraught with hazard. Eighteenth-century debates about imitation and 'literary property' positioned Milton right in the middle of this landscape: he was both a common good, and a piece of literary property. That is a further reason why he became at once such a powerful resource for later poets and potentially also a source of anxiety.

This had a profound influence on Milton's most ambitious imitator, William Wordsworth (one of the main subjects of Chapter 9). Wordsworth sought, as he put it, 'to imitate, and, as far as possible, to adopt the very language of men'.[31] The object of imitation, he claimed, was not the language or practice of another poet, or Miltonic poetic diction, but a language common to all. But Wordsworth too was an imitating author. His aspiration to represent in enhanced and elevated form the experiences of common men went along with an elaborate refashioning of one of the oldest metaphors for the imitative poet: that of someone who follows in the footsteps of an earlier author. The master-image of Wordsworth's writing is that of a poet who wanders across a landscape which is criss-crossed with roads and public rights of way, which might lead on to sublime spaces of unknown nature. As he moves through that landscape he attempts to transform its common elements, its breezes and waters, all of which are the common, shared experiences of mankind, into the substance of his own experience and the inspiration for his verse. All the while, however, those landscapes are haunted by the shades, and by the language and linguistic mannerisms, of Milton.

Wordsworth responded to the arguments about the relationships between *imitatio* and intellectual property over the previous centuries by fashioning a landscape in which the common goods of the earth—breezes, waters,

---

31. William Wordsworth and Samuel Taylor Coleridge, *Lyrical Ballads: with Pastoral and Other Poems, in Two Volumes*, 2 vols. (London, 1802), p. xviii.

public highways—subsist alongside proprietorial spaces over which other poets or landowners might have control. Wordsworth's attempts to remake the epic tradition in *The Recluse* and *The Prelude* are thus repeatedly shaped by the changing legal and critical language in which arguments about imitation were conducted.

Thinking about *imitatio* has never been entirely insulated from thinking about a wide range of concepts with which it is close kin. Chapter 9 shows how arguments about literary property and copyright radically reshaped the theory and practice of literary imitation. Chapter 10 turns to a rather different but equally influential area. It argues that the long history of writing about the manufacture of artificial human beings—which was a central component in Enlightenment arguments about the relationship between body and spirit—also had a profound influence on the way in which *imitatio* was understood in the nineteenth century and beyond. Could a human artist not just imitate an earlier poem, but create a mechanical creature which could imitate life so completely that it could use language in the same way as a human being, or even a poet?

That was a threatening question on many levels, since if the answer were affirmative it would destroy the traditional view of human beings as immaterial souls harnessed to material bodies. Human beings would be all matter, a mechanically replicable machine without a ghost or soul inside it, and consequently entirely imitable agents. The process of imitating, of reassembling materials from past texts into new, living form, has long had associations with necromancy and with the uncanny reawakening of the dead. Those associations run right back to the *nekyia* or summoning up the spirits of the dead in Book 11 of the *Odyssey*, in which the poet of the *Odyssey*—who was in all probability an artful imitator of the *Iliad* poet—describes the ghosts of the dead drinking the blood of a sacrifice, which reanimates the heroes of the *Iliad*.[32] That association between imitation and the revival of the dead was given further strength by Milton's extraordinary creation of the monstrous shadow that actually *is* Death, who was himself a kind of reanimation of Virgil's ghost of Hector, whose lethal vitality derived from the long-established tendency to regard a malign imitation as a *simulacrum* or shadow of a formerly living *exemplum*. Combine these with the arguments about artificial persons and the elements were all in place for the creation of an imitated being who was at once a *simulacrum* of life and a mortal threat to its creator.

32. For imitations of the *Iliad*, see M. L. West, *The Making of the Odyssey* (Oxford, 2014), esp. p. 25. On the *nekyia*, see Glenn Most, 'Il poeta nell'Ade: catabasi epica e teoria dell'epos tra Omero e Virgilio', *Studi italiani di filologia classica* 10 (1992), 1014–26.

When Mary Shelley set about to imitate German gothic tales in the summer of 1816 that creation staggered into life. Frankenstein's monster, a being made from dead limbs that lives and talks, draws its life from a long series of arguments about the ways in which matter could be made to live, fused with centuries of argument about what it is to imitate an earlier author. Mary Shelley's creation imitates both Milton's Satan and Milton's Eve. The monster reads *Paradise Lost*, and describes how he learnt what he was through a direct imitative transformation of Milton's Eve, and of the moment when Eve looks at herself in a pool and creatively imitates Ovid's Narcissus. And the mysterious processes used by Frankenstein to animate his monster are a gothic reimagining of the central problem in the tradition of imitative writing: how does new autonomous life emerge from an assimilation or digestion of past authors?

That uncanny afterlife of Milton also reflects a much wider tendency. Once an authorial *corpus* is regarded as a 'body' of work which displays identifiable and potentially quantifiable characteristics—a preference for particular verbal collocations, a disposition to describe characteristic kinds of scene—that corpus might be seen as extensible after the death of its principal creator, and as replicable thing. It might be brought to life again by a 'formula' derived from statistical analysis of the 'corpus' of prior works, from which further texts could be generated. The possibility of mechanically replicating a text or a human being in turn raises in stark form the recurrent question about the relationship between the visible series of texts ascribed to a single person and the invisible *ingenium* or talent or genius which is believed to have produced them.

That relationship had been on the edges of discussions about *imitatio* from early modernity onwards, when lexica and concordances began to make it possible to generate texts that closely resembled the verbal mannerisms of Cicero. Discussions of the different styles of authors, from Cicero onwards, implicitly raise the question 'what distinguishes this writer from that writer?' That question could be answered by saying 'it is a disposition to write in this way', or 'that was the nature of his talent or *ingenium*'; or it could be answered in a more quantifiable manner, by noting the frequency with which Cicero ends a sentence with 'esse videatur', or by compiling statistical analyses of his habitual collocations. If those quantificatory methods of stylistic analysis are combined with a heightened version of the tendency in early discussions of *imitatio* to emphasize the inimitable, lost *ingenium* or talent of a past author they have the potential to generate a profound perplexity. When these two myths collide an author might be regarded as at one and the same time a unique, inimitable talent and as an algorithm that could generate more works of a similar kind. Those two concepts not only seem to be but actually are radically incompatible.

I suggest at the end of the book that this perplexing fusion of concepts, the partial genesis of which can be tracked back through the history of *imitatio*, is particularly evident in our own cultural moment. Human behaviour is increasingly seen as predictable by machines, and yet we are also repeatedly told that human beings make choices—as consumers, as lovers, and as writers. Machines can replicate and anticipate many of our choices, of what we buy, of who we are likely to love, and of the word which we are most likely to write next. The ghost and the machine have never seemed more closely allied, and yet have never been so widely separated. The machine mimics the ghost, and the ghost cries out that it nonetheless has a choice, that it is more than the machine. Poetry has frequently been regarded as a product of the human spirit, of the *ingenium* or unquantifiable genius of the author. But now poetry, or at least verse of a kind, can be produced by online bot-poetry engines at the click of a mouse. Could a machine imitate the unreplicably human thing we call genius? Could a computer replicate the practices of a human imitator of earlier poems?

Although I believe that the answer to those questions for now and for a long time to come is 'no', I do argue in the Postscript to this book that the long-running history of arguments about *imitatio* has fed indirectly into a range of contemporary philosophical and fictional conundrums and creative anxieties about the boundaries between the human and the non-human. Those arguments play a part in Alan Turing's influential discussions of what he termed 'the imitation game', in which a computer is programmed to replicate the behaviour of human language users.[33] They also have a shaping influence on the rich body of science fiction (in fiction and in film) about clones and replicants. These children of Frankenstein's monster, who was himself an offspring of Milton, raise in new forms questions which run through the history of authors imitating authors: can a replicant reproduce whatever it is that is peculiar to its original? They also directly address the question which has been a preoccupation of philosophers at least since Descartes: could human consciousness be imitated by a machine which simply sought to replicate the outward linguistic behaviours of human beings?

Those questions have generated a rich body of both philosophical discussion and fiction since the 1950s. The story of the android that can biologically reproduce itself and become indistinguishable from a human being (in *Blade*

33. A. M. Turing, 'Computing Machinery and Intelligence', *Mind* 59 (1950), 433–60.

Runner 2049), or (in Kazuo Ishiguro's *Never Let Me Go*) of the clone who wishes to create rather than merely to imitate, are fables which arise from the long story of *imitatio*. And they are fables which speak to our present concerns. The unsettling conjunction in classical writing about *imitatio* between the vanishing marvel that is the mind of Cicero and the possibility of replicating that mind through imitating his words is made into a creative *dis*junction in clone fictions; and the insistence in the tradition of writing about *imitatio* that the 'true' or 'good' or 'successful' imitator is an autonomous being who resembles an *exemplum* as a child resembles its parent, rather than a mere replicant of an earlier text, is one which, with much mutating of mutandorum and indeed mutating of mutants, has become one of the master tropes of contemporary culture. The fear and curiosity that artificial humans can produce is the product of a different world from Virgil's imitations of Homer or Ennius or Lucretius. But the long and rich history of *imitatio* creates a sinuous path that ties these phenomena together. So the story I am telling is not simply one about how highly educated poets imitated and thought about other highly educated poets in past centuries. It is finally about how we think about what it is to be a human agent today.

★

The pages that follow offer a broadly historical account of *imitatio*, beginning with early Greek philosophical and literary texts, and running onwards towards futurity. I aim to tell a coherent story which connects with present-day concerns rather than to provide a comprehensive history. I concentrate on a set of recurrent issues (adaptive imitation, formal imitation, the relationship between imitation and plagiarism), a set of key texts which are repeated objects of imitation (the ghost of Hector arises repeatedly from the dead in the pages that follow), and a repertoire of metaphors which repeatedly animate both the practice and the theory of *imitatio* (chiefly the opposition between the 'living' assimilation of texts by digestion or rebirth as against the creation of ghostly replicants or *simulacra*).

There are many major areas which I do not consider—Shelley's imitations of Greek poetry, for instance, or Wyatt's imitations of Petrarch, Ezra Pound's 'Homage' to Sextus Propertius, or indeed the endlessly multiplying 'imitations' of classical texts in the eighteenth, nineteenth, and twentieth centuries—because it would be impossible to cover all this terrain in a single book.[34] Hoccleve and Lydgate and Henryson and Spenser all imitated Chaucer;

---

34. Patrick Cheney, Rita Copeland, Philip Hardie, David Hopkins, Charles Martindale, Norman Vance, and Jennifer Wallace, eds., *The Oxford History of Classical Reception in English Literature*, 5 vols. (Oxford, 2012–) offers comprehensive coverage.

Chaucer and Gower imitated Ovid and Virgil;[35] Dante imitated Virgil and Ovid and Statius. Throughout the middle ages responses to classical texts—often mediated through commentaries and through pedagogical practices derived from the classical rhetorical tradition—generated a wealth of fictions, as Rita Copeland has explored in a series of brilliant studies.[36] These are all versions of imitation.

The central arguments of the later sections of this book, however, are closely connected with the reception history of a group of rhetorical texts—the later rhetorical works of Cicero and the complete text of Quintilian's *Institutes*—which were not rediscovered until the fifteenth century. They provided the metaphors which were so vital to later imitating authors, and they provoked detailed rhetorical analysis of earlier texts and of the styles of earlier authors. Because of my focus on the reception history of these texts I have not included a chapter on fourteenth-century, or 'Ricardian', poets as imitators.[37] I would not wish this to be taken as a sign that I am yet another credulous believer in the humanist myth that the middle ages were dark days of ignorance, in which scholars and poets sat waiting for the light from Troy to bring a new dawn. It will be clear from my discussion of Petrarch in Chapter 4 that this was a myth by which humanists sought to exaggerate the differences between their practices and those of the immediate past. Medieval authors had a rich understanding of the classical tradition, but it is a rather different kind of understanding from that which runs through the particular story that I am telling.

There is a huge amount that could be said about other areas too. Supplementation, forgery, centos, and the ways in which spurious works are insinuated into an authorial canon all could be regarded as versions of imitation. An endless book could be written about the ways in which non-European cultures have imitated and transformed canonical works from the

35. See, e.g., Andrew Galloway, 'Ovid in Chaucer and Gower', in John F. Miller and Carole E. Newlands, eds., *A Handbook to the Reception of Ovid* (Chichester, 2014), 187–201, James G. Clark, Frank Thomas Coulson, and Kathryn L. McKinley, eds., *Ovid in the Middle Ages* (Cambridge, 2011). For an argument that responses to Ovid before 1547 are freer than those of the later period, see James Simpson, *Reform and Cultural Revolution* (Oxford, 2002), pp. 131–60. On Virgil, see, e.g., Christopher Baswell, *Virgil in Medieval England: Figuring the Aeneid from the Twelfth Century to Chaucer* (Cambridge, 1995), John Watkins, *The Specter of Dido: Spenser and Virgilian Epic* (New Haven, 1995), and Marjorie Curry Woods, *Weeping for Dido: The Classics in the Medieval Classroom* (Princeton, 2018).

36. Rita Copeland, *Rhetoric, Hermeneutics and Translation in the Middle Ages: Academic Traditions and Vernacular Texts* (Cambridge, 1991) and Rita Copeland, ed., *The Oxford History of Classical Reception in English Literature: Volume 1, 800–1558* (Oxford, 2016).

37. See J. A. Burrow, *Ricardian Poetry: Chaucer, Gower, Langland and the Gawain Poet* (London, 1971).

countries that have dominated them or which they have dominated. Imitation is so central to the processes of identity-formation both for individuals and cultures that the topic has no self-evident conceptual, historical, or geographical boundaries. It is a key way in which a subaltern culture can reconfigure the influences which have come to dominate it, and through which it can appraise its status as a replicant of an earlier culture, as a subversive mimic which questions the values of that culture, or as an autonomous entity.

Imitatio was, after all, one means by which the most powerful yet culturally subject nation of all—Rome—addressed its relations to Greece, and vice versa. As Horace put it: 'Greece, the captive, made her savage victor captive, and she brought the arts into rustic Latium' ('Graecia capta ferum victorem cepit et artis | intulit agresti Latio', *Epistles*, 2.1.156–7). Those lines can themselves be transposed to describe multiple different cultural relationships, as the imitation of them by Alexander Pope illustrates very neatly: 'We conquer'd France, but felt our captive's charms; | Her arts victorious triumph'd o'er our Arms.'[38] The imitative relationship between the conquering Rome and its Greek-speaking subject peoples, however, was not simply a matter of a colonizer adopting the culture of the conquered. As Tim Whitmarsh has said of Greek writers under the Roman empire, imitation was 'not simply a means of marking a stable relationship between two fixed co-ordinates, the present and the past; it was a locus of conflict between various groups trying (vainly) to define that relationship in different ways'.[39] The empire could write back.

The practice of imitation has, from at least the mid-twentieth century onwards, been subjected to critique and critical transformation by writers who wish to position themselves outside the dominant canon of European writing. It is not hard to see why. *Imitatio* could readily be seen as an engine of patrilinear supremacy, which ensures the replication of a dominant set of values, descending from fathers to sons. Citizens of nations that were governed for generations by white men trained to compose Virgilian hexameters have particularly strong reasons to see imitation in that light, and to be suspicious of it as an ideological instrument.

38. Text from Alexander Pope, *The Poems: A One-Volume Edition of the Twickenham Text with Selected Annotations*, ed. John Butt (London, 1963).
39. Tim Whitmarsh, *Greek Literature and the Roman Empire: The Politics of Imitation* (Oxford, 2001), p. 29.

My emphasis on the unruliness of and potential contradictions within *imitatio*, however, is aimed to present it not as a practice which leads to personal or cultural self-replication, but one which enables change, and which also contains within itself the possibility of a derivative authority which interrogates that of the source. An imitator does not need to mimic what is admirable in an imitated text, but can reflect back a sinister double of its failings, or make a monster of her master, as Mary Shelley so influentially did. That makes imitation powerfully double-edged, and potentially a tool of psychological and also political resistance. But it also perhaps makes it inescapable even for those who resist it, which, indeed, is a pervasive feature of the mechanisms by which European culture has perpetuated itself. When post-colonial critiques of imitation are overtly presented as acts of resistance to a wider Greco-Roman tradition they can sometimes fall subject to the general rule that oppositional acts themselves imitate and mirror the structures that they oppose. So Frantz Fanon argued at the conclusion of *The Wretched of the Earth* (1961) that the imitation of European models should be set aside by post-colonial writers:

> Let us decide not to imitate Europe; let us combine our muscles and our brains in a new direction. Let us try to create the whole man, whom Europe has been incapable of bringing to triumphant birth.
>
> Two centuries ago, a former European colony decided to catch up with Europe. It succeeded so well that the United States of America became a monster, in which the taints, the sickness and the inhumanity of Europe have grown to appalling dimensions.[40]

Fanon's Marxist and Hegelian intellectual foundations make him resist the dialectical mirroring of master and slave, of black and white, implicit in the cultural imitation of Europe by its former colonies. His political belief that decolonization requires active resistance to colonizing powers and his hostility to imitation are several worlds away from Quintilian. But, as Fanon himself acknowledges, 'deep down in the brain' of the 'colonized intellectual' 'you could always find a vigilant sentinel ready to defend the Greco-Latin pedestal' (p. 45). His opposition between a 'manly' rebirth of 'l'homme total' on the one hand and the Frankenstein's monster imitation of Europe that

---

40. Frantz Fanon, *The Wretched of the Earth*, trans. C. Farrington (Harmondsworth, 1967), pp. 312–13 ('Décidons de ne pas imiter l'Europe et bandons nos muscles et nos cerveaux dans une direction nouvelle. Tâchons d'inventer l'homme total que l'Europe a été incapable de faire triompher. Il y a deux siècles, une ancienne colonie européenne s'est mise en tête de rattraper l'Europe. Elle y a tellement réussi que les États-Unis d'Amérique sont devenus un monstre où les tares, les maladies et l'inhumanité de l'Europe ont atteint des dimensions épouvantables').

is the United States of America on the other is deeply indebted to the Greco-Roman European traditions described in this book: the live birth of an independent being continues to do battle with its *simulacrum*.

By imitating aggressively or subversively or appreciatively writers can establish both their own relationships to and independence from those whom they have read, and can also address wider relationships between their nation and language and other nations and languages. From Derek Walcott's Caribbean reimagining of epic in *Omeros* (1990) to J. M. Coetzee—an imitator of both Defoe and Dostoevsky, who has in *Elizabeth Costello* (2004) woven a series of thoughts about imitation and the classical tradition into reflections about what might be involved in imagining the consciousness of another person—imitation is a key component in post-colonial Anglophone literature and theory. For Homi Bhabha colonial 'mimicry'—an imitation of a dominant culture that is unsettlingly not quite the same as that which it imitates—can produce not servility to a hegemonic culture, but a potentially destabilizing double of that culture.[41]

To see these arguments as all stemming from European discussions of the freedom of the imitator would be reductive. They are the product of particular geopolitical configurations and political conflicts. But the larger discourse described in this book—a discourse that flows out from Plato and Aristophanes, through the rhetorical tradition, and into the foundational texts of the Western canon—is perhaps impossible to escape in any part of the world that has been subjected to any significant European cultural or political influence. That is why the wider issues raised by *Imitating Authors* radiate off in so many directions. The only realistic way to shape the topic into a manageable form is to try to provide an internally coherent framework for thinking rather than anything which resembles a comprehensive history, and to suggest ways in which that framework might be developed in new directions. This is what I have sought to do. As my footprints trail off I hope others will continue along the path, or trace new ways through the gaps (which can indeed be wide) between my steps.

★

What does *Imitating Authors* add to the much-studied subject of *imitatio*? Much has been written about the topic in the last forty years, but Thomas Greene's *The Light in Troy* has throughout that period remained a key

---

41. See Homi K. Bhabha, *The Location of Culture* (London, 1994), pp. 85–92 ('Of Mimicry and Man: The Ambivalence of Colonial Discourse').

reference-point.[42] Greene offers many suggestive analyses of relationships between particular texts, but also presents a taxonomy of modes of *imitatio* that has rightly been described as 'too *dirigiste*'.[43] Imitations need not fit Greene's fourfold division into 'sacramental' (imitations which pay homage to texts unassimilable to modernity), or 'eclectic', or 'heuristic' (a mode of imitation which Greene suggests creates a distance between a text and its models), or 'dialectical' (in which imitated and imitation are mutually critical), though they can do.[44] Greene's Renaissance is a period chiefly defined by 'historical solitude', or yearning for a lost classical past, the retrieval of which necessarily generates a sense of dislocation or of lack and loss. Ben Jonson is presented as marking the end of a period of discomforting but creative alienation (in which texts are imitated 'heuristically' to discover truths about both the past and the present) and as the beginning of a period in which the classics were 'domesticated', in which 'imitation becomes an updating', and in which the past has lost its 'proper strangeness'.[45]

Greene's treatment of the early modern period as a self-contained unit principally distinguished from what comes before and after by historical self-consciousness now seems highly questionable, and his decision to end his story before Milton and Dryden is regrettable on many counts. Leonard Barkan's study of Renaissance sculpture, *Unearthing the Past* (now twenty years old, but still wonderfully fresh) provides a very different model of *imitatio*, which implies that early modernity was characterized by a combination of rediscovery, supplementation, and creative forgery, of simultaneously unearthing past artworks and making (as it were) the missing arms of a broken statue of Venus. Artists performed these acts of practical retrieval in an environment in which it was contemporary artists, rather than the ancients, who were the main objects of rivalry.[46] I am more in sympathy with Barkan's way of thinking about imitation than I am with Greene's; but

42. Thomas M. Greene, *The Light in Troy: Imitation and Discovery in Renaissance Poetry* (New Haven and London, 1982).

43. Patrick Cheney and Philip R. Hardie, eds., *The Oxford History of Classical Reception in English Literature: Volume 2, 1558–1660* (Oxford, 2015), p. 18. See pp. 13–21 in that volume for a helpful overview of imitation in the period.

44. Greene, *Light in Troy*, pp. 38–45.

45. Greene, *Light in Troy*, p. 293. A radical alternative to his view of 'domesticated' imitation in the age of Dryden is offered in Paul Hammond, *Dryden and the Traces of Classical Rome* (Oxford, 1999).

46. Leonard Barkan, *Unearthing the Past: Archaeology and Aesthetics in the Making of Renaissance Culture* (New Haven and London, 1999), esp. pp. 273–96.

I wish to explore how the reception of this aspect of the classical tradition permeates our thinking now.

Anyone working on the topic of *imitatio* will be in debt to a series of articles by G. W. Pigman, which have also been influential for a long time, and will regret that those essays did not become a monograph—though that gap has partially been filled by splendid discussions by Terence Cave and Martin McLaughlin of imitation in early modern French and Italian writing, as well as by a host of innovative work by more recent critics.[47] Like Greene, Pigman adopts a taxonomical approach to the unruly body of thinking about *imitatio*. He divides imitation into three broad types: the transformative, the dissimulative, and the eristic.

This triad is a helpful tool for thinking, but also has limitations. Pigman tends to stress the dissimulative (the hiding of sources) and the eristic (the overgoing of sources) forms of imitation over other kinds. He does so because his understanding of the subject is underpinned by a Freudian model of literary relations: sources are to be hidden or fought with, rather than texts to be learnt from, adapted, and absorbed into the practice of a new author. Pigman was a graduate at Yale (where Greene was also on the Faculty of Comparative Literature) shortly after Harold Bloom had published *The Anxiety of Influence* (1973), in which agonistic Freudian struggles between authors are everywhere, and in which (it sometimes appears) the humble process of learning from an earlier example—which lies at the heart of *Imitating Authors*—appears to be only for the weak. Indeed Bloom's descriptions of the rivalry which he believes drives along literary history can sometimes fuse Freudianism together with the ethos of competitive capitalism in a manner which, nearly half a century on, seems to make of it a toxic zero-sum game: 'Where generosity is involved, the poets influenced are minor or weaker; the more generosity and the more mutual it is, the poorer the poets involved.'[48]

Pigman's historically sensitive work is far removed from Bloom's stridency—although Greene's description of 'dialectical' imitation, in which a new text

47. G. W. Pigman, 'Imitation and the Renaissance Sense of the Past: The Reception of Erasmus' *Ciceronianus*', *The Journal of Medieval and Renaissance Studies* 9 (1979), 155–77, G. W. Pigman, 'Versions of Imitation in the Renaissance', *Renaissance Quarterly* 33 (1980), 1–32, G. W. Pigman, 'Barzizza's Treatise on Imitation', *Bibliothèque d'Humanisme et Renaissance* 44 (1982), 341–52; Cave, *Cornucopian Text*, Martin L. McLaughlin, *Literary Imitation in the Italian Renaissance* (Oxford, 1995); more recent material on English authors includes Loewenstein, *Possessive Authorship*, Lyne, *Memory and Intertextuality*, and Victoria Moul, *Jonson, Horace and the Classical Tradition* (Cambridge, 2010).
48. Harold Bloom, *The Anxiety of Influence: A Theory of Poetry* (Oxford and New York, 1973), p. 30.

'had to expose the vulnerability of the subtext while exposing itself to the subtext's potential aggression' clearly is not.[49] But even Pigman is, to revert to Bloom's commercial metaphor, heavily invested in the association between imitation and rivalry as well as in the connection between psychic defence mechanisms and the absorption of earlier texts.[50]

My own intellectual roots lie in the Cambridge English Faculty in the late twentieth century. From that (often combative) environment I have carried away a desire to think about literature across wide spans of time and space, but also to treat texts as particular objects. I have learnt from the work of Quentin Skinner and the methods of the 'Cambridge School' of intellectual history to attend to the ways in which vocabularies change and persist through time, as they are tested and transformed by their usage at specific historical junctures. These strands of influence are complicated by my long-standing interest in reception history. New situations and different cultural horizons make texts change their appearance and open up new possibilities for their readers and imitators. They also transform complex concepts such as *imitatio*.

Imitating Authors argues that *imitatio* is continually being redefined in new ways, and that the concept and the practice are subjected to continual metamorphoses as a result of multiple influences—some material, some intellectual, some the result of innovative and irreverent thinking or practice. *Imitatio* is such a complex process and such a multiplex concept that no one who imitates can be expected ever to be quite sure what they are doing, or how exactly they stand in relation to their textual origins; and (*pace* Bloom and Greene) if you do not know who your adversary actually is it is rather hard to pick a fight with him or her, let alone win it. By linking *imitatio* closely to wider processes of learning from what one reads *Imitating Authors* shows how it *can* go along with love for or rivalry with an earlier author, or a desire to occlude a debt to a prior author, but that it also can be accompanied by the gentler marks of affinity or admiration for, or a sense of kinship with, writers from the past.[51] We live with our pasts and we try also

49. Greene, *Light in Troy*, p. 45.
50. For his Freudianism, see G. W. Pigman, *Grief and the English Renaissance Elegy* (Cambridge, 1985).
51. On relationships of paternity between authors, see Christopher Ricks, *Allusion to the Poets* (Oxford, 2002), Tom MacFaul, *Poetry and Paternity in Renaissance England: Sidney, Spenser, Shakespeare, Donne and Jonson* (Cambridge, 2010), and Helen Cooper, 'Choosing Poetic Fathers: The English Problem', in Lukas Erne and Guillemette Bolens, eds., *Medieval and Early Modern Authorship* (Tübingen, 2011), 29–50.

to live beyond them, and we might even learn things that matter a great deal to us from people whom we do not admire.

My interest in *imitatio* as a process of acquiring competences, and as a form of learning, has been informed by the recent work of philosophers and experimental psychologists who have written about imitative and emulative learning.[52] This has enabled me to perceive larger connections between the history of thinking about *imitatio* and more recent arguments about machine learning—between which and the work of experimental psychologists there are strong synergies at present. Superb work by Kathy Eden on the history of style and of intellectual property has also enabled me to perceive a longer narrative than that presented in earlier studies of this topic.[53]

I have also sought to incorporate theoretical work on allusion and influence by classicists into a wider understanding of the history of Western literature.[54] The Pisan school of classical studies, and in particular the work of Gian Biagio Conte and Alessandro Barchiesi, still has a great deal to teach those studying vernacular European literatures.[55] Conte's earlier work, and Barchiesi's study of the relationship between Homer and Virgil, show that *imitatio* can reach behind particular textual relationships between authors to the structural principles and generative grammar which underlie those texts. A competent imitator is a practitioner who has mastered what Barchiesi has termed 'the traces of the model', or its shapes and structures as

52. See, e.g., Cecilia Heyes, *Cognitive Gadgets: The Cultural Evolution of Thinking* (Cambridge, Mass., and London, 2018), S. L. Hurley and Nick Chater, eds., *Perspectives on Imitation: From Neuroscience to Social Science*, 2 vols. (Cambridge, Mass., and London, 2005), Chrystopher L. Nehaniv and Kerstin Dautenhahn, eds., *Imitation and Social Learning in Robots, Humans and Animals: Behavioural, Social and Communicative Dimensions* (Cambridge, 2007), Arbib, *How the Brain got Language*. For a more systematic use of experimental psychology to examine the processes of imitation, see Lyne, *Memory and Intertextuality*.

53. Kathy Eden, *Friends Hold all Things in Common: Tradition, Intellectual Property, and the Adages of Erasmus* (New Haven and London, 2001), Kathy Eden, *The Renaissance Rediscovery of Intimacy* (Chicago, Ill., 2012), and Kathy Eden, 'Cicero Redivivus and the Historicizing of Renaissance Style', *Nottingham Medieval Studies* 56 (2012), 143–69. The fine analytical work of Peter Mack on traditions of Northern European rhetoric has also played a vital part in the genesis of this study: see Peter Mack, *Elizabethan Rhetoric: Theory and Practice* (Cambridge, 2002), and Peter Mack, *A History of Renaissance Rhetoric, 1380–1620* (Oxford, 2011).

54. Notably Hinds, *Allusion and Intertext*, Philip R. Hardie, *The Epic Successors of Virgil: A Study in the Dynamics of a Tradition* (Cambridge, 1993), Philip R. Hardie, *Ovid's Poetics of Illusion* (Cambridge, 2002), and Philip R. Hardie, *Lucretian Receptions: History, the Sublime, Knowledge* (Cambridge, 2009).

55. Conte, *Rhetoric of Imitation*, Conte, *On Imitation*; Alessandro Barchiesi, *La traccia del modello: effetti omerici nella narrazione virgiliana* (Pisa, 1984), translated as Alessandro Barchiesi, *Homeric Effects in Vergil's Narrative*, trans. Ilaria Marchesi and Matt Fox (Princeton, 2015).

well as its words; and a competent imitator (as I suggest in the Postscript to this book) might also have grasped, and can on occasion refashion, the internal dynamic within a tradition by which one author relates to and transforms a predecessor or set of predecessors.

An imitating author therefore can be someone who understands a textual tradition in a way akin to that in which a language user grasps a linguistic practice: an imitator gives as a criterion of understanding an earlier author or a genre a performance of that competence in the form of a poem which is not identical to that which is imitated. And because an imitator of an earlier author by doing so in effect transforms that earlier author into a genre, a *kind* of writing with recurrent characteristic features rather than a finite body of texts, the act of imitating an author is not simply a matter of one individual responding to another's work. Imitating an author entails interpreting an earlier text and grouping it with other texts and kindred ways of writing. It also entails thinking about the distinctive features of the earlier author's works that make them imitable, and in turn thinking about how to make one's own texts bear a similarly distinctive character, which might enable them to be imitated by others.

Imitating authors consequently do not simply mimic what they read; they are drivers of literary history. They can constitute earlier authors as reifiable entities by highlighting imitable features in those authors; but they can also play a part in disassembling prior authors by fusing them together into a wider generic group, and subordinating them to the creation of a new form or style that can itself be subsequently imitated. Imitating authors are therefore makers, unmakers, and remakers of earlier authors.

PART I

Antiquity

I

From *Mimēsis* to *Imitatio*

Before and After Plato

Brekekekex koax koax.[1]

'Pretty Polly.'[2]

Come, my Celia, let us prove,
While we may, the sports of love;
Time will not be ours for ever:
He, at length, our good will sever.
Spend not then his gifts in vain.
Suns that set may rise again:
But if once we lose this light
'Tis, with us, perpetual night.[3]

E ach of these utterances might be called an 'imitation' in one sense or another. In the first Aristophanes imitates the sound of frogs. In the second a parrot imitates what a human being has said to it, and does so, in the common idiom, 'parrot-fashion'. The third is described by the most recent editor of Ben Jonson's poems as 'an imitation of Catullus 5'. These three examples may illustrate quite how broadly and variously the words 'imitation' and its cognates are used today.

None of these examples is as simple as it might seem. Aristophanes imitates the sound of frogs as they sounded to literate Athenians in the fifth century. If an English person today were to imitate the sound made by a frog he or she would probably croak or ribbit rather than brekkek. Parrots, as we say, parrot: they repeat sounds which they hear. In calling them 'imitators' or

---

1. Aristophanes, *Frogs*, 209.   2. © Parrots, passim.
3. Ben Jonson, *The Cambridge Edition of the Works of Ben Jonson*, ed. David M. Bevington, Martin Butler, and Ian Donaldson, 7 vols. (Cambridge, 2012), 5.222–3. The editor of the poems, who parrots common opinion, is Colin Burrow.

'mimics' we are implicitly saying that they do not understand the meaning
of the sounds they utter. Polly may say 'Pretty Polly', but she does not know
that she is being narcissistic as she does so. But imitation is never an entirely
straightforward concept. At least one experimental psychologist has believed
that at least one parrot, called Alex, was what we call a language user rather
than a parroter. Alex was said to be able to pick out a red piece of leather
when asked to do so, and, it was claimed, could generalize the concept 'red'.
He was also, much more contentiously, claimed to have the concept of
wanting.[4] He did have reassuringly bird-like aspects, however: apparently he
was better able to recognize objects after he had chewed them.[5] Alex has
been seen as an exceptional bird (and the claim that he was 'properly' a
language user has been often challenged), but he has an extensive genealogy.
A widely discussed passage in John Locke's *Essay Concerning Human
Understanding* (to which I return in Chapter 10) describes a prodigious
parrot which Sir William Temple said could conduct conversations in
perfect Brazilian. It said 'Lord, what a company of white men are here'
when it met Prince Maurice of Nassau. Locke said this was 'sufficient to
countenance the supposition of a rational parrot', although the evidence
from Temple's memoir involved a translator who glossed the parrot's words,
and the parrot seemed rather suspiciously Polly-lingual.[6]

   That anecdote illustrates two of the central questions about imitation.
When does an imitator become an understander? And how does one distinguish an imitation of a piece of behaviour from a performance by an
autonomous practitioner of an achieved skill? How do we know that Polly
does not know that she is pretty, or mean 'red' when she says 'red'? In the
Doctor Doolittle books there is a parrot called Polynesia, who is the wisest
and most thoughtful character in a world in which we are allowed to
imagine that it is possible to talk to the animals. In the days when my
children were young enough not to be plugged into headphones in the car
we all listened to Alan Bennett read one of the Doctor Doolittle books on
tape. He quite clearly, or so it seemed to me, imitated Polynesia in the voice
of Dame Edna Everidge. So a clever parrot came to be not just a mimic of
human sounds, but a sophisticated speaker whose voice was then mimicked
by an actor mimicking a very clever mimic. This is the kind of *mise en abyme*

4. Irene M. Pepperberg, *The Alex Studies: Cognitive and Communicative Abilities of Grey Parrots*
   (Cambridge, Mass., and London, 1999).
5. Pepperberg, *The Alex Studies*, p. 47.
6. John Locke, *An Essay Concerning Human Understanding*, ed. P. H. Nidditch (Oxford, 1975), p. 333.
   See pp. 376–7 in this volume for the philosophical implications of this parrot.

which imitation tends to create, where a question—what is it to understand a language rather than simply to repeat a set of sounds?—generates around it a set of echoes which prevent the question quite being heard, let alone answered. And as for Ben Jonson, do we call his imitation of Catullus in *Volpone* an imitation rather than a translation, and if so, why do we do so? Where does imitation begin and end?

The word 'imitation' is used to describe a whole spectrum of ways in which the productions of human agency resemble the world—painting, poetry, drama, papier mâché, and plastic artefacts could all be said to imitate something outside themselves. The word is also used today of a variety of social, commercial, and cognitive processes. A generation of philosophers and experimental psychologists (notable among them the late Susan Hurley) has given the word 'imitation' further resonances, positioning imitative behaviour at the centre of our processes of learning, of our interpersonal lives, and of our ability to read the minds and intentions of others.[7] Experimental studies have suggested that when a macaque monkey sees another monkey performing a particular activity, 'mirror neurons' in its brain fire up as though the observer monkey is performing the activity it watches—although some experimental psychologists wisely insist that analogous reactions in humans are likely to be products of complex pro-cesses of acculturation.[8] Are we, an imitative species, able to understand others and learn from others because we too have these 'mirror neurons', which hard-wire imitative behaviour into our brains, and which give us an internal sense of what another being is experiencing when we see them performing an action or displaying a gesture of pain? Do these neurons play a part in core aspects of human social evolution, such as mutual instruction, tool use, the ability to read other minds, and language acquisition?

These studies, inconclusive as they appear to be, have done much to reinvigorate interest in a wide range of imitative acts or processes. That is, the word 'imitation' is presently being used in explanations of how human beings and higher primates learn and communicate, and in explorations of

7. S. L. Hurley and Nick Chater, eds., *Perspectives on Imitation: From Neuroscience to Social Science*, 2 vols. (Cambridge, Mass., and London, 2005).

8. Michael A. Arbib, *From Action to Language: The Mirror Neuron System* (Cambridge, 2006), p. 3. See Marco Iacoboni, Jonas Kaplan, and Stephen Wilson, 'A Neural Architecture for Imitation and Intentional Relations', in Chrystopher L. Nehaniv and Kerstin Dautenhahn, eds., *Imitation and Social Learning in Robots, Humans and Animals: Behavioural, Social and Communicative Dimensions* (Cambridge, 2007), pp. 71–87, and Celia Heyes and Geoffrey Bird, 'Correspondence Problem and Mechanisms—Imitation: Thoughts about Theories', in ibid., pp. 23–34, as well as the wide-ranging discussion in Cecilia Heyes, *Cognitive Gadgets: The Cultural Evolution of Thinking* (Cambridge, Mass., and London, 2018), pp. 116–43.

how human beings respond to the emotions of others. However, our language in this area remains extremely slippery. While imitation as process is moving towards the centre of our sense of what it is to be a learning, social animal, uses of the word to describe an object or an outcome still carry a strong negative charge. We call perfumes or handbags 'imitations' or 'fakes' when they proclaim themselves to be Givenchy but have not been made in the authentic sweatshop where the 'real thing' is made. There has been a small wave of attempts recently to defend the idea of imitating or copying within commercial and artistic contexts,[9] but these have not dispelled the popular and post-Romantic suspicion that there is something intrinsically inauthentic, 'unoriginal', and perhaps even illegal or plagiaristic about things called imitations. And that fear of inauthenticity carries across to imitation as process: no one would say that when they grow up they want to parrot their teachers. We might talk instead of 'role models' or people who represent generic patterns of achievement— becoming the first woman Speaker of the House of Commons—that we wish to emulate.

Studies of 'imitation' by experimental psychologists tend to focus on the behaviour of children rather than adults, and some of these experimental findings provide striking evidence that we are an imitative species. Infants as young as 42 minutes have been said to be able to imitate gestures and expressions they see—though this claim has been decisively contradicted by more recent experimental work.[10] Experimental psychologists routinely distinguish 'imitation' of this kind, which entails gestural replication, from 'emulation', in which an imitator grasps the purpose of the task which they are witnessing and seeks to achieve that end rather than imitating accidental gestures which do not contribute to that task. It has been claimed that human children are more prone than infant chimpanzees to engage in what is called 'over-imitation': that is they will adopt inessential sub-routines of a task they are set to imitate. The fact that such studies focus on children is a consequence of what may or may not be an illusory belief that it is possible to exclude the influence of other learnt behaviours from observations of

9. Marcus Boon, *In Praise of Copying* (Cambridge, Mass., 2010); Marjorie Perloff, *Unoriginal Genius: Poetry by Other Means in the New Century* (Chicago, Ill., and London, 2010).

10. Alvin I. Goldman, 'Imitation, Mind Reading, and Simulation', in S. L. Hurley and Nick Chater, eds., *Perspectives on Imitation: From Neuroscience to Social Science*, 2 vols. (Cambridge, Mass., and London, 2005), 2.79–93 at p. 81. For the counter-case, see Heyes, *Cognitive Gadgets*, p. 128.

newly-born children as one could not if investigating the behaviour of adults. It also may reflect a deep-seated cultural tendency to associate imitative behaviour with immature or not-quite autonomous 'adult' behaviour: we are prone to believe that children and perhaps some animals 'imitate', while adults do something different.

It is tempting to play the analytic philosopher here and say by 'imitation' we mean too many things and that what we really need to do is to slice through the confusions with a fine edge of distinction. However I very much do not want to do that. 'Imitation' is an important concept because it is one which has never been completely broken down into its constituent elements. It is a revealing way into human and literary history *because* it is so unruly. This book is concerned chiefly with what is sometimes called 'the imitation of artists' or the imitation of one author by another, or *imitatio*. This subject cannot be hermetically sealed off from other kinds of imitation. From the earliest surviving usages the vocabulary associated with 'imitation' and related terms tends to combine several different senses. Those combinations of senses may well tell us as much about what we are as language users and human beings as the efforts of experimentalists and philosophers to tease out the separate filaments of mind and sense. The theory and practice of literary imitation repeatedly raises wider questions—about how we learn practices from others, about how we learn languages, about how we understand the emotions or characters of another person, about how we grasp a style or a way of writing.

This first chapter explores the origins of the idea of literary imitation. It presents some detailed philological investigation, the principal aim of which is to break down a fairly widespread narrative about the origins of *imitatio*, the imitation of texts. According to this narrative, the idea of *imitatio* as a practice whereby one author learns from and imitates another develops relatively late in the literary tradition, and effectively has its origins in rhetorical theory and practice. That narrative is not absolutely false, but it is over-simplified. The earliest usages of the word *mimēsis* and its related verb (the words which are the roots of our verb to 'imitate') have been written about extensively before, but on the whole from the perspective of that other kind of *mimēsis*, the imitation of reality in art. What might a close look at those early usages tell us about *imitatio* or the imitation of texts? My argument will be that there is a continual and close interaction between *mimēsis* as the imitation of things or events in the world and *mimēsis* in the sense of the imitation of texts and authors.

Early uses of '*mimēsis*'

Gerald Else, in an influential essay on the history of the word *mimēsis*, has related it to *mimoi*, mimes. He locates its roots in a theatrical conception of mimicry, which might sometimes convey deception or disguise.[11] Homer uses no form of the word, which seems almost certainly to have entered the Ionic-Attic dialect from Dorian origins along with a wave of abstract terms with a philosophical heritage ending in *-sis*.[12] Else suggests that the *mimēsis* word-group gradually migrates from theatrical senses—enacting in gesture and mime—to include representation, and thence it takes on what he terms a rather colourless sense of 'to do as another person does'.[13]

There is a beguiling persuasive kind of philological history here: imitation begins on the stage, with a tightly circumscribed cultural practice—mimicry by actors—and is gradually generalized outwards to more abstract senses. That history has the scent of fabrication to it, of a belief that there is simple equation between abstraction and lateness and sophistication of sense. Else's idealized history of *mimēsis* has been criticized by Stephen Halliwell, who finds much more range and a much less clear historical progression in the use of this word-group than Else.[14]

Two points might be added to this story, both of which endorse Halliwell's opinion that *mimēsis* is extremely complex in sense from its earliest recorded occurrences. The first is a very simple observation. The sense-range in early uses of the word *mimēsis* and its cognates appears to be determined at least as much by genre as it is by chronology. So usages in Pindar's odes are almost all linked to representation of actions through music and dance because music and dance matter for odes.[15] In Aristophanes, as we shall see, usages of the word *mimēsis* tend to imply mimicry or theatricality. This is probably what you would expect in a play.

The second point is less self-evident. If the early usages of the word *mimēsis* are looked at from the viewpoint of someone investigating the history of *imitatio*, of how texts imitate other texts, some of them look rather

---

11. Gerald F. Else, 'Imitation in the Fifth Century', *Classical Philology* 53 (1958), 73–90; his view is broadly endorsed by Andrew Laughlin Ford, *The Origins of Criticism: Literary Culture and Poetic Theory in Classical Greece* (Princeton, 2002), pp. 93–6.
12. Else, 'Imitation in the Fifth Century', pp. 78, 86.
13. Else, 'Imitation in the Fifth Century', p. 82.
14. Stephen Halliwell, *The Aesthetics of Mimesis: Ancient Texts and Modern Problems* (Princeton, 2002). I am greatly indebted to this superb study.
15. See *Pythian* 12.21, Frag. 94b l.15, Frag. 107a.

more self-conscious and complex than they do if they are positioned within a history of arguments about how artworks represent reality. That is a rather knotty way of saying that literary genealogists like to believe that the imitation of authors is a late and sophisticated development which emerges out of the earlier and more straightforward concept that literature imitates reality. That claim giddily rotates in a hermeneutic circle. If you believe imitation of reality precedes imitation of texts the evidence appears to support that belief. But the imitation of texts and of the world are not simply separable, and, within the textual record, it is impossible to be sure which comes first. This dense and difficult passage of Theognis, from around the fifth century BC illustrates the point:

> οὐ δύναμαι γνῶναι νόον ἀστῶν ὅντιν᾽ἔχουσιν·
> οὔτε γὰρ εὖ ἔρδων ἀνδάνω οὔτε κακῶς·
> μωμεῦνται δέ με πολλοί, ὁμῶς κακοὶ ἠδὲ καὶ ἐσθλοί·
> μιμεῖσθαι δ᾽ οὐδεὶς τῶν ἀσόφων δύναται.   (367–70)

I can't understand the city's attitude: they're hostile whether I do right or wrong. Yes, plenty criticize me, both good men and base, but not one of the fools can match my style (*mimeisthai*).[16]

Commentators note the pun here on *mōmeuntai* and *mimeisthai*: everyone can criticize the poet but none of the unwise can imitate him. Else passes quickly over this example because of the uncertainties surrounding the chronology and authorship of the corpus ascribed to Theognis. There may be good reason for doing so, but doing so is also suspiciously convenient, because the passage clearly does not fit Else's historical argument that early usages of the word are theatrical in force. Theognis says 'No one is able to imitate me'. That is clearly not a theatrical usage. Given the implied civic context of the extract it could be a claim to singular political virtue, but it could also convey a claim to singular poetic skill: I am inimitable, in a literary sense.[17] Literary historians tend to exclude that sense for reasons that have a suspicious resemblance to a *petitio principii*: Theognis is assumed to be early, therefore he cannot be interested in literary imitation, which is a secondary

16. Translation from M. L. West, ed., *Greek Lyric Poetry* (Oxford, 1993), p. 70; text from M. L. West, ed., *Iambi et Elegi Graeci ante Alexandrum Cantati*, 2 vols. (Oxford, 1989), 1.192.
17. Halliwell, *Aesthetics of Mimesis*, p. 15 resists the claims of Gregory Nagy, 'Early Greek Views of Poets and Poetry', in George A. Kennedy, ed., *The Cambridge History of Literary Criticism: Volume 1, Classical Criticism* (Cambridge, 1989), 1–77, p. 48, that the passage refers to poetic re-enactment; he sees it instead as a piece about behavioural re-enactment. It is hard to see any grounds for this beyond Halliwell's belief that imitation of an author is subsequent to and derivative from the notion of ethical emulation.

or belated activity; if this passage shows signs of being interested in literary imitation it must therefore be late.[18] We might also note that the verb *mimeisthai* is in the infinitive and is governed by a word meaning 'be able'. The carping critics are not able to imitate him. This could well be important. For Theognis imitating is not what macaque monkeys are said instinctively to do when they see one of their species crack a nut. It is associated with skill, with possessing or lacking a quite specific *technē*. It also here is associated with how one is situated within a larger state or community of critics and potential rivals.

With these points in mind, let us inch forwards, so far as the chronology can be determined, to the Homeric *Hymn to Apollo*. Here the relevant passage, which has also been much debated, comes from the first part of the hymn, known as the Delian part, which probably dates from around 586 BC. The poet is talking about the Delian maidens, who are exceptionally skilled in *mimēsis*:

> μνησάμεναι ἀνδρῶν τε παλαιῶν ἠδὲ γυναικῶν
> ὕμνον ἀείδουσιν, θέλγουσι δὲ φῦλ' ἀνθρώπων.
> πάντων δ' ἀνθρώπων φωνὰς καὶ κρεμβαλιαστὺν
> μιμεῖσθ' ἴσασιν· φαίη δέ κεν αὐτὸς ἕκαστος
> φθέγγεσθ'· οὕτω σφιν καλὴ συνάρηρεν ἀοιδή   (160–4)[19]

They remember men and women of old and they sing a hymn, and they charm the tribe of men. They know how to imitate the voices [possibly 'accents'] of all men and their rattling with castanets [or in other texts the onomatopoeic word *bambaliastun*, which means stammering or babble], and anyone might think it was he himself speaking, so well is their song constructed.[20]

This is a passage of high-self-consciousness. It cannot be taken as evidence that early uses of the verb *mimeisthai* were simply associated with theatrical representation.[21] There is a clear attempt to incorporate echoic mimeticism into a passage about aural mimeticism with the noun *krembaliastun*, or, in

---

18. For a dating of the Theognidea to 640–479 BC, see Thomas J. Figueira and Gregory Nagy, eds., *Theognis of Megara: Poetry and the Polis* (Baltimore, 1985), p. 1.

19. Text from N. J. Richardson, ed., *Three Homeric Hymns: To Apollo, Hermes, and Aphrodite, Hymns 3, 4, and 5* (Cambridge, 2010).

20. Translation from M. L. West, ed., *Homeric Hymns, Homeric Apocrypha, Lives of Homer* (Cambridge, Mass., and London, 2003).

21. Richard Janko, *Homer, Hesiod, and the Hymns: Diachronic Development in Epic Diction* (Cambridge, 1982), p. 105: 'This root is not otherwise attested (except for Theognis 370) until Pindar and Aeschylus, and ... may indicate a cultural change that postdates Homer.'

other texts, *bambaliastun*.[22] Because the passage is so early—because, remember, 'early' means 'prior to the terrible sophistications brought about by literary criticism and other wicked tools of cultural complexity'—critics have been reluctant to recognize how strange it is. The act of imitating presses on the bounds of personal identity: the imitation is so good that people think they themselves are speaking. Are the women imitating the sounds of a crowd or the vocal mannerisms of particular individuals, or the dialects of particular groups? Or perhaps in the act of imitation this distinction between individual and collective voice collapses?[23]

The urge to disambiguate this passage extends to even the most sophisticated commentators. Alexander Nehamas argues that the earliest senses of *mimeisthai* are principally associated with speech and behaviour rather than with pictorial representation, and that its primary sense is to 'act like' someone, without a connotation of either mimicry or of moral deception.[24] That claim is extremely plausible in its general outlines, but it downplays the evident vitality and range of the word in its earliest usages. It is hard to believe that the author of the Delian *Hymn to Apollo*, the unnamed rhapsode, is not also at some level reflecting on his own relation to Homer: the women, in recalling men and women of old, are doing what he is himself doing or about to do in reciting a passage from the Homeric poems. And the rhapsode himself is of course composing a poem in a style which is full of Homeric echoes, as they are now called, and so his voice is only partially distinguishable from that of Homer.[25] Remarkably enough, this passage precedes the ending of what is generally regarded as the 'Delian' section of the hymn, which concludes with an appeal to the maidens in the voice of the poet himself. He is blind, and asks the maidens to remember him in future, and name him as their favourite poet. It seems reasonable to agree with Richard Janko that this is an attempt at a self-portrait-by-proxy of

22. See Halliwell, *Aesthetics of Mimesis*, p. 18; Alexander Nehamas, *Virtues of Authenticity: Essays on Plato and Socrates* (Princeton, 1999), p. 258; for the reading *bambaliastun*, see Stephen C. Colvin, *Dialect in Aristophanes: and The Politics of Language in Ancient Greek Literature* (Oxford, 1999), pp. 46–7.

23. Cf. the description in Seneca's 84th Epistle comparing imitation to the blending of multiple voices in the choir, discussed on pp. 86–7 in this volume.

24. Nehamas, *Virtues of Authenticity*, pp. 258–9.

25. The maidens are described as 'charming' (*thelgousi*) their audience. The same verb is used twice in Eumaeus's description of the disguised Odysseus (17.514, 521), who is compared to a minstrel performing in his hall 'charming' those who listen. This association may be significant in a context in which a poet is pretending to be Homer. See Andrew M. Miller, *From Delos to Delphi: A Literary Study of the Homeric Hymn to Apollo* (Leiden, 1986), p. 59.

Homer himself. Janko also may well be right to suppose that the poem was composed by one of the Homeridae at Chios.[26]

Whatever its precise sense in these early usages, the verb *mimeisthai* tends to trigger or accompany reflections about how individuals relate to others, to a contemporary crowd, as well as to the past, and to poetic traditions. And this is a usage, we should recall, from the sixth century BC. This passage also should put pressure on the comfortable narrative that is sometimes trotted out to the effect that the rhapsodes of the Hymns thought of themselves as 'part of a Homeric tradition', and that there is some distinction between 'being part of a tradition' and being an imitator—the latter being later, probably Alexandrian, and probably also somehow inferior to unreflective and instinctive immersion in a continuous oral tradition, which is healthy because unselfconscious and *völkisch*. There is nothing primal about this passage at all: it is pulling together the senses of *mimēsis* in an extraordinarily suggestive way. Aural *mimēsis* combines with literary *imitatio*. It is also worth pausing over the fact that the verb *mimeisthai* is again in the infinitive: the women do not just instinctively parrot. They know (*isasin*) how to imitate. *Mimēsis* is (as it is implicitly in Theognis, too) a craft, a *technē*; and it is already a craft which creates uncertain relationships between archetype and imitation, and between self and other.

Greek drama

Given what I have said about the interrelationship between how *mimēsis*-related words are used and the genre in which they appear, it is perhaps unsurprising that the earliest uses of *mimēsis* and related verbs in the surviving corpus of Greek drama tend to associate it with disguise and vocal mimicry. Orestes tells Pylades that they must imitate or put on the accent of the Phocians when they return home in Aeschylus's *Choephoroi* (450 BC; 1. 564). It does not appear to be until 412 BC, however, that dramatists unequivocally blend the vocal-mimetic usage of *mimēsis* with the theory and practice of

26. Janko, *Homer, Hesiod, and the Hymns*, p. 115: 'The pious fraud is at once comprehensible, indeed familiar, in an oral tradition, where poets may claim to be singing the song of a great predecessor, while altering that predecessor's song substantially during free oral recomposition-in-performance. In Chios, a close-knit guild of followers and descendants endeavoured to preserve the deeds and poems of their founder; so, in this Hymn, the honoured bard is surely Homer, and it is one of the Homeridae of Chios who bestows on him the praise which he deserved, but would surely have hesitated to utter himself.'

textual imitation. The crucial surviving text is Euripides's *Helen* of 412. This play has the premise that the Trojan War was fought not over the real Helen, but over a thing variously called a *mimēma* or *eidōlon* of her, which was present at Troy while the real Helen was in fact chastely in Egypt. Helen was of course one of the earliest vocal mimics in Greek literature: she is described by Menelaus in *Odyssey* 4.279 as circling the Trojan horse calling out the names of the Greek heroes 'likening (*iskous'*) your voice to the voices of all the wives of the Argives'.[27] The word *mimēsis* and its related verbs are never used by Homer, as we have seen, and the verb used of the Homeric Helen's imitative skill is *iskō*, 'to make like'. In this Homeric passage, interestingly enough, even the concept of vocal *mimēsis* is sufficient to unsettle commentators and make them suspect that the line was an interpolation by a later writer. The description of Helen as mimic was objected to by the scholiast and may have been athetized by Aristarchus.[28] Is mimicry late or is it just believed to be late because of a very long-standing belief that imitation is intrinsically secondary? Euripides's *mimēma*-Helen also grows from two phantasms in Homer: that of Aineas (*Iliad*, 5.445–53), and perhaps also the appearance to Penelope of Iphthime (*Odyssey*, 4.795–801). The *Helen* as a whole is also some species of intervention in the idea of literary history, where a false creature, who, as it were, is and is not Helen, is positioned at the heart of the central events of the Homeric poems. Does the presence of this *mimēma* make the heroic tradition into a kind of ghostly charade?

In the year following Euripides's *Helen* Aristophanes wrote *Thesmophoriazusae*, probably for the City Dionysia.[29] This play brings Euripides himself, or at least a *mimēma* of him, onstage. It also repeatedly quotes words written by Euripides and, as we now say, parodies his style. *Thesmophoriazusae* is sometimes represented as a simple conservative attack on Euripides. That is a simplification.[30] The play strongly suggests that Aristophanes was drawn to

27. The verb *iskō* can in later verse mean simply 'say', but in the *Odyssey* it can connote moral unease: at 19.203 Odysseus 'made the many falsehoods of his tale seem (*iske*) like the truth'. Homer's Helen is a mistress of likenesses: rather than simply recognizing Telemachus at 4.141–6 she says that she has never seen anyone who looks as much like Telemachus as this young man.

28. Alfred Heubeck, Stephanie West, J. B. Hainsworth, Joseph A. Russo, and Manuel Fernández-Galiano, eds., *A Commentary on Homer's Odyssey*, 3 vols. (Oxford, 1988), 1.211. Her imitation of the voices is described as 'laughable' and 'impossible' by the scholiast, and editors sometimes suggest that the line is a later interpolation.

29. For the possibility it was staged at the Lenaia of 411, see Aristophanes, *Thesmophoriazusae*, ed. Colin Austin and S. Douglas Olson (Oxford, 2004), pp. xli–xliv.

30. M. S. Silk, *Aristophanes and the Definition of Comedy* (Oxford, 2000), p. 52, is more considered: 'Aristophanes is never hostile to Euripides *tout court*, but is content to seem ambivalent about the great tragedian's experiments.'

Euripides's recent experiments with the concept of *mimēsis* in the *Helen*, and by an awareness of its potential for mischief. Aristophanes' Euripides is accused of misogyny by the council of women at the festival of Thesmophoria. The playwright needs someone to pretend to be a woman in order to go among the council and defend him against these charges. Euripides initially chooses as his brief the outrageously camp playwright Agathon, who is rolled onto the stage on the *ekkuklēma*, or rolling trolley, in highly effeminate dress. Agathon is a full-body imitator. He declares that 'To be a poet, a man must suit his behaviour to the requirements of his plays. If, say, he's writing plays about women, his body must partake of women's behaviour' (149–52), and continues by saying 'Qualities which we do not have must be sought by *mimēsis*' ('ha d'ou kektēmetha, | mimēsis ēdē tauta sunthēreuetai', 155–6).[31] The context of these remarks—uttered onstage by a satirical portrait of a dramatist who is tagged as effeminate—suggests that by 411 BC the word *mimēsis* was being used by playwrights in theoretical justifications of their art, and that Aristophanes was sending up a particular school of thought which does not survive except through his parody.[32] The Loeb translator reasonably enough renders *mimēsis* in the passage just quoted by 'mimicry', but on Agathon's honeyed lips the word becomes richer than that. It is a kind of mimicry which transforms the body and the person. It is not a single specific skill at catching a mannerism or representing someone else's speaking voice. Euripides's sidekick, called the Kinsman, gets the idea of this super-literal form of imitation when he says 'let me know when you're writing about satyrs; I'll get behind you with my hard-on and tell you how to do it' (157–8). Writing plays, Agathon suggests, depends on behavioural *mimēsis* and that kind of *mimēsis* is self-transformational. The kinsman's comic phallus nails that self-transformation to some kind of reality, and associates it with not quite being an adult male: *mimēsis* turns men to women, or at the very least into passively homosexual men. The association between imitation and childishness or not quite perfect maleness runs very deep in Western literature: Helen, Agathon, even the Delian maidens, are doing things that make men feel a little uneasy about themselves.

31. Text and quotations from *Aristophanes*, trans. Jeffrey Henderson, 5 vols. (Cambridge, Mass., and London, 1998).
32. Douglas M. MacDowell, *Aristophanes and Athens: An Introduction to the Plays* (Oxford, 1995), p. 256: 'Probably Aristophanes is mocking a theory that someone had actually propounded, arguing that a dramatist by physical imitation could feel his way into a character's natural speech and behaviour; there is, however, no other evidence for this theory in Aristophanes' time.' A similar notion of *mimēsis* is apparent in Aristophanes' *Acharnians*, 410–13: Euripides writes about beggars because he prefers to wear ragged clothes himself.

Thesmophoriazusae 'imitates' Euripides in various ways, and perhaps part of the joke of the play is its unsettling multiplication of different kinds of imitation: Aristophanes gives us a *mimēma* of the playwright onstage, whose voice repeatedly pastiches Euripidean phrases. He also directly imitates scenes from Euripides's lost *Telephos*, as well as from his *Andromeda* and his *Helen*, both of which had been staged the year before *Thesmophoriazusae* in 412.[33] When Euripides's kinsman is captured by the women he tries to use tactics imitated from Euripides's plays in order to escape. He says 'I will imitate the new Helen' ('*tēn kainēn Helenēn mimēsomai*', 850)—a phrase which is finely poised: it could mean both 'I will pretend to be the new Helen (the character)' and (primarily) 'I will mimic that recent play called *Helen*'.[34] He does both: he dresses up as Helen and he also quotes from Euripides's play (855–919). Euripides himself then enters pretending to be Menelaus from his own play, but entirely fails to perform a heroic rescue—despite making some fine speeches, which are imitated, of course, from Euripides. This is a paradigmatic example of what was to become in later literary tradition a basic feature of parodic imitation: extremely close verbal replication is combined with the complete neglect of the narrative context and effects of the words replicated. Direct textual replication is accompanied by clear higher level textual signals that the intent in replication is not simple theft or appropriation, but critical mockery.

In this gloriously comical way Aristophanes delivers a one-two to *mimēsis*. The biggest joke of the play is the boundless inconsistency of its implied argument, which is chiefly constructed so as to make sure that a poet committed to *mimēsis* loses both ways. Theatrical mimicry has a sudden and radical effect on personal identity: dress up as a girl and you become womanish.[35] Imitate a satyr and you end up buggering or being buggered by the person in front of or behind you. The only way imitation moves is (in Greek terms) down: the arts of travesty and transvestism teach you no kind of skill, because if you try to imitate the words of an onstage hero you do not suddenly acquire the ability to do the same deeds that he performed. As a result Aristophanes

---

33. Aristophanes, ed. Austin and Olson, *Thesmophoriazusae*, pp. xxxiii–xxxvi; lvi–lxiv.
34. Aristophanes may call Euripides's version of the myth 'new' in order to associate Euripides with dangerous novelty: see Euripides, *Helen*, ed. William Allan (Cambridge, 2008), p. 67.
35. Silk, *Aristophanes*, p. 243: 'It is a sufficient, though not a necessary condition of recreative figuration that it should involve figures whose external condition is decisive for their being. It follows that if such figures are disguised, they change…hence the wonderful repeated joke in the second half of *Thesmophoriazusae*, that by appearing to be Menelaus, Euripides can rescue Mnesilochus, if Mnesilochus appears to be Helen.'

implies that imitation is hyper-effective in its sexually degenerative effects but entirely ineffective as a means of practical self-elevation. A playwright pretending to be a girl does indeed become effeminate, but a playwright dressed up as a mythical hero and voicing the words of a stage hero does not acquire the powers of that hero, but becomes instead a textual imitation of heroism which has no practical effect.

Aristophanes also conjoins *mimēsis*-as-gestural-replication with *mimēsis*-as-textual-imitation much more forcefully, and perhaps with much more deliberate artistry, than any surviving earlier author. An attempt to use a direct literary imitation of a tragedy as a means of resolving a practical problem becomes parody of a tragedy, because obviously it is impossible to learn how to act like Menelaus by writing as though you are Menelaus or by reciting words put into the mouth of a fictional Menelaus by a playwright. *Mimēsis* as a result becomes a glorious comic mess. It is psychologically transformative but ethically and practically useless. It leads to transpositions across genres and across space and time in ways that destabilize tone and intent, and is strongly linked with movements between genders in directions that are typically unmanly. Aristophanes is not crudely attacking Euripides, but is liberating the comic potential which underlies Euripides's methods of literary allusion in the *Helen*. And the joke on *mimēsis* goes all the way down: *mimēsis* of an author cannot even be really degenerative, because otherwise Aristophanes in imitating Euripides would be becoming Euripides, and would be sharing his vices rather than displaying them for mockery. His comical recreation of Euripides-as-character is a clear sign that Aristophanes has not in any simple sense *become* Euripides-as-author. It is other imitators apart from him who are contaminated by imitating. A playwright can imitate another playwright without succumbing to his vices, provided he does it to render him absurd.

Plato

There is a particularly strong reason for dwelling on the literary events of 412–411 BC. At that date a young Athenian called Plato was about sixteen years old. He was probably too young to attend the city Dionysia even as an ephebe, but he was old enough to hear about or to read the onstage debates. These plays clearly circulated in written form: Aristophanes' particular kind of intimate parody is dependent on access to a written text of Euripides, rather than just memory of his words.[36] Whether read or witnessed, or just absorbed second-hand, Aristophanes' comic *mimēsis* of *mimēsis* in action had a profound influence on Plato, and through him on the entire subsequent history of literary imitation. Indeed conventional literary histories that begin arguments about imitation with Plato should take a step backwards and begin the story with Aristophanes: Aristophanes and Agathon, of course, both appear, more or less affectionately presented, in Plato's *Symposium*, which is set at the house of Agathon. It is possible that Aristophanic comedy provided Plato with his first serious engagement with the word *mimēsis*, and the word is there associated with sodomy, with emasculated males, and with parodic imitations of Euripides.

That presents a slightly new way of gripping the prickliest and hoariest literary-critical chestnut of all time. Why did Plato banish the poets from his ideal commonwealth? Why was he so uneasy, and perhaps confused, about the mimetic arts generally? Given the heritage of the word *mimēsis* it is not surprising that Plato should have felt the Guardians of his republic should minimize their exposure to mimetic art of all kinds. Plato's treatment of *mimēsis* in the *Republic* is of course one of the most contentious and complex aspects of his philosophy. Plato discusses *mimēsis* in Books 2–3 of the *Republic* and again in Book 10. Scholars argue over the compatibility of his arguments at these different points, over the meanings of *mimēsis* for Plato, and over whether he banishes all poets from his ideal republic, or only poets who indulge in *mimēsis*, or only poets who indulge in *mimēsis* of vicious behaviour.[37] Stephen Halliwell, in the most perceptive study of the topic, has rightly suggested that for Plato the meaning of *mimēsis* is 'fluctuating and constantly revised', and that is certainly true.[38]

There is no room here for a discussion of Plato's arguments about how art does or does not imitate reality, but the crucial part of *The Republic* so far as the history of *imitatio*, or the imitation of authors by other authors, is concerned is the passage in Book 3 in which Plato discusses *lexis*, or diction. In this section he makes a very influential distinction between *mimēsis* and

---

36. Euripides, ed. Allan, *Helen*, p. 83.
37. The best starting-point is Halliwell, *Aesthetics of Mimesis*; see also M. F. Burnyeat, 'Culture and Society in Plato's *Republic*', *Tanner Lectures in Human Values* 20 (1999), 215–324, Nehamas, *Virtues of Authenticity*, 'Plato on Imitation and Poetry in *Republic* X', pp. 251–78, J. Tate, '"Imitation" in Plato's *Republic*', *Classical Quarterly* 22 (1928), 16–23, J. Tate, 'Plato and "Imitation"', *Classical Quarterly* 26 (1932), 161–9. See also the clear account in Christopher Janaway, *Images of Excellence: Plato's Critique of the Arts* (Oxford, 1995), pp. 106–57.
38. Halliwell, *Aesthetics of Mimesis*, p. 38.

diegēsis. Mimēsis in this context means the representation by a poet of a
person through direct speech—Agamemnon talking, or perhaps even a
character called Euripides talking. *Diegēsis* is narrative in the poet's own
voice (392c–395b).[39] For Plato in this passage *mimēsis* entails assimilating the
poet's own lexis to that of the person represented, as well as taking on what
he terms the voice or accent, *phonē*, and appearance, *schēma*, of the person
imitated (393c). It also risks taking on his vices.

Plato's distinction between *mimēsis* and *diegēsis* may well have been a
response to the conventions and language of Greek comedy. A running joke
in Aristophanes' representations of Euripides is that theatrical *mimēsis* is
absolute and unprovisional, and ascends or descends directly to the author's
behaviour: Euripides wrote about characters who wore rags so he wore rags.
The idea that imitating a person's appearance or *schēma* may have ethical
consequences is also an element in comic drama. At one point in Aristophanes'
Frogs (405 BC, l. 462) Xanthias tells Dionysus, who is dressed like Hercules in
order to enable him to undergo his *katabasis*, to knock at the door of the
underworld and show 'Heracles' guts as well as his garb (*schēma*)'—that is, do
more than simply display his *schēma*, his mere outward appearance.

The distinction between *mimēsis* and *diegēsis* is perhaps designed to create
a form of literary presentation which is ethically safe: *diegēsis* allows for the
description of virtuous actions without any risk of adopting the voice or
ethos of an inferior or wicked person. The distinction appears not to have
been explicitly made by Plato before the *Republic*, and it is not one that he
finds it easy to sustain in practice in his own highly theatrical dialogues. The
dialogue of the *Symposium*—which of course consists of an artful *mimēsis*
of different voices, of Socrates, of Agathon the playwright, of Aristophanes
the comedian, and in which 'it is remarkable how many of the speeches . . . contain elements of parody'[40]—is introduced with the verb *diēgēsasthai* (174a). It
is as though Plato is attempting to present his dialogues as the narration
(*diegēsis*) of mimetically represented voices, and thereby insulate himself
from contamination by the process of mimetically representing voices
within the dialogue. But that distinction proves very permeable: when
Socrates, who claims he lacks the encomiastic skill to present a speech in
praise of love, relates a *mimēsis* of the voice of Diotima he blurs the divide
between *mimēsis* and *diegēsis* by having Diotima allude to the myth of the

39. References to and translations from Plato, *The Republic*, trans. Paul Shorey, 2 vols. (Cambridge,
    Mass., 1930).
40. Nehamas, *Virtues of Authenticity*, p. 307.

hermaphroditic origin of mankind, which Diotima, whose voice he is merely imitating, could not have heard because she is not actually present (204d–e).

However, after attempting to give a firmer foundation to the porous distinction between *mimēsis* and *diegēsis* in *The Republic*, Plato asks the question whether we should allow poets to imitate at all. His answer is that his guardians should be men who excel in the single skill of governing, rather than people who possess multiple abilities. They should therefore not write literature themselves and should only imitate good and pious men. For, Socrates says, 'have you not observed that imitations, if continued from youth far into life, settle down into habits (*ethē*) and (second) nature in the body, the speech, and the thought? ... We will not then allow our charges, whom we expect to prove good men, being men, to play the parts of women and imitate a woman young or old wrangling with her husband, defying heaven, loudly boasting' (395d). Philosophically speaking this is the nub of Plato's discussion of *mimēsis* as distinct from *diegēsis*, and it is reasonable to regard it as the centre of Plato's ethical objection to theatre. It perhaps also motivates his more metaphysical attack on *mimēsis* in Book 10: the supersensible ideas which are presented as the true objects of imitation in the later book are at least in part an attempt to stabilize the dangerous plurality of the word *mimēsis* by providing an ontologically secure entity the imitation of which might be intrinsically good.

Certainly the argument in Book 3 seems constantly to slide beyond its immediate occasion. The argument here addresses the imitation of style, or *lexis*, in the *mimēsis* of a particular character. And yet for Plato the imitation of the *lexis* of a woman or a madman, or (he goes on) smiths or neighing horses becomes habit, and that habit becomes in turn morally degenerative. As Halliwell has noted, part of the context of Plato's argument is the immersive nature of Greek musical and literary art. Plato does not think audiences just watch; he believes that they participate emotionally in the performance.[41] Hence witnessing a *mimēsis* of a woman weeping might be expected to produce womanishness in the same way that writing in the voice of a woman or pretending to be a woman might do—as when Odysseus weeps like a woman in a sacked city when he hears Demodocus sing about the fall of Troy in the *Odyssey* (8.521–34). That is a good historical justification of Plato's argument. But contextualizing it in this way also suggests that this

---

41. Halliwell, *Aesthetics of Mimesis*, p. 52.

part of Plato's argument is less than fully rational. Underlying it is the Aristophanic model of imitation as potentially degenerative.

Socrates's statement 'have you not observed that imitations, if continued from youth far into life, settle down into habits' has led Myles Burnyeat, in one of the most profound and also entertaining readings of *The Republic*, to suggest that Plato was worried by *mimēsis* because culture influences the mind 'by a gradual, often unnoticed accumulation of images that come in at a level below, and relatively independent of, reason's activities of judgment, evaluation, and belief-formation'.[42] As a result 'What you imitate regularly is what you become, so from childhood on the Guards must imitate appropriate models of courage, temperance, and other virtues.'[43] Plato is hostile to *mimēsis* according to Burnyeat because he fears the slow process of habitual seepage by which art can corrupt a culture. This would make Plato's hostility to imitation rational, but it may make it more rational than it actually is, since habituation is perhaps less Plato's concern than something which we might call inculcation, or the belief that a poem leaves an impress on its reader.

Early in his discussion of poetry Plato associates it with *paideia*, and says that poetry presents what he calls a *tupos*, a type or stamp, which can be impressed upon what we still call the 'impressionable' minds of youths very easily (377b). These *tupoi* can become ineradicable (*ametastata*, 378e). The imitation of unmanly *tupoi* unmans and penetrates the body, just as Agathon on his couch becomes womanish by writing imitations of women's voices. Crucially, that same word *tupos* comes back into play towards the end of the section in which Plato is discussing *lexis*. The man of the right sort, the *metrios anēr*, will indulge sparingly in *mimēsis*, and will not want to liken himself to someone who is his inferior and 'will be embarrassed both because he is unpractised in the mimicry of such characters, and also because he shrinks in distaste from moulding and fitting himself to the types [*tupous*] of baser things' (396d). *Tupos* can mean a blow, the impress of a seal, the outline, the model, or a system of doctrine. It is used in Plato's discussion of memory in the *Theaetetus*, in which he compares the operation of memory to the impressing of a seal in wax:

> whenever we wish to remember anything we see or hear or think of in our own minds, we hold this wax under the perceptions and thoughts and imprint them upon it (*apotupousthai*), just as we make impressions from seal rings…It is impossible for anyone to think that one thing which he knows and of which

42. Burnyeat, 'Plato's *Republic*', 227.   43. Ibid., 280.

he has received a memorial imprint [*tupos*] in his soul, but which he does not perceive, is another thing which he knows and of which he also has an imprint, and which he does not perceive. (*Theaetetus*, 191d–192a)[44]

A *tupos* in that context has a slightly narrower sense than it comes to bear in *The Republic*, since it means effectively the memorial imprint left by specific sensory experience. It seems in the *Theaetetus* almost to function as a synonym for the word *sēma* (impress, seal, or sign). In *The Republic* a *tupos* is a moral imprint which can affect the entire soul, and for that reason the word *tupos* plays a central part in Plato's unease with *mimēsis*. It, as it were, seals his account of *mimēsis* as a descendant of that of Aristophanes. Imitating another person's voice moulds, it stamps a character.

This may be the result of long habituation and cultural seepage, as Burnyeat implies in his benevolent interpretation of what Plato meant. But when Plato talks in the *Republic* of the impression made by a *tupos* on the mind he tends to treat it as instant and exact, in a manner that is closely akin in its operation to the usage of the word to describe the act of remembering a thing or a person in the *Theaetetus*. A *tupos* impresses instantly, perhaps as it does so feminizing the recipient of its mark. The immediacy of this imprint is particularly emphasized in *The Republic* in cases where the *tupos* imitated is female or homosexual. Impressions which Plato regarded as base seem to strike the soul more deeply than noble ones. There is remarkably little in *The Republic* about *how* exposure to imitation in practice changes the soul, and there is surprisingly little too about the role of habituation in this transformation. Surely even an actor has to practise in order to be able to imitate the gesture and style of a woman? That may indeed be why Plato comes back anxiously to the topic of imitation from a more metaphysical perspective in Book 10. His efforts to supply a higher metaphysical explanation of why *mimēsis* is intrinsically undesirable may result from sneaking recognition that it cannot be quite as instantaneously transformative and corrupting as it appears to be in Book 3.

Whatever the larger movement of Plato's thinking about the imitative arts in general, the concept of a *tupos*—a type or a stamp—is essential to understanding his attack on *mimēsis*, and also to understanding the legacy of problems and opportunities which Plato left for subsequent writers who

44. Text and translations from Plato, *Theaetetus; Sophist*, trans. Harold North Fowler (London, 1921). See Myles Burnyeat, *The Theaetetus of Plato*, trans. M. J. Levett (Indianapolis and Cambridge, 1990), pp. 90–101.

discussed literary imitation. The word *tupos* enables Plato to move directly from considering *lexis* to ethics. You adopt the *lexis* of a woman and your words become womanlike, and you also have womanishness stamped into your soul.

A central feature of Plato's attack on poetry is a tendency to equate gestural and linguistic emulation with ethical transformation. He does not sustain a stable distinction between what we might want to call mimicry and what we might call practical transformation, or the acquisition of skills and mannerisms to the point at which they become learnt and habitual behaviour. Indeed the failure to distinguish between these two things is central to Plato's attack on *mimēsis* in *The Republic*. He is prone to believe, he was primed by Aristophanes to believe, that there are no inverted commas in the moral life. You speak like a woman and you become womanish. This manifests a social prejudice. But it also points towards a wider truth. The imitation of an external mannerism and the acquisition of a skill or habit are intrinsically hard to distinguish. The following short imitation of a Socratic dialogue might clarify this point:

SOCRATES: You would agree, would you not, that I could adopt the verbal and physical mannerisms of a carpenter? I could talk of noggins and tenons, carry a Workmate and wear a toolbelt, and stick a pencil behind my ear? But when I was asked to cut a dovetail joint, would imitating these features of a carpenter's behaviour help me?

ARISTOPHANES: Certainly not, oh Socrates.

SOCRATES: But would you agree that an apprentice in the art of carpentry may adopt the mannerisms of master workman, by tucking a pencil behind his ear and so on, while he seeks to acquire the skill of his master, and that he could show his admiration and respect for his master by doing so, as well as manifesting his desire eventually to equal him in skill?

ARISTOPHANES: Certainly, oh Socrates.

SOCRATES: And do we call that imitation?

ARISTOPHANES: Even I wouldn't be thick enough to do otherwise.

SOCRATES: Now consider the apprentice who watches a skilled carpenter cutting a dovetail joint on EuTubos.[45] Surely he can then re-enact what he sees in order to learn how to do it himself? He can learn by watching

---

45. From other references in Greek literature this appears to have been a repository of misinformation and entertainment, chiefly concerning cats, but no textual traces of it survive.

a master craftsman that the correct angle at which to incline a saw in cutting a dovetail joint in hardwood is 1:8?

ARISTOPHANES: EuTubos is the place where we Greeks learn all there is to learn, oh Socrates. But I believe dovetail joints were invented by the Egyptians.

SOCRATES: By the dog (and I learned that oath from the Egyptians too) that's beside the point, Aristophanes. I am not concerned with history here. Don't we also call that process of learning through watching 'imitation'?

ARISTOPHANES: I am overwhelmed by your perspicacity, oh Socrates.

SOCRATES: Would you agree that we might want to distinguish here two types of imitation. Let us call the apprentice tucking a pencil behind his ear gestural replication. The other kind of imitation we might want to call 'skill acquisition by imitative behaviour', or 'emulative learning' or some such?

ARISTOPHANES: That seems jolly sensible, oh Socrates. How do you make this stuff sound so easy? You really ought to write plays, you know.

SOCRATES: Shut up. I do the irony round here. Let me continue. These two types of imitation overlap, but are not coextensive?

ARISTOPHANES: For God's sake don't get too technical with me. I am a man of the boards and of the strap-on phallus. Explain what you mean in simple words.

SOCRATES: If I carry a Workmate every day and put on my toolbelt every morning will it not eventually give me the lopsided walk of a carpenter, and perhaps even give me carpenterlike callouses on my delicate and philosophical hands? I might assume these physical mannerisms as part of the process of becoming a carpenter, but they would not be enough in themselves to enable me to make a couch.

ARISTOPHANES: Ah! So long as you stick to talking about couches I will understand you, oh Socrates. You mean not all people who wear check shirts and tuck pencils behind their ears are actually carpenters. I once had a carpenter like that...

SOCRATES: And is it not true that imitating the style of a Socratic dialogue will not give me the wit or the wisdom of Socrates?

ARISTOPHANES: Of course, Socrates. How could a mere imitation of Socrates's manner of delivery enable anyone to equal the inimitable philosophic greatness and rigour of the original?

And here we come to a crunch. It is possible to sustain some sort of distinction between gestural replication and skill acquisition when talking about a material skill such as couch-making. But this distinction becomes extremely cloudy when a person attempts to imitate someone of whom they have only a textual record. By imitating a turn of phrase, or by adopting the lexis of a particular writer, have I also acquired his *technē*, his skill? Could I also acquire his virtue or be influenced by his wickedness as a result of this form of *mimēsis*? Or have I simply acquired something analogous to a carpenter's manner of walking rather than his skill?

Plato does not of course explicitly discuss *imitatio*, the imitation of authors, at all. But his unease about *mimēsis* in *The Republic* is partly caused by an intrinsic problem which becomes much more of a problem when it is transferred to the processes by which one writer imitates another. Human beings are animals who tend initially to acquire skills by seeing other human beings perform actions. We are also animals who are acutely aware of the gestures and mannerisms which individuate other members of the species, or which characterize particular groups within the species. We may attempt to replicate those too, as part of the processes by which we get on in the world, or move from one group to another. That means that these two kinds of imitation, which we might distinguish as behavioural imitation and technical emulation, are often quite hard to distinguish. It is extremely difficult to distinguish *mimēsis*-as-pretending-to-be from *mimēsis*-as-*technē*-acquisition (and every time a child plays she is rejoicing in the difficulty of making that distinction).

The line between the two is perhaps impossible to draw without making some kind of extrinsic judgement. We might use moral judgements to prise the two apart: Plato might think that being skilled at pretending to be a women is less good for a man than being skilled at making couches, so *mimēsis*-as-pretending is intrinsically less valuable than *mimēsis*-as-*technē* acquisition. But if one applies pressure to the distinction it instantly seems more slippery than this simple opposition would suggest. A person who imitates a carpenter with the aim of mastering the art of making a couch will at some point be called a carpenter rather than a person pretending to be a carpenter. He will have acquired a skill, and we will pay him to perform his skill. The distinction between the pretend carpenter and the carpenter who has mastered the art is, it might seem, a practical one: dovetail joints made by a carpenter hold together; those made by a person who is capable only of imitating the gestures and mannerisms of a carpenter do not. But it is also a distinction which depends on social conventions and practices: at some point—the end of an apprenticeship, the end of ephebe-hood—a culture decides that someone has learnt how to be a carpenter and is no longer imitating a carpenter.

It is not simply a cultural decision, however. As learners we probably know when we have ceased to feel as though we are pretending. We sink in the saw without overtly recalling the angle at which our teacher has done so. But who judges the point when gestural imitation stops and technical competence begins? And if we can learn a skill through imitation which has a clear criterion to mark the attainment of the skill, what happens if we imitate it 'in sport'? Might we not become what we pretend to be in just the same way that a would-be carpenter comes to be a carpenter by imitating the behaviour of a master-carpenter? Or might we just acquire the vicious external mannerisms of a lower order of being whilst learning nothing of their skill?

In imitating a person who is known to us only through texts the distinction between 'imitation-as-gestural-replication' and 'imitation-as-skill-acquisition' becomes exceptionally hard to discern. Do we seek to capture the turn of phrase of an author, or to capture and replicate his style and lexis? Do we, as we say, parrot him or her? Or do we seek to replicate the technical skill a poet has used in making a particular poem? And even if we do this kind of reverse engineering how can we acquire the *skill* of making through the act of dismantling? To revert to couches for a moment, a novice carpenter can pull a couch apart and see how it fits together, but that does not give him the skill to cut a tenon or gouge out a mortice. What skill, therefore, do we need to imitate a text, and what do we learn from doing so?[46]

That is not a question which Plato formulates directly, but it may partly again underlie the arguments about *mimēsis* in Book 10 of *The Republic*. These arguments are largely about how artists do or do not imitate reality, rather than about how poets imitate other poets or the voices of other people, and so are extraneous to the subject of this book. But the arguments in Book 10 do implicitly build on the mimicry/skill distinction, or perhaps what should rather be called the mimicry/skill indistinction.

Plato's argument in Book 10 of the *Republic* runs roughly along these lines: objects differ from different viewpoints (598b). The artist represents a thing as

46. On *technē* in Plato's philosophy, see John Gould, *The Development of Plato's Ethics* (Cambridge, 1955), pp. 3–46. Gould argues that for Plato *aretē* (virtue) rests on 'a form of moral *ability*, comparable in some respects to the creative or artistic ability of potters, shoemakers and the like', p. 7.

it appears. So does he represent the thing itself or a phantasm (*phantasmatos ē alētheias ousa mimēsis*)? Plato answers that question by saying that *mimēsis* represents *phantasmata*, unreal appearances. Again Plato's vocabulary for describing the limitations of literature might be traced back to the dramas of 411 and 412. In Euripides's *Helen* the real Helen was away in Egypt; the one over which the Homeric heroes fought was a *mimēma*, a *phantasma*, a fake. That vocabulary of insubstantiality permeates Plato's critique of *mimēsis*. He insists that *mimēsis* creates *phantasmata* which are ontologically inferior to the Forms. God is the natural creator who really makes things. He is, as it were, the real carpenter who does not just know how to represent couches but how to make them. Writing and artistic representation cannot teach these skills. And in a way that has an incalculable influence on the later history of literary imitation Plato attaches vocabulary deriving from natural generation to God: he is the *phoutourgos*, the nature-worker, the generator of real things. The artist on the other hand is left with a vocabulary deriving from perception and mental representation, a vocabulary which is close kin to dreams and magic. He creates delusions, *phantasmata*, *eidōla*, things which are not. But the artist for Plato also lacks the skills which he represents: he does not have the *technē* of making a couch but only the ability to represent the way a couch appears from one particular angle. Those who experience the artwork cannot acquire those technical skills from it.

These arguments are connected to a crucial passage in *The Sophist* which may gloss and develop Plato's earlier attack on the imitative arts in *The Republic*. In this passage Plato distinguishes between likeness-making (which is acknowledged to be a good thing) and the fashioning of mere illusions and *eidōla*. The Eleatic Stranger, who is the principal speaker in this later dialogue, says 'I see the likeness-making art as one part of imitation. This is met with, as a rule, whenever anyone produces the imitation by following the proportions of the original (*tou paradeigmatos summetrias*) in length, breadth, and depth, and giving, besides, the appropriate colours to each part' (235d–e). That phrase 'following the proportions of the original' is couched in quasi-mathematical language (a register which will become increasingly significant for later stages of this literary history). Presumably the Eleatic Stranger is here principally referring to statues or portraits which exactly reflect the dimensions of their sitter, and which can therefore be opposed to pictorial representations of very large scenes in which an artist must illusionistically distort proportion so as to convey the appearance rather than the actual dimensions of what is represented. But his language is significant: *tou paradeigmatos summetrias* could be translated as 'the proportions of the paradigm', or the mathematical relationships between the different elements of the object represented. These could be (and the mathematical register of the language here rather suggests that they should be) imagined as ratios between different elements of the thing represented—say a particular ratio of arm-length to leg-length or of brow to chin in the sitter. This in turn means that the Eleatic Stranger is suggesting that good imitation is true to the underlying mathematical structures of the thing represented.

This passage is significant for a number of reasons. It shows a characteristically late Platonic concern with number as a means to convey and preserve truths. But perhaps the most important thing of all about it is that it uses the word *paradeigma*, which was to become the central term used in the rhetorical tradition after Plato to describe the thing or person imitated by a *verbal* imitator. That word *paradeigma* Plato sometimes used in later dialogues of the Forms, especially when they are considered as means to practical action. It was also used in the art of building to refer to 'a sample capital which the builder uses as a model for all the others'.[47] It is therefore associated with a proportional example from which subsequent copies could be generated. It was generally translated in the Roman rhetorical tradition by the word *exemplum*, and in the later Anglo-Saxon tradition of literary criticism it has generally come to be rendered by the word 'model' (the genealogy of that usage is explored in detail in Chapter 8). It is a helpful word for the imitator, because it suggests a way in which Plato might not simply be critical of the imitative arts: if an imitation corresponds to the mathematical ratios of that which is represented, to the proportions of a *paradeigma*, there might be a relationship of truth between imitation and the reality which it represents. The imitator of objects in the world is intrinsically inferior to God, the *phoutourgos* (597d), the single maker of nature and of the forms, because he imitates many different things, none of which he knows how to make. He cannot make reins or couches like a saddler or a carpenter. He creates *eikones* or *phantasmata* of reins or couches which may not preserve the actual proportions of their *paradeigma*. The creations of the illusionistic imitator are as insubstantial as the ghosts and tricks summoned up by conjurors and *mimetes*. But if the imitator were to replicate the proportions of the paradigm, he might show that he understands its actual quasi-mathematical form and therefore that he

---

47. Rachel Barney, 'The Carpenter and the Good', in Douglas Cairns, Fritz-Gregor Herrmann, and Terrence Penner, eds., *Pursuing the Good: Ethics and Metaphysics in Plato's 'Republic'* (Edinburgh, 2007), 293–319, p. 317.

has both a practical skill (that of reproducing a paradigm) and theoretical knowledge of what is good (through an understanding of its proportions).

Plato did not develop this potential consolation for the imitator. Rather he left to his successors a radical problem for the theory and practice of *imitatio*: where, if anywhere, is a line to be drawn between imitating-as-pretending-to-be and imitating-as-acquiring-a-skill? Even Aristotle (about whom this book has little to say because he has almost nothing to say about how writers imitate each other) does not really address this problem, despite having a far more sophisticated vocabulary for describing habituation and the process of moral learning than Plato. Aristotle famously stated that 'it is an instinct of human beings, from childhood, to engage in *mimēsis*',[48] by which he meant both the imitation of other humans and the making of images and representations, and he insisted that poetry was an art of imitation. He also (in the words of Myles Burnyeat) is aware of 'our ability to internalize from a scattered range of particular cases a general evaluative attitude which is not reducible to rules or precepts'.[49] He was well equipped to discuss how writers might learn to imitate each other, but never did so. Indeed perhaps the biggest gap in the history of Western literary criticism is not Aristotle's lost treatise on comedy, but the entirely unwritten Aristotelian theory of how one writer by learning from an earlier writer might come to acquire the habits, the skills, the *technai*, and perhaps even the deliberative desires of that earlier writer.

After Plato

It is often said that *imitatio*, the imitation of texts or authors, emerged from earlier Greek literary criticism via the rhetorical tradition. The analysis of very early usages of the word-group above suggests if there was such an emergence it should not be expected to display a simple teleology.[50] The imitation of authors and the imitation of other people's actions were deeply entangled from the earliest uses of the word *mimēsis*. But the traditional

48. Aristotle, Longinus, and Demetrius, *Aristotle Poetics; Longinus On The Sublime; Demetrius On Style*, trans. Stephen Halliwell, D. A. Russell, W. Hamilton Fyfe, and Doreen Innes (Cambridge, Mass., and London, 1995), p. 37 (1448b).
49. M. F. Burnyeat, 'Aristotle on Learning to be Good', in Amélie Oksenberg Rorty, ed., *Essays on Aristotle's Ethics* (Los Angeles, 1980), 69–92, p. 72.
50. See Richard McKeon, 'Literary Criticism and the Concept of Imitation in Antiquity', *Modern Philology* 34 (1936), 1–35.

story conveys a simple truth. The word *mimēsis* was used by Plato of moments when a playwright or narrative poet represented direct speech through a persona. That usage was historically significant. The belief that it was possible to create a representation of the way another person talked enabled the word *mimēsis* to encompass the idea that one poet could imitate another. A rhapsode could adopt the voice of Homer. A playwright could satirically represent the work of another playwright onstage.

It does appear to have been a rhetorician, Isocrates, however, who developed these associations. He used the word *mimēsis* of the process by which a young orator learns from his teachers to speak in a particular way. In a fascinating passage in *Against the Sophists* he weaves together the broadly Platonic language of *tupoi*, moulds, paradigms, and habituation to create one of the most significant statements about *imitatio* from antiquity:

> For the rest he [the teacher] must in himself set such an example (*paradeigma*), that the students who are moulded (*ektupoun*) by him and are able to imitate (*mimēsasthai*) him will, from the outset, show in their speaking a degree of grace and charm greater than that of others.[51]

Isocrates's verb *ektupoun*—to stamp out—suggests that the *paradeigma* (the practice of the exemplary practitioner) is impressed on his pupils like a seal on wax. We might note too that this passage is about imitation as an educational practice, rather than a purely textual one. It is dependent upon the physical presence of a charismatic teacher, whose example imposes itself upon those whom he teaches almost instantly ('from the outset'). That conception of bodily presence which generates charisma ('grace and charm') in the pupil remained a massively significant component in discussions of *imitatio* in the later rhetorical tradition.[52] It suggests that a charismatic teacher provides simultaneously conceptual instruction and a radiant influence which transmits itself to his pupils.

But even when, and perhaps especially when, imitation is presented as an educational process there is still a profound question to ask of it. What happens when the charismatic influence passing from teacher to pupil is mediated by texts, and the *paradeigma* is not a present teacher, but a textual authority? The

51. *Against the Sophists*, 18. Text from Isocrates, *Isocrates*, trans. George Norlin (London, 1982). See E. Fantham, 'Imitation and Evolution: The Discussion of Rhetorical Imitation in *De Oratore* 2, 87–97', *Classical Philology* 73 (1978), 1–16, p. 12.
52. See C. Stephen Jaeger, *Enchantment: On Charisma and the Sublime in the Arts of the West* (Philadelphia, 2012), p. 23: charisma 'inspires imitation; it awakens the desire to be like the charismatic person'.

person who gave the most systematic and influential attention to this question was Dionysius of Halicarnassus, whose surviving rhetorical works were composed in Rome between 29 and 10 BC.[53] Dionysius's *Peri Mimēseōs* (*On Imitation*) survives only in an epitome and in an extended quotation from it in the *Letter to Pompeius*.[54] Stephen Halliwell, who treats *imitatio* as (literally) only a footnote to the study of *mimēsis*, the imitation of reality, suggests that Dionysius developed the elements within Plato's theory of *mimēsis* which were concerned with theatrical mimicry, and adapted them to the imitation of one authorial style by a later writer.[55] Practitioners of *imitatio* are therefore a subspecies of mimic. The general outlines of this explanation are likely to be accurate, and given the fragmentary nature of the evidence it is unlikely that we will ever be able to piece together a much better one. Sadly it appears that Dionysius abandoned his treatise on imitation (as several of those working on this topic have done) just as it got interesting: Book 3, which addressed 'the question of how imitation ought to be done', was never written, and the remainder was lost.[56]

It is impossible to reconstruct the argument of Dionysius's *Peri Mimēseōs*, but it is possible to offer some plausible conjectures about its scope and nature. Dionysius was in all his literary works interested in the minutiae of style. His treatise *Peri Suntheseōs* (usually translated as 'On Literary Composition', but perhaps more accurately as 'On Word-Order', since it is chiefly concerned with how to order words so as to achieve a particular stylistic effect) is one of the earliest works to perform extended rhetorical analysis on passages of verse and prose. In *Peri Suntheseōs* Dionysius is also interested in a number of broadly 'mimetic' effects—how Homer's language can represent echoically the rolling back of Sisyphus's rock, for example. Throughout his works

---

53. George Alexander Kennedy, *A New History of Classical Rhetoric* (Princeton, 1994), p. 262. For discussion, see Tim Whitmarsh, *Greek Literature and the Roman Empire: The Politics of Imitation* (Oxford, 2001), pp. 72–5.

54. See 'Letter to Gnaeus Pompeius', ch. 3 in Dionysius of Halicarnassus, *The Critical Essays*, trans. Stephen Usher, 2 vols. (Cambridge, Mass., and London, 1974), 2.370–98; the treatise is also mentioned in 'On Thucydides' ch. 1, Dionysius of Halicarnassus, *The Critical Essays*, 1.462. The relationship between the extract in the Letter to Pompeius and the epitome is discussed in Malcolm Heath, 'Dionysius of Halicarnassus On Imitation', *Hermes* 117 (1989), 370–3 and Gavin Weaire, 'The Relationship between Dionysius of Halicarnassus' *De imitatione* and *Epistula ad Pompeium*', *Classical Philology* 97 (2002), 351–9.

55. Halliwell, *Aesthetics of Mimesis*, p. 293, n. 21.

56. 'The first of these [three books] concerns an enquiry into the nature of imitation itself. The second discusses the question of which particular poets and philosophers, historians and orators, should be imitated. The third, in which the question of how imitation should be done, is as yet incomplete.' Dionysius of Halicarnassus, *The Critical Essays*, 1.370.

Dionysius was keen to make stylistic differentiations between authors. On the whole these are quite rudimentary: he offers epithets to describe a particular writer's style—so the style or *lexis* of Thucydides is described as 'beautiful', while that of Herodotus is both beautiful and sweet.[57] This interest in stylistic characterization is a symptom of something larger.

Dionysius clearly held that individual authors have stylistic characters. He had evidently read the lost treatise by Theophrastus *On Style (Peri Lexeōs)*, in which Theophrastus may have developed a scheme for dividing compositions into different levels of styles—what came to be called the plain, the middle (or mixed), and the grand.[58] These levels of style, whether by Theophrastus or some earlier writer, were often called *charactēres*.[59] The work for which Theophrastus is now chiefly remembered, his *Characters*—or thumbnail sketches of different types of person—repeatedly suggests a relationship between different styles of speech and different *charactēres*. Theophrastus regularly begins his *Characters* with a formula like this: 'The flatterer is the kind of person who says things like "only you could have written such an inimitably wonderful book".' Part of what Theophrastus means by a 'character' is a disposition to say or do a particular kind of thing in a particular way. It might be reasonable to speculate, though it is probably not possible to do more than this nor to verify the speculation, that post-Theophrastan peripatetics might have made a connection between *charactēres* in this sense and idiosyncratic styles of speech, which then fed into the rhetorical tradition:[60] certainly by the first century BC what we term a 'style' could be described as a *charactēr* in the sense of being an imprint of a particular type of person, or a particular set of repeating characteristics of style.

---

57. Dionysius of Halicarnassus, *On Literary Composition: being the Greek Text of the De Compositione Verborum*, ed. W. Rhys Roberts (London, 1910), p. 120 (ch. 8).

58. Doreen C. Innes, 'Theophrastus and the Theory of Style', in William W. Fortenbaugh, ed., *Theophrastus of Eresus: On his Life and Work* (New Brunswick, NJ, 1985), 251–67 and G. M. A. Grube, 'Theophrastus as a Literary Critic', *Transactions of the American Philological Association* 83 (1952), 172–83 are sceptical; George A. Kennedy, 'Theophrastus and Stylistic Distinctions', *Harvard Studies in Classical Philology* 62 (1957), 93–104 less so; see also Kennedy, *A New History of Classical Rhetoric*, pp. 84–8. There is strong association going back at least until the fourth century BC between style and character: Diogenes Laertius (6.15) ascribes to Antisthenes (4th century BC) a treatise *On Style, or on the Characters (Peri lexeōs ē peri Charactērōn)*. But 'The history of these concepts is extremely complicated and by no means fully known', D. A. Russell, 'Rhetoric and Criticism', in Andrew Laird, ed., *Oxford Readings in Ancient Literary Criticism* (Oxford, 2006), 267–83, p. 276.

59. Demetrius of Phalerum (a pupil of Theophrastus) regularly refers to the different types of style as *charactēres*, Demetrius, *Demetrius on Style: The Greek Text of Demetrius De Elocutione*, ed. W. Rhys Roberts (Cambridge, 1902), p. 86 (2.36).

60. Liddell and Scott, s.v. *charactēr*, 5.

It is also likely—though again we can say no more—that the vogue among rhetoricians from the second sophistic of the second century BC for declamations which were rich in *ēthopoeiai*, or representations of the character and the stylistic mannerisms of particular types of person—misers, or aggrieved husbands—further associated particular manners of speech with specific types of people.[61] It was a small step from this kind of careful stylistic representation of a particular character-type to a belief that authors had stylistic characters of their own, which could become *paradeigmata*, or textual objects which could be analysed and imitated.

Dionysius certainly makes a connection between the word *charactēr* and the style of individual authors. His late treatise on Thucydides, for instance, aims to discuss 'the character of his style in all its aspects' (*tou charactēros tōn logōn*). He also describes Thucydides's impartiality and his avoidance of myth as beautiful principles worthy of imitation (*kala kai mimēseōs axia*). And 'worthy of imitation' or 'imitable' there refers primarily to *imitatio*, literary imitation,[62] although, as is increasingly the case in the rhetorical tradition, *imitatio* is more or less inseparable from ethical emulation: a *charactēr* is at once a style and set of ethical principles. This is why the word *zēlōsis*, which can mean both 'emulation' and 'love', often accompanies the notion of literary imitation in Dionysius's treatise: the imitator aspires not simply to reproduce the verbal style of another author, but is also driven by desire to understand and to re-instantiate the moral virtues of the *paradeigma*. The word *axia* also may suggest that for Dionysius a style is determined by abstract and more or less extra-linguistic principles, by a set of underlying virtues and vices which are manifested in speech or writing. Here he may show a debt to Plato's conception of a *paradeigma*, which Dionysius appears to be adapting to literary *imitatio*. For Plato a *paradeigma* can be a quasi-mathematical model of the proportions of an object which could be imitated in various forms. Dionysius's *axia* are perhaps analogous: they are principles which can be extrapolated from the style of a writer which can then provide the principles for new texts, or imitations as Dionysius would call them.

This developing vocabulary for describing the styles of individual writers had a profound effect on the relationship between *imitatio* and the cluster of concepts covered by the word *mimēsis*. In particular it enabled a reassessment

---

61. D. A. Russell, *Greek Declamation* (Cambridge, 1983), esp. pp. 87–105.
62. Dionysius of Halicarnassus, *The Critical Essays*, 1.468; ch. 8. On Dionysius's methods for categorizing styles, see Stanley F. Bonner, *The Literary Treatises of Dionysius of Halicarnassus: A Study in the Development of Critical Method* (Cambridge, 1939), pp. 21–4.

of Plato's highly influential distinction between *diegēsis* and *mimēsis* (*Republic*, 392c–395b). As we have already seen, Plato used *diegēsis* of third-person narrative in the voice of the poet himself (393a) and opposed to it *mimēsis* in the sense of 'direct representation of a particular person's voice'. So for Plato when Agamemnon stops speaking in *The Iliad* Homer stops doing *mimēsis* and starts doing *diegēsis* or narrative, a form of imitation which, in *Republic* 3 at least, is less objectionable than *mimēsis*. For Dionysius things are rather different. For him Thucydides has a Thucydidean *charactēr* even when he is purportedly relating the speech of a general to his troops, as well as in the not-explicitly-mimetic bits in between. He has a style, a character, that runs through the whole work. That style is potentially reducible to axioms and could become the object of imitation, just as Homer imitated the speech of an old man in Chryses's speeches in *Iliad* 1 (393a–394b). Again we might here look back to Theophrastus, whose sole surviving use of the word *diegēsis* pushes it towards the sense 'characteristic style of narration': in describing the character of a chatterbox he claims that 'idle chatter' (*adoleschias*) is a *diegēsis* of prolonged and unpremeditated words.[63]

This does not mean that Dionysius or Theophrastus simply collapse Plato's distinction between *diegēsis* and *mimēsis*. They do not. But by the age of Augustus it does appear that *diegēsis*—narrative which does not seek to represent the voice of a character within the fiction—could manifest the 'character' of an author in the same way that direct *mimēsis* of a voice could represent a character within the fiction. That made it possible to think of imitating a passage of *diegēsis* by selectively adopting its style and manner in the same way that one might imitate the lexis or physical mannerisms of a particular person, or of an old man, or a Phocian, or Euripides. These developments partly result from the fact that Dionysius was writing about and for orators and historians rather than about and for poets. He wanted to encourage young orators not to produce the cut and thrust of dialogue, but to produce an imitation of the overall tenor, style, and character of an earlier writer or speaker. As a result Dionysius makes it possible to perform a secondary imitation of texts by imitating a *charactēr* of style, a character which might run through both the *diegēsis* and the *mimēsis*, the narrative and the dialogue, of a particular author. That, I would suggest, is one crucial enabling condition

---

63. Theophrastus, *Characters*, trans. Ian Campbell Cunningham, A. D. Knox, and Jeffrey S. Rusten (Cambridge, Mass., and London, 1993), p. 60 (ch. 3).

for the emergence of *imitatio*, the imitation of texts, as a semi-autonomous field from *mimēsis*, the representation of people or events.

There is an additional twist here, although the evidence for it is tantalizingly thin. Dionysius was a teacher of rhetoric as well as a historian.[64] He was interested in the processes of training and habituation which enable an orator to acquire linguistic fluency and to win cases. As a distant heir to a peripatetic tradition he regards the acquisition of a *hexis* or habit as an intrinsic part of the process of learning to write. This in turn leads him to connect his notion of stylistic imitation very closely with pedagogical practice. At one point in the *Peri Suntheseōs* Dionysius discusses how Demosthenes learnt to write: 'when long training had issued in perfect mastery, and had graven on his mind forms and impressions (*labousa tupous*) of all that he had practised, he henceforth produced his effects with the utmost ease from sheer force of habit (*hexeōs*)'.[65]

This is a particularly important passage, because it shows a post-Aristotelian emphasis on the role of training and practice in instilling *tupoi* in the mind. These stamps or impressions are no longer just imprinted in the minds of tender youths, as Plato had suggested. Imitation is the acquisition of a *hexis* or a *habitus*, of learning how to write like someone else as the result of a long process of reading and writing and training. Because Dionysius of Halicarnassus had a broadly Aristotelian conception of the role of habit in education he treated the inculcation of *tupoi* not as a sudden exposure to a degenerate imprint, as Plato might have done, but as a gradual process of habituation. For Dionysius learning from an author is not a stamping of an impress into the mind. It is a matter of gradually acquiring a competence. This in turn breaks down the Platonic distinction between the morally destructive effects of imitating other people's mannerisms on the one hand, and the positive benefits of learning the *technē* of a carpenter on the other. For Dionysius lexical imitation is an aspect of moral emulation, and rhetorical success is the result of combining these two things together. You can learn how to replicate the style of Demosthenes by reading Demosthenes and by exercising a *zēlos* to be like him. And by painstaking analysis of his word-order and vocabulary it is possible to acquire the *hexis*, the habit, of writing like an earlier author. A person's stylistic character consequently becomes a skill that can be acquired.

64. Bonner, *Dionysius of Halicarnassus*, p. 2.
65. Dionysius, ed. Roberts, *On Literary Composition*, p. 269 (ch. 25).

This gradual shift towards a theory of learning which emphasizes habit (*hexis*), practice, and induration is the foundation of imitative theory in rhetorical writings in the first century BC. We should not see this as either a complete transformation of literary criticism, in which *imitatio* suddenly and simply comes to be regarded as a both an autonomous field and a good thing, however. Problems remain. In particular they continue to surround the concept of a *paradeigma* or a model. What is it that an imitator learns from a *paradeigma*? If a young orator or historian wants to imitate the style of Thucydides, for instance, what is he to do? Does it entail mastering the vocabulary and syntax of Thucydides and using only words that he uses? Does it mean inferring the political and ethical principles which lie behind the works of Thucydides and writing from those inferred positions? Theorists including Dionysius are clear that imitation involves some kind of judge-ment about what is good to imitate and what is not, and so is a critical exercise in selection. Your choice of *paradeigma* as well as the way you imi-tate it are moral matters: you do not imitate faults but seek to bring out what is good through imitation of what is good.

Writers in the rhetorical tradition tend not to put pressure on these problematic areas. They are more interested in outcomes and results than in explaining processes. Following the example of Demosthenes in winning a case is the aim, rather than explaining what kind of cross-cultural under-standing and interpersonal understanding is involved in imitating an earlier writer. The crucial questions behind the emergence of *imitatio* from the larger conceptual realm of *mimēsis* as a result remained substantially unarticulated. What is the object of literary imitation? Is it a particular set of texts, is it a particular moral character, is it a set of quasi-mathematical axioms or algo-rithms that can be understood to underlie the work of an earlier writer, or is it a literary character that can be assumed to have generated those texts? And if the latter, what *is* a literary character?

In this area both the vocabulary and the conceptual apparatus, if there is such a distinction, of Augustan and post-Augustan critics are extremely unclear. Dionysius defines imitation in his first book in a sentence of mind-blowing obscurity. It is 'an activity (*energeia*) reproducing [the verb used, *ekmassō*, can mean 'mould in wax'] the model (*paradeigma*) through theoretical principles (*theōrēmatōn*)'.[66] Given that this gnomic sentence survives only as a fragment

---

66. Dionysius of Halicarnassus, *Opuscules Rhétoriques*, ed. Germaine Aujac, 5 vols. (Paris, 1992), p. 27. This fragment is difficult to gloss because it has no context: see D. A. Russell, 'De Imitatione',

one might reasonably shrug one's shoulders and say that it is impossible to do more than conjecture what it might mean. But what it probably means is something along these lines: imitation entails determining the principles of composition which underlie the *paradeigma* and following those.[67] The moulding of the style of the new orator to the *tupos* of the old requires theoretical extrapolation of the habits of the earlier writer from the earlier author's texts and an attempt to replicate them. This is done through practice, so that the imitator eventually comes to acquire the *hexis* and the *lexis*, the habits of writing and the style, of the *paradeigma*, or *exemplum*. This notion we might call dispositional imitation, since it entails learning the dispositions (moral and political as well as stylistic) of an earlier author rather than simply echoing his or her words. The really crucial point about this theory, though, is that neither Dionysius nor anyone else in his tradition managed to articulate it in a manner that was both abstract and lucid.

This is not simply the result of the woeful state of the text of the *Peri Mimeseōs*. It was the result of the deep problem of explaining how stylistic emulation could convey a *technē*, or shape the character and skill of the imitator. That question, though, 'How does "dispositional imitation" work?' is one of the most crucial and fertile unanswered questions in the Western literary tradition. In Chapter 2 I shall suggest that this unanswered question encouraged Roman orators to describe *imitatio* not through systematic argument, but chiefly through a set of metaphors. These metaphors were to run through the practice of imitative poetry, in the Augustan period, in the Renaissance, and beyond.

---

in David West and Tony Woodman, eds., *Creative Imitation and Latin Literature* (Cambridge, 1979), 1–16, p. 10.

67. Cf. Alessandro Barchiesi, *La traccia del modello: effetti omerici nella narrazione virgiliana* (Pisa, 1984), p. 95: 'Si potrebbe anche dire ... che propriamente non esiste imitazione che si limiti ai testi (o si dovrebbe parlare allora soltanto di riproduzione). Ciò che veramente si imita sono stili, convenzioni, norme, generi. Imitare un testo, allora, presuppone che in via preliminare si costruisca un modello—parola, appunto, terribilmente ambigua: applicabile a un testo, visto come una totalità concreta, ma anche a un insieme di tratti distintivi, a una struttura generativa.' ('One may add also that generally speaking there is no imitation that limits itself to the text (otherwise it would be a case of sheer reproduction). What one really imitates are styles, conventions, norms, genres. To imitate a text, then, presupposes at the outset that it has been constructed as a *model*—a terribly ambiguous word, of course. It can be applied to a text, viewed as a concrete totality, but also to a set of distinctive features, a generative structure.') Alessandro Barchiesi, *Homeric Effects in Vergil's Narrative*, trans. Ilaria Marchesi and Matt Fox (Princeton, 2015), p. 73. That *terribilmente ambigua* word 'model' will figure large in Chapter 8.

2

Building Bodies

Imitatio and the Roman
Rhetorical Tradition

A t the start of the extant epitome of Dionysius of Halicarnassus's treatise
Peri Mimēseōs ('On Imitation') there is an anecdote which is supposed
to explain how prolonged exposure to good writing can make a writer
come to resemble the *charactēr* of what he reads. Dionysius or his epitomist
relates that there was once an ugly farmer who feared that his children
would be ugly too. So he made beautiful images (*eikones*) and made his wife
look at them for a long period. When he slept with her (*sungenomenos*) she
conceived a son who took on the beauty of the images.[1] The belief that the
appearance of children was influenced by what their mother happened to

1. Dionysius of Halicarnassus, *Opuscules Rhétoriques*, ed. Germaine Aujac (Paris, 1992), 5.32
   (Epitome, 2). Wendy Doniger and Gregory Spinner, 'Misconceptions: Female Imaginations and
   Male Fantasies in Parental Imprinting', *Daedalus* 127 (1998), 97–129 discuss the wider history of
   this belief, tracing it through to Heliodorus's *Ethiopian History*, Maimonides, and Talmudic
   scholarship. Cf. Soranus, *Soranus' Gynecology*, trans. Owsei Temkin (Baltimore, 1956), pp. 37–8:
   'What is one to say concerning the fact that various states of the soul also produce certain
   changes in the mould of the fetus? For instance, some women, seeing monkeys during intercourse, have borne children resembling monkeys. The tyrant of the Cyprians who was misshapen,
   compelled his wife to look at beautiful statues during intercourse and became the father of
   well-shaped children; and horse-breeders, during covering, place noble horses in front of the
   mares.' Cf. Empedocles [A 81], cited in Hermann Diels, *Doxographi Graeci* (Berolini, 1965),
   p. 432: 'How do offspring come to resemble others rather than their parents? . . . Foetuses are
   shaped by the imagination of the woman around the time of conception. For often women
   have fallen in love with statues of men and with images and have produced offspring which
   resemble them.' For further examples, see M. D. Reeve, 'Conceptions', *Proceedings of the
   Cambridge Philological Society* 215 (1989), 81–112, which includes, pp. 95–6, the sad tale of Mary
   Tofts, who in 1726 was frightened by a rabbit and was subsequently delivered of a rabbit. For
   later treatments, see also Marie-Hélène Huet, 'Monstrous Imagination: Progeny as Art in French
   Classicism', *Critical Inquiry* 17 (1991), 718–27. For discussion of this passage in the context of
   Greek relations to Roman literature, see Tim Whitmarsh, *Greek Literature and the Roman Empire:
   The Politics of Imitation* (Oxford, 2001), p. 75.

look at during intercourse was widespread in antiquity. Soranus's *Gynecology*, from the second century AD, records a woman who looked at monkeys during sex and had children who resembled monkeys—and of course it just had to be monkeys, that proverbially imitative species, who figure in that anecdote.

As Chapter 1 showed, Plato had made a distinction between the life-giving creativity of God the *phutourgos* on the one hand and the shadowy reproductions of the forms, the *eikones* and *phantasmata*, brought about by the mimetic artist on the other.[2] Dionysius's story of the ugly farmer makes mischief, and probably deliberate mischief, for Plato's distinction. Dionysius implies that image-making imitation can be non-degenerative, or re-generative, and even biologically productive. Make good pictures and you could have beautiful children.

The logic is not perfect, and the biology is by present-day standards decidedly questionable. But Dionysius's tale of the farmer is extremely revealing about the treatment of literary imitation in Rome. He conducts a defence of literary imitation by image and story rather than by argument. Dionysius is trying here to explain what I have termed 'dispositional imitation'. That is, his story is an effort to explain how prolonged study of a *paradeigma* can enable an imitator to mould himself to its character. The detail of this process—the practices and activities it requires—remain unexplained in the sections of the treatise which survive. But he offers a vivid image instead of the physical power of beautiful works of art to generate people who resemble them. His anecdote seeks to explain how an imitator could resemble the creations of an earlier author (as Seneca put it in his enormously influential 84th Epistle) 'as a child resembles its father'.

The association between biological resemblance and imitation runs through the history of thinking about *imitatio* in Rome, and could serve as a metaphorical substitute for abstract discussion of how one author learns from another. This chapter is principally concerned with the genesis and development of this and a series of other interconnected metaphors for *imitatio* within discussions of Roman rhetorical theory. Running races, building bodies, breeding: these metaphors were to become central to the theory

2. Cf. Jacques Derrida, *Dissemination*, trans. Barbara Johnson (London, 1981), p. 150: 'Here is the analogy: simulacrum-writing is to what it represents (that is, true writing—writing which is true because it is authentic, corresponds to its value, conforms to its essence, is the writing of truth in the soul of him who possesses the *episteme*) as weak, easily exhausted, superfluous seeds giving rise to ephemeral produce (floriferous seeds) are to strong, fertile seeds engendering necessary, lasting, nourishing produce (fructiferous seeds).'

and practice of *imitatio* in early modern Europe. Why did these metaphors become so pervasive within the Roman rhetorical tradition?

The *Ad Herennium*

One kind of answer to that question can be found in the surviving rhetorical handbooks, into which discussion of *imitatio* fitted rather awkwardly. The traditional division of rhetoric into five distinct elements, *inventio* (finding out the matter of a speech), *dispositio* (arranging it), *elocutio* (style), *memoria* (memorizing it), and *actio* (performance) did not instantly provide a heading under which imitation could be discussed, since the imitation of an author could entail following the practice of that author in any or all of these skills. The anonymous author of the earliest surviving Roman art of rhetoric, the *Rhetorica Ad Herennium*, treats *imitatio* as one of the three foundational techniques by which all the constituent elements of the art of rhetoric may be learnt. The five elements of rhetoric can be acquired, he declares, 'By art or theory, by imitation, and by practice. Art or theory means learning by precepts or rules, which give a definite method and system of speaking. Imitation is that by which we are impelled, in accordance with a careful method, to flourish in speaking by being like others. Practice is continuous exercise and habit in speaking' ('arte, imitatione, exercitatione. Ars est praeceptio, quae dat certam viam rationemque dicendi. Imitatio est qua impellimur, cum diligenti ratione, ut aliquorum similes in dicendo valeamus esse. Exercitatio est adsiduus usus consuetudoque dicendi', *Ad Herennium*, 1.2.3).[3]

The sentence about *imitatio* is hard to translate accurately, and is particularly obscure. The author uses vocabulary which implies that imitation is founded on clear principles: it is practised 'cum diligenti ratione', with careful method. The word 'ratio' makes it appear that imitation can be accommodated within a theoretical model of rhetoric, and that there might be rationally apprehensible principles underlying it. But *imitatio* is then presented not as a systematic practice but as a drive, by which we are impelled (*qua impellimur*) to be like another person in speaking. The rational principles behind this drive are never explicated in the *Ad Herennium*, which, apart from this very obscure passage, has little to say on the subject.

---

3. Quotations from [Cicero], *Rhetorica ad Herennium*, ed. Harry Caplan (Cambridge, Mass., and London, 1954). For the traditional opposition between rule-following and imitation, see George Alexander Kennedy, *The Art of Persuasion in Greece* (Princeton, 1963), pp. 332–3.

There is, however, the shadow of a further discussion of *imitatio* at the start of the fourth book of the *Ad Herennium*, which deals with *elocutio* or style. If imitation is a matter of speaking like another person, then it might reasonably be treated principally as an aspect of style and as naturally falling within a discussion of how particular authors use particular figures. The fourth book of the *Ad Herennium* duly begins with a long discussion of the use of *exempla* of different kinds of style in rhetorical treatises. But the way the author treats that topic is rather surprising. He offers a prolonged argument against the way that Greek authors of rhetorical handbooks present examples of different registers of style. According to the *Ad Herennium* the Greek theorists gather together *exempla* of the different types of rhetorical style (which the author defines in the traditional manner as the high, the middle, and the low) from different ancient sources. The author then says that the Greeks should instead have written their own new examples to illustrate the types of style. This use of earlier *exempla* in the Greek rhetorical manuals, he argues, confuses their pupils, since an expert in an art ought to be able to produce new examples of his own rather than simply reproducing passages which illustrate different styles from earlier texts.

This section of the *Ad Herennium* is curiously insistent that it is transcending the Greek manuals from which it presumably derived, and one way of explaining its stridency is to suppose that this section of the treatise occupies the position—at the start of a discussion of style—in which some Greek rhetoricians discussed the imitation of both single and multiple *exempla*, and in which others took pre-existing examples to illustrate the different kinds of style. Rather than running in a race themselves in the Olympics, the author of the *Ad Herennium* complains, these Greek rhetoricians just stand there talking about how good the runners of old were. He then goes on to deploy a series of biological metaphors in order to explain how a master of the *ars rhetorica* ought himself to be able to produce new instances of particular rhetorical styles. At 4.3.5 he says 'You are writing a treatise of your own; you are creating new precepts for us; but these you cannot confirm yourself: you take examples from others' ('artem tuam scribis; gignis novas nobis praeceptiones; eas ipse confirmare non potes; ab aliis exempla sumis').[4] The creation or 'birth' (*gignis*) of precepts is not matched by a fertility in examples. The person who chooses examples from others, he claims, does so

---

4. Cf. John T. Kirby, 'Ciceronian Rhetoric: Theory and Practice', in William J. Dominik, ed., *Roman Eloquence: Rhetoric in Society and Literature* (London, 1997), p. 14: 'The greatest rhetorical genius of the Greeks, to generalize somewhat, was theory; that of the Romans, practice.'

when he ought to be 'conceiving, creating, and bringing forth' ('non tum cum parere et ipsi gignere et proferre debent', *Ad Herennium*, 4.4.7). This is itself a moment in which a highly imitative rhetorical theorist becomes innovative: the author of a Roman *ars rhetorica* differentiates his practice from that of the Greeks and asserts the superiority of Rome not by simply gathering examples culled from earlier exponents of the different styles of rhetoric but by actually writing those examples himself. Precept and example become new praxis; and that moment is marked by a fanfare of biological language. Rebirth is consequently presented as a primary goal of imitation.

This passage at the start of the fourth book of the *Ad Herennium* is highly significant. It associates the power to produce new examples to illustrate precepts and principles with two kinds of physical potency: the power to run (and implicitly with a power to outrun Greek rhetorical theorists) and with the ability to bring forth a new birth. These metaphors were to be central to most discussions of *imitatio* in the Roman rhetorical tradition. The *Ad Herennium* also insists that those who offer precepts for others to follow should be practitioners and successful imitators, and those who do not deploy their own bodily and mental vigour to create new works are consequently deficient in the art of rhetoric. But in making these claims it notably fails to provide an explicit explanation of the *ratio* of *imitatio*—the methodical principles determining how, when, and why a writer might imitate another.

How do we explain this failure? A self-evident reason is that it is intrinsically challenging to reduce *imitatio* to a series of precepts. It is very much easier to describe the processes by which a student might construct an *exordium* or develop a probable argument, or to provide precepts explaining the appropriate situations in which to use particular tropes, than it is to prescribe how, when, and why one orator might imitate another.[5] But the conceptual thinness with which imitation is considered in the *Ad Herennium* is connected with a number of further problems which are intrinsic not so much to the concept itself as to the history of rhetoric.

One of these problems was a question about the art of rhetoric itself. The word *ars*, like the Greek word *technē*, can mean 'a systematic body of knowledge and practical techniques, an art or science' (*OLD*, 5), and so imply that an 'art' is a codification of practices. But the same word can be used of 'professional, artistic, or technical skill as something acquired and exercised in

---

5. On the ideal combination of theory and practice in an expert artist, see Aristotle, *Metaphysics*, 1.981b7–10 and D. Blank, 'Philodemus on the Technicity of Rhetoric', in Dirk Obbink, ed., *Philodemus and Poetry* (Oxford, 1995), 178–88.

practice' (*OLD*, 1), and therefore can describe the practice itself. Was the root aim of the *artes rhetoricae* to explain methodically to students the rules they should follow in order to construct good speeches (*ars* in the sense 'instruction manual'), or was it intended to illustrate and explain a practice which was beyond all rules and codification (*ars* in the sense of 'skill')?[6] The majority of handbooks of rhetoric in the ancient world were composed by teachers, whom Cicero terms 'praeceptores dicendi' (makers of the rules of speaking, *De Inventione*, 2.7). More introductory works on rhetoric tend to assume that the provision of precepts is a central element in an 'art' of rhetoric. Cicero's very early and fragmentary treatise called the *De Inventione* (which was probably written at about the same time as the *Ad Herennium*), repeatedly talks of *praecepta*, the guidelines or precepts by which the experience of earlier orators could be encapsulated in the form of a rule.[7]

The question of whether an 'art' is a practice or a codification of practice leads on to a wider set of questions about the social status of those who taught rhetoric. *Grammatici*, who taught the rudiments of grammar, tended to be of relatively low social status, and might indeed be Greeks or ex-slaves. *Rhetores*, who taught the *ars rhetorica*, were generally free-men of some social standing:[8] Quintilian, the most successful of the *rhetores* and the author of the longest surviving Roman rhetorical treatise, was ultimately awarded consular rank.

This created a social problem which interacted with the conceptual question about what constituted an 'art', since the final stage of training for elite orators took the form of a quasi-apprenticeship to a more senior figure, who might be of high rank and standing. Cicero, the greatest orator of Rome and the most influential writer on rhetoric, was trained by Lucius Licinius Crassus. This method of learning through apprenticeship to a practised orator was formalized through what was known as the *tirocinium fori* (induction of the inexperienced into the ways of the forum), in which young men of high social status were handed over at about the age of sixteen to an older

6. Quintilian, *Institutio*, 6.2.25 insists that his aim is not to reproduce *praecepta* but to 'bring to light the secret principles of this art . . . giving the result not of teaching received from others, but of my own experience and the guidance of nature herself [*experimento meo ac natura ipsa*]'. All references to Quintilian, *The Orator's Education*, trans. Donald A. Russell (Cambridge, Mass., and London, 2001).

7. On the *technai*, see Thomas N. Habinek, *Ancient Rhetoric and Oratory* (Malden, Mass., and Oxford, 2004), pp. 44–52.

8. On the social origins of *grammatici* (who appear frequently to have been freedmen) and *rhetores*, who were in general not of servile origin, see Charles McNelis, 'Grammarians and Rhetoricians', in William Dominik and Jon Hall, eds., *A Companion to Roman Rhetoric* (Oxford, 2007), 285–96.

friend or relative to learn from example how to speak in public.[9] These high-level practitioners taught their charges principally by example. For them the 'art' of rhetoric was not a set of precepts or codifiable techniques. It was an achieved skill which was embodied in what they did. They sought the kind of influence described by Isocrates in *Against the Sophists*, 18: a teacher 'must in himself set such an example (*paradeigma*), that the students who are moulded (*ektupoun*) by him and are able to imitate (*mimēsasthai*) him will, from the outset, show in their speaking a degree of grace and charm greater than that of others'. Grace and charm, those uncodifiable virtues, were the chief qualities conveyed by the imitation of a living teacher.

Discussions of *imitatio* therefore encountered problems which might be loosely described as both conceptual and social. Explaining how a young writer becomes an accomplished and independent performer through imitation in the form of precepts was in itself not easy, but it also ran the risk of demystifying the personal relationship between an elite, charismatic teacher and his pupil. It might even blur the division between those men and the slaves and freedmen who undertook the inculcation of grammatical and rhetorical principles to younger students. It is these pressures that underlie that strange claim in the *Ad Herennium* that *imitatio* 'impels' us to be like others, but also has a *ratio*. The author of that treatise presents *imitatio* as simultaneously within and beyond the art of rhetoric: it is subject in theory to rationally apprehensible precepts, but is in practice a matter of arcane personal affinities and drives, in which a *tyro* learns a whole manner of behaving from his master, rather than just a set of techniques.

Cicero

In the mature and later rhetorical works of Cicero, these problems were addressed in highly distinctive ways. The fact that *imitatio* defied codification was crucial to Cicero because it distinguished a class of great and successful orators—of which he considered himself to be perhaps the greatest

---

9. See Jean-Michel David, *Le patronat judiciaire au dernier siècle de la République romaine* (Rome, 1992), pp. 336–41. See also Stanley F. Bonner, *Education in Ancient Rome: From the Elder Cato to the Younger Pliny* (London, 1977), pp. 84–5. Tacitus's *Dialogus De Oratoribus* does not directly discuss *imitatio*, but in 34–5 describes the practice of apprenticeship as having been lost after the decline of republican eloquence, and presents it as exemplifying the principle that theory and practice must be linked in good oratory. Tacitus deplores the replacement of this system of practical and exemplary learning by schooling under *rhetores*.

example—from the mere technicians who possessed an understanding only of what he scornfully terms an *artificium* ('The rules or theory of an art, a prescribed method or system', *OLD* 3). The orators who were true masters of the art, on the other hand, and who were worthy of imitation, had something—an *ingenium*, a rhetorical power, or a distinctive inner strength which Cicero frequently calls *vis*—which no one else could match, even if their apprentices might seek to imitate that talent. Their brilliance could not be reduced to *praecepta*.

Cicero's fullest discussion of *imitatio* is found in the second book of his mature rhetorical treatise the *De Oratore*, a dialogue which he began to write around 56 BC, but which was set almost half a century earlier.[10] The preamble to Cicero's discussion of *imitatio* is worth detailed consideration, since it shows the deep association between discussion of *imitatio* and the opposition between learning by precept and learning from the practice of a particular person. In that preamble Antonius describes the power of the orator. Catulus then asks him by what principles and precepts such great *vis* or rhetorical power can be acquired ('quibusnam rationibus quibusque praeceptis ea tanta vis comparetur', *De Oratore*, 2.18.74).[11] Catulus insists, however, that he has no need of a Greekling professor to provide him with hackneyed precepts ('pervulgata praecepta', *De Oratore*, 2.18.75). Such men are as foolish as the philosopher Phormio, Catulus says, who lectured Hannibal on the principles of being a general despite never having led an army into battle.

Antonius responds by setting out the broad principles of rhetoric according to the Greeks. He sees sense in some of them, he says, but the Greeks err in assuming that oratory is an *artificium* in which all practice can be presented in the form of rules. He goes on to consider the example of Sulpicius, who as a young man spoke too quickly and impetuously, and was led to do so by his *ingenium*. Antonius valued his youthful *fecunditas* (a word which can convey sexual fecundity as well as mental agility), and urged him to choose Lucius Crassus as a master to train and direct his rampant *ingenium*. A year later Sulpicius had become a new orator: 'Surely Nature herself was leading him towards the grand and glorious style of Crassus, but this alone would not have been enough, if he had not pressed forward on that same way by careful imitation, and formed the habit of speaking with every thought and

---

10. See Elaine Fantham, 'Imitation and Evolution: The Discussion of Rhetorical Imitation in *De Oratore* 2, 87–97', *Classical Philology* 73 (1978), 1–16.

11. Quotations from Marcus Tullius Cicero, *De Oratore*, trans. E. W. Sutton and H. Rackham (Cambridge, Mass., and London, 1942).

all his soul fixed in contemplation of Crassus' ('Omnino in illud genus eum Crassi magnificum atque praeclarum natura ipsa ducebat: sed ea non satis proficere potuisset, nisi eodem studio atque imitatione intendisset atque ita dicere consuesset, ut tota mente Crassum atque omni animo intueretur', *De Oratore*, 2.21.89).[12]

The description here is vague about method but deliberately intense in its evocation of the spiritual relationship between master and pupil: the whole mind and entire soul of the imitator must be fixed upon his master. The aim, Antonius, continues, is to emulate the excellence of the *exemplum* rather than to reproduce his quirks and idiosyncrasies, and this requires practice or *exercitatio*: 'then practice is required, by which he may by imitating reproduce and express (*exprimat*) the person whom he has chosen to imitate, not in the way that many imitators I have known have done, who pursue in their imitation those things which are obvious or even those which are abnormal or vicious. There is nothing easier than to imitate a person's style of dress or pose or gait' ('tum accedat exercitatio, qua illum, quem delegerit, imitando effingat atque ita exprimat, non ut multos imitatores saepe cognovi, qui aut ea, quae facilia sunt, aut etiam illa, quae insignia ac paene vitiosa, consectantur imitando. Nihil est facilius, quam amictum imitari alicuius, aut statum, aut motum', *De Oratore*, 2.22.90–1). Antonius continues, apparently on a new tack, to ask why each age appears to have its own favoured kinds of speech ('genera dicendi', *De Oratore*, 2.22.92), and offers a rapidly sketched history of Greek oratory. The dominance of one style in each age is, he argues, the result of the dominance of a particular orator as an object of imitation.

The discussion of *imitatio* in the *De Oratore* shows how labile this topic was. It intersects with discussion of how individual styles develop. It stands in an uneasy relationship to the wider question of whether one learns through precepts, through practice, or through observation of others. The whole discussion also shows how central the notion of direct personal influence was to Cicero's understanding of *imitatio* by around the mid-50s BC. It is a commonplace to say that Cicero's later rhetorical works are more Platonic than *De Oratore*, but in the case of his discussions of imitation this is a simplification: Cicero is very clear in the *De Oratore* that imitation is soul-work, which requires judgement; and he is also clear that imitation of external attributes—dress, gesture, and the other characteristics of theatrical mimicry deplored by Plato in his discussion of *mimēsis*—are not what he has in mind

---

12. See Elaine Fantham, *The Roman World of Cicero's De Oratore* (Oxford, 2004), pp. 240–1.

when he uses the verb *imitari*. The whole soul and mind is engaged in the process of learning from charismatic instruction.

Cicero's later works on rhetoric, the *Brutus* and the *Orator* (both from 46 BC) added a further dimension to his treatment of *imitatio*. His overall ambition in these later works was to present rhetoric as a quasi-political skill which might help renovate Rome, or at least preserve its ancestral republicanism during a period when it was under terminal strain. This context changed the implications of imitating earlier authors. It became a political act, which had the potential to bring back orators from the past to influence their successors as though they were still alive. As with the *De Oratore*, Cicero set the *Brutus* in an earlier period and presented it as a Platonic dialogue. By doing this he aimed to create the impression that earlier orators were still in effect rhetorically present, or akin to the living masters whom a young orator could imitate. *Imitatio* in these later works consequently becomes entangled in nostalgia for a past world of orators who survive only as texts, but who are imagined as presences who can still influence contemporary rhetoricians. It also becomes potentially a means of resisting the state of the present by reviving the skill of the past.

The later rhetorical works of Cicero have a further distinctive preoccupation. They develop the association between *imitatio* and the cultivation of a style characteristic of a particular person or of a particular period. Book 4 of the anonymous *Ad Herennium* had presented the ability to produce speeches in each of the high, middle, and low styles as an index of rhetorical skill.[13] Theophrastus, as we saw in Chapter 1, appears to have used the word *charactēr* for each of these registers of speech. In Rome the usual term for the different registers of style was *genera dicendi* (kinds of speech): Aulus Gellius in his *Noctes Atticae* directly translates Theophrastus's word *charactēres* by this phrase (6.14),[14] and Cicero also talks of the 'genera dicendi' in the *Orator* (5.20). Very confusingly, however, the *Ad Herennium* refers to the 'characters of style' as the 'figurae', the figures of style (4.8.11) or as the kinds of figures ('genera figurarum', 4.10.15), or indeed individually as a 'kind of speech' or *genus orationis* (4.11.16). The word *genus* is a common element in this tangle of terminology, and it too is rich with potential for confusion. *Genus* is ancestor both of our botanical word 'genus' and of our literary word 'genre', but it can be used by Cicero in an entirely non-technical

---

13. See *Ad Herennium*, 4.10.15–16; *De Oratore*, 3.45.177; 3.51.199.
14. Text and translation from Aulus Gellius, *The Attic Nights of Aulus Gellius*, trans. John Carew Rolfe (London and New York, 1927).

sense to mean 'kind', as in a more or less throwaway term such as 'hoc genus omne'—all that type of thing.

Cicero defines 'genus' in *De Oratore* as 'that which embraces two or more species, resembling one another in some common property while differing in some peculiarity' ('Genus autem id est, quod sui similes communione quadam, specie autem differentes, duas aut plures complectitur partes', 1.42.189). But in his discussions of style Cicero sometimes talks of a *genus* in a casual way to mean something very close to the 'type of speech used by a particular person'.[15] He does this in *De Oratore* 3.7.27 when he says that equal praise can be given to Aeschylus, Sophocles, and Euripides despite the fact that they write in 'dissimili tamen genere' (in different ways). In the discussion of imitation in the *De Oratore* 2.21.89 he refers to 'Crassus's splendid and noble way of speaking' ('illud genus Crassi magnificum atque praeclarum') in a manner that appears to collapse together Crassus's distinctive form of eloquence and a wider class of the grand style. The exact implication of these phrases is hard to judge, but 'genus' could here be taken to imply that the greatest orators effectively have their own manner of speech, or even their own *genera dicendi* in a quasi-technical sense. This would mean that there is not just a high, low, and middle style but Sophoclean and Aeschylean and Crassan *genera dicendi* too. As *De Oratore* puts it 'perhaps there might be as many ways of speaking as there are orators' ('fore ut quot oratores, totidem paene reperiantur genera dicendi', 3.9.34). In the *Brutus* Cicero states that 'Antony's style of speech is much more suited for lawcourts than the forum' ('Antoni genus dicendi multo aptius iudiciis quam contionibus', 165).[16] The term *genus* thus can blur the divide between formal *genera dicendi* on the one hand and idiosyncratic types of speech on the other. There is an Antonine way of speaking, which is a virtual *genus* specific to a particular speaker.

This sounds like a rather arcane point about vocabulary, but it was significant for the history of *imitatio*. It relates to Gérard Genette's apparently paradoxical claim that '*it is impossible to imitate a text*, or—which comes to the same—*that one can imitate only a style: that is to say, a genre*'.[17] Imitation

15. See Elaine Fantham, 'On the Use of Genus-Terminology in Cicero's Rhetorical Works', *Hermes* 107 (1979), 441–59. Fantham's principal concern is to determine Cicero's exact meaning; mine is to bring out the opportunities for later interpreters in his ambiguous terminology.

16. Quotations from Marcus Tullius Cicero, *Brutus; Orator*, trans. George Lincoln Hendrickson and H. M. Hubbell (Cambridge, Mass., and London, 1952).

17. Gérard Genette, *Palimpsests: Literature in the Second Degree*, trans. Channa Newman and Claude Doubinsky (Lincoln, Neb., 1997), p. 83.

does not entail grasping and reusing the words of a prior text, but forming a conception of the principles underlying those words. It entails understanding the *kind* of writing an earlier text or speech is, rather than simply taking over its words. Presenting an author as akin to a *genus* therefore was one conceptual foundation for this form of *imitatio*, which treated an individual orator as a 'kind of speech'. An author's individual style might be identifiable with a particular register in a similar way to the high, middle, and low styles; hence it could subsequently become an object of imitation akin to the voice of a character within literary representation.

In the *Orator* there is a further peculiarity of idiom, which was to become significant for Cicero's later readers and commentators. The dialogue is explicitly Platonic, but it shies away from describing the form of the ideal orator: 'It is always difficult to describe the form (*formam*) [of an ideal orator], for which the Greek word is *charactēr*, because different people have different notions of what is best' (*Orator*, 11.36). Cicero then goes on to say that each writer is good in his own kind.

The word *charactēr* is a striking one for Cicero to have chosen at this point, since it is by no means Plato's commonest word for what we now call a 'Platonic idea' or a 'form'. The same word could be used for more or less what we now call a 'character', in the sense of a distinctive manner of speech and behaviour, or indeed of a fictional person in a literary text who speaks in an idiosyncratic way. Aulus Gellius, immediately after he translates the Greek word *charactēres* as meaning 'kinds of speaking' ('genera dicendi'), goes on to suggest that each of the three *genera dicendi* is appropriate to a different 'character' in the modern sense in Homer's *Iliad*: he says 'But in early days these same three styles of speaking were exemplified in three men by Homer: the grand and rich in Ulysses, the elegant and restrained in Menelaus, the middle and moderate in Nestor' ('Sed ea ipsa genera dicendi iam antiquitus tradita ab Homero sunt tria in tribus: magnificum in Vlixe et ubertum, subtile in Menelao et cohibitum, mixtum moderatumque in Nestore', *Noctes Atticae*, 6.14.7).[18]

That overlap in senses is significant for the history of *imitatio*. A particular author, or a speaker mimetically represented within a fiction, might have his or her own 'genus dicendi', which might mean something as loose as 'way of talking' or something as precise as 'a distinctive style'. An author consequently might be akin to a character, in having a 'genus' of style distinctive to that author.

---

18. Leofranc Holford-Strevens, *Aulus Gellius: An Antonine Scholar and his Achievement* (Oxford, 2003), p. 222, describes this passage as 'entirely derived from Varro'.

However, combining this notion that a personal style could be analysed as though it were a particular kind of speaking with the belief that each great orator had his own distinctive *ingenium* leads to a profound problem. The object of imitation was a style or character of speech that was rooted in the *ingenium* and perhaps also in the body and the historical circumstances of a particular author. If this was the case, what should an imitator actually be imitating? A way of putting together exordia? A manner of structuring proofs? A particular rhythm of speech or a particular vocabulary? Or should they be seeking to refine their own *ingenium* by choosing one author with whom they felt an elective affinity and then studying all aspects of his style and manner of proceeding?

These questions are in every sense rhetorical. Furthermore, within the social context of Roman oratory it was undesirable to answer them in a theoretical form, since that might threaten the uncodifiable charismatic relationship between exemplary teacher and pupil. *Imitatio* was a process by which charisma might be transmitted from person to person and across the generations, rather than a matter for the precepts of Greekling grammarians. A character of style, an impress of *ingenium*, was consequently at once the object of imitation and the ineffable lost quality of a past speaker which could not be recaptured.

That final point is crucial. Someone who had directly witnessed Crassus plead a case would in some sense 'know' the object of imitation, since Crassus was standing there and speaking, as a living *exemplum* of a particular kind of rhetorical practice. He might move his audience or be loved and admired by them. But how can that relationship be transferred to the imitation of an author who is present only as a textual record?

Seneca and metaphors for *Imitatio*

As writers on the art of rhetoric believed themselves to be further and further removed from the distinctive performances by individual orators which were the ideal objects of imitation, so the description of *imitatio* became increasingly rich in metaphors. Biological metaphors were particularly common. This was because they could serve three functions at once. They could provide a substitute for the act of personal witnessing required by the 'apprenticeship' model of imitation by suggesting that the excellence of past orators could, metaphorically, be 'reborn' through careful study of their speeches. They were also a means of explaining how an accomplished and independent adult speaker could emerge from a child who initially struggled over the basic rules of rhetorical composition: a child might 'digest' an earlier author, or even grow strong by wrestling with him. They also bridged a temporal gulf. Instead of learning to imitate Demosthenes by hearing him speak, or following his rules, you might emulate his power and his force by reading him, and seek to resemble him as a child resembles its father.

The most metaphorically rich discussion of *imitatio* in the Roman world occurs in the 84th Epistle of the philosopher and statesman Lucius Annaeus Seneca (*c.*4 BC–65 AD). It was also to become the most influential single text on the subject, partly because Macrobius quoted substantial parts of it in the preface to the *Saturnalia* (probably composed sometime after 430 AD).[19] As a result Seneca's views on *imitatio* were widely disseminated through the Christian middle ages, and had a shaping influence on arguments about imitation in the Italian quattrocento.[20] Although literary historians have tended to treat Seneca's epistle as in effect another theoretical piece of writing about *imitatio* which falls squarely within the rhetorical tradition, it is potentially misleading to do so. It is found not in a technical manual of oratory, but in an epistle from Seneca to his friend Lucilius, which was included in a collection of philosophical letters probably composed in the early to middle 60s AD. The letters in the collection are variable in their ends and their rhetorical methods.[21] Many of the distinctive features of what Seneca says about *imitatio* derive from the fact that the work is an epistle rather than a rhetorical treatise. In Epistle 84 Seneca is attempting to create a Stoic and philosophical account of imitation in a deliberately casual and discursive manner, whilst with equal casualness using and transforming the terminology used to discuss the topic within the rhetorical tradition. Seneca was the younger son of a teacher of rhetoric. He was immersed in the technical vocabulary and practice of the art of rhetoric, and often echoes his father's phrasing and teaching;[22] but in this epistle he subordinates a rhetorical account of imitation to a philosophical and highly Stoic view of what

---

19. See Ambrosius Aurelius Theodosius Macrobius, *Saturnalia*, trans. Robert A. Kaster (Cambridge, Mass., and London, 2011), Pr. 5–10 and pp. 145–6 in this volume.

20. See Martin L. McLaughlin, *Literary Imitation in the Italian Renaissance* (Oxford, 1995), pp. 22–7.

21. See Thomas N. Habinek, *The Politics of Latin Literature: Writing, Identity, and Empire in Ancient Rome* (Princeton, 1998), pp. 137–50 for Seneca's use of the conventions of the exhortation.

22. E. Rolland, *De l'influence de Sénèque le père et des rhéteurs sur Sénèque le philosophe* (Gand, 1906), pp. 17–18 notes that both Senecas have a 'système éclectique' with respect to imitation. See Lucius Annaeus Seneca (the elder), *Declamations*, trans. Michael Winterbottom (Cambridge, Mass., and London, 1974), I.pr.6: 'non est unus, quamvis praecipuus sit, imitandus'—'no single person, no matter how outstanding, should be imitated'.

reading and imitating should be, and does so in a way which displays the casual intimacy of a letter to a friend.

He begins by saying that we should 'imitate the bees', who gather or digest honey. That metaphor leads him to drift off into a discussion of whether bees simply gather or in some way ferment and transform their honey, before he returns to the point: we should blend savours from our reading into one compound in a way that resembles digestion, when food turns into physical strength ('tum demum in vires et in sanguinem transeunt', *Epistles*, 84.6). He insists that we should 'digest' our reading, otherwise it passes merely into our memory, rather than becoming part of our *ingenium* or natural talent. He then considers imitative relationships to individual writers, which he says should be concealed. Even if there is in what you write a resemblance to one person whom you particularly admire 'I would have you resemble him as a child resembles its father not as a picture resembles its original, for a picture is a dead thing' ('similem esse te volo quomodo filium, non quo-modo imaginem; imago res mortua est', *Epistles*, 84.8). When his imagined interlocutor asks 'but won't it be seen whose speech, whose method of reasoning, whose pungent sayings you are imitating?' Seneca goes on to insist:

> I think that sometimes it is impossible for it to be seen who is being imitated, if a greatly talented man stamps his own form upon all the features which it has drawn from what we may call the archetype [*exemplar*], in such a way that they are combined into a unity.
>
> Puto aliquando ne intellegi quidem posse, si magni vir ingenii omnibus quae ex quo voluit exemplari traxit formam suam inpressit, ut in unitatem illa conpetant.[23]

The passage contains a textual crux surrounding the phrase 'magni vir inge-nii'. Some manuscripts read 'si magni viri nec enim'; some modern editions (including the Loeb) adopt Marvig's emendation of 'magni viri' to 'imago vera'. This emended text would make the word *imago* function at first as a negative term for an exact replica—'an *imago* is a dead thing'—a mirror image or portrait of an earlier writer—and then as (in the words of the Loeb transla-tor) 'a true copy'. That is implausible, but it illustrates that the kinds of confu-sion which surround the practice of *imitatio* can generate textual confusion.[24]

<hr />

23. Here I follow the text of Lucius Annaeus Seneca, *L. Annaei Senecae ad Lucilium epistulae morales*, ed. Achilles Beltrami (Rome, 1949).
24. The emendation has embedded itself anachronistically even within a study of imitation which is principally concerned with anachronism: see Thomas M. Greene, *The Light in Troy: Imitation and Discovery in Renaissance Poetry* (New Haven and London, 1982), p. 75.

The unemended text is also curious, because it reverses the traditional Platonic metaphor of being moulded *by* a text that one imitates. Instead a man of great talent stamps his own form on what he reads. The word *exemplar* can mean 'something which is copied', like a manuscript text which is replicated by its scribe. It is also, curiously but significantly, one of the words Roman philosophers could use to translate a Platonic 'form'. And it can also mean the copy that is produced from an exemplar. That further unsettles the relationship between the man of great *ingenium* and his original, into which he is stamping his own image, and which therefore bears the imprint of him. Seneca then bustles on to make a further comparison between imitation and a choir, in which many voices blend into one. He concludes by saying:

> I would have my mind of such a quality as this; it should be equipped with many arts, many precepts, and patterns of conduct taken from many epochs of history; but all should blend harmoniously into one. 'How,' you ask, 'can this be accomplished?' By constant effort; by doing nothing without the approval of reason and by avoiding nothing without the approval of reason.
>
> (Epistles, 84.10–11)
>
> Talem animum esse nostrum volo; multae in illo artes, multa praecepta sint, multarum aetatum exempla, sed in unum conspirata. 'Quomodo,' inquis, 'hoc effici poterit?' Adsidua intentione; si nihil egerimus nisi ratione suadente, nihil vitaverimus nisi ratione suadente.

The vocabulary here recalls the traditional tripartite method by which rhetoric is acquired: the acquisition of skills by art, by imitation, and by practice is paralleled by Seneca's 'many arts, many precepts, and many examples'; but that tidy division of methods is subordinated here to a higher method: the assiduous attentions of reason. That in turn is described by the biological metaphor of 'conspirata', which might be translated as 'welded together by breathing'.

The whole epistle reflects the practical and dialogic ethics embodied in Seneca's philosophical essays, in which the Stoic life according to reason is an overarching goal, but in which the casual idiom of a familiar letter allows for constant changes of tack and of mind. As Catharine Edwards has suggested, in the *Epistles* a Stoic self is a piece of work-in-progress, in whom divergent currents of belief and behaviour are repeatedly being corrected. That presentation of personal identity is matched in the *Epistles* by a mode of address in which Seneca at one moment corrects the behaviour of his addressee Lucilius and at the next confesses his own weaknesses, blending the role of *praeceptor* and student.[25] The image of imitation as a choir of voices, breathing together (another sense of 'conspirata') as one, is intimately linked with Seneca's conception of selfhood as a bundle of urges and appetites which the sage seeks to unite into one. And that image of the choir is also Seneca's way of breaking from the notion that the *ingenium* of a trainee orator should be subordinated to imitation of a single rhetorical master through the *tirocinium fori*. We should instead, he implicitly argues, absorb multiple examples, whilst remaining more or less single ourselves through the diligent subordination of our reading to the scrutiny of our reason. Seneca attempts in this epistle, as it were casually, to move beyond the apprenticeship model of rhetorical *imitatio* to a mode of reading in which several things taken from several places can be absorbed into a single person, and in which reason, perhaps enforced by the heavy imprint of *ingenium*, should ultimately be the master, and stamp its image on what is read.

What Seneca's epistle offers as a substitute for conceptual clarity is a series of powerful metaphors. The claim that the *ingenium* can be fed by reading which is properly absorbed by the reason is secured by the biological metaphor of digestion: 'we must digest our reading: otherwise it will pass into our memory, but not into our *ingenium*' ('Concoquamus illa: alioquin in memoriam ibunt, non in ingenium'). The epistle offers a trio of biological metaphors— be like a bee, resemble your exemplar as a child resembles his father, digest your reading—which had immense influence over later writers.

Seneca's discussion of imitation also tallies with the view of style which is presented in his *Epistles*. Earlier histories of Latin style typically and often crudely oppose a Senecan style to the Ciceronian. Seneca's view of individual style in the *Epistles* is as pragmatic and fluid as his Stoicism. He is prepared to accept that individuals write in different ways that reflect their individual natures. He is, however, extremely tolerant of authors who subordinate rhetorical shaping to a persuasive familiarity of style, which conveys instruction without oppressing those who might wish to emulate it. He defends the workaday style of Papirius Fabianus (*Epistles*, 100.6) against Lucilius's criticisms by describing it as 'a good house to live in' ('domus recta est') which conveys honest opinions ('sensus honestos'). Fabianus's style follows his content like the shadow follows its substance ('ille rerum se magnitudini addixit, eloquentiam velut umbram non hoc agens trahit', *Epistles*,

---

25. Catharine Edwards, 'Self-Scrutiny and Self-Transformation in Seneca's Letters', in John G. Fitch, ed., *Seneca* (Oxford, 2008), pp. 84–101.

100.10). Seneca goes on to say that this familiar style is defensible because it encourages imitation without making its would-be imitators despair of ever equalling it ('imitationem sui evocarent sine despiratione vincendi', *Epistles*, 100.12).[26] The imperfect Stoic, striving to compile one rational agent out of many influences, and striving in a practical manner to make other agents grasp the principles of virtue, approves of a less than Ciceronian rigour of style, since 'it is disheartening to inspire in a man the desire and to take away from him the hope of imitation' ('Deterret enim qui imitandi cupiditatem fecit, spem abstulit', *Epistles*, 100.12). The august ideal of Ciceronian rhetoric is not the explicit opponent of this defence of an inartificial style, but Seneca wants it to be known that both style and the art of imitation are entirely subordinate to the process of educating people in virtue and enabling them to aspire towards stylistic goals which are attainable; and that might entail compromising on the notion that the *ingenium* of one author and his character of writing should be the single object of imitation.

As this discussion of Seneca implies, by the close of the first century AD there was not a single 'Roman theory of imitation'. Rather different writers responded variously to the inherited problematics of *imitatio*. The practice was crucial to the perpetuation of a rhetorical tradition and was a valuable means of keeping Roman oratory in touch with the primal political values of the republic, but it was so flanked with conceptual problems that the problems came to be central to the concept itself. How does an imitation combine resemblance to that which it imitates with difference from it? How do we distinguish or not distinguish gestural or stylistic imitation from 'properly' learning a *technē*? And what in practice is an imitator doing? Does an imitator seek to use the same *lexis* as an earlier writer, or does he make inferences about the ethical character and priorities of an earlier writer and attempt to produce a resemblance of what such a person might have written?

Quintilian

Although Marcus Fabius Quintilianus, or Quintilian as he is generally known, presents himself as Seneca's adversary, the discussion of *imitatio* in the tenth book of his massive treatise on the art of rhetoric, the *Institutio Oratoria*, shows that both writers inherited and responded to a similar set of

---

26. Rolland, *De l'influence*, pp. 19–20 notes that Seneca's father said similar things about Fabianus in II.pr.1. Compare *Moral Epistles*, 29.22.5.2 where Seneca attacks the over-elaborated style.

problems.[27] Quintilian's treatise, written in or around 94–5 AD, contains in the second chapter of its tenth book the fullest surviving discussion in Latin on the subject of *imitatio*. This was written about thirty years after Seneca's *Epistles*, and seeks in several respects to correct Seneca's view of the topic. Quintilian positions his chapter on imitation immediately after the section of the *Institutio* which is about *elocutio*, or style, which is in itself significant: it encodes within the structure of the work an association between *imitatio* and the understanding of what an individual style might be.

Quintilian was born in 35 AD, almost eighty years after Mark Antony had had Cicero's hand and head cut off and nailed to the rostra in the forum in 43 BC. Nonetheless Quintilian imitated Cicero's example as a theorist and practitioner of rhetoric, and he necessarily did so from Cicero's published texts rather than from direct personal contact. He therefore responded actively to the historical and political nostalgia for the republic which had pervaded Cicero's later rhetorical works: Cicero's conviction that the great age of republican oratory had died and was in urgent need of revival paralleled Quintilian's own conviction that Cicero embodied a lost age of perfection in Roman oratory.

Two further points about Quintilian's intellectual origins are germane to this discussion. He attempted to sum up and to some degree fix the entire rhetorical tradition. Consequently he was willing to offer rules or *praecepta* in the manner of a humbler codifier of the *ars rhetorica* akin to the author of the *Ad Herennium*. But his main priority was to preserve the Ciceronian (and originally Catonian) ideal of an orator as a *vir bonus dicendi peritus* (a good man skilled in speaking, *Institutio*, 12.1) who might influence the law and the state through his eloquence.[28] As a result Quintilian more explicitly than any earlier Roman writer on the art of rhetoric fuses together what might crudely be called the elite and the pedagogical conception of what an 'art' of rhetoric might be: he conceives rhetoric as both an achieved practice instantiated in the works of Cicero and as a technical skill which can be grasped by following a systematic method. A further point worthy of note is that it is generally accepted that Quintilian's discussion of *imitatio* was indebted to Dionysius of Halicarnassus.[29]

---

27. See Elaine Fantham, 'Imitation and Decline: Rhetorical Theory and Practice in the First Century after Christ', *Classical Philology* 73 (1978), 102–16.
28. See the excellent account of Quintilian's aims in Quintilian, *Institutio Oratoria. Book 2*, ed. Tobias Reinhardt and Michael Winterbottom (Oxford, 2006), esp. pp. xxxiv–xlv.
29. D. A. Russell, '*De Imitatione*', in David West and Tony Woodman, eds., *Creative Imitation and Latin Literature* (Cambridge, 1979), 1–16.

One of the main ways in which it appears Quintilian departed from his major source and guide, however, was in the richness of metaphorical language he used to describe *imitatio*. The particular metaphors which Quintilian used in his discussion of imitation often share Seneca's association between imitation and biological processes, although Quintilian gives a distinct twist to those metaphors. Underlying his discussion of *imitatio* and indeed much of the *Institutio* is an ideal of Roman manliness, which leads him to describe both rhetoric and imitation in quasi-military terms, or as a form of physical contest. This is not in itself surprising. An eristic and competitive element was intrinsic to the art of rhetoric: litigators want to win, and regularly present what they do in court as a kind of battle, or as a sporting contest, or gladiatorial contest, and rhetorical practice, as Thomas Habinek has eloquently shown, is intimately connected with the cultural replication of 'manly' speakers.[30]

Quintilian, however, heightens that association. He does so for three main reasons. The first was that he saw himself as belonging to a late and slack age that needed renovation by looking back to the powerful orators of the past.[31] The second is that by emphasizing the muscle of Roman oratory he could imply that it conquered the Greek orators from whom it derived. A third is that metaphors of athletic exercise and of warfare could bring to his *ars rhetorica* a substitute for bodily presence and direct charismatic influence. That is to say, those metaphors enabled him to suggest that an imitator should seek to imitate in an *exemplum* not just a set of precepts or a set of texts, but a body and a whole style of being.[32]

Quintilian's ideal imitator is very similar to his ideal orator, a *vir bonus dicendi peritus*, a good man skilled in speaking. He is in search of *exempla* who can give him what Quintilian variously calls *vis dicendi*, power of speaking, or *robor viris* ('truly masculine strength', *Institutio*, 10.1.43). Imitation is one method to be used in pursuit of that aim of quasi-physical rhetorical power. Right at the start of Book 10 Quintilian states: 'Eloquence will never be mature and robust unless it develops strength by much practice [*multo stilo*] in writing' ('Nam neque solida atque robusta fuerit umquam eloquentia nisi multo stilo vires acceperit', *Institutio*, 10.1.2).

---

30. Habinek, *Ancient Rhetoric*, esp. pp. 65–8.   31. Fantham, 'Imitation and Decline'.
32. It is misleading to claim that 'In Roman discussions of *imitatio* during the first century B.C., metaphorization is a good deal denser in poetry than in the prose rhetorical treatises where the subject most commonly arises', Greene, *Light in Troy*, p. 60. Significantly this remark accompanies a very cursory discussion of Quintilian.

The *stilus* is a pointed piece of metal, but also the Roman equivalent of a pen, as well as the word for 'style'. That accidental fusion of senses enables the use of the *stilus* to be presented as akin to athletic exercise, which builds up the manly strength on which successful oratory depends.[33] The *stilus* can bring 'at once the most labour and the most profit' (*Institutio*, 10.3.1), and practising your *stilus* is akin to working out with a javelin to acquire a skill. Writing is a kind of *exercitatio*—which is also a key term in Cicero's rhetorical works, and was of course one of the three ways in which the art of rhetoric could be acquired for the author of the *Ad Herennium*—a physical exercise that strengthens the body and the tongue by practice.[34] And it is practice that enables the orator to go beyond merely following precepts, since, as Quintilian states at the very start of Book 10, it is through practice that an orator acquires a habitual ability to speak well:

> But these rules of style, while part of the student's theoretical knowledge, are not in themselves sufficient to give him oratorical power (*vim*). In addition he will require that assured facility which the Greeks call *hexis*.
>
> Sed haec eloquendi praecepta, sicut cogitationi sunt necessaria, ita non satis ad vim dicendi valent, nisi illis firma quaedam facilitas, quae apud Graecos ἕξις nomitatur, accesserit. (*Institutio*, 10.1.1)

James Murphy does not overstate the case when he says 'The whole operational theory of the *Institutio* is that men can be habituated, through exercise, into both skill and virtue...I believe that *hexis*, habit, is the key to the whole *Institutio oratoria*.'[35] Practice, or physical exercise, transcends the precepts which might be imparted by a vulgar grammarian, because it leads to a *hexis*, a habit, or (more exactly) a stably possessed power and disposition to

33. 'Rhetorical training should be regarded not just as acquisition of knowledge and technique but as a more complex and wide-ranging "process of acculturation".' William J. Dominik and Jon Hall, eds., *A Companion to Roman Rhetoric* (Malden, Mass., and Oxford, 2007), p. 309. Cf. Habinek, *Ancient Rhetoric*, p. 61: 'it is helpful to regard rhetorical training not just as acquisition of knowledge, but more generally as a process of acculturation. Indeed we might go so far as to say that rhetoric becomes its own culture into which the student is gradually initiated.'
34. Elaine Fantham, *Comparative Studies in Republican Latin Imagery* (Toronto, 1972), p. 141 discusses Cicero's use of images from the *palaestra* in *De Oratore* 1.73 and 1.81 and comments on the military overtones of *exercitatio* in *De Oratore*, 2.187, and *Brutus*, 139 on p. 158. Fantham's discussion of Cicero's imagery of the body associated with the ideal of being *ornatus* concludes that Cicero's favoured words for describing achieved rhetorical skill (*sanguis, ossa, lacerti, nervi*) 'have no equivalent in the Greek metaphorical vocabulary of the rich style'. Quintilian adopts this vocabulary, and in his writing 'Greek aesthetic pleasure has been displaced by Roman emphasis on training and the strength which it produces', pp. 173–4.
35. James J. Murphy, 'The Key Role of Habit in Roman Rhetoric and Education, as Described by Quintilian', in Tomás Albaladejo Mayordomo, Emilio Del Río, and José Antonio Caballero López, eds., *Quintiliano: historia y actualidad de la retórica* (Logroño [Spain], 1998), 141–50, p. 145.

do. It is not clear quite how technical or quite how Aristotelian Quintilian's understanding of that term might be (which he may well have derived from Dionysius of Halicarnassus), but a *hexis* presumably means a habit of healthy fluency which is modelled on the practices of the writer(s) who is imitated.

Although Quintilian uses a Greek word to describe the goal of achieving practical skill, his objective was to create distinctively Roman rhetorical warriors. He insists that orators are not like poets because they subsist in the eristic environment of the law-courts: 'But we, let us not forget, stand armed in the front line, fight for high stakes, and strive for victory' ('nos vero armatos stare in acie et summis de rebus decernere et ad victoriam niti', *Institutio*, 10.1.30). He even advises young writers to revise their works while their mind is still warm, so that it 'recovers strength and gathers fresh impetus' ('recipit ex integro vires', *Institutio*, 10.3.6), just as people take a run up for the long-jump or when they throw javelins. This pervasive military imagery is underpinned not simply by a belief that orators fight and win in the courts, but by a larger cultural programme. Roman oratory must learn from its Greek originals how to defeat those originals. Hence Cicero is not just the best orator to imitate. He is the one who can powerfully oppose the Greeks, and defeat the best of them in a cultural battle: 'I would happily pit Cicero forcefully against any of the Greeks' ('nam Ciceronem cuicunque eorum [Graecorum] fortiter opposuerim', *Institutio*, 10.1.105).

Quintilian overlayers that cultural battle with an implied economic battle. For as well as being a martial man, Quintilian's orator seeks 'riches' or 'abundance', which he variously terms *opes* or *copia*. These words, which were again central to Cicero's rhetorical writings, also straddle a boundary between the physical and the metaphorical, since wealth and abundance of goods was in Rome, as now, a foreseeable consequence of a legal career. The copious orator has a rich store of material at his command which are *propria*, things which are his own and not someone else's. This *vir* is clearly a property-holding citizen, possessed of his own *propria* which he can use to augment the qualities he finds in his *exemplum*: 'But it is the man who also adds his own good qualities [*propria*] to these, making good the deficiencies and cutting out any superfluities, who will be the perfect orator we are seeking' ('Qui vero etiam propria his bona adiecerit, ut suppleat quae deerant, circumcidat, si quid redundabit, is erit, quem quaerimus perfectus orator', *Institutio*, 10.2.28).

The words *propria* and *bona* here mean the orator's own peculiar virtues, which are not present in the copious riches of his *exemplum*; but they are also the orator's very own goods or wealth.[36] And that in turn connects indirectly back to the concept of possessing a *hexis*, or a permanently owned disposition, since the noun *hexis* derives from the Greek verb 'to have'. Being in debt to others, to be lacking in personal possessions or *propria*, is an evil: 'are we', Quintilian asks at one point, 'to have nothing that is not a gift from strangers?' ('sed nihil habebimus nisi beneficii alieni', *Institutio*, 10.2.6)? Underlying this question are two parallel fears: that of personal financial dependency and that of cultural dependency. Are we Romans to be dependent, economically and culturally, and are we therefore condemned to performing mechanical labours of replication?

The image Quintilian uses to develop this fear is highly significant. It is that of the copyist of the visual arts: 'That would make us like certain painters, who study only to learn how to copy pictures by means of measurements and lines' ('Quemadmodum quidam pictores in id solum student, ut describere tabulas mensuris ac lineis sciant', *Institutio*, 10.2.6). Is a Roman orator to resemble a lowly artisan or freedman who spends his life merely copying artworks by reproducing their proportions? That is not simply a reverse colonial cringe, in which the pupil nation Rome disowns its debts to Greek oratory. It also alludes to the more humdrum aspects of the *ars rhetorica*, the codification and dissemination of rules and precepts which Cicero disparagingly termed *artificium*. Imitating in a way that develops your independent strength is a means of transcending the mechanical skill of a copyist or a grammarian who draws up rules for rhetorical practice. That skill adds *propria*, matter of one's own, to the skill of a mechanic artist who measures each limb of a statue in order to be able to carve a replica for a patron. Quintilian does not want to think of himself as someone who delivers rules for replication, as an upmarket *grammaticus*-cum-tutor in rhetoric. And he does not want to think of Romans as mere copyists of Greek artefacts either: he wants rather to think of Roman orators as rich, breeding, independent athletic bodies.

This focus on Roman orators as in effect rhetorical body-builders rather than statue-makers or replicators explains one curious absence from Quintilian's discussion of *imitatio*. He shies away from the more technical language used

---

36. Cf. the discussion in Habinek, *Politics of Latin Literature*, pp. 57–9 of how the word *exemplum* came to be transferred from an economic to a moral register in Terence. The occult ways in which imitation of an *exemplum* informs the practice of an orator parallel the mysterious way in which he acquires *copia* and *propria*—a full style which is all his own whilst not being quantifiable in the manner of a material possession.

by Dionysius of Halicarnassus when he enigmatically described *imitatio* as 'an activity (*energeia*) reproducing the model (*paradeigma*) through theoretical principles (*theōrēmatōn*)'.[37] That language was Greek, not only in its abstraction, but also in its implications: the word *theōrēmatōn* might imply that an imitator should be analysing or measuring an *exemplum*, as a sculptor who wished to reproduce a statue from an original might do.

As well as avoiding the technicality of Dionysius's Greek, Quintilian's sharp-edged and eristic model of imitation was also designed to make Seneca (whom he openly attacks in *Institutio*, 10.1) sound round-bellied and slack, a bit too keen on imitation as a matter of rationally musing and munching and digesting texts, and not quite the kind of rippling mean rhetorical machine Quintilian himself sought to foster.[38] Seneca himself says that his love of literature makes him 'lazy and careless about his body' ('pigrum me et neglegentem corporis litterarum amor faciat', *Epistles*, 84.1). Quintilian is willing to associate imitation with eating, but when he does so he stresses what hard work it is to 'digest' a text: 'Let us go over the text again and work on it. We chew our food and almost liquefy it before we swallow, so as to digest it more easily; similarly, what we read must not be committed to the memory for subsequent imitation while it is still in a crude state, but, as it were, softened and reduced to a pulp by frequent repetition' ('Repetamus autem et retractemus, et ut cibos mansos ac prope liquefactos demittimus, quo facilius digerantur, ita lectio non cruda, sed multa iteratione, mollita et velut confecta, memoriae imitationeque tradatur', *Institutio*, 10.1.19).

But the strangest features of Quintilian's writing on *imitatio* occur when he relaxes his emphasis on bodily regimen. At these moments his relentless focus on activity and exercise can slip away. So history can be just a fruitful source of nourishment: 'History also can nourish the orator with its rich, sweet sap' ('Historia quoque alere oratorem quodam uberi iucundoque suco potest', *Institutio*, 10.1.31). *Sucus*, the word Russell translates as 'sap', can also mean 'vital principle' (*OLD*, 3b), or the principle of style; and *uber*, which derives from the Latin word for 'breast', can mean 'rich'. Quintilian imagines that we imbibe a vital juice from our reading which is something akin to breast-milk for the mind. Indeed Quintilian's interest in *vis* and virility is

---

37. Dionysius of Halicarnassus, ed. Aujac, *Opuscules*, p. 27. See Russell, '*De Imitatione*', p. 10 on the difficulty of this passage.

38. On Quintilian's ideal of a fit male body, see Michael Winterbottom, 'Quintilian the Moralist', in Albaladejo Mayordomo et al., *Quintiliano: historia y actualidad de la retórica*, 317–34. For a comparison of Seneca and Quintilian on this point, see Fantham, 'Imitation and Decline', pp. 110–11. On Quintilian's hostility to Seneca, see Dominik, *Roman Eloquence*, pp. 50–7.

matched and offset by a quality which he tends to call *ubertas*—fertility, an abstract noun which also derives from the word for 'breast'. He writes with a real passion of Cicero's most blessed fertility of mind, for instance:

> It seems to me, in fact, that Cicero, having devoted himself entirely to the imitation of the Greeks, succeeded in reproducing the forcefulness of Demosthenes, the abundance of Plato, and the elegance of Isocrates. But he did more than reproduce by study the excellences of each: most, or rather all, of his virtues are the self-generated product of the happy richness [*ubertas*] of his immortal genius. He does not, as Pindar says, 'collect the rainwater', but wells forth a living flood.

> Nam mihi videtur M. Tullius, cum se totum ad imitationem Graecorum contulisset, effinxisse vim Demosthenis, copiam Platonis, iucunditatem Isocratis. Nec vero quod in quoque optimum fuit, studio consecutus est tantum; sed plurimas vel potius omnes ex se ipso virtutes extulit immortalis ingenii beatissima ubertas. Non enim pluvias, ut ait Pindarus, aquas colligit, sed vivo gurgite exundat. (*Institutio*, 10.1.108–9)

Ubertas (fertility) and *vivo* (living) are the words that stand out of this passage. Quintilian on the whole associates *ubertas* with agrarian cultivation and natural fertility, rather than with a capacity for sexual reproduction or with the mothering energies of the breast: the force of steel cutting through the land is more often than not in the background when he talks of fertility, partly because his beloved word *exercitatio* can mean both 'practice' and 'the working (of soil in agriculture), cultivation' (*OLD*, 1.b)—and we might also recall that *stilus*, a style, a stylus, can also mean a sharp tool that can be used in weeding and in grafting plants (*OLD*, 1).[39]

But *exercitatio*, practice, is the keyword of Book 10 of the *Institutio*. Quintilian uses it more than seventy times in the whole work, but fourteen of those usages occur in Book 10 alone, which is about twice as many as would be expected from an even distribution of the word across the entirety of the *Institutio*. It comes to connote exercise on the battlefield, the digging of soil, cultivation, energizing labour. It consequently unites the notion that the imitative orator is a hard-working soldier with the idea that he is also

---

39. Catherine Connors, 'Field and Forum: Culture and Agriculture in Roman Rhetoric', in Dominik, *Roman Eloquence*, p. 71 explores the conflict between rhetorical contempt for rustic speech and Roman admiration for cultivation in Roman rhetorical writing, in *De Oratore*, 2.88 and 2.131 in particular. Teresa Morgan, *Literate Education in the Hellenistic and Roman Worlds* (Cambridge, 1998) discusses agrarian metaphors in educational theory, pp. 256–60. See also Elaine Fantham, 'The Concept of Nature and Human Nature in Quintilian's Psychology and Theory of Instruction', *Rhetorica* 13 (1995), 125–36.

fertile of novelty. He has a kind of military-industrial-agricultural womb of his own, an *ubertas* that comes from *exercitatio* in the double sense of military exertion and georgic labour. The classic statement of this belief is in 10.3:

> As deep digging makes the soil more fertile for the germination and growth of seeds, so progress which is not sought by superficial means yields the fruits of study more generously and retains them more faithfully... Above all, let us develop a strength which will be sufficient for the fatigues of our battles, and will not be exhausted by continual use. Nature herself has willed that no great thing can be brought about in a moment; she has set difficulties in the way of every noble work—she even made it a law of birth [*nascendi legem*] that bigger animals should stay longer within the mother's womb.

> Nam ut terra alte refossa generandis alendisque seminibus fecundior, sic profectus non a summo petitus studiorum fructus et fundit uberius et fidelius continet... Vires faciamus ante omnia quae sufficiant labori certaminum et usu non exhauriantur. Nihil enim rerum ipsa natura voluit magnum effici cito praeposuitque pulcherrimo cuique operi difficultatem; quae nascendi quoque hanc fecerit legem, ut maiora animalia diutius visceribus parentis continerentur.

> *(Institutio, 10.3.2–4)*

This is in every sense a fertile passage. Our Roman man of virtue or *vir virtutis*, digging, doing his *exercitatio* on the land, developing strength to fight his battles, has a fecund mind, and the aim of his labours, which grows with their duration, is to produce a mighty birth.

Running alongside this curious mixture of muscle and breast, of botanical and biological growth, is another metaphor: that of the race. That metaphor again suggests that the acquisition of rhetorical skill is analogous to the acquisition of physical strength on the Campus Martius. But, like the image of the fertile body, it is also potentially an awkward metaphor to use in the context of *imitatio*. Temporally speaking the imitator's predecessors are behind him, and yet they are unsurpassable because that also means they were the first to arrive at their destination. The imitator has to run fast to catch up: 'no one can draw level with a man in whose footsteps he feels bound to tread. The follower is inevitably always behind' ('Eum vero nemo potest aequare, cuius vestigiis sibi utique insistendum putat; necesse est enim semper sit posterior qui sequitur', *Institutio*, 10.2.10).

The language here draws on the recurrent metaphor of imitation as a journey or race, but it also takes us back to the comparison in the *Ad Herennium* of Greek rhetorical theorists to mere spectators at the Olympic games. And it goes along with a kind of historical reversal which energizes cultures that come later: if 'posterior' and 'sequitur' are taken in a spatial sense, as they would be in describing a running-race, then the follower lags behind, tracking the footsteps of the leader, sniffing at a scent, and unable to catch up. If they are taken in a temporal sense, however, being *posterior* does not simply mean coming last. It might also mean coming afterwards in a way that implies an advance on a prior position. Does the imitator 'follow' from behind (spatially) or in front (temporally); and temporally speaking which *is* the front and which is behind?[40]

Quintilian regards coming afterwards as potentially beneficial. He makes this clear when he presents a reassuring natural law of unlikeness. It is easier to be unlike than it is to be alike an earlier example:

> Furthermore, it is generally easier to improve on something than simply to repeat it. Total similarity is so difficult to achieve that even Nature herself has failed to prevent things which seem to match and resemble each other most closely from being always distinguishable in *some* respect.
>
> Adde quod plerumque facilius est plus facere quam idem. Tantam enim difficultatem habet similitudo ut ne ipsa quidem natura in hoc ita evaluerit, ut non res quae simillimae, quaeque pares maxime videantur, utique discrimine aliquo discernantur.   (*Institutio*, 10.2.10)

That potentially is consoling, and its consolation is related to the concern of Cicero's later rhetorical works with the diversity of styles: each orator, even an imitative orator, will be different from previous orators because it is impossible to be identical with the object of imitation. *Exercitatio* has as its aim and consequence the cultural distinctness of Latin writing from Greek; it generates the health and strength of the individual orator; it brings forth new births; and it is assisted by the law of necessary unlikeness which states that an attempt at replication will intrinsically differ from that which it attempts to replicate.

Consequently practice in imitating a predecessor necessarily establishes an independent body, which departs from its *exemplum* even as it imitates it. Hence being *posterior*, coming afterwards in the race, has difference as its rich consolation prize. This presents an alternative to the bleak vision of imitation proposed by the elder Seneca in the preface to his *Declamations*, where he puts forward a superficially similar thought: 'Don't imitate a single person, no matter how outstanding he is, because the imitator never becomes the equal of the original author. This is the nature of the matter: likeness

---

40. See Pernille Harsting, 'Quintilian, Imitation and "Anxiety of Influence"', in Albaladejo Mayordomo et al., *Quintiliano: historia y actualidad de la retórica*, 1325–36.

always falls short of the truth' ('Non est unus, quamvis praecipuus sit, imitandus, quia numquam par fit imitator auctori. haec rei natura est: semper citra veritatem est similitudo', *Controversiae*, 1.pr.6).

But if *exercitatio* is the keyword of Quintilian's discussion of *imitatio*, the words *vis* and *ingenium* are the rub. As for Cicero *vis* can mean 'rhetorical power' or 'bodily force'. It could also be used of a power of style which was manifested by some writers more than others. *Vis* can mean muscular strength of the kind that can be developed by practice, by *exercitatio*; but it can also in Quintilian mean something very close to 'spirit'. The word can also be used to mean the intrinsic nature of something, its quiddity, its whatness, the power by which it is itself and not another thing (*OLD*, 17). And *vis* in that sense, like the unique *ingenium* or character of an author's style, presents a necessary outer limit to what is imitable.[41]

So Quintilian says of Demosthenes 'Of these Demosthenes was far the greatest, almost a law of oratory in himself: such is his force, the concentration of his thought, his muscular firmness, his economy, his control—one feels there is nothing lacking and nothing superfluous' ('Quorum longe princeps Demosthenes ac paene lex orandi fuit; tanta vis in eo, tam densa omnia, ita quibusdam nervis intenta sunt, tam nihil otiosum, is dicendi modus, ut nec quod desit in eo nec quod redundet invenias', *Institutio*, 10.1.76). *Vis* is here aligned with an unquestionable and political authority: Demosthenes is an emperor of eloquence, who embodies all the laws of eloquence. Homer, too, is unemulably himself: 'It takes a great mind, I will not say to rival, for that is impossible, but simply to appreciate [*sequi*, literally 'to follow'] his virtues' ('ut magni sit viri virtutes eius non aemulatione, quod fieri non potest, sed intellectu sequi', *Institutio*, 10.1.50).

Quintilian's repeated emphasis on the distinctive *vis* of earlier orators makes sense of one startling further feature of his vocabulary. In the surviving corpus of classical Latin there are only four occurrences of the word 'inimitabilis' (inimitable). Three of these are in Quintilian's *Institutio Oratoria*.[42] Paradoxically, inimitability is a key concept for Quintilian, that great theorist of imitation. The principal qualities of an orator include *vis*, energy/vitality, *ingenium* or unique talent, which cannot be acquired simply by practice:

---

41. Fantham, 'Concept of Nature', p. 132, considers the relationship between natural talent and imitation to be 'the most problematic part of Quintilian's theory'.

42. *Institutio*, 1.10.7; 2.16.16; 8.3.25. The other is Velleius Paterculus 2.97.3. Quintilian also describes (e.g.) Pindar as imitable by no one (10.1.62).

'Again, the greatest qualities of an orator are inimitable: his talent, invention, force, fluency, everything in fact that is not taught in the textbooks' ('Adde quod ea, quae in oratore maxima sunt, imitabilia non sunt, ingenium, inventio, vis, facilitas et quidquid arte non traditur', *Institutio*, 10.2.12). This thought seems to be tacked lazily on to the preceding discussion by Quintilian's favoured way of conjoining thoughts, 'and also' ('adde quod'), but it is in fact central to Quintilian's thinking. In the *Institutio Oratoria* imitation leads to a recognition that the central defining qualities of a writer are not only inimitable, but cannot be encapsulated by art, *ars*, or in a rhetorical text-book. Like Cicero, Quintilian wishes to preserve the notion that rhetoric is a living art with a power of its own that cannot be codified or captured in precepts. Great orators can inspire practice; but they also have a reserve of uniqueness that makes it impossible to replicate their achievements. Imitation therefore necessarily leads towards the inimitable as both its origin and its goal.

As a result the imitator, unable fully to reproduce the *vis* and *ingenium*, the distinctive force and talent, of his inimitable *exemplum* might become no more than a maker of shadows or reflections, or what Plato termed *eidōla*: 'Again, whatever resembles another object is bound to be less than what it imitates, just as the shadow is less than the body, the picture less than the face, and the actor's performance less than the emotions of real life' ('Adde quod, quidquid alteri simile est, necesse est minus sit eo, quod imitatur, ut umbra corpore et imago facie et actus histrionum veris adfectibus', *Institutio*, 10.2.11). Difference can be consoling: I am not like Demosthenes because my natural *ingenium* differs from his. But difference is also potentially the imitator's bad dream: despite my constant desire to become like Demosthenes, I manage only to become an image or shadowy replicant of him. I differ from him (as Seneca would put it) not as a son does from his father, but as an *imago* or shadow does from a living body. Quintilian then offers a startling and vivid comparison in order to describe these failed imitations:

> And even those who have judgement enough to avoid faults should not be satisfied with producing an image of excellence, a mere outer skin, as it were, or rather a 'shape' like those which Epicurus says are given off by the surfaces of bodies.
>
> Nec vero saltem iis, quibus ad evitanda vitia iudicii satis fuit, sufficiat imaginem virtutis effingere et solam, ut sic dixerim, cutem vel potius illas Epicuri figuras, quas e summis corporibus dicit effluere.   (*Institutio*, 10.2.15)

This takes us into the Roman version of Plato's cave: the imitation of another writer might produce only ghostly images.[43] But there is a very significant twist. Those ghostly images are akin to the thin films of atoms which Epicurus believed were emitted from bodies, and which, he believed, gave rise both to perceptions and to illusions such as ghosts and spirits. As Chapter 3 will show, the principal word used by Lucretius for that phenomenon is *simulacrum*; Quintilian the rhetorician prefers the richly ambiguous term *figura*. That in turn suggests that the imitator will never quite achieve the power of Dionysius's farmer, and create *eikones* which will enable him to breed beautiful living sons. An imitation *should* be a thriving exercised body, capable of conquering and controlling, which is rich in fertility, which has absorbed the excellences of others into its body and which consequently strengthens and enriches its own *vis* and *ingenium*. But in practice it is likely to be a shadow or a figure of its original, which fails to capture the intrinsic properties of that which it imitates. Seek to develop your own *vis* through *imitatio* and you might end up producing no more than a *simulacrum* of the *vis* of another.

At no point does Quintilian offer the imitator a clear criterion for distinguishing between a *simulacrum* and living imitation, except by his insistence that the two are distinct. Quintilian's account of the entire topic is trapped within the Roman rhetorical tradition: the inbuilt resistance of that tradition to any 'Greekish' attempt to codify the mysterious talent by which a great orator influences his pupil means that according to Quintilian the imitator might be alive, energetic, and possessed of a distinctive *ingenium*, or he might simply be a *simulacrum*, a pale semblance of the paradigm towards which he aspires.

The consequences of this could be seen from several points of view. One would be brutally negative: Roman 'theories' of *imitatio* simply fail to explain what it is, beyond insisting that it should result in a strong and well-developed *ingenium*. But that is a superficial view. The failure of the Roman rhetorical tradition to provide clarification of the relationship between imitator and the imitated *exemplum* had immense literary value. It generated a mystery.

---

43. The word *imago* could be used of the death masks of predecessors worn at a Roman funeral and theatrically brought to life to mark that occasion: see Habinek, *Ancient Rhetoric*, p. 78. Both *imagines* and *simulacra* could also be used of the images created by the artificial memory of an orator when he sought to associate particular arguments with particular places. See *Ad Herennium*, 3.16.29 and Cicero, *De Oratore*, 34.157. Aulus Gellius, *Attic Nights*, 6.14.4, ascribes to each of the three characters of style a corresponding defect which he describes as arising from an attempt to mimic their manner and character in a false appearance ('quae earum modum et habitum simulacris falsis ementiuntur').

It made *vis* and *ingenium* objects of aspiration and admiration. And instead of providing methods of replicating them it offered a series of powerful metaphors, and a set of potentially powerful anxieties. Can a child equal his father? Can an imitator be more than a *simulacrum*?

Longinus

Later chapters of this book will show just how influential and productive those questions and the accompanying metaphors were. But before we consider how poetic practice interacts with thinking about *imitatio* in the rhetorical tradition, we might pause in the age of Quintilian, and shift perspective. How might a Greek have responded to the metaphorical riches and conceptual poverty of the Roman tradition of thought about *imitatio*, so much of which directly or indirectly related to the attempted cultural supremacy of Rome over Greece?

An answer to that question can be glimpsed in the treatise *Peri Hypsōs* or, *On the Sublime*, which is ascribed to Dionysius Longinus. Given the uncertainties about the date and authorship of this treatise it is impossible to be sure of its relationship in chronology or influence to Quintilian. It is generally agreed to have been written by a Greek-speaking subject of the Roman empire, and seems most likely to have been composed in the late first century AD.[44] The fact that it is written by a Greek matters a great deal, as several recent studies have shown: it treats rhetorical *paideia* and cultural authority in ways that often lie distinctively athwart the traditions of Roman rhetoric.[45] Indeed Longinus's celebration of the wild and ungovernable rhetorical power of the sublime is an example of the empire fighting—or at least talking—back to Rome.

On the Sublime begins with that simple question which is so foundational to the rhetorical tradition: whether art (*technē*) or nature produces the sublime style. Longinus's answer to that question is to emphasize the role played

---

44. D. A. Russell resists any date after 100 AD in Aristotle, Longinus, and Demetrius, *Aristotle Poetics; Longinus On The Sublime; Demetrius On Style*, trans. Stephen Halliwell, D. A. Russell, W. Hamilton Fyfe, and Doreen Innes (Cambridge, Mass., and London, 1995), p. 145. Despite the doubts over the identity of the author I shall refer to him simply as Longinus.
45. See Whitmarsh, *Politics of Imitation*, pp. 57–75, who argues that for Longinus the sublime is a means by which late Greeks under Roman rule can use their secondariness to positive effect. Yun Lee Too, *The Idea of Ancient Literary Criticism* (Oxford, 1998), pp. 187–217 argues for its tropically dislocating effect.

by natural power: he argues that *hypsos* or sublimity requires an extreme form of natural talent, which he denotes by the word *megalophuē* (2.1), or greatness of nature, and which he insists is born not made. Although he does draw on the methods of a *technologia* or practical manual of instruction on style in offering advice about the figures to use at moments of sublimity, he goes beyond any Roman rhetorician in explaining sublimity in a style which itself seeks to instantiate the qualities which it describes and commends.[46] As a result Longinus produces at once a technical manual and a text which itself seeks to become a model for imitation as an instance of the sublime style.

On the Sublime picks up and develops many of the metaphors and *aporiai* which had become central to Latin discussions of imitation, and throws those questions back at Rome in extreme, awkward, and sometimes distorted forms. In a comparison between Cicero and Demosthenes, for instance, Longinus insists that 'our' Greek, Demosthenes, is able to defeat the Roman orator with his great force (*biē*—the closest Greek equivalent to the Latin word *vis*), which is compared to a lightning-bolt (*Sublime*, 12.4).[47] The *vis* of the Roman rhetorical tradition is defeated by an overwhelming destructive power which is natural rather than simply biological.

When Longinus moves on to discuss *imitatio* it is as though he is deliberately seeking to remove from it all traces of the traditionally 'Greek' method of teaching through precepts. He begins with a light allusion to the metaphor of the path: one road (*hodos*) to the sublime, he says, is imitation and emulation (*mimēsis kai zēlōsis*, *Sublime*, 13.2). That road leads, not to Rome as all roads proverbially do, but to the inspired centre of Greek religion, the Pythian oracle at Delphi. It is possible to be inspired by an earlier author, Longinus declares, as the Pythian priestess 'becomes impregnated with the divine power and is at once inspired to utter oracles; so, too, from the natural genius of those old writers (*apo tēs tōn archaiōn megalophuias*) there flows into the hearts of their admirers as it were an emanation from those holy mouths' (*Sublime*, 13.2).

This priestly description of imitation as a kind of inspired birth develops Longinus's earlier assertion that the true sublime elevates its readers and makes them believe that they themselves had created it (*hōs autē gennēsasa hoper ēkousen*, *Sublime*, 7.2). The keyword here is *gennēsasa*: the creation of the sublime is a kind of birth, which spreads by inspiration from author to

46. G. B. Walsh, 'Sublime Method: Longinus on Language and Imitation', *Classical Antiquity* 7 (1988), 252–69.
47. The image had been used of Demosthenes by Cicero himself, *Orator*, 70.234.

reader, and which is implicitly ungovernable by principle or rule. That profoundly Greek image of the Pythian priestess impregnated by divine power is an estranged and amplified version of the Roman rhetoricians' biological images of imitation as akin to biological reproduction. And it stamps Longinus's view of imitation as defiantly Greek. He draws on the inspirational poetics of Plato's *Ion* in order to qualify the hostility of Plato to *mimēsis* in *The Republic*.[48]

To stamp the point home Longinus draws on a further piece of Platonic vocabulary when he states that 'Such borrowing is no theft; it is rather like the reproduction of good character by sculptures or other works of art' (*Sublime*, 13.4). The word here translated by 'reproduction' (and there is some uncertainty about how best to gloss the text here) is *apotupōsis*, or 'the stamping out'.[49] As we saw in the last chapter, the notion that poetry could stamp the soul like a *tupos* or a seal was a significant element in Plato's hostility to *mimēsis*: bad images could be deeply and permanently impressed on the soul by mimicry. Longinus follows Plato and challenges him at one and the same moment: imitation of a prior writer can be inspired and can infuse the soul of the past into the present, and it can also stamp out from the exemplar multiple images of virtue.

And, Longinus continues, Plato would not have achieved his own kind of sublimity 'had he not striven, with heart and soul, to contest the prize with Homer, like a young antagonist with one who had already won his spurs, perhaps in too keen emulation, longing as it were to break a lance, and yet always to good purpose' (*Sublime*, 13.4). The Roman rhetorical discussions of imitation as an *agōn*, a struggle and race and a gladiatorial battle, are here used to describe the relationship between the greatest of the Greeks; and that description is written by a Greek who is himself imitating Plato in an ostentatiously eristic way. Longinus is radically revising the Platonic view of *mimēsis*, by suggesting that imitation can be morally beneficial, while retaining elements of Plato's vocabulary and argument.

48. *Ion* 533D. See Russell's note in Longinus, *On the Sublime*, ed. D. A. Russell (Oxford, 1964), ad loc.
49. Russell in Longinus, *On the Sublime*, glosses as either concerned with 'the imitation of good *mores* in works of art' or 'the formation of the mind by the imitation of good *mores* or works of art'. Walsh, 'Longinus', p. 265, notes that *apotypōsis* 'is a standard term for the influence of parents upon children: see Plato *Leg.* 681B5'; it was also common in educational writings: see Morgan, *Education*, pp. 259–60. Too, *Ancient Literary Criticism*, p. 210 glosses the word as 'remodelling'.

He also, crucially, draws for his account of imitation on the metaphors of bodily strength and feminine creative energy which were used by Roman writers on the art of rhetoric in the first century AD. These, rather than the stereotypically 'Greek' registers of technique and analysis, dominate his discussion. He draws on them with an extreme rhetorical force which is connected to his view that 'the use of metaphor, like all the other beauties of style, always tempts writers to excess' (*Sublime*, 32.6). Instead of resembling an exemplar as a child resembles a father, the imitator should be creatively inseminated by the earlier author. The imitator should resemble not a gladiator or a runner on the Campus Martius, but the inspired priestess of the oracle of Delphi, at the very centre of Greece, or Plato as he struggles with Homer like a tyro wrestling to overcome his master.

Longinus's transformation of *imitatio* is a deliberately transgressive response by a Greek author to problems and images which were present in the Roman tradition. *On the Sublime* subjects the key metaphors of Roman imitation theory in the first century to the intensity of the grand style, which ratchets the metaphors used by Roman writers on the subject to the highest pitch of intensity. *Imitatio* becomes as a result an inspired and generative force, a power akin to lightning, a force sufficient to defeat Plato. Because Longinus discussed the sublime in a style that is itself sublime we seem to have broken through the conceptual problems which haunt the Roman rhetorical tradition onto a new plane in which a sublime artist actually creates a new birth.

But Longinus, despite his preference for Demosthenes over Cicero, shared the Ciceronian and post-Ciceronian belief that outstanding rhetorical practice lay in the past. *On the Sublime* ends with a description of the cultural decline of the present which has led to the end of sublime writing: greed and the death of republican liberty mean that 'really sublime and transcendent natures are no longer, or only very rarely, now produced' (*Sublime*, 44.1). Longinus's discussion of *imitatio* suggests that such natures can be brought back to life, in a similar way to the magic by which Dionysius of Halicarnassus's farmer's wife brought forth handsome sons by looking on images. We should ask ourselves 'How might Homer have said this same thing, how would Plato or Demosthenes or (in history) Thucydides have made it sublime? Emulation (*zēlos*) will bring those great characters before our eyes, and their shining presence will lead our thoughts to the ideal standards of perfection' (*Sublime*, 14.1).

Those ideal standards of perfection, however, seem almost unattainable. It is a Greek past which Longinus seeks to revive, rather than a Roman one, and the age of Greek liberty is well gone. The example of Longinus, strange and aberrant as it may appear to be within the wider history of rhetoric, illustrates a vital truth: although Roman writing on *imitatio* might be seen as, in the words of Gian Biagio Conte, 'collectively disappointing' when considered purely as argument, nonetheless its limitations, confusions, and metaphorical evasions were potentially sources of enormous power—and not only to the Greek subject peoples of Rome, as Chapter 3 will show.[50]

---

50. Gian Biagio Conte, *Stealing the Club from Hercules: On Imitation in Latin Poetry* (Berlin and Boston, 2017), p. 8.

3

Dreamitation

Lucretius, Homer, Virgil

There have been many attempts to interpret Latin poetry and the poetry of the Renaissance in the light of the theory of *imitatio*.[1] The discussion of *imitatio* in the Roman rhetorical tradition in Chapters 1 and 2 may indicate some of the potential frustrations of seeking to do so. It is metaphor rich and concept poor. The conceptual fuzziness of writing about imitation, however, makes it a powerful literary resource. The relation of the 'theory' to the 'practice' of imitation is not either simply hierarchical—theory generates or explains practice, or alternatively that practice is the foundation of theory— or uni-directional. The poetic and the rhetorical traditions are partially autonomous, but they share a set of conceptual underpinnings and a set of uncertainties and metaphorical resolutions of those uncertainties. Many of the metaphors used to describe *imitatio* in the rhetorical tradition are present not just in passages of Latin poetry which are about imitation, but also in many passages which *are* imitations.[2] An epigrammatic statement of what this and the preceding chapter attempt to achieve would be that they attempt to put the poetry back into poetics, by presenting the 'theory' of literary imitation as raising a set of conceptual problems and metaphorical quasi-resolutions of those problems which can be traced through imitative poetry too. The

---

1. David Alexander West and A. J. Woodman, *Creative Imitation and Latin Literature* (Cambridge, 1979), G. W. Pigman, 'Versions of Imitation in the Renaissance', *Renaissance Quarterly* 33 (1980), 1–32, and Thomas M. Greene, *The Light in Troy: Imitation and Discovery in Renaissance Poetry* (New Haven and London, 1982) explore a range of relationships between theory and practice.
2. For a related study, see Colin Burrow, '"Full of the Maker's Guile": Ovid on Imitating and on the Imitation of Ovid', in Philip Hardie, ed., *Ovidian Transformations: Essays on Ovid's Metamorphoses and its Reception* (Cambridge, 1999), 271–87. I would dissent from the claim in Gian Biagio Conte, *Stealing the Club from Hercules: On Imitation in Latin Poetry* (Berlin and Boston, 2017), p. 9, that 'there is a disparity in attitude between critics (grammarians and commentators) on the one side, and poets on the other'.

question of who drives whom in this reciprocal relationship is irresolvable. It would hardly be contentious to claim that all Latin poets had a sophisticated rhetorical training and that this influenced their practice as imitators.[3] It would also be entirely plausible to suggest the reverse: that rhetoricians had read and thought about poets, their interrelationships, and their imitative practices, and that this informs their discussions of *imitatio*.

But even if this relationship was reciprocal it was not fully symmetrical. Orators might sometimes directly allude to the words of earlier orators, or signal their relationship to earlier writers by alluding to the setting or other features of an earlier discursive work—as Cicero does, for example, in his allusions to the Platonic dialogues in his *Orator*. Poets tend as a matter of course, however, both to imitate in the many senses of that term in the rhetorical tradition and simultaneously to mark those larger acts of imitation by local allusions. In the poetic tradition therefore the intellectual and metaphorical energy of *imitatio* is often combined with what came to be called in the tradition of learned commentary 'imitations', or the production not just of writing which resembled the practice of an earlier writer, but of clear local parallels to a previous text. This chapter explores some of the ways in which such local imitations are coloured by themes and metaphors which abound in the larger history of imitation, and it does so chiefly by exploring the interrelationship between Lucretius, Virgil, and Homer. Since Lucretius wrote more vividly about imitation than any other Latin author, it is with Lucretius—whose *De Rerum Natura*, probably composed in the mid-50s BC, predates most of the Roman writing on imitation discussed in Chapter 2— that we begin.

Lucretius

The prologue to Book 3 of the *De Rerum Natura* combines together in one place most of the major ways of metaphorically describing the relationship between a poet and his predecessor. Lucretius here presents himself following the footsteps of his great master, the Greek philosopher Epicurus:

---

3. 'Virgil had to be considered no less an orator than a poet, seeing that he was shown to be so skilled in the ways of oratory and so keen a student of rhetoric' ('Vergilium non minus oratorem quam poetam habendum pronuntiabant, in quo et tanta orandi disciplina et tam diligens observatio rhetoricae artis ostenderetur'), Ambrosius Aurelius Theodosius Macrobius, *Saturnalia*, trans. Robert A. Kaster, 3 vols. (Cambridge, Mass., and London, 2011), 5.1.1.

E tenebris tantis tam clarum extollere lumen
qui primus potuisti inlustrans commoda vitae,
te sequor, o Graiae gentis decus, inque tuis nunc
ficta pedum pono pressis vestigia signis,
non ita certandi cupidus quam propter amorem
quod te imitari aveo; quid enim contendat hirundo
cycnis, aut quidnam tremulis facere artubus haedi
consimile in cursu possint et fortis equi vis?
tu pater es, rerum inventor, tu patria nobis
suppeditas praecepta, tuisque ex, inclute, chartis,
floriferis ut apes in saltibus omnia libant,
omnia nos itidem depascimur aurea dicta,
aurea, perpetua semper dignissima vita.   (*DRN*, 3.1–13)[4]

You, who out of deep darkness first was able to raise a torch so clear, shedding
light upon the true joys of life, it is you I follow, you glory of the Greek race,
and in your deepset prints firmly now I plant my footsteps, not in eager
emulation, but rather for love, because I long to imitate [*imitari*] you; for how
could a swallow rival swans, or what might kids with trembling limbs
accomplish in a race which might compare with the stout strength of a horse?
You are our father, the discoverer of truth, you supply us with a father's
precepts, and from your pages, our hero, even as bees in flowery glades sip
every plant, we in like manner browse on [lit. 'devour'] all your sayings of
gold—yes, of gold—and worthy of perpetual life.

Lucretius presents Epicurus as an origin, a route-finder, an *inventor* or finder
out. He dispels the shadows—and the word *tenebrae* for Lucretius means not
just darkness in general but the illusions of the mind, the fears of death that
they create, and the darkness of self-deception. Lucretius also emphasizes
that Epicurus comes first, and re-emphasizes that priority by describing him
as a person who provides *prae-cepta*, or the truths which precede perception.
Elsewhere he is repeatedly described as *primus*, as at 1.66–7: 'primum Graius
homo mortalis tollere contra | est oculos ausus primusque obsistere contra'—
'a man of Greece first dared to raise his mortal eyes to meet her (*religio*) and
first dared to stand against her', and as the man who reveals the *prim-ordia
rerum*, the first principles of things. He is also the *pater* of Lucretius.

That individual relationship is extended by line 9 of the prologue to Book 3,
when the first person singular gives way to the plural form. At this point
the Greek philosopher seems also to become the paternal spirit of Rome,
who issues foundational precepts for the whole nation ('patria praecepta').

4. Text and translations (modified) from Titus Lucretius Carus, *Titi Lucreti Cari de rerum natura libri
sex.*, ed. Cyril Bailey, 3 vols. (Oxford, 1947), unless otherwise indicated.

The word 'patria' can mean both 'paternal' (*OLD*, 2) and 'native' (*OLD*, 4). Lucretius's readers are invited here to think of Epicurus as so much of an *inventor* and a father of philosophy that he almost becomes a male parallel to the 'alma Venus' (mother Venus) whom Lucretius had invoked at the very opening of the poem as the 'genetrix' (female generator) of men, and gods, and of the race of Aeneas. Elsewhere Epicurus is given a generative power akin to that of Plato's *phoutourgus*, who can give birth to achievements which are 'born out of his own bosom' ('pectore parta suo', *DRN*, 5.5).

The central image of the passage, though, is that of the path, which begins as the poet follows in the footsteps ('pedum...vestigia') of Epicurus, but which Lucretius—for whom puns and etymological relationships are a vital means of conveying the nature of the universe—turns into the foundation of the whole passage.[5] The Greek philosopher 'suppeditas', supplies, the underpinning advice of a father. The world 'suppedito' derives from 'sub-pedes'—literally 'underfooting'—and that etymological connection is extended to suggest that Epicurus is akin to Nature, who a few lines later 'supplies everything the gods need' ('omnia suppeditat', *DRN*, 3.23). The notion that Epicurus not only supplies principles but that those principles are equivalent to the ground beneath our feet is picked out four lines later by the description of things 'which are carried on underneath through the void below our feet' ('*sub pedibus* quaecumque infra per inane geruntur', *DRN*, 3.27). Lucretius is not simply following the path beaten by Epicurus; rather the philosopher makes the very ground beneath our feet, the principles on which we stand, the road along which we move.

Lucretius, meanwhile, follows. That simple statement draws attention to the most striking absence from this virtuoso aria on imitation, which is particularly apparent when it is compared to the discussions of imitation in the rhetorical works from the first century AD considered in Chapter 2. Lucretius's discussion of the relationship between imitator and imitated is ostentatiously free from the competitive edge which runs through Quintilian's discussion of the topic in Book 10 of the *Institutio*. Lucretius is not imitating Epicurus like an athlete who is refining his javelin-throwing in the gym, nor does he seek to dash eagerly past his master into a new understanding of the world. The emulous love or *zēlōsis* of an imitator for his *exemplum* which Longinus was to bring to the fore in his discussion of imitation is explicitly denied: Lucretius claims that he is *not* eager to surpass his *pater*.

5. See André Thill, '*Alter ab illo*': *recherches sur l'imitation dans la poésie personnelle à l'époque augustéenne* (Lille, 1976), pp. 587–94.

The physical and metaphorical environment of the prologue to Book 3 is designed to suit that counter-eristic impulse. It creates a virtual geography of imitation: it begins with tracking the footsteps 'ficta' (made, perhaps also invented) by the master, and follows (as commonly in didactic poetry) a 'via' or pathway which has previously been travelled by the teacher or *praeceptor* (literally, the person who has grasped something beforehand).[6] The risk of that metaphor hardening into a hunt for or a desire to overtake the original as he strides into the unknown spaces of the cosmos then prompts the comparison of swallows to swans, which implies that Lucretius is light and darting rather than purposive and strong, a chirruper rather than a poet who sings powerfully a mortal tune.[7] Any suggestion that a swallow might actually be more agile than a heavy swan is then cancelled out by the image of Lucretius as a kid on wobbly legs, who is set beside the mature strength of a racehorse, and who seeks to emulate its *vis* despite being visibly unable to do so. Then he metamorphoses into an assimilative bee (and at the same time as he makes that change into a hive-dwelling and cooperative creature he becomes a 'we' rather than an 'I'), darting to and fro, drawing honey from the flowers of Epicurus.[8] The description of that honey as 'gold' intimates that this precious resource is simply gathered directly from Epicurus's writings, rather than being produced by the digestive and assimilative activity of the bees themselves, as Seneca was to imply in his 84th Epistle.[9]

The prologue to Book 3 is however by no means the only passage about imitation in the *De Rerum Natura*. The introduction to the very next Book appears to present a very different view of the imitator's activity, which emphasizes the priority of Lucretius himself:

> Avia Pieridum peragro loca nullius ante
> trita solo. iuvat integros accedere fontis
> atque haurire, iuvatque novos decerpere flores
> insignemque meo capiti petere inde coronam
> unde prius nulli velarint tempora musae.   (*DRN*, 4.1–5)

---

6. See Don Fowler, 'The Didactic Plot', in Mary Depew and Dirk Obbink, eds., *Matrices of Genre: Authors, Canons, and Society* (Cambridge, Mass., and London, 2000), 205–19. On the importance of the metaphor of the path to Epicurus, see Diskin Clay, *Paradosis and Survival: Three Chapters in the History of Epicurean Philosophy* (Ann Arbor, 1998), pp. 140–1.

7. On the race as a metaphor for imitation, see Thill, *'Alter ab illo'*, pp. 594–6.

8. For the bee simile as a metaphor specifically for poetic composition, see J. H. Waszink, *Biene und Honig als Symbol des Dichters und der Dichtung in der griechisch-römischen Antike* (Opladen, 1974). See, e.g., Pindar, *Pythian*, 10.53–4; Horace, *Epistles*, 1.3.20–1, *Odes*, 4.2.27–32.

9. For a perceptive reading of this passage as one which presents Epicurus as a poet whom Lucretius is imitating, see Katharina Volk, *The Poetics of Latin Didactic: Lucretius, Vergil, Ovid, Manilius* (Oxford, 2002), pp. 107–16.

I traverse the distant haunts of the Pierides, never trodden before by the foot of man. It is my joy to approach those untasted springs and drink my fill, it is my joy to pluck new flowers and gather a glorious crown for my head from places from which the muses have never before gathered a wreath for the forehead of any man.

Here again imitation occurs within a virtual landscape.[10] It is 'avia', or path-less, with not even the footsteps of a predecessor to guide the poet; and yet he goes forward towards the source of inspiration to drink his fill, and along the way plucks a garland for his own temples. Throughout the poem foot-prints and tracking are used as metaphors for discovery: like a keen-scented hound the acute pupil can pursue even the lightest footprints towards under-standing ('verum animo satis haec vestigia parva sagaci | sunt per quae possis cognoscere cetera tute', DRN, 1.402–3), and a comparison between visible and invisible phenomena, such as between the movement of dust-motes in a sunbeam and the movement of atoms through the void, can provide 'vestigia notitiai', traces of a concept (DRN, 2.124). Those who err in doctrine wander from the path (DRN, 1.711), or are themselves trackless, or 'avius' (DRN, 2.82, 2.229), or, like a confused hunting dog, wander around looking for the footprints (vestigia) of the trail ('errant saepe canes itaque et vestigia quaerunt', DRN, 4.705). Lucretius himself pursues the 'vestigia' of Epicurus who is the philosopher who 'viam monstravit' (DRN, 6.27), showed the way. And as you follow the footsteps of a predecessor into understanding of the nature of things you proceed 'pedetemptim' (DRN, 5.533), step by step. But in the prologue to Book 4 Lucretius seems to step out alone, and to gener-ate his own path.

There is a clear potential contradiction between the prologue to Book 3 and that to Book 4: in the earlier prologue Epicurus comes first and makes the path, while at the start of the very next book Lucretius is said to do the same. That contradiction is more apparent than actual, since Roman poets regularly claimed to be 'first' when they were in fact the first poet to attempt a particular genre in Latin which already had a first founder in Greek: so Horace,

10. The passage alludes to Callimachus's advice not to 'drive your chariot upon the common tracks of others, nor along a wide road, but on unworn paths (keleuthous atriptous)', Aetia, Fr.1.27–8, while the fountains probably recall 'the trickling stream that springs from a holy fountain, pure and undefiled, the very crown of waters', Callimachus, Hymn, 2.111–12. For the influence of Callimachus on Lucretius, see Robert D. Brown, 'Lucretius and Callimachus', Illinois Classical Studies 7 (1982), 77–97. Texts from Callimachus, Aetia, Iambi, Lyric Poems, trans. C. A. Trypanis (Cambridge, Mass., and London, 1958) and Callimachus and Lycophron, Hymns and Epigrams, trans. A. W. Mair and G. R. Mair (Cambridge, Mass., and London, 1955): see Volk, Latin Didactic, p. 87.

having condemned the 'slavish herd' of imitators, goes on immediately to boast that 'I did not stick to others' tracks' and 'I first brought epodes | to Latium'.[11] The programmatic 'proem in the middle', which outlines the poet's principles, was an established convention in antiquity, and one which Lucretius follows here.[12] But the separation of the two claims in the *De Rerum Natura*— to be a follower and a person who comes first—and their juxtaposition in the prologues to successive books does encourage readers to see a degree of conflict between them: in Book 4 Lucretius is a Latin leader, while in Book 3 he was the humble kid, hobbling after a Greek racehorse.

The relationship between these two passages is complicated by the fact that there is a notorious textual problem with the prologue to Book 4. Lucretius's claim to be the first drinker at the well of didactic poetry at the start of Book 4 duplicates, with a few verbal variants, a passage which had already appeared at the end of Book 1 (*DRN*, 1.926–50). As a result Lucretius declares himself to come 'first' both before and after the modest prologue to Book 3.[13] Scholars disagree over the reasons for this duplication, and there is no clear consensus as to whether it is deliberate or the accidental result of imperfect revision. However the start of Book 4 is a particularly significant place for a repetition of the claim that Lucretius is the first to make a path through the trackless wastes, for what might at first appear to be the unlikely reason that Book 4 of the *De Rerum Natura* begins by outlining in full detail the Epicurean theory of vision. This theory had a surprisingly powerful influence on the history of thinking about imitation, and indeed may also help to explain why Lucretius's claim to priority is repeated nearly verbatim at the start of Book 4.

The theory in brief is this. According to Epicurus all bodies are made up of minute atoms, which are surrounded by a void. All bodies shed thin films

11. *Epistles*, 1.19.20–5. Translations from Horace, *Horace: The Epistles, Translated into English Verse with Brief Comment*, trans. Colin Macleod (Rome, 1986). Cf. also Virgil, *Georgics*, 3.10–11. For discussion of Horace's claim, see Siobhán McElduff, *Roman Theories of Translation: Surpassing the Source* (New York, 2013), pp. 136–9 and D. C. Feeney, 'Horace and the Greek Lyric Poets', in Niall Rudd, ed., *Horace 2000: A Celebration. Essays for the Bimillennium* (London, 1993), 41–63.

12. See Gian Biagio Conte, *The Poetry of Pathos: Studies in Virgilian Epic* (Oxford, 2007), pp. 219–31.

13. Monica Gale, *Myth and Poetry in Lucretius* (Cambridge, 1994), p. 138 argues that the repetition is deliberate, and emphasizes Lucretius's departure from strict Epicurean hostility to poetry and myth. Volk, *Latin Didactic*, pp. 86–7 disagrees on the grounds that the passage is longer than other repeated passages and does not contain specifically Epicurean doctrine in need of reiteration. Cf. Bailey's note on 1.921–50. The lines were imitated in Virgil, *Georgics*, 3.289, and the imitation was noted by Servius, and in Macrobius, *Saturnalia*, 6.2.2—although Thomas in Virgil, *Georgics*, ed. Richard F. Thomas, 2 vols. (Cambridge, 1988), p. 97 argues the primary debt is to Callimachus, *Aetia* 1, Fr. 1.25–7. The lines which follow on sugaring the didactic pill were quoted by Quintilian, *Institutio*, 3.1.4 and *DRN*, 4.1/1.926 were quoted by him at 8.6.45.

of atoms from their surfaces, which Epicurus generally terms *eidōla*, and which Lucretius compares to the skins of snakes.[14] These are thinner than gossamer replicas of the objects from which they constantly stream, and they move with great speed through the void. The *eidōla* give rise to perception, as well as to mental delusions, such as the belief in fantastical monsters (which arise from the accidental fusion of *eidōla* of different creatures) as well as optical effects such as shadows and reflections. The word Lucretius generally uses for these *eidōla* is 'simulacra', which derives from 'simul', the Latin word for 'at the same time', or 'in close physical conjunction'. The same word can be used to mean 'visual representation' (*OLD*, 2) and 'ghost' (*OLD*, 4). The principal ethical purpose of the *De Rerum Natura* is to remove the fear of death, and the Epicurean theory of vision contributes in a significant way to this aim: when a person appears to see a ghost, either while waking or asleep, that does not provide perceptual evidence of an afterlife; rather it is the result of seeing the *simulacra* or resemblances of dead people which have reached the perceiver after the death of the person whose form they represent (*DRN*, 4.749–76; 5.62–3).

This set of beliefs about vision and perception are relevant to thinking about imitation in several ways. The first is that Lucretius explicitly links *simulacra* with the vocabulary of imitation—and it is presumably that association which prompted Quintilian to compare the imperfect imitator to 'a "shape" like those which Epicurus says are given off by the surfaces of bodies' (*Institutio*, 10.2.15). When Lucretius explains shadows and reflections by reference to the theory of *simulacra* he describes those visual effects as 'imitating' our behaviour, and he does so in a passage which brings together two of his relatively rare uses of the verb to imitate (*imitari*):

> indugredi porro pariter simulacra pedemque
> ponere nobiscum credas gestumque imitari...   (*DRN*, 4.318–19)

You would believe that the *simulacra* [in a mirror] move step by step with us and imitate our gestures...

> umbra videtur item nobis in sole moveri
> et vestigia nostra sequi gestumque imitari   (*DRN*, 4.364–5)

Shadows also seem to us to move in the sunshine and follow our footprints and imitate our gestures.

---

14. On Lucretius's evolving vocabulary for translating Epicurus's *eidōlon*, see D. N. Sedley, *Lucretius and the Transformation of Greek Wisdom* (Cambridge, 1998), pp. 39–42.

Shadows and reflections appear to imitate, but are actually products of simulacral perception; and they are further associated with *imitatio* by the fact that in both cases they are described, like good imitators, as following in the footsteps (*vestigia*) of that which they imitate.

The repetition of Lucretius's claim to come 'first' at the start of Book 4 may be simply a textual accident, but both the repetition and the claim itself have a particular appropriateness positioned as they are, shortly before the discussion of the various ways in which objects in the world endlessly reproduce semblances of themselves. The prologue to Book 4 itself might appear to be a *simulacrum* of an earlier passage from the poem, which returns to haunt the reader.[15] And this might be related to a wider aspect of the doctrine expressed in and the method of construction of Lucretius's poem. The different elements of the *De Rerum Natura*, from letters, to words, to phrases, to more extended sections of text, can appear, like the atoms which they describe and of which they are made, to be continually recurring and recombining. More than once Lucretius makes use of the fact that the Latin word 'elementa' can mean both 'letters of the alphabet' and 'atoms'.[16] Hence the repetition of Lucretius's claim to priority has an eerie appropriateness. It seems as though the poem is shadowing itself or following its own footsteps.

But what makes the repetition of the prologue to Book 4 unsettling is that the fact of its repetition conflicts with its overt argument: that Lucretius is singular and comes first, and that he journeys alone to the haunts of the Muses. A claim to singularity that is duplicated, and which is then followed by a discussion of how all objects are continually emitting diaphanous replicas of themselves has a curious claim to truth.[17] At the moment Lucretius insists that he is no *simulacrum*, no mere shadow cast by the bright light of Epicurus, but a creator of his own path, he goes on to suggest that everything has near infinite numbers of replicas in circulation. The leader in the race may be a replicant, or a generator of replicants, or both.

15. There is a large secondary literature exploring how the *DRN* might itself in various ways be a *simulacrum* of the universe, which uses letters like atoms to construct a world and which begins with birth (in Venus) and then dissolves to death in the plague at Athens. See notably Alessandro Schiesaro, *Simulacrum et imago: gli argomenti analogici nel De rerum natura* (Pisa, 1990) and Eva M. Thury, 'Lucretius' Poem as a Simulacrum of the Rerum Natura', *The American Journal of Philology* 108 (1987), 270–94.
16. See *DRN*, 1.196–8 and Bailey *ad loc.*
17. On Lucretius as 'first' in the sense of being the first person to imitate Epicurus in Latin verse, while also being 'second' in the sense of following Epicurus, see Volk, *Latin Didactic*, pp. 115–16. On the Latin desire to be 'first' in this sense, see Thill, *'Alter ab illo'*, pp. 1–36.

This discussion of Lucretius's emphasis on his own priority and the nature of his beliefs about *simulacra* enables us to turn to the most influential of all his writings about imitation, which is the prologue to Book 1 of the *De Rerum Natura*. I have delayed discussion of this passage to this point because its full significance is easier to grasp in the light of Lucretius's physical and epistemological thinking, and because it had a greater influence on Virgil, to whom the second half of this chapter will be devoted, than any other passage in Lucretius's poem. In Book 1 Lucretius describes the early Roman epic poet Ennius (*c*.239–*c*.169 BC) meeting Homer, who informs him of the nature of things.[18]

> etsi praeterea tamen esse Acherusia templa
> Ennius aeternis exponit versibus edens,
> quo neque permaneant animae neque corpora nostra,
> sed quaedam simulacra modis pallentia miris;
> unde sibi exortam semper florentis Homeri
> commemorat speciem lacrimas effundere salsas
> coepisse et rerum naturam expandere dictis.   (*DRN*, 1.120–6)

And yet despite this [his belief in reincarnation], Ennius sets forth in the discourse of his immortal verse that there is besides a realm of Acheron, where neither our souls nor bodies endure, but as it were images [*simulacra*] which are extraordinarily pale; and thence he tells that the form of Homer, ever green and fresh, rose to him, and began to shed salt tears, and to reveal the nature of things in conversation.

This passage brings together, in a manner typically Lucretian for being both brilliant and brutal, two of the most pervasive metaphors for *imitatio*—metaphors that can be traced right back to the Platonic dialogues. Ennius, the primary Roman epic poet and perhaps also the first Roman didactic poet, is presented as having incompatible beliefs about his relationship to Homer. In the prologue to his epic about early Roman history called the *Annales* Ennius described himself receiving instruction from the ghost of Homer. It also appears that Ennius had claimed to have brought Homer back to life in a very literal way by being a reincarnation of the Greek poet.

---

18. On Ennius, see William Fitzgerald and Emily Gowers, eds., *Ennius Perennis: The Annals and Beyond* (Cambridge, 2007), and in particular Emily Gowers, 'The *Cor* of Ennius', pp. 17–37. On Lucretius and Ennius, see Stephen Harrison, 'Ennius and the Prologue to Lucretius DRN 1 (1.1–148)', *Leeds International Classical Studies* 1 (2002), 1–13. On the significance of this passage for Lucretius's afterlife, see Philip R. Hardie, *Lucretian Receptions: History, the Sublime, Knowledge* (Cambridge, 2009), p. 4, and on Ennius's reception, see Nora Goldschmidt, *Shaggy Crowns: Ennius' Annales and Virgil's Aeneid* (Oxford, 2013).

Lucretius in this passage presents Ennius as a radical mess. He implies, with some reason, that Ennius entertained incompatible beliefs: it is hard to see how the spirit of Homer could simultaneously be infused into Ennius and also be visible to him as a ghost. And both of these incompatible beliefs rest, according to Lucretius, on philosophical error. Ennius's belief that he was a reincarnation of Homer presupposes the existence of an extra-physical soul, which is incompatible with the Epicurean belief that personal identity was a consequence of a particular combination of atoms, which dissolved after death. Ennius's belief that he has met a ghost of Homer is the product of another kind of error: he has failed to understand the Epicurean doctrine of *simulacra*, or the films of atoms shed by all bodies as they move through space and time, which explain in material form the appearance of ghosts.[19]

The rhetorical power and historical influence of this passage partly derive from the zeal with which it destroys an earlier poet's conception of literary genealogy by reference to philosophical principles. But Lucretius's passage on the meeting between Homer and Ennius also is highly significant for another reason. Despite its overt aim to assail Ennius's mistaken beliefs about his relationship to Homer it actually preserves them. And as it does so it forcibly conjoins the image of an imitator as a kind of rebirth with the image of the imitator as someone who lives in realm of shadows and ghosts, of *eidōla* and *simulacra*.[20] That presentation of *imitatio* as simultaneously a kind of rebirth and an encounter with a substanceless shadow had, as we shall see in later chapters, a profound influence on later Latin, and indeed European Renaissance, writing.

The power of that influence derived from several causes. The incoherence which Lucretius attributes to Ennius's representation of Homer, as both spectral vision and actual rebirth, has a deep affinity with the problems which we have seen running through theoretical writings on *imitatio* in the rhetorical tradition: is an imitator a rebirth of an earlier author or a mere shade? But it also has deep connections with the other aspects of Lucretius's poem. We have already seen how that passage anticipates the discussion of ghosts and *simulacra* in Book 4. But it also taps into the larger thematic

19. See the rich and suggestive survey of *eidōla* and dreams in ancient poetry, W. R. Hardie, 'The Dream of Ennius', *The Classical Quarterly* 7 (1913), 188–95.
20. Bailey notes this passage is imitated in Virgil's apparition of Hector, and had an extensive influence on Virgil: 'simulacra modis pallentia miris' is adopted in *Georgics*, 1.477. See Virgil, *Georgics*, ed. R. A. B. Mynors (Oxford, 1990). For the additional echo of Ennius, *Annales*, Fr. iv, see Quintus Ennius, *The Annals of Q. Ennius*, ed. Otto Skutsch (Oxford, 1985), pp. 154–7.

concerns of the poem. The *De Rerum Natura* repeatedly and programmatically conjoins the substanceless with the overwhelmingly vital. Lucretius calls his atoms the *semina rerum*, the seeds or original principles of life. The atoms and their swerving movement through the void are the source of all life in the universe, and Lucretius, albeit hypothetically, imagines the possibility that after our own bodies have dissolved time might re-gather our substance into the same shape—although such a new being would be nothing to us because we would feel no connection with it after the dissolution of our soul (*DRN*, 3.847–51). The whole poem, as a result, could be seen as a giant materialist account of how the world constantly disassembles and over the very long term might replicate itself.

The atoms swirl through the void, generating life and material objects, which emit showers of *simulacra* or likenesses of themselves, and then separate in death, and then, in due course, might recombine to recreate a new world or even a new Lucretius. That account is shorn of the mistaken Pythagorean belief in the permanence of the soul or the continuity of experiences in different material formations of a person, to be sure, but it offers a surging confirmation of the perpetually recombinatory power of the world to produce resemblances of itself.

And that world, although it teems with sexual energy and a power to recreate itself through endless recombination of elements, and although it is relentlessly material, is also full of void. Coexisting with the 'corpus', body, or physical matter of the atoms, there was according to Epicurean philosophy also a 'vacuum' or void, which Lucretius regularly describes as 'inane' or empty. Physical objects and even psychological and perceptual phenomena depend not only upon the combination of different atoms, or 'seeds of things', but also the presence of void between their interconnections. As a result of this physical model of the universe Lucretius was prone to use verbal collocations which conjoined bodies with nothingness. Other philosophers err for not mixing 'the void into their notion of bodies', and striking collocations of the word body (corpus) or 'thing' (res) with 'inane' or void are quite frequent (e.g. *DRN*, 1.330, 1.369, 1.382, 1.386, etc.). The adjective 'inanis', empty, can be used of philosophical authorities who are void of truth (as of Heraclitus at *DRN*, 1.639).

The *simulacra* are also material things on the boundary of immateriality: they are usually called 'rerum simulacra' (*DRN*, 1.1060, 4.30, 4.50, 4.127, 4.130, 4.164, etc.), the likenesses of *things*, and that phrase not only insists on their materiality despite their superfine tenuosity of substance but also links them with the 'rerum natura', the nature of things, which is Lucretius's overall subject-matter. So although Lucretian poetics appear to be founded on a declaration that Ennius was misguided to believe himself a reincarnation of Homer or that he could converse with the insubstantial spirit of Homer, Lucretius himself in a range of ways appears to endorse a distant parallel to the reincarnational and spectral poetics that he criticizes in Ennius: living seeds surrounded by nothingness hurl themselves around, constantly de-creating and recreating life, constantly generating showers of spectral resemblances of objects which are simultaneously body and void, and constantly generating new birth. Although Lucretius strenuously insists that matter is eternal and that it cannot die and then be repeatedly reborn from nothing (a claim repeated in variants of the formula 'de nihiloque renata vigescat copia rerum', that everything would be reborn and flourish out of nothing, at *DRN*, 1.542, 1.674, 1.757) he does in effect produce the outlines of a renaissance poetics, in which elements are recombined and reborn (*renata*) in new forms continually, and in which primary acts of creation and birth coexist with shadowy replication.

There is no doubt that Lucretius's poem and its treatment of *imitatio* had an influence on the Roman rhetorical tradition. As we have seen, Quintilian explicitly compared a lifeless imitation to the kind of *simulacra* that Epicurus believed emanated from bodies.[21] Quintilian's emphasis in *Institutio*, 10.3 on the generative powers of nature and the long gestation of large bodies in the earth (above, p. 96), may also be a recollection of Lucretius's creation story in Book 5 of the *De Rerum Natura*, in which beasts pull themselves free of the soil, born from earth, driven by the creative force of the seeds of things. Quintilian does after all say that the nature of things herself ('rerum ipsa natura', *Institutio*, 10.3.4) wishes it so, as though to signal an allusion to the *De Rerum Natura*.

These metaphors of birth twinned with images of shadowy resemblance create, as we have seen, some internal conflicts in Quintilian's discussion of *imitatio*, in which his powerful Roman orators seem shadowed by mere replic-ants of the rhetorical tricks of earlier writers. Those conflicts are anticipated in Lucretius. The poetics and physics of the *De Rerum Natura* combine a

---

21. The connection between Quintilian, *Institutio*, 10.2.15 and *DRN*, 4.42–3 is noted in John J. Savage, 'Quintilian and Lucretius', *The Classical Weekly* 46 (1952), 37. On connections between Lucretius and contemporary rhetoric, see Alessandro Schiesaro, 'Lucrezio, Cicerone, l'oratoria', *Materiali e discussioni per l'analisi dei testi classici* 19 (1987), 29–61.

fascination with the material and generative with the ghostly and evanescent. The influence of Lucretius in the history of Western poetics is in large measure due to the sophisticated way in which he enfolded metaphors of imitation within a larger vision of the cosmos.

Lucretius himself seems sometimes only barely able to control the richness and the plurality of that vision, and seems also only barely able to tread a path across the fecund universe without reproducing the errors of his predecessors. For his imitators—and particularly for successors who attempted to write narrative poetry—he generated a series of immensely fertile problems, which were deeply interwoven with the conceptual problems we have already explored within the rhetorical and philosophical traditions. Did an imitator produce a mere *simulacrum* of an earlier body or a fit and living being? How can the difference between these two things be established? How can an imitator claim to come first whilst also acknowledging that a predecessor in another tongue has also come first? The passage in which Lucretius criticized Ennius for believing himself to be both a reincarnation of Homer and someone who mistakenly took Homer's *simulacrum* for his spirit forced these conceptual problems right into the centre of Roman literary tradition. Ennius, the old master, who was to become the touchstone of heavy Roman virtue: was his relationship to Homer that of a reincarnation or of a bad dream? Should a Roman poet strike out boldly across the void or follow in the footsteps of the Greeks?

Virgil's ghosts

These questions are all central to Virgil's *Aeneid*.[22] Virgil's poetics, his relationship to Homer, and his relationship to Lucretius are all vast and complex subjects. I will make some suggestions about each of these areas by concentrating on one particular aspect of his greatest poem: representations of dreams and ghosts in the *Aeneid*.

We have seen that the vocabulary of *mimēsis* from its earliest theoretical and practical explorations in Athens brought with it a set of ghosts and visions—Euripides's *mimēma* of Helen, the *eidōla* made by the poet in Plato's *Republic*. This group of insubstantial imitations has a distinctive vocabulary,

---

22. For excellent discussion, see Hardie, *Lucretian Receptions* and Philip R. Hardie, *Virgil's Aeneid: Cosmos and Imperium* (Oxford, 1986). On Virgil and Epicureanism, see note 53 in this chapter.

of *eidōla, phantasmata, simulacra*, things of nothing. It is this squadron of insubstantial horrors that Quintilian's muscly embodied view of rhetorical imitation sought to resist. This set of metaphors for imitation, which moved uneasily between the generative force of nature and its shadowy semblances, was vital for Lucretius; and because he drew on it in his seminal description of the encounter between the first epic poet—Homer—and the first *Roman* epic poet—Ennius—it came to haunt (and that verb has something like a literal force) the subsequent epic tradition. We might therefore expect the dream, or the vision of a *simulacrum* of a person, to have a particular significance in epic poetry.

There are indeed good grounds for regarding dreams as one of the many markers used in Roman and later classically derived fictions to signal that an imitation is going on. Markers of substantiality—of embodiment or dreamlike disembodiment—might be added to what have been called 'Alexandrian footnotes', or occasions on which phrases such as 'I remember' are used to indicate moments when poets are alluding to earlier poets in Alexandrian and post Callimachean poetics.[23] I also want to make two more tendentious claims: that the opposition between an imitation as a mere *eidōlon* and imitation as a substantial, renewed body which has digested the past writer into its own substance, should be regarded as a significant and signifying aspect of the language of the *Aeneid*; and that the turbulence created by Lucretius's poetics and by his physics for the language used to describe *imitatio* carries over into the many irresolutions and uncertainties in Virgil's epic.

With those thoughts in mind let us plunge directly in to Book 2 of the *Aeneid*. Aeneas is asleep while Troy is being sacked.[24] The figure of Hector appears to him:

> Tempus erat, quo prima quies mortalibus aegris
> incipit et dono divum gratissima serpit.
> in somnis, ecce, ante oculos maestissimus Hector

---

23. See David O. Ross, *Backgrounds to Augustan Poetry: Gallus, Elegy, and Rome* (Cambridge, 1975), p. 78 and Stephen Hinds, *Allusion and Intertext: Dynamics of Appropriation in Roman Poetry* (Cambridge, 1998), pp. 1–4. See also the discussion of allusion as textual memory in Gian Biagio Conte, *The Rhetoric of Imitation: Genre and Poetic Memory in Virgil and Other Latin Poets*, trans. Charles Segal (Ithaca, NY, and London, 1986), pp. 60–3. The older and more conservative Conte, *On Imitation*, p. 56, slaps the wrists of the 'fantasizing interpreter' who seeks metapoesis in allusions.

24. Poulheria Kyriakou, 'Aeneas' Dream of Hector', *Hermes* 127 (1999), 317–27 notes the parallels with Achilles' dream of Patroclus, *Iliad*, 23.60–108. See the fine essay by Emily Wilson, '*Quantum Mutatus ab Illo*: Moments of Change and Recognition in Tasso and Milton', in Michael Clarke, Bruno Currie, and R. O. A. M. Lyne, eds., *Epic Interactions: Perspectives on Homer, Virgil, and the Epic Tradition* (Oxford, 2006), 273–99.

visus adesse mihi largosque effundere fletus,
raptatus bigis, ut quondam, aterque cruento
pulvere perque pedes traiectus lora tumentis.
ei mihi, qualis erat! quantum mutatus ab illo
Hectore, qui redit exuvias indutus Achilli
vel Danaum Phrygios iaculatus puppibus ignis!
squalentem barbam et concretos sanguine crinis
vulneraque illa gerens, quae circum plurima muros
accepit patrios.   (*Aen.*, 2.268–79)[25]

It was the hour when for weary mortals their first rest begins, and by grace of the gods steals over them most sweet. In slumbers, lo! Before my eyes there seemed to stand Hector, most sorrowful and shedding floods of tears; torn by the chariot, as once of old, and black with gory dust, his swollen feet pierced with thongs. Ah me! What aspect was his! How changed from that Hector who returns after donning the spoils of Achilles or hurling on Danaan ships the Phrygian fires! With ragged beard, with hair matted with blood, and bearing those many wounds he got around his native walls.

The dream of Hector and its later imitations have been persuasively read by Emily Wilson.[26] She sees the episode of the dream as one which asks the question 'How different can we be from our literary origins and still be part of the same tradition?' How *mutatus* can an imitator be before he or she ceases to belong to a tradition? That is a very suggestive view of the episode and its afterlife. But the most remarkable feature of this description is how pointedly *un*-dreamlike the vision of Hector is. Hector is crudded in blood; he is different, *mutatus*, even *mutilatus*, from the living Hector, but he is certainly a body, and is indeed much more physically real than one might expect a dream or a ghost to be. Translators have often been unable to stomach how carnal he is: Dryden reads 'When Hector's Ghost before my sight appears: | A bloody Shroud he seem'd, and bath'd in Tears' (2.352–3).[27] But a ghost he is not. He does not flit away murmuring or vanish through a gate of ivory or horn, or slip through a keyhole, as dreams in Homer can do. And he certainly

25. Quotations from Virgil, *Virgil*, trans. H. Rushton Fairclough, 2 vols. (Cambridge, Mass., and London, 1978).
26. 'How different can a hero be, and still be a hero? How much can Virgil swerve from Homer, and still follow the tradition of Homeric epic? The encounter between Aeneas and Hector uses the motif of an altered character— Hector—to mark the alteration which epic and epic heroism itself must undergo, as Virgil draws on but alters his Homeric models', Wilson, '*Quantum Mutatus*', p. 291.
27. Quotations from John Dryden, *The Works*, ed. Edward Niles Hooker, H. T. Swedenberg, and Vinton A. Dearing, 20 vols. (Berkeley, 1956–2000).

is not wearing the sheet or shroud with which Dryden coyly clothes him. Hector speaks, and then Aeneas simply wakes up and is instantly in reality.

In these respects the dream Hector is pointedly mutated, not just from his living appearance, but also from the several dreams in the Homeric poems from which he is clearly imitated. When the dead appear in Homeric dreams they tend to be termed *eidōla*, though sometimes they are also *psuchai*. These dream ghosts tend to be insubstantial enough to hover over someone's head and then vanish like smoke into the earth. But as Michael Clarke has shown, ghosts and the *eidōla* of dreams in Homer can also be quite substantial presences when the narrative context allows, and can on these occasions speak as though they were embodied people, so that the poet seems to forget that they are a ghost.[28] They can also carry a strong metapoetic charge, as most notably in the visit to the House of the Dead in *Odyssey* 11, where the pale gibberers crowding round a basin of blood as they search for sustenance from the living come not only to live again and speak but also, as Glen Most has argued, to encapsulate all the different forms of epic in archaic Greece on which the *Odyssey* poet drew.[29]

The dream of Hector is principally an imitation of Achilles' dream of the dead Patroclus in Book 23 of the *Iliad*. If we compare Virgil's imitation with that particular passage it is evident that Hector is pointedly transformed from Patroclus. He is in particular transformed by being *unlike* his living self. Homer explicitly says that the ghost/dream *eidōlon* of Patroclus is 'like his live self in all aspects—his stature, his fine eyes, | his voice; and even the clothes he had on were the same' (*Iliad*, 23.65–7).[30] The dream Patroclus is unmartial, clad as for a friendly conversation.[31]

And on this point the narrator and Achilles are at one. When he awakes (*Iliad*, 23.107) Achilles describes the 'spirit' and 'phantom', the *psuchē chai eidōlon*, of Patroclus as 'looking marvellously like his living self'. Virgil's Hector is a body, both more bloodily real and more different from how he

---

28. Michael Clarke, *Flesh and Spirit in the Songs of Homer: A Study of Words and Myths* (Oxford, 1999), p. 193: 'Just as Homer is ambivalent over whether the dead in Hades are empty images or dead men of substance, so his conception of their ability to think and speak like living men appears and disappears in different contexts.'

29. See Glenn Most, 'Il poeta nell'Ade: catabasi epica e teoria dell'epos tra Omero e Virgilio', *Studi italiani di filologia classica* 10 (1992), 1014–26. For Virgil's imitation of this aspect of Homer, see Stephen Harrison, 'Vergil's Metapoetic Katabasis: The Underworld of *Aeneid* 6 and the History of Epic', in H.-C. Günther, ed., *Virgilian Studies: A Miscellany Dedicated to the Memory of Mario Geymonat* (Nordhausen, 2015), 169–94.

30. Translations from Homer, *The Iliad*, trans. Peter Green (Oakland, Calif., 2015).

31. Ruth Bardel, 'Eidola in Epic, Tragedy, and Vase Painting', in N. Keith Rutter and Brian A. Sparkes, eds., *Word and Image in Ancient Greece* (Edinburgh, 2000), 140–60, p. 146.

was in life than its Homeric original—*mutatus* as it were conceals within it *mutuatus*, borrowed, and cancels the debt with the mutation of a ghost into a mutilated body. He is tangibly mortal, battered by Achilles' abuse of his corpse. Virgil is insisting that this is a *corpus*, a real body, not just an *eidōlon* or a *simulacrum*: it is Hector as he is in death, who *visus*, is seen, appeared— Hector as he was made to become by battling with the Greeks.

There is an overt ethical purpose to this transformation, which is the principal reason why Virgil is so pointedly un-Homeric in his description of the dream Hector. Hector is delivering to Aeneas the classically unheroic advice to run away—to leave Troy and pursue the founding of Rome. If Virgil had given to this dream revival of a Homeric figure any traces of the insubstantiality of Homeric dreams that message might be contaminated by a fear that Aeneas was being addressed by a mere illusion or an *eidōlon*. That would compromise the larger ethical aim of the passage, and its higher level aggressive transformation of Homer, which is to suggest that a Roman hero can be heroic even when fleeing, provided his motivation for doing so is solid enough, steeped in blood and physical presence.[32] The exclusion of the conventions of ghostliness from the ghost of Hector, that is, is part of what the scene *means*, and acts as a marker of a wider transformation of the epic tradition. It gives the dream vision the *enargeia*—the visual force—of a real blooded body, a kind of deadly *vis*. It also of course charges the imperial warning with blood and death; but that may be the price of being new. I change (*muto*) and I borrow (*mutuor*) derive from the same root, and there can be a cost to borrowing as to changing form.

Hector also owes some of these features to Ennius. 'Visus adesse mihi' echoes 'visus Homerus adesse poeta' from the prologue to the *Annales*, and the tears of Hector probably also recall the tears of Ennius for the dead Homer.[33] Behind the dream of Hector is also Lucretius: no Roman reader would fail to see this as a variant version of the appearance of Homer to Ennius at the start of the *Annales*; and that would necessarily bring with it something of Lucretius's sceptical treatment of that passage in the *De Rerum Natura*. Part of what Virgil is doing in this scene is exorcizing the ghostly *simulacrum* of Ennius's Homer as seen by Lucretius from his imitation: he

32. On the moral authority of Hector, see the classic account in Richard Heinze, *Virgil's Epic Technique*, trans. David Harvey, Hazel Harvey, and Fred Robertson (London, 1993), pp. 16–18.
33. For the echoes, see Virgil, *P. Vergili Maronis Aeneidos, liber secundus*, ed. R. G. Austin (Oxford, 1980), p. 129, and for the fragments of Ennius, see Ennius, ed. Skutsch, *The Annals of Q. Ennius*, p. 70. On the general influence of Ennius on Virgil's dreams, see Hans-Rudolf Steiner, *Der Traum in der Aeneis* (Bern, 1952).

brings Hector back to life in full carnal substance in order to insist that he is not a mere imitative *simulacrum* but a heroic body.

This episode might prompt a general law of *simulacra*, which like all literary laws is a heuristic aid rather than an immutable truth. The law is this: the metaphors used to describe *imitatio* permeate the practice of imitation, and the way those metaphors are used is part of the illocutionary force of an imitation.[34] To turn a person who in your *exemplum* was an insubstantial *eidōlon* into a substantial presence constitutes a claim to have made something new and strong. To create an imitation which is an insubstantial spectre, on the other hand, allows the potential ineffectiveness of the process of imitation to leak through into the ethical standing of the thing imitated.

In the dream of Hector that general law cooperates with Virgil's pressing need to justify Aeneas's departure from Rome. A bodily Hector who tells Aeneas to leave Troy does not have the moral and ontological dubiety of the *eidōlon* of Nestor that Zeus sends to Agamemnon in a dream in *Iliad* 2, who tells Agamemnon (falsely) that if he attacks Troy now it will fall, but the appearance of which (curiously) leads Agamemnon to test the resolve of the Achaians by telling them to return home. That ethically shady dream becomes a bleeding piece of truth in the *Aeneid*.

The law of *simulacra* operates in a rather different way at the other end of the *Aeneid*, where we encounter effectively the antitype of Aeneas's dream of Hector. In Book 10 Juno is allowed by Jove to lure Turnus from the battlefield in order to delay his death. To achieve this, Juno creates an Aeneas who is all ghost, in the description of whom the insubstantiality is layered on as thick, or as thin, as can be:

> tum dea nube cava tenuem sine viribus umbram
> in faciem Aeneae (visu mirabile monstrum)
> Dardaniis ornat telis, clipeumque iubasque
> divini adsimulat capitis, dat inania verba,
> dat sine mente sonum gressusque effingit euntis;
> morte obita qualis fama est volitare figuras
> aut quae sopitos deludunt somnia sensus.
> at primas laeta ante acies exsultat imago
> inritatque virum telis et voce lacessit.
> instat cui Turnus stridentemque eminus hastam
> conicit; illa dato vertit vestigia tergo.   (*Aen.*, 10.636–46)

---

34. Cf. the discussion of how metaphors used to describe translation permeate the practice in Matthew Reynolds, *The Poetry of Translation: From Chaucer and Petrarch to Homer and Logue* (Oxford, 2011), esp. pp. 46–55.

Then the goddess makes an insubstantial, strengthless phantom of hollow cloud in the shape of Aeneas, a wonder marvellous to behold, and decks it out with Trojan weapons; she counterfeits the shield and crests on the godlike hero's head, gives it empty words and mindless utterance, and fashions for it the step of a walking man, just like the shades which are said to flit about after death, or the dreams that delude the slumbering senses. And the phantom prances exultantly before the front ranks, and provokes the hero Turnus with its weapons and challenges him with its shouting. Turnus goes for it, and at long range throws his whirring spear; the phantom turns tail and wheels its steps about.[35]

This imitation-Aeneas is also an imitation of Homer. Aineias in *Iliad* 5 is briefly replaced on the battlefield by what Homer terms an *eidōlon*, an image of the hero, who is made by Apollo. Peter Green in his fine translation of the poem renders this as 'a phantom... a clone of Aineias himself, with his kind of armour' (*Iliad*, 5.450)—and that translation neatly connects the beginning of the story told in this book with its end, since, as we shall see in Chapter 10, much of the language used in and many of the anxieties relating to discussions of imitation in the classical tradition emerge transformed in twentieth-century writing about human cloning. Homer's Aineias is particularly prone to be involved in episodes where the gods protect their favourites: he is rescued by Aphrodite earlier in Book 5 (311–17) and in Book 20 is hurled away from the battle through the air by Poseidon (*Iliad*, 20.318–39).[36] While the 'clone' of him is left on the battlefield the real Aineias is taken off to a rest-cure in the temple of Apollo, from which he emerges revived and refreshed. The *eidōlon* simply lies there while the warriors fight over him or it.[37]

This episode of the false Aineias in Homer was a major influence on one of the examples of imitation briefly mentioned in Chapter 1. When Euripides suggested that the whole Trojan war was fought over an *eidōlon* or *mimēma* of Helen he was building an entire ghostly alternative plot for the

---

35. Translation from Virgil, *Aeneid 10: With Introduction, Translation and Commentary*, ed. Stephen Harrison (Oxford, 1991).

36. There are also references to Aineias's being saved by Zeus at 19.291–4, 20.89–96, 20.189–94.

37. Harrison (Virgil, ed. Harrison, *Aeneid 10*, p. 226) suggests a further debt in the fashioning of the phantom from the air to Euripides's *Helen*, 34. He also notes the relationship between 641 and the phrasing of Lucretius *DRN*, 1.135 and 2.380, so the line is substantially Lucretian. Thomas van Nortwick, 'Aeneas, Turnus, and Achilles', *Transactions of the American Philological Association* 110 (1980), 303–14, pp. 304–5 detects a reference to the deception of Achilles by the apparition of Agenor (although van Nortwick confuses him with Hector), who is really Apollo disguised (*Iliad*, 21.599–611). In Homer an *eidōlon* can be untrustworthy: when Odysseus fails to embrace the spirit of his mother he fears that she might be nothing more than an *eidōlon* sent by Persephone to augment his grief (*Odyssey*, 11.213–14).

Trojan war partly from this episode in the *Iliad*, in which a *simulacrum* generates an entire alternative narrative.

That association between *mimēmata* or *eidōla* and parallel worlds which bring with them potentially spurious kinds of heroism, or at least alternative forms of behaviour, is also present in Virgil's episode of the phantom Aeneas. He creates not just a false Aeneas but one which mimics the external behaviour of heroism (he makes loud noises, he carries the right arms) rather than its substance. The phantom imitation of Aeneas is consequently introduced into the poem more or less in scare quotes. Virgil's imitation of the *eidōlon* of Aineias in the *Iliad* is a hyperactive fleering jeering *simulacrum* of Aeneas. It is not just an *umbra* but a *tenuis umbra*. It has an excess of *vis* but no bodily substance. Its words are empty, its armour seems more or less empty too, and its words are *sine mente*, mindless, without intent—and we are not even told what it says. This phantasm (Dryden calls it as it vanishes a 'guileful Phantom', 10.935) makes noise not speeches.

Moreover it is not just compared to a ghost or a dream, but to both. And to cap it all, the ghost to which the false Aeneas is compared does not even have the dignity of existing, since it is itself only a rumour. It has been recognized at least since Macrobius's *Saturnalia* in the early fifth century that the description of the phantom Aeneas is indebted to Lucretius: Virgil's 'morte obita' is a direct quotation from the description of delusive dreams in Book 1 of the *De Rerum Natura:* '[Therefore we must give good account of...] what thing it is that meets us and affrights our minds in waking life, when we are touched with disease, or again when buried in sleep, so that we seem to see and hear hard by us those who have met death, and whose bones are held in the embrace of earth' ('et quae res nobis vigilantibus obvia mentis | terrificet morbo adfectis somnoque sepultis, | cernere uti videamur eos audireque coram, | morte obita quorum tellus amplectitur ossa', *DRN*, 1.132–5).[38] That little allusion to Lucretius adds a twist to the larger imitation of Homer in this episode. Virgil alludes to a passage in which Lucretius not only discusses the illusory appearance of ghosts but also where he insists on the material reality of death: our minds see ghosts, but the dead are 'bones', physical remains. That passage of Lucretius in summary form reprises

---

38. Macrobius, trans. Kaster, *Saturnalia*, 6.1.48. 'The episode of the phantom Aeneas is a strange piece of writing in Virgil's most fantastic and imaginative style, owing as much to Lucretian theories of *imagines* as to Homer', K. W. Gransden, *Virgil's Iliad: An Essay on Epic Narrative* (Cambridge, 1984), p. 149.

Ennius's vision of Homer: we may be tempted to see Homeric ghosts, but we are wrong to do so. There is no body there.

I describe this episode as a complement to the super-bodily vision of Hector in Book 2 of the *Aeneid* because it seems as though at this moment Virgil is evacuating all the quasi-bodily elements from Homeric *eidōla* in order to make something that is purest nothing, an imitative being that is all *simulacrum* and no body. Given this, it is no coincidence that the phantasm Aeneas shows its *vestigia*, its footprints, to Turnus, condemning him to follow it in the race like an imitator. Turnus struggles to overtake its hissing *vis*, and is led off the battlefield into a magical ship which carries him to Ardea. The complete removal of substance from this particular imitation again has an almost over-encoded intent behind it. This Aeneas, like the Aeneas in Book 2, runs away. But that unheroic action is stripped of any moral danger in Book 10 because this Aeneas is a fake. Completely, insubstantially only a likeness and not really Aeneas at all, he's just an 'imitation' in the sense of a delusory perceptual replication of the real Aeneas who founds the Roman people.

I have presented the false Aeneas in Book 10 as the complement to the powerfully embodied dream of Hector in Book 2 because both episodes deploy familiar metaphors for describing *imitatio*, deliberately or unconsciously, as a means of establishing the rhetorical effect of a particular act of imitation. There is potentially an extremely crude opposition between the two. Body-like dream imitations speak truth. Phantoms do not, and they can carry a hero off in a wild chase for the footprints or traces of the past. But we should not be tempted to suppose that Virgil *simply* uses 'bodily' imitations to signify moments that should be taken seriously, while 'phantasms' are created to mark 'non-heroic' moments, and indeed should recall that close and intimate link established by Lucretius between body and void. Both imitations cross wires between the substantial and the insubstantial: Hector is dead yet vividly present; the phantasm Aeneas is given an overdose of the vitality which the *eidōlon* of Aineias in the *Iliad* seemed to lack. There is perpetual and electrifying leakage between a 'good' substantial imitation and a 'bad' simulacral imitation in this poem, and that creates hermeneutic noise. Where does the life of the poem lie? With the increasingly taciturn Aeneas or with the super-lively phantasm of him?

The fact that the *simulacrum* of Aeneas is made by Juno, a goddess with no great affection for the Trojan cause, may also be significant. Virgil often ensures that bodily substance is removed from imitations which are feminine productions. It is almost as though he shrinks away from the idea that an imitator can give birth, in womanly ways, to a 'living' version of an original, or that a quasi-feminine *ubertas*—fertility—is the main quality to be sought in an imitator.

This observation further complicates the temptingly simple opposition between a ghostly imitation, which is ethically and physically an object of uncertain status, and a bodily presence which is thick, substantial, full of living force, and trustworthy. That simple opposition would suggest that an imitative poet could in a relatively simple way use and control the metaphors of imitation. But the unruly hoard of metaphors that go along with attempts to explain what *imitatio* might be is not fully controllable.

And here we might move from meta- and intra-poetic questions to rather larger and more traditional ones. Readers have often found a sense of vanity in Virgil's *Aeneid*. The 'Harvard school' has famously emphasized the illusory nature of divine promptings, the tendency of images of loved ones to vanish, and the way imperial ambitions tend to bring with them shadows of ghostly regret.[39] These features of the poem may derive from some unease, articulated or repressed, which the historical Virgil had about the historical Augustus or about Roman imperial politics. They might even imply a sense of the spectral emptiness of the imperial projects of Rome. But these political readings should not be simply separated from Virgil's imitative practices, nor are they separable from the language in which those practices are conducted, nor should we unreflectively claim any simple hierarchical relationship between the two. The unanswerable question 'what is a living *imitatio*?' has its political implications too. How *real* is a cultural edifice such as Rome, which is founded on difference from a culture on which it declares itself also to be grounded?[40] How much *vis* of its own does that culture have, and how much of its claim to *vis* finally looks like a claim either to violence or to insubstantial mimicry?

These questions have a particular bite when they are applied to the episode which it is orthodox to regard as the chief parallel to the dream Hector in Book 2: the episode in which a *simulacrum* of Aeneas's wife Creusa appears to the hero while he is seeking her through the flaming ruins of Troy. Creusa

---

39. A crisp summary is in Philip R. Hardie, *Virgil* (Oxford, 1998), pp. 94–5. For antecedents of pessimistic readings of the poem, see Craig Kallendorf, *The Other Virgil: 'Pessimistic' Readings of the Aeneid in Early Modern Culture* (Oxford, 2007), and for recent reassessments of the school and its influence, see the articles gathered in the special issue of *Classical World* 111.1 (2017).

40. For a related exploration, see Paul Hammond, *Dryden and the Traces of Classical Rome* (Oxford, 1999).

has mysteriously gone missing during the flight from Troy, and the search for her has prompted Aeneas to trace and retrace, not the footsteps of some mighty predecessor, but his own *vestigia* ('repeto et vestigia retro | observata sequor'—'I go back and retrace my own footsteps', *Aen.*, 2.753–4). While he remains in Troy searching for his wife Aeneas is in danger of becoming a compulsive self-imitator, tracking back and tracking back, and that fact is marked by the curiously strong association between Creusa and footprints: Aeneas has earlier said 'longe servet vestigia coniunx' ('let my wife follow our steps afar', *Aen.*, 2.711), and a little before that she has stopped him leaving the house by grabbing his feet in supplication.

Somewhere behind these references may be a flicker of self-referentiality. Aeneas's wife was sometimes named Eurydica in historical sources, including in Ennius's *Annales*.[41] In representing a hero seeking this lost wife at the risk of his own death Virgil was perhaps in danger of retracing his own steps, retreading ground already covered in the tale of Orpheus and Eurydice in the *Georgics*.[42] Generic movement onwards requires a poet to avoid treading the same ground: making a ghost out of an old story is one way of avoiding the peril of becoming stuck in one's own literary past. When the ghost of Creusa appears and echoes Hector's order to move on and leave Troy she is partly issuing an appeal to break out of the cycle of repetition that comes from simply following the path laid down by one's own footsteps.

Underlying the episode though is also a set of more complex engagements with the metaphors of imitation. Creusa is the mother of Aeneas's child, a source potentially of life and of physical replication, and of cultural continuity in the form of biological continuity. There is also nothing ethically dubious about her: she offers advice to Aeneas which is broadly similar to that offered by Hector, to flee from Troy, stop feeling, move on. All of these aspects of her role in the poem would make it natural for her to appear to Aeneas like Hector, in quasi-bodily form as a voice of moral authority. But she is a woman, and Aeneas is relating this narrative to Dido, another flesh and blood woman. So when Creusa appears to Aeneas in Book 2 she is not just

41. Ennius, ed. Skutsch, *The Annals of Q. Ennius* (1.34–7); Skutsch's note, p. 197, gives full details.
42. See J. Heurgon, 'Un exemple peu connu de la *retractatio* Virgilienne', *Revue des études latines* 9 (1931), 258–68, W. W. Briggs, 'Eurydice, Venus and Creusa: A Note on Structure in Virgil', *Vergilius* 25 (1979), 43–4; on intertexts with *Georgics* 4, see Luca Grillo, 'Leaving Troy and Creusa: Reflections on Aeneas' Flight', *The Classical Journal* 106 (2010), 43–68 and Monica Gale, 'Poetry and the Backward Glance in Virgil's "Georgics" and "Aeneid"', *Transactions of the American Philological Association* 133 (2003), 323–52.

a ghost. She forces Virgil to crush almost all the vocabulary of perceptual error, ghostliness, *simulacra*, all into a couple of lines:

> infelix simulacrum atque ipsius umbra Creusae
> visa mihi ante oculos et nota maior imago.   (*Aen.*, 2.773–4)

There rose before my eyes the sad phantom and ghost of Creusa herself, a form larger than her wont.

She may be bigger than her usual form, but she is a *simulacrum* and an *umbra* and an *imago* too—and the intensity with which she is presented as not really there at all may mark unease at presenting a woman offering counsel to a man, or, indeed, seek to erase the horror of what is likely to have happened to a woman who has been lost in a city that is being sacked.[43] She is a percept, a representation, a thin film, something pointedly lacking in either *vis* or *ubertas*. Hugged, she is air, or a winged dream, something much closer to a Homeric *eidōlon* than any other dream presence in the poem. The Creusa episode exploits the turbulence within the language of imitation—a turbulence which in Virgil is often linked with questions of gender. There is an urgent attempt here to disembody, to enforce emptiness and vanity on the voice of female authority. Avoiding treading in your own footsteps again and again entails turning a body of a woman into a mere *imago* which can be left behind.

There is still a tendency in literary criticism to filter out what we might call transmissional noise—that is, to regard 'reception studies' and 'influence' as a separate category of activity from understanding what a text is doing. Processes of textual genesis (frivolous, literary) can still often be artificially distinguished from political meanings (dark, serious) or from gender politics (often dark and certainly serious). These distinctions are profoundly misleading. It is impossible entirely to separate what a text says or seeks to do from questions about where a text comes from and the ways in which it articulates and obscures its own origins. Virgil's use of the metaphors of *imitatio* is part of the conscious or unconscious language of the *Aeneid*, but it also becomes part of the uneasy politics of the poem. Making an empire

---

43. Contrast the ghost of Anchises at *Aen.*, 5.719–40. He vanishes like smoke, but his arrival is not marked by any of the vocabulary of ghostliness: 'visa dehinc caelo facies delapsa parentis', 'there seemed to glide down from heaven the likeness of his father Anchises', as Fairclough translates: but *visa* can mean 'appeared' rather than 'seemed', and *facies* can mean 'face' or 'physical appearance' rather than 'likeness'. *OLD* cites *Aeneid*, 3.310 'verane te facies, verus mihi nuntius adfers' to support the sense 'A body, etc., w. respect to its outward appearance, form (esp. as seen in dreams or visions)'; but at this moment Andromache is using the word emphatically to ask 'are you a real presence rather than a ghost?', so even this sense connotes substantial being.

entails making dead bodies and live children, as well as making ghosts of the past, and attempting a ghostly revival of past epic. The fashioning of a substantial being from earlier heroes and the creation of *simulacra* necessarily shadow such a process.

So we might add to the first law of imitative *simulacra* another suggestion. That a characteristic of Latin poetry is to be suffused by the metaphors of *imitatio* and to seek urgently and vainly to control them. The difficulty of understanding what exactly is involved in literary imitation produces metaphorical richness. That metaphorical superabundance in turn makes a language of such complexity that it can generate chaos under the illusion of controlling it. And the corollary of this is that perhaps the presence of 'other' and 'further' voices, vain spectral figures who seem to carry a surplus of ethical charge, in the *Aeneid* are in part artefacts of the language of imitation, and they, ironically enough, rather than the soberly embodied rhetorical warriors whom Quintilian sought to create, were to become primary to its influence. A poetics grounded in replication with variation has as its shadow a poetics in which an endless series of *simulacra* are generated from an earlier text, who might in the larger span of literary history run away with the garland of Apollo. Is an imitation more like a *simulacrum* or like a rebirth? Does it necessarily partake disturbingly in both?

Those questions come to a head in the final book of Virgil's *Aeneid*, and its particularly brilliant interweaving of Homeric and Lucretian influences. In Book 12 the Rutuli violate the truce with the Trojans, and Aeneas is wounded with an arrow. When Aeneas is eventually cured from his wound by the help of Venus he returns to the battlefield, and intends to finish the war by punishing Turnus for his breach of the truce. As has been frequently observed, the hero Aeneas and his adversary are in many respects doubles, whose actions repeatedly reflect and parallel each other, not least in the unique double *aristeia* in which each warrior successively overgoes the actions of his rival.[44] Macrobius suggested 'that the whole of Virgil's poem is shaped as a kind of mirror-image of Homer',[45] and an imitation of an earlier narrative which seeks to distinguish its own ethical foundations from those of an earlier text whilst retaining much of its actions must almost necessarily

44. Virgil, *Aeneid. Book XII*, ed. R. J. Tarrant (Cambridge, 2012), pp. 9–16. The echo of 'solvuntur frigore membra' between Turnus (12.951) and Aeneas (1.92) is the most explicit of these links. The double *aristeia* is at 2.500–47. See Richard F. Thomas, 'The Isolation of Turnus', in Hans-Peter Stahl, ed., *Vergil's Aeneid: Augustan Epic and Political Context* (London, 1998), 271–302.
45. Macrobius, trans. Kaster, *Saturnalia*, 5.2.13.

also include internal mirrorings, as one character replicates the actions from the earlier text which the author sees as misguided, while another produces a divergent version of those actions for which the author is seeking the approval of his readers. Polarized imitations result, in which characters shadow each other, and seem by virtue of their comparability to resemble each other and consequently to qualify the ethical distinctions which their comparability was designed to establish.

Aeneas follows Turnus's footprints, tracking him down through clouds of dust on the battlefield. Like that great tracker of truth Epicurus, he seeks him through the darkness: 'solum densa in caligine Turnum | vestigat lustrans, solum in certamina poscit' (*Aen.*, 12.466–7). The verb 'vestigo' (I follow in the footsteps) is only used by Virgil in this final book of the poem, and it is used repeatedly and emphatically. Aeneas is driven to follow in the footsteps of Turnus again and again. At 12.557 he is 'tracking Turnus here and there throughout the host' ('ille ut vestigans diversa per agmina Turnum'). The same verb 'vestigo' recurs again when Aeneas is compared to a shepherd who is smoking bees out from their hive ('inclusas ut cum latebroso in pumice pastor | vestigavit apes fumoque implevit amaro', *Aen.*, 12.587–8). That combination of bees and tracking stamps these episodes as imitations which draw on the language of imitation. Where Lucretius just described himself following Epicurus and taking golden honey from him in the prologue to Book 3 of the *De Rerum Natura*, Aeneas hunts down the hive with destructive intent. The potentially predatory implications of following in a predecessor's footprints which Lucretius had so notably suppressed from his discussion of *imitatio* here become the main driver of the narrative: Aeneas is a hunter-killer aggressively tracking his prey, a shepherd driving the bees from their honey so he can possess it himself.

While Aeneas purposively pursues the 'vestigia' of Turnus (and he is compared explicitly to a hunting dog at *Aen.*, 12.749–55), Turnus becomes increasingly isolated.[46] Allusions to the death of Hector in Book 22 of the *Iliad* cluster around him, but so do (with increasing frequency) direct quotations from Lucretius. Indeed in his final moments Turnus is presented as more or less exactly the kind of person whom the *De Rerum Natura* was designed to help—a mortal who is subject to perceptual illusion and to the fear of death. He is guided around the battlefield by a shape-shifter who can assume whatever 'forma' she likes, Juturna his charioteer. He wears a helmet

---

46. Thomas, 'The Isolation of Turnus'.

bearing the figure of a Chimaera, a mythical beast explicitly associated by Lucretius with delusional beliefs.[47] He cannot see properly through the mist of war, and is confused by the 'appearances of things' rather than what is actually before him ('obstipuit varia confusus imagine rerum', *Aen.*, 12.665)—and 'imagine rerum', conjoining substance of a thing with the airiness of a perception, is such a Lucretian phrase that it is remarkable that Lucretius never actually used it.

One of the Dirae is then sent to terrify him in the form of an owl, 'suddenly shrinking to the shape [*figuram*] of that small bird' ('alitis in parvae subitam collecta figuram', *Aen.*, 12.862). Like one of the unenlightened religious believers whom Lucretius mocked for their superstition and perceptual blindness, Turnus is terrified by this illusory visitation and succumbs to *horror* and *torpor*. And at this point in the endgame of the poem its imitations of Homer and of Lucretius explicitly converge. Turnus picks up a huge stone, like Homer's Aineias during his encounter with Achilles in *Iliad*, 20.285–7, and hurls it 'through the empty air' ('vacuum per inane', *Aen.*, 12.906). The allusion to the *Iliad* is enough to imply things are going badly for Turnus, since Aineias never actually gets to throw the stone, and it is said that had he done so Achilles would have killed him (he has a lucky escape since Poseidon decides to hurl him bodily from the battlefield).

But the direct quotation of 'vacuum per inane' from *De Rerum Natura* 2.202 has perhaps an even more sinister effect.[48] When Lucretius uses that phrase he is arguing that objects can never move themselves upwards, even if like a flame or a plank of wood pressed down below the surface of water, they may appear temporarily to do so. Everything, he insists, falls: stars, fire, all. That makes the allusion particularly cruel.[49] Turnus is a warrior at the end of his life, who is desperately heaving the last of his force together in order to hurl a mighty stone and to do what the Greek Aineias had failed to do: to kill his adversary with a gigantic effort. But stones, like all things, necessarily fall through the void. The whole physical foundation of the cosmos is against Turnus. He is destined not to overcome the centric weightedness of stones, and is bound for the emptiness that is death. And at exactly this

47. *DRN*, 5.890–906; 2.705.
48. Tarrant notes that phrase has 'a Lucretian ring', Virgil, ed. Tarrant, *Aeneid. Book XII*, ad loc., but does not record the direct parallel.
49. On Lucretius's general hostility towards warfare and his use of military imagery to describe the triumphs of Epicurus over the warlike ethos of Rome, see Stephen Harrison, 'Epicurean Subversion? Lucretius's First Proem and Contemporary Roman Culture', in David Norbrook, Stephen Harrison, and Philip Hardie, eds., *Lucretius and the Early Modern* (Oxford, 2015), 29–43.

moment Virgil introduces the final dream in the *Aeneid*. It is, like so many of his dreams, a direct imitation of Homer—a dreamitation—and it is a version of the worst Homeric dream of all, the dream that Hector has when he is fighting Achilles for the last time:

> ac velut in somnis, oculos ubi languida pressit
> nocte quies, nequiquam avidos extendere cursus
> velle videmur et in mediis conatibus aegri
> succidimus; non lingua valet, non corpore notae
> sufficiunt vires, nec vox aut verba sequuntur:
> sic Turno...   (*Aen.*, 12.908–13)

And as in dreams of night, when languorous sleep has weighed down our eyes, we seem to strive vainly to press on our eager course, and in mid effort sink helpless: our tongue lacks power, our wonted strength fails our limbs, nor voice nor words ensue: so to Turnus...

As in a dream one can't overtake the quarry one's chasing—
the fugitive can't get away, nor his pursuer catch him—
So Achilles could not catch up, nor Hektōr get clear away...
(*Iliad*, 22.199–201)

With that dream Turnus truly enters the realm of the insubstantial, and in effect becomes himself a *simulacrum*. As Richard Tarrant notes, the phrase 'in somnis' (*Aen.*, 12.908) is generally used in the *Aeneid* to mark the start of a dream or vision (*Aen.*, 1.353, 2.270. 3.151, 4.353, and 4.466). The description of Turnus's paralysis draws repeatedly and deeply on the language of Lucretius.[50] Not only is Turnus doomed by the gods and by the literary parallels that connect him to Hector. He is also caught in a dream which destroys his bodily strength, and removes from him the energy that keeps a 'living' imitation from collapsing into a mere *simulacrum*.

As living and dreaming blend, Turnus experiences a fatal loss of *vis*: 'our tongue lacks power, our wonted strength (*vires*) fails our limbs' ('non lingua valet, non corpore notae | sufficiunt vires', *Aen.*, 12.911–12). The Homeric simile describes a dream of a hunt in which pursuer and pursued track each other in an endless chase.[51] That hunt seems in the *Aeneid* almost to have

---

50. At 12.908–9 Tarrant cites parallels from Lucretius (5.887: an exhausted old horse; 4.453–4 which describes dreams as evidence for the unreliability of sensual impressions); at 12.910 on 'velle videmur' he cites the continuation of Lucretius's passage on dreams, *DRN*, 4.455–7; on 'succidimus' in 12.911 he cites *DRN*, 3.152–8, a passage on the somatic nature of fear which underlies much of the description of Turnus; on 12.912 'nec vox aut verba sequuntur' he cites *DRN*, 4.533 and 4.549–79, a passage on the corporeality of speech.
51. Green's translation highlights the metaphor of the hunt more than the original; but Homer does repeat the word 'to pursue or hunt', διώκειν, at the end of successive lines.

been exploded outwards into the surrounding narrative: Aeneas relentlessly tracks the footsteps of Turnus, while Lucretian dream lore fills up the void left behind in the simile. And the hunt is also made pointedly one-sided, for in the Virgilian version of it there is only one hunter: Aeneas, the relentless tracker of Turnus. His victim by contrast is condemned to the world of dreams and shadows. But Turnus is also in the dream simile, as Richard Thomas has noted, one of us:[52] 'velle videmur', says Virgil: *we* seem to want to run. The imitator's aggression is being amplified and embodied in the relentless tracker Aeneas, while the human perceptual weaknesses evoked with such vividness by Lucretius finally engulf Turnus.

It is sometimes argued that Virgil's *Aeneid* is an Epicurean poem.[53] In the examples explored here it is not Epicurean doctrine that Virgil takes from Lucretius but an imaginary praxis. The *Aeneid* responds at a profound fictive level to the fusion of Epicurean physics and epistemology with the poetics of imitation which Lucretius presented in the *De Rerum Natura*. In the latter part of the poem Virgil effectively fashions a Homeric narrative out of the perceptual goals of Lucretius's poem. Aeneas becomes the relentless tracker across the darkness of the void; Turnus becomes the man subject to the terror of death, who finally fades into a Homeric dream, without substance or *vis* or even voice of his own.

There is an overt Roman imperial coding here: the tracker, the hunter, the warrior of body and substance kills the insubstantial ghost of a Homeric hero. But there is also a built-in counter-narrative: the aggression removed from the act of imitation by Lucretius becomes the victorious, and finally a destructive force; meanwhile the imperfections of mortal experience, which Lucretius had so powerfully evoked that many readers have found in him an *anti-Lucrèce chez Lucrèce*, arguing implicitly against his own certitude that death was not to be feared, are increasingly loaded onto Aeneas's adversary Turnus. The perceptual failings, the dreams and delusions and desires that all mortals feel are what lose. And those delusions seem finally to be generated by the forces which destroy them. *Imitatio* is a duplicitous tool: an attempt to re-embody a past text will always generate ghosts of the earlier text within itself.

---

52. 'He has become one of us, a very human creature, who has just realized that the cosmic order is against him', Thomas, 'The Isolation of Turnus', p. 291.
53. On which, see David Armstrong, *Vergil, Philodemus, and the Augustans* (Austin, 2004), Viviane Mellinghoff-Bourgerie, *Les incertitudes de Virgile: contributions épicuriennes à la théologie de l'Enéide* (Bruxelles, 1990), Leah Kronenberg, 'Mezentius the Epicurean', *Transactions of the American Philological Association* 135 (2005), 403–31, and Julia T. Dyson, 'Dido the Epicurean', *Classical Antiquity* 15 (1996), 203–21.

PART II

Early Modernity

4

Petrarchan Transformations

The ghost of Virgil's Hector puts in a fleeting appearance in a letter from the Florentine humanist Poggio Bracciolini to Guarino Veronese in December 1416:

> He was sad and dressed in mourning, as people are when doomed to death; his beard was dirty and his hair caked with mud, so that by his expression and appearance it was clear that he had been summoned to an undeserved punishment. He seemed to stretch out his hands and beg for the loyalty of the Roman people, to demand that he be saved from an unjust sentence, and to feel it a disgrace that he who had once preserved the safety of the whole population by his influence and his eloquence could now not find one single advocate who would pity his misfortunes and take some trouble over his welfare and prevent his being dragged off to an undeserved punishment.[1]

> Moestus quidem ipse erat ac sordidatus, tanquam morti rei solebant: *squalentem barbam gerens ac concretos pulvere crines*: ut ipso vultu atque habitu fateretur ad immeritam sententiam se vocari. Videbatur manus tendere, implorare Quiritum fidem, ut se ab iniquo judice tuerentur; postulare et indigne ferre quod qui quondam sua ope, sua eloquentia multorum salutem conservasset, nunc neque patronum quempiam inveniret, quem misereretur fortunarum suarum, neque qui suae consuleret saluti, aut ad injustum rapi supplicium prohiberet.[2]

The prisoner described here was not Virgil's Hector but Quintilian, of whose *Institutio Oratoria* Poggio and a group of fellow humanists had discovered a complete manuscript in the church next to the monastery of St Gall. Poggio trumpets his find by an allusion to Hector ('squalentem barbam et concretos sanguine crinis', *Aen.*, 2.277), whom he artfully transforms into an orator pleading for his liberty, who can exploit the full range of *actio* (the hand gestures used by a trained orator) to support his petition for release. That transformation of a warrior into an orator plays on Quintilian's

---

1. Poggio Bracciolini and Niccolò Niccoli, *Two Renaissance Book Hunters; the Letters of Poggius Bracciolini to Nicolaus de Niccolis*, ed. Phyllis Walter Goodhart Gordan (New York, 1974), p. 194.
2. Poggio Bracciolini, *Poggiana, ou la vie, le caractere, les sentences, et les bons mots de Pogge florentin, avec son Histoire de la republique de Florence*, ed. Jacques Lenfant, 2 vols. (Amsterdam, 1720), 2.311.

repeated association between the art of rhetoric and physical and military prowess, and the passage as a whole draws deeply on Quintilian's repeated metaphorical association of texts with physical beings. It simultaneously represents and enacts the rediscovery of the *Institutio*.

The use of such corporeal language to describe acts of textual discovery and reconstruction was a deep characteristic of humanist rhetoric, and it has played a foundational role in critical attitudes towards imitation and its relationship to that thing still often called 'the Renaissance'—'the rebirth of learning'—over the past forty years. A. Bartlett Giamatti and Thomas M. Greene—who might be referred to as the 'Yale school', since they shared not only an institution but also a way of talking about humanism—developed a very influential model of humanist poetics which was substantially indebted to the heroic self-representations of early humanist scholars. A manuscript could be metaphorically embodied as a mutilated person and restored to full life and freedom by the healing and liberating hand of scholarship.[3] Meanwhile, it was argued, the scholars and poets who were engaged in such acts of retrieval had a clear historical sense which enabled them to perceive the alterity of those texts even as they restored them to life. As a result, the humanist was characterized by a sense of historical exile, a longing for a past which he knew to be a different world from his own, but which nonetheless he sought constantly to recover. Giamatti describes the 'romance of early humanism' as 'the secondary culture's deep belief that, despite distance and loss, it might become primary; the conviction that, through effort and emulation, the copy might become an original, the removed might restore the beginning, the exile might—through purposeful wandering—become a point, or recapture the point, of origin'.[4] Thomas Greene's study of imitation, *The Light in Troy*, which remains a reference-point in work on this subject today, presented Petrarch as 'the first to notice that classical antiquity was very different from his own medieval world' and as the first writer to develop a theory and practice of imitation that would at once mark and bridge that historical divide.[5] For

---

3. See A. Bartlett Giamatti, *Exile and Change in Renaissance Literature* (New Haven and London, 1984), pp. 12–32.

4. Giamatti, *Exile and Change*, p. 16.

5. Thomas M. Greene, *The Light in Troy: Imitation and Discovery in Renaissance Poetry* (New Haven and London, 1982), esp. p. 90. For a robust attack on this view, see James Simpson, 'Subjects of Triumph and Literary History: Dido and Petrarch in Petrarch's *Africa* and *Trionfi*', *Journal of Medieval and Early Modern Studies* 35 (2005), 489–508 and Martin Eisner, 'In the Labyrinth of the Library: Petrarch's Cicero, Dante's Virgil, and the Historiography of the Renaissance', *Renaissance Quarterly* 67 (2014), 755–90.

Greene Petrarch's poetry stands at the beginning of early modernity because it encourages 'sub-reading', in which an implied conversation with a past text is conducted beneath the surface. And for Greene, as for Giamatti, 'exile' characterizes the relationship of a humanist to the past: he knows that the classical past is distinct from his own world, and yet he simultaneously longs to return to and recreate it.

That view of Petrarch corresponds more closely to Petrarch's self-representations than to his actions. Indeed it corresponds far more closely to a historiographical tradition that represented 'the Renaissance' as the origin of an awareness of historical difference between the present and the classical past than it does even to Petrarch's highly misleading descriptions of his own activities. The aim of this chapter will be to argue that, however sophisticated Petrarch's understanding of historical difference and of chronology might have been, that understanding was not the foundation of his imitative poetics. Petrarch was indeed keen to present himself as an innovator, and without doubt he did display an awareness of literary chronology that was unusual before the mid-fourteenth century. But in his writing about imitation, and (as we shall see later in this chapter) in his Latin poetry too, the vast majority of his innovations were aided and abetted not by a desire to be illuminated by the pure light of classical learning, but by his extremely adroit (and sometimes deliberately deceptive) use of late antique and medieval sources. I will aim in this chapter, that is, to emphasize the medieval aspects of Petrarch. I will suggest he was not the psychologically tormented being evoked by the Yale school, who sought an impossible retrieval of the past which he knew to be irretrievable, but someone who was very good at using what he happened to know, and who was very good at concealing his debts to other people.

Humanist rediscoveries?

Before turning to Petrarch, let us stay for a moment with the 'rediscovery' of Quintilian. That event shows very clearly how humanist scholars in the generation after Petrarch represented their activities in ways that did not quite correspond to the facts. Scholars did not simply find mutilated lost texts, blow off the dust of corruption which had accumulated through centuries of monkish neglect, and bring them to the world in rejuvenated form. Poggio Bracciolini knew that the discovery of a complete Quintilian was a perfect occasion for representing himself as a hero of textual renovation. He knew that not because he had achieved a radical break with the immediate past, but because a conceptual space already existed for his discovery. Quintilian was already known, read, and admired, but in a form that was known to be imperfect. The Florentine Chancellor Coluccio Salutati had tried and failed to obtain a complete text of the *Institutio* in 1396, and Gasparino Barzizza (who wrote a treatise on imitation) had apparently even attempted to write the missing sections of the text.[6] There was also in a near literal sense a pre-existing space for Poggio's textual discovery, since fourteenth-century manuscripts of Quintilian often included blank areas on their pages to indicate missing sections of the text.[7] Petrarch acquired a manuscript of Quintilian of this type in 1350, which textual scholars still refer to as 'mutili', or mutilated copies.[8] That word is one of the many relics of humanist ideology which remains alive within the present-day language of textual scholarship, and conveys both an extremely misleading picture of these manuscripts and a deeply prejudicial view of medieval scribes. It could be taken to imply that incomplete manuscripts of Quintilian displayed in their physical form evidence of their mistreatment by earlier generations, in the form of pages missing and torn out. In fact many of the so-called

---

6. Carl Joachim Classen, *Antike Rhetorik im Zeitalter des Humanismus* (Munich, 2003), pp. 156–7. For the treatise, see G. W. Pigman, 'Barzizza's Treatise on Imitation', *Bibliothèque d'Humanisme et Renaissance* 44 (1982), 341–52.

7. For earlier use of blank spaces as paratextual markers of missing or illegible material, see Justin A. Stover, 'Space as Paratext: Scribal Practice in the Medieval Edition of Ammianus Marcellinus', in M. J. Teeuwen and I. Van Renswoude, eds., *The Annotated Book in the Early Middle Ages: Practices of Reading and Writing* (Turnhout, 2017), 305–21. James Jerome Murphy, *Rhetoric in the Middle Ages: A History of Rhetorical Theory from Saint Augustine to the Renaissance* (Berkeley and London, 1974), pp. 123–30 describes how the brief revival of interest in Quintilian in the twelfth century, particularly in Chartres, was followed by two centuries of neglect. For a detailed study of the influence of Quintilian in commentaries on Cicero before the discovery of the complete text by Poggio in 1416, see Priscilla S. Boskoff, 'Quintilian in the Late Middle Ages', *Speculum: A Journal of Medieval Studies* 27 (1952), 71–8, C. J. Classen, 'Quintilian and the Revival of Learning in Italy', *Humanistica Lovaniensia* 43 (1994), 77–98.

8. Remigio Sabbadini, *Le scoperte dei codici latini e greci ne'secoli XIV e XV*, 2 vols. (Firenze, 1905), p. 13 lists the contents of the *mutili*. A more detailed discussion is in Murphy, *Rhetoric in the Middle Ages*, pp. 123–30, which is substantially indebted to the helpful history of the reception of Quintilian, *M. Fabii Quintiliani Institutionis Oratoriae liber I*, ed. F. H. Colson (Cambridge, 1924), pp. xliii–lvi; pp. lx–lxiii relate the state of and use of the *mutili*, the main group of which, including Petrarch's manuscript (now Codex Parisinus Latinus 7720), omitted Proem. 1–1.1.6; 5.14.12–8.3.64; 8.6.17–8.6.67; 9.3.2–10.1.107; 11.1.71–11.2.33; 12.10.43 to the end. Petrarch's commentary and notes were particularly rich on the section of Book 10 which he had. See Pierre de Nolhac, *Pétrarque et l'humanisme: d'après un essai de restitution de sa bibliothèque* (Paris, 1892), pp. 281–90, and for transcriptions of Petrarch's notes, see M. Accame Lanzillotta, 'Le postille del Petrarca a Quintiliano (Cod. Parigino lat. 7720)', *Quaderni Petrarcheschi* 5 (1988), 1–201.

'mutili' were carefully designed by their scribes to alert their readers to the deficiencies and lacunae in the text they were reading. Petrarch's manuscript of Quintilian (now Codex Parisinus Latinus 7720 in the Bibliothèque nationale), for instance, breaks off mid-sentence at the very end of 9.2, during Quintilian's discussion of the figures of speech. A column and a half is then left blank by the scribe in order to indicate that material is missing (fol. 87v). Then the text resumes (in rather faded ink) on the next page, at 10.1.108, right in the middle of a passage in which Quintilian is comparing Cicero to Demosthenes.

These lacunae signalled by a careful scribe mattered to Petrarch almost as much as the text which surrounded them. In one of his series of letters to classical authors composed in around 1351 and included in the final book of his *Familiarium Rerum Libri* (Books of Familiar Letters) he addressed Quintilian himself, and described his manuscript of the *Institutio Oratoria* as 'the dismembered limbs of a beautiful body', at the sight of which 'my mind was overcome by admiration and grief; perhaps someone now possesses you in your entirety who is doubtlessly unaware of his guest's renown'.[9] In that letter Petrarch set out the tune on which many later humanist composed variations. Poggio Bracciolini, who 'rescued' Quintilian from the cellars of St Gall, was a pupil of Giovanni Malpaghini, who had helped Petrarch with the editing of the collection in which the letter to Quintilian appeared. He was therefore a direct heir to Petrarch's rhetoric about the 'mutilation' of Quintilian. This small fact prompts a larger observation: what we call 'the Renaissance' had its roots in the classicism of the later middle ages, and the careful ways in which scribes and scholars drew attention to deficiencies and gaps in their knowledge. 'Humanist' scholars—who earned their livings by presenting themselves as innovators and discoverers who broke decisively with the past—were very adept at occluding this fact.[10]

From 1350 onwards Petrarch had access to Quintilian's discussion of imitation in Book 10, chapter 2 of the *Institutio*. In his manuscript (as in subsequent printed editions) this chapter was headed 'De imitatione', and

9. Francesco Petrarca, *Letters on Familiar Matters: Rerum familiarium libri*, trans. Aldo S. Bernardo, 3 vols. (Baltimore and London, 1975–85), 3.329. 'Vidi formosi corporis artus effusos; admiratio animum dolorque concussit; et fortasse nunc apud aliquem totus es, et apud talem forsitan qui suum hospitem habet incognitum', Francesco Petrarca, *Le familiari*, ed. Vittorio Rossi and Umberto Bosco, 4 vols. (Firenze, 1933), 4.241. Parenthetical references are to these editions.

10. For some detailed examples, see Francisco Rico, 'Petrarca e il medioevo', in Accademia dei Lincei, ed., *La cultura letteraria italiana e l'identità europea: sotto l'alto patronato del Presidente della Repubblica (Roma, 6–8 aprile 2000)* (Rome, 2001), 39–56.

Petrarch paid close attention to it. When Quintilian insisted that 'Total similarity is so difficult to achieve that even Nature herself has failed to prevent things which seem to match and resemble each other most closely from being always distinguishable in *some* respect' (10.2.10, fol. 89r) Petrarch marked the passage with a pointing finger in the margin. In his familiar letter addressed to Quintilian himself, Petrarch allowed that the rhetorician did not merely follow in the footsteps of Cicero but found out doctrine of his own: 'following in his footsteps you acquired a new renown not from imitation but from your own learning, which gave birth to your remarkable work' ('post tanti viri [i.e. Cicero's] vestigia novam non imitationis sed doctrine proprie preclarique operis gloriam invenisti', *Fam.*, 24.7).[11] He took seriously Quintilian's injunction to follow several authorities rather than one, and jotted a note to himself to remember the injunction that 'imitation does not consist solely in words' (*Institutio*, 10.2.27).[12]

Petrarch, however, tended to regard Quintilian as a source of local observations about imitation rather than of an entire educational system which trained students how to imitate from the very start of their careers. This was the main distinction between him and the later generations of humanists discussed in Chapter 5. One reason for this rather selective view of Quintilian was that Petrarch came to him relatively late: in 1350 when he acquired his manuscript of the *Institutio* he was 46. The manuscript he obtained at that date also had one very significant feature: it lacked the crucial sentence from the start of Book 10 in which Quintilian said that an orator should attempt to learn not precepts but the entire *hexis*, the habitual practices, of a predecessor:

> But these rules of style, while part of the student's theoretical knowledge, are not in themselves sufficient to give him oratorical power (*vim*). In addition he will require that assured facility which the Greeks call *hexis*.
>
> Sed haec eloquendi praecepta, sicut cogitationi sunt necessaria, ita non satis ad vim dicendi valent, nisi illis firma quaedam facilitas, quae apud Graecos ἕξις nomitatur, accesserit.   (*Institutio*, 10.1.1)

In that sentence Quintilian grounded his entire discussion of imitation in learned habituation in the practices of a predecessor, rather than in local allusion. And that sentence Petrarch never read. As a result Petrarch tended

---

11. Petrarca, *Letters*, 3.329.
12. 'Lege, Silvane, memoriter' ('Read, Silvanus, so as to remember'). See Lanzillotta, 'Le postille', pp. 96–7 and Martin L. McLaughlin, *Literary Imitation in the Italian Renaissance* (Oxford, 1995), p. 24.

to present Quintilian—as he did in his letter to him—as a trainer of youth rather than someone who set out a programme for acquiring the skill and habit of a mature orator.

Much of Petrarch's writing about imitation is concentrated in three of his familiar letters: 1.8 to Tommaso da Messina (one of a trio of letters about learning and style, which, from the frequency of their allusions to Quintilian, must date from after 1350), and two slightly later letters to Boccaccio: 22.2 from October 1359, and 23.19 composed in around 1366.[13] Although Petrarch does discuss education and rhetorical training in several of those letters, the language he uses to talk about *imitatio* is much less indebted to Quintilian than it is to Seneca's 84th Epistle. The language of 1.8 is characteristically Senecan. That same letter also contains a particularly revealing reference to another intermediate source for Petrarch's thinking on the topic:

> His loftiest advice about invention is to imitate the bees which through an astonishing process produce wax and honey from the flowers they leave behind. Macrobius in his *Saturnalia* reported not only the sense but the very words of Seneca so that to me at the very time he seemed to be following this advice in his reading and writing, he seemed to be disapproving of it by what he did. For he did not try to produce honey from the flowers culled from Seneca but instead produced them whole and in the very form in which he had found them on the stems.[14]

> Cuius summa est: apes in inventionibus imitandas, que flores, non quales acceperint, referunt, sed ceras ac mella mirifica quadam permixtione conficiunt. Eius autem non sensum modo, sed verba Macrobius in *Saturnalibus* posuit; ut michi quidem uno eodemque tempore quod legendo simul ac scribendo probaverat, rebus ipsis improbare videretur; non enim flores apud Senecam lectos in favos vertere studuit, sed integros et quales in alienis ramis invenerat, protulit.[15]

Critics have often been too ready to trust what Petrarch says about the fifth-century author Macrobius here.[16] It is true that Macrobius does

13. See McLaughlin, *Literary Imitation*, pp. 22–34. See also Cornelia C. Coulter, 'Boccaccio's Knowledge of Quintilian', *Speculum: A Journal of Medieval Studies* 33 (1958), 490–6.
14. Petrarca, *Letters*, 1.41.   15. Petrarca, ed. Rossi and Bosco, *Le familiari*, 1.39.
16. Gerard Paul Passannante, *The Lucretian Renaissance: Philology and the Afterlife of Tradition* (Chicago, Ill., and London, 2011), p. 54; John Ahern, 'Good-Bye Bologna: Johannnes Andreae and *Familiares* IV 15 and 16', in Teodolinda Barolini and H. Wayne Storey, eds., *Petrarch and the Textual Origins of Interpretation* (Leiden and Boston, 2007), 185–204, at p. 195, and Kathy Eden, *The Renaissance Rediscovery of Intimacy* (Chicago, Ill., 2012), p. 61. Ronald G. Witt, *In the Footsteps of the Ancients: The Origins of Humanism from Lovato to Bruni* (Leiden, 2000), p. 261 (committed as he is to Greene's view of Petrarchan imitation) simply omits the reference to Macrobius from the quotation. G. W. Pigman, 'Versions of Imitation in the Renaissance', *Renaissance Quarterly* 33 (1980), 1–32 at pp. 5–6 is the noble exception.

substantially quote Seneca's comparison of imitators to bees in his prologue to the *Saturnalia*. But it is not true that he did so *verbatim*. He in fact departed from Seneca's language at one particularly significant moment. Seneca said the bees combine all they gather 'in unum saporem', in one flavour. Macrobius, by contrast, wrote that they create a single flavour 'mixtura quadam et proprietate spiritus sui mutant' (*Saturnalia*, Pr. 5), 'by blending in the peculiar quality of their own spirit'.[17] The addition of that single word *proprietas* connects the activities of the bees with textual ownership, and with the creation of a new entity; and it did so by using a word that Petrarch was highly attuned to notice. As Kathy Eden has shown, after Petrarch's discovery of Cicero's familiar letters in 1345 he developed a particular interest in texts which displayed a 'personal' or 'domestic' or intimate style, for which a key Latin term was 'proprietas'.[18] Macrobius also used an indefinite relative pronoun to describe the mysterious transformative action of the bees: *quadam*, a certain (unspecified) mixture, a 'something' personal. This again directly influenced Petrarch's language: he echoes Macrobius's indefinite pronoun when he says that the bees transform what they gather by 'a kind of miracle-working mixture' ('mirifica *quadam* permixtione'). That small verbal detail has larger implications. It shows the unreliability of Petrarch's explicit self-representations. He did not return *ad fontes* to Seneca. Nor did he by his own miraculous power of transformation turn Seneca into something new. Rather he Macrobianized Seneca's discussion of *imitatio* at the very moment he was criticizing Macrobius.

Imitatio and plagiarism

When Petrarch accused Macrobius of simply reproducing Seneca's words, however, he did foreground a feature in his thinking about imitation which differentiates his writing on the subject from that of most of his classical sources in the rhetorical tradition. All of his letters about *imitatio* display a marked fear of theft from or of servitude to a source. That, however, was not a sign that Petrarch belonged to a new era, but rather an indicator that he was an exceptionally careful reader of Macrobius's *Saturnalia*, which was one of the first and favourite manuscripts which he owned. Macrobius's

17. Text and translations from Ambrosius Aurelius Theodosius Macrobius, *Saturnalia*, trans. Robert A. Kaster, 3 vols. (Cambridge, Mass., and London, 2011).
18. See the brilliant discussion in Eden, *Intimacy*, pp. 49–72.

Saturnalia was the principal text from the later ancient world to explore relationships between *imitatio* and textual appropriation, or what we now call plagiarism. Although there are uncertainties about the date of Macrobius's work, it was probably (like Augustine's *City of God*, which was also at the heart of Petrarch's early reading) written in the 430s AD, during the aftermath of and in response to the sack of Rome in 410. It relates a civilized dialogue from the late fourth century which was designed to evoke the culture of Rome before that traumatic event.[19] It is indeed itself a piece of cultural retrieval and reconstruction. In the fifth and sixth books of the *Saturnalia* Macrobius dramatized a discussion about the sources of Virgil, in the course of which he quoted passages from a number of authors whom Virgil had closely imitated, including Homer, Ennius, Naevius, Lucretius, and even Cicero. At the start of the sixth book the participants in the dialogue take stock of what Virgil has borrowed from Homer, and wonder if he is guilty of literary theft, or the appropriation of another's goods ('usurpatio alieni', *Saturnalia*, 6.1.2).

In the rhetorical tradition the direct replication of another orator's words was generally presented as a mark of ineptness rather than as an act of theft: to repeat Cicero's words verbatim might show an orator had not grasped the key skill of the rhetorician, which is to adapt words to suit particular occasions and audiences. In poetry and drama, however, the line between imitation and appropriation was thin and porous. Direct quotation (or even the imitation in Latin of a Greek source text which had previously been imitated by a Roman writer) could be stigmatized as a 'furtum' or theft.[20]

It has been plausibly argued that Macrobius's discussion of Virgil responded to a series of lost attacks on the poet which presented him as a literary thief.[21] At the start of Book 6 Macrobius sets about refuting those allegations in earnest. Virgil, it is argued by Rufius Albinus, did not steal. His imitations were praiseworthy, since they prevented the ancient texts which he imitated from being forgotten. This argument was calculated to have a particular strength in a period immediately after the cultural catastrophe of the sack of Rome, when the continuity of a literary tradition might be perceived to be under threat. It also had a strong resonance for Petrarch,

19. 'Not only was Macrobius one of the earliest writers possessed by Petrarch, but he was one of the most frequently cited ones in Petrarch's personal notations in the margins of his Virgil', Aldo S. Bernardo, *Petrarch, Scipio and the 'Africa': The Birth of Humanism's Dream* (Westport, Conn., 1978), p. 111.
20. See notably the prologue to Terence's *Eunuchus*, and pp. 344–6 in this volume.
21. Scott McGill, *Plagiarism in Latin Literature* (Cambridge, 2012), pp. 182–209.

working as he did from manuscripts which were in many cases visibly imperfect records of their archetypes. Rufius continues by saying that Virgil improved what he imitated, and that many of his apparent borrowings from Homer were in fact borrowings from other authors who had also borrowed from the same source (*Saturnalia*, 6.1.6–7). Virgil was therefore not guilty of appropriation, but simply borrowed from a common stock ('rerum communio', *Saturnalia*, 6.1.5).

Macrobius's very keenness to refute the charge of literary theft keeps it constantly in his readers' minds; and in the chapters that follow he presents extensive quotations from earlier Latin poetry followed by quotations of Virgil's (often very close) 'imitations' of them. These implicitly raise the question of how and how fully Virgil had assimilated those prior texts just as Macrobius is defending him against the charge of textual appropriation. The influence of Macrobius on early modern commentaries on Virgil— which came routinely to annotate local 'imitations' or 'borrowings', many of which derived from those listed by Macrobius—cannot be overstated. He made it commonplace for scholars to think about where poems come from, and to think of what might be lost and gained through poetic imitation. He was also the main authority from late antiquity who encouraged authors and editors to think of imitation as a localized phenomenon, in which one particular passage recalled an earlier one.

The influence of Macrobius on Petrarch is also hard to overstate, but it is also sometimes hard to see, since it was a partially occluded influence, and it pulled Petrarch in several directions at once. Macrobius gave powerful and conflicting messages about imitation in the *Saturnalia*. On the one hand (according to Petrarch at any rate) he was willing in his preface to borrow Seneca's discussion of imitation word for word. On the other hand he carefully attempted to develop a vocabulary of 'borrowing' (*mutuandi*) from a common store, and of *imitatio* as an act of retrieval and improvement. These were supposed to make a moral distinction between *imitatio* and textual appropriation. Petrarch's writing on the topic of imitation responds to all these aspects of the *Saturnalia*. It is the *Saturnalia* that generates the combination of corporeal specificity with conceptual cloudiness that runs through Petrarch's second letter on the subject to Boccaccio:

> An imitator must take care to write something similar yet not identical to the original, and that similarity must not be like the image to its original in painting where the greater the similarity the greater the praise for the artist, but rather like that of a son to his father. While often very different in their individual

features, they have a certain something our painters call an 'air', especially noticeable about the face and the eyes, that produces a resemblance; seeing the son's face, we are reminded of the father's, although if it came to measurement, the features would all be different, but there is something subtle that creates this effect... It may all be summarized by saying with Seneca, and Flaccus before him, that we must write as the bees make honey, not gathering flowers but turning them into honeycombs, thereby blending them into a oneness that is unlike them all, and better. (*Fam.*, 23.19)[22]

curandum imitatori ut quod scribit simile non idem sit, eamque similitudinem talem esse oportere, non qualis est imaginis ad eum cuius imago est, que quo similior eo maior laus artificis, sed qualis filii ad patrem. In quibus cum magna sepe diversitas sit membrorum, umbra quaedam et quem pictores nostri aerem vocant, qui in vultu inque oculi maxime cernitur, similitudinem illam facit, que statim viso filio, patris in memoriam nos reducat, cum tamen si res ad mensuram redeat, omnia sint diversa; sed est ibi nescio quid occultum quod hanc habeat vim... Standum denique Senece consilio, quod ante Senecam Flacci erat, ut scribamus scilicet sicut apes mellificant, non servatis floribus sed in favos versis, ut ex multis et variis unum fiat, idque aliud et melius.[23]

This is evidently rich in Senecan metaphors, but it is also infused with the language of approximation which Macrobius used in the prologue to the *Saturnalia*. Mere measurement cannot reveal the true nature of a family resemblance, for there is a 'nescio quid', a 'je ne sais quoi', or a 'something' in the resemblance between a father and a son or of a portrait and its sitter which cannot be quantified.[24] That association between imitation and an indefinable family resemblance is capped by the word Petrarch uses to describe the 'air' of resemblance between a son and a father: it is *vis*, power. That word had played a central part in Quintilian's discussions of the distinctive and inimitable powers of particular rhetoricians, and Petrarch uses it here to evoke the unique power of 'creative' imitation. Again we see the fertility (if in this context the metaphor can be forgiven) of the language of imitation: the difficulty of distinguishing imitation from illicit textual appropriation generates a strong metaphorical register of bodily assimilation, and that is combined with a strategic vagueness about what an imitator actually brings to the text that is imitated. The same letter also goes on to consider the fine line between imitation and *furtum* or theft, since Petrarch proceeds to record how his young scribe, Giovanni Malpaghini, had spotted three

---

22. Petrarca, *Letters*, 3.301–2.   23. Petrarca, ed. Rossi and Bosco, *Le familiari*, 4.206.
24. On the history of this idea, see Richard Scholar, *The Je-Ne-Sais-Quoi in Early Modern Europe: Encounters with a Certain Something* (Oxford, 2005).

words in the *Bucolicum Carmen* which were directly repeated from Virgil's *Aeneid*, a repetition which made Petrarch fear that he might be accused of having stolen the phrases.[25]

The central topic of his other letter to Boccaccio about *imitatio* (*Fam.*, 22.2) was Petrarch's revisions to his *Bucolicum Carmen*, which, he records, had in its earlier form included several three-word phrases (and we should note that phrases of this length seem for Petrarch to have crossed the line between imitative assimilation and appropriation) which were uncomfortably close to texts by Virgil and Ovid, and which he wished to revise away. Again the discussion of imitation is inseparable from an attempt to defend himself against the charge of textual appropriation. And this passage also shows the extent to which Petrarch's thinking about *imitatio* was connected to his awareness that his own readers—learned men like Malpaghini and Boccaccio—had also read the texts which he had read and might catch him in an act of verbal appropriation:

> I have read Virgil, Flaccus, Severinus, Tullius not once but countless times, nor was my reading rushed but leisurely, pondering them as I went with all the powers of my intellect; I ate in the morning what I would digest in the evening, I swallowed as a boy what I would ruminate upon as an older man. I have thoroughly absorbed these writings, implanting them not only in my memory but in my marrow, and they have so become one with my mind that were I never to read them for the remainder of my life, they would cling to me, having taken root in the innermost recesses of my mind. But sometimes I may forget the author, since through long usage and continual possession I may adopt them and for some time regard them as my own; and besieged by the mass of such writings, I may forget whose they are and whether they are mine or others'.[26]

> Legi apud Virgilium apud Flaccum apud Severinum apud Tullium; nec semel legi sed milies, nec cucurri sed incubui, et totis ingenii nisibus immoratus sum; mane comedi quod sero digererem, hausi puer quod senior ruminarem. Hec se michi tam familiariter ingessere et non modo memorie sed medullis affixa sunt unumque cum ingenio facta sunt meo, ut etsi per omnem vitam amplius non legantur, ipsa quidem hereant, actis in intima parte radicibus, sed interdum obliviscar auctorem, quippe qui longo usu et possessione continua quasi illa prescripserim diuque pro meis habuerim, et turba talium obsessus, nec cuius sint certe nec aliena meminerim.[27]

---

25. 'Atque intonat ore' (*Ecloga*, 6.193) repeated the end of *Aen.*, 6.607 verbatim. That repetition prompts him to wonder if he has 'stolen' (*rapui*).
26. Petrarca, *Letters*, 3.212–13 (22.2).
27. Petrarca, ed. Rossi and Bosco, *Le familiari*, 4.106.

Again Petrarch enriches Seneca's images in order to force the distinction which is so difficult to make in abstract theoretical terms between imitative assimilation and textual appropriation. He insists on his own agency by using a string of verbs in the first person, runs a series of variations on the image of reading as a form of digestion, and then talks of his *possessio* or ownership of the works that he has read.

Petrarch then goes on to reveal another aspect of his debt to Macrobius. He quotes Lucretius's declaration that he was the first to lead Roman writing onto the path of didactic poetry, 'Avia Pyeridum...'. This programmatic passage, repeated in both Book 1 and Book 4 of the *De Rerum Natura*, was a major statement of the view that it was possible to be at once a leader and an imitator: the 'first' person to compose a particular genre in Latin could legitimately claim to be the first in that language even if he was following a Greek example. Petrarch's knowledge of this passage did not come directly from a manuscript of Lucretius—whose *De Rerum Natura* was not rediscovered until Poggio Bracciolini came across a manuscript in Germany in 1417—but from Macrobius's *Saturnalia* (6.2.3). Lucretius had been kept alive in the minds of medieval readers as a member of a literary category which was of crucial significance to Petrarch and his contemporaries: he was what we might call a lost imitand, a text which was known through selective quotation in rhetorical and discursive texts and through its imitation by other authors. He was at once a lost text and a path-maker, an innovator.

Through Macrobius's quotations from the *De Rerum Natura* Lucretius was also known to have given rise to a number of imitations by Virgil; but he—like a manuscript text of Quintilian with blank spaces marked out to indicate what was not there—was a known unknown, since he was known to be not known in full. He survived, we still say, in 'fragments'; but again this relic of the language of humanistic textual recovery is an extremely misleading word to use of the passages of Lucretius known to Petrarch. They were not akin to potshards, or pieces of the past which were unearthed in physically decayed form. Rather they were textual extracts which had been carefully recorded because they gave rise to subsequent imitations, and were known and thought about in relation to that practice. That meant Lucretius, like Quintilian, was a text for whom a partial pathway to rediscovery and influence was already sketched out for late medieval readers well before Poggio's rediscovery of the *De Rerum Natura* in 1417: he was preserved in the *Saturnalia* as an object of imitation, or as a pre-text to Virgil's poems, and as a path-finder who was himself lost. That made Lucretius, like Quintilian, at once a text to be sought after among uncatalogued manuscripts in monastic libraries *and* a space in which the reconstructive imagination could operate.

After quoting Lucretius on the pathless ways of the muses, Petrarch then quotes Virgil's imitation of that passage in the *Georgics*, 3.292–4, which Macrobius describes as an imitation 'as though in a mirror' ('quasi de speculo', *Saturnalia*, 2.1), of Lucretius. He then goes on to insist that he wishes neither to follow others nor to lead the way:

> I am one who intends to follow our forebears' path but not always others' tracks [*vestigia*]; I am one who wishes upon occasion to make use of others' writings, not secretly [*furtim*] but with their leave, and wherever possible I prefer my own; I am one who delights in imitation and not in sameness, in a resemblance that is not servile, where the imitator's genius [*ingenium*] shines forth rather than his blindness or his ineptitude; I am one who much prefers not having a guide than being compelled to follow one slavishly. I do want a guide who leads me, not one who binds me to him, one who leaves me free use of my own sight, judgment, and freedom; I do not want him to forbid me to step where I wish, to go beyond him in some things, to attempt the inaccessible, to follow a shorter or, if I wish, an easier path, and to hasten or stop or even to part ways and to return.[28]

> Sum quem priorum semitam, sed non semper aliena vestigia sequi iuvet; sum qui aliorum scriptis non furtim sed precario uti velim in tempore, sed dum liceat, meis malim; sum quem similitudo delectet, non identitas, et similitudo ipsa quoque non nimia, in qua sequacis lux ingenii emineat, non cecitas non paupertas; sum qui satius rear duce caruisse quam cogi per omnia ducem sequi. Nolo ducem qui me vinceat sed precedat; sint cum duce oculi, sit iudicium, sit libertas; non prohibear ubi velim pedem ponere et preterire aliqua et inaccessa tentare; et breviorem sive ita fert animus, planiorem callem sequi et properare et subsistere et divertere liceat et reverti.[29]

This passage is often quoted on its own, decoupled from its surrounding concerns with verbal debts. That makes it sound like a declaration of poetic independence, rather than a slightly desperate attempt to thrash out a poetics which would allow Petrarch to learn from his reading without being accused by his readers of simply echoing another's words. It is a richly allusive passage, which in a very Petrarchan way does not quite reveal the sources which clearly underlie it. There is a flash here of Quintilian's remarks about the necessary difference between an imitation and that which it imitates, against which Petrarch had drawn a pointing finger in the margin of his manuscript. The description of an imitator following a path but taking

---

28. Petrarca, *Letters*, 3.214.   29. Petrarca, ed. Rossi and Bosco, *Le familiari*, 4.108.

short cuts and occasionally taking an easier route gives Petrarch's imitator much of the geographical freedom of Seneca's bees, who range around an entire landscape in search of nectar, and may obliquely acknowledge that the initial topic of Seneca's 84th Epistle is travel. But Petrarch is also concerned here not to imitate *furtim*, secretly, like a thief, and he insists on that crucial distinction between what is another's (*alienus*) and what is his own. Here he does not rely on indefinite pronouns to describe the miracle that is transformative imitation, but on abstract nouns of extremely elastic sense. One of those words is *ingenium*—that distinctive talent which Quintilian had presented as an 'inimitable' quality of an orator. Petrarch's phrase 'the light of talent', *lux ingenii*, is also striking. It might appear to anticipate the subsequent assimilation of the rhetorical concept of *ingenium* into that of 'genius', the main term used in the eighteenth century for the transformative power of the creative artist, whose radiant power was frequently figured as a source of illumination.[30] The combination of *ingenium* with *libertas*, freedom, suggests that a 'proper' or individual style, *ingenium*, and liberty all naturally accompany each other, since all are associated with autonomy: a writer who has his 'own' style, which is akin to a possession or a piece of property, has the freedom to range off a path set down by a predecessor, to act in a semi-autonomous relationship to his *duces* (leaders or masters), and to display his own distinct talent.

That description of a poet guided exclusively by his own judgement and concerned with his own freedom might sound like an endorsement of Jacob Burkhardt's influential identification of 'Renaissance man' with individualism. But we should remember that the whole letter has its roots in the embarrassment of a learned poet writing for a learned audience. Petrarch knew that his addressee Boccaccio, and the audience of learned future readers for whom he compiled his collection of letters, might recognize the unfortunate fact that some of the words of his *Bucolicum Carmen* derive from Virgil and Ovid. By emphasizing his *libertas* Petrarch is excusing himself for his accidental servility to the words of others. He was also writing in an extremely allusive way, in the knowledge that Boccaccio would pick out the deliberate irony of a declaration of *libertas* which was itself a transformative imitation of a series of classical and medieval authorities.

---

30. M. H. Abrams, *The Mirror and the Lamp: Romantic Theory and the Critical Tradition* (New York and London, 1958).

His ideal of literary *libertas* is an equivalent for the implied ethos which underlies Quintilian's writing about *imitatio*: that of the free male Roman citizen, physically powerful and skilled in body and mind, who goes beyond the merely servile labour of simply replicating the dimensions of a Greek archetype. That is what Petrarch wants *libertas* to connote. But his description of being free to follow his own intellect as though it were his 'dux' also strongly suggests another literary authority whose influence Petrarch sought through much of his life to downplay: the figure of Dante in the *Inferno*, who literally and patiently follows in the footsteps of Virgil, who is regularly referred to in the *Commedia* as 'duca mio', my leader.[31]

That faint ghost of Dante behind the passage is one which Boccaccio of all people would have recognized. It was in a letter to Boccaccio from 1359 that Petrarch explicitly denied envying Dante or having read him early in life, and in which he protested that 'if any of my vernacular writings resembles, or is identical to anything of his or anyone else's, it cannot be attributed to theft or imitation, which I have avoided like reefs, especially in vernacular works, but to pure chance or similarity of mind, as Tullius calls it, which caused me unwittingly to follow in another's footsteps' (*Fam.*, 21.15, 3.204). In that letter too he reports that Boccaccio had referred to Dante (whom Petrarch never names in the course of the entire letter: he had a radical tendency not to want directly to acknowledge debts) as 'your first guide and light of your youthful studies' (*Fam.*, 3.202: 'studiorum *dux* et prima fax', *Fam.*, 4.94, my italics).

The echoes of Dante go right down to the apparently Burkhardtian conclusion of the passage: so when Virgil leaves Dante in *Purgatorio* 27 he suggests that his follower has arrived at the point where his own pleasure can be his 'duce' ('Tratto t'ho qui con ingegno e con arte; | lo tuo piacere omai prendi per duce', 'I have brought you here with understanding and with art. Take henceforth your own pleasure for your guide').[32] Petrarch's belief that a poet should adopt his own judgement (*iudicium*) as a *dux* or guide is consequently an artful allusion to a late medieval near contemporary. And one could press this further. Allegorical commentators on the *Commedia* from Dante's son Pietro onwards, identified Dante's 'duca' Virgil with

---

31. On Petrarch's guarded relationship to Dante, Aldo S. Bernardo, 'Petrarch's Attitude toward Dante', *PMLA* 70 (1955), 488–517 is still valuable. More sophisticated accounts are in Eisner, 'In the Labyrinth of the Library', and Zygmunt G. Baranski and T. J. Cachey, *Petrarch and Dante: Anti-Dantism, Metaphysics, Tradition* (Notre Dame, Ind., 2009).

32. *Purgatorio*, 27.130–1. Quotations and translations from Dante Alighieri, *The Divine Comedy*, ed. Charles Southward Singleton, 3 vols. (Princeton, 1982).

Reason.[33] Petrarch's 'individualist' account of imitation consequently is in part a reliteralization of an allegorical gloss on a medieval vernacular epic which Petrarch famously denied having read until late in his life. Virgil is not your guide; Dante is not your guide. But 'reason' is. The 'Renaissance individual' who appears in Petrarch's letters is therefore an artefact fashioned from extremely careful concealment of prior authorities.

'Africa' and the lost imitand

Petrarch's writing about imitation is consequently itself a mélange of sources both classical and post-classical, some acknowledged and some occluded. Throughout that body of work Petrarch weaves together texts ancient and modern, and swerves light-footedly away from direct verbal replication.

A very similar pattern of mind can be discerned in his Latin writings, where of course the risk of displaying a debt to a classical author by direct quotation was far more acute than it was in the vernacular. The exemplary instance is Petrarch's unfinished Latin epic about the second Punic war, the *Africa*. Petrarch claimed to have been inspired to write his epic on Good Friday 1338 or 1339. Some part of it was complete by the time of his laureation in Rome in 1341, and the lament for his patron at that laureation, King Robert of Naples, in Book 9 must have been composed around 1343. Petrarch complained of his problems in completing the work: 'For me indeed it would be simpler to count the sands of the sea and the stars of the heavens than all the obstacles envious fortune has put in the way of my labours' (*Fam.*, 7.18, 1.385). Envious fortune never ceased presenting him with obstacles, with the result that nine books of the epic were left incomplete and unpublished at his death. Coluccio Salutati received a copy in 1377 and lamented that its narrative was incomplete, either because Petrarch had rough drafts which he never revised, or because, like an imperfect text of a classical author, passages were omitted from the text from which it was copied.[34] Although the poem was not printed until 1501, the *Africa* was more deeply connected to Petrarch's image of himself as both a laureate

---

33. 'Through human reason, represented in the figure of Virgil' ('Per rationem humanam, in personam Virgilii figuratam'), Pietro Alighieri, *Comentum super poema Comedie Dantis*, ed. Massimiliano Chiamenti (Tempe, Ariz., 2002), p. 99.
34. Coluccio Salutati, *Epistolario di Coluccio Salutati*, ed. Francesco Novati, 4 vols. (Rome, 1891), 1.253.

poet and an imitator of the classical past than any other work. Although no one would argue it is in any sense a perfect work, it does display powerful and complex intellectual ambitions which are directly comparable to those which operate in Petrarch's writings about imitation.

The *Africa* drew on Petrarch's extensive editorial work early in his life on the text of Livy, who is its main source for Roman history. But it also took its frame and much of its inspiration from Macrobius. Petrarch owned a manuscript of Macrobius's *Commentary* on the *Somnium Scipionis* from early in his life, and this, like most manuscripts of that work, included the 'fragment' of the sixth book of Cicero's *De Republica* relating Scipio's dream. Much of the first two books of the *Africa* relate a dream vision in which Publius Cornelius Scipio appears to his son Scipio Africanus the elder. This is a version (nudged back through the generations) of the dream related in Cicero's *De Republica*, in which Scipio Africanus the elder appeared to the younger Scipio. This Macrobian frame to the epic served a purpose which has a fascinating parallel to Petrarch's writing on imitation: it enabled Petrarch to rework and elaborate a 'fragmentary' text by Cicero—the *De Republica*, which survived in partial form through Macrobius's commentary. It also drew him to the necromantic side of imitation, since when Petrarch describes Scipio the elder being visited by the ghost of his father he conjures up yet another version of the ghost of Virgil's Hector:

> celoque emissa silenti
> Umbra ingens faciesque patris per nubila raptim
> Astitit ostendens caro precordia nato
> Et latus et multa transfixum cuspide pectus.   (*Africa*, 1.161–4)

> Then lo, from the calm welkin high above,
> clad in a cloud, appeared to him the shade
> and visage of his noble sire, who there
> displayed to his beloved son his heart
> and breast and flank, transfixed by countless spears.   (1.220–4)[35]

The scene—a wounded ghost appears—is founded on the apparition of Hector's ghost. But the language in which the apparition is described calls to mind two other Virgilian ghosts. The first is that of Aeneas's father Anchises ('there seemed to glide down from heaven the likeness of his father Anchises', 'visa dehinc caelo facies delapsa parentis', *Aen.* 5.722). The

---

35. Quotations from Francesco Petrarca, *L'Africa*, ed. Nicola Festa (Firenze, 1926); translation from *Petrarch's Africa*, trans. Thomas Goddard Bergin and Alice S. Wilson (New Haven, 1977).

second is that other ghost vision which appears to Aeneas as Troy burns: the 'umbra' of Creusa, whose *simulacrum* appears to the hero larger than life.

The ghost visions from Book 2 of the *Aeneid* are overlayered in this way because of the simple fact that *Africa* was composed in Latin verse, which necessarily alerted Petrarch to the danger of producing a *cento* of quotations. To avoid that risk Petrarch tends *either* to use Virgilian language *or* to evoke a Virgilian episode, but tends not to do both at the same time: so 'caelo delapsa' (fallen from the sky) in the description of the descent of Anchises becomes 'caelo emissa' (sent out of the sky) to avoid the appearance of excessive verbal dependency. That goes along with a curious feature of the *Africa*. Petrarch avoids using Virgil's name or directly including him in any of his versions of the literary canon evoked in the poem.[36] It has been suggested that some of his revisions to the poem were aimed at removing or reducing direct verbal echoes of Virgil in particular,[37] and certainly at times the *Africa* invites a very curious version of what Greene calls 'sub-reading', or reading for a text which is not quite the text before our eyes: at almost every moment it seems to be erasing direct verbal evidence of the texts from which it manifestly derives. This is, however, not a manifestation of Petrarch's historical consciousness or of his sense of exile from classical antiquity. It rather illustrates quite how profoundly his poetic practice was influenced by Macrobius's unease about textual appropriation, and by his awareness that his own readers would recognize the texts from which— often at the last minute—he swerves.

The most vivid example of this tendency to flinch from imitation-as-verbal-allusion occurs in the episode of Massinissa and Sophonisba which occupies Book 5 and the start of Book 6 of the *Africa*. This is a tragic love story based on the episode of Dido and Aeneas in the *Aeneid*, in which

---

36. See Andrew Laird, 'Re-inventing Virgil's Wheel: The Poet and his Work from Dante to Petrarch', in Philip Hardie and Helen Moore, eds., *Classical Literary Careers and their Reception* (Cambridge, 2010), 138–59, esp. pp. 147–57, and Craig Kallendorf, *In Praise of Aeneas: Virgil and Epideictic Rhetoric in the Early Italian Renaissance* (Hanover, 1989), p. 54.

37. Vincenzo Fera, *La revisione petrarchesca dell'Africa* (Messina, 1984). The 210 alleged verbal borrowings from Virgil listed in Richard Seagraves, *The Influence of Vergil on Petrarch's 'Africa'* (Ann Arbor, 1977), pp. 303–44 include only four instances where Petrarch uses more than two words in the same case positioned at the same point in a line. Three of the exceptions to this rule occur in the first book (*Africa*, 1.166/*Aen.*, 4.280; *Africa*, 1.262/*Aen.*, 9.131; *Africa*, 1.387/*Aen.*, 9.641; *Africa*, 4.367/*Aen.*, 12.103), which indicates that Petrarch was increasingly keen to avoid repeating three-word collocations from classical texts for fear of being accused of theft (see note 25 in this chapter). Seagraves does not record a fifth instance: *Africa*, 7.780/*Aen.*, 2.271, discussed below, where, as Festa notes (ad loc.), the Virgilian echo 'Visus adesse mihi' is found in MS Laur. Ashburnham; the metrically aberrant but non-Virgilian 'Apparuit michi quam' is found in other MSS.

Petrarch, keen to make his hero Scipio as morally exemplary as possible, devolves the love affair to a minor character, the Numidian King Massinissa. The episode, like Dido's story, concludes with the suicide of Sophonisba, after which her soul disappears to the underworld. This is described in the very last line of Book 5. Nobody reading this line, given its position, sense, and narrative context, could fail to expect an echo of the final line of the *Aeneid*, in which the soul of Turnus 'fugit indignata sub umbras' (*Aen.*, 12.952), a line which in turn echoes Dido's plea at the moment of her suicide ('sic, sic iuuat ire sub umbras', 'thus, thus, it pleases me to go into the shadows', *Aen.*, 4.660) and which was anticipated in the description of Camilla's death by an exact verbal echo (*Aen.*, 11.831). It is Virgil's line for a pathetic death.

Petrarch, however, deliberately swerves away from these words in order to provide a paraphrastic alternative to them. As Sophonisba dies, her 'violent spirit seeks the Tartarean shades' ('Tartareasque petit violentus spiritus umbras', *Africa*, 5.773). This might be called a deliberately neutered allusion, or an allusion via conspicuous avoidance: Petrarch does not simply rewrite the line, but does so—given the non-echo of two of the most famous lines in the most famous poem in the world—in a way that is designed to call to mind the words that are *not* there. The result is, like quite a lot of the *Africa*, uncomfortable: Petrarch, sensitized by Macrobius to the dangers of exact verbal borrowing, sometimes seems to flinch so far from Virgil's style that he sounds almost like a late medieval glossator or paraphrast of a classical text. Absent texts, as it were, float behind the glosses and circumlocutions by which he avoids simply repeating the words of earlier writers. That was not a consequence of his developing awareness of historical anachronism. It was the result of a Macrobian fear of verbal theft.

Another kind of absent text preoccupied Petrarch in both his critical writings and in the *Africa*. These were texts which had either been lost or which had never been written, but about which enough evidence remained for them to be reinvented. For a writer who had been sensitized by Macrobius's *Saturnalia* to the dangerous proximity of imitation and plagiarism the appeal of such ur-texts is obvious: writing an 'imitation' of an unwritten or lost text necessarily carries zero risk of improper verbal borrowing, since its words were by definition not known.

There is a particularly delicious passage in Petrarch's Letter to Homer (*Fam.*, 24.12) which associates one such unwritten text with the danger of unacknowledged quotation. In that letter Petrarch attempts to placate Homer's irritation at having been imitated so extensively by Virgil. As he does so he makes a brief but inevitable reference to Macrobius, the author who had alerted him to the possibility that Homer might have been irritated by his successor's free way with his texts: 'even though in the *Saturnalia* there is the unsettled controversy on the question of superiority between yourself and the one about whom you most complain, Virgil' (3.345). He then goes on to address the accusation that Virgil never directly acknowledged Homer by name in the *Aeneid* in the way that Statius acknowledged Virgil at the end of the *Thebaid*. Statius, of course, humbly records that he is following in Virgil's footprints ('vive, precor; nec tu divinam Aeneida tempta, | sed longe sequere et vestigia semper adora', 'Live, I beg you; but do not attempt to rival the divine *Aeneid*, but follow at a distance and revere its footsteps', *Thebaid*, 12.816–17). Petrarch claims that Virgil had intended to write a similar acknowledgement of his debt to Homer: 'He would have done so, believe me, having been the gentlest and most modest of men, and, as we find written of him, "a man of irreproachable life," were it not that death interfered' (3.346). That fantasy of a thirteenth book of the *Aeneid* containing a full list of acknowledgements, or a coda in which Virgil confessed that he did no more than follow humbly in the footsteps of Homer, shows how deeply later Latin literature shadowed Petrarch's view of the *Aeneid*. For him the absence of a Statian coda to the poem—a footnote, as it were, acknowledging the footsteps of a prior authority—was a mark of its incompleteness.

The final book of the *Africa* was in many respects Petrarch's own attempt to write this almost unimaginable piece of creative footnoting, in which an imitator explicitly greets and acknowledges his predecessor. But it is a curiously oblique and evasive version of such an episode, since in the final book of the *Africa* Petrarch does not acknowledge his own debts to Virgil— though he may indeed have sought to imitate Virgil in *not* recording his most substantial debt—or to that other major influence on the poem, Lucan's *Pharsalia*.[38] Instead he dramatizes a parallel scene of literary acknowledgement in which the early epic poet Ennius confesses his debt to Homer.

This is in effect Petrarch's way of displacing his own debts to Virgil onto another writer. Ennius is a character in Petrarch's poem, who voyages back

---

38. See the expert summary, Philip Hardie, 'After Rome: Renaissance Epic', in A. J. Boyle, ed., *Roman Epic* (London and New York, 1993), 294–313. Richard T. Bruère, 'Lucan and Petrarch's *Africa*', *Classical Philology* 56 (1961), 83–99, cites many parallels with Lucan, and the elusive nature of many of these testifies to the rigour with which Petrarch the imitator followed the three-word rule set out in the previous note. On Petrarch's complex attitudes to Lucan's Caesar, see Matthew Leigh, 'Petrarch's Lucan and the *Africa*', in S. J. Heyworth, P. G. Fowler, S. J. Harrison, and Don Fowler, eds., *Classical Constructions: Papers in Memory of Don Fowler, Classicist and Epicurean* (Oxford, 2007), 242–57.

to Rome with Scipio Africanus after the defeat of Hannibal at the battle of Zama. Bringing Ennius himself into his poem in this military context allowed Petrarch explicitly to address relationships between the poetic laurel and the laurels granted to military victors, and to incorporate a long defence of poetry into his poem. But it also enabled him to enter an enormously fruitful zone for imitation. It enabled him to evoke 'texts which were not there' in a much more powerful way than through deliberate non-quotation. Ennius's *Annales* was known to Petrarch chiefly through the passages which Virgil imitated closely enough for Macrobius to have cited them in the *Saturnalia*, and from short quotations in the works of Cicero. Those traces were enough to enable Petrarch to track back through time and imagine a poem which did not survive. Petrarch is himself described as another Ennius (*Africa*, 2.443); and both he and Ennius seek to follow the footsteps of fame back into the earliest time:

> Vestigia Famae
> Rara sequens, quantum licuit per secula retro
> Omnia pervigili studio vagus ipse cucurri,
> Donec ad extremas animo rapiente tenebras
> Perventum primosque viros, quos Fama perenni
> Fessa via longe ignotos post terga reliquit.   (*Africa*, 9.133–8)

> I have traced back through ancient years,
> as best I might, the tenuous spoor of fame.
> At length, spurred on by my inquiring mind,
> I reached the furthest shades, the first of men,
> whom Time, grown weary of the lengthening road,
> had long abandoned to oblivion.   (9.183–8)

To imitate the first men (*primosque viros*) whom Fame has forgotten from the early Roman Republic was for Petrarch a guarantee of *libertas* in two overlapping senses of the word. Ennius wrote in a period of *libertas* for Rome, and about a period in which its energetic activities abroad (in Petrarch's view of it at least) guaranteed freedom at home. But writing about Ennius also enabled Petrarch's own authorial *libertas* because the *Annales* existed in such a fragmentary state that servitude to, or debt to, his words was not an option.[39] A track with no footprints, a verbal trace without words: that is the space towards which Petrarch voyages in the final book of the *Africa*.

---

39. Jonathan Foster, 'Petrarch's *Africa*: Ennian and Vergilian Influences', *Papers of the Liverpool Latin Seminar* 2 (1979), 277–98 (pp. 281–2) notes only one echo of the fragments of Ennius that Petrarch knew, at *Africa*, 6.345–52, which echoes a passage recorded in Cicero's *De Officiis*. Other examples are noted below.

The allure of rewriting a lost but primal text is immense: it enables writing to become both an act of retrieval and a means of opening up a new pathway for others to follow. But it is symptomatic of Petrarch's uneasy concern with textual authority that he signals his desire to recreate a lost work by a surprisingly direct verbal allusion to that other early republican author whose text he never knew as a whole: Lucretius. In the invocation to the muses which precedes the battle of Zama (the crucial defeat of Hannibal) Petrarch explicitly echoes Lucretius's claim to track across the 'avia', the trackless ways, and attempt a new genre: 'Avia Castalie sitiens convexa pererro; | Urget amor fameque trahit spes blanda decore' ('Thirsting I roam Castalia's lonely ways, | impelled by love of fame and hope of glory', *Africa*, 7.504–5/670–1). The original of this passage was well known to Petrarch as an exemplification of both the theory and the practice of *imitatio*, since he had transcribed it (from Macrobius's *Saturnalia*) into his manuscript of Virgil next to the passage in the *Georgics* in which Virgil imitated it.[40] And his willingness to allude so openly to Lucretius's desire for the trackless ways in the *Africa*—despite his overt denial in his letter to Boccaccio that he had any such desire to beat out a new path alone—was the result of his knowing that it was a fragment of a lost text which had been already imitated by Virgil. Petrarch was returning not *ad fontes*, to the Castalian springs of learning, in humanist fashion, but to a common store of previously borrowed material—the body of texts which Macrobius calls *rerum communio* (*Saturnalia*, 6.1.5). This body of texts, which included largely lost texts by Ennius and Lucretius, was the one from which it was possible to imitate without circumscribing the *libertas* of his *ingenium* or appropriating the property of another author.

The climax of the *Africa* is shaped by the ultimate text that is not there. Ennius relates to Scipio Africanus how Homer appeared to him in a dream. This is certainly the most ambitious passage in the *Africa* and it deserves to be regarded as one of the greatest things Petrarch ever wrote. It is a recreation of the encounter which Lucretius had described in Book 1 of the *De Rerum Natura*, in which the ghost of Homer appeared to Ennius.[41] Petrarch knew about that episode not from Lucretius (the *Saturnalia* does not quote that section of the *De Rerum Natura* because Virgil never imitated it closely

40. See the facsimile of Biblioteca Ambrosiana Codex A. 49 inf, in *Francisci Petrarcae Vergilianus codex: ad Publii Vergilii Maronis diem natalem bis millesimum celebrandum quam simillime expressus atque in lucem editus*, ed. Giovanni Galbiati (Mediolani, 1930), fol. 39v.

41. Nora Goldschmidt, 'Absent Presence: Pater Ennius in Renaissance Europe', *Classical Receptions Journal* 4 (2012), 1–19.

enough for Macrobius to have recorded it as a parallel) but from Cicero's
Somnium Scipionis, the text of which Petrarch possessed in a manuscript
principally devoted to Macrobius's commentary on it.[42] Petrarch took that
tantalizing allusion to an entirely lost text within a fragment of a largely lost
text by Cicero, and he constructed from it a great imagining of literary
tradition as a meeting between ghosts:

> Hic nocte sub alta
> Aspicio adventare senem, quem rara tegebant
> Frusta toge et canis immixta et squalida barba.
> Sedibus exierant oculi. Cava frontis ymago
> Horrorem inculta cum maiestate ferebat.
> Dirigui...
> 'Aspice qualis erat quondam dum vixit Homerus.
> Huc ego vix tandem reserato carcere Ditis
> Emersi, tacite perrumpens viscera terre.'   (*Africa*, 9.166–77)

> Then in the depth of night—behold, I saw
> an aged man draw near, his body wrapped
> in fragments of a toga, with a beard
> unkempt, his grizzled hair with strands of white.
> His sockets had no eyes. That spectral face,
> hollowed and gaunt, bore a crude majesty,
> yet moved my heart to horror...
>   ... 'Here stands what your heart
> and mind have so long yearned for, here behold
> Homer as he appeared in living flesh.
> Hither I come, fresh from the cell of Dis
> but recently unbarred. I've made my way
> in silent upward through the bowels of earth.'   (9.226–41)

Ennius's vision of Homer is couched in the necromantic and corporeal
metaphors which had played such a vital part in both Petrarch's discussions
of *imitatio* and in the Roman rhetorical tradition. Homer is at once an old
body and a ghostly *imago*. He is also a digest of various aspects of Petrarch's
reading. At a structural level he resembles Virgil's Anchises in Book 6 of the
Aeneid, who offers a vision of the future. At the level of Petrarch's anxious
habit of not-quite-verbatim allusion his unkempt beard or 'squalida barba' is
at once near enough to and far enough away from the 'squalentem barbam'

42. Petrarch's manuscript of Cicero's *Somnium* with Macrobius's commentary is British Library
    Manuscript Harley 5204. See Nicholas Mann, *Petrarch Manuscripts in the British Isles* (Padua,
    1975), p. 493. For a list of other references to the episode, see Quintus Ennius, *The Annals of
    Q. Ennius*, ed. Otto Skutsch (Oxford, 1985), pp. 150–3.

(*Aen.*, 2.277) of Virgil's Hector to indicate the connection while making the charge of direct textual appropriation just about deniable.

And curiously enough the confluence of Homer, Ennius, and the ghost of Virgil nudges Petrarch again towards what Macrobius called the *rerum communio*, the common body of texts, which Virgil had established through his imitation of earlier texts. Petrarch's Homer echoes Virgil's 'qualis erat' (such he was). Petrarch knew that phrase was not just 'Virgil's' words used to describe the apparition of Hector's ghost. Servius (whose commentary on the *Aeneid* was well known to Petrarch) recorded that the phrase derived from Ennius—or, to use Servius's exact phrase, was 'Ennii versus', a verse of Ennius.[43]

And to illustrate further the bizarre displacements of debt and influence that run through the *Africa* we might note one further point at which Petrarch exploits the 'common store' of words from Ennius which had been subsequently imitated by Virgil. One of his rare direct borrowings of a three-word phrase from the *Aeneid* occurs at *Africa* 7.780, where he uses the phrase 'visus adesse mihi'. This is the phrase used to describe the appearance of Hector in the *Aeneid* (2.271). Petrarch had reason to believe that this phrase was an imitation of Ennius because Cicero quotes 'visus Homerus adesse poeta' during a discussion of dreams in the *Academica* (2.51).[44]

The vision of the humanist poet, who attempts to gather the scattered limbs of a dead poet and bring them back to life, with which this chapter began, seems both very close to what Petrarch attempts here and at the same time very far away. Phrases of Ennius are gathered and collated from a range of intermediate sources, in a way that does make Petrarch appear to be an Aesculapius of the classical past, reassembling the severed limbs of an ancient poet. But at the same time he is fracturing allusions to episodes from and words written by other poets whose works do survive, in order to avoid accusations of literary theft. The reconstruction of what an early Latin historical epic 'might have sounded like' entailed hypothetical thinking and conjecture. It involved dreaming what the past might have been. Petrarch also thought that it required him to draw as far as possible on a 'common store' of phrases and epithets which had already been freely exchanged

---

43. Hardie, 'Renaissance Epic', at p. 297. In the same essay pp. 294–302 are the best pages on the *Africa*. Maurus Servius, *Servii Grammatici qui feruntur in Vergilii Carmina Commentarii*, ed. G. Thilo and H. Hagen, 2 vols. (Leipzig, 1878–83), 1.265: 'Ennii Versus'.

44. See Foster, 'Petrarch's *Africa*', p. 293. For Petrarch's use of Cicero's *Academica* to acquire knowledge of lost texts, see *Fam.*, 3.18. Skutsch in Ennius, *The Annals of Q. Ennius*, ed. Skutsch, pp. 153–4 suspects Cicero was misquoting.

between earlier writers, and the consequence of that was avoiding phrases which could be pinned down to a single *auctor*. The result is a massive paradox which runs through the encounter between Homer and Ennius in the *Africa*: this great scene insists on continuity in the literary tradition, at the same moment that Petrarch strikingly fails to acknowledge his own manifest debts.

And those debts are multiple as well as manifest. When Ennius sees Homer he bows down to kiss his feet:

> Procubui voluique pedes contingere pronus:
> Umbra fuit nudeque heserunt oscula terre.   (*Africa*, 9.178–9)

> Prostrate I fell and in humility
> sought to embrace his feet. My lips, alas,
> brushed but the naked ground; he was a shade.   (9.242–4)

That detail shows an unmistakable debt to the meeting between the shades of the dead poets in Dante's *Purgatorio* 21, in which Statius attempts to embrace the feet ('abbracciar li piedi') of Virgil, but is told that he is just a shade.[45] Dante's episode was one of the structural templates from which Petrarch sought to reinvent the lost meeting of Ennius and Homer,[46] and without doubt he knew it well. In the first of his two letters to Cicero he compares the orator to 'a wayfarer at night carrying a lantern before him, you revealed to your followers the path where you yourself stumbled most wretchedly' (*Fam.*, 24.3; 3.317). That is the mirror image of Statius's description of Virgil in the *Purgatorio*: 'Facesti come quei che va di notte, | che porta il lume dietro e sé non giova, | ma dopo sé fa le persone dotte' ('You were like one who goes by night and carries the light behind him and profits not himself, but makes those wise who follow him', *Purgatorio*, 22.66–9)—although again this image was itself part of the *rerum communio*, or common store, of antiquity, with parallels in Ennius and in Augustine.[47]

---

45. *Purgatorio*, 21.130. See Giuseppe Velli, 'Il Dante di Francesco Petrarca', *Studi petrarcheschi* NS 2 (1985), 185–99, esp. pp. 194–9 and, for verbal echoes, Francesca Galligan, 'Poets and Heroes in Petrarch's *Africa*', in Martin L. McLaughlin, Letizia Panizza, and Peter Hainsworth, eds., *Petrarch in Britain: Interpreters, Imitators, and Translators over 700 Years* (Oxford, 2007), 85–93.

46. Kevin Brownlee, 'Power Plays: Petrarch's Genealogical Strategies', *Journal of Medieval and Renaissance Studies* 35 (2005), 467–88 argues a different case: that Petrarch deliberately attempts to exclude Dante's vernacular epic from the true genealogy of Neo-Latin heroic verse.

47. Cicero in *De Officiis*, 1.16.51 quotes a passage of Ennius about a traveller who lights his followers, and Augustine in *De Symbolo*, 4.4 used the comparison of the Jews.

But the episode in which Ennius and Homer meet in the *Africa* does not and could not even present the faintest trace of a possible debt on Petrarch's part to Dante or to anyone else: one of the poets in this scene of mutual acknowledgement—Homer—Petrarch could not read because his Greek was not good enough to do so, and the other—Ennius—he could not imitate because the *Annales* existed for him only in extracts quoted by commentators on Virgil or in brief quotations in the works of Cicero. The scene of imitative acknowledgement, that is, pointedly excludes reference to Petrarch's own most substantial literary debts—to Virgil, or to Dante. It displays the same characteristics as the letter to Tommaso da Messina, in which he exposes Macrobius's unacknowledged debt to Seneca whilst occluding his own profound debt to Macrobius. Petrarch was drawn to the lost texts of the distant Roman past not out of a sense of exile and longing for classical antiquity. The fact that those texts were not known except through detached phrases or their imitations by later authors was profoundly useful to him: they enabled him to highlight *other* poets' debts in order to distract attention from his own.

The dream Homer then presents Ennius with a vision, in which he sees Petrarch himself in the future, at work on the *Africa*. The language Ennius uses to describe this work strikingly recalls Petrarch's description in the letter to Boccaccio (*Fam.*, 23.19) of what an imitator adds to the texts he is imitating: 'Nescio quid, nisi fallor, enim sub pectore versat | Egregium altumque nimis' (*Africa*, 9.220–1), 'he is turning over in his breast an I don't know what, unless I'm mistaken, of excellence and sublimity'.[48] To *seek* to write poem which displays an 'I don't know what' of singular excellence comes very close to attempting a logical contradiction: it is to be driven by a sublime idea of unreachable perfection which is necessarily unreachable. But that is what Petrarch attempted in the *Africa*. And Ennius's prophecy of the poem which Petrarch will write ends in an unseeably distant futurity: 'He will by his song call back the exiled muses, and, at the end of time, will recall the sisters to Helicon' ('Ille diu profugas revocabit carmine Musas | Tempus in extremum, veteresque Elicone Sorores | Restituet', *Africa*, 9.229–31). It is scarcely surprising that the *Africa*, steeped in futurity, conceived as a 'nescio quid' which would be added to the stock of Petrarch's

---

48. Stephen Hinds, 'Petrarch, Cicero, Virgil: Virtual Community in Familiares 24, 4', *Materiali e discussioni per l'analisi dei testi classici* 52 (2004), 157–75 at p. 172 relates the phrase to Propertius's 'nescio quid maius nascitur Iliade', and makes many suggestive connections with Petrarch's second letter to Cicero.

reading, direct testimony of which he persistently sought to avoid giving in
the words of the poem itself, remained itself fragmentary after Petrarch's death.

★

Attempting to position Petrarch in relation to 'the Medieval' and the
'Renaissance' is an intrinsically absurd exercise for two reasons. The first
is that Petrarch was not representative, and cannot serve as a cipher for
a period. The second is that many people mean different things by 'the
Renaissance' or 'Medieval', and most critics would now want to blur or
dissolve the boundaries between those periods, even if they were supposed
to be distinct in the first place.[49] Attempting to place an item that is *sui
generis* in one of two indefinable categories might provide a recipe for an
unwritten chapter in *Alice in Wonderland*, but it can only make for frustration
in literary history. However, some general conclusions can be drawn from
this discussion. In many respects Petrarch was much less different from his
immediate predecessors than he wanted to appear. Throughout his writing
on *imitatio* and in much of his imitative writing he made far more extensive
use of familiar late antique and early medieval authorities than he admitted.
He had a stronger awareness of textual ownership and of the impropriety of
direct verbal quotation than many of his predecessors, but he was also in
some respects surprisingly 'medieval' in his attitudes to literary authority.
The climactic meeting of Homer and Ennius in the *Africa* may be an
elaborate attempt to transform Dante's description of the meeting of the
poets in the *Purgatorio*, but it also reveals that Petrarch had one profound
point in common with Dante: like his predecessor (and, indeed, like Chaucer
in the *House of Fame*) he tended to embody textual *auctoritates* as people,
who could meet and try to touch each other, and who could be imitated
not just as texts but treated as moral *exempla* and guides for conduct. This
representation of classical authorities as embodied persons tends to be
avoided by later writers. Milton does not do it at all in relation to his classical authorities. The figures of Chaucer and Lydgate are regularly presented
as physical beings that can be embraced by later fifteenth- and early
sixteenth-century English authors. Ben Jonson was to bring classical poets
onto the stage in *Poetaster*, but they exist, fictionally speaking, in their own
world, and he would not have sought to kiss their feet or embrace their

---

49. See, e.g., Brian Cummings and James Simpson, eds., *Cultural Reformations: Medieval and
Renaissance in Literary History* (Oxford, 2010).

bodies. Jonson's verse tends to register influence by local allusions to prior writers or by overt structural debts. And by the seventeenth century, in England at least, it tends to be vernacular writers (Ben Jonson himself was to become the most notable example) who are represented as embodied authorities, rather than classical authors.

But other aspects of Petrarch's practice are characteristic of what came to be called 'humanist' textual scholarship. Petrarch inherited and developed this form of scholarship from his immediate predecessors.[50] He was attuned by Macrobius to avoid the direct appropriation of sequences of words from his reading. The culling of *auctoritates* word for word into a new text was consequently something which, in his Latin verse at least, he sought to avoid. He was prompted by Macrobius's *Saturnalia* to think about a common store of ancient texts which were known only through fragments, and on which Virgil drew freely; and he was also prompted by his reading of Macrobius to think about, and seek to reconstruct, texts such as Ennius's *Annales* which had been lost. This marks a division between him and Dante. Petrarch's attempt to recreate the lost encounter between Homer and Ennius from the *Annales* was strikingly different from Dante's preferred modes of textual allusion: it was neither a direct verbal reference to a prior text nor an uninhibited invention. It was an effort to create a new poem in the space of an earlier poem that was known to be lost.

In all of these respects Petrarch was remarkable and distinctive as both a theorist and a practitioner of *imitatio*. But it is more accurate to describe him as distinctive than as the originator of a movement or the inventor of a new age or practice. Indeed one could argue that Petrarch's mode of imitation was a kind of false start, so crippled was Petrarch's attempt to write a Latin epic by the influence of Macrobius. It is hard to read *Africa* without wincing at the attempts to avoid or eradicate direct quotations from earlier poems: 'Petrarch's style' in the poem seems as a result to be chiefly defined negatively as 'not the same words in the same order as Virgil or Lucan'. That was in turn the consequence of the particular phase of thinking about *imitatio* of which he is the most vocal spokesman. *Imitatio* was for him a combination of a strong body of metaphors plus a persistent fear of textual appropriation. That made writing a Latin poem, and giving it a 'nescio quid' that differentiated it from its predecessors, exceptionally difficult.

---

50. For Petrarch as a 'third generation' humanist, see Witt, *Footsteps*, pp. 231–89.

Chapters 5 and 6 will attempt to explain what, as it were, Petrarch lacked; or, to put that in a positive form, they explore some of the concepts and texts which later writers and thinkers brought to the theory and practice of *imitatio*, and which made it easier (the comparative is important: it was never *easy*) to imitate an earlier author's way of writing than it had been for Petrarch. Much of the theoretical material which prompted these developments was indeed already present within that 'mutilated' manuscript of Quintilian which Petrarch had acquired in 1350. Some of it was supplied by the fuller texts of that work, which were copied, read, and then printed and widely disseminated by later scholars. And some of it was developed from the later rhetorical writings of Cicero which were largely unknown to Petrarch and to his age. Later generations of writers on *imitatio* had more time than Petrarch fully to digest the system of education that Quintilian set out, which enabled an orator not just anxiously to chew his quill as he tried to add a *nescio quid* of his own to what Cicero said, but to learn how to speak in a distinctive style, and to learn how to analyse in detail the style of earlier authors. For the generation after Lorenzo Valla, *imitatio*, if it was not to swerve between the avoidance of verbal repetition and a warm, embodied glow of metaphorical fuzziness, had to be embedded in an entire pedagogical practice. That long tale of educational change, infused by the rhetorical texts rediscovered in their entirety by the generation immediately after Petrarch's, had a profound influence on the history of English and European poetry in the sixteenth and seventeenth centuries.

5

Adaptive Imitation

Ciceronians, Courtiers, and Quixotes

In 1421, five years after Poggio's discovery of a complete text of Quintilian's *Institutio Oratoria* at St Gall, there was another discovery of rhetorical texts. The Bishop of Lodi in Northern Italy, Gerardo Landriani, discovered in his Cathedral archive a manuscript which included Cicero's *De Inventione* and the *Ad Herennium*, as well as complete texts of *De Oratore* and of the *Orator*. This was a major find, since both of the latter had previously been known in copies which omitted substantial passages. The big prize, however, was a complete copy of Cicero's *Brutus*, which was previously unknown.[1] The manuscript was conveyed to Gasparino Barzizza who had it copied. By the close of the sixteenth century more than thirty editions of the *Brutus* had been printed and more than forty of the *Orator*.[2]

The discovery of those texts was rapidly enlisted to support a narrative of the renaissance of lost knowledge: Guarino Veronese wrote to Gasparino Barzizza in July 1422 declaring that 'Cicero chose you as his first host when he returned from the gods of the underworld, or more truly the Elysian fields, as he was reborn [*renascens*] to the light of the upper world' ('ab diis manibus vel verius Elysiis campis renascens ad superos Cicero [te] primum

---

1. The discovery is termed 'un'importissima risurezione' in Remigio Sabbadini, *Le scoperte dei codici latini e greci ne'secoli XIV e XV*, 2 vols. (Firenze, 1905), 1.100. Previously known MSS of *De Oratore* lacked 1.129–56; 1.194–65; 2.1–19; 2.50–9; 2.91; 2.246–367; 3.18–109; *Orator* lacked 1–90; 191–231. James Jerome Murphy, *Rhetoric in the Middle Ages: A History of Rhetorical Theory from Saint Augustine to the Renaissance* (Berkeley and London, 1974), p. 360.
2. These very rough figures are based on Lawrence D. Green and James Jerome Murphy, *Renaissance Rhetoric Short-Title Catalogue 1460–1700* (Aldershot, 2006), pp. 107–26. The figures are comparable to those for Quintilian's *Institutes*, but Cicero's *De Oratore* was reprinted roughly twice as frequently.

delegit hospitem').[3] Guarino then went on to make a slightly different point. He said to Barzizza, 'you imitate Peisistratus [who was believed to have reassembled the text of Homer] and Lycurgus [who according to Plutarch edited the Homeric poems], those rediscoverers and digesters of Homer'.[4] Guarino, that is, emphasizes Barzizza's actions not only as one who recovered texts but also as one who edited and disseminated them. Discovery is significant, but dissemination may matter more in the long term.

The greatest changes in the literary culture of the fifteenth and sixteenth centuries were brought about not simply by the rediscovery of ancient rhetorical texts but by the ways in which they were understood, disseminated, and printed. Quintilian in particular became by the early sixteenth century the foundation of an entire pedagogical system, which aimed to train students from their first steps in the Latin language into models of eloquence.

For Lorenzo Valla (1407–57), Quintilian's main appeal was the very aspect of his work which had made Petrarch value him less than Cicero: rather than providing a charismatic *exemplum* to be imitated, he set out an entire programme of rhetorical training from early youth.[5] That meant the imitation of Cicero could become not a matter of local verbal echoes, but a lifetime's pursuit through the acquisition and development of rhetorical techniques. Desiderius Erasmus, the greatest editor and educational reformer of the sixteenth century, recognized that the distinctive merit of Quintilian over Cicero for writers on rhetoric and education was that he 'starts with the rudiments and sets out all the successive stages, the theory of rhetoric, its application, and the development of proficiency, including quite a lot of material that Cicero either omitted or merely touched on in passing'.[6]

3. Guarino Veronese, *Epistolario di Guarino Veronese*, ed. Remigio Sabbadini, 3 vols. (Turin, 1959), 1.345.

4. 'Imitare Pisistratum et...Lycurgum...Homeri repertores et digestores', Veronese, *Epistolario di Guarino Veronese*, ed. Sabbadini, 1.346. For Peisistratus as responsible for reassembling the Homeric poems, see *De Oratore*, 3.137; for Lycurgus, see Plutarch's 'Life of Lycurgus', 4.4 in Plutarch, *Plutarch's Lives*, trans. Bernadotte Perrin, 11 vols. (Cambridge, Mass., and London, 1914–26), 1.215.

5. See the discussion in Carl Joachim Classen, *Antike Rhetorik im Zeitalter des Humanismus* (Munich, 2003), pp. 153–75. On early modern rhetoric, see Brian Vickers, *In Defence of Rhetoric* (Oxford, 1988), pp. 254–93, esp. pp. 178–81, on Valla.

6. Desiderius Erasmus, *Collected Works of Erasmus. Vol. 28, Literary and Educational Writings 6: Ciceronianus*, ed. A. H. T. Levi (Toronto, 1986), p. 427. Parenthetical references are to this edition and to the Latin text in Desiderius Erasmus, *Opera omnia Desiderii Erasmi*, ed. J. H. Waszink, L. E. Halkin, C. Reedijk, and C.M. Bruehl, 30 vols. (Amsterdam, 1969–), 2.1.599–710.

The phenomenon which might be called the institutionalization of the *Institutio* had profound effects on the way in which *imitatio* was both thought about and practised. Quintilian's *Institutio*, when turned into a programme of education, provided not just an influential chapter on the theory of imitating, but an entire system for reverse-engineering Ciceronian orators from their earliest years onwards through training in every aspect of the art of rhetoric.

That process of turning Quintilian into a programme of education, however, depended on the technology of print. This enabled not only the dissemination of systematized rhetorics, but also the public and heated dissemination of *rival* systems of rhetoric, which were grounded on different principles and distinct interpretations of the texts of classical antiquity. Print also enabled the long, slow educational revolution of the later fifteenth and early sixteenth centuries in Northern Europe to produce, in far greater volume than had been possible before, pedagogical aids to the process of learning from the ancients. These tools might be apparently simple ones, such as the index, which readily enabled the systematic gathering of allusions, or the concordance, or neatly presented marginal annotations which drew attention to the parallels between one text and another, or books of commonplaces, which provided phrases and circumlocutions which a student could deploy in his own texts. None of these tools was entirely new with the age of print, but all of them became far more readily available and far more routine elements in the processes of reading and of writing than they had been in the fourteenth, thirteenth, or twelfth centuries.

The consequence of all these broad currents of change was that a pupil born in the early sixteenth century would have experienced the practice and the concept of *imitatio* in several conflicting forms. On the one hand it was the laborious acquisition of a practical skill at speaking, which involved both grasping rules and principles as well as imitating examples of rhetorical and poetic excellence. Acquiring that 'possessed skill' or *hexis* which Quintilian saw as central to the art of rhetoric required endless labour to habituate one's lexis in the idiom of the ancients. Implicitly accompanying those practices was a concept of an author as inhering in a particular kind of stylistic excellence, the imitation of which was an all but unattainable aspiration.

But on the other hand sixteenth-century readers and learners also experienced 'imitation' as something far more local and identifiable. The editions they read laid bare the mechanics of textual production by noting allusions and parallel passages, which absorbed and added to the parallels which

Macrobius had noted between Homer and Virgil, for instance. These might
be presented to the readers of those texts as 'imitations', which in this sense
were specific and local acts of identifiable textual allusion. A text or an
entire *oeuvre* could be turned into a concordance, and the more sacred and
influential the text the more likely its words were to be presented in alpha-
betical form or indexed: so in 1470 appeared the first printed concordance
of the Bible (though manuscript concordances had been produced since the
thirteenth century). By 1535 the Italian humanist scholar Marius Nizolius
had produced a lexicon-cum-concordance of Ciceronian Latin, which
grew into a massive 1,500 page index and dictionary of Ciceronian vocabulary, to which was grudgingly added a mere ten page appendix of 'Barbarous
Words' not used by Cicero along with elegant Ciceronian circumlocutions
for them.[7] This created a massive stress line right through the middle of the
unfortunate Cicero. He was supposed to be at once a huge searchable lexicon of words which any schoolboy could use. But he was also supposed to
be a living *exemplum* of rhetorical excellence.

These forces within the educational and scholarly culture of sixteenth-
century Europe also put intense pressure on the concept of *imitatio* as it had
been explored in the rhetorical tradition, and indeed exaggerated the longest
and deepest fissure within that concept. This is best illustrated by returning
to the passage from *Against the Sophists* in which Isocrates stated that teaching
rhetoric consisted in both the inculcation of principle and the provision of
a living example, and imagining how it might sound in the age of print:
'The teacher, for his part, must so expound the principles of the art with the
utmost possible exactness as to leave out nothing that can be taught, and,
for the rest, he must in himself set such an example [*paradeigma*] of oratory
that the students who have taken form under his instruction and are able to
pattern [*mimēsasthai*] after him will, from the outset, show in their speaking
a degree of grace and charm which is not found in others.'[8] The side of this
concerned with the extraction and inculcation of principles was perfectly
attuned to the era of print: mass-produced manuals which set out the principles of rhetoric could potentially mass-produce pupils well-versed in the
precepts for attaining rhetorical excellence.

7. Mario Nizolio, *Observationum in M. T. Ciceronem prima [et secunda] pars* (Ex Prato Albuini, 1535);
   frequently reprinted under the more transparent title of *Nizolius sive Thesaurus Ciceronianus*.
8. Isocrates, *Isocrates*, trans. George Norlin and Larue Van Hook, 3 vols. (London and New York,
   1928), 2.175, 'Against the Sophists', 17–18.

But what of that element of charismatic influence, the 'grace and charm' with which a teacher is supposed to equip his charges? Those virtues suggest direct contact with a teacher, or at least a mode of transmission which conveys the force of the exemplum's mode of speech. Could that be conveyed through printed texts? Or do those words denote exactly what an able student, equipped with his Nizolian textbook listing every word ever used by Cicero, would *not* be able to reproduce from Cicero?

These questions rumbled beneath what have come to be called 'the Ciceronian controversies' of the later fifteenth and early sixteenth centuries. These were a series of arguments between humanists about the best way to imitate the ancients. Some contributions to this debate were tedious, some were brutal, and many were both. The details of the arguments, particularly as they unfolded in Italy and France, have been well set out elsewhere, so do not need to be rehearsed in detail here.[9] Crudely put, writers tend to be called 'Ciceronians' if they advocated the imitation of Cicero alone as the best way to achieve perfect eloquence. Their opponents are rather misleadingly called 'anti-Ciceronians', but they were not in any simple sense anti-Ciceronian. Rather, most of them followed Quintilian in arguing that dispositions vary among authors, and so an imitator should take the best things from many *exempla* and imitate eclectically. As it had for Quintilian, that belief could go along with great reverence for Cicero.

In each place and in each time the particular points at issue in the Ciceronian controversies varied greatly, and sometimes the debates were proxies for religious or political disagreements. But the arguments used on both sides repeatedly drew on the rich metaphorical legacy of the classical discussions of *imitatio*: good imitators are like bees, who make a new savour from many flowers, or like children who resemble their father in an unspecifiable way, or like good artists who capture the spirit of what they represent; bad imitators are like apes, or parrots, or shadows, or *simulacra*. Much of this metaphorical language was a deep element within the materials actually imitated as well as being replicated and reflected in the works which sought to conceptualize *imitatio*.

9. Martin L. McLaughlin, *Literary Imitation in the Italian Renaissance* (Oxford, 1995), pp. 185–274; Terence Cave, *The Cornucopian Text: Problems of Writing in the French Renaissance* (Oxford, 1979), pp. 39–56; John Monfasani, 'The Ciceronian Controversy', in Glyn P. Norton, ed., *The Cambridge History of Literary Criticism, Volume 3: The Renaissance* (Cambridge, 1999), 395–401, and Chapter 6 in this volume. The earlier work by Izora Scott, *Controversies over the Imitation of Cicero* (New York, 1910) has been thoroughly superseded. The major contributions are well edited and translated in JoAnn DellaNeva, ed., *Ciceronian Controversies* (Cambridge, Mass., and London, 2007).

The Ciceronian debates shaped the main ways for thinking about not only *imitatio* but also authorship in the centuries ahead. They encouraged thinking about how to distinguish the style of one person from that of another, and about how to identify differences between the writing of the past and of the present. Chapter 6 will explore some ways in which the debates also encouraged early modern readers and writers to think about the 'form' of what they read, and to treat that as an object of imitation. But this chapter concentrates on one key issue which arose out of the debates, and which is central to renaissance poetics: how can an imitation of an ancient text or a past author meet the primary requirement of an orator's speech, that it should be 'apt' to its occasion?[10] The later part of this chapter will show how that question works itself out through the sixteenth-century epic tradition, and how it contributed to the emergence of the novel from that tradition, via Don Quixote's potently inept imitation of Amadis de Gaul. But the generative power of these apparently rather sterile debates about the imitation of authors is best displayed in two texts which appeared in 1528 (something of an *annus mirabilis* for thinking about *imitatio*): Erasmus's *Ciceronianus* and Castiglione's *Book of the Courtier*—the latter of which came to be one of the most widely disseminated works in sixteenth-century Europe.[11]

Erasmus's Ciceronianus

Erasmus was the most notorious opponent of those who argued that it was best to imitate Cicero alone, and exclusively to restrict one's vocabulary to words used in the extant corpus of his works. The core of Erasmus's argument against such people was very simple: they rendered themselves unable to talk of Christ or the crucifixion, and so made themselves into virtual pagans. This was a deliberately tactless assault on the Italian Ciceronian scholars attached to the papal court, who responded in force to Erasmus's attack.[12] Erasmus compounded this insult by concluding with a survey of contemporary scholars and their claims to be 'Ciceronian'. His extended

---

10. The topic has been brilliantly explored in Kathy Eden, 'Cicero Redivivus and the Historicizing of Renaissance Style', *Nottingham Medieval Studies* 56 (2012), 143–69, to which (as well as to conversations with Prof. Eden) I am much indebted.
11. See Peter Burke, *The Fortunes of the Courtier: The European Reception of Castiglione's Cortegiano* (Cambridge, 1995).
12. Luca D'Ascia, *Erasmo e l'umanesimo romano* (Firenze, 1991).

attack on Christophe de Longueil, a French humanist who had been born in Italy, generated anti-Erasmian polemic on both sides of the Alps. These later and increasingly *ad hominem* attacks tended to obscure the key conceptual issues at stake in the controversy.[13]

Erasmus's most constructive contribution to the Ciceronian debates was that he embodied the arguments for and against in a set of memorable characters and images. He presented the most vivid polemical portrait of the obsessive Ciceronian in the figure of the crazed Nosoponus, who at the start of the dialogue has spent seven years desperately in love with Cicero, and in reading nothing but Cicero. Nosoponus has sought so eagerly to purge his vocabulary of any word or grammatical form which does not appear in the writings of his master that his own bodily substance is wasting away. He enters the dialogue as an almost bodiless presence: 'that look, that emaciated face, suggests something ominous'.[14] By its end he claims to be nearly cured of the wasting disease of Ciceronianism. That portrait was vivid but its substance was by no means new. Indeed, as Erasmus acknowledged, his obsessively literalistic Ciceronian had in effect been invented by Quintilian. Quintilian had attacked nameless orators who believed that if they ended sentences with 'esse videatur' they would be writing as Cicero would have written, or reproducing what Quintilian calls the *genus* or kind of writing which Cicero practised:

> Those who are tame and listless, if only they can produce long enough periods, swear that this is just the manner in which Cicero would have spoken. I have known some who thought that they had produced a brilliant imitation of the style [*genus*] of that divine orator, by ending their periods with the phrase *esse videatur*.[15]
>
> otiosi et supini, si quid modo longius circumduxerunt, iurant ita Ciceronem locuturum fuisse. Noveram quosdam, qui se pulchre expressisse genus illud caelestis huius in dicendo viri sibi viderentur, si in clausula possuissent *Esse videatur*. (*Institutio*, 10.2.18)

In those remarks, much cited in the early phases of the Ciceronian debates, Quintilian was following the lead of Cicero himself. Cicero in the *Brutus* (the rhetorical treatise which had been rediscovered at Lodi in 1421) includes an attack on superficial imitators who think they are Atticists

13. On the French arguments with Erasmus, see notably Cave, *Cornucopian Text*, pp. 35–77.
14. Erasmus, ed. Levi, *Ciceronianus*, p. 343.
15. Quintilian's passage is duly echoed by Poliziano, in DellaNeva, ed., *Ciceronian Controversies*, p. 3 and by Erasmus in *Ciceronianus*, p. 370.

because they imitate the asperity of Thucydides. Cicero insists, in a sentence that was to have enormous influence over the theory and practice of imitation in the sixteenth century and after, that 'If Thucydides himself had been alive at a later date he would have been more mellow and less harsh' ('Ipse enim Thucydides si posterius fuisset, multo maturior fuisset et mitior', *Brutus*, 83.288).[16] In that passage Cicero presents an author as a transhistorical principle that can be described in the subjunctive. Doing so implies that an author is not a lexicon or a set of stylistic mannerisms, but a *genus* or kind of writing. An author, that is, is an adaptive principle which might speak or write in a different way in response to changing circumstances.

Cicero's subjunctivization of authorship, if such an ungainly phrase may be used of the prince of eloquence, was to become a strong element in the understanding of imitation and indeed of translation in later centuries. It was most famously adapted by John Dryden when he claimed in his 'Dedication of the Aeneis' (1697) that in translating Virgil he had 'endeavour'd to make *Virgil* speak such *English* as he wou'd himself have spoken, if he had been born in *England*, and in this present Age'.[17] Erasmus's main contribution to the history of *imitatio* was that he fully grasped the implications of Cicero's remark, which requires one to think of an *oeuvre* not as a fixed body of texts, but rather as akin to a genre in that it is a series of instantiations of an underlying set of skills and dispositions. Each particular text is produced from the interaction between those skills and dispositions and a particular occasion, be that a set of historical events, or an audience with distinctive needs and interests. The series of actually existing works by a particular author therefore does not delimit the possibility that there might be more.

What made it relatively natural for writers in the rhetorical tradition to regard an author in this way as a non-finite series of texts which manifest similar genetic principles was that it could be very readily assimilated to a concept which was central to the art of rhetoric: decorum. Decorum required an orator not always to use the same words or registers, or to keep within predetermined bounds, but to speak aptly, both to the circumstances of the utterance and to the needs of the audience—or as Cicero put it in his influential discussion of decorum in *Orator*, 20.71: 'the same style and the same thoughts must not be used in portraying every condition in life, or

---

16. Texts and translations from Marcus Tullius Cicero, *Brutus; Orator*, trans. George Lincoln Hendrickson and H. M. Hubbell (Cambridge, Mass., and London, 1952).

17. John Dryden, *The Works*, ed. Edward Niles Hooker, H. T. Swedenberg, and Vinton A. Dearing, 20 vols. (Berkeley, 1956–2000), 5.330–1.

every rank, position or age, and in fact a similar distinction must be made in respect of place, time and audience'.

It is relatively easy to move from the belief that authors necessarily adapt themselves to circumstance to the principle that authors who imitate other authors have to imitate not just the words but the adaptive practice of the person they are imitating. Even hard-line advocates of imitating the single example of Cicero had to confess that he was not the best example to imitate for people who were attempting to write an epic poem or an elegy, because the decorum of these genres was different from that of a speech of persuasion or a treatise of philosophy. The extension of this argument from decorum into the notion that authors should be regarded as *transhistorically* adaptable entities is the central insight of Erasmus's *Ciceronianus*.[18]

As Erasmus's Bulephorus put it in a series of killer Socratic questions to his skeletal Ciceronian adversary Nosoponus, it can be generally agreed 'that no one deserves the fair title of Ciceronian unless he can speak as Cicero does':

NOSOPONUS Quite so.
BULEPHORUS And moreover that a man doesn't speak well, if he doesn't speak appositely [*apte*].
NOSOPONUS That too.
BULEPHORUS And that we only speak appositely if what we say is appropriate to present persons and circumstances?
NOSOPONUS Certainly.   (p. 383/p. 636)

Nosoponus is reduced by these questions to the most simple-minded of Socratic stooges. He has to confess that Cicero is the master of apt speech. If he also accepts that Ciceronian vocabulary is not apt to the present day, then he is sunk.

He does, and he is. And that enables Bulephorus to embark on the most famous passage in the *Ciceronianus*:

You say that no one can speak well unless he reproduces [*exprimat*] Cicero; but the very facts of the matter cry out that no one can speak well unless he

---

18. For the development of Erasmus's interest in historical decorum, see G. W. Pigman, 'Imitation and the Renaissance Sense of the Past: The Reception of Erasmus' *Ciceronianus*', *The Journal of Medieval and Renaissance Studies* 9 (1979), 155–77, and Eden, 'Cicero Redivivus'. Cf. Erasmus's claim in a letter of 6 May 1526: 'in an age that has seen a revolution in religion, government, public offices, place names, buildings, dress, and manners, could anything be more absurd than to be afraid to express oneself differently than Cicero? If Cicero himself were to come back to life, he would laugh at this band of Ciceronians', Desiderius Erasmus, *The Correspondence of Erasmus*, ed. R. A. B. Mynors, D. F. S. Thomson, Wallace K. Ferguson, Alexander Dalzell, Charles Fantazzi, and James Martin Estes, 17 vols. (Toronto and London, 1974), 12.195.

deliberately and with full awareness abandons the example of Cicero. Wherever I turn I see everything changed, I stand on a different stage, I see a different theatre, a different world. What am I to do? I am a Christian and I must talk of the Christian religion before Christians. If I am going to do so in a manner befitting my subject, surely I am not to imagine that I am living in the age of Cicero, and speaking in a crowded senate before the conscript fathers on the Tarpeian height, and scrounge a few poor words, figures and rhythms from speeches which Cicero delivered in the Senate?   (p. 383/p. 637)

As Kathy Eden has shown, this passage builds on Cicero's argument in the *Brutus* that a rhetorician should speak aptly to the times, and more generally upon the guiding assumption of the later works of Cicero that styles vary through time and space.[19] This awareness of decorum as a transhistorical principle which required change, or 'ad-aptation', within the history of eloquence was for Erasmus amplified by the profound contrast between pagan and Christian beliefs and vocabularies, a contrast which generates an urgent rhetorical need to adapt words to new times: 'a man who speaks in a manner inappropriate to his subject certainly does not speak well' ('nec bene dicit qui non dicit apte'), he declared, and in the second edition of *Ciceronianus* he added a coda to this crucial statement: 'This cannot be said too often' (pp. 406–7/p. 655).

Erasmus unobtrusively exemplifies his own argument by the vocabulary he uses. When his spokesman Bulephorus describes the characteristics of Cicero which make him so difficult to imitate—his particular skill in arranging speeches or his exceptional talent—he very often uses words which Cicero himself never used. So he insists with Quintilian that an imitator has to have natural *ingenium*, and as he does so he describes Cicero as *inimitabilis*. That word had been used by Quintilian, but never by Cicero himself: 'if you do not have the natural gifts which will enable you to reproduce that *inimitable* flair for the perfect expression, what is more stupid than torturing yourself over the unattainable?' (p. 439/p. 702). He also talks of Cicero's *genius*, a word which Cicero also never used in the sense of 'unique talent', and which appears to have been first used in this way by Gianfrancesco Pico in a contribution to the Ciceronian debates in 1513.[20] So, a poor imitation is a mere *simulacrum* or image which lacks 'that genius endowed with its own mysterious energy' ('ubi genius ille peculiarem et arcanam adferens energiam', p. 376/p. 631) which Cicero possessed.

---

19. Eden, 'Cicero Redivivus'.   20. DellaNeva, ed., *Ciceronian Controversies*, p. 20.

Those lexical details defeat the obsessive Ciceronian Nosoponus just as completely as the overt arguments of Bulephorus: the very thing that one is trying to imitate—the unique and inimitable genius of Cicero—could not even be *described* if the imitator did not depart from Cicero's own vocabulary. Being 'apt' in describing Cicero himself requires one to depart from the Ciceronian lexicon. And Erasmus's insistence on the 'apt', on writing and speaking that suits its occasion, is the core of his understanding of what it is to be 'Ciceronian'. Cicero is better described as a practice or a set of priorities which are subjunctive and adaptable to different occasions than as a sum of words or as a set of specific stylistic tricks which work on all occasions and in all contexts.

This had a wide range of secondary consequences. Imitators should be aware of and speak aptly not only to their immediate audience but also the ambient customs of their day. Consequently they not only could but *should* occlude verbal debts to their *exempla* as part of the process of adaptation to the present moment. This necessarily diminished the anxiety about plagiarism which had beset Petrarch in his writing about *imitatio*: changing circumstances require new and apt words, therefore the avoidance of verbal replication is a natural consequence of adaptive imitation. Concealment of one's *exempla* by avoiding replication of their vocabulary was not for Erasmus so much an end in itself, as an enabling precondition of adaptive emulation: new things need new words.[21]

The principal end of adaptive imitation should be to recreate the features of an *exemplum* which Quintilian had described as inimitable (power, force, *ingenium*, or, in Pico and Erasmus's word, 'genius') within a distinct vocabulary that is apt to the times. All of these would enable an imitator to address an occasion in ways which show an achieved skill rather than simply a grasp of a set of rules. And when Erasmus articulates this core principle of adaptive emulation he deploys a wide range of metaphors of life, alongside which we also find their familiar opposing doubles, the vocabulary of shadows and *simulacra*. As Bulephorus puts it:

> I am pleading not only Cicero's case, but ours too: Cicero's, in that I hope to prevent us producing a bad copy of him that will give him a bad name, just as a portrait by an incompetent painter who cannot reproduce the features properly makes the sitter an object of ridicule; and ours, in that I want to save us

---

21. Cf. G. W. Pigman, 'Versions of Imitation in the Renaissance', *Renaissance Quarterly* 33 (1980), 1–32, at pp. 9–10.

from misplacing our affections, and suffering a fate as humiliating and miserable as Ixion's, who, according to the story, embraced an empty cloud-form [*nubis inane simulacrum complexus est*] instead of his desired Juno; or Paris', who fought a war for ten years for the Helen he had carried off and all the time was embracing a false image of Helen [*mendax Helenae simulacrum*], because the real Helen had of course been carried off to Egypt by a stratagem of the gods. What could be more miserable and humiliating for us, if after all our efforts we found ourselves in possession of nothing but an empty counterfeit semblance of Cicero [*inanem ac fallacem Ciceronis umbram*].   (p. 360/p. 619)

The parallels for failed imitation here are classical, erotic, and tragic, and in them erotic desire is directed at a *simulacrum* rather than a substantial body. The biological metaphors used by Quintilian to describe imitation have multiplied: failed imitators love only a *simulacrum*, and either fail to produce offspring at all (as Paris did in the version of the story of Helen apparently originating with Stesichorus, in which he abducts a *simulacrum* of Helen and the whole Trojan war is fought over a phantom),[22] or offspring who are monsters. Ixion slept with a cloudy replicant of Juno made by her husband Jove, and from their union generated the race of Centaurs. When *imitatio* becomes the reproduction of a *simulacrum* it proliferates insubstantial and non-human entities.

In describing superficial imitation Erasmus contrasts it forcefully with the bodily presence which a true imitator should seek to create from the act of imitation—an act which Erasmus clearly regarded as a form of reincarnation:

Where are the brain, the flesh, the veins, the sinews and bones, the bowels, blood, breath humours? Where are life, movement, feeling, voice, and speech? Where finally are man's special characteristics, mind, intelligence, memory, and understanding? The painter in fact finds it impossible to represent the most distinctive features of a person ... Something very different is required of us if we wish to represent [*exprimere*] the whole Cicero. If the picture [*simulacrum*] we paint of Marcus Tullius is devoid of life, movement, feeling, sinew, and bone, our representation of him will be completely unconvincing.

(p. 375/p. 631)

It would be easy to represent both of these passages as no more than copious elaborations of Seneca's injunction that an imitator should resemble an original

---

22. Euripides, *Helen*, ed. William Allan (Cambridge, 2008), pp. 18–22; for the textual record, see Stesichorus, *The Poems*, ed. Malcolm Davies and Patrick Finglass (Cambridge, 2014), pp. 299–343. See also Leonard Woodbury, 'Helen and the Palinode', *Phoenix* 21 (1967), 157–76.

as a portrait resembles a sitter or as a child does its parents, or of Cicero's emphasis on the 'sinews' and 'nerves' required of a successful orator.[23]

But they go beyond that, and they do so for several reasons. Erasmus displays here traces of a sixteenth-century reformer's iconophobia, which adds a threat of irreligion to the simulacral recreation of an ancient author. Erasmus's stridency here, however, principally arises from his own position within a wider culture of publication and education. He was the single greatest disseminator of handbooks which codified and disseminated rhetorical training throughout Northern Europe. The exacting replication of Ciceronian vocabulary embodied in Nosoponus therefore had a particular horror for him because it was a parodic version of his own enterprise. Indeed one can see in Erasmus a highly intensified version of the problem which had beset Roman theorists of *imitatio*. Erasmus's Roman predecessors, as Chapter 2 showed, used heightened metaphorical language to describe *imitatio* in order to avoid presenting the relationship between imitator and imitated in the form of precepts. This was a means of preserving the charismatic process by which an elite orator was imitated by his pupils. For Erasmus, a one-man machine for producing classical texts and pedagogical manuals, whose manual of handy Latin phrases the *De Copia* was among the most reprinted books in the century, the problem was analogous to but even more acute than it had been for his Roman predecessors.[24] How could the charismatic and quasi-bodily relationship between imitated and imitator be transferred to the medium of print? And how could that model of authorship survive in a culture which abounded in short-hand methods for learning words from prior authors?

What Erasmus urgently needed to do was bring charisma, life, and bodily coherence to a practice of imitation. But the whole enterprise of printed humanistic pedagogy—in which he was such a central figure—was against him. Hence the intensity of his imagery here, and hence too the procreative energy of his description of an achieved imitation:

> imitation which does not immediately incorporate into its own speech any nice little feature it comes across, but transmits it to the mind for inward digestion, so that becoming part of your own system, it gives the impression not of something begged from someone else, but of something that springs from

23. Elaine Fantham, *Comparative Studies in Republican Latin Imagery* (Toronto, 1972), pp. 173–4.
24. On the influence of the *De Copia*, see Cave, *Cornucopian Text*, pp. 3–34. On Erasmus and charisma, see Lisa Jardine, *Erasmus, Man of Letters: The Construction of Charisma in Print* (Princeton, 1993).

your own mental processes, something that exudes the characteristics and force of your own mind and personality. Your reader will see it not as a piece of decoration filched from Cicero, but a child sprung from your own brain [*foetum e tuo natum cerebro*], the living image of its father [*vivam parentis imaginem*], like Pallas from the brain of Jove. Your speech will not be a patchwork or a mosaic, but a lifelike portrait [*spirans imago*] of the person you really are, a river welling out from your inmost being.   (pp. 441–2/p. 704)

Imitation enables parthenogenesis, a live birth of wisdom from your own brain; but it also generates a pagan goddess and a *spirans imago*, a breathing replica. The conceptual evasions and the rich metaphorical legacy of classical discussions of *imitatio* primed Erasmus to identify its successful forms with biological reproduction; but the unmarried scholar, a secular monk steeped in the ideals of homoerotic companionship and the psychological identity between friends which were the staple components of classical and early modern discussions of love and friendship, almost necessarily saw that ideal of sexually reproductive replication as simultaneously an enrichment of his distant relationship with his readers and pupils and a kind of threat or diminution: Pallas springs without sexual union from the brow of Jove, a lifelike portrait, or perhaps an airy image. The educator from the age of print who sought to replicate the charismatic relationship between pupil and teacher from the early stages of the history of rhetoric does so by piling metaphor of life on metaphor of image and reproduction in various forms and senses.

We might here return to Erasmus's praise of Quintilian, with which this discussion began, and extend the quotation given in the introduction to this chapter a little further. Having said that Quintilian 'starts with the rudiments and sets out all the successive stages, the theory of rhetoric, its application, and the development of proficiency, including quite a lot of material that Cicero either omitted or merely touched on in passing', Erasmus then goes on to say we should not be obsessively or narrowly concerned with *praeceptiones* (which the Toronto translation of the *Works* renders by 'theory', but it would be better translated as 'rudimentary principles'), because 'Our skilful expositor will teach much more than a textbook' (p. 404).

That is on the face of it a straightforward restatement of the principle central to discussions of *imitatio* in the Latin tradition: pupils learn more from personal example than they do from simply following rules. But Erasmus's Latin here is very surprising: 'Index ille peritus, multo plus contulerit, quam praeceptiones';[25] literally, 'that skilled index is far better than precepts', or 'one who shows and points the way can achieve more than a series of rules'. 'Index' occurs here in a context where the expected word might be 'iudex', a living judge possessed of discretion and skill, who could act as a living example to imitate. But 'index' is not a misprint: it is repeated in all editions of *Ciceronianus* printed during Erasmus's lifetime. In two minims it collapses the judicious and distinctive voice of Erasmus the *iudex* back into the nightmare of a text which has been rendered infinitely replicable and fragmented by the textual convenience of an index. How does the ability of an orator to speak aptly to circumstance coexist with the world of indices, codifications of precepts, and mechanical reproduction? Erasmus's response to that question was to heighten the metaphors used to describe imitation, and to make of it a power akin to that of birth. When combined with his insistence on imitation that was 'apt' to the times it made his *Ciceronianus* the second most influential offshoot of the Ciceronian controversies. The most influential, however, was another text published in 1528 which is also concerned with adaptive imitation: Castiglione's *Il Cortegiano*.

Castiglione: *sprezzatura* and the courtier's mastery

Although Baldassare Castiglione's *Il Cortegiano*, or *The Book of the Courtier*, appeared in the same year as Erasmus's *Ciceronianus*, the two works probably do not influence each other. But they share a common genesis. The extended composition of Castiglione's dialogue about how to be a perfect courtier covered the period during which the debate between Castiglione's friend Pietro Bembo and Gianfrancesco Pico about how best to imitate Cicero was being disseminated in print (1513–24). Bembo was a hard-liner in the Ciceronian controversies, who in 1513 gave his 'strong approval to those who, intending to write prose, resolve to imitate Cicero alone'.[26] In 1518 Castiglione had sent a draft of *Il Cortegiano* to Bembo for comment, and Bembo is both a character within the dialogue and one of those responsible for editing the final version of Castiglione's text.[27]

25. Desiderius Erasmus, *De recta Latini Graecaeque sermonis pronuntiatione dialogus. Eiusdem dialogus cui titulus, Ciceronianus, siue, De optimo genere dicendi* (Basel, 1528), p. 337.
26. DellaNeva, ed., *Ciceronian Controversies*, p. 67.
27. Brian Richardson, *Print Culture in Renaissance Italy: The Editor and the Vernacular Text, 1470–1600* (Cambridge, 1994), pp. 62–3.

Nonetheless in both the text and the dedicatory epistle of the printed version Castiglione departs in significant ways from Bembo's austere Ciceronianism. Despite not addressing the Ciceronian debates directly, *Il Cortegiano* is the most powerful response to the conceptual problems within the concept of *imitatio* to which those debates drew attention. That question, 'How can one imitate in a way that is *apt* to the times?' exerts a shaping force over its argument. The keyword of Castiglione's first book, and which has come to encapsulate the doctrine of the treatise as a whole, is the great untranslatable: *sprezzatura*, a word which Castiglione himself describes as 'new' and which has often been taken to epitomize the effortless ease with which the courtier is supposed to act. The principal speaker of Book I, Count Ludovico, introduces the word as part of an attempt to explain what 'grace' is:

> But having wondered to myself many times whence this 'grace' is born [*nasca*], leaving aside those who have it just from the stars, I find a completely universal rule, which it appears to me to be more valid than any other in relation to this in all human affairs concerning saying or doing, and that is to avoid affectation as far as is possible, as though it were the sharpest dangerous rock. And, to say what is perhaps a new word, to use in all actions a certain 'sprezzatura' or effortless ease, which hides art and which shows that which one does and says to have been done without effort and without reflection.

> Ma avendo io già più volte pensato meco onde nasca questa grazia, lasciando quelli che dalle stelle l'hanno, trovo una regula universalissima, la qual mi par valer circa questo in tutte le cose umane che si facciano o dicano più che alcuna altra, e ciò è fuggir quanto più si po, e come un asperissimo e pericoloso scoglio, la affettazione; e, per dir forse una nova parola, usar in ogni cosa una certa sprezzatura, che nasconda l'arte e dimostri ciò che si fa e dice venir fatto senza fatica e quasi senza pensarvi.   (I.26; p. 124)[28]

The word *sprezzatura* was not an entirely new coinage, but, as Castiglione indicates, it appears not to have been used in this sense before.[29] It is notoriously difficult to translate: Thomas Hoby, the first translator of *The Book of the Courtier* into English in 1561, rendered it as 'recklessness', which attempted to capture the sense 'acting with effortless ease'.[30] *Sprezzatura* has often been seen as a courtly adaptation of the art that conceals art which Cicero

---

28. My translation. Quotations from Baldassarre Castiglione, *Il cortegiano, con una scelta delle opere minori*, ed. Bruno Maier (Turin, 1955).
29. Burke, *Fortunes of the Courtier*, p. 31.
30. Baldassarre Castiglione, *The Courtyer of Count Baldessar Castilio*, trans. Thomas Hoby (London, 1561), sig. E2r.

describes in his *Orator* ('quaedam etiam neglegentia est diligens', 23.78).[31] But *sprezzatura* is also a word for something akin to what we now call a 'skill', or the ability to act instinctively in a way that is appropriate to a particular occasion without necessarily being able to formulate in theoretical form the grounds for one's actions.[32]

Eduardo Saccone has suggestively related it to Aristotle's discussion in *Nicomachean Ethics* 2 of the virtue of truthfulness (*alētheia*), which is a mean between 'ironical' utterance and 'boastful speech', and suggests that *sprezzatura* is a reserved and ironical version of truthfulness which is designed to impress an elite group by suggesting that the performer has additional inner reserves.[33] This perceptive observation may go too far. Castiglione's *sprezzatura* describes the quality possessed by someone who inhabits his place and time perfectly, who has internalized a rule as a practice or habit, and who can therefore simply do what is appropriate without having to make an effort to do so. The effortless ease of a courtier's actions is consequently analogous to the ability of Aristotle's man of practical wisdom, who can simply act in the right way at the right time, without conscious effort at self-control.[34] *Sprezzatura* is a word for someone who has gone beyond grasping precepts and, who, as Quintilian put in that influential Aristotelianizing sentence at the start of the tenth book of the *Institutio*, has grasped a *hexis* or a habituated pattern of practice through imitation of prior examples.

Castiglione adapts arguments which had been conducted within the rhetorical tradition to a wider social setting. That is in large measure the source of *Il Cortegiano*'s extraordinary international success: it suggests that a learnt style of aristocratic behavioural fluency could be acquired by imitation. And that adaptation of arguments from the rhetorical sphere runs right through the work. It begins with a direct allusion to Cicero's *Orator*, which underlies the aim of the treatise to present the 'forma' (I.1; p. 79) or idea of the perfect courtier, and references direct and oblique to the *De Oratore* and

31. Cf. *De Oratore*, 2.156, 2.177; Quintilian, *Institutio*, 4.1.57; Samuel Holt Monk, 'A Grace Beyond the Reach of Art', *Journal of the History of Ideas* 5 (1944), 131–50; Rudolph Wittkower, 'Genius: Individualism in Art and Artists', in Philip P. Wiener, ed., *Dictionary of the History of Ideas: Studies of Selected Pivotal Ideas*, 5 vols. (New York, 1973), 2.297–312.
32. Richard A. Lanham, *The Motives of Eloquence: Literary Rhetoric in the Renaissance* (Eugene, Oreg., 1976), pp. 149–50.
33. Eduardo Saccone, 'Grazia, Sprezzatura, Affettazione in the *Courtier*', in Robert W. Hanning and David Rosand, eds., *Castiglione: The Ideal and the Real in Renaissance Culture* (New Haven, 1983), 45–67.
34. See Tarik Wareh, *The Theory and Practice of Life: Isocrates and the Philosophers* (Boston, Mass., and London, 2012), p. 201.

to Quintilian's *Institutio* are found throughout the dialogue, which presents in effect at once a poetics and a rhetoric of living. The 'esercizi' on the tiltyard which Count Ludovico is so keen to commend as means by which the courtier can acquire his unaffected ease are direct descendants of the rhetorical *exercitationes* which enabled Quintilian's tyro orator to become a practised rhetorician who displays the effortless skill of a warrior or athlete.

The specific connections between *sprezzatura* and earlier sixteenth-century arguments about *imitatio*, though, are instantly apparent from the context in which Castiglione introduces the word.[35] *Sprezzatura* is presented as the alternative to *affettazione*. Affectation in the rhetorical tradition is frequently associated with a vice which Quintilian calls *kakozēlon*—literally 'bad imitative zeal'—a Greek term which Quintilian renders by the Latin phrase 'mala adfectatio', or bad affectation (*Institutio*, 8.3.56). For Quintilian it is one of the worst vices in an author because it displays a radical failure of judgement and an inability to grasp the virtues of style.

Sprezzatura is the inverse of this 'bad imitation' or ineptness. And as though to signal its proximity to arguments about *imitatio* Castiglione positions his discussion of *sprezzatura* immediately after a passage that explicitly addresses how people learn from their masters. Count Ludovico says (in Thomas Hoby's translation) 'He therfore that wil be a good scolar, beside the practysing of good thinges, must evermore set al his diligence to bee lyke his mayster, and (if it were possible) chaunge himself into him' ('Chi adunque vorrà esser bon discipulo, oltre al far le cose bene, sempre ha da metter ogni diligenzia per assimigliarsi al maestro e, se possibil fosse, transformarsi in lui', sig. E1v–E2r/I.26; p. 123). Ludovico's insistence here that we should follow a singular exemplar or 'maestro' gives a courteous nod to Castiglione's Ciceronian friend Pietro Bembo, who had claimed that an imitator should follow the single example of Cicero. But it is followed almost immediately by a quite contrary emphasis on the value of eclectic imitation:

> And when he begins to feel that he has learned the rudiments, it is of great benefit to see diverse teachers, and, governing himself with that good judgment which he always has as a guide, to go making a selection of various qualities now from one and now from another. And like the bee in the green fields, which always goes gathering the flowers among the grass, so our courtier

---

35. On the connection between *sprezzatura* and *imitatio*, see Clare Lapraik Guest, *The Understanding of Ornament in the Italian Renaissance* (Boston, 2016), pp. 259–75.

will be able to steal this grace from those who will provide it for him and from each that part which will be most praiseworthy.

E quando già si sente aver fatto profitto, giova molto veder diversi omini di tal professione e, governandosi con quel bon giudicio che sempre gli ha da esser guida, andar sceglidando or da un or da un altro varie cose. E come la pecchia ne' verdi prati sempre tra l'erbe va carpendo i fiori, così il nostro cortegiano averà da rubare questa grazia da que' che a lui parerà che la tenghino e da ciascun quella parte che più sarà laudevole. (I.12; p. 123, my translation)

The bee, now so freighted with the nectar of many authors that it is no longer Seneca's but a piece of common property, marks this as a passage concerned with *imitatio*. And that bee flies around attempting to 'steal its grace', *rubare questa grazia*, from others. Ludovico goes on to argue that we should not be like the unnamed person whom he says his audience knows, who imitates the twitches of Ferdinando II of Naples rather than his noble nature (which is itself a transformative adaptation of a commonplace that imitators should not reproduce the warts on the faces of their originals).[36] He then states his completely universal rule ('regula universalissima') that the courtier should do everything with *sprezzatura*. That concept consequently emerges from a discussion of how an imitator should acquire a set of abilities from someone else without either simply following a set of prescriptions or affectedly following the mannerisms of a prior *exemplum*— in the way that literal-minded Ciceronians reproduced the lexis of Cicero. The courtier grasps the principles beneath his exemplars' conduct, and acts and speaks with instinctive appropriateness and aptness to his occasion, and thereby avoids *kakozēlía*, or the affected and inept use of another person's words.

He is, that is to say, like Erasmus's imitator, a master of apt speech. He is also aware of his times. In one of the earliest manuscript versions of the

---

36. Cf. Pico's letters to Bembo in DellaNeva, ed., *Ciceronian Controversies*, pp. 26–7 and 106–7. It is likely that the first of these passages influenced Castiglione here, since it contrasts imitating moles and scars with imitating 'muscles, living strength and grace'. Cf. Plutarch, *Moralia*, 'How to Tell a Flatterer from a Friend', 9, which also contrasts the changeable imitation of superficial mannerisms by a flatterer to the stability of a true friend: 'In a similar way it is said that close acquaintances used to copy Plato's stoop, Aristotle's lisp, and King Alexander's twisted neck as well as the harshness of his voice in conversation. In fact, some people unconsciously acquire most of their peculiarities from the traits or the lives of others. But the flatterer's case is exactly the same as that of the chameleon ... even as bad painters, who by reason of incompetence are unable to attain to the beautiful, depend upon wrinkles, moles, and scars to bring out their resemblances, so the flatterer makes himself an imitator of licentiousness, superstition, passionate anger', *Plutarch's Moralia*, trans. Frank Cole Babbit, 16 vols. (Cambridge, Mass., 1927–69), I.287–9.

Cortegiano Castiglione qualified his discussion of imitation by saying that the imitator should imitate 'accommodandosi sempre a l'uso de' suoi tempi'[37]— 'always accommodating himself to the custom of his time'. That deleted phrase shows that from the earliest stages of composition Castiglione, like Erasmus, was aware that decorum has a transtemporal aspect, since orators must speak aptly to the occasion, and as customs change their language must change too.

This interest in apt speech continued to grow as Castiglione worked on the dialogue. In its final version the deleted phrase about 'accommodating himself to the custom of his time' was extended into a lengthy debate about the kind of language a courtier should use. According to the hard-line Bemboist Federico a courtier should follow the idiom of Petrarch and Boccaccio. Ludovico argues the contrary case, that the courtier should adopt a more contemporary and common (*commune*) style. The debate between the two speakers becomes an abbreviated version of the extensive debates which came to be called the *questione della lingua*, which concerned the appropriateness of using Tuscan forms of Italian in literary works.

But that set debate is once more adapted to suit the particular rhetorical concerns of a courtier, as it were enacting Castiglione's insistence on the adaptive nature of successful imitation.[38] Ludovico argues that the avoidance of affectation, which is an enabling condition of *sprezzatura*, requires the use of contemporary language, while Federico presents what is in its outline the conservative approach to linguistic usage which had been advocated by Pietro Bembo in his *Prose della volgar lingua*, that Petrarch and Boccaccio should provide the norms of usage. This debate on linguistic decorum is foregrounded in the dedicatory epistle to the printed text of *Il Cortegiano*, and in the dialogue itself becomes so extended that eventually Lady Emilia has to interrupt and tell Federico and Ludovico to move on.[39]

---

37. Olga Pugliese, Lorenzo Bartoli, Filomena Calabrese, Adriana Grimaldi, Ian Martin, Laura Prelipcean, and Antonio Ricci, eds., 'The Early Extant Manuscripts of Baldassar Castiglione's *Il libro del cortegiano*' (2012), <https://www.researchgate.net/publication/277867222_The_Early_Extant_Manuscripts_of_Baldassar_Castiglione%27s_Il_libro_del_cortegiano_transcriptions>, p. 144. Accessed February 2018.

38. On Castiglione's debt to G. B. Pio in this area, see Carlo Dionisotti, *Gli umanisti e il volgare fra Quattro e Cinquecento* (Firenze, 1968), pp. 92–3.

39. On the revisions to this section, see Uberto Motta, 'La "questione della lingua" nel primo libro del *Cortegiano*: dalla seconda alla terza redazione', *Aevum* 72 (1998), 693–732, and Olga Zorzi Pugliese, *Castiglione's The Book of the Courtier (Il libro del cortegiano): A Classic in the Making* (Naples, 2008), pp. 45–6.

But the swelling debate enables Ludovico to articulate a view of imitation analogous to that of Erasmus: he insists language changes and times change, and that speaking aptly to the times—with effortless ease that will not alienate an audience—requires the courtier/orator *not* simply to use the words of speakers from an earlier age, but to adopt *consuetudo*, or custom, as a guide. The authority of custom should be such that even ancient authors would themselves not sound like themselves were they to write in the present day. Ennius and Virgil avoided verbal echoes of their predecessors: 'and Cicero says that Ennius scorned (*sprezzò*) his predecessors in several places, in such a way that if we wanted to imitate the ancients we should not imitate them. And Virgil, whom you say imitated Homer, didn't imitate him in his language' ('e dice che Ennio ancor sprezzò in alcune cose i suoi antecessori, di modo che, se noi vorremo imitar gli antichi, non gli imitaremo. E Virgilio, che voi dite che imitò Omero, non lo imitò nella lingua', I.32; p. 138).

That echo of the noun *sprezzatura* in the verb *sprezzò* is illuminating in both directions. It suggests that an imitator does not just 'scorn' a predecessor's words, but displays 'an effortlessly easy grasp on contemporary rhetorical practice' in doing so; conversely it suggests that behaving with *sprezzatura* does entail a degree of potentially contemptuous neglect of the exact source of one's action, if that source is out of harmony with present custom. Ludovico goes on to declare (in a sentence that is not found in the earlier versions of the work) that 'if Petrarch and Boccaccio were alive in the present time they would not use many words which we find in their works, hence it is inappropriate to imitate their vocabulary' ('Se 'l Petrarca e 'l Boccaccio fossero vivi a questo tempo, non usariano molte parole che vedemo ne' loro scritti: però non mi par bene che noi quelle imitiamo', I.36; p. 145). 'Non usariano': Ludovico's verb is in the subjunctive, and that is a non-trivial detail. For him—and here he is in effect speaking for Castiglione and against the dogmatic Bemboist Federico—as for the Cicero of the *Brutus*, and as for the Erasmus of the *Ciceronianus*, an author becomes a subjunctive operator when that author is imitated. What an author *would or might* write aptly to the present occasion is as much a part of what is imitated as what was actually written.

Ludovico returns, albeit indirectly, to the topic of imitation in I.37—a section of *Il Cortegiano* which draws repeatedly on the discussion of imitation in Quintilian's *Institutio* 10.2. He had earlier said that a young disciple should assimilate what he terms a *maestro* so that he becomes a very he. He uses the word *maestro* again immediately after the discussion of how to avoid linguistic affectation, but he does so with a revealing shift of emphasis. The *maestro* turns from an external authority into an internal power: 'their true *maestro*, I believe, should be *ingegno* and their own natural judgment' ('Ma il lor vero maestro cred'io che fosse l'ingegno ed il lor proprio giudicio naturale', I.37; p. 147). Castiglione is here once more adapting the language of the rhetorical tradition: it is *ingegno*, the Italian equivalent of *ingenium*, native talent, which is to be a student's true *maestro* rather than an external authority.[40] And that again takes us back to one of Quintilian's key statements about *imitatio*: 'the greatest features of an orator are not imitable: *ingenium*, invention, force, facility, and whatever art cannot be learnt from art' ('ea quae in oratore maxima sunt imitabilia non sunt, ingenium, inventio, vis, facilitas et quidquid arte non traditur', *Institutio*, 10.2.12). But Castiglione again adapts Quintilian to the political environment of an Italian city state: the final end of a courtier (as Book V of the *Cortegiano* explains) is not simply to display *ingenium* in a way that is apt to the times, but to offer frank, plain spoken advice to his ruler, without affectation or circumlocution—to become, if not a master of his political master, then at least someone who can contribute to the government of a city state by offering effective political counsel.

Book I of *Il Cortegiano* lays out the foundations for that political art of quasi-autonomous frankness: the courtier possesses an *ingegno* which enables him to speak aptly to all occasions and which enables him to become his own *maestro*. As Quintilian's orator displays the autonomy of a property-holding, physically athletic male citizen of Rome, so Castiglione's courtier displays the achieved skill of an inhabitant of an early modern court. The key skill in that environment is the ability to speak plainly, which entails a measure of 'scorn' for the affected language of prior speakers. If that skill is acquired the courtier can himself become a *maestro* in two senses: he is both 'his own ruler' and 'one who can teach others'.

Castiglione's use of the word *proprio* in the same passage ('il lor proprio giudicio naturale') marks an allusion to the tradition which saw *proprietas*, or speaking words suitable to oneself, as the governing criterion of rhetorical excellence.[41] Every person is their own *maestro*; every person rules their own

---

40. For direct (though unacknowledged: Castiglione's own *sprezzatura* requires him to bury the debts) borrowings from Quintilian in 1.37, see Motta, 'La "questione della lingua" ', p. 699.
41. Cf. Quintilian, *Institutio*, 10.2.28: 'But the man who to these good qualities adds his own [*propria*], that is to say, who makes good deficiencies and cuts down whatever is redundant, will be the perfect orator of our search' ('Qui vero etiam propria his bona adiecerit, ut suppleat quae deerant, circumcidat, si quid redundabit, is erit, quem quaerimus, perfectus orator').

speech by internalizing the speech of many *maestri*. We should adopt a language which is *commune*, embedded in the *consuetudo* or custom of our times, and turn it, with effortless ease or *sprezzatura*, into our own, proper discourse. The result is mastery.

This aspect of Castiglione's argument was one of the reasons for the extraordinary success of the *Cortegiano* in sixteenth-century Europe. Castiglione did not simply replicate the debates about imitation and linguistic propriety from the previous decades, or rehash the Ciceronian debates. He generated from them a script for the self-determination of an aspirant aristocratic class.[42] And unlike Erasmus he managed in effect a codification of charisma. Castiglione's courtier is the imitator as gracious native and master of the authority he has learnt from others: he is ever apt, he perfectly internalizes his *exempla* or *maestri*, he learns from them technique rather than vocabulary, and uses those skills to influence the powerful by frank, unaffected persuasion.

Epic adaptations and novel creations

The wisest historian of *imitatio* in the Renaissance, G. W. Pigman, has suggested that Erasmus's arguments about historical decorum in the *Ciceronianus* suffered 'almost total neglect' in subsequent treatises on *imitatio*.[43] Pigman notes that among those who did respond to Erasmus's arguments, some, including the Spanish humanist Juan Luis Vives, saw in them a threat to the exemplary function of history and by implication of literature more generally. For literature and history to have a morally exemplary function it is necessary to assume that past texts have an ethical content which is to some degree transhistorical, and which could remain valuable in new circumstances without being 'adapted', or rendered apt, to the customs of the present.[44] Erasmus's emphasis on adaptive *imitatio* brought out the potential division between imitation of a textual object on the one hand and ethical emulation

---

42. See Jennifer Richards, 'Assumed Simplicity and the Critique of Nobility: Or, How Castiglione Read Cicero', *Renaissance Quarterly* 54 (2001), 460–86.

43. Pigman, 'Sense of the Past', p. 161.

44. See Pigman, 'Sense of the Past', pp. 176–7 and Juan Luis Vives, *Io. Lodouici Viuis . . . opera* ed. Huldericus Coccius (Basel, 1555), pp. 505–6: 'nimirum negare nemo potest, omnia esse mutata, & mutari quotidie' ('it is impossible for anyone to deny that everything is changed, and changed daily'). On the end of humanist ideas of historical exemplarity and its literary consequences, see Timothy Hampton, *Writing from History: the Rhetoric of Exemplarity in Renaissance Literature* (Ithaca, NY, 1990).

on the other—a distinction which the very word *imitatio* tended to collapse. If you could imitate Cicero you could also imitate Christ, or Virgil's Aeneas. But how could a belief in the ethically instructive value of literature from the past survive the notion that everything—vocabulary, social mores, ethical priorities—changed, that Cicero today would not be as he once had been? As many scholars have noted, there is a profound threat to humanist notions of the exemplary function of literature and history hidden within the historically contextualist aspects of humanism.[45] In *Ciceronianus* these two aspects of the humanist synthesis do indeed appear to be on a collision course.

Pigman is quite correct that that collision was seldom contemplated directly in the Neo-Latin treatises explicitly about *imitatio* which directly responded to Erasmus. But the concept of adaptive *imitatio* (whether directly derived from Erasmus or developed independently from the same rhetorical texts which he and Castiglione had read) nonetheless had a profound influence on the theory and practice of imitating one classical genre in particular: that of epic. The reason why this genre became a particular focus for thought about adaptive imitation is not hard to find. Epic was routinely regarded as a species of epideictic rhetoric, or the rhetoric of praise. Epic was believed to praise its heroes for possessing distinctive virtues that its readers were in turn encouraged to regard as ethical *exempla*. This made it the genre to which (with history a close second) the exemplary function of literature was most central. As Sir Philip Sidney put it (defending heroical literature with an instance of its potential for ethical emulation which is so extreme as to approach comedy): 'Who readeth Aeneas carrying old Anchises on his back, that wisheth not it were his fortune to perform so excellent an act?'[46] Epic heroes were supposed to be imitated.

But despite being regarded as a genre founded on an exemplary idea of heroism, epic was also the literary genre in which early modern readers could most readily find evidence that what is regarded as exemplary behaviour changes through time. This was because epic was the clearest example of a classically derived genre in which students could make a full and detailed comparison between a complete set of Greek texts (Homer) and what a Roman author (Virgil) did to those texts. This enabled inferences

45. See notably Hampton, *Rhetoric of Exemplarity*.
46. Sir Philip Sidney, *An Apology for Poetry or the Defence of Poesy*, ed. Geoffrey Shepherd (Manchester, 1973), p. 114. See also Brian Vickers, 'Epideictic and Epic in the Renaissance', *New Literary History* 14 (1983), 497–537.

to be drawn from the comparison between these two authors about the ethical differences between both them and the wider cultures whose priorities they represented.

The ethical changes already visible through a comparison of the classical examples of this archetypically exemplary genre were powerfully amplified by the way in which the epic genre was transformed from the late fifteenth century onwards. The epic romances of Matteo Maria Boiardo and Ludovico Ariosto freewheelingly incorporated overt allusions to Virgil into narratives which had multiple heroes and multiple strands, which drew on vernacular prose and verse romances, and in which love became a driving motivational force.[47] By combining a structural transformation of the single narrative line of classical epic with an ethical transformation of heroism these poems implicitly pressed for an identification between their formal and ethical features: heroes who are lovers keep on seeing new objects of desire, and their narrators keep on multiplying love stories as they defer the dynastic marriages for which they are ultimately bound. That form indicated the co-dependency of ethos and structure in epic, and implied that those co-dependent features achieved a distinctively modern form in epic romances. It also implied that genres survive by adaptive imitation.

Furthermore, epic, adaptively imitated in this way, had the potential to give immense weight to the metaphorical accretions which had grown up around *imitatio*. In particular it could give a deep explanatory power to the opposition to which Erasmus had given such emphasis, between successful imitation as the live birth from the brain on the one hand, and failed imitation as the creation of a mere *simulacrum* of an original on the other. Indeed epic romance had the potential to turn that metaphorical opposition into a central driver of plot, structure, and ethics. With Ariosto the explicit (though by no means readily realized) goal of the epic hero became dynastic marriage.[48] Hence the heroes of epic romance could be regarded as bringing past texts and past values back to a new life in a very literal way, through fathering children and new dynasties. Meanwhile the delusive visions associated with a failed imitation could acquire a corresponding association with dilation and delay, as heroes fell repeatedly for delusive semblances of the ideal goal of recreative *imitatio* of epic through dynastic marriage, by

47. Colin Burrow, *Epic Romance: Homer to Milton* (Oxford, 1993); Patricia A. Parker, *Inescapable Romance: Studies in the Poetics of a Mode* (Princeton, 1979).
48. Andrew Fichter, *Poets Historical: Dynastic Epic in the Renaissance* (New Haven, 1982).

running after a fleeting glimpse of the lovely pagan Angelica, or by seeing imaginary semblances of past lovers which pull them away from what is supposed to be their exemplary course.

Those distracting semblances and *simulacra* of the good could also take on new religious overtones in these new times: very often in Italian epic romances the ghosts and delusions of the classical epic tradition are represented as products, not of divine intervention, but of sorcery, witchcraft, diseased imaginations, or of Satan himself. Boiardo's *Orlando innamorato* set the tone. Boiardo transformed the episode in which Juno created a ghostly phantasm of Aeneas which drew Turnus away from the battlefield into one in which the hero Ranaldo is tricked into fighting a demon who has been disguised as his adversary Gradasso by the mage Malagise (*Orlando innamorato*, 1.5.13–56).[49] The simulacral and diabolical could unite.

It was in Torquato Tasso's *Gerusalemme liberata* of 1581 that the creative tension resulting from the adaptive imitation of epic reached a climax. In the ill-omened Canto 13 of Tasso's poem the enchanter Ismeno attempts to prevent the Christian forces who are besieging Jerusalem from making siege engines from a nearby wood. He does so by summoning a mass of demons and 'fantasma orrendo' to protect the forest (*GL*, 13.25.5).[50] These terrify the Christian forces. Eventually the hero Tancred is sent into the enchanted wood. He bursts through what Tasso describes as the 'simulacro' of flame (*GL*, 13.36.6), but then sees a cedar tree that speaks to him with the voice of his dead pagan love Clorinda. This *simulacrum*, which is imitated from the episode of the talking tree Polydorus in Book 3 of Virgil's *Aeneid* (3.13–68), is presented as at once a delusion and a powerful generator of emotion. Its ontological status reflects the uneasy status of the exemplary epic: to create the perfect neoclassical hero Tasso wishes to strip away the accretions of romance and even of the more marvellous episodes in the *Aeneid* from his hero's very mind, and with them too the errors of pagan religion; but those accretions are the very stuff of which his hero's experience and his own plot is built.

The result is one of the great moments in Western imitative fiction, in which the imitator and his central character are both at once in love with

---

49. On Boiardo and the phantom Aeneas, see Dennis Looney, *Compromising the Classics: Romance Epic Narrative in the Italian Renaissance* (Detroit, 1996), pp. 77–90: 'in his imitation the Renaissance poet uses romance narrative techniques to lure the reader away from the epic source of his scene in the *Innamorato*', p. 77.

50. Quotations from Torquato Tasso, *Gerusalemme liberata*, ed. Lanfranco Caretti (Turin, 1980).

the simulacral imitation of an ancient text and ethically committed to destroying it. Tancred in the enchanted forest is caught in a nightmare in which his entire experience becomes a *simulacrum* of reality:

> Qual l'infermo talor ch'in sogno scorge
> drago o cinta di fiamme alta Chimera,
> se ben sospetta o in parte anco s'accorge
> che 'l simulacro sia non forma vera,
> pur desia di fuggir, tanto gli porge
> spavento la sembianza orrida e fera,
> tal il timido amante a pien non crede
> a i falsi inganni, e pur ne teme e cede.   (*GL*, 13.44)

As the sicke man that in his sleepe doth see
Some oughly dragon or some chimere new,
Though he suspect or halfe perswaded bee,
It is an idle dreame [*simulacro*], no monster trew,
Yet still he feares, he quakes, and strives to flee,
So fearefull is that wondrous forme to vew;
      So feard the knight, yet he both knew and thought
      All were illusions false by witchcraft wrought.[51]

The episode of Tancred in the haunted wood is exemplary in many respects. It illustrates how the epic when adapted to Christian and dynastic purposes is pulled in multiple directions: the vivid imaginings which arise from imitating a pagan poem create what is in effect an illusory alternative reality. This simultaneously generates overwhelming emotion and an awareness that those emotions arise from entities which are fictional. That in turn generates a desire to destroy these illusions of the mind, which are explicitly associated at once with sorcery, with imitations of classical epic, with the conventions of romances, and with the process of adapting epic to present customs.

The allusive and psychological processes that result are profoundly complex. The apparently simple desire to pare away the simulacral accretions of romance in order to create a hero who is adapted to the purposes of a dynastic epic entails destroying the very substance of the fiction which has been created by adapting past epic to the present. And as if to mark that hideous tension, both the poet and the hero in the passage quoted above enlist a very surprising ally to assist them: the voice of that arch illusion-buster and enemy to organized religion, Lucretius. It was Lucretius who insisted that

---

51. Translation from Torquato Tasso, *Godfrey of Bulloigne: A Critical Edition of Edward Fairfax's Translation of Tasso's Gerusalemme liberata*, ed. Kathleen M. Lea and T. M. Gang (Oxford, 1981).

neither Chimaeras nor centaurs could exist, and that such hybrid beings were the products of the conjunction of *simulacra*, the thin films of atoms which flow from objects and enable them to be perceived, of distinct species flitting into the air (*DRN*, 4.722–48; 5.855–987). And with a profound irony it is this voice of pagan scepticism that helps Tancred, the Christian hero, in his attempt to drive imitative *simulacra* from his mind.

In later epic romances the suppression of the ghostly doubles of epic and of the illusory imitations of true purpose (which frequently are given female form), becomes both a principle of ethics and a driver of the narrative. Phantasms and *simulacra* of real women spring up with particular vigour in Protestant adaptations of epic, where they tend to be associated with not only paganism but also Catholic idolatry. One of the most vivid members of this legion of ghostly beings is encountered early in Edmund Spenser's *Faerie Queene* (1590–6). This is a robotic sprite who is summoned from the cave of Morpheus and instructed by the (implicitly Catholic) Archimago (whose name suggests he is at once a mage and an arch maker of images or semblances) to replicate Una, the destined partner of the Red Cross knight. That ghostly replicant is herself the product of a long series of imitations of Ovid's description of the Cave of Morpheus.[52] But her literal creator is Archimago, who

> made a Lady of that other Spright,
> And fram'd of liquid ayre her tender partes
> So liuely, and so like in all mens sight,
> That weaker sence it could haue rauisht quight:
> The maker selfe for all his wondrous witt,
> Was nigh beguiled with so goodly sight: (*FQ*, 1.1.45)[53]

The imitator of nature makes a bodiless double of the 'real' heroine, which is all air and nothing more, and which 'He taught to imitate that Lady trew'. This sprite he instructs to allure the hero into a carnal union that reduces the structure of dynastic epic itself to a *simulacrum*: the Red Cross knight is tempted to indulge in a mock marriage with a piece of 'liquid ayre'; and

---

52. For the role of this episode in the genesis of the mock heroic poem in England, see Colin Burrow, '"Full of the Maker's Guile": Ovid on Imitating and on the Imitation of Ovid', in Philip Hardie, ed., *Ovidian Transformations: Essays on Ovid's Metamorphoses and its Reception* (Cambridge, 1999), 271–87.

53. Text from Edmund Spenser, *The Faerie Queene*, ed. A. C. Hamilton, Hiroshi Yamashita, and Toshiyuki Suzuki, 2nd edn (Harlow, 2001).

that mock marriage can result in no birth because it is a union with a substanceless semblance.

That *simulacrum* of epic romance goals is replicated repeatedly in the multiplications of false Florimels and deceptive women who people Spenser's poem. These are not just re-embodiments of the ghosts and phantasms of Virgil's *Aeneid*; they are rather consciously Protestant reimaginings of those ghosts, which build on Virgil's reluctance to give substantial life and authority to female characters like the ghost of Creusa. They become creatures who fuse idolatry and lustful imaginings with the falsity inherent to beings who derive from acts of imitation. In sixteenth-century epics—which are consciously adapting an ancient genre to new linguistic and religious environments—the metaphors by which theorists of *imitatio* sought to differentiate a 'living' imitation from a mere shadow become generative principles of plot, and at once enable and justify a transformation of the narrative structure of epic. A goal of generative marriage combines with a multiplication of *simulacra* of that main plot. And that made early modern epic romances structurally, ethically, and thematically distinct from ancient epic in ways that were instantly apparent to their readers.

Epic was therefore by the later sixteenth century the perfect test-bed for practical and theoretical reflection about adaptive imitation. The 'new' genre, that adapted epic to the age of romance, became a centre not just of innovative thinking but of thinking about how to be new. Giraldi Cinthio's treatise on romances from 1554 contains relatively conventional discussions of *imitatio* and decorum, but (*pace* Pigman) shows clear signs of having absorbed Erasmus's concerns with historically adaptive imitation into its wider argument.[54] Indeed Cinthio insists that adaptation to new customs and occasions has always been central to the epic tradition. So Virgil, whom Cinthio regards as a model of decorum, adapted Homer, since 'What was drawn from [Homer] needed to be better digested and brought to that perfection which would be entirely consonant with the time in which it was written, so that what was drawn from him would be improved. Cicero

---

54. Giambattista Cinzio Giraldi, *Giraldi Cinthio on Romances: Being a Translation of the Discorso intorno al comporre dei romanzi*, ed. Henry L. Snuggs (Lexington, 1968), pp. 126–33. The discussion of decorum, pp. 56–62, notes that romance writers who place their work in antiquity may use the names of pagan gods with decorum. For fuller discussion of the critical arguments about romance, see Daniel Javitch, *Proclaiming a Classic: The Canonization of Orlando Furioso* (Princeton, 1991) and Bernard Weinberg, *A History of Literary Criticism in the Italian Renaissance* (Chicago, Ill., 1961), pp. 954–1073.

taught us this when he said that the Romans borrowed many things from the Greeks but then made them better' (p. 32).

The writings of Greece, and the epic poetry of Ennius, Cinthio argued, came to be regarded as 'inept' or 'unapt' (*inetto*) as later refinements of them emerged. Cinthio places great emphasis on that word *inetto*: indeed he digresses to consider whether the Greeks had a word which corresponded to it.[55] The gist of Cinthio's overall argument is that the multi-stranded many-heroed form of the romance *is* the modern equivalent of the epic genre, duly adapted to the changed conventions of the present, and that ancient epic unadapted to the times would no longer be apt to the occasion. Cinthio, that is, put the principle of historical decorum which Erasmus had outlined in *Ciceronianus* to the service of vernacular literary theory, and made it both the principal foundation of arguments for generic change and a marker of value: the unapt imitation is the inept, a failure to remake a genre in new times is a marker of poetic ineptitude.

According to Cinthio, however, there are decorous limits even to historical adaptations of the epic genre. He is content for Ariosto to imitate both Virgil and Boiardo, and for the epic to acquire multiple heroes and to concern itself with love, since in doing these things it is avoiding the 'inetto'. But he also imposes boundaries of ethical decorum on the genre of epic romance. This he does because a heroic poem is both a work in which an author imitates an earlier text and one in which an author describes a hero who himself could be imitated as an *exemplum* of behaviour by a reader. This dual form of imitation, in which the author's transformative imitation of an earlier text is delimited by the requirement to provide an ethically imitable hero, imposes transtemporal boundaries on the range of behaviour that could be considered heroic.

In setting out those boundaries Cinthio tends to contrast vernacular verse epic romances with romances in prose, which, to his eyes, overstep the limits of ethical decorum. Cinthio is uneasy in particular about some moments of unheroic behaviour in the Spanish prose romance *Amadís de Gaula*. Ariosto, he says, would have been criticized if he had incorporated into his romance the moment when Amadis faints at the sight of his Oriana in battle. For 'it seemed to Ariosto that, even if perhaps those things were fitting either to the nation or the times in which *Amadís* was written, they

---

55. Giambattista Cinzio Giraldi, *Discorsi intorno al comporre de i romanzi, delle comedie, e delle tragedie, e di altre maniere di poesie* (Venice, 1554), p. 36.

did not suit his own times (*non convenissero*) or the people whom he brings into his Romances' (p. 33/p. 37). An imitator of classical epic who replicated everything that happens in a prose romance, without moral discrimination in making the adaptation, might create absurdity.

This simple claim, coming out of very traditional concerns for the apt and the decorous in the art of rhetoric, and combined with the equally trad-itional concern for the exemplary in epic, points forward to one of the greatest literary consequences of Erasmus's arguments about historical decorum. Erasmus had implied that *un*-adaptive *imitatio* would only produce fleshless, substanceless anachronisms like his mad Ciceronian Nosoponus. Cinthio had taken an example from *Amadís de Gaula* to insist that the practice of historically adaptive imitation also had ethical limits.

From the combination of these two claims by sixteenth-century writers on imitation one can see the dim outlines of a new genre emerging. In 1605 appeared the first volume of Cervantes's *Don Quixote*, a work which began, in effect, as a study of unapt and inept *imitatio*. Don Quixote is one of the world's great literalistic imitators. He imitates exactly the text from which Cinthio had taken his example of an episode which could *not* decorously be adapted to the genre of epic: Quixote follows Amadis de Gaul in his dress, his speech, and in the reality which he delusively believes himself to inhabit.[56] His failure to adapt his vocabulary or his conduct to his times, to his own social status, or to the brute facts of his world is matched by his affection for phantasms of the mind, his Dulcinea and his windmill giants. These in turn show a deep-seated debt to Tasso's association between the conventions of romances and the delusive processes of the imagination.

Don Quixote's obsessive *imitatio* of the singular example of Amadis de Gaul is, however, also a vernacular calque of the obsessive imitation of the singular example of Cicero in the Neo-Latin tradition. 'The lankness of his body...the thinness and pallor of his face' are physical marks of the obsessive imitator, and make him a true heir of Erasmus's obsessive Ciceronian imitator Nosoponus.[57] The Don has 'dried up flesh and withered

56. Kenneth P. Allen, 'Cervantes'"Galatea" and the "Discorso intorno al comporre dei Romanzi" of Giraldi Cinthio', *Revista Hispánica Moderna* 39 (1976), 52–68 argues for the influence of Cinthio on Cervantes (who was in Italy, 1569–75). See also Alban Forcione, 'Cervantes, Tasso, and the Romanzi Polemic', *Revue de Littérature Comparée* 44 (1970), 433–43.

57. Miguel de Cervantes Saavedra, *The Ingenious Hidalgo Don Quixote de la Mancha*, trans. John Rutherford (London, 2000), p. 584. Citations are from this edition. For a general account of Cervantes and Erasmus, see Marcel Bataillon, *Érasme et l'Espagne: recherches sur l'histoire spiritu-elle du XVIe siècle* (Paris, 1937), pp. 819–44. He notes the dissemination of *Ciceronianus* in Spain on p. 340.

face' (p. 25), as Cervantes describes him: his withered shanks ostentatiously lack the kind of muscular skill which Quintilian had so strongly associated with a successful, well-exercised orator and with the successful imitator. Quixote himself shows he is aware of this aspect of his genesis when he insists to Sancho Panza in the Sierra Morena that Amadis de Gaul was unique, and should be the sole object of *imitatio*:

> A fig's end for Don Belianis and for all those who say that he was in any way the equal of Amadis, because I swear they are mistaken. Let me add that when a painter wants to become famous for his art, he tries to copy originals by the finest artists he knows. And this same rule holds good for nearly all the trades and professions of importance that serve to adorn a society; and so what a man must do and what a man does if he wishes to achieve a reputation for prudence and long-suffering, is to imitate Ulysses, in whose person and labours Homer painted for us a living portrait of these two qualities, just as Virgil showed us in the person of Aeneas the courage of a dutiful son and the sagacity of a brave and able captain, not describing or revealing them as they were but as they should have been, to leave models of their virtues for future generations. In this same way Amadis was the pole star, the morning star, the sun of brave and enamoured knights, and we who serve under the banner of love and chivalry should all imitate him. If, then, this is so, as it is, I consider, friend Sancho, that the knight errant who best imitates [*imitará*] Amadis will be the closest to attaining perfection in chivalry.   (p. 207)

Cervantes was a genius at spotting the intellectual elisions and confusions within the major debates of his age. The Don's speech elegantly reiterates most of the conflations of thought which ran through sixteenth-century arguments about *imitatio*, but pointedly says nothing about adapting a prior text to new time. This is despite the fact he hurls together so many other versions of imitation from the commonplace book of his mind: he conflates ethical emulation with the acquisition of skills, and even combines imitation in the sense of pictorial representation with imitation in the sense of reproducing a moral exemplar. The great unspoken counter-truth beneath his tissue of cliché, however, is Erasmus's main argument in the *Ciceronianus*. *Imitatio* without aptness generates insubstantial absurdity.

The whole of *Don Quixote* prises apart the two main senses of the verb to 'imitate' in early modern poetics. In theory an author who adaptively imitated Virgil might create a hero who was himself an *exemplum* worthy of imitation in new times. That would, in theory at least, produce a synergistic relationship between an imitating author's own (literary) imitation of an earlier author and his readers' (ethical) imitation of the principles embodied in the imitation. In *Don Quixote* this ideal synthesis—which had since the start of the sixteenth century always been more an ideal than something actually achieved—is made to collapse. Cervantes took the *simulacrum*, redefined as the historically unapt and physically inept imitation, and turned it into the generating force behind what was to become a new genus or kind of fiction. The mad Ciceronian became an obsessive follower of Amadis, mounted a horse, and tilted at the simulacral giants of his imagination. Meanwhile the author Cervantes imitated earlier romances adaptively, and described in graphic detail the changed world which makes a mockery of the knight's imitation of Amadis. *Don Quixote* takes what Erasmus says literally: the whole stage of the world has changed (there *are* no magicians, no damsels, no castles), but this hero still follows exactly in the hoof-prints of Amadis.

Not only does Quixote imitate Amadis de Gaul. This Spanish hidalgo also demonstrates in practical form the fears that the Spanish humanist Juan Luis Vives had expressed in the immediate aftermath of Erasmus's *Ciceronianus*: with his first tilt at the windmills he demonstrates that the requirement to imitate so as to adapt old texts and ethical systems to new times necessarily *does* lead to the collapse of the naïve view that fiction is in a simple way morally exemplary.[58] Literally imitating Aeneas when he carries Anchises on his shoulders might make the imitator look a touch absurd. But imitating Don Quixote in the way he imitates Amadis would not just be bad for windmills; it would be madness. Inept as a knight, an imitator of language and behaviour rather than a reanimator of past *ingenium* or *vis*, unapt to his own times, he is askew from his world.

But *Don Quixote*, the novel in which he appears, was far more than a simple attack on imitation that failed to adapt to the times. Indeed imitation is hard to attack because it is never a stable target—and that is one reason why the Ciceronian debates were debates rather than a school or a single doctrine. *Imitatio* can unsettle relationships between a text and its prototypes, between a text and its readers, and between past and present. Cervantes positioned a literalistic imitator within an adaptive imitation of a romance, but that conjunction does not simply generate a satire directed against the literalistic imitator. It enabled Don Quixote the character to occupy

---

58. See Hampton, *Rhetoric of Exemplarity*, pp. 237–96, for the view that 'Cervantes depicts a world in which the imitation of models has run amok, but where the concern for virtue so central to humanist ideology has virtually vanished' (p. 238).

the exact point of convergence between madness, pathos, idealism, and
originality. It was also one thing that made *Don Quixote* a work which later
authors wanted to imitate. If an imitating author creates a text in which an
inept imitator reaches perfect identity with the object of his imitation in
completely changed times, then suddenly the scale of ineptitude flips round,
and the imitating author who represents the failed imitator becomes himself
a new and indeed even 'original' phenomenon.

Something similar happens within the fiction itself. Literalistic imitation
becomes the agent of forced historical disjunction, and can enable a comic
dialectic between present and past which unsettles both present and past
values. Don Quixote, the imitator within the text, is as a result not simply
an absurd embodiment of inept *imitatio* like Nosoponus: he can also seem to
be an idealistic and noble throwback to a world bigger and better than that
of the present. The genius of Cervantes—that is to say the distinctive achievement which so many generations of his later imitators among authors of
romances and novels wanted to follow—lay in making the inept *so* inept that
it became apt. That ineptness is a core principle of the Don, and it brings
with it the thickening of the detail with which the world around him is
described that came to be called 'realism'. It goes further than that, though.
The Don becomes a character who does not even always remain apt to himself. With remarkable frequency he says things which do not accord with the
expectations about his character held by those around him: sometimes he
sounds crazy, but then he has moments of extraordinary pathos, wisdom, and
lucidity. Repeatedly readers and audiences within the novel have to adjust
their view of him. What kind of ethical agent is he? And could one, actually,
define Don Quixotism, given his inconsistent nature? That principle of
complete unpredictability gives him the edge of inimitability, the aura of a
distinctive 'character' in the fictional sense, which made so many later authors
wish to imitate him. Cervantes transformed the merely gestural imitator into
what might in various senses be called a 'novel' creation.

As a result *Don Quixote* opens up wider reflections on the double attitudes to past writing which underlie the imitation of earlier authors.
Imitating authors value the past, but they also struggle to preserve the value
of that past in a world which has changed, and to which the works they
imitate no longer appear apt. The imitator consequently seeks to reconcile
change and nostalgia, and desires at once that the imitated texts should
mutate *and* that they should remain stable archetypes or paradigms of conduct or composition. In that respect all imitating authors potentially have a

trace of Don Quixote: they seek to follow an ancient example within times that have irreversibly changed.

Jorge Luis Borges recognized this aspect of *Don Quixote*, of course: his Pierre Menard 'did not propose to copy' *Don Quixote* but 'his admirable ambition was to produce pages which would coincide—word for word and line for line—with those of Miguel de Cervantes'.[59] 'To be, in some way, Cervantes and to arrive at *Don Quixote* seemed to him less arduous—and consequently less interesting—than to continue being Pierre Menard and to arrive at *Don Quixote* through the experiences of Pierre Menard' (p. 33). But Menard's word-for-word copy of *Don Quixote* would be a different thing from Cervantes's *Don Quixote* because it was produced in an entirely different world. When Borges wrote 'Pierre Menard, Author of *Don Quixote*' in 1938 he presumably could not have appreciated the almost miraculous coincidence that in 1971 Erasmus's *Ciceronianus* would be edited for the *Opera Omnia* by the French scholar named Pierre Mesnard—although Mesnard was in post at the University of Poitiers by 1937 and was working on the *Ciceronianus* when he died, and Borges had sensitive tentacles. But it is from the dilemmas of inept replication explored in *Ciceronianus* that *Don Quixote* derives much of its force.

I have suggested that the medium of print intensified a desire to preserve the impress of authorial uniqueness at exactly the same time as it enabled mass mechanical reproductions of a text. Not only that, but the language of uniqueness ('expression', 'form', 'character') had rich etymological associations with the techniques of mechanical reproduction. Given all of that, it is not surprising that Don Quixote, ineptly driven by the desire to re-express the actions recorded in printed books of romances, became himself at once unique and the object of imitation and replication. In the second volume of his adventures he reads false records of his actions produced by Cervantes's own imitators (2.59). Nor is it entirely a surprise that he should visit a print-shop in which he sees his own apocryphal adventures being printed (2.62),[60] or that he is greeted in Barcelona as the *real* Don Quixote 'not the fraudulent, fictitious, apocryphal recently displayed to our gaze in false histories' (p. 904; 2.61), or that other characters in the novel pretend to be him. *Simulacra* surround the imitator.

59. Jorge Luis Borges, *Ficciones* (London, 1993), p. 32.
60. See Roger Chartier, *Inscription and Erasure: Literature and Written Culture from the Eleventh to the Eighteenth Century* (Philadelphia, 2007), pp. 28–45.

These moments in his adventures might take us back to one of the most quoted, but also the most double-edged passages, in *Ciceronianus*. Bulephorus insists that

> Cicero doesn't exist in his entirety, as we made plain enough earlier; he is hardly half there in fact, whether we think of vocabulary, idiom, rhythms, or corpus of writings.
>
> NOSOPONUS: Where does he exist in his entirety then?
>
> BULEPHORUS: Nowhere except in himself. But if you want to express [*exprimere*] the whole Cicero you cannot express [*exprimere*] yourself, and if you do not express yourself [*exprimis*] your speech will be a lying mirror [*mendax speculum*]. (p. 399/p. 649)

A superficial reading of this passage might see it as being about 'self-expression' as against imitation: avoid servility to Cicero and you will be able to 'express' yourself. But that verb 'exprimo' is not as simple as it appears. Erasmus routinely uses it to describe someone who attempts to 'replicate' or 'imitate' Cicero. He and his contemporaries could also use the same verb in the sense 'print' or 'replicate'. The great humanist and editor is in this passage suggesting not only that it is desirable to do more than simply replicate the words of Cicero, but also that because many works of Cicero are lost it is simply impossible to 'express' or 'print' the totality of what he is. What appears to be a statement about 'self-expression' is shadowed by a Borgesian *simulacrum* of itself: 'even if you wished to print the whole of Cicero all over again and identify yourself with it you would still be missing several pieces'. Cicero is a mould or a model or a form that can never be fully replicated by that which copies it, because the mould itself is partially incomplete. And if that is the case, can we *ever* 'stamp out, print, express' that which is inside *ourselves*? What is it that enables an author to produce words that are *more* than a 'lying mirror', and which print, 'express', or press out the totality of that author?

The genesis of Don Quixote consequently lies not just in *Amadís de Gaula* and *Tirant lo Blanc*, but in the rich foundational paradox of renaissance poetics: you must both be like an archetype and yet unlike it in being apt to an age that is immeasurably different from the age inhabited by that archetype; and, like the archetype itself, you might yourself be an imperfect work in progress, which could be supplemented by others. Don Quixote himself is the paradigm instance of what might be called the revenge of the *simulacrum*. The failed imitation, which is a mere specular delusion lacking in substance, transforms itself by virtue of its very deficiency as a 'living' imitation into a source of creative energy, and acquires a 'je ne sais quoi' of its specular and satirical own by virtue of its unaptness to its age. Imitate with conscious and deliberate ineptness or unaptness to your times and suddenly you may create a text so original that it can be endlessly replicated through the printing press, and may even generate an entirely new genre. The impossible prescriptions of *imitatio*—resemble an author and yet be like yourself, be at once apt to your times and to your original, be at once a 'character' and someone who can adapt to unexpected new occasions, express your genius and carry the impress of your source—were presented with such power and authority to the youth of sixteenth-century Europe that those who absorbed those principles more or less had to work the paradoxical and self-contradictory energies of those prescriptions out into fiction.

Castiglione's courtier, perfectly adapted to and master of his courtly environment, seems as different as it is possible to be from the inept Don Quixote. But those two great creations of early modernity are mirror images of each other. The Don, a provincial hidalgo determined to enter a social and imaginary realm which belongs to another age and a social group of which he can never hope to be a part, pursues imitation with painstaking literalism. He replicates Amadis, he duplicates his words, he reruns his actions, and over and over again he fails to replicate his skill because he has imitated un-aptly. Meanwhile his author became the star creator of a new genre, while the literalistic imitator whom he invented seems almost a shadow of his author's own nostalgia for an earlier world.

The mass appeal of both *Il Cortegiano* and *Don Quixote* depended on the way in which they reconfigured arguments about *imitatio* explicitly to address the aspirations of different social groups in the vernacular. *Don Quixote* did so by constructing its audience as canny, worldly and highly literate people, who could perceive both the incompetence of the Don and the implied critique of the social world which he and they inhabit, but who also (they are reading an adaptation of romance, after all) shared his love of romances. *Il Cortegiano* did so by suggesting that through *imitatio* it was possible to acquire a skilled lexical and political independence which was perfectly suited to articulate citizens who inhabited a public sphere. Both creations were radically dependent on the concept of adaptive *imitatio*, the complexities and contradictions of which repeatedly stimulated sixteenth- and early seventeenth-century imitating authors to make it new.

6

Formal Imitation

The 'Leaden-Headed Germans' and Their English Heirs

The story told in this chapter requires us initially to move back in time from the wonderful year of 1528, and from the creative consequences of that year in *Don Quixote* and the theory of adaptive imitation, to the immensely fertile early phase of the Ciceronian debates in the first decade of the sixteenth century. Those debates not only raised questions about what it was to imitate an earlier text so as to 'adapt' it to the times, but also stimulated wider speculations about what the characteristic and imitable features of an author were. The arguments between Castiglione's friend Pietro Bembo and Gianfrancesco Pico in particular encouraged later European writers to think about the 'form' of earlier authors' texts—in various senses of the word 'form'—as something which could be imitated. The narrative presented in this chapter is intricate, but it rests on a very straightforward claim. The Ciceronian controversies stimulated a complex range of thinking about how to imitate the 'form' rather than the words of an earlier author; and that thinking developed, through the work of Philipp Melanchthon, Johannes Sturm, and Roger Ascham, into a view of *imitatio* which stressed how imitating authors should read the texts they imitated with an eye to how those texts were structured. That encompassed 'form' in many levels and senses, from the choice of rhetorical figures and tropes, through sentence structure, right up to the ways in which arguments were set out. The focus on formal analysis encouraged by this view of *imitatio* had a huge influence on the practice both of imitation and of authorship in later sixteenth-century England. It enabled and encouraged later English Elizabethan authors—John Lyly is one powerful instance, but also Ben Jonson, who is the subject of Chapter 7—to develop highly distinctive, and indeed imitable styles of their own.

Pico and Bembo

One of the most frequently reprinted exchanges from the Ciceronian debates was that between Gianfrancesco Pico and Pietro Bembo in 1512–13.[1] This group of letters was first published in Rome soon after their composition, probably in 1513. The letters were then republished at Basel in a larger edition of Pico's works by Erasmus's friend and publisher Johann Froben in 1518.[2] They therefore reached a wide readership in both Southern and Northern Europe.

Gianfrancesco Pico was an advocate of eclectic *imitatio*—that is to say the imitation of many authors rather than of the single example of Cicero—who had absorbed the Platonizing arguments of Cicero's *Orator*. He insisted that the 'idea' of a perfect orator can either be intuited or abstracted from many different examples, and that this 'idea', rather than a single author, should be the object of imitation. To support his argument Pico indulges with delicious excess in many of the metaphors associated with imitation. He argues that Nature is not exhausted in the modern world, but remains capable of strong birth of new *ingenium*;[3] but as a result of an excessive devotion to the single example of Cicero 'some talents have been so wasted and devoured as if by disease ... that they present themselves more in the likeness of a phantom and vanishing shade (*simulachri et evanidae umbrae magis quam vivi animi effigiem*) than in that of a living soul' (p. 30). The word *simulacrum* there becomes a figure for the obsessive reader and imitator of Cicero, like Erasmus's Nosoponus or Cervantes's Don Quixote, who reduces his own bodily substance to a mere shadow by obsessive focus on a single corpus of texts.

Pico also brought to the traditional opposition between body and shadow a highly distinctive version of the notion that *imitatio* entailed following in the footsteps of the ancients. This, he argued, is not a good way of proceeding for the simple reason that foot sizes vary; so unless we could find the 'lasts' or moulds which were used in an ancient shoe-shop to make shoes for

1. For the wider quattrocento background to the debate, see Martin L. McLaughlin, *Literary Imitation in the Italian Renaissance* (Oxford, 1995), pp. 249–74. McLaughlin emphasizes the significance of Bembo's arguments, which had extensive influence in Italy; from a wider European perspective Pico was arguably more influential.

2. Giovanni Francesco Pico della Mirandola, *Io. Francisci Pici Mirandulae domini ... Physici libri duo, i. De appetitu primae materiae ... ii. De elementis. Et Rhetorici duo, De imitatione, ad Petrum Bembum. P. Bembi de imitatione liber unus* (Basel, 1518), pp. 53–123.

3. JoAnn DellaNeva, ed., *Ciceronian Controversies* (Cambridge, Mass., and London, 2007), p. 28. Citations and translations from this edition.

every different size of foot we will end up slipping around in or spilling over the edges of the footsteps of the ancients (p. 31). That apparently trivial detail in his argument is highly significant. The word Pico uses for 'lasts' or moulds is *formulae*, little moulds. That word is notably double-edged. It implies that each foot has its own proportions and needs its distinctive 'pattern' to make shoes that would fit it. But it can also mean both a scalable model or paradigm (and those senses lie behind the present-day mathematical usage of the term) and what we still call a 'formula' of words that can be used without variation in a particular context.

The word implies that Pico regarded what is now called a literary 'model' or example as a thing of its own size and peculiar shape, but also as something which might by quasi-mathematical means produce a replica of the same proportions but different dimensions. It may also suggest a kind of replication which had the potential to become (as we would say) formulaic.[4] Pico argued that it is in practice impossible without adaptation to make the 'formula', or the little mould, of an earlier author fit the feet of a new one, since everyone has a *genius*—and Pico appears to have been the first person to have used this word as a substitute for *ingenium*—and natural propensity ('genium propesionemque naturae', p. 22) which is distinctive to themselves.

Those distinctive qualities were for Pico partly what would now be called formal characteristics. He defends Virgil against the charge of excessive imitation by insisting that he had his own form of versification, his own features (*lineamenta*—both the outlines of a face, and perhaps too 'lines' considered as geometrical features) and in particular had his own and proper way of arranging material ('suos ipse habet numeros, propria tenet lineamenta, dispositionemque in primis peculiarem et maxime propriam', p. 18). The possession of these made him an emulator and not merely an imitator of the ancients.

Towards the end of his first letter Pico re-emphasizes the distinctiveness of an author's structural techniques: he locates the character of an author not just in *elocutio*, or the choice of words, which can be imitated, but in other elements of rhetoric—in *inventio*, the discovery of matter for a speech, and in *dispositio*, the arrangement of its elements in order. Since all of these are distinctive to a particular author, he argues, an individual author is in effect inimitable (p. 34). This goes significantly beyond Quintilian, who had

---

4. Cicero uses *formula* when discussing the 'type and pattern of each genre of speaking' in *Orator*, 75.23.

associated imitation principally with word-choice but had urged an imitator also to attend to a range of features which were not lexical (the ways an earlier orator uses the exordium, his control over the emotions of the audience, and the way he uses popular applause to win a case).[5]

Pico's principal significance in the history of *imitatio* is therefore perhaps not so much his very visible Platonizing tendencies (though those provide powerful evidence that the Platonizing Cicero of the *Orator* was thoroughly absorbed into thinking about imitation by the early sixteenth century), as his view of what is *in*imitable: the lost 'formula', or little mould, the pattern, the paradigm, of an earlier author's skill inheres as much in a structure as in word-choice. It is what he terms the *constructio* (p. 36), or the way in which a work is put together, that makes it distinctive to a particular author. This means even if one were to use only words deployed by Cicero one would never write quite like Cicero.

Pico also insists that different people are drawn to different 'characters' of style (p. 36), and, moreover, that individual authors may have their own characters of style which are not reproducible. When discussing this area Pico is prone to use the language of literally 'expressive' replication—a stamp or a mould or a 'character' or a 'form' that presses out a reproduction—in the service of idiosyncrasy. A writer has his own 'forma'; the 'formula' of his foot size is particular to him; a 'character' or stamp of style is not generic but specific to an individual. These aspects of Pico's vocabulary carry the form

---

5. *Institutio*, 10.2.27: 'We must consider the appropriateness with which those orators handle the circumstances and persons involved in the various cases in which they were engaged, and observe the judgment and powers of arrangement which they reveal, and the manner in which everything they say, not excepting those portions of their speeches which seem designed merely to delight their audiences, is concentrated on securing the victory over their opponents. We must note their procedure in the exordium, the method and variety of their statement of facts, the power displayed in proof and refutation, the skill revealed in their appeal to every kind of emotion, and the manner in which they make use of popular applause to serve their case, applause which is most honourable when it is spontaneous and not deliberately courted. If we have thoroughly appreciated all these points, we shall be able to imitate truly' ('Illuc intendenda mens, quantum fuerit illis viris decoris in rebus atque personis, quod consilium, quae dispositio, quam omnia, etiam quae delectationi videantur data, ad victoriam spectent; quid agatur prooemio, quae ratio et quam varia narrandi, quae vis probandi ac refellendi, quanta in adfectibus omnis generis movendis scientia, quamque laus ipsa popularis utilitatis gratia adsumpta, quae tum est pulcherrima cum sequitur, non cum arcessitur. Haec si perviderimus, tum vere imitabimur'). There is a clear echo of this claim in Erasmus's *Ciceronianus*: how can we imitate Cicero's 'skill in arrangement [*dispositionis ratio*], his development of propositions, his judgment in handling arguments [*consilium in tractandis argumentis*], his effectiveness in stirring the emotions [*vis in movendis affectibus*], the charm that captivated his audience', Desiderius Erasmus, *Collected Works of Erasmus. Vol. 28, Literary and Educational Writings 6: Ciceronianus*, ed. A. H. T. Levi (Toronto, 1986), p. 376/631.

and pressure of the medium in which his treatise came to be disseminated: the way of describing the distinctive voice of a new author is stamped, in print, out of an earlier language of mechanical replication. *Exprimo* is a standard word for the printing of books in early modern Latin usage.[6] A text is the impress of a prior character or *modulus*, a little mould which is *ex*pressed through its physical impression.

Pietro Bembo's reply to Pico was the single most influential expression of the position that came to be called 'Ciceronian'. Bembo insisted that one author should be imitated, and for him that meant Cicero. Bembo also regarded *imitatio* as a matter of transferring the likeness of another person's style into your own writing ('alieni stili similitudinem transferre in tua scripta', p. 56), and so at least implicitly regarded it as principally concerned with word-choice. Over and above this central point of disagreement, however, Bembo and Pico share some significant common principles. Bembo's main ground for advocating the imitation of Cicero alone was not simply a dogmatic belief that Cicero was the best orator. He had a conception of the totality of a text which is analogous to Pico's belief that the distinctive way a piece of writing is put together is part of what makes it characteristic of its author. And for Bembo too that concept of integrity leads him to talk of a work's 'form': 'Imitation, however, embraces the entire form [*formam*] of any piece of writing and demands that one follow the individual parts of that form' (p. 58). That form is a quasi-bodily unity which is spread throughout the structure and body of a text ('in universa stili structura atque corpore versatur', p. 58).

Indeed much of Bembo's argument against eclectic imitation rests on the belief that the work of a particular author is akin to a body or *corpus* to which the *forma* is integral. Once alien elements are imported from other authors in a hybrid imitation that 'form' is compromised; hence eclectic imitation is misguided because it violates the integrity of the *exemplum*.

Bembo's argument with Pico was consequently not just a debate about whether one author or many should be imitated, or whether Cicero is king of the orators. It was grounded on differing conceptions of what the word 'forma' means, and of what is distinctive to an author's style. To put the opposition in crude terms, Pico appears to have regarded 'forma' as a principle of structuration that is intrinsically inimitable, and so each orator should look

---

6. René Hoven, Laurent Grailet, Coen Maas, and Karin Renard-Jadoul, *Lexique de la prose latine de la Renaissance* (Leiden and Boston, 2006), s.v. *exprimo*.

to his own nature, read widely and develop his own 'idea' (or quasi-Platonic 'form') of writing which would suit his own genius, and from which he might produce works which manifested that 'form'. For Bembo, on the other hand, the 'form' of a piece of writing is intrinsic to it and nothing can be added to it or taken away. Hence the only viable imitation is of a single author, whose individual 'forma' would be the object of *imitatio*.

Erasmus claimed not to have read the argument between Pico and Bembo when he composed the first edition of *Ciceronianus*. This may not have been entirely disingenuous, since for the early part of 1518, when Froben's edition of those texts appeared, Erasmus was living not at Froben's house in Basel but at Louvain, and he was during this period hard at work on the second edition of his New Testament. By the time of the second edition of *Ciceronianus*, however, Erasmus had clearly read not just the debate between Bembo and Pico, but also the earlier exchanges between Angelo Poliziano and Paolo Cortese. Nonetheless even the revised version of *Ciceronianus* did not consider the implications of what Pico and Bembo had to say about 'form'. Yet Bembo and Pico in particular had a profound influence on later sixteenth-century attitudes to imitation, and, in ways less visible than but arguably just as profound as Erasmus's *Ciceronianus*, on literary practice too.

Melanchthon

That influence was largely because Bembo's debate with Pico fed into the thinking of the reformer and rhetorician Philipp Melanchthon, whose writings about *imitatio* were to permeate the theory and practice of later sixteenth-century English authors in particular.[7] Melanchthon's work on imitation was written shortly before and after the appearance of Erasmus's *Ciceronianus*, and is found in three places: in a short commentary on Cicero's *De Oratore* (first published in 1525 and much reprinted), at length in the two-book *Elementa Rhetorices*, which came to final form in 1531, and in a

---

7. I am indebted to the reappraisals of Melanchthon in Kathy Eden, *Hermeneutics and the Rhetorical Tradition: Chapters in the Ancient Legacy and its Humanist Reception* (New Haven and London, 1997), pp. 79–89 and Peter Mack, *Renaissance Argument: Valla and Agricola in the Traditions of Rhetoric and Dialectic* (Leiden, 1993), pp. 320–33, as well as to the helpful survey of German Ciceronian scholarship in the sixteenth century, C. J. Classen, 'Cicero inter Germanos Redivivus, II', *Humanistica Lovaniensia* 39 (1990), 157–76. Quotations are from *Philippi Melanthonis Opera quae supersunt omnia*, ed. Karl Gottlieb Bretschneider, Heinrich Ernst Bindseil, and C. A. Schwetschke und Sohn, 28 vols. (Halle, 1834).

posthumously printed commentary on Book 10 of Quintilian, which included a *Commonefactio*, or short essay, on imitation.

The key points of Melanchthon's theory of imitation remain substantially the same in all three works, though one might perhaps detect a distant anti-Erasmian flavour as his thinking develops, perhaps because of the disparaging remarks Erasmus made about him towards the end of *Ciceronianus*.[8] Melanchthon distinguishes in all his writing on imitation between what he terms *imitatio generalis* and *imitatio specialis*. *Imitatio generalis* is the imitation of words and phrases (*formulae*) from a particular period of Latin literature ('est imitatio verborum ac phrasis, seu formularum latini sermonis', 16.722). *Imitatio specialis*, on the other hand, is imitation of a particular author's style. The separation of these two forms of *imitatio* was a significant move. It was designed to cut the ground from beneath the feet of the philological Ciceronians: *imitatio generalis* acknowledged that a detailed understanding of Latin idioms from a specific period was the foundation of writing in a classical style; but lexical and stylistic fidelity to a particular period did not (as the narrowly lexical Ciceronians were thought to believe) restrict imitation to the vocabulary of a single author.

What Melanchthon says about *imitatio specialis* is more significant, and in many respects more original. The imitation of a particular person's style for Melanchthon chiefly entailed determining how that author put things together. The word Melanchthon repeatedly uses for this is *collocatio*.[9] This is an unusually ambiguous word even within the lexicon of rhetorical terms, which abounds in terminology of elastic or multiple sense. 'Collocatio' can mean the ordering or juxtaposition of words, but it can extend upwards to encompass the ways an author structures sentences or his habitual methods of connecting arguments together. Indeed Marius Nizolius, in his lexicon of Ciceronian vocabulary, defined the word simply as 'dispositio', or the skill a rhetorician uses in structuring a speech.[10] Nizolius cites several instances from Cicero's *Orator* which do indeed use 'collocatio' as a near synonym for *dispositio*,[11] but Cicero also uses the word in the phrase *collocatio verborum* to refer to specific conjunctions of words.[12]

8. Erasmus, ed. Levi, *Ciceronianus*, p. 427.   9. On which, see Eden, *Hermeneutics*, pp. 81–3.
10. Marius Nizolius, *Nizolius, sive Thesaurus Ciceronianus* (Basel, 1559), col. 355.
11. e.g. *Orator*, 15.50, 17.54, 70.232; collocation is linked with 'cohaerentia' and used to mean 'ordering of words' at 44.149.
12. *De Oratore*, 1.151, 3.172.

That range of senses—extending through both the structure of an argument and the specific detail of word-order in a habitual phrase—is the foundation of what Melanchthon terms throughout his writing on imitation *imitatio specialis*, or imitation of a particular writer. As he put it 'The rationale of *imitatio specialis* lies in the juxtaposition of words, in the shaping of arguments and in the sequence of sentences' ('Specialis quaedam imitationis ratio est posita in collocatione verborum, in absolvendis argumentis et in ordine periodum', 16.723).

That interest in *collocatio* in all of these senses was enriched by Melanchthon's general concern with what he terms *cohaerentia*, or the way in which speeches and sentences and arguments hang together. That conjunction of collocation with coherence is again probably something that Melanchthon took (probably filtered through the rhetorical works of Rudolph Agricola) from the later works of Cicero, and which he in turn applied to his own analysis of Cicero's style. So Cicero has something distinctive (*peculiaris*) about his *collocatio* (13.494–5). He structures sentences in particular ways. He favours certain ways of ordering his figures of speech. Melanchthon argues that the imitator should not imitate Cicero's vocabulary but this peculiar manner of collocation and of structuration.

This aspect of Melanchthon's thought on the topic derived principally from the exchange between Pico and Bembo. And it suggested that the chief difference between successful emulative imitation and simian replication was that the successful imitator had a distinctive mode of *dispositio*, of structuring arguments, as well as distinctive verbal collocations.[13] Melanchthon further extends the analysis of style as an object of imitation from word-choice and a preference for certain figures of speech through to the habitual methods of structuring a sentence or (via the association between *collocatio* and *dispositio*) an entire work. Melanchthon consequently includes *dispositio*, or the arrangement of material as an object of *imitatio*, as well as word-choice or *elocutio*. His conception of *imitatio specialis* indeed requires one to think of an author not as subjunctive principle of adaptation, or as a huge lexicon of words, but as a series of habitual ways of structuring form, or of patterns of structuration.

In the *Elementa* of 1531 Melanchthon made a further step. He identified what I have termed the 'patterns of structuration' of Cicero's writing with

13. Pico not only states that Virgil 'has his own rhythms, his own features and above all an individual and distinctive arrangement', but also discusses distinctive ways of arranging material later in his treatise: see DellaNeva, ed., *Ciceronian Controversies*, p. 18. and pp. 26–8.

what he refers to as Cicero's 'forma': 'How much better would our teachers have counselled us if they had taught and accustomed their pupils in the reading of Cicero not only to take words from him, but also to imitate phrases and the entire form (*formam*) of his speech, that is, his order of sentences and of ornaments' ('Quanto melius consuluissent nobis praeceptores, si et ad Ciceronis lectionem discipulos assuefecissent et docuissent, non solam verba ex Cicerone excerpere, sed etiam phrasin imitari, et totam orationis formam, hoc est, sententiarium ordinem atque ornamenta effingere', 13.503). That is Melanchthon's crispest and most powerful expression of what he thinks an imitator should do. But it is powerful because its precise sense is so unclear. What in particular is meant by the *forma* that should be the object of imitation?

The word *forma* of course has a complex history. It appears in its earliest usages to have meant something like 'mould'; hence it shares its genealogy in part with the Greek word *tupos*, as a term for a shape which can give rise to multiple instances of the same shape, and which gives rise in due course to our use of the term 'type-faces' to describe the mechanical reproduction of texts. But in Melanchthon's usage it takes on some of the senses which we would now include within the word 'form' when it is used of a text. Given Melanchthon's preoccupation with the structuring of discourse, it is likely that he principally means by *forma* Cicero's habitual methods of collocation, Cicero's way of putting things together, or the structuring principles which underlie Cicero's writing.

In using that word of Cicero Melanchthon also drew on that vital passage about the ideal orator from Cicero's late work the *Orator* (46 BC), which was discussed above (pp. 82–3) but to which we should briefly return here. In that passage Cicero is explicitly Platonic. He attacks the misguided imitators of Thucydides, as he had done in the *Brutus*. Then Cicero returns to the question of how to describe the ideal orator (*Orator*, 11.36), and uses the Greek word *charactēr* to mean 'Platonic form'. He says 'It is always difficult to describe the form (*formam*) of the best [i.e. of an ideal orator], for which the Greek word is *charactēr*, because different people have different notions of what is best' ('Sed in omni re difficillimum est formam, qui χαρακτήρ Graece dicitur, exponere optimi, quod aliud aliis videtur optimum'). Cicero's use of *charactēr* as a Greek equivalent for the Latin *forma* is understandable, since a primary sense of *charactēr* is an 'impress, stamp on coins and seals' (Liddell and Scott, II), which takes it close in sense to 'forma' as a word for a 'type', or a replicable example. But, as we also saw in Chapter 2, the word *charactēr* had been used by Theophrastus to describe what Roman rhetorical theorists came to call the *genera dicendi*, or the different registers of speech.[14] The same word could be used to describe what we now call a 'character', in the sense of a distinctive manner of speech and behaviour, or indeed of a fictional person in a literary text who speaks in an idiosyncratic way; and that usage was assisted by Aulus Gellius's influential statement that different characters in Homer were associated with different ways of speaking, or *genera dicendi*.[15] Cicero's unstable vocabulary therefore enabled a convergence between the ideal orator in the abstract—the Platonic perfect orator who should be the sole object of imitation—and a particular orator's distinctive style. That convergence between the ideal and the distinctively particular was facilitated by Cicero's confession in the same passage that judgements about what is best vary from person to person. An imitable *forma* or *charactēr* therefore might not be a universal ideal, but an imitable idiom distinctive to each orator.

The more or less accidental overlap in sense between these terms, *forma*, *genus dicendi*, and *charactēr*, is of immense significance for the history of theories of style, and for the history of ideas about *imitatio*, and indeed for the history of ideas about authorship. A particular author, or a speaker mimetically represented within a fiction, might have a distinctive way of speaking or 'genus dicendi', which might mean something as loose as 'way of talking' or something as precise as 'a distinctive style'. For Melanchthon in particular, given his preoccupation with *collocatio* and the formal aspects of literary imitation, that 'way of talking' would be as much a structure as a vocabulary. Cicero, understood in this way, provided a means of thinking of an author not as a 'Platonic' form which subsisted in the realm of ideas and which an author might seek to imitate because of its singular excellence, but as a mode of structuring materials which was distinctive to that author. That mode of structuring materials a later author trained in the art of rhetoric might both identify and imitate.

---

14. See Heinrich Lausberg, David E. Orton, and R. Dean Anderson, eds., *Handbook of Literary Rhetoric: A Foundation for Literary Study* (Leiden, 1998), pp. 471–6 (§1079).

15. 'But in the early days these same three styles of speaking were exemplified in three men by Homer: the grand and rich in Ulysses, the elegant and restrained in Menelaus, the middle and moderate in Nestor' ('Sed ea ipsa genera dicendi iam antiquitus tradita ab Homero sunt tria in tribus: magnificum in Vlixe et ubertum, subtile in Menelao et cohibitum, mixtum modera-tumque in Nestore', *Noctes Atticae*, 6.14.7). Text from Aulus Gellius, *The Attic Nights of Aulus Gellius*, trans. John Carew Rolfe, 3 vols. (London and New York, 1927).

The association between the 'form' of a writer's speech and his rhetorical 'character' is given a further tweak in Melanchthon's later work.[16] His final major statement about imitation came in his commentary on Quintilian. This was not published until 1570, a decade after his death. In the *Commonefactio de imitatione* appended to that commentary Melanchthon states that imitators should hold an 'idea' of Cicero in their mind ('Then the Idea of a certain pure and ancient orator will surround our soul, from which we should not depart far, even if we cannot straight away express the lineaments of one particular example'; 'Deinde Idea quaedam purae ac veteris orationis circumferatur animo, a qua non multum discedamus, etiamsi non unius tantum lineamenta prorsus exprimere possimus').[17] This again recalls the Platonism of Cicero's *Orator* (2.7–10), and by using the verb 'exprimere', express, print out, Melanchthon suggests that the aim of imitation is to actualize the impress of a Platonic *forma*. By using that word 'lineamenta'— outlines, characterizing lines of a face—he also may display his continuing debt to Pico's letter to Bembo.

Melanchthon elsewhere claims that an 'idea' derives from an act of intellection in which elements are taken from a range of instances, rather than being an abstraction which subsists in a supra-sensible world outside the mind. This in all likelihood reflects his work as a commentator on Aristotle's *Nicomachean Ethics* during exactly the years in which he developed his thinking on *imitatio*, since it implies that he took a broadly Aristotelian line on the relationship between a form and instantiation.[18] The 'idea' of an orator is consequently in effect an abstract pattern of a rhetorician's practice which is derived from observation of that practice. It is a mental conception of an orator as a particular way of ordering material, which can in turn be 'expressed' by another orator; and when positioned within Melanchthon's

---

16. Melanchthon's note on the word *character* in his commentary on the *Orator* says 'this is evidently the same as what he termed *idea* above' ('est plane idem quod supra ideam vocavit'), Marcus Tullius Cicero, *Marci Tullii Ciceronis De oratore libri tres. Eiusdem de perfecto oratore ad M. Brutum liber*, ed. Philipp Melanchthon (London, 1573), p. 431.

17. Philipp Melanchthon, *Erotemata dialectices* (Wittenberg, 1593), p. 23 states 'an *idea* or form of a beautiful body subsists in the mind of the artist. This form is not a thing external to the understanding, but the very act of understanding itself, painting that imaginary figure' ('in mente pictoris formam seu Ideam pulcri corporis humani inclusam esse. Haec forma non est res extra intellectionem, sed ipse actus intelligendi, pingens hanc imaginationem.'). He criticizes Plato explicitly for treating ideas as 'common natures, flying about, who knows where' ('communes naturas, nescio ubi volitantes').

18. Erwin Panofsky, *Idea: A Concept in Art Theory*, trans. J. J. S. Peake (New York, 1975), pp. 6–7. For the commentary, see Melanchthon, *Opera*, 16.279–415, esp. 290–1.

earlier writing on *imitatio* it suggests that he came close to identifying *forma* with *collocatio*, or an author's habitual practices of disposition and structure.

This dual emphasis on the significance of structure and on the formation of an idea of an earlier author was not unique to Melanchthon. It has roots, as we have seen, in Pico's neo-Platonizing letters on imitation to Bembo, and is perhaps also informed by Bembo's responses to them; but it was through Melanchthon's widely reprinted texts that this way of thinking about *imitatio* entered the daily lives of Northern European school-children. Melanchthon extracted from the debates about Cicero in the sixteenth century and from Quintilian's writing about imitation, hybridized with Cicero's later rhetorical works, a very distinctive conception of what an author is, and what it is that an imitator should seek to imitate. Cicero is for Melanchthon a writer who practises a particular form of *collocatio* of words drawn from the usages specific to his period. What you should seek to imitate in him are not his particular phrases but his *hexis*, his habit of style, and the habitual collocations that follow from that *hexis*.[19]

The passage at the very start of Book 10 of the *Institutes* in which Quintilian talks about the *hexis*, the habitual practices, of an earlier orator (a passage which had been missing from Petrarch's manuscript of Quintilian) consequently was vital to post-Erasmian thinking about imitation in Northern Europe. In seeking to replicate the practice of an earlier author an imitator might also refine and express the *idea* of him which had been extrapolated from his practice, of which the dominant characteristic is his *forma*, the structure of his style at all levels, from the arrangement of the speech right down to the individual *kōla* that make up his writing and his sequencing of rhetorical figures. Cicero has a particular way of putting things together, a kind of *collocatio* and, at a higher level, a particular kind of *cohaerentia* which gives rise to a particular kind of form—a 'form' which can be both abstracted from the works and imitated by a student who laboured to acquire a *hexis* analogous to that of Cicero.

Melanchthon's thinking about imitation was probably more influential than that of Erasmus in Northern Europe as a whole, and was certainly more influential in England. His final thoughts on imitation were included in a variorum commentary on Book 10 of Quintilian's *Institutio* edited by Stephan Reich, which was printed in 1570.[20] Melanchthon's notes are always

---

19. See Eden, *Hermeneutics*, pp. 81–2.
20. Stephan Reich, ed., *In M. Fabij Quintiliani Institutionum librum decimum, doctissimorum virorum annotationes, nempe P. Melanthonis . . . in ordinem digestæ & æd. per M. Riccium* (Leipzig, 1570).

placed first in this edition, and he leads off the commentary by reiterating what were by now the firmly established principles of *imitatio*: that precepts alone do not make a skilled artificer in any activity, unless they are supplemented by practice (*exercitatio*) and use (p. 2). He then provides a long note explaining in both Latin and German what Quintilian meant by *hexis*, which Melanchthon defines as an established facility, *firma facilitas* (p. 6) which arises from both practice and a 'natural aptitude' (*naturali quodam impetu*). That edition included Melanchthon's *Commonefactio* on imitation, which was to at least one early modern reader of more interest than the text of Quintilian itself, and which was itself treated within the volume as a text which required glossing and elaboration.[21] The *Commonefactio* on imitation by Johannes Velcurio (the soubriquet of Johannes Bernhardi) adopted Melanchthon's distinction between general and particular imitation, and went on to emphasize the imitation of structures of sentences and arguments, of *constructio* and *connexio*.[22] The *Parerga* on imitation by Johann Stigel was also included in the volume, and that too followed Melanchthon in emphasizing *imitatio constructionis*, or structural imitation of both sentences and arguments (fol. 143v). Volumes such as this kept Melanchthon's thinking on imitation wrapped right around the interpretation of Quintilian through to the late sixteenth century, and nudged it in the direction of formal imitation.

But that process had begun as early as the 1530s. A collection of writings about imitation by several learned men (*De imitatione eruditorum quorundam libelli*) appeared in Strasbourg in 1535.[23] That volume reprinted the early Italian Ciceronian debates between Calcagnini and Giraldi, between Poliziano and Paolo Cortese, and between Gianfrancesco Pico and Pietro Bembo. These Italian Ciceronian debates are followed in the 1535 volume by Melanchthon's *De Imitatione*, which is directly reprinted from his *Elementa*. Reproduced immediately after Melanchthon's *De Imitatione* at the very end of the volume is the text of Quintilian's *Institutio* 10.2, which is also entitled (as this crucial chapter usually was in the sixteenth century, and as it had been in Petrarch's manuscript) 'De imitatione'. This volume presented the Ciceronian

21. In the copy shelf-marked Corpus Christi College, Oxford O.14.13 (part of the bequest from the seventeenth-century headmaster of Eton, John Rosewell) a contemporary hand is particularly prone to underline passages concerning order and *cohaerentia* in the *Commonefactio* (e.g. fol. 134r, fol. 135r, fol. 136v).

22. Reich, ed., *In Librum Decimum*, fol. 143r. On Velcurio, see Sachiko Kusukawa, *The Transformation of Natural Philosophy: The Case of Philip Melanchthon* (Cambridge, 1995), p. 110.

23. Celio Calcagnini, *De imitatione eruditorum quorundam libelli…puta, Caeli Calcagnini…super imitatione commentatio* (Strasbourg, 1535). There is no indication of who edited the volume.

controversy as effectively a series of commentaries on Quintilian, of which the climactic end was not Erasmus (who does not figure in the volume at all), but Melanchthon.

Sturm

The year after this collection of works on imitation appeared at Strasbourg Melanchthon's pupil Johannes Sturm moved to that city. By 1538 Sturm was established as the rector of Strasbourg's new gymnasium.[24] Sturm probably had a greater influence on the evolution of thought about imitation in Northern Europe than any other person apart from Melanchthon, and was the main channel by which continental discussion of imitation reached England.[25] Sturm, however, was, like his master Melanchthon, not just interested in *imitatio*. He had a life-long concern with the work of later Greek rhetoricians who described what were sometimes called the 'characters' of style and sometimes the 'ideas' of style—the terms which, as we have seen, were playing a significant but profoundly ambiguous role in Melanchthon's discussions about *imitatio*.

In 1550 Sturm printed an edition of the remarkable discussion of style by the Augustan Greek rhetorician Dionysius of Halicarnassus. This was called *Peri Suntheseōs*, or 'on word order'. Sturm gave to this treatise a Latin title which has a distinct savour of Melanchthon: he called it the *De collocatione verborum*, concerning the collocation of words. Sturm also translated and was strongly influenced by the rhetorician Hermogenes, whom he repeatedly cites in his writing on imitation in order to explain the difference between distinct stylistic registers—an interest in later Roman rhetoricians which Sturm shared with Gianfrancesco Pico.[26] The section of Hermogenes' rhetoric devoted to different styles was, significantly, called 'on the ideas of style'; and perhaps equally significantly Sturm was never quite sure how to

---

24. Peter Mack, *A History of Renaissance Rhetoric, 1380–1620* (Oxford, 2011), pp. 132–4. A brief biography is in Johannes Sturm, *Johann Sturm on Education: The Reformation and Humanist Learning*, ed. Lewis William Spitz and Barbara Sher Tinsley (St. Louis, Mo., 1995), pp. 19–44; see also Charles Guillaume A. Schmidt, *La vie et les travaux de Jean Sturm* (Strasbourg, 1855).
25. See Marion Trousdale, 'Recurrence and Renaissance: Rhetorical Imitation in Ascham and Sturm', *English Literary Renaissance* 6 (1976), 156–79.
26. DellaNeva, ed., *Ciceronian Controversies*, p. 41; on Hermogenes, see Annabel M. Patterson, *Hermogenes and the Renaissance: Seven Ideas of Style* (Princeton, 1970), pp. 17, 36. It is noteworthy that the final section of Melanchthon's *Elementa Rhetorices*, immediately after the section 'De Imitatione', is about the 'characters' of style.

translate Hermogenes' word 'ideai': on the title page it is *De Dicendi Generibus sive formis orationum* ... ('On the characters of style or the forms of speeches'); on the first page of the translation itself 'ideas' becomes 'figures of speech' (*De Dicendi Generibus, sive figuris orationis*).[27] In the work of Sturm there is a convergence of interests which was to have a profound influence on later sixteenth-century English writing. He brought together an interest in imitation with an interest in the 'characters' or 'ideas' or 'forms' of style in various senses of the word.

Sturm was also concerned, as Melanchthon had been, with the underlying rhetorical and structural principles of a text, and his conception of imitation was designed to enable students to produce new variants on those underlying patterns or 'forms' or 'ideas'.[28] Sturm could sometimes represent those forms and patterns diagrammatically, as though illustrating the architecture or underlying design beneath a work: so he maps the rhetorical structures of Virgil's first Eclogue, for instance, in *A Rich Storehouse*.[29] His concern with the detail of style—of word-choice and word-order—fused together with an interest in how one might 'characterize' an individual author through an abstract form. An author therefore became imitable as a way of arranging and structuring material, rather than just as a source of content, or a producer of words that could be echoed or transposed. It was an author's habitual collocations, in various senses ranging from overall structure to specific verbal conjunctions, which made that author distinctive. That insight influenced not only students of classical literature and their understanding of style, but also vernacular writers in prose and in verse who sought themselves to acquire a style that could be regarded by their readers as distinct to them.

Sturm's main work on *imitatio*, his *De imitatione oratoria* (1574), states categorically that imitators should imitate the best author, and that the best orator is Cicero, and so Cicero should be imitated ('Cicero imitandus: quia optimus').[30] This might make Sturm sound like a throwback to the Ciceronian zealots who advocated imitating a single author, such as Pietro Bembo in 1513 or Étienne Dolet in the 1530s. But there is a profound

27. Johannes Sturm, *Hermogenis ... de dicendi generibus siue formis orationum libri ii, Lat. donati et scholis explicati atque illustr. a J. Sturmio* (Strasburg, 1571), p. 3. The running-titles are 'De form. orat.' On Hermogenes' use of Platonic vocabulary to bring an appearance of philosophical method to rhetoric, see Ian Rutherford, *Canons of Style in the Antonine Age: Idea-Theory in its Literary Context* (Oxford, 1998), pp. 14–18.
28. Trousdale, 'Recurrence and Renaissance'.
29. Johannes Sturm, *A Ritch Storehouse or Treasure for Nobilitye and Gentlemen*, trans. Thomas Browne (London, 1570), p. 26.
30. Johannes Sturm, *De Imitatione Oratoria Libri Tres* (Strasburg, 1574), fol. B4.

difference between Sturm and these earlier Ciceronians. The goal of imitation for Sturm was not replicating the vocabulary or even the ethical qualities of the *exemplum* or *paradeigma*. It was rather to turn the *communia*, the common features of discourse, such as individual words or phrases, the tropes and figures of style, features such as the rhythmic endings of sentences known as *clausulae*, into things of your own, or into *propria*.

Kathy Eden has traced the origins of the idea of a *proprietas* of style through the rhetorical tradition, and has shown that the prehistory of our ideas of intellectual property lies in that tradition.[31] A concern with textual ownership, as we have seen in relation to Petrarch and Macrobius, was always entangled with the history of imitative poetry, which repeatedly is haunted by the possibility of *furtum* or plagiarism. Sturm, however, is concerned with the practical details of what it might mean to have a style which sounds distinctive to the speaker. Cicero imitated Demosthenes. But he did so not like a child, by taking over phrases from him, and he therefore (as the author's notes to the *De Imitatione* make explicit) did not commit 'furtum' or a theft (sig. T1r) from his original. Instead he covertly transformed his *exemplum*, and dissimulated his borrowings by a variety of acts of substitution and transformation.[32] As Quintilian had argued in that crucial second chapter of the tenth book of the *Institutio*, 'total similarity is so difficult to achieve that even Nature herself has failed to prevent things which seem to match and resemble each other most closely from being always distinguishable in *some* respect' (*Institutio*, 10.2.10), so imitation necessarily implies differentiation.

Hence an imitator could consequently take *communia*, or the shared elements of discourse, and make them his own by omitting, reordering, and restructuring. The result is the concealment of that which is being imitated. As Sturm had put it in his earlier work on imitation, the *Nobilitas Literata* of 1549:

> Nevertheless an Imitator must hide all similitude and likenesse: which is never praysed but when it is comparable with the patterne, and yet cannot be perceived by what means and in what places, and examples it cometh to passe. But this meanes of hyding standeth in three things: In addition, ablation, alteration, and changing

31. Kathy Eden, 'Literary Property and the Question of Style', in Hall Björnstad and Kathy Eden, eds., *Borrowed Feathers: Plagiarism and the Limits of Imitation in Early Modern Europe* (Oslo, 2008), 21–38.
32. On this aspect of Sturm, see G. W. Pigman, 'Versions of Imitation in the Renaissance', *Renaissance Quarterly* 33 (1980), 1–32 (esp. p. 11).

Veruntamen obtegenda imitatori omnis est similitudo: quae tum demum
laudatur: cum par gloria scriptorem sequitur: quo modo vero & quibus in locis
atque exemplis comparata sit non potest deprehendi. Occultandi vero modus
in tribus consistit: additione, ablatione, mutatione.[33]

By the time of his later and larger work *De Imitatione* Sturm had augmented
the list of methods of occluding a source to include 'appositio, detractio,
transpositio, immutatio, copia et brevitas' (sig. H6r)—adding things, taking
things away, changing the collocation of elements, changing words, copious expansion or compression. He also, like Petrarch, emphasized the 'libertas' that could come to an imitator by imitating in this way; and that is
in part a product of his interest in the way that an author can transform
'communia'—common things—into 'propria'—or things that were his own.
We should imitate, he declares,

> Not so that we become slaves of an earlier writer as though of a master, and
> not even as it were freedmen of a patron, but so that we might be equal to
> those well born with talent, who are born free and with talent. Towards that
> end must this faculty be directed: imitation consists more in unlikeness than
> in likeness.
>
> ut, ne simus servi primi scriptoris, tanquam domini, nec etiam liberti, tanquam
> patroni: sed ut simis pares ingenuis, qui ingenui nati sunt. Eo dirigenda est haec
> facultas: imitatio magis consistit in dissimulitudine, quam similitudine.[34]

Sturm keeps his vocabulary carefully close to Latin social divisions by
talking of slaves and freedmen. He avoids the word 'dux', which Petrarch
had used to describe how an imitator should seek to become a leader rather
than a follower. But he does deliberately play on the words 'ingenuus' (well
born) and 'ingenium' (talent), from the fusion or confusion of which the
later conception of 'creative genius' was to emerge.[35] He does so in order to
advocate a form of imitation that guaranteed a freedom equivalent to that
adumbrated in Quintilian's discussions of imitation, and which we have

---

33. Sturm, *Storehouse*, fol. 37v; Johannes Sturm, *Ad Werteros Fratres, Nobilitas literata* (Strasburg,
   1556), fol. 42v. See G. W. Pigman, 'Barzizza's Treatise on Imitation', *Bibliothèque d'Humanisme
   et Renaissance* 44 (1982), 341–52, who argues that Barzizza's treatment of imitation in around
   1417 anticipates Sturm and Ascham's emphasis on dissimulative imitation. That notion is however of some antiquity: Macrobius says Virgil sometimes 'dissimulatively imitates by changing
   the arrangement of the passages he is imitating' at *Saturnalia*, 5.16.12.
34. Sturm, *De Imitatione Oratoria Libri Tres*, sig. T2r. My translation.
35. Rudolph Wittkower, 'Genius: Individualism in Art and Artists', in Philip P. Wiener, ed.,
   Dictionary of the History of Ideas: Studies of Selected Pivotal Ideas (New York, 1973), 2.297–312.

seen repeatedly remade in writing on *imitatio*, not least by Petrarch and Castiglione: it enabled the imitator to be a free, property-holding citizen in the republic of letters, rather than a slave or prisoner to his richer ancestors.

There is a further aspect to Sturm's theory of imitation which makes it more than a process for the invisible assimilation of *communia* into the corpus of a free independent writer. Like Melanchthon before him, he was more interested in the principles underlying acts of imitation than their outcomes. Sturm is happy to recommend the imitation of Cicero because for him Cicero was not simply a body of texts but a *genus dicendi*, a way of speaking that constituted both an 'idea' of style and a set of exemplary processes for the further transformation of texts. That is to say, Sturm held that the imitator of Cicero needs to know how Cicero read Demosthenes and how Cicero transformed what he read (*De Imitatione*, sig. I4). Cicero was for Sturm not just a set of texts and principles, but a pattern of difference that made him not Demosthenes. This made Cicero not just an advocate of republican liberty in his prose, but a manifestation of the *libertas* that an imitator might possess through the transformation of prior *exempla*. Structural transformation rather than verbal replication enables liberation.

Like Melanchthon, Sturm also has room for the *idea* of an orator. And here the influence of Hermogenes' 'ideas' or principles of style has a small but significant part to play in the development of his thinking about *imitatio*.[36] An 'idea' of an author, for Sturm (as for Melanchthon), is not quite a Platonic idea, but is an idealized conception of an orator derived from instantiations of his work. Sturm in his commentary on Hermogenes' *De Formis Orationum* says there are two kinds of idea or forms. The first is a supra-mental 'idea' in the Platonic sense. The second is 'seen, read, heard: the Demosthenic oration, the Platonic dialogue, the speeches of Aeschines. The orator ought always to have these two kinds of Forms placed before his eyes for imitation... but the first kind is deduced from the second; and we see what kind of words and conceptual frameworks Demosthenes used, and from this we deduce the imperceptible ideal: because his style is almost that of the perfect orator'. ('Haec duo genera formarum orator in imitando semper ad oculos posita habere debet: Sed a posteriore initium est sumendum: & videmus Demosthenes, quibus generibus verborum & sententiarum

---

36. On Sturm and Hermogenes, see Walter J. Ong, *Ramus, Method, and the Decay of Dialogue* (Cambridge Mass., and London, 1983), p. 232.

utitur, & ab hoc accendum est, ad illud *aoraton*: quod paene est perfectissimi
Oratoris.')[37] An idea of an orator that can be imitated has first to be abstracted
from careful analysis of an author's practice.

Ascham

Although Sturm spent the bulk of his later career in Strasbourg, his influence
on England was exceptionally deep. His discussion of imitation in *Nobilitas
Literata* was translated into English in 1570 as *A Ritch Storehouse or Treasure
for Nobilitye and Gentlemen*, and the emphasis on nobility and gentlemanly
status in the title reminds us of the intimate connection between imitation
and social aspiration in this period—which was a foundational strand of
Castiglione's *Il Cortegiano* and, in its way, of *Don Quixote* too. Sturm's work
on sentence structure, the *De Periodis*, although it was never translated,
enjoyed even greater favour: it was dedicated to Princess Elizabeth, the
future Elizabeth I, in 1550. That work on the minutiae of style was printed
in a twin volume which also contained Sturm's edition of Dionysius of
Halicarnassus's *Peri Suntheseos*. This was the text to which Sturm had given
that title with a Melanchthonian ring to it, the *De Collocatione Verborum*.
That work was also dedicated to the future Queen.

The dedication was prompted by the famous English educational humanist
Roger Ascham, who had served as Elizabeth's tutor from 1548–50. Ascham
had extensive correspondence with Sturm from 1550–62, and his love for
Sturm was so great that he named his unfortunate son Sturm Ascham—an
act of friendship which does not seem to have prompted Ascham junior to
great things.[38] In 1568 Ascham begged to see Sturm's discussion of *imitatio*
in what was to become *De Imitatione Oratoria Libri Tres*. Ascham made his
request in a long letter that appears to have been in effect a first draft
towards his own proposed, though unwritten, book on imitation.[39] Ascham's
letter to Sturm was not a private exchange between obscure late sixteenth-
century Ciceronians. It was printed at the very start of the collected edition

---

37. Hermogenes, *Hermogenis . . . de dicendi generibus siue formis orationum libri ii, Lat. donati et scholis
    explicati atque illustr. a J. Sturmio*, ed. Johannes Sturmius and Jan Kocìn (Strasburg, 1571), p. 11.
38. Roger Ascham, *Letters of Roger Ascham*, ed. Alvin Vos (New York, 1989), p. 221. On Ascham's
    form of Ciceronianism, see Alvin Vos, ' "Good Matter and Good Utterance": The Character of
    English Ciceronianism', *Studies in English Literature 1500–1900* 19 (1979), 3–18.
39. Roger Ascham, *English Works*, ed. William Aldis Wright (Cambridge, 1904). He refers to the
    unwritten book on p. 274; pp. 264–95 are headed 'Imitatio'.

of Ascham's correspondence, a volume which went through four editions in England between 1576 and 1590.[40]

In his discussion of imitation Ascham was very close to Sturm, although he was less technical in his vocabulary. Cicero, Ascham argued, is best understood by grasping how Cicero is unlike his sources. 'If I should want to write a poem, I could not find anyone more divine than Virgil, more learned than Horace. But for rhetoric I want Cicero himself—if not him alone, certainly him in preference to others. And I must have Cicero the imitator as my model, not the imitator of Cicero... For the one who intelligently observes how Cicero followed others will most successfully see how Cicero himself is to be followed.'[41] The aim is Sturmian meta-imitation, which imitates Cicero's modes of imitation rather than Cicero's language or phraseology. Cicero is treated as a principle of generative change rather than a fixed model to follow, and he becomes too part of a process of continuing educational reconstruction: 'If I should desire to become another Cicero... what approach would be better than the approach Cicero took to make himself Cicero?'[42]

In his vernacular treatise on education called *The Scholemaster* (posthumously published in 1570) Ascham devotes a substantial and characteristically garrulous section to *imitatio*, which is laden with praise of Melanchthon and Sturm in particular. He praises those who list practical examples of imitations, but insists that the real task for a writer on the topic should be to explain the relationships between the imitator and the imitated. He condemns those who have written about the subject like 'common porters, and bringers of matter and stuff togither. They order nothing... They busie not themselves with forme of buildyng' (p. 276). That emphasis on ordering and on 'form'—the compositional practices and modes of arrangement that change one text into another—marks Ascham's deep debt to Sturm, a debt that is confirmed by the fact that his discussion of *imitatio* concludes with a section on the different characters of style and genres of discourse.

The notions that an author should be regarded as a *forma*, a particular mode of collocation, or as a set of principles for the transformation of texts,

---

40. Lawrence V. Ryan, *Roger Ascham* (Stanford and London, 1963), pp. 265–70. See Roger Ascham, *Familiarium epistolarum libri tres*, ed. Edward Grant (London, 1576), pp. 1–12. For a survey of English Ciceronianism, see J. W. Binns, 'Ciceronianism in Sixteenth Century England: The Latin Debate', *Lias* 7 (1980), 199–203.

41. Ascham, ed. Vos, *Letters*, p. 271.

42. Ascham, ed. Vos, *Letters*, p. 273. This is a close allusion to Erasmus, ed. Levi, *Ciceronianus*, p. 401: 'Let us imitate him as he imitated others.'

were all readily available to writers in England in the later sixteenth century, either through Ascham's letters, Sturm's treatises, or (more pervasively) through Melanchthon's *Elements of Rhetoric*. That accessible rhetorical textbook as well as some of Melanchthon's other writings about imitation began to have a major influence in England in the 1570s, just as Ascham's correspondence with Sturm, and Ascham's *Scholemaster* (of which there were three editions between 1570 and 1573) enjoyed their peak of popularity. In 1573 a printer called John Kingston issued the first edition of Cicero's *De Oratore* in England, which appeared along with Cicero's late Platonic work the *Orator*. The edition was accompanied by the notes on both texts by Philipp Melanchthon, and included his extended note headed 'De imitatione' in the *De Oratore*. There is strong evidence that William Shakespeare among others read this commentary.[43]

This means that the later Platonizing vocabulary of Cicero, which fuses together the words *idea* and *character*, has a very distinctive history. It was rediscovered in the 1420s, fully incorporated into a pedagogical discussion of imitation in the 1520s and 1530s by Melanchthon, wrapped around and into Quintilian and the rhetorical writings on style by Hermogenes and Dionysius of Halicarnassus, and disseminated by Sturm and Ascham in the 1550s and 1560s. By the early 1570s an English printer could bring out an edition in the hope of ensuring a wide readership—just as Sturm's ideas of style and Ascham's writing on Ciceronian imitation were coming to the height of fashion. Indeed John Kingston was in the early 1570s printing not just school textbooks—Erasmus's *De Copia* and Mantuan's *Eclogues*—but also works which had their roots in the Ciceronian controversy, including Longolius's, or Christophe de Longueil's, commentary on the *Ad Herennium*. Kingston had earlier printed Richard Rainolde's *Foundation of Rhetoric* (1563) and had reprinted Thomas Wilson's *Art of Rhetoric* in 1560. It was not surprising that in February 1577 he was chosen to become printer to the University of Cambridge.[44] Here he would have become perhaps the main supplier of books to Christopher Marlowe and Thomas Nashe. The schoolroom texts printed by Kingston in the 1570s were the core of a slow-burning stylistic and rhetorical revolution.

43. I have argued that Shakespeare knew the commentary on the *De Oratore* before he wrote *Hamlet*: see Colin Burrow, 'Shakespeare's Authorities', in Katie Halsey and Angus Vine, eds., *Shakespeare and Authority: Citations, Conceptions and Constructions* (London, 2018), 31–53 (pp. 42–6).
44. David McKitterick, *A History of Cambridge University Press*, 3 vols. (Cambridge, 1992), 1.58–62.

This cluster of texts directly shapes the intellectual foundations of high Elizabethan literature during the period 1580–1600. These are the books and ideas about style which shaped the educational experience of Spenser, Shakespeare, and Marlowe, and which also appealed to the young Sir Philip Sidney—on whom the influence of Melanchthon in particular was strong and deep.[45] The influence of this tradition has, however, been partially occluded by a series of historiographical accidents. The first was the Ciceronian debates themselves. The Quintilianic German and English 'Ciceronians' were very different from the philological Italian Ciceronians of the early sixteenth century (or at least they differed from the parodic representations of those figures by their enemies): they did not believe that Cicero alone should be imitated, and they were not simply concerned with word-choice. And yet because they were a *kind* of Ciceronian it was easy to stigmatize them by the same pejorative label. Certainly by 1594 Sturm and Melanchthon were such easy targets that Thomas Nashe, whose eagerness to be at the forefront of fashion was second only to his appetite for jibes at the unfashionability of others, could suggest that no reason on earth would compel him to shiver and snore through what he called 'the leaden headed Germanes' who, according to Nashe, first originated Ciceronianism, while 'wee Englishmen have surfetted of their absurd imitation'.[46]

Ramus, Harvey, and English 'stylism'

The other reason why these post-Erasmian theorists of imitation became unfashionable by the end of the sixteenth century was the growing attention given to the logic and rhetoric of Petrus Ramus. Ramus made a great deal of noise about his originality, and launched attacks on the rhetorical theory of Cicero and Quintilian. He insisted that 'invention, arrangement,

45. See Robert E. Stillman, *Philip Sidney and the Poetics of Renaissance Cosmopolitanism* (Aldershot, 2008).
46. Thomas Nashe, *Works*, ed. Ronald B. McKerrow and F. P. Wilson, 4 vols. (Oxford, 1958), 2.251. McKerrow's note reflects Anglophone neglect of the German tradition of Ciceronianism, knowledge of which Nashe took for granted: 'I can only suppose Nashe took Longolius, one of the most prominent of the Ciceronians, for a German; he was, however, a Belgian, native of Malines. Apart from him the excessive worship of Cicero seem to have been almost confined to Italy ... or was Nashe really thinking of Sturmius?', 4.275. Given that Sturm wrote a preface to Antonius Schorus's *Thesaurus Ciceronianus* in 1570, and so was directly associated with Ciceronian reference works, McKerrow had no need to hesitate.

and memory belong to dialectic and only style and delivery to rhetoric'.[47] The simplification of rhetoric and logic which resulted from separating style and delivery from the other elements of rhetoric created widespread tensions in later sixteenth-century universities, particularly in Ramus's native France.[48]

For all Ramus's self-proclaimed radicalism, however, his treatise called *Ciceronianus* (1557) was surprisingly retrograde. Ramus insisted that Cicero never advocated a form of imitation that limited itself to the vocabulary of an *exemplum*, and so those who imitate him in this way are not Ciceronian.[49] Indeed (in a terrifying transformation of the notion that imitators should resemble their original as a child resembles its father) Cicero would act like an angry father towards those who seek to imitate him in his words alone, and will disinherit them, because it would be impossible to equal his example (p. 39). Truly to imitate Cicero would be to imitate his virtues, his political activity, and even, Ramus appears to suggest in the latter part of the treatise, the actions of his life. Ramus in effect argues that Cicero should be regarded as a living model for conduct.

The reasons for this literal-minded approach to the imitation of Cicero lie in Ramus's *Rhetoricae Distinctiones in Quintilianum* of 1549. Here Ramus had argued that a student who wished to imitate a text should first perform 'analysis' on it, which meant breaking it down into the logical categories on which it was founded, and then should attempt on the basis of that analysis to perform what Ramus called 'genesis': so 'first of all we must understand the use of the art in representative examples, and then we must fashion our own like them'.[50] The best 'representative examples', Ramus argued, were oral performances rather than written texts. These would inspire young aspirant orators by example and encourage them to replicate Cicero's methods of speaking and his behaviour. Cicero is consequently best regarded as a speaking person. Hence imitation of Cicero for Ramus reverts to something akin to the *imitatio Christi*: the whole life of Cicero, rather than simply his language and style, should be the object of analysis and imitation.

47. Petrus Ramus, *Arguments in Rhetoric against Quintilian: Translation and Text of Peter Ramus's Rhetoricae Distinctiones in Quintilianum (1549)*, ed. James J. Murphy and Carole E. Newlands (DeKalb, Ill., 1986), p. 104.
48. See Mordechai Feingold, 'English Ramism: A Reinterpretation', in Mordechai Feingold, Joseph S. Freedman, and Wolfgang Rother, eds., *The Influence of Petrus Ramus: Studies in Sixteenth and Seventeenth Century Philosophy and Science* (Basel, 2001), pp. 127–76.
49. Petrus Ramus, *Ciceronianus* (Paris, 1557), p. 35.
50. Ramus, ed. Murphy and Newlands, *Arguments against Quintilian*, p. 155.

Also underpinning that revival of an exemplary view of imitation was Ramus's attack on Quintilian's arguments about *imitatio*. The master self-publicist Ramus trumpeted that *imitatio* need not be restricted to the choice of words or lexis, but could be extended to include the analysis and genesis of an author's *inventio*. This attack was supposed to pierce the heart of Quintilian's supposed confusion of rhetoric with dialectic. But it was in many respects a noisy development of the interest of earlier theorists, who seldom in practice restricted *imitatio* to word-choice, and who also had encouraged imitators to replicate the argumentative structure as well as the words of their originals. Gianfrancesco Pico had principally limited *imitatio* to style, but had also insisted that what makes a writer distinctive is a particular way of putting materials together; Melanchthon had implied that *imitatio* extended into disposition and arrangement of sentences and of arguments. Even writers such as Jacobus Omphalius, who inclined to see imitation as primarily a matter of *elocutio* or style, included among the features which should be imitated sentence structure and collocations (and Omphalius even tabulates the latter in ways which visually anticipate the analytical trees of Ramistic logic).[51] Ramus had attended lectures given by Johannes Sturm on Cicero and on logic at Paris in 1529, and the imprint of Sturm was visible even in his later writing about imitation.[52] Ramus encouraged subsequent imitators to replicate the argumentative structures of the texts which they imitated, and in this, as in every other area of his work, he was deeply dependent on the work of his teachers. But his principal influence lay in his noisy condemnation of those who sought to be 'Ciceronian' in their word-choices. His zealous opposition to merely elocutionary imitation had a powerful effect on later writers—if only to make them identify the word 'Ciceronian' with 'windy idiot'.

Ramus's most vocal English spokesman, Gabriel Harvey, leapt onto the bandwagon with two speeches which presented the development of his thinking about the imitation of Cicero.[53] Harvey described his own growth away from a Sturmian Ciceronianism, and towards a Ramistic emphasis on

51. Jacobus Omphalius, *De elocutionis imitatione ac apparatu liber vnus* (Basel, 1537), p. 225. This work was dedicated to Jean du Bellay, cousin of the more famous Joachim. Cf. Giambattista Cinzio Giraldi, *Giraldi Cinthio on Romances: Being a Translation of the Discorso intorno al comporre dei romanzi*, ed. Henry L. Snuggs (Lexington, 1968), p. 127: the imitator 'ought also to consider the order, the terms, the joining of the words, and the positions in which, as in their own place, the one he chose to imitate lodged these words in expressing his thoughts'.

52. Schmidt, *Sturm*, pp. 10–11; Ramus praised Sturm in Petrus Ramus, *P. Rami Scholae In Tres Primas Liberales* (Frankfurt, 1581), pp. 9–10.

53. See Binns, 'Ciceronianism'.

the analysis and imitation of content—a personal narrative which had
become a commonplace by the later sixteenth century.[54] He insisted that
imitators should attend to the 'argumentorum cellulas', divisions of arguments, in an author: 'For those who point the finger only to flashy tropes
and polished figures, rather than the divisions of argument, the treasure
houses of concepts, and the ordering of the structure, these indeed seem to
me to display a most beautiful and elegant body, but one that is deprived
of sense and life' ('Nam qui digitum tantummodo ad troporum lumina,
figurarumque expolitiones intenderunt; nec argumentorum cellulas, nec
argumentationum thesauros, nec ordinis structura indicarunt: perinde mihi
facere videntur, ac si corpus pulcherrimum, venustissimumque ostentarent,
sed sensu privatum atque vita').[55]

Harvey is here transforming the long-standing idea that an imitator seeks
to replicate not just a text but the life behind it: those who fail to attend to
argument and structure (as Sturm had doubtless taught Ramus to do, and as
Ramus had taught Harvey) will replicate only a dead body rather than
produce a living imitation. Gabriel Harvey and Ramus in effect killed off
Ciceronianism at the same time as drinking deeply from the life-blood of
Northern European Ciceronians.

Their very public attacks were then reinforced by Francis Bacon, in what
often used to be regarded as his 'anti-Ciceronian' excursus in *The Advancement
of Learning*, in which he says 'then did Sturmius spend such infinite and
curious pains upon Cicero the orator and Hermogenes the rhetorician,
besides his own books of periods and imitation and the like. Then did Carr
of Cambridge, and Ascham, with their lectures and writings, almost deify
Cicero and Demosthenes.'[56] Historians of literary style who have naïvely
followed Morris Croll have argued that Bacon marked a break from an elaborate Ciceronian 'Asiatic' style towards the 'Attic' or plain style.[57] Bacon was,
however, voicing what was by the early seventeenth century a commonplace

---

54. Cf. Justus Lipsius, *Principles of Letter-Writing: A Bilingual Text of Justi Lipsii Epistolica Institutio*, ed.
    R. V. Young and M. Thomas Hester (Carbondale, Ill., 1996), p. 36, where he describes himself
    as an adherent of Ciceronianism when he was 'paullo juvenilius', a little younger.
55. Gabriel Harvey, *Gabrielis Harueij Ciceronianus, vel Oratio post reditum* (London, 1577), p. 49.
56. Francis Bacon, *Works*, ed. James Spedding, Robert Lesley Ellis, and Douglas Denon Heath,
    14 vols. (London, 1857–74), 3.283–4. On Bacon's debts here to the Ciceronian controversies,
    see Brian Vickers, 'The Myth of Francis Bacon's "Anti-Humanism"', in Jill Kraye and
    M. W. F. Stone, eds., *Humanism and Early Modern Philosophy* (London and New York, 2000),
    135–58.
57. See the convincing attack on that approach in Brian Vickers, *Francis Bacon and Renaissance Prose*
    (Cambridge, 1968), pp. 96–115.

caricature of later sixteenth-century rhetorical theory. The 'leaden-headed Germans' did not just sink into oblivion, but had their heads forcibly thrust beneath the waters by people who had learnt from them.

There is a general rule in literary and intellectual history: people lie, even to themselves. Those who claim to be new are usually deeply indebted to the people whose influences they most strongly disavow. Most writers who had received a classical education in the 1560s or 1570s or 1580s were steeped in the work of Sturm and Ascham and Melanchthon either directly or through their teachers, or through one of Melanchthon's editions of Ciceronian rhetorical treatises. They may then have read Ramus, or read Nashe insisting that Sturm and Ascham were infinitely passé, and changed how they presented themselves accordingly. But that did not mean that the influence of the 'leaden-headed Germans' was extinct by the mid-1580s. Indeed by the 1580s the ideas of *imitatio* disseminated by those leaden-headed Germans played a constitutive role in constructing the kind of literature which C. S. Lewis famously but wrong-headedly described as 'golden'.[58] Their association of style with distinctive rhetorical patterns and syntactic structures had a deep and permanent influence on ways of writing and on ways of thinking about imitation and authorial identities in the last quarter of the sixteenth century and beyond. They attuned an entire generation to think closely about word-order and sentence structure, and to regard those as characteristic of particular genres and even of particular authors.

John Lyly is the most obvious example. His *Euphues* (1578), with its concern for the shaping or misshaping of a native wit by education, has clear and evident connections with the arguments about education developed in Roger Ascham's highly Sturmian *Scholemaster*. Indeed *Euphues* could be regarded as *The Scholemaster's* bastard child, since Ascham not only describes the dangers of over-flexible wit but does so in a style which anticipates that of Lyly's fiction: 'Euphues' is defined by Ascham as 'he, that is apte by goodnes of witte, and appliable by readines of will, to learning' (p. 194); and when he describes that apt and over-adaptable wit Ascham's usually orderly and mundane similes are allowed to frolic off as though the author has been grazing on the rich pasture of Pliny's *Natural History*: 'For, the pure cleane witte of a sweete yong babe, is like the newest wax, most hable to receive the best and fayrest printing: and like a new bright silver dishe never

58. C. S. Lewis, *English Literature in the Sixteenth Century, Excluding Drama* (Oxford, 1954), pp. 318–535.

occupied, to receive and kepe cleane, anie good thyng that is put into it'
(p. 200), wrote Ascham. 'As, therefore, the iron being hot receiveth any form
with the stroke of the hammer, and keepeth it being cold for ever, so the
tender wit of a child, if with diligence it be instructed in youth, will with
industry use those qualities in his age', wrote Lyly.[59]

Lyly's style, itself a kind of imitation of Ascham, also declared a debt to
those 'leaden-headed Germans' Sturm and Melanchthon. Again and again
he reiterates his own peculiar form of sentence structure and *collocatio*.
Anyone who read more than a page of *Euphues* and who had a schoolroom
knowledge of rhetoric would know that if they wanted to sound like Lyly
they should write sentences which consisted of three correlative clauses, at
least two of which alliterated and at least one of which sounded as though
it contained recondite information drawn from Pliny's *Natural History* (even
if that information was actually made up), and that ideally most of these
should also be similes. The creator of that style, John Lyly, knew from his
reading in Ascham, Sturm, and it is reasonable to suppose (given that he
probably began his education at King's School, Canterbury, and then
certainly proceeded to Magdalen College, Oxford) in Melanchthon too
that the obtrusive display of habitual syntactic structures was a central defining characteristic of the 'idea' of an author. Euphuism was consequently not
just a style invented by John Lyly, and it was not in any reductive sense
'Ciceronian'. It was made by, and also designed to be noticed by, people
who were familiar with Northern European arguments about *imitatio*. It
impressed its readers just as much as it expressed the idea of John Lyly's style.

By the 1590s England was struck by an extraordinary vogue for stylistic
'-isms': that good Ramist Gabriel Harvey lamented that by the early 1590s
there was 'no Arte, but Euphuisme; no witt, but Tarletonisme; no honesty,
but pure Scogginisme; no Religion, but precise Marlowisme'[60] and that 'To
be a Ciceronian, is a flowting stocke' (p. 17). The rise of what might be
called 'stylism' in this period had an immediate local impulse behind it:
the anti-prelatical pamphleteer Martin Marprelate (who may have been a
stylistic manner adopted by more than one author) through the later 1580s
produced pamphlets in an instantly recognizable fusion of low-brow and
high-brow registers, and provoked repeated attempts on the part of the

---

59. John Lyly, *Euphues: The Anatomy of Wit and Euphues and His England*, ed. Leah Scragg
    (Manchester, 2003), p. 35. For Lyly's influence on markets for print and ideas of authorship, see
    Andy Kesson, *John Lyly and Early Modern Authorship* (Manchester, 2014).
60. Gabriel Harvey, *Pierces Supererogation, or a New Prayse of the Old Asse* (London, 1593), p. 149.

authorities to discover the identity of the 'Martinist' author(s). But behind the rise of stylism in the 1580s and 1590s was also a wider European story. It was in large measure a product of a tendency to reify distinctive styles as syntactic and structural rather than merely lexical phenomena. That tendency had its roots in earlier sixteenth-century rhetorical handbooks, but also in arguments about *imitatio*.

That point takes us back to the deep mutual involvement between arguments about *imitatio* and the practices of print authorship. The pre-Ramistic generation of Northern European rhetoricians gave later Elizabethan writers two key things. The first was a notion that structure—rhetorical structure, sentence structure, and narrative structure—was the main feature of an earlier text on which an imitating author should concentrate. It was by having a 'forma' or 'character' in the sense of a distinctive repertoire of structural characteristics that one author became imitable by another, and so could be said to have an individual and distinctive style. But the second thing they gave to writers in this period was on almost a direct collision course with the first. They encouraged those who *read* any author, including their contemporaries, not only to grasp the structure, the 'form' or 'idea' or 'character' of a writer's style, but also to imitate it. Because readers and writers of vernacular texts were to a substantial degree grounded on the same intellectual foundations, readers could readily reverse-engineer what they read, and either imitate it or analyse its rhetorical characteristics with such clarity that they could subject it in its turn to either imitation or to parody.

These two impulses were thrown violently together by the expansion of the market for vernacular literary texts at the close of the sixteenth century in England. John Lyly wanted to write in a way that sounded like John Lyly. But the idea of style, the particular form of *collocatio*, that he invented was also a marketable commodity: there were at least sixteen editions of Lyly's *Euphues* and *Euphues and his England* between 1578 and 1600. The consequence of the success of the 'Euphuistic' style was that almost every other author of prose fiction wanted to sound like John Lyly too, or to imitate at least his success in fashioning an idea of style. Euphuism as a result became not an inimitable, individual style which expressed (and once more the printerly overtones of that word are significant) the unique *ingenium* of John Lyly. It so clearly displayed the structures of its own genesis that it rapidly became a replicable commodity, and ultimately a target for parody. Others wrote sequels to *Euphues* or strove to write like John Lyly—notably Thomas Nashe and Robert Greene; or, more accurately they aimed to give a twist to

Lyly's style that might make it sound like Nashe's style or Greene's style. This urge to become a stylistic 'ism' had its deep roots in the most powerful 'ism' of all: Ciceronianism. Because this generation of authors was trained to observe how an author imitated, to note the rhetorical structures in an earlier text and its habitual forms of collocation, they sought to make a stylistic signature for themselves which was founded on these structural features.

This does not simply give a recipe for the emergence of an individual style which is 'proper' to its author and distinct from common discourse, since in the world of *imitatio* substance and shadow, form and its expression, tend to be mutually generative. Rather it fed into the commodification of style, and, indeed, was the enabling condition of endless battles over whose style was genuinely distinctive. It was a recipe for the major literary quarrels which dominated the English literary scene in the 1580s and 1590s—for the slanging matches between Nashe and Gabriel Harvey which frequently turned on the nature of each other's style: as Nashe spluttered at the height of his dispute with Harvey 'Hee bids the world examine the Preamble before the Supplication to the divell, and see if I doo not praise my selfe, and that the tenour of the stile & identity of the phrase proves it to be mine.'[61] It also paved the way for the attacks launched by Ben Jonson on more or less everybody else in the so called 'war of the theatres', in which 'propriety', in the double sense of 'ownership of texts' and the possession of an individual style, were key terms of debate.[62] And it is to the greatest of all English imitators of classical texts, Ben Jonson, that we should turn our attention next.

---

61. Nashe, ed. McKerrow and Wilson, *Works*, 3.127, and later on the same page 'He needed not go so far about to sent [scent] me out by my stile and my phrase, for if he had ever overlookt it he would have seene my name to it'.
62. On which, see James P. Bednarz, *Shakespeare and the Poets' War* (New York, 2001).

7

Ben Jonson

Formal Imitation

It is very easy to be taken in by Ben Jonson. This is because he often presents apparently plain and direct statements of truths which appear to interpret themselves. 'Language most shows a man; speak, that I may see thee', he declared in *Discoveries*,[1] and visible Ben seems indeed to shine through his words. Jonson is still regularly presented as master of the 'plain style', and this tempts critics to do little more than expound what he has said and believe that he meant it. A line of criticism extending from the 1970s and still influential today presents Jonson's poetry as enacting with varying degrees of smoothness its own moral and stylistic precepts. Thomas Greene argued that Jonson valued a 'centred self', to which was opposed the fluid identities of those who could not digest and absorb their reading into a single whole, just as Jonson had urged Sir Thomas Roe to 'Be always to thy gathered self the same' (Epigram 98.9).[2] Edward Partridge established a similar distinction in the *Epigrams* between the 'named' (aristocrats or friends, who embodied virtue) and the 'nameless'—figures of undefinable identity who, like the 'Something that walks somewhere' of Epigram 11, represented the horror of sin, distraction, and a morally uncentred life.[3] These ethical readings of Jonson had a powerful influence on Richard Peterson's *Imitation and Praise in the Poetry of Ben Jonson*, which argued that Jonson sought to absorb the texts he imitated into a stable personal identity, which stood firm against the world. Peterson argued that Jonson's poetry of

---

1. Ben Jonson, *The Cambridge Edition of the Works of Ben Jonson*, ed. David M. Bevington, Martin Butler, and Ian Donaldson, 7 vols. (Cambridge, 2012), 7.567. All quotations from this edition.
2. Thomas M. Greene, 'Ben Jonson and the Centered Self', *Studies in English Literature* 10 (1970), 325–48.
3. Edward Partridge, 'Jonson's *Epigrammes*: The Named and the Nameless', *Studies in the Literary Imagination* 6 (1973), 153–98.

praise, founded on the imitation of Seneca, Horace, Plutarch, and other classical authorities, sought to generate images of praiseworthy people which might themselves become objects of ethical emulation.[4] Peterson related these ethical features of Jonson's verse in elegant and persuasive ways to his recurrent imagery—of circles, of buildings, of 'turning', and 'standing'—and to Jonson's own statements about imitation. But the wider outcome of his study was to imply that Jonson's conception of *imitatio* was principally a moral ideal: you digest your reading in classical authors into a 'centred self' which brings that classical reading back to life by creating an exemplary moral persona, or by composing a panegyric to an embodiment of virtue. These exemplary figures in turn invite imitation, in the sense of 'ethical emulation'.

That creation of a community of exemplary virtue became something close to a grand tautology in a celebrated and still much cited essay by Stanley Fish, which argued that Jonson's verse sought to establish the merit of its author by creating a closed loop of virtue which united the poet, his addressee, and his readers.[5] This picture of Jonson as the manufacturer of great moral tautologies has had a long life. There has been outstanding historical and contextual work on Jonson's later poetry since the 1980s.[6] Joseph Loewenstein has explored how complex connections between the history of the book and thinking about plagiarism and imitation helped to form what he terms Ben Jonson's 'bibliographic ego'. Raphael Lyne has thought vividly about relationships between recent work on memory in the cognitive sciences and Jonson's practices as an imitator, and Victoria Moul has brought to life Jonson's engagements with Horace; but there has not been a major reappraisal of how Jonson's poetry in general and his *Epigrams* in particular relate to wider histories of thinking about *imitatio* since Peterson's study.[7]

---

4. Richard S. Peterson, *Imitation and Praise in the Poems of Ben Jonson* (New Haven, 1981). The 2011 edition of Peterson remains a reference point in recent discussions of imitation: see, e.g., Janet Clare, *Shakespeare's Stage Traffic: Imitation, Borrowing and Competition in Renaissance Theatre* (Cambridge, 2014), pp. 8–9.
5. Stanley Fish, 'Author-Readers: Jonson's Community of the Same', *Representations* 7 (1984), 26–58.
6. See, e.g., Martin Butler, 'The Dates of Three Poems by Ben Jonson', *Huntington Library Quarterly* 55 (1992), 279–94, Annabel M. Patterson, *Censorship and Interpretation: The Conditions of Writing and Reading in Early Modern England* (Madison, Wis., 1984), pp. 120–58.
7. See Joseph Loewenstein, *Ben Jonson and Possessive Authorship* (Cambridge, 2002), Raphael Lyne, *Memory and Intertextuality in Renaissance Literature* (Cambridge, 2016), pp. 43–75, and Victoria Moul, *Jonson, Horace and the Classical Tradition* (Cambridge, 2010).

The main aim of this chapter is to suggest some ways in which we might think differently about both the theory and practice of imitation in Jonson's poetry. Jonson's highly derivative prose remarks about *imitatio* in *Discoveries* and his own statements about the ethical aims of his poetry look like secure guides to his practice. But they are not. His principal innovation as an imitator of classical writing in England was his extremely observant responses to the style—to both the rhetorical structures and the formal characteristics—of the authors that he imitated. I shall suggest that in developing a style based on *formal* imitation Jonson was the main English heir to the wider history of thinking about *imitatio* in Northern Europe that was set out in Chapter 6. That history shaped Jonson's way of imitating and his ways of establishing his own distinctive poetical character. It enabled him to imitate not just poems but styles, and to make in the process a style which was itself imitable. Indeed he established the dominant mode of imitating classical poetry in England for the next century and a half. Jonson was also an heir to the arguments about style in the 1590s: his mode of imitating particular poems was often driven by rivalry with other vernacular imitators, whose style and manner of imitating Jonson aimed to overgo.

Justus Lipsius and Jonson on imitation

It might appear counter-intuitive to argue that a major part of Jonson's intellectual genesis lay in the work of German and English Ciceronians of the sixteenth century, and their close attention to rhetorical figures and to the characteristics of style. Could the notoriously 'plain' style of Ben Jonson owe anything to the Ciceronian debates? The short answer to that question is 'yes'. Wesley Trimpi argued many years ago that Ben Jonson was an advocate of the 'plain' or 'styleless style whose models are the familiar letter and urbane conversation'.[8] The rise of that style has often been linked with the short treatise on letter-writing by Justus Lipsius, called the *Epistolica institutio*, of 1590, which is often said to have marked the death of Ciceronianism and the rise a prose style which is conversational, unornamented, individual,

---

8. Wesley Trimpi, *Ben Jonson's Poems: A Study of the Plain Style* (Stanford, 1962), pp. 58, 74–5. The foundation of Trimpi's study is Morris W. Croll, *Style, Rhetoric, and Rhythm: Essays*, ed. J. Max Patrick (Princeton, 1966), pp. 51–101; for a criticism of which, see Brian Vickers, 'The Myth of Francis Bacon's "Anti-Humanism"', in Jill Kraye and M. W. F. Stone, eds., *Humanism and Early Modern Philosophy* (London and New York, 2000), 135–58.

and suited for both political resistance and philosophical discourse between men.[9] Lipsius's treatise did indeed have an influence on Jonson, but that treatise was not simply 'anti-Ciceronian'. Although Lipsius was very keen to present himself as marking a new era in the history of style, much of what he said about imitation was rooted in the concerns with form and sentence structure of later sixteenth-century European Ciceronians.[10]

Like Gabriel Harvey and Ramus before him, Lipsius insisted that being simply Ciceronian was infantile, or a mere propaedeutic to the acquisition of an individual style that he describes as 'virilis', or manly. He describes Italian Ciceronians as vain and fussy ('vani et fastidiosi', p. 34) and confesses that when he was a bit younger ('paulo juvenilius') he was attracted to their teaching.

But despite these protests Lipsius both knew and learnt from the authors with whom he presented himself as disagreeing. In a letter decrying the excesses of Ciceronianism in 1596 he grudgingly described Melanchthon as 'not despicable' (*haud aspernabilis*).[11] The praise is predictably muted given Lipsius's Catholicism and Melanchthon's association with reform, but Lipsius was keenly aware of Sturm and Melanchthon's work on *imitatio*. He had absorbed their emphasis on the imitation of formal structures in a prior author's texts into both his theory and practice of style.

Lipsius's own later prose style was unmistakable: short clauses and abrupt sentences displayed their lack of concern for Cicero's elegantly constructed periods. Lipsius's critics immediately before and after his death described that style as 'inimitable', despite the fact that many attempted to imitate it.[12] Daniel Heinsius in his funeral oration on Joseph Justus Scaliger said that Lipsius's pupils at Leiden 'foolishly desired to follow models which they could not successfully copy... sentences hopped along; a lean and jejune speech, juiceless and meagre, broken by some short phrases and plays on words, or by abrupt clauses and short questions, occasioned nausea

---

9. Justus Lipsius, *Principles of Letter-Writing: A Bilingual Text of Justi Lipsii Epistolica Institutio*, ed. R. V. Young and M. Thomas Hester (Carbondale, Ill., 1996) presents this text as bearing out the claim of Croll, *Style*, that Lipsius was 'anti-Ciceronian'. For political implications, see Andrew Eric Shifflett, *Stoicism, Politics, and Literature in the Age of Milton: War and Peace Reconciled* (Cambridge, 1998), pp. 24–30.

10. For an alternative genealogy of the 'familiar' style, see Kathy Eden, *The Renaissance Rediscovery of Intimacy* (Chicago, Ill., 2012).

11. Justus Lipsius, *Iusti Lipsii epistolarum selectarum centuria quarta (quinta) miscellanea postuma* (Antwerp, 1613), 3.28.

12. Trimpi, *Plain Style*, p. 58, cites *Orator* 23.76 on the difficulty of imitating the plain style.

and disgust'.[13] That criticism (inverting as it does the traditional ideal of 'digesting' a source through imitation) cannot be taken entirely straight, since Heinsius was praising Scaliger, who was Lipsius's successor at Leiden, and whose table-talk records criticisms of Lipsius's later style.[14] But it does point towards a truth: Lipsius fostered a style that declared its distinctiveness, and invited others to imitate it, even though it was a style very far from Ciceronian. By having such a distinctive character it invited *formal* imitation, or imitation at the level of clausal and sentence structure.

In that respect Lipsius's mature prose style develops from the discussions of *imitatio* in his *Epistolica institutio.* So, he allows that younger pupils might indeed profitably read nothing but Cicero without suffering permanent damage, but insists that even at this early stage they should pay attention to the 'contextus orationis' (p. 36), or the putting together of his speeches. That concern with the structure of speeches was widely emphasized by early seventeenth-century discussions of *imitatio* which were influenced by Lipsius.[15] But Lipsius also advocates compiling a commonplace book specifically devoted to what he calls 'formulae' (p. 42). That word had been used by Gianfrancesco Pico to mean 'little patterns for making shoes', and again by Melanchthon to mean 'characteristic combinations of words'.[16] For Lipsius a 'formula' is an established structural device—a way of beginning, continuing, or ending speeches (p. 43).

Children should follow these *formulae,* and they might lace the speeches structured by the use of these devices with verbal borrowings from Cicero: 'first, in the composition as a whole imitate formulae mainly and the well-known commonplaces; second, the form, rhythm, features, and texture of the Ciceronian oration' ('ut formulas imprimis et communia illa contextus totius imitere: secundo, ut ductum, numeros, lineamenta et faciem Tullianae orationis', pp. 46–7). Lipsius here shares the concern of earlier German theorists with imitation which seeks to resemble the 'contextus' or the overall shape of Ciceronian speeches, and that concern is evoked here in

13. George W. Robinson, ed., *Autobiography of Joseph Scaliger: with Autobiographical Selections from his Letters, his Testament and the Funeral Orations by Daniel Heinsius and Dominicus Baudius* (Cambridge, 1927), p. 83.

14. See Joseph Juste Scaliger and Jean Daillé, *Scaligerana* (Cologne, 1667), p. 142: 'Lipsius did not glorify Virgil and Terence, because they wrote proper Latin and their sentences were coherent rather than Lipsian' ('Virgilium Lipsius non magnificat & Terentium, quia Latine scribunt & eorum periodi cohaerent, non vero Lipsianae').

15. See, e.g., Bartholomaeus Keckermannus, *Systema Rhetoricae* (Hanover, 1608), p. 907.

16. Cicero tends to use 'formula' to mean something like 'guiding pattern or rule', as in *De Optimo Genere,* 4.15 and *Orator,* 11.36 and 23.75.

language that dissolves textual structure into the physical appearance of a person: *lineamenta et faciem* suggests both 'the features and texture' of Cicero's speeches and 'the characterizing lines and face (*facies*) of Cicero himself'— language most shows a man, indeed.

Adult imitators, he argues, ought to be freer in their method of imitation, and should not replicate phrases from earlier authors. But above all they ought, just like the courtier in Castiglione's *Book of Courtier*, to avoid *affectatio* in their phrasing (p. 48). These elements in Lipsius's treatment of imitation show that he did not simply mark a sudden revolution against earlier forms of Ciceronianism. Rather, like Ramus before him, he had absorbed the formal concerns of earlier German theorists of *imitatio* into his critique of hard-line Ciceronianism, and had fused that with his interest in later Latin prose style.

This helps contextualize Jonson's position within the wider sixteenth-century debates about *imitatio*. He occupies a similar position to Lipsius in relation to earlier theorists. By education and training he was habituated to notice and to aspire to imitate not the lexis but the form and the structure of the texts he read. This, as we shall see, was a vital element in his practice of imitation. But before we turn to Jonson's practice, we should first consider his own remarks on imitation in his *Timber or Discoveries*, since these have typically provided the prologue to discussions of what Jonson actually did with his reading.

Discoveries is often described as a 'commonplace book', and its contents have long been identified as more or less a tissue of translations from a range of authorities, ranging from Seneca and Quintilian, through to the early sixteenth-century Spanish humanist Juan Luis Vives, and right on to Jonson's contemporary John Hoskyns—whose extensive borrowings from Lipsius, duly borrowed by Jonson, have led many scholars to regard *Discoveries* as the clinching piece of evidence that Jonson sought a consciously 'plain' or style-less style.[17] But we should be cautious in using *Discoveries* as a guide to Jonson's own ways of imitating throughout his life. A number of references to datable texts position the majority of the *Discoveries* very late in his career (in the later 1620s and 1630s), and Jonson, despite his protestations about his own moral fixity, changed a great deal in the course of his career in response to the criticisms and also the practices of his contemporaries.

---

17. Notably in Trimpi, *Plain Style*, whose thesis remains a strong influence on Lorna Hutson's introduction to *Discoveries* in *The Cambridge Edition of the Works of Ben Jonson*, 7.483–94.

The main discussion of *imitatio* in *Discoveries* occurs in a section which begins 'It pleased Your Lordship of late to ask my opinion touching the education of your sons' (7.554). The Lord in question is generally supposed to be William Cavendish, Earl of Newcastle. This would place the treatise very late indeed in Jonson's career, since Cavendish's second surviving son was not born until 1630, only seven years before Jonson's death. Whether or not *Discoveries* is quite *that* late in Jonson's career is a moot point. But the form of address to a noble patron should alert us to the rhetorical purpose of the section of *Discoveries* about education. It does not set out Jonson's beliefs about or codify his own practice of imitation. It aims to present Ben Jonson as an elite instructor of the elite, who adapts the rhetorical works of Quintilian and the humanistic treatises of Vives into the vernacular in order to establish that he is perfectly qualified to advise a nobleman on the best way of instructing his sons. So throughout most of his discussion of education Jonson moves easily back and forth between the early books of Quintilian (which concern elementary education) and the key passages about reading and imitation in the early chapters of the tenth book. He does this because his aim is to sound like a skilled teacher, a rhetorician who might himself provide an example to imitate for the sons of a nobleman.

Much of what Jonson culls from Quintilian is conventional: 'For a man to write well, there are required three necessaries: to read the best authors, observe the best speakers, and much exercise of his own style' (7.556; cf. *Institutio*, 10.3.1). But throughout the *Discoveries* Jonson often brings a metaphorical point even to apparently flat statements drawn from Quintilian. Exercise—*exercitatio*—to develop a 'style' always had a particular point, even a barb, for Jonson. He was alive (as Quintilian and Horace had also been) to the fact that a 'stilus' could be both a 'characteristic way of writing' and a writing implement or spike. At the very start of the seventeenth century Jonson declared 'this my style no living man shall touch...But, like a sheathèd sword, it shall defend | My innocent life' (*Poetaster*, 3.5.65–8), and that association between style and the arts of quasi-military training continues through *Discoveries*:[18] 'Periods are beautiful when they are not too long, for so they have their strength too, as in a pike or javelin' (7.565). Jonson translates Quintilian's observations about revision with a relish for the association between rewriting and *exercitatio* or physical practice: 'As we

---

18. Cf. Horace, *Satires*, 2.1.39–41: 'sed hic stilus haud petet ultro | quemquam animantem et me veluti custodiet ensis | vagina tectus' and Peterson, *Imitation and Praise*, pp. 22–3.

see in the contention of leaping, they jump farthest, that fetch their race largest; or, as in throwing a dart or javelin, we force back our arms to make our loose [throw] the stronger' (7.556–7; cf. *Institutio*, 10.3.6).

This might go to support the view that the 'plain' style was overtly masculine, and that its rise was linked to the emergence of homosocial forms of discourse between men.[19] But Jonson's ideal imitator was not just a man who exercised so he could excel in the courtroom or the palaestra: he also makes use of the feminine generative imagery which was also such a strong component in classical theories of *imitatio*. Jonson shares Quintilian's interest in the physically creative power of an author to give birth to something new: 'For all that we invent doth please us in the conception or birth' (7.557), he states. The association between literary invention and childbirth was common in the period,[20] but here it gives a burst of animation to the verb 'invent', which Jonson uses not simply to refer to the rhetorical skill of *inventio* ('to discover of pre-existing materials'), but in the sense 'to produce something new by mental activity'. There is implicitly an entire biography of growth running through the discussion of imitation in *Discoveries*: a rhetorical birth of the mind is honed and trained to become a strong and independent body with a sharp and combative *stilus* of its own, which is simultaneously a procreative body capable of further invention.

Quintilian also guides Jonson's vocabulary in interesting directions a little later on in *Discoveries*: 'such as accustom themselves and are familiar with the best authors, shall ever and anon find somewhat of them in themselves, and in the expression of their minds, even when they feel it not; be able to utter something like theirs, which hath an authority above their own' (7.557; cf. *Institutio*, 2.7.3). The whirl of pronouns here ('them . . . themselves . . . their . . . they . . . theirs . . . their own'—whose exactly?) is combined with arresting shifts in sense: what does it mean to 'find' something of another author in oneself even if one does not 'feel' it? That implies discovering retrospectively and with surprise a debt to something to which one is 'accustomed' and 'familiar' (cf. *familiaria*, *Institutio*, 2.7.3)—and both those words are used with extreme deliberateness to suggest both habituation in and a family relationship to a source text.

19. Lorna Hutson, 'Liking Men: Ben Jonson's Closet Opened', *ELH* 71 (2004), 1065–96, and Patricia Parker, 'Virile Style', in Louise Fradenburg and Carla Freccero, eds., *Premodern Sexualities* (London, 1996), 199–222.

20. For this image, see Katherine Eisaman Maus, 'A Womb of His Own: Male Renaissance Poets in the Female Body', in James Grantham Turner, ed., *Sexuality and Gender in Early Modern Europe: Institutions, Texts, Images* (Cambridge, 1993), 266–88.

The phrase 'in the expression of their minds' might also appear to press *imitatio* towards an expressivist aesthetic—though, here, as in the passage from Erasmus's *Ciceronianus* which argued that 'if you want to express [*exprimere*] the whole Cicero you cannot express [*exprimere*] yourself' (p. 399/p. 649), it is likely that the literal sense of 'making an external impression from the mould or form that is one's mind' is what makes it appear that Jonson has travelled so far in that direction. And he moves in that direction because he is nudged by Quintilian to do so. So the passage which Jonson is adapting or remembering here states 'and so without being conscious of doing so they will express the form of that speech which they had received deeply into their mind' ('et iam non sentientes formam orationis illam, quam mente penitus acceperint, exprimerent', *Institutio*, 2.7.3). Quintilian's use of the word 'forma' in conjunction with 'exprimerent' carries across to Jonson's vocabulary of 'expression': imitation is a matter of registering and then expressing a 'form' that is impressed upon your mind. But the elasticity of Quintilian's language here also allows that the metaphor of imitation as the 'expression' of a pre-existing 'mould' or type might be extended. Texts could be regarded as replicable structures or general outlines ('forms') rather than just seals or types which are then stamped out in identical copies. That is borne out by Quintilian's insistence in the same passage that imitators grasp not just the 'forma' of a speech, but also its 'compositio' and its 'figurae', its structure and both its rhetorical figures and the character of its style.[21]

So Jonson read and translated Quintilian later in his life with vigour. He drew out of Quintilian's metaphors a view of imitation as akin to a physical process of training or of birth, and responded actively to Quintilian's suggestion that imitators 'express the form' of their originals rather than simply replicating it. Jonson's inclination towards biological and physical imagery also comes through in the ways in which the *Discoveries* draw on sources other than the *Institutio*. Jonson owed a great deal to Juan Luis Vives's *De Ratione Dicendi* (1533), and was prone to echo Vives when Vives in turn used the corporeal imagery on which Quintilian had relied so strongly in his discussion of imitation and style. And curiously, as scholars have often

---

21. 'They will have a plentiful and choice vocabulary and a command of artistic structure and a supply of figures which will not have to be hunted for, but will offer themselves spontaneously from the treasure house, if I may so call it, in which they are stored' ('Abundabunt autem copia verborum optimorum et compositione et figuris iam non quaesitis sed sponte et ex reposito velut thesauro se offerentibus'), *Institutio*, 2.7.4.

44 IMITATING AUTHORS

remarked, passages drawn directly from Vives are also often the moments at which Jonson seems to sound most like Jonson. Jonson's digest of a passage from the start of the second book of Vives's *De Ratione Dicendi* (with which this chapter began) is the strongest example:

> Language most shows a man: speak, that I may see thee. It springs out of the most retired and inmost parts of us, and is the image of the parent of it, the mind. No glass renders a man's form or likeness so true as his speech. Nay it is likened to a man; and as we consider feature and composition in a man, so words in language: in the greatness, aptness, sound, structure, and harmony of it. Some men are tall and big, so some language is high and great. Then the words are chosen, their sound ample, the composition full, the absolution plenteous and poured out, all grave, sinewy, and strong. Some are little, and dwarfs; so of speech, it is humble and low, the words poor and flat, the members and periods thin and weak, without knitting or number. The middle are of a just stature. (7.567–8)

The start of this is a more or less a straight translation of Vives, before Jonson begins to paraphrase Vives's extended parallels between the different characters of style and distinct human bodily types:

> Wherefore speech arises from the most inward recesses of our hearts, where the true and unadulterated man resides. And it is the image of its parent, the mind, and to this extent of the universe of man. So that there is no mirror which more exactly reflects the likeness (*simulacrum*) of a man than speech. Nor is that Greek proverb wrong which states that 'a man's life is like his speech.' Therefore they apply the same terminology [to kinds of style] as we are accustomed to use in describing the human mind and body... Therefore let us work our way through the aspects of the human body, beginning with those which are most obvious to the senses. First of all we speak of stature, which can be seen most clearly in the size and sound of words and of structure. From this, high speech is termed 'grand', 'sublime', or 'elevated': in which the words are sophisticated and cultured, and their sound loud, magnificent, the composition full, and the completeness all worked together, lest it wanders licentiously.

> Quippe oratio ex intimis nostri pectoris recessibus oritur, ubi verus ille ac purus homo habitat. Et imago est animi parentis sui, atque adeo hominis universi. Ut non sit ullum speculum, quod hominis simulacrum certius reddat, quam oratio. Nec iniuria Graeco proverbio iactatur, talem esse quemquam, qualis sit eius oratio. Ergo easdem appellationes indiderunt, quas in hominis solemus usurpare ex animo, & corpore... Progrediamur igitur per humana omnia a corporeis ordientes, quae maxime sunt exposita sensibus. Primum omnium de statura, quae spectatur potissimum in magnitudine et sono verborum ac structurae. Ex illa appellationes has sumit oratio magna, grandis, sublimis,

celsa: in qua verba sunt urbana et culta, sonus eorum amplus, magnificus, compositio plena, absolutiones fusae, modo ne licentiose evagentur.[22]

Instead of developing the traditional contrast between successful imitation as a source of strength and growth on the one hand and imitation as a mere *simulacrum* on the other, Vives collapses it (and he is not alone in doing this): language is such an accurate image of its parent that it creates an *imago* or *simulacrum* of the mind, in the sense of a 'perfect likeness'.

In the *De Ratione Dicendi* Vives goes on to explore at some length the 'characters' of style, which he extends beyond the conventional triad of the high, middle, and low styles, because, he argues, there are as many different sizes of body as there are characters of style. Jonson massively compresses Vives's discussion of style, in order (he was himself a man of superior bulk, shall we say) to re-enforce its corporeal imagery. And when Jonson returns later in the *Discoveries* to the subject of imitation, in a section devoted to poets and poetry, he is again insistently corporeal:

> The third requisite in our poet or maker is imitation, to be able to convert the substance or riches of another poet to his own use. To make choice of one excellent man above the rest, and so to follow him till he grow very he, or so like him as the copy may be mistaken for the principal. Not as a creature that swallows what it takes in crude, raw, or indigested, but that feeds with an appetite, and hath a stomach to concoct, divide, and turn all into nourishment. Not to imitate servilely, as Horace saith, and catch at vices, for virtue: but to draw forth out of the best and choicest flowers with the bee, and turn all into honey, work it into one relish, and savour, make our imitation sweet; observe how the best writers have imitated, and follow them. How Virgil and Statius have imitated Homer, how Horace, Archilochus; how Alcaeus, and the other lyrics, and so of the rest. (7.582)

In this passage Jonson switches away from Vives, and is generally said to have turned to Jacobus Pontanus's *Institutio Poetica* (an epitomized version of which was printed in London in 1624). Given that Pontanus was himself digesting familiar remarks about imitation, from the *Ad Herennium* to Seneca's epistles, it is difficult to be entirely sure either about the source itself or which version of it Jonson actually consulted.[23]

22. My translation. Text from Juan Luis Vives, *Io. Lodouici Viuis . . . opera*, ed. Huldericus Coccius (Basel, 1555), 1.103–4. On this treatise, see Peter Mack, 'Vives's *De Ratione Dicendi*: Structure, Innovations, Problems', *Rhetorica* 23 (2005), 65–92.

23. Johann Buchler and Jacob Pontanus, *Sacrarum profanarumq[ue] phrasium poeticarum thesaurus* (London, 1624), pp. 440–1. Peterson, *Imitation and Praise*, pp. 6–10 argues (following Donald Lemen Clark, 'The Requirements of a Poet: A Note on the Sources of Ben Jonson's "Timber",

The insistent syntax of Jonson's passage appears to support the traditional view of him as a voracious assimilator, who seeks to absorb all substance into himself, and avoid the moral perils of instability and change.[24] It also suggests that as a result of his reading in Quintilian—though we should not discount Jonson's personal delight in food—he was instinctively inclined to equate good writing with a body which had capacious digestive powers.[25] Imitation is described through a series of infinitive verbs, 'To make choice', 'to follow', 'to draw forth', 'to work', 'to turn' (a feature of the passage which strongly suggests Jonson had the shorter version of Pontanus before him). But that repeated grammatical structure is unbalanced by the mixture of metaphors suggested by those verbs: 'to follow him' suggests the metaphor of the path, and yet the very next verb, 'till he grow', transforms following into biological development, and then is rapidly supplanted by the vocabulary of copying, and then of feeding. The argument too is dispersive whilst appearing to go in one direction. At its start an author is supposed to be following one person; by its end, however, the imitator is urged to consider how a number of authors have imitated their *exempla*. The goal is a single body, but that single body has radial connections to several different sources of reading, and it is a body that seeks to follow a path that does not go simply in one direction.

Although Jonson is in *Discoveries* attempting to sound like a master rhetorician who has organically developed from his reading the skill to make the sons of the nobility thrill with rhetorical vigour, he is himself following many different textual paths in that work. And the traces of his own earlier education sometimes shine through the facade of anglicized European humanism which he sought to create. The injunction to 'observe how the best writers have imitated, and follow them' in the passage just quoted merits particular attention. It certainly does not come from either version of Pontanus's *Institutio* or from any other readily identifiable authority. An exact verbal source for the phrase may yet come to light; but

Paragraph 130', *Modern Philology* 16 (1918), 413–29) that Jonson referred to the full version of 1600 rather than to Buchler's paraphrase. The paraphrase, however, is closer to the repeated infinitives of Jonson here. The longer version refers, as Jonson does but the Buchler version does not, to Horace's 'O imitatores servum pecus' (Jacobus Pontanus, *Jacobi Pontani . . . poeticarum institutionum libri iii* (Ingolstadt, 1600), p. 30), but that passage is so familiar that Jonson would not have needed a source.

24. See Greene, 'Centered Self'.
25. See Bruce Thomas Boehrer, *The Fury of Men's Gullets: Ben Jonson and the Digestive Canal* (Philadelphia, 1997).

whether or not such a source is eventually discovered, Jonson's words are absolutely in line with the Northern European Ciceronian tradition as embodied in Ascham and Sturm, who had argued that an imitator should imitate not just an author, but the way in which that author has imitated others. As Ascham put it 'But for rhetoric I want Cicero himself—if not him alone, certainly him in preference to others. And I must have Cicero the imitator as my model, not the imitator of Cicero... For the one who intelligently observes how Cicero followed others will most successfully see how Cicero himself is to be followed.'[26]

This gives us a wider perspective on Jonson's supposed 'anti-Ciceronianism' and on his attitudes to *imitatio* more generally. Even at this very late point in Jonson's career the voices of his own schoolmasters can be heard echoing through the gaps between the texts which he stitched together in *Discoveries*. Underlying Jonson's thinking about and practice of *imitatio* was a deep stratum of later sixteenth-century Ciceronian theory: Sturm, Ascham, and Melanchthon—the latter of whom was praised by Vives as providing a key guide to practice alongside Cicero's *De Oratore*, *Orator*, and *Brutus*.[27]

That is not surprising; indeed it is what we should expect. Jonson attended Westminster School from about 1579. Ascham's letters to Sturm about imitation were edited by Edward Grant, who was in 1579 the headmaster of Westminster School. The printed editions of Ascham's Sturmian letters on imitation also contained a dedicatory poem by Jonson's own master William Camden. The later German Ciceronians are a deep stratum in the development of Jonson's poetics. Giving them their due weight within the formation of his style enables us to appreciate a key fact about his particular mode of imitation. Jonson was acutely sensitized by his education to the imitation of *form* in a wide range of senses: he was trained to think about an author's overall character of style as inhering in *collocatio*, in word-order and the structure of argument. He was trained not just to stamp out a copy of an earlier author or to fashion centred, manly speech from his reading, but to 'express' the 'form' of a prior model or mould, and to seek himself to become such a form, which could be expressed by others.

And we might note here that the word 'express' here has a strange reciprocality: both the wax and the seal 'express' the image, one by yielding and the other by pressing. 'Expressing' an original might be an active process of

26. Roger Ascham, *Letters of Roger Ascham*, ed. Alvin Vos (New York, 1989), p. 271.
27. Juan Luis Vives, *Vives: On Education: a Translation of the De Tradendis Disciplinis*, trans. Foster Watson (Cambridge, 1913), p. 183; Vives, ed. Coccius, *Opera*, p. 491.

fashioning or a passive one of receiving a 'seal' from that original. And either
way the 'expression' of a source, if it was considered as a 'form', would
not entail replicating its language but grasping its structural features. As
Bartholomaeus Keckermann put it 'imitation is particularly important in
inventio, collocatio, and the structuring of words' ('Praecipue autem imitatio dominatur in inventione, collocatione et structura verborum').[28] Hence
in formal imitation, *imitatio* might mean imitating the rhetorical figurations
of an earlier author rather than his words, or it might entail imitating the
way in which an earlier author had imitated his sources—the consequence
of which would be necessarily to occlude the relationship between the origin text and its imitation.

Formal imitation

Jonson the poet did not 'digest' his sources as though they were so much
ethical matter from which he sought to build the stable moral body of
Ben Jonson, author. He read his authors, pen in hand, with an eye to their
rhetorical figuration, their generically distinctive features, and the way they
were put together. He wrote poems based on those exacting formal observations. His tendency to do this is most visible in what might appear to be
an unlikely place: what are often called Jonson's 'literal' translations of
classical texts. Jonson completed a very close verse translation of Horace's
Ars Poetica in the early seventeenth century, which he then revised sometime after 1610 in the light of Daniel Heinsius's reordering of Horace's text.
The translation was not printed until 1640, and has generally enjoyed low
critical esteem. It is traditionally placed at the other end of the scale from
Jonson's 'free' imitations of Martial or Seneca or indeed of Horace.

The main reason for treating Jonson's *Ars Poetica* in this way does not lie
in its nature, but in the particularities of its reception history. John Dryden
in his 'Preface' to the translation of Ovid's epistles of 1680 presented Jonson's
Ars Poetica as the primary example of 'metaphrase', or 'turning an Author
word by word, and Line by Line, from one Language into another'. Dryden
(at that date still a member of the English Church) presented his own
favoured form of 'paraphrase', or 'translation with latitude', as a *via media*
between the extremes of superstitiously faithful metaphrase (for which one

28. Keckermannus, *Systema Rhetoricae*, p. 908.

might read 'Popish devotion to the arbitrary power of the original') and the licentiousness of imitation. Dryden takes imitation to be 'an Endeavour of a later Poet to write like one who has written before him on the same Subject: that is, not to Translate his words, or to be Confin'd to his Sense, but only to set him as a Pattern, and to write, as he supposes, that Author would have done, had he liv'd in our Age, and in our Country' and sees it as potentially 'the greatest wrong which can be done to the Memory and Reputation of the Dead'.[29]

Dryden's division of translation into these three types was massively influential, but it should not be forgotten that it was at least in part a work of self-defence, designed to align his own relatively free practice as a translator with latitudinarian currents in the English Church. No part of it accurately describes Jonson's methods of translating or imitating. Indeed Jonson translated in ways that were very close structural kin to his methods of imitating. He both translated 'literally' and imitated 'freely' with acute awareness of word-order and rhetorical structure. Although Jonson's translation of the *Ars Poetica* aspires towards compression, and includes frequent Latinate disruptions of expected English word-order, it has more in common with what Dryden describes as 'imitation' than with Dryden's description of metaphrastic word by word translation:

> 'Tis hard to speak things common properly,
> And thou mayst better bring a rhapsody
> Of Homer's forth in acts than of thine own
> First publish things unspoken and unknown.
> Yet common matter thou thine own mayst make,
> If thou the vile, broad-trodden ring forsake.
> For, being a poet, thou may'st feign, create;
> Not care, as thou wouldst faithfully translate,
> To render word for word; nor with thy sleight
> Of imitation leap into a strait
> From whence thy modesty, or poem's law,
> Forbids thee forth again thy foot to draw.　　(183–94)

> 　　　Difficile est proprie communia dicere, tuque
> Rectius Iliacum carmen deducis in actus,
> Quam si proferres ignota, indictaque primus.
> Publica materies privati iuris erit, si

29. John Dryden, *The Works*, ed. Edward Niles Hooker, H. T. Swedenberg, and Vinton A. Dearing, 20 vols. (Berkeley, 1956–2000), 1.114–17. See Paul Hammond, *Dryden and the Traces of Classical Rome* (Oxford, 1999), pp. 143–50.

> Nec circa vilem patulumque moraberis orbem:
> Nec verbum verbo curabis reddere fidus
> Interpres; nec desilies imitator in artum,
> Unde pedem proferre pudor vetet aut operis lex...   (128–35)

This may look 'literal', or as critics are fond of saying 'painstakingly literal';
but in the extract quoted above, which translates Horace's warning against
being a mere 'faithful translator', Jonson inserts a phrase which insists on the
free creative power of a maker: 'being a poet, thou may'st feign, create'. That
is apparently an intrusion of procreative poetics analogous to that phrase
from *Discoveries* 'For all that we invent doth please us in the conception or
birth'. The insertion appears completely at odds with the careful attempt
in the translation as a whole to reproduce the concision of Horace's style, a
care which extends to a preference for English words which are cognate
with the Latin ('common', 'properly', 'acts', 'vile', 'render'), and which leads
Jonson to replicate the form if not the exact plosive effect of Horace's alliterative triplet 'pedem proferre pudor' in 'Forbids thee forth again thy foot'.

But Jonson's Horace should not be regarded as a 'literal translation'. It
attempts to reproduce the verbal collocations, word-order, and structure of
the *Ars Poetica*, as well as to unfold in English, even at the cost of occasionally expanding the original, the key principles which it sets out. This gives
the translation both bounds and licence. It is licensed to extrapolate the
sense of the original by additions ('thou mayst feign, create'), as well as seeking to replicate the rhetorical shaping of the translated text. For these reasons
it should not be positioned within a tradition of 'word for word' translation,
but rather in a long tradition of translation that sought to reproduce the
rhetorical figures and the underlying character of the translated author. That
tradition goes back to an extremely influential, but also extremely obscure,
passage in Cicero's *De Optimo Genere Oratorum*, in which Cicero describes
how he translated speeches by Aeschines and Demosthenes:

> And I did not translate them as an interpreter, but as an orator, keeping the
> same ideas and the forms, or as one might say the 'figures' of thought, but in a
> language which conforms to our usage. And in so doing, I did not hold it
> necessary to render word for word, but I preserved the general style and force
> of the language.
>
> nec converti ut interpres, sed ut orator, sententiis isdem et earum formis tam-
> quam figuris, verbis ad nostram consuetudinem aptis. In quibus non verbum
> pro verbo necesse habui reddere, sed genus omne verborum vimque servavi.[30]

30. Text from Marcus Tullius Cicero, *De Inventione; de Optimo Genera Oratorum; Topica*, trans.
    H. M. Hubbell (Cambridge, Mass., 1949), 5.14. For discussion, see Siobhán McElduff, *Roman*

Cicero's discussion of translation relies on several keywords from the tradition of writing about *imitatio*: he seeks to preserve the form (*forma*), kind (*genus*) of writing, and its force, or *vis*. That implicit association between translation and imitation frequently became explicit in sixteenth-century discussions of the topic. From Denys Lambin's edition of the *Ars Poetica* in 1561 onwards it became common for commentators to cite this passage from Cicero as a gloss on Horace's injunction not to translate as a 'fidus interpres'. Lambin, indeed, glosses the passage from the *Ars Poetica* as an invitation to imitate not like a mere interpreter, but 'so that it will look as though we are drinking from the same sources, from our judgement and understanding' as our originals. He then goes on to cite the extract from the *De Optimo Genere* quoted above to explain what he means.[31]

Jonson certainly knew Cicero's remarks, which had been central to arguments about the nature of translation through the early middle ages and onwards, and which could also figure in arguments about *imitatio*. So St Jerome's *Epistle* 57 juxtaposed Cicero's discussion of translation with Horace's injunction not to be a 'fidus interpres', but also very influentially associated translating word for word with the rhetorical abuse termed *kakozēlía* or 'slavish imitation'. As we have seen, that rhetorical vice had been condemned by Quintilian as 'bad affectation', and it is the vice which Castiglione's courtier seeks to avoid by his internalization of rhetorical and social practices into his effortless *sprezzatura*.[32] In the sixteenth century there was a general preference for translating 'like an orator', but there was extensive debate about what Cicero meant by this phrase. What did it mean to preserve the 'figurae' and 'formae' of the original? Did Cicero mean by 'figurae' the figures of speech used by the author who was being translated?

Theories of Translation: Surpassing the Source (New York, 2013), pp. 96–121, and for its early influence, see Rita Copeland, *Rhetoric, Hermeneutics and Translation in the Middle Ages: Academic Traditions and Vernacular Texts* (Cambridge, 1991). Sheldon Brammall, *The English Aeneid: Translations of Virgil, 1555–1646* (Edinburgh, 2015) is particularly helpful on translation theory in the period.

31. 'Monet igitur hoc loco Horatius, ne eos, quos nobis proposuimus imitandos, aut e quibus argumentum scribendi petimus, ita sequamur, ut interpres, sed potius ut e fontibus eorum, iudicio, arbitrioque nostro, quantum, quoque modo videbitur, hauriamus', *Q. Horatius Flaccus, ex fide atque auctoritate decem librorum manuscriptorum, Opera*, ed. Denys Lambin (Venice, 1566), fol. 196r–v. I cite from a copy which formerly belonged to Ben Jonson's friend Dudley Digges (Codrington Library, All Souls College, Oxford, b.11.16(2)). Surprisingly Lambin does not record the parallel in his edition of Cicero from 1566, a copy of which was owned by Jonson. On the relationship between Horace and Cicero's theories of translation, see McElduff, *Roman Theories of Translation*, p. 145.

32. Jerome, *Epistles*, 57.5.2–3 in *Liber de optimo genere interpretandi (Epistula 57)*, ed. G. J. M. Bartelink (Leiden, 1980), pp. 13–14; see Erika Rummel, *Erasmus as a Translator of the Classics* (Toronto, 1985), pp. 27–8. The fear of *kakozēlía* is also found in discussions of translation by Englishmen: see Laurence Humphrey, *Interpretatio Linguarum* (Basel, 1559), p. 248.

Or was the word 'figura' used in the sense which Cicero himself preferred, to refer to a particular 'character' of style?[33]

In the fullest sixteenth-century discussion of Cicero's gnomic remarks, the Italian scholar Sebastiano Fausto da Longiano concluded that by 'forma' and 'figura' Cicero probably meant 'l'ordine delle cose', the way in which arguments and sentences are sequenced in a speech. He also favoured taking the word 'figura' as referring to the rhetorical 'schemes' or figures of the source text,[34] but he allowed that Cicero's 'formis tanquam figuris' were completely mysterious words ('tutte parole di misterio').[35] In order to explicate those mysterious words he makes a connection between this passage and the section of the *Orator* (11.36) in which Cicero connects the *forma* of an author with the word 'character'—a passage which we saw in Chapter 6 was crucial in encouraging an association between 'the ideal form of an orator' and the more humdrum sense of 'the formal aspects of a speech'. Fausto also noted (and this was not unusual in the period) that translating 'ut orator' was extremely close to *imitatio*.

These debates about the fine line between translation and imitation are highly suggestive aids to understanding Jonson's practice as a translator. He translated Horace not just 'faithfully', like a Catholic clinging to the very words of the Bible, but 'as an orator', with a concern for the *forma* and *figura* of his original in all the senses of those flexible and ambiguous terms. At one moment he closely follows the rhetorical shape of his source text, while at another he flexes away from it to incorporate thoughts which a *forma*—an abstract idea, even perhaps a Platonic idea—of Horace might have had. The aim to preserve what Cicero calls the 'vis' or 'force' of the original allowed for the insertion of expansions or glosses (such as 'thou mayst feign, create') which reinforced its argument.

If the aim of 'rhetorical' translation was to replicate the 'form' in the sense of 'the disposition of materials' of an original this also explains one apparently strange feature of Jonson's revisions to his translation of Horace. The version of the translation published in the second Folio of 1640 followed Daniel Heinsius's rearrangement of the poem from his edition of 1610. The revision was not simply a sign of Jonson's admiration for

---

33. On the early history of 'figura', see Erich Auerbach, *Scenes from the Drama of European Literature*, trans. Paolo Valesio (Manchester, 1984), pp. 11–28.

34. Sebastiano Fausto, *Dialogo del Fausto da Longiano del modo de lo tradurre d'una in altra lingua segondo le regole mostrate da Cicerone* (Venice, 1556), fol. 20v.

35. Fausto, *Dialogo*, fol. 16r. Fausto is discussed in Glyn P. Norton, *The Ideology and Language of Translation in Renaissance France and their Humanist Antecedents* (Geneva, 1984), pp. 198–203.

Heinsius—although he did both admire his work and meet the man himself.[36] Heinsius's reordering affected the overall structuration of Horace's poetic treatise, its disposition and arrangement, or its *forma* in the wider sense of the arrangement of its argument. Heinsius's own justification for his reordering was the requirement that the argument of the text cohere. It was to the inner coherence and the structure of his Latin originals—their *forma* and their *figura* in the widest senses—that Jonson was especially attuned. This shaped his work both as a translator and as an imitator.

Jonson's *Epigrams*

Jonson's *Epigrams* appeared in the Folio of his works of 1616. Both the form of the book and individual poems within it are imitations from Martial, whose fourteen volumes of epigrams were written in the first century AD.[37] There were many reasons why Jonson should have been drawn towards Martial's epigrams in the early seventeenth century. Martial's books created what William Fitzgerald has aptly called a 'panegyrico-scoptic world' by combining panegyrics on the great with satirical attacks on Roman types and customs.[38] By 1616, or by 1612, when a lost edition of Jonson's *Epigrams* may possibly have appeared, Jonson had more or less by accident accumulated a similarly miscellaneous body of poems in praise of patrons and in scorn of unnamed contemporary types. To turn these into a literary statement by gathering them into a book modelled on Martial's made sense.

But the affinity between Jonson and Martial went beyond expediency. Martial was (and remains) a supremely imitable poet because his abrupt and pointed style, with its penchant for tropes and turns on words as well as for figures of ordered repetition, is every inch a *stilus*: poem after poem is designed, honed, and rhetorically pointed to sink into the flesh of its victims. In addition, Martial is relatively unusual among classical authors for being identified with a single sub-genre: the epigram. The genre of the epigram is itself unusually multiplex and extensible: Martial himself offers epigrams about dodgy goings on in bathhouses, epigrams in praise of rulers,

36. David McPherson, 'Ben Jonson Meets Daniel Heinsius, 1613', *English Language Notes* 14 (1976), 105–9.
37. On Jonson's reconstructions of classical volumes of verse, see Richard C. Newton, 'Jonson and the (Re-)Invention of the Book', in Claude J. Summers and Ted Larry Pebworth, eds., *Classic and Cavalier: Essays on Jonson and the Sons of Ben* (Pittsburgh, 1982), 31–55.
38. William Fitzgerald, *Martial: The World of the Epigram* (Chicago, Ill., and London, 2007), p. 115.

epigrams which are invitations to dinner, epigrams which are social ripostes, and epigrams which aspire to become epitaphs, which lament the death of a slave or scribe. In writing several of each of these sub-kinds Martial not only identified his own work with the genre of the epigram but also in effect encoded the process of generative rewriting into his own *oeuvre*. He often seems to be rewriting his own poems, which fall into recognizable groups which answer, extend, and respond to each other, as though contributing to infinitely extensible sub-genres or groups within his own body of work. That practice made the epigram an unusually accommodating form for imitators: it provided an open invitation to Martial's successors to continue the series.

What makes Martial a particularly piquant author to imitate is that he is also famous for having insisted that those who copy and recite his poems should recognize that they are his property. He was the first (and only) Latin poet to call someone who stole his verses a *plagiarius* (1.52.9), or kidnapper, and repeatedly attacks those who appropriate his verse as their own.[39] His sharp style, ringing the changes on the forms and possible senses of verbs, and punctuating those experimental transformations of a word by sentences of explosive brevity, of course gave stylistic support to his overt claims to ownership over his verses by establishing a style which seemed entirely 'his own'—despite his own deep and recurrent debts to Catullus. The epigram as practised by Martial combined an unusually rich version of generic openness to imitation with a directly conflicting insistence on textual ownership—an insistence which is a particularly surprising companion for poems which often present themselves as jokes and put-downs, or as adaptable social performances which might be used by other people in similar situations. Bridging those two incompatible elements was a *style* with its own character: a repertoire of rhetorical characteristics that made a Martial epigram seem not just to be an epigram, but a *Martial* epigram.

All of this made Martial the best possible poetic master for Ben Jonson, an imitative poet who was consistently preoccupied with his ownership of his writings. As Joseph Loewenstein has shown, Jonson derived the roots of his 'bibliographic ego', or his preoccupation with preserving his own textual identity in an age of mechanical reproduction, from Martial:[40] Jonson's attacks on 'Prowl the Plagiary' (Epigram 81), on hack poets, and 'On

---

39. All quotations from Martial, *Epigrams*, trans. D. R. Shackleton Bailey, 3 vols. (Cambridge, Mass., and London, 1993).
40. See Loewenstein, *Ben Jonson and Possessive Authorship*.

Playwright', for whom 'Five of my jests, then stol'n, passed him a play' (Epigram 100), are all continuations of Martial's attempt to use accusations of plagiarism both to control the spread and circulation of his own writing techniques, and to mark them as his own. But Jonson also imitated Martial's 'form' and 'figure'—his syntax, and his favoured rhetorical figurations.

Here again Jonson's practice as a translator is the best guide to his work as an imitator. Around the end of the first decade of the seventeenth century Jonson translated Martial's poem on the happy life (10.47).[41] The poem does not seek to drive a pointed *stilus* into the flesh of victim, since it was addressed to Martial's friend Julius Martialis—although early modern editors believed it was a soliloquy by the poet to himself:

> The things that make the happier life are these,
> Most pleasant Martial: substance got with ease,
> Not laboured for, but left thee by thy sire;
> A soil not barren; a continual fire;
> Never at law; seldom in office gowned;   5
> A quiet mind; free powers; and body sound;
> A wise simplicity; friends alike-stated;
> Thy table without art, and easy rated;
> Thy night not drunken, but from cares laid waste;
> No sour or sullen bed-mate, yet a chaste;   10
> Sleep that will make the darkest hours swift-paced.
> Will to be what thou art; and nothing more:
> Nor fear thy latest day, nor wish therefor.

> *Vitam quae faciant beatiorem,*
> *Iucundissime Martialis, haec sunt:*
> *Res non parta labore, sed relicta;*
> *Non ingratus ager, focus perennis;*
> *Lis numquam, toga rara, mens quieta;*   5
> *Vires ingenuae, salubre corpus;*
> *Prudens simplicitas, pares amici;*
> *Convictus facilis, sine arte mensa:*
> *Nox non ebria, sed soluta curis:*
> *Non tristis torus, attamen pudicus:*   10
> *Somnus, qui faciat breves tenebras:*
> *Quod sis, esse velis nihilque malis:*
> *Summum nec metuas diem, nec optes.*

---

41. Herford and Simpson printed the poem at the end of *The Underwood*. There is no textual authority for doing so, and in my edition in *The Cambridge Edition of the Works of Ben Jonson*, 4.220 it appears among ungathered verse.

The translation is constructed so as to spill as little as possible over the form of its original's thirteen lines, and is repeatedly exact. The superlative 'iucundissime' becomes 'most pleasant'; the comparative 'beatiorem' is rendered by 'happier'. Only the need to expand and gloss a specifically Roman custom and make it apt to his times (as Cicero advised in his description of how to translate 'as an orator') leads to an expansion: 'toga rara', is unpacked into 'seldom in office gowned'. Even here, however, Jonson is trying to think in Latin, since he gives to the word 'office' some of the Latinate weighting that it has in Cicero's *De Officiis*, of offices and public duties. This is a translation driven by the desire to preserve the *forma* of its original with careful but minimal adaptation to Jonson's times.

Jonson's 'imitations' of Martial display a skill which is closely analogous to that displayed in the 'literal' translation. Indeed some of his most 'original' or sourceless epigrams appear to have been created not from an understanding of particular poems by Martial but from a grasp of his general stylistic character, his habitual syntactic practices, the snaps and returns of his syntax, the bite of his style. They imitate Martial as a *genus dicendi*, a way of writing. A good example is Epigram 12 on Lieutenant Shift:

> Shift, here in town not meanest among squires
> That haunt Pict-Hatch, Marsh-Lambeth and Whitefriars,
> Keeps himself with half a man, and defrays
> The charge of that state with this charm: 'God pays'.
> By that one spell he lives, eats, drinks, arrays
> Himself: his whole revenue is 'God pays'.
> ...
> Then takes up fresh commodity for days;
> Signs to new bond; forfeits, and cries 'God pays'.
> That lost, he keeps his chamber, reads *Essays*,
> Takes physic, tears the papers; still God pays.
> ...
> Not his poor cockatrice but he betrays
> Thus; and for his lechery scores 'God pays'.
> But see! th' old bawd hath served him in his trim,
> Lent him a pocky whore. She hath paid him.

A favourite technique of Martial's is to make one of his victims repeat a catch-phrase which the poet spins round against the victim at the end of the poem. He does this with the set phrase 'what's it to you?' ('quid ad te') in Epigram 7.10. Martial plays a similar trick with a repeated phrase in 4.71, in which he says that 'no girl says no' ('nulla puella negat'), which he then turns about to say that even a chaste one doesn't say no; she just doesn't do anything. Jonson takes over that trope, in which a phrase returns and then turns on its victim, and uses it in a piece of imitation which it seems appropriate to call 'formal' or even 'figural', since it is grounded in identifying and then replicating a characterizing figure of speech from an earlier author. But his imitation is also adaptive to Jonson's times. It takes Martial's rhetorical figure and embeds it in a poem so steeped in the customs of early seventeenth-century London that it seems to be entirely the product of its own times. Locations, fashions, even Shift's consolatory reading-matter of *Essays* (Florio's translation of Montaigne's *Essays* appeared in 1603) pin the poem exactly to the first decade of the seventeenth century.

That combination of formal/figural and adaptive *imitatio* is crucial to Jonson's wider project of insisting that his poems are his and not another person's. His imitation of Martial is at once lacking in visible debt to its original because it is 'formal', based on a grasp of Martial's characteristic figurations, and because it is so adaptive to the circumstances of the present. As a result it seems to be simply Ben Jonson talking to and of his age. It might be tempting to identify Jonson's practice here with the form of imitation which G. W. Pigman has called 'dissimulative', which seeks to occlude its own source texts, or even to demur with Gian Biagio Conte that 'to allege an imitation without being able to point to convincing traces and proofs would be a serious betrayal of the intertextual method'.[42] But formal imitation and adaptive imitation are intrinsically 'dissimulative' but are so *per accidens*, since they render the source text a transposable structure which can be re-embedded in new times. Jonson was not driven by a desire to occlude a poetic father, but to take over the structural relationships of the parent texts. Jonson's imitations are not motivated by a desire to *conceal* a source, but rather by a desire to display *how* he has read it. *Pace* Conte, that *is* a form of *imitatio*. His epigrams are so deeply grounded in rhetorical analysis of his source texts that the source vanishes into a matrix of figures which can be rendered 'apt' (ad-apted) to Jonson's own times. As a result the style declares rather than conceals a debt to Martial. It cries out that Jonson has grasped Martial's 'form' and has adapted that form to his own purposes, and invites its readers to applaud the rebirth of the old texts in new forms.

---

42. Gian Biagio Conte, *Stealing the Club from Hercules: On Imitation in Latin Poetry* (Berlin and Boston, 2017), p. 2; G. W. Pigman, 'Versions of Imitation in the Renaissance', *Renaissance Quarterly* 33 (1980), 1–32.

Regarding Jonson as a formal or figural imitator in this sense clarifies several apparently perplexing features of his 'own' verse. His poems are both famously imitative and display a style which telegraphs its distinctiveness. Jonson will have no nonsense, and he will say it straight, and he will always be the first to tell you that he is doing so. He will also probably say that he is either the first to have done something (be it writing plays that obey the laws of comedy or writing classically inspired epigrams) or that he is the first to do it properly if it so happened that another vernacular author had preceded him. He will make these claims even if they are patently untrue. The epigraph from Horace's *Epistles* (1.1.922) which he attached to the 1600 quarto of *Every Man Out of his Humour* says it all: 'I did not press down my foot in another's tracks' ('non aliena meo pressi pede'). This quotation comes from the influential passage in which Horace attacks the slavish herd (*servum pecus*) of imitators, and it is one to which Jonson's imitative writing frequently either explicitly or implicitly recurs.

The desire to make a new impression—to establish a new imprint on the shape of English by 'expressing' an earlier form—is central to Jonson's ambition as a poet. In Epigram 18 he declares his novelty by directing his stylus at his 'Meer English Censurer', to whom he insists that his is the right and true and first way of writing epigrams:

> To thee my way in epigrams seems new,
>   When both it is the old way and the true.
> Thou say'st that cannot be, for thou hast seen
>   Davies and Weever, and the best have been,
> And mine come nothing like. I hope so. Yet,
>   As theirs did with thee, mine might credit get,
> If thou'ldst but use thy faith as thou didst then
>   When thou wert wont t'admire not censure men.
> Prithee believe still and not judge so fast:
>   Thy faith is all the knowledge that thou hast.

Characteristic of Jonson's verse is a deep moral falsity beneath a thick carapace of honesty. It all seems so direct, so steeped in good solid English monosyllables like 'true' and 'new' (rhymed, lest you fail to notice them) that no one could suspect his plain good sense of duplicity—and 'plain good sense' are the three monosyllabic epithets that his writing seems most to crave. But the duplicity here runs so deep that it is hard to quantify or pin down. 'To thee my way in epigrams seems new' adopts a very un-English word-order which sounds merely as though it is echoing Latin ('tibi novum est'); but the reason for the inversion is to allow a scornful emphasis to fall on 'To *thee*' (compare the friendly positioning of 'to thee' at the end of a line of Epigram 96 to John Donne: 'Who shall doubt, Donne, whe'er I a poet be, | When I dare send my *Epigrams* to thee'). Only an ignorant critic would suppose that Jonson's epigrams are 'new'. That claim manages to sound self-deprecating at the same time as it suggests that Jonson was the one and only true writer of epigrams in English.

Jonson was actually less of a path-breaker in writing English epigrams than he wanted his readers to believe. He followed in the footsteps, and indeed stepped on the heels, of a number of other authors. Both John Davies and John Weever had published volumes of epigrams in the 1590s which combined poems adapted from Martial with panegyrics on named noblemen. They had also, like Jonson, adapted the epigram to an aggressively topical London landscape. So when Jonson declares 'And mine come nothing like. I hope so' he is saying the truth in several ways. It sounds as though he is simply delivering a plain-speaking rebuttal of the critic, stabbing the point home with the bullet-pointed stylistic brevity of Martial's 'nec ego' ('not me', 4.72). But at the same time the meaning 'I actually do *hope* so, since I am not completely sure that they are different from everyone else's' is not entirely erased. 'The *old* way and the true' is another simple statement which vigorously tropes simple words into complex interpersonal senses. It has meaning on two historical timeframes at once: for a *mere* English censurer, one who reads only in the vernacular, 'old' might be a term of dispraise— old-fashioned, last year's style. That is a deliberate allusion to the title of Weever's volume of epigrams called *Epigrammes in the Oldest Cut and Newest Fashion* (1599), which was prefaced with an apology that the poems it includes are last year's fashions: 'Epigramms are much like unto Almanacks serving especially for the year for the which they were made, then these (right judging Readers) being for one year pend, and in another printed: are past date before they come from the Presse.'[43] Jonson took over that mono-syllable 'old' and made it open up millennia of antiquity which lie far beyond the gaze of the mere English censurer. 'Old way' declares 'I am not like those passé peddlers of almanac-like epigrams Davies and Weever'; but it also implies 'Yes, I am so old that I am like Martial'.

Using Martial's syntax with such martial aggression against his rival epi-grammatists was such a Jonsonian trick that it seems to have permeated

---

43. John Weever, *Epigrammes in the Oldest Cut, and Newest Fashion* (London, 1599), sig. A8r.

even his conversation. William Drummond of Hawthornden reported of Jonson that he put down his rival epigrammatist Sir John Harington by saying 'That when Sir John Harington desired him to tell the truth of his epigrams [i.e. give him a true judgement on his epigrams], he answered him that he [i.e. Harington] loved not the truth, for they were narrations, and not epigrams' (5.361). The real point of the put-down was that it was itself an imitation of Martial, though the imitation has gone unremarked because Jonson completely absorbed Martial into the texture and structure of his speech:

> 'Dic verum mihi, Marce, dic amabo;
> nil est, quod magis audiam libenter.'
> sic et cum recitas tuos libellos,
> et causam quotiens agis clientis,
> oras, Gallice, me rogasque semper.
> durum est me tibi, quod petis negare.
> vero verius ergo quid sit, audi:
> verum, Gallice, non libenter audis.   (8.76)

'Tell me the truth, Marcus, now please do. There's nothing I would hear more gladly.' So you beg of me Gallicus, so you always ask, when you are reciting your little books or pleading a client's cause. It is hard for me to refuse your request. So hear what is truer than true: the truth, Gallicus, you do not gladly hear.

Martial's epigrams became part of the turns, stabs, and occasional explosions and recoils of Jonson's own characteristic style.

The critical tradition has tended to locate Jonson's imitations of Martial in rather more obvious places: in poems which have a clear relation to one or more classical source poem, and which adapt the source poems to a contemporary world. These are poems which eighteenth-century editors would refer to as 'imitations', since they signal their status as adaptations of particular source poems by allusion or verbal reminiscence. These are, however, a narrow subset of the products of *imitatio* as practised by Jonson. Critical discussion of those poems has tended to perpetuate the illusion (which Jonson was so keen to create) that he was a solitary humanist in his study who pored over the poems of Martial, digested them into his single and stable identity, and built a new poem from them. But both the epigram to 'My Mere English Censurer' and Jonson's conversational put-down of Sir John Harington's epigrams should remind us that he did not work alone. He fashioned his mode of figural imitation partly by contrast with his contemporaries. Indeed it would be only a slight exaggeration to say that Jonson's relationship to classical authors is always triangulated by a relationship with English rivals. He wants to be the real classic, the person who sees and reanimates the shape and structure of ancient discourse. And both the consequence and the enabling condition of that desire is that others are *not* the real classic.[44]

That habit goes back at least as far as *Poetaster* (1601), in which Jonson does not just represent himself as Horace, but also represents his contemporaries John Marston and Thomas Dekker as emphatically *not* classics.[45] That penumbra of rivalry is less overtly visible in his imitations of Martial, but it is a constitutive element in their creation. 'To Captain Hungry' (Epigram 107) is a case in point. This poem may have played a part in the arguments with Dekker and his contemporaries which preceded the composition of *Poetaster* and which precipitated the so-called 'war of the theatres' around 1599–1601, and may date from an earlier and more eristic stage in Jonson's career. It evidently responds to the shape and structure of Martial's epigram 9.35, but also evidently adapts that poem to Jonson's times. The Martial poem looks like this:

> Artibus his semper cenam, Philomuse, mereris,
>   plurima dum fingis, sed quasi vera refers.
> scis, quid in Arsacia Pacorus deliberet aula,
>   Rhenanam numeras Sarmaticamque manum,
> verba ducis Daci chartis mandata resignas,
>   victricem laurum quam venit ante vides,
> scis, quotiens Phario madeat Iove fusca Syene,
>   scis, quota de Libyco litore puppis eat,
> cuius Iuleae capiti nascantur olivae,
>   destinet aetherius cui sua serta pater.
> tolle tuas artes; hodie cenabis apud me
>   hac lege, ut narres nil, Philomuse, novi.   (9.35)

---

44. Cf. Leonard Barkan, *Unearthing the Past: Archaeology and Aesthetics in the Making of Renaissance Culture* (New Haven and London, 1999), p. 313: 'The relations of the modern artist to antiquity and to contemporary artists are thus mutually mediating; and the act of reproducing an ancient work is always partly informed by the system of relations . . . that ties artists to their immediate contemporaries', and compare René Girard's conception of mimetic desire, René Girard, *Deceit, Desire, and the Novel: Self and Other in Literary Structure*, trans. Yvonne Freccero (Baltimore, 1976). See also George E. Rowe, *Distinguishing Jonson: Imitation, Rivalry, and the Direction of a Dramatic Career* (Lincoln, Neb., 1988).

45. For the wider context of the ways in which rivalrous relations between early modern dramatists shaped their treatment of sources and genres, see Clare, *Stage Traffic*.

These are the arts, Philomusus, by which you always earn your dinner: you invent a deal of news but retail it as though it were true. You know what Pacorus is deliberating in his Arsacian palace, you number the Rhenish and Sarmatian hosts, you unseal words that the Dacian chieftain has put to paper, you see the victorious laurel before it comes. You know how many times dusky Syene is drenched by Pharian rain, you know how many ships leave the Libyan shore, for whose head the Julian olives are born, to whom the celestial Father destines his wreaths. Away with your arts! You shall dine with me this evening on one condition, Philomusus, that you tell me no news.

Jonson's version is aggressively topical, so apt to its times that it is dizzying:

Do what you come for, Captain, with your news,
    That's sit and eat: do not my ears abuse.
I oft look on false coin, to know't from true,
    Not that I love it more than I will you.
Tell the gross Dutch those grosser tales of yours,   5
    How great you were with their two emperors,
And yet are with their princes. Fill them full
    Of your Moravian horse, Venetian bull.
Tell them what parts you've ta'en, whence run away,
    What states you've gulled, and which yet keeps you in pay.   10
Give them your services and embassies
    In Ireland, Holland, Sweden (pompous lies),
In Hungary, and Poland, Turkey too;
    What at Leghorn, Rome, Florence, you did do:
And in some year all these together heaped,   15
    For which there must more sea and land be leaped,
If but to be believed you have the hap,
    Than can a flea at twice skip i' the map.
Give your young statesmen (that first make you drunk,
    And then lie with you closer than a punk,   20
For news) your Villeroys and Silleries,
    Janins, your Nuncios, and your Tuilleries,
Your archduke's agents, and your Beringhams,
    That are your words of credit. Keep your names
Of Hannau, Scheiterhuysen, Popenheim,   25
    Hans-spiegle, Rottenberg, and Boutersheim
For your next meal: this you are sure of. Why
    Will you part with them here unthriftily?
Nay, now you puff, tusk, and draw up your chin,
    Twirl the poor chain you run a-feasting in.   30
Come, be not angry: you are Hungry; eat.
    Do what you come for, Captain: there's your meat.

The source poem in Martial nearly vanishes into the conspiratorial fancies of Captain Hungry in a kind of imitation one might call hyper-adaptative: English customs and Euro-gossip overwrite the solid foundations of the poem in Martial, as it adopts the 'Venetian bull' of the hungry soldier and begins to speak proper Dutch. But the poem also responds to the implied invitation from Martial, that great self-imitator, to make another poem of the same kind, or to answer his poems, since it also reads as much like an English sequel to Martial's poem as an imitation of it. Jonson tells Hungry not to spout his news right from the start, as though he is beginning where Martial left off. The poem appears to be anchored in a first-person of scrupulous judgement, who deals in true English monosyllables: 'I oft look on false coin, to know't from true.'

But by line 25 these certainties are starting to dissolve. The carefully localized events and places of Hungry's fake news have become Euroland fantasies over which the Captain can skip as though they are a tiny representation on a map: Scheiterhuysen means 'Shit-house', Boutersheim means 'Butterburg', and neither place exists. Apt and present knowledge of contemporary Europe gradually grows and swells in the course of the imitation into a gorgeous fiction which occludes both real events in the Low Countries and the poem's source in Martial, with its realistic Roman imperial place names. Hungry offers a mere simulacrum of news.

Jonson's imitation of Martial is, however, clearly not just based on reading Martial. It is triangulated against another imitation of the same Latin poem that had been produced in around 1594 by Sir John Davies. This version of Martial adapted him very precisely to Davies's own times:

> The smell feast Afer Travailes to the Burse
> Twice every day the flying newes to heare,
> Which when he hath no money in his purse,
> To rich mens Tables he doth often beare:
>   He tels how Gronigen is taken in,
>   By the brave conduct of illustrious Vere:
>   And how the Spainish forces Brest would win,
>   But that they do Victorious Norris feare.
> No sooner is a ship at Sea surprisde,
> But straight he learnes the newes and doth disclose it,
> No sooner hath the Turke a plot devisde
> To conquer Christendom, but straight he knows it.
>   Faire written in a scrowle he hath the names,
>   Of all the widowes which the plague hath made,

And persons, Times and places, still he frames,
  To every Tale, the better to perswade:
We cal him Fame, for that the wide-mouth slave
Will eate as fast as he wil utter lies:
For Fame is saide an hundreth mouthes to have,
And he eates more then woulde five score suffice.[46]

As T. K. Whipple observed almost a century ago, Davies 'has learned from Martial how to treat London as Martial treated Rome'.[47] The English Afer goes to places such as the Burse, built in 1566 by Thomas Gresham; he knows about the siege of Gröningen in July 1594 and the recapture of Brest by Sir John Norreys in 1593–4. Martial is made to speak from Davies's times, and that means not simply Elizabethan England but the spur of a moment in the latter end of 1594. It is not an entirely happy transformation: Davies's translation-cum-imitation of Martial finally resorts to a translingual pun which barely works in English. Latin 'Fama' means rumour or Fame, and 'fames' means hunger, so being Fame obsessed and being Famished, Davies wants us to believe, go together.

Jonson read this poem critically alongside Martial, and it influenced his imitation of Martial's poem. His chief response to Davies's way of imitating was simple but brilliant. Jonson prevented his own adaptation becoming instantly outdated by turning the specific rumours and datable allusions in Davies's imitation into general ones. That transformed Martial's Philomusus into a creator of fictions which were more or less timeless fantasies. Then he responded to Davies's bad trans-linguistic pun on *fama* and *fames* and made it an English joke about the name of his victim: Captain 'ungry is urged not to be Captain Angry. Both puns derive from Martial's poem: Philomusus, whose name means he is a lover of or perhaps beloved by the muse, is evidently someone who likes making things up. But Jonson's pun is not a response to Martial's name, but a vernacular response to Davies's. It implicitly claims that Jonson can do Martial in English better than the celebrated Inns of Court wit, Sir John Davies. Jonson not only imitated Martial. He sought to imitate him in a way that trampled violently over the path beaten before him by previous vernacular imitators.

---

46. John Davies, *The Poems*, ed. Robert Krueger (Oxford, 1975), p. 147.
47. T. K. Whipple, *Martial and the English Epigram from Sir Thomas Wyatt to Ben Jonson* (Berkeley, 1925), p. 338.

Jonsonian reincarnations

I have argued that the conventional digest of passages about imitation contained in *Discoveries* should not be treated as a definitive guide to Jonson's practice as an imitator, and that Jonson was much more indebted to major currents in German Ciceronianism than he confessed. The concerns with structural and formal imitation which had run through the work of Melanchthon and Sturm, and which in turn resonated with Cicero's remarks about translating as an orator, were foundational to his practice. Jonson imitated an author as though he were an aggregate of figures and structures. He saw the form beneath a poem, and it was around that form that he moulded his imitations. He also did not commune directly with his classical authorities as *Discoveries* suggested an imitator should do. He adapted ancient poems to his times with an acute awareness of how his contemporaries and predecessors had imitated them.

But this is not the whole story. As we have seen, in *Discoveries* Jonson responded vigorously to the metaphors used by Quintilian and Valla to describe the mysterious processes by which one author might nourish another. When Jonson urges his readers to imitate 'Not as a creature that swallows what it takes in crude, raw, or indigested, but that feeds with an appetite, and hath a stomach to concoct, divide, and turn all into nourishment' (7.583) he was not simply reiterating a commonplace or manifesting his own delight in food. The metaphors habitually used to describe the act of literary imitation frequently nourish (if the metaphor can be forgiven in this context) Jonson's practice. They can give flesh to the outline form and figure of the author whom he is imitating. In the *Discoveries* Jonson offers a short discussion of what (following Vives) he terms in a marginal note '*Figura*' or 'the figure and feature in language'. In that discussion he insists that the 'figure' of an author needs to be coated in flesh: 'We say it is a fleshy style, when there is much periphrasis... It hath blood and juice, when the words are proper and apt' (7.569). Those metaphors suggest a fleshly reincarnation of the figure of an earlier author, where 'apt' imitation gives life and power without surplus bulk.

We can see what it might mean to create a fleshly reincarnation of the *figura* of an earlier poem in Jonson's sequel to or imitation of the series of poems that Martial composed to invite friends to dine with him—a sequence

which itself seems to offer an open invitation to imitators. These include
Martial's 5.78 and 11.52, as well as 10.48, which happens to be right next to
the poem on the happy life, 10.47, which Jonson had translated so literally.
This series of poems Jonson digested and adapted into Epigram 101, 'Inviting
a Friend to Supper', which retrospectively turns Martial's series of invitation
poems into something akin to a genre:[48]

> Tonight, grave sir, both my poor house and I
>   Do equally desire your company;
> Not that we think us worthy such a guest,
>   But that your worth will dignify our feast,
> With those that come, whose grace may make that seem   5
>   Something, which else could hope for no esteem.
> It is the fair acceptance, sir, creates
>   The entertainment perfect, not the cates.
> Yet shall you have, to rectify your palate,
>   An olive, capers, or some better salad,   10
> Ush'ring the mutton; with a short-legged hen,
>   If we can get her, full of eggs, and then
> Lemons and wine for sauce: to these a cony
>   Is not to be despaired of for our money.
> And, though fowl now be scarce, yet there are clerks,   15
>   The sky not falling, think we may have larks.
> I'll tell you of more, and lie, so you will come:
>   Of partridge, pheasant, wood-cock, of which some
> May yet be there, and godwit, if we can:
>   Knat, rail, and ruff too. Howsoe'er, my man   20
> Shall read a piece of Virgil, Tacitus,
>   Livy, or of some better book to us,
> Of which we'll speak our minds amidst our meat;
>   And I'll profess no verses to repeat.
> To this, if aught appear which I know not of   25
>   That will the pastry, not my paper show of.
> Digestive cheese and fruit there sure will be;
>   But that which most doth take my muse and me

---

48. Jonson's poem follows exactly the structure—invitation, menu, entertainment—set out in
Lowell Edmunds, 'The Latin Invitation-Poem: What Is It? Where Did It Come From?', *The
American Journal of Philology* 103 (1982), 184–8. It may also echo the downmarket transformation of the invitation in the *Cena Trimalchionis* of Petronius, 46.2 (which refers to chickens and
eggs) and 39.3. Jonson translated an epigram ascribed to Petronius as Underwood 88. For discussion of its relations to its sources, see Lyne, *Memory and Intertextuality*, pp. 52–7 and Robert
Cummings, 'Liberty and History in Jonson's Invitation to Supper', *Studies in English Literature,
1500–1900* 40 (2000), 103–22. For Horatian resonances, see Moul, *Jonson, Horace*, pp. 54–63.

Is a pure cup of rich Canary wine,
    Which is the Mermaid's now, but shall be mine: 30
Of which had Horace or Anacreon tasted
    Their lives, as do their lines, till now had lasted.
Tobacco, nectar, or the Thespian spring
    Are all but Luther's beer to this I sing.
Of this we will sup free, but moderately,   35
    And we will have no Poley or Parrot by,
Nor shall our cups make any guilty men:
    But, at our parting, we will be as when
We innocently met. No simple word
    That shall be uttered at our mirthful board   40
Shall make us sad next morning, or affright
    The liberty that we'll enjoy tonight.

This poem has been read as more or less an allegory of receiving Martial in English by Thomas Greene,[49] and by Joseph Loewenstein as the work of a poet who is struggling for control over his words in an age of mechanical reproduction. Poley and Parrot, the spies, threaten to spread and misinterpret Jonson's words, and his printed poems (Loewenstein argues) show up at the feast used as wrappings for the pastries at the end of the meal.[50] Jonson's invitation also grows in part from the language of classical imitation theory, which gives flesh to the figure of Martial. Jonson's poem is not simply a continuation of Martial's invitation poems, but one that offers a measure of life which far exceeds that of its originals. Martial offers deliberately humble fare in 5.78 ('cheap Cappadocian lettuce and smelly leeks', 'viles Cappadocae gravesque porri') and in 10.48 ('a chicken and a ham that has already survived three dinners', 'pullus ad haec cenisque tribus iam perna superstes'). Jonson, by contrast, serves up a near-excess of life in that chicken packed with eggs.

Indeed one might say he coats Martial's fare with a fine layer of crispy better: 'Some better salad' is echoed in 'some better book'. It is as though the generative vitality so long associated with successful *imitatio* is suffusing even the representation of food which is presented as dead for consumption in an imitative poem. That excess of life is ready to be eaten. 'For all that we invent doth please us in the conception or birth': the concept underlying the cultural metaphor of 'renaissance' is that an imitation can bring new life

49. Thomas M. Greene, *The Light in Troy: Imitation and Discovery in Renaissance Poetry* (New Haven and London, 1982), pp. 282–3.
50. Joseph Loewenstein, 'The Jonsonian Corpulence; Or, The Poet as Mouthpiece', *ELH* 53 (1986), 491–518.

to an original. And this metaphor of digestive assimilation and rebirth allows Jonson to overlayer Martial's poems with a faint suggestion of a Christian triumph over a feast of pagan learning: the Mermaid's wine, promising eternal life, has more than a hint of the sacrament, transcending the beer of Germany and Lutheranism, and implicitly also the Falernian wine of the classical symposium.

But the poem is modestly poised. Imitation can reanimate and transform an earlier set of poems. But—as Don Quixote discovered—it can also generate illusions. There is not exactly a ghost at Jonson's feast, but there is a shadow of the *simulacrum* in the air, since so much of what Jonson has to offer is not actually present. The cold sausage and beans offered by Martial— not grand food, but nutritious—vanish into a puff of copious words: 'And god-wit, *if we can*' (19). Jonson's feast is determinedly subjunctive, where all manner of riches—food, eternal life, potable God and edible god-wit—are at once promised and withheld. The fare on offer sounds ruggedly Anglo-Saxon: 'Knat, rail, and ruff'—and these gruff monosyllabic fowl replace the 'duck and mallard' of the manuscript witnesses which preserve an early authorial version of this poem, perhaps because Jonson wanted a phonic echo of the 'rum, ram, ruf' which Chaucer had associated with the northern vernacular alliterative tradition.[51] But the more apparently abundant and solid and Anglo-Saxon the food on offer becomes, so the more non-existent it appears to be.

There is a strong analogy here with the epigram 'To Captain Hungry': that poem is also nourished by Martial, and represents hunger as an onto-logical condition, and is also another version of the poetical invitation to dinner which turns the contemporary world into a hyperbolic illusion. The adaptation of an earlier poem to current customs may build an entirely new structure on the earlier form; but the fabric of verbiage layered so fulsomely over the classical text might be pure persiflage, pure Venetian Bull, a succu-lent contemporaneity which tempts and deceives without offering any actual nourishment. That stops Jonson's 'Invitation to Supper' being merely a triumphalist transcendence of the group of Martial poems with which it aligns itself. The poem shimmers between worlds, alluring a reader into 'some better' place, and then modestly confessing that the new enhanced

---

51. British Library, Harley MS 6917, fol. 84r–v and Folger, MS V. a. 276, Part II, fols. 20v–21v; cf. 'The Parson's Prologue', l. 43 in Geoffrey Chaucer, *The Riverside Chaucer*, ed. Larry Dean Benson and F. N. Robinson (Boston, 1987).

reality on offer may be an illusion after all. The imitation is at once a vital rebirth and a duplicitous shadow of its original.

The sons of Ben

Jonson regularly wrote the motto 'like an explorer' ('tamquam explorator') on the title pages of his books. He also insisted that the ancients went before 'as guides, not commanders' (7.504).[52] Those phrases suggest that he wished to be regarded as at once a leader and a follower, simultaneously a subaltern following in the footsteps of his classical guides and a bold venturer who sets off into the unknown. The imitating author can have it both ways: an imitator who adapts an earlier author's practice to a new language simultaneously follows earlier footprints and breaks new ground. Jonson's insistence on his own singular ability as a path-finder made him brutal in his treatment of his contemporaries. But his methods of imitation were surprisingly generous to his successors. The *formulae*, the little moulds, the rhetorical patterns, that his footprints created were extremely accommodating to later footsteps.

The chief reason for this was that the principles on which Jonson wrought his transformations of what he read were so apparent in what he produced. Imitators of Jonson did not have to echo Jonson's words. They had instead to grasp his *figura*, the rhetorical structures which underlay his style, the structures by which he transformed his reading. An epigram after Jonson had to swirl and shift in sense. It had to transpose customs from Rome to London in a way that left an uneasy flavour of hyperbole surrounding present-day manners. It might turn on apparently simple monosyllables, whose sense appeared to slip from solidity into insubstantiality in the course of reading the poem. The clarity with which he displayed his own transformations of his reading was one reason for the enormous popularity of Jonson himself as an *exemplum* for later poets. Writers who wished to be identified as the 'sons of Ben' did so not by imitating Jonson's words, but by imitating Jonson's ways of imitating Martial, or Horace, or Anacreon, or by imitating Jonson's grammatical structures, or Jonson's favoured genres, or Jonson's stanzaic forms, or his ways of beginning poems, as well as the wider, looser class of Jonsonian *genera dicendi*: stiff true speech, gruff criticism of

52. Peterson, *Imitation and Praise*, pp. 9–11.

others, a twinkle of self-conscious hyperbole around a solid bulk of truth. He in effect constructed a vernacular tradition around himself by establishing not only a personal style but articulating that style through a formal and a syntactic mode of imitating.

When combined with Jonson's aggressively adaptive transformations of classical originals this had a radical and long-term effect on the ways in which classical poems were imitated in the English vernacular. In many respects Jonson helped to free *imitatio* from its associations with direct verbal replication and with plagiarism: if the object of imitation was not the words of an original but its form and figure, then imitation could readily be regarded as an activity dependent on the analytical acuity of the imitator rather than on illegitimate appropriation of the words of an earlier author. The *forma* or *figura* of an author may be a difficult thing to define, but it is distinct from the *words* of that author, since it inheres in generic principles—choosing *these kinds* of words, or *this kind* of sentence structure, using *these kinds* of rhetorical figure, or imitating other authors in *this kind* of way, or, indeed, imitating an earlier author's experiment in a particular genre or literary kind. And if a *forma* is imitated and adapted to a new time and a new place in new words and new customs there is no reason to feel that anything which resembles a theft or an illicit appropriation of an earlier text has occurred. What has happened is one poet learning from another to make a new poem in new times from a common set of rhetorical principles. To return to that vital insight from Gérard Genette: '*it is impossible to imitate a text*, or—which comes to the same—*that one can imitate only a style: that is to say, a genre.*'[53] When an author becomes a genre—a set of underlying rhetorical principles and a group of methods for transforming prior texts—that author becomes imitable without creating anxieties about plagiarism.

Generic imitation, however, is not a panacea. Indeed it had close and intimate links with fears of plagiarism even in the Roman tradition. Roman poets generally sought to maintain a porous but sustainable distinction between intra- and trans-linguistic imitation. Imitation across languages was relatively free of stigma, since it could be an act which enlarged the native repertoire of Latin verse. Latin imitators of other Latin texts, however, could be accused of literary theft. Terence and Martial in particular associate literary theft or plagiarism with two particular classes of activity. The first is

---

53. Gérard Genette, *Palimpsests: Literature in the Second Degree*, trans. Channa Newman and Claude Doubinsky (Lincoln, Neb., 1997), p. 83.

what we now tend to call plagiarism: intra-linguistic borrowing in which exactly the same words are used in two texts in the same language. The second is a particular source of concern for Terence, and is more subtle. An imitator could be accused of theft if he imitated a Greek text which had already been adapted by another earlier Roman author.[54] The chief means of insulating generic imitation from the charge of theft was to insist that being the first to practise a particular genre in Latin deserved particular praise. This allowed Horace, for instance, to imitate Greek lyric while claiming also to be an originator. But it had a price. It wrought a close quasi-proprietorial bond between particular genres and the first poets to practise them in a particular language. When Jonson began his career English poets were adopting a similarly proprietorial attitude towards generic originality. So Jonson's contemporary Joseph Hall boasted at the start of his book of satires called *Virgidemiarum Liber* (1598) that he was the first English satirist:

> I First adventure, with fool-hardie might
> To tread the steps of perilous despight:
> I first adventure: follow me who list,
> And be the second English Satyrist.[55]

Like Lucretius before him, Hall claimed to have opened up a path into a new genre. Hall was much criticized by his rivals for making this claim. He was also (and not coincidentally) a bitter critic of contemporaries who also wrote satires founded on classical examples. Indeed it was Hall who by a narrow margin beat Jonson to be the first English poet to have used the word 'plagiary' in print. Hall refers to a sonneteer who imitates Petrarch's poems as a 'Plagiarie sonnet-wright' (4.2.84). The reason he does so is that by 1590 the sonnet genre was so hackneyed that even if an imitator of Petrarch was in theory imitating trans-linguistically between English and Italian he could be regarded as a 'plagiary': he would be borrowing from earlier English imitations of Petrarch.

Jonson's keenness to operate in new genres and to establish his own way of speaking developed against this background. Indeed Jonson amplified the contradictions of his contemporaries by insisting that no one plagiarize his plainly imitative writings. All of this made Jonson's emphasis on formal

---

54. Terence, *Self-Tormenter*, Prologue 16–19, *The Eunuch*, Prologue 19–34, *The Brothers*, Prologue 6–14. Cf. *De Oratore*, 1.154, where Cicero reports Crassus saying that when he attempted to paraphrase Latin poetry he found that Ennius had often already used (*occupasset*) the best word.
55. 1.Pr.1–4. Text from Joseph Hall, *The Poems*, ed. Arnold Davenport (Liverpool, 1969).

imitation a less successful technique for separating *imitatio* from plagiarism than it could in theory have become. Indeed among Jonson's successors plagiarism tended to haunt imitation like an evil twin. Ian Donaldson has explored the historical irony that Jonson could fume and thunder against plagiarism of his own writings by his contemporaries and yet himself borrow so extensively from classical authors that he came himself to be regarded as a plagiarist.[56] Dryden described Jonson as 'a learned plagiary' who 'has done his Robberies so openly, that one may see he fears not to be taxed by any Law. He invades Authors like a Monarch; and what would be theft in other Poets, is only victory in him.'[57]

Dryden's remarks highlight a significant cultural shift in the later seventeenth century, by which time the fragile distinction between intra- and trans-linguistic imitation had more or less broken down. Jonson played a major part in both making and breaking that distinction. On the one hand he developed a mode of formal imitation which was potentially free of direct verbal debt; but on the other he calibrated his own imitations against those of his contemporaries, encouraged his followers to imitate his own methods, and excoriated those who borrowed directly from him. As a result, formal imitation never entirely separated itself off from rivalrous literary relationships, or from textual ownership.

This complex is very evident in Jonson's vernacular influence. He founded something akin to a literary genealogy. By the 1640s it was common for poets to claim to be his 'sons'.[58] This might seem inevitable as at once a consequence and consummation of the language of paternity and birth which runs through imitation theory. But it is also peculiarly Jonsonian, since Jonson's own name was remarkably polyphiloprogenitive: 'Ben' is Hebrew for 'son' and 'Jon-son' translates the Hebrew first-name into the final syllable of the surname. The lapidary Epigram 45, 'On My First Son', plays on those names by referring to Jonson's dead son as the 'child of my right hand' (which literally translates the name 'Ben-jamin')

---

56. Ian Donaldson, '"The Fripperie of Wit": Jonson and Plagiarism', in Paulina Kewes, ed., *Plagiarism in Early Modern Europe* (Basingstoke, 2003), 119–33. See also Stephen Orgel, 'The Renaissance Artist as Plagiarist', *ELH* 48 (1981), 476–95 and the elderly but still helpful Harold Ogden White, *Plagiarism and Imitation during the English Renaissance: A Study in Critical Distinctions* (Cambridge, 1935).

57. Dryden, *The Works*, 17.21, 57.

58. Claude J. Summers and Ted Larry Pebworth, eds., *Classic and Cavalier: Essays on Jonson and the Sons of Ben* (Pittsburgh, 1982); Paula Blank, 'Jonson's Family Values', in Amy Boesky and Mary Thomas Crane, eds., *Form and Reform in Renaissance England: Essays in Honor of Barbara Kiefer Lewalski* (Newark and London, 2000), 127–49.

as 'BEN. | JONSON his best piece of poetry'. This phrase delicately plays on Martial's epigram 1.101, in which Martial describes his dead scribe as 'once the faithful amanuensis [lit. 'hand'] of my studies' ('Illa manus quondam studiorum fida meorum'), but seems completely embedded in Jonson's own life and biological identity.

All of this forged a powerful association between Ben Jonson's name, parenthood, and writing—an association which was not lost on his successors. But in his relations with poets in the next generation Jonson himself was far less promiscuous in claiming poetic fatherhood than is sometimes suggested.[59] Underwood 69 (possibly addressed to Lucius Cary) is called 'Epigram: To a Friend and Son', but it insists that the author's relationship to his addressee rests on 'Freedom and truth, with love from those begot' (5), rather than 'profit or chance', let alone from a genealogical relationship. In the late Horatian epistle 'Answering to One that Asked to be Sealed of the Tribe of Ben' (Underwood 47) poetic paternity is also presented as a matter of sharing virtue with a follower. In that poem Jonson declares that he loves only those 'led by reason's flame' (69), and that he 'seals', or marks out for favour, his follower in the same way that members of the tribe of Benjamin are sealed on the forehead in Revelation 7.8 as 'the servants of our God':

> These I will honour, love, embrace, and serve,
>   And free it from all question to preserve.
> So short you read my character, and theirs
>   I would call mine...   (71–4)

Jonson frequently echoed Juvenal's assertions that virtue was the sole nobility, and that family trees mattered not at all.[60] It is a shared and legible 'character'—a word which could of course mean 'the impress on a stamp or seal' as well as a 'moral nature' or 'a style of speaking'—rather than a shared genealogy which leads him to 'seal' other poets as members of his tribe. Jonson not only became in effect a genre of imitative writing. He also insisted that being part of his tradition was a matter of learning to 'read my character', bearing the impression of the form of Jonson. By that he meant becoming a member of his tribe required his imitators to understand and

---

59. Tom MacFaul, *Poetry and Paternity in Renaissance England: Sidney, Spenser, Shakespeare, Donne and Jonson* (Cambridge, 2010), pp. 188–225, argues that Jonson presents himself as an asexual godfather.

60. See headnote to *Underwood* 84.8 in *The Cambridge Edition of the Works of Ben Jonson*.

acquire a style as well as to follow his example. The stamp, form, seal, or character of Ben Jonson was available for anyone who had the skill to replicate it from his works.

This was one reason why after Jonson's death so many poets were keen to be regarded as his 'sons': to be a son of Ben was to claim a retrospective seal of quality, and to share in Jonson's poetical character—which rapidly came to be identified not just with a set of stylistic features but with a particular kind of virtue which was at once social and self-contained. It also brought with it an implicit claim to be the legitimate heir to Jonson's poetic techniques, and hence their owner. Many of the elegies to Jonson which appeared the year after his death in *Jonsonus Virbius* (1638) present their authors as Jonson's offspring, which resemble him as a child resembles its father. Jonson became 'Father of poets', as William Cartwright termed him, or 'father Ben', in the words of Shackerley Marmion, while those who remained were, as John Rutter put it, 'like greedy Heires, | That snatch the fruit of their dead Fathers cares', or were left wishing with Clement Paman 'might I but be thy Posthume son'.[61] After Jonson's death the genealogical relationship between his classical forebears and his vernacular offspring also rapidly became a sprawling and comically extended family tree, as when Thomas Randolph wrote a poem to thank Jonson for 'adopting him to be his Son' (and the only evidence that Jonson did this is Randolph's own poem):

> I am a kinne to *Hero's* being thine,
> And part of my alliance is divine.
> Orpheus, Musaeus, Homer, too; beside
> Thy Brothers by the Roman Mother's side;
> As Ovid, Virgil, and the Latin Lyre,
> That is so like thy *Horace*; the whole quire
> Of Poets are by thy Adoption, all
> My uncles...[62]

This is Jonsonian plain and visible comic hyperbole: declarative, rich in the plainest of plain verbs ('am...is...is...are'), it states plain untruths in a very Jonsonian manner.

61. Brian Duppa, *Ionsonus virbius: or, The memorie of Ben: Iohnson revived by the friends of the Muses* (London, 1638), pp. 34, 47, 40. See Ian Donaldson, *Jonson's Magic Houses* (Oxford, 1997), pp. 162–79. For a fine contrast between the plurality of Jonson's sons and Dryden's preoccupation with primogeniture, see Christopher Ricks, *Allusion to the Poets* (Oxford, 2002), pp. 16–19.
62. Thomas Randolph, *Poems; With the Muses Looking-Glasse* (London, 1638), p. 22.

Robert Herrick, who did not directly claim to be one of the sons of
Ben, though he did write a jocular prayer to 'Saint Ben', displays all the
characteristics of a writer who had actively sought to read Jonson's 'character'
and imitate it. Many of Herrick's poems are generated from applying to
Ben Jonson's poems the principle that you imitate an author's methods of
imitation as well as his distinctive syntactic structures. So when Herrick
imitated in 'The Invitation' the same group of poems by Martial which
Jonson had imitated in 'Inviting a Friend to Supper', he did so while simultaneously imitating Ben Jonson:

> To sup with thee thou didst me home invite;
> And mad'st a promise that mine appetite
> Sho'd meet and tire, on such lautitious meat,
> The like not *Heliogabalus* did eat:
> And richer Wine wo'dst give to me (thy guest)
> Then Roman Sylla powr'd out at his feast.
> I came; (tis true) and lookt for Fowle of price,
> The bastard *Phenix*; bird of *Paradice*;
> And for no less then Aromatick Wine
> Of *Maydens-blush*, commixt with *Jessimine.*
> Cleane was the herth, the mantle larded jet;
> Which wanting *Lar*, and smoke, hung weeping wet;
> At last, i'th'noone of winter, did appeare
> A ragd-soust-neats-foot with sick vineger:
> And in a burnisht Flagonet stood by
> Beere small as Comfort, dead as Charity.
> At which amaz'd, and pondring on the food,
> How cold it was, and how it child my blood;
> I curst the master; and I damn'd the souce;
> And swore I'de got the ague of the house.
> Well, when to eat thou dost me next desire,
> I'le bring a Fever; since thou keep'st no fire.[63]

'I curst the master; and I damn'd the souce'. The syntactic parallelism is *echt*
Jonson—and a whisper in the ear from Sigmund Freud may have made
Herrick rhyme 'house' with 'souce' here. It suggests 'a drinking cup' (*OED*
n.2) but perhaps also a 'sauce' which suffuses his poem in his Jonsonian
'source' by recalling Jonson's 'Lemons and wine for sauce'. Although
Herrick's poem is simultaneously a tribute to both Martial's invitation

63. Robert Herrick, *The Complete Poetry*, ed. Tom Cain and Ruth Connolly, 2 vols. (Oxford, 2013),
    I.249.

poems and an answer to Jonson's imitations of them, it is driven by the logic of emulation into two corners at once. Jonson had made his fowl as English as could be in 'Inviting a Friend to Supper', and so Herrick rebounds back to a classicising antiquity of language: he provides the only cited instance in *OED* of the deliberately over-Latinate 'lautitious', and then piles on Heliogabalus and Sulla to make the feast as Latin as possible. By adding the Phoenix to the pyre of expected foods he raises the rhetorical threshold of the invitation to the classical skies. But those classical skies have Jonson twinkling in them as their lodestar. Underlying Herrick's poem are not only Jonson's imitation of Martial, but also Volpone's hyperbolical promises to Celia while he offers her if she sleeps with him 'The heads of parrots, tongues of nightingales, | The brains of peacocks and of ostriches | Shall be our food; and, could we get the phoenix, | Though nature lost her kind, she were our dish' (3.7.201–4). Then for the actual feast Herrick again goes for the ultimate in Jonsonian grossed out monosyllabic yuk: 'A ragd-soust-neats-foot with sick vinegar'. The poem shows how imitators imitating Martial after Jonson had also to imitate Jonson, and Jonson's methods of imitating: the 'master' and 'the source' were necessarily encountered together. And that was partly too an imitation of Jonson's habitual way of triangulating his imitations of classical texts against those of his vernacular predecessors.

In this way Ben Jonson invented a tradition. He impressed his seal and character on a generation of poets. But he also remained a haunting presence. Did his heirs really inherit the right to imitate him? Or were they merely *simulacra* of the master? These questions explain why Jonson enjoyed a surprisingly vivid afterlife not only as a poetical father but also as a ghost. The spirit of this mighty eater and mighty speaker was, predictably enough, not a mere attenuated *simulacrum* of the kind that we have encountered radiating outwards from Lucretius's *De Rerum Natura* and Virgil's *Aeneid*. He was a ghost who could clip those who survived him round the ear, or claim to be sole favourite of Apollo. William Cavendish's 'To Ben Jonson's Ghost' presents him as the lost spirit of English poetry, in comparison to whom surviving poets are 'as light as straws and feathers'.[64] By 1650 Andrew Marvell in 'Tom May's Death' presented Jonson's ghost as arbiter of taste in the underworld, where he is 'for corpulence and port' about as far removed from the attenuated spectre of Virgil's Hector as it is possible to imagine.

64. Timothy Raylor, 'Newcastle's Ghosts: Robert Payne, Ben Jonson, and the "Cavendish Circle"', in Claude J. Summers and Ted Larry Pebworth, eds., *Literary Circles and Cultural Communities in Renaissance England* (Columbia and London, 2000), 92–114.

He is a completely corporeal being, who 'shook his grey locks' (32) and 'whipped [May] o'er the pate' (37) with a laurel wand.[65] The physical authority of Jonson's ghost did not mean that Jonson's successors were simply haunted by his past example, or burdened by the past he represented, or beaten by his example into submission. They heard him speak to them, whether it was in convivial 'Sessions of the Poets' as imagined by Sir John Suckling, or in the underworld as imagined by Andrew Marvell, because his style was so sharply defined in its rhetorical character. But his successors were aware of the *figura* of his verse more or less every time they attempted to imitate a classical poem.

The extent of Jonson's influence on the practice of *imitatio* indicates that we should be very cautious in accepting the argument of Thomas Greene that after Jonson antiquity had been in effect received into England, and that the anachronistic pleasures of Renaissance *imitatio* died with him.[66] What happened was something very different from this. Jonson embedded the imitation of classical texts in the vernacular within a complex of rela-tionships—generic, genealogical, ethical, stylistic—between contemporary English writers and their recent predecessors. He also allowed *imitatio* to come very close indeed to the skill required of a translator who was alive to the figurations of his originals. This made him a profound influence on the nature of influence. He made *imitatio* a process of inventing a poetical char-acter for yourself which would differentiate you from your contemporaries at the same time as establishing a relationship with classical writers. That relationship was generic in a way that was also genealogical: it could in turn be replicated in the relationship between the writing of his followers and their followers. But he also stamped a seal of possessive authorship over the act of imitation. Jonson warned that 'Greatness of name in the father oft-times helps not forth but o'erwhelms the son' (7.514). He gave later poets a character to live up to: he was an imitator whose ghost might beat up his own imitators if they let him down, an imitator who became himself both a figure of style and a stamp of authority.

For all his insistence on the 'centred self' as a moral ideal, Jonson also left a legacy of stylistic instability which had a huge influence on the subsequent

---

65. Quotations from Andrew Marvell, *The Poems*, ed. Nigel Smith (London, 2003). See further Ian Donaldson, 'Talking with Ghosts: Ben Jonson and the English Civil War', *Ben Jonson Journal* 17 (2010), 1–18, esp. p. 14.
66. Greene, *Light in Troy*, pp. 292–3. Presumably Greene makes this claim because he wants his book to end with Jonson.

history of English classicism. He generated a classical style that veered between hyperbole and hyper-realism, between hyper-classicism and a near disgust with the vernacular. His influence is everywhere in high Augustan poetry of the later seventeenth and earlier eighteenth century. Translations which look like imitations, imitations which absorb the works of antiquity so completely into the turbulent literary marketplace of London that both the present and the past seem destabilized by the combination—these are all Jonsonian legacies to the world of Dryden and Pope. Jonson's successors had to be as English as can be, and they had at the same time to sound as completely classical as they could, while defensively enclosing themselves within a boundary that would distinguish their own practice as imitators from those of rival lineages. The mania of Alexander Pope's *Dunciad*, which presents almost all modern literary production as plagiarism and filth with the single magical exception of Pope and his friends, is a product of Jonson's insistence that he and those who bear his seal are the virtuous, while the rest are aberrations. Jonson's careful positioning of his own practices as an imitator in relationship to the practices of his contemporaries, indeed, explains what is to many innocent readers the most surprising feature of later English neoclassicism. Alexander Pope's rich fascination with the filthiest aspects of contemporaneity, which he often transforms into muck which can be flung at his fellow poets, is a direct descendant of Jonson, who made 'being classical' synonymous with 'being unlike one's contemporaries'. But as we shall see in Chapter 8, John Milton's powerful and idiosyncratic contribution to the history of *imitatio* also had a major part to play in the future of the concept and of the practice.

PART III

Milton and After

8

Milton

Modelling the Ancients

Milton is such a gigantic figure in the history of classical reception that he tends to be positioned at beginnings or endings, rather than, as here, towards the middle. He is often treated as an end-point in stories about imitation, and with some reason. As the first section of this chapter shows, in *Paradise Lost* many of the metaphors used in discussions of *imitatio* in the rhetorical tradition are associated with a range of Satanic creatures, from Sin and Death to Satan himself. That might make it appear that, despite Milton's many artful imitations of classical and vernacular authors, he was the imitating author who finally made *imitatio* appear to be an intrinsically corrupting practice. It is therefore tempting to position him at the start of a new story about inspiration and originality, in which the Holy Spirit or a poetic genius allowed pure unmediated divinity to flow from the pen of the poet.

But, as the first section of this chapter also shows, Milton was deeply divided in his treatment of *imitatio*. One of the larger questions raised by the act of imitation—how does one create a free and living new body from the corpus of an earlier author?—feeds into the human argument of the poem in relatively benign form. Eve is at once mother of mankind and an imitator of Ovid; and the ethical and theological issue over which angels and mortals repeatedly anguish—how it is possible to obey a loving authority who is one's origin without being entirely subsumed to his will?—mirrors in the language of theology a central question about the relationship between imitator and imitated. How does one absorb an earlier text, or breed a new 'living' work from it, in a manner which is at once free from and indebted to it? Questions about the nature of *imitatio* ripple through every level of *Paradise Lost*, from its human relationships and theological arguments to the texture of its verse, which displays not just artful Latinity, but the fact that Milton created a style so distinctive that it positively invited imitation itself.

Although Milton was a giant, he also rested on the shoulders of others. This chapter resists the tendency to see him as a singular marvel who turned the destructive gunpowder of Christian theology against the pagan epic and the pagan practice of *imitatio*. Milton's attitudes towards *imitatio* and antiquity alike were complex. And that complexity was the result of multiple currents in his age. As the second section of this chapter shows, Milton responded to the way that seventeenth-century commentaries printed what were explicitly called 'imitations'—clear parallels in the work of earlier authors—in the margins of classical texts, and invited their readers to make evaluative comparisons between the imitation and the text which it imitated. He reflected a growing unease with imitation among readers of Quintilian in the period, and he responded to changing currents in education. He also reacted to emergent fashions in formal and adaptive imitation in the later seventeenth century.

But, as the third section of this chapter suggests, perhaps Milton's most significant contribution to the wider history of imitating authors was his tendency to treat classical texts as 'models' in a distinctively seventeenth-century sense—as akin to architectural templates on the foundations of which later works could be built. This was a significant development from earlier arguments that an imitator should imitate the 'form' of prior texts. It was liberating, since a 'model' provided a set of proportional relationships rather than a body of text on which to draw. A 'model' could therefore be imitated without verbal debt. It also enabled Milton to present his own work as a vast elaboration of his classical 'models', which by comparison could seem like tiny archetypes of *Paradise Lost*. However, regarding ancient poetry as a 'model' from which later works could be imitated also granted to those texts a structuring authority akin to that of an architectural model. A 'model' is at once a tiny precursor and the structural determinant of a later text. This double perspective, I suggest, underlies some of the bewildering shifts of scale which can surround Milton's imitations of classical works. The simultaneous reduction and magnification of the classical world that comes from regarding it as 'model' combines in *Paradise Lost* with an internal battle between *imitatio* as enabling freedom and *imitatio* as a form of Satanic servitude, which traps the imitator in a world of *simulacra*. Those tensions within the ways Milton thought about imitation were vital not just to *Paradise Lost* itself, but also (as later chapters will show) to its influence—and they constitute strong reasons for positioning that poem at the middle rather than at the end of a story about imitation.

The sin of imitation?

Satan's first words in *Paradise Lost* are addressed to Beelzebub as the two fallen warriors welter in the flaming lake of hell:

> If thou beest he; but O how fallen! how changed
> From him, who in the happy realms of light
> Clothed with transcendent brightness didst outshine
> Myriads though bright...   (*PL*, 1.84–7)[1]

As Thomas Newton noted in 1749, Milton here 'imitates Isaiah and Virgil at the same time'. The Virgilian episode imitated is of course Aeneas's meeting with the ghost of Hector, how changed from the old Hector ('quantum mutatus ab illo | Hectore', *Aen.*, 2.274), the episode to which Poggio Bracciolini had compared his sad encounter with a dusty text of Quintilian. That episode is itself transformed by being combined with the words of the prophet Isaiah as he describes the fall of Lucifer: 'How art thou fallen from heaven, O Lucifer, son of the morning! how art thou cut down to the ground, which didst weaken the nations!' (Isaiah, 14:12). That combined imitation reveals a great deal in little about Milton's practices and priorities as an imitator. Isaiah's 'how fallen' precedes Virgil's 'how changed'.

This implicitly gives priority to the biblical text; and that priority gives a powerful irony to Satan's words. Isaiah is describing the fall of Lucifer himself, rather than that of his companions. Satan seems unknowingly to allude to his own fallen state while attempting to present Beelzebub as a fallen Homeric or Virgilian hero. Milton knew exactly what he was doing here. He knew—because more or less every commentator on Virgil since Servius had said so—that Aeneas's encounter with the ghost of Hector was based on the moment at the start of Ennius's *Annales* when the first Roman epic poet described his meeting with the ghost of Homer. It was with an allusion within an allusion to this great incipatory literary encounter that Milton began the speaking career of his Satan. Layering the voice of the prophet Isaiah over those reverberating echoes of classical texts suggests that it is the prophet rather than Satan himself who really knows what is going on in this scene. Satan's echo of Virgil seems like an afterthought, an attempt to cover over his biblical fall with epic allusions.

---

1. Quotations from John Milton, *Paradise Lost*, ed. Alastair Fowler (Harlow, 1998).

In Book 2 of the *Aeneid*, Virgil's imperial hero escapes from the flames of Troy. He is warned by the ghost of Hector and by a vision of his wife to pursue his imperial quest and to found a new civilization. *Paradise Lost* also begins with imperial hero who leaves one flaming civilization to look for a new home, and who is helped on his way by creatures of dubious ontological status. Milton's Satan sets out from the 'nether empire' of hell in Book 2 of *Paradise Lost* in search of what he later calls 'honour and Empire with revenge enlarged' (*PL*, 4.390). At the gateway to his flaming prison he meets two creatures. The first of them is a snaky-tailed woman, who is girded around by hell-hounds, who 'when they list, would creep, | If aught disturbed their noise, into her womb' (*PL*, 2.656–7). This figure is monstrously fecund, surrounded by her brood of offspring. We learn she is called Sin. The other shape looms through the darkness:

> The other shape,
> If shape it might be called that shape had none
> Distinguishable in member, joint, or limb,
> Or substance might be called that shadow seemed,
> For each seemed either; black it stood as night,
> Fierce as ten Furies, terrible as hell,
> And shook a dreadful dart; what seemed his head
> The likeness of a kingly crown had on.   (*PL*, 2.666–73)

This phantasm that blurs the division between substance and shadow is Death. Satan learns that Sin is his own daughter, who sprang living from his brow like Athene from the brow of Jove. He was then attracted by his own 'image' in her, and raped her. Death, that 'phantasm' (*PL*, 2.743)—who takes much of his insubstantial but brutal being from the *eidōlon* of Hercules, described in *Odyssey*, 11.601–16—is Satan's son, begotten of his own daughter, who is the product of his own mind.

The episode of Sin and Death was seldom appreciated by early readers and commentators on the poem: Samuel Johnson rumbled that 'Milton's allegory of Sin and Death is undoubtedly faulty', because of the way it blurs divisions between the literal and the allegorical.[2] Nonetheless it also came to be regarded as one of the key examples of Milton's sublime art. And to see sublimity in it is entirely true to its literary origins, since this shadowy episode was adumbrated by what the chief ancient theorist of the sublime,

---

2. Samuel Johnson, *The Lives of the Most Eminent English Poets; With Critical Observations on their Works*, ed. Roger Lonsdale, 4 vols. (Oxford, 2006), 1.291.

Longinus, says about imitators who are inspired by ancient authors. Longinus says that sublime imitators can be impregnated like the Pythian priestess by the 'conceptions' of an earlier author, or as the translation of Longinus by Milton's admirer John Hall put it:

> many are so rapt and transported with the conceptions of another, that they are possessed like the Pythia raving upon her Tripos, where there is a cleft of the earth breaths up (as they say) a strong inspiring vapour, which seizing the prophetesse shakes her, and fils her with such divine furies that she raves out mysteries and prophesies accordingly. Such kind of airs and vapours shoot themselves from the admirable writings of ancient Authors, as it were from some secret cave, which breath upon the souls of their imitatours though possibly not made for such high transports, and swell them up into a greatnesse like their own.[3]

The swelling inspiration of present authors by the ancients makes them, in Longinus's word, 'pregnant' (*egkumona*).[4] The impregnation of Sin by Satan makes the episode teem with imaginative life. But it does so in ways that cast dark light on both 'life' and on what it is to be 'imaginative': Satan spawns Sin, who spawns Death, who rapes his mother and spawns a generation of hell-hounds. A single person creates a whole breed of monsters by turning his imagination and his sexual desires inward on himself.

Sin has a messy literary genealogy. She is evidently related to Spenser's monster Errour in *The Faerie Queene*, and to the imitation of Errour in Phineas Fletcher's Hamartia (who is identified by a marginal note as 'Sinne') in *The Purple Island* (1633), who is vomited up from the 'detested maw' of Satan.[5] All of Sin's vernacular ancestors are themselves descendants of Ovid's Scylla—whom Milton describes as being 'far less abhorred' than Sin. Representing Sin in this way is a dark Miltonic joke: she is, quite definitely, not 'original' in any literary sense, even if she might claim to embody the

---

3. Longinus, *Peri Hypsous, or, Dionysius Longinus on the Height of Eloquence*, trans. John Hall (London, 1652), p. XXIX. On Hall, see Annabel M. Patterson, *Reading Between the Lines* (Madison, Wis., 1993), pp. 258–70.

4. Aristotle, Longinus, and Demetrius, *Aristotle Poetics, Longinus On The Sublime, Demetrius On Style*, trans. Stephen Halliwell, D. A. Russell, W. Hamilton Fyfe, and Doreen Innes (Cambridge, Mass., and London, 1995), p. 210 (13.2).

5. *The Purple Island*, 12.27 in Giles Fletcher and Phineas Fletcher, *Poetical Works*, ed. F. S. Boas, 2 vols. (Cambridge, 1908), 2.157. For echoes of Shakespeare, see David Hopkins, 'Milton's Sin and Shakespeare's *Richard III*', *Notes and Queries* 29 (1982), 502–3; William Poole, *Milton and the Making of Paradise Lost* (Cambridge, Mass., and London, 2017), p. 261 adds Hesiod, *Theogony*, 924–9 to the mix.

original sin that infects the will of mankind.[6] And underlying the fictional history of Sin and Death is again a spare biblical truth. As Jonathan Richardson noted in 1734, the episode is 'a kind of Paraphrase on those words of St. James I. 15 "Then when Lust hath conceived, it bringeth forth Sin: and Sin, when it is Finished, bringeth forth Death".'[7] As with Satan's allusion to Isaiah, this biblical under-presence gives a potentially corrosive irony to the scene: the biblical archetype of the episode seems even to threaten the physical existence of Satan's creations by turning them into a series of grotesque allegorical incarnations of the plain moral words of Saint James.

The creation of Sin and Death was also massively indebted not just to the practice of imitation, but to the language habitually used to describe it. That language is just as much a 'source' of this episode as Spenser, or Ovid, or Fletcher. Sin and Death are a dark retort to the traditional view, established by Quintilian and Seneca and commonplace by the seventeenth century, that an imitator could be compared to a strong, independent body, who resembled the imitated writer as a child resembles its parent. Indeed they seem almost to be a direct response to the most vivid early modern reanimation of those ideas and metaphors from the classical tradition in Erasmus's *Ciceronianus* (1528). Bulephorus favours a way of imitating Cicero

> which does not immediately incorporate into its own speech any nice little feature it comes across, but transmits it to the mind for inward digestion, so that becoming part of your own system, it gives the impression not of something begged from someone else, but of something that springs from your own mental processes [*ex ingenio tuo natum*], something that exudes the characteristics and force of your own mind and personality. Your reader will see it not as a piece of decoration filched from Cicero, but a child sprung from your own brain, the living image of its father [*vivam parentis imaginem*], like Pallas from the brain of Jove.[8]

Sin's fecund energy is a dark travesty of this belief that successful imitation is a kind of rebirth. Her fate turns Erasmian *imitatio* grotesquely against itself: she is not the product of achieved and absorbed literary digestion which

---

6. Maureen Quilligan, *Milton's Spenser: The Politics of Reading* (Ithaca, NY, 1983), pp. 79–128 notes at p. 90: 'The great saving humility that Milton achieves in this episode is that in predicating Sin's character on Errour's, he avoids making Satan's mistake: he pays due respect to his original, to Spenser.' See also Victoria Kahn, 'Allegory and the Sublime in *Paradise Lost*', in Annabel Patterson, ed., *John Milton* (London, 1992), 185–201.

7. Jonathan Richardson, *Explanatory Notes and Remarks on Milton's Paradise Lost* (London, 1734), p. 71.

8. Desiderius Erasmus, *Collected Works of Erasmus. Vol. 28, Literary and Educational Writings 6: Ciceronianus*, ed. A. H. T. Levi (Toronto, 1986), pp. 441–2.

leads to a rebirth of the past. Rather she springs from Satan's head like a parody of Pallas from the brain of Jove, and then becomes a feast for her own offspring. Death, she says, 'Tore through my entrails', and her children (who are simultaneously her grandchildren) have 'My bowels, their repast.' This is itself an imitation of the brood of Spenser's Errour, who 'sucked vp their dying mothers blood, | Making her death their life, and eke her hurt their good' (*FQ*, 1.1.25.8–9), but it goes further, indeed into the very bowels and womb of Sin. This was a powerful move. In creating Sin Milton not only graphically literalized the metaphors of imitation. He also turned them around. He absorbed and partially digested Spenser's Errour, and from her generated a scene which shows what it might be like to create something that exists to be eaten and absorbed by its own offspring. Underlying the episode is a simple biblical truth about the birth of sin from death; but underlying it too is a grotesque allegory of textual production in an age of imitation. You digest your reading to create a new birth. That new birth then ingests its parents. And that process continues endlessly.

Hanging over this potently deviant representation of imitation is the dark shadow of Death. He too is a massive amplification and universalization of problems inherent to *imitatio*. As we have seen, Quintilian was prone to present the *ingenium* or *vis* or power of an earlier author as individual, indefinable, and inimitable; consequently the imitator might produce no more than a shadow or *simulacrum* of an earlier text, a dream or a nightmare. Seneca, in his 84th Epistle, stated explicitly that a mere picture or 'image' of an earlier text is a dead thing, *imago res mortua est* (Epistles, 84.8). Milton's Death is a chiastic transformation of that thought, which flips Seneca's description of failed *imitatio* around. If an image is a dead thing then the terms could be reversed: *mors imago est*, Death is a shadow, a thing without substance, a kind of nothing. Seneca also, of course, argued that the imitator should resemble the imitated as a father does his son. Death, the rapist of his mother, is the image of his father; and Sin herself is such a perfect resemblance of her 'author' Satan that, as she puts it, 'Thy self in me thy perfect image viewing | Becamest enamoured, and such joy thou took'st | With me in secret, that my womb conceived | A growing burden' (*PL*, 2.764–7). And the dutiful daughter declares later on 'Thou art my father, thou my author, thou | My being gavest me; whom should I obey | But thee, whom follow?' (*PL*, 2.864–6).

Sin's desire to 'follow' her author again gives a literal force to the metaphors habitually used to describe *imitatio*: Longinus's discussion of imitation and emulation begins by terming it 'another road (*hodos*) to sublimity'

(*Sublime*, 13.2), and Lucretius had suggested an imitator can beat a path over areas hitherto untrodden in his own language as he follows a predecessor in Greek (*DRN*, 3.1–13). After the fall of man Sin and Death give a hyper-literal force to that metaphor too: in a huge feat of engineering they fashion a veritable motorway from earth to hell by building a bridge across Chaos 'by wondrous art…following the track | Of Satan' (*PL*, 10.312–15). In Milton's hell imitation seems to have become a monstrous parody of creation. It generates a violently physical version of birth which generates a thing without a shape, the *simulacrum* that is death, who haunts us all. It seems too that the invitation to follow the path of an author across a trackless waste could create a terrible and corrupting bridge between worlds, which takes past authors and refashions them into evil.

But *imitatio* is not simply a dark art for Milton. Rather it is deeply duplicitous. Imitation can generate shadows and reflections, but it can also be the foundation of new beings; and it is not simply a patrilineal force in which daughters and sons resemble and obey their father. Eve's account of her first moment is the best illustration of the potentially positive use of *imitatio* in Milton's poem:

> As I bent down to look, just opposite,
> A shape within the watery gleam appeared
> Bending to look on me, I started back,
> It started back, but pleased I soon returned,
> Pleased it returned as soon with answering looks
> Of sympathy and love; there I had fixed
> Mine eyes till now, and pined with vain desire,
> Had not a voice thus warned me, What thou seest,
> What there thou seest fair creature is thyself,
> With thee it came and goes: but follow me,
> And I will bring thee where no shadow stays
> Thy coming, and thy soft embraces, he
> Whose image thou art, him thou shall enjoy
> Inseparably thine, to him shalt bear
> Multitudes like thyself, and thence be called
> Mother of human race: what could I do,
> But follow straight, invisibly thus led?   (*PL*, 4.460–76)

The very first moment of Eve's being is an exceptionally close imitation of Ovid's story of Narcissus:

> quid videat, nescit; sed quod videt, uritur illo,
> atque oculos idem, qui decipit, incitat error.

credule, quid frustra simulacra fugacia captas?
quod petis, est nusquam; quod amas, avertere, perdes!
ista repercussae, quam cernis, imaginis umbra est:
nil habet ista sui; tecum venitque manetque;
tecum discedet, si tu discedere possis!   (*Met.*, 3.430–6)

He does not know what he sees, but what he sees, he burns for, and error urges on the same eyes that it deceives. Foolish boy! Why do you try in vain to catch these fleeting *simulacra*? What you seek is nowhere: look away and what you love will vanish. It is the shadow of a reflected shadow. It has no substance of its own: with you it came and stays; and it will go away with you too, if you *can* leave![9]

There is an obvious difference between Milton's and Ovid's versions of the story of Narcissus. Eve is prompted to get up and move away from her image to become 'mother of human race' where Narcissus pines with vain desire into a flower. There is also a less obvious difference between the two passages. Milton massively contracts the mocking language of *simulacra* and shadows which plays such a large part in Ovid's description of Narcissus, almost as though that vocabulary belongs to the Satanic parody of imitation in hell rather than to Eve's world.[10] Milton's representation of Eve's creation has been read in various ways as a fable about identity formation.[11] For Eve the 'I' of her emerging consciousness meets an 'it' in the image of her own reflection. She is then led on by that mysterious voice, imitated from Ovid's narratorial voice, but in Milton's retelling audible to Eve, to the recognition that there is a world beyond her own mind and her own body. The passage has also been read delicately and persuasively by Maggie Kilgour as being implicitly about the formation of Milton's own poetic identity: as Eve goes beyond Narcissus, leaving behind her own image, so 'Milton's transformation of his Ovidian source suggests too how artistic reflection...must include change and difference from the original'.[12]

Eve's account of her first moments is about what it might feel like to become a person who reaches beyond herself into a world outside. That

9. Text from Ovid, *Metamorphoses*, trans. Frank Justus Miller and G. P. Goold, 2 vols. (Cambridge, Mass., and London, 1977).
10. See Philip R. Hardie, *Ovid's Poetics of Illusion* (Cambridge, 2002), pp. 143–72.
11. See notably Linda Gregerson, *The Reformation of the Subject: Spenser, Milton, and the English Protestant Epic* (Cambridge, 1995), pp. 148–63.
12. Maggie Kilgour, '"Thy perfect image viewing": Poetic Creation and Ovid's Narcissus in *Paradise Lost*', *Studies in Philology* 102 (2005), 307–39 (p. 332); developed in Maggie Kilgour, *Milton and the Metamorphosis of Ovid* (Oxford, 2012), pp. 165–228. See also Richard J. DuRocher, *Milton and Ovid* (Ithaca, NY, 1985), pp. 85–93, and Mandy Green, *Milton's Ovidian Eve* (Farnham, 2009), pp. 23–51.

ethical reading is replicated at a metapoetic level: the episode also reflects on
what it might be like for a poet to create something that seems to lift itself
up and go beyond its source. But quite remarkably, as well as all these things,
it is also a moment where Milton signposts his imitation of Ovid by 'metaphrase', or word-for-word translation, as Charles Martindale has eloquently
shown.[13] Milton does not just imitate here. He translates almost as accurately
as in his painstaking translation of Horace's Ode 1.5, even to the extent of
mirroring the tenses of the Ovidian original: 'with thee it came and goes',
which renders 'tecum venitque manetque' (*Met.*, 3.435). This gives rise to a
simple question. How does this passage manage to be all of these things, to
appear at once to be both a fable of ego-formation and an extremely close
'metaphrase' or translation?

The answer to that question lies in the particular shape of Milton's
response to the traditions of imitation. His imitation of Ovid is not just
steeped in the metaphors of resemblance and bodily replication which run
through classical imitation theory. It attempts to sift apart the more or less
indistinguishable good and bad forms of *imitatio*. Love of an image, a
simulacrum, an *imago*, is supplanted by a birth, a promise of 'Multitudes like
thyself'. Milton's narrative moves from the metaphors associated in the
classical tradition with failed imitation—which are realized in the shadowy
replicants of hell—to those associated with success. Those metaphors drive
the narrative movement, from *imagines* to procreation, from a shadow to a
promise of birth.

The fact that Renaissance theories of *imitatio* are chiefly about pedagogy,
about how an orator or poet forms a stylistic identity from reading earlier
authors, is also highly relevant here. This is why the metaphors used to
describe *imitatio* can so readily leak into wider questions about the formation of identity and poetic identity. Eve learns to become Eve by moving
away from an *imago*, towards birth, breeding substantial life. Milton becomes
Milton by doing one side of an exercise in double translation and then
moving on beyond Ovid. He makes Eve/Narcissus stop reflecting on her
own image and instead breed living images of herself. The passage contains
a near metaphrase of Ovid, but the whole episode is a kind of answer to the
question 'who am I?' for both Eve and Milton. It suggests that the act of

---

13. Charles Martindale, *John Milton and the Transformation of Ancient Epic* (London, 1986), p. 167:
    'the slight awkwardness in the tenses of "With thee it came and goes" (469), which gives
    the words a curious Miltonic power, is due to exact imitation of the tenses of the Ovidian
    original (434–6).'

imitating is a primary stage in learning, a moment which is an education in personal identity and embodied being. You begin close to your text, an *imago* of Narcissus; then independent life supervenes on the imitation, as you learn to be separate from an earlier text. That gives to imitation a profound positive charge: done in the right way it can be what makes you live.

But as Milton observed in *Areopagitica* 'Good and evill we know in the field of this World grow up together almost inseparably' (*CPW*, 2.514). Quintilian noted the duplicity inherent to imitative replication: 'In addition whatever is like another thing is necessarily less than that which is imitated, as a shadow is less than a body and as an image is less than a face, and as the performance of an actor is inferior to real emotions' ('Adde quod, quidquid alteri simile est, necesse est minus sit eo, quod imitatur, ut umbra corpore et imago facie et actus histrionum veris adfectibus', *Institutio*, 10.2.11). That thought brings a vital instability to the argument of *Paradise Lost*, which is foundational to its complexity and richness. Eve is not a sole source of what is good. Her shadow or prefiguration is Sin, whose image Satan has loved, whose children have torn her entrails and fed upon her, and who herself seems to be grotesque embodiment of a plain biblical truth that the offspring of sin is death. The type and the antitype, the shadows of narcissism and the energies of creative love, are mutually involved to such an extent that it is impossibly simplistic to claim that Eve's movement towards loving another rather than loving herself is simply separate from and preferable to its hellish double, or that human breeding and replication is a benign alternative to its Satanic twin.[14] The two forms of replicating shadow each other.

This leads on to one of the main claims of this chapter. It is, perhaps like the best sort of claim, not *always* true; but it is true surprisingly often of major moments when Milton is imitating a classical text in *Paradise Lost*, and particularly in its early books. The small claim is that for Milton the metaphorical legacy of imitation theory plays a structural part in the process of imitating. That is, the metaphors used by classical writers to describe what happens when people imitate successfully or unsuccessfully do not simply colour Milton's practice. They give his imitations a larger ethical resonance, and even generate some of the central questions in *Paradise Lost* about the relationships between image and substance, between creator and his image and likeness, between self and other. Being Milton is as perilous as

---

14. On the relationship between imitation and doubling in *PL*, see Poole, *Making of Paradise Lost*, pp. 243–63.

being Eve, since imitation is duplicitous. It can generate a mass of deadly insubstantial shadows, like Death. Or it can generate a person with her own strength and spirit and ability to replicate, like Eve.

Imitatio in the seventeenth century

That is one way in which Milton is highly responsive to earlier writing about *imitatio*. But what has been less often appreciated is the extent to which he was also responsive to arguments about imitation which were going on around him, and which developed alongside his writing career. Milton was not just special, but said he was special, a poet with his garland and singing robes about him who enjoyed a peculiar grace;[15] and critics as a result have sometimes been a little too willing to believe that he was special in the way that he wants us to believe.

It is often said that Milton is a poet who fears that his own art, imitative of God's true creativeness, is potentially Satanic. This high-level theological anxiety is often read into moments such as Eve's creation and Sin's Satanic origins: how can a created being do more than merely parody the creative activity of God? Milton's anxiety about this question is generally said to be a product of his Christianity. How can a created being claim to create an original poem without becoming like Satan, or claim to create something more than a *simulacrum* of the world created by God? It is also sometimes suggested that Milton's relation to classical writing is in effect triumphalist, or that he is a heroic conqueror of the ancients, who turns his pagan sources into weak prefigurations of his Christian epic. This story sometimes has welded onto it another story: that Milton effectively lies at the end of a poetics grounded on *imitatio* and at the beginning of a poetics which stresses originality. And this in turn creates anxious analogies between his own creative capacities and those of Satan. David Quint has put this position clearly and well:

> By relegating his poetic predecessors to a secondary human status vis-à-vis the originary Holy Spirit which dictates his own unpremeditated verse, Milton is able, with one and the same gesture, to affirm both his unique authority and his authorial uniqueness. An inevitable analogy thus arises between Satan's attempts to be original, dramatized and criticized by *Paradise Lost*, and the poem's own brilliantly successful assertion of originality.[16]

15. See Stephen M. Fallon, *Milton's Peculiar Grace: Self-Representation and Authority* (Ithaca, NY, and London, 2007).
16. David Quint, *Origin and Originality in Renaissance Literature: Versions of the Source* (New Haven, 1983), p. 214.

This points towards some of the central preoccupations of Milton's poem, and to many of the features of it which have made it matter to its readers over the centuries. But in its emphasis on Milton's uniqueness and his ability to 'relegate' his predecessors it plays Milton's own game too willingly by accepting his own account of his poetics. It is indeed the case that often, as William Poole has recently put it, 'epic imitation in Milton carries with it a subtle incrimination of what it imitates', but the subtlety is all.[17]

The particular way that Milton practised and thought about imitation was not simply the product of his genius or of a singularly intimate relationship to the Holy Spirit, or of a conviction that Christian poetics and ethics were necessarily superior to their classical predecessors. It can be traced to much wider currents in the history of classical scholarship and education in the seventeenth century. In what follows I will not seek to explore in an exhaustive way the texts Milton imitates and what he does with them. There are many excellent book-length studies which do that, and more will doubtless follow.[18] Rather I will seek to situate Milton within arguments about literary imitation in seventeenth- and early eighteenth-century England. This will provide another way of explaining why *imitatio* was such a particularly fraught and creative issue for him.

Earlier chapters have emphasized that the main discussions of how one author should imitate another in Rome were concerned with oratory and education. They dwelt on the means by which a new orator learnt to speak from reading his *exempla*, his *paradeigmata*, the texts and authors which we might now describe as his 'originals' or 'models'. Classical writing about *imitatio* was, that is, chiefly about education. Young orators should start off trying to write like Cicero or Demosthenes, and by seeking out *exempla* that were suited to their individual dispositions they might become independent practitioners. Milton learned this the hard way. Throughout the sixteenth and seventeenth centuries, the grammar schools that educated Shakespeare, Milton, and Dryden remained enormously indebted to the classical theorists of rhetoric.

Those writers were brought up in an environment which assumed that imitating classical texts was how you learnt to write and to think. The underlying rationale for this (which was not always evident to the poor boys

17. Poole, *Making of Paradise Lost*, p. 191.
18. See, e.g., Martindale, *Transformation*, Francis C. Blessington, *Paradise Lost and the Classical Epic* (Boston, 1979), David Quint, *Inside Paradise Lost: Reading the Designs of Milton's Epic* (Princeton, 2014), and, for illuminating explorations of Milton's imitations of Apollonius Rhodius and Valerius Flaccus, Poole, *Making of Paradise Lost*, pp. 190–200.

themselves) was that if you mastered a good Latin style you might replicate the virtue of Cicero, and become, as Quintilian put it, quoting Cato, a good man skilled in speaking ('vir bonus dicendi peritus', *Institutio*, 12.1.1). Grammar schools evolved with grinding slowness. Educational treatises, from Roger Ascham's *Schoolmaster* (1570) to Charles Hoole's *New Discovery of the Old Art of Teaching Schoole* (1659), relied heavily on their predecessors. And again and again these treatises insist that imitation is central to the educative process. Hoole, for instance, insists that the imitation of Aesop and Erasmus's *Colloquies* will ultimately enable his pupils 'to speak their mindes upon any occasion'—and that intersection between something apparently personal and direct ('speak their mindes') and something impersonal (the occasion to which speech must be 'apt') was at the heart of a rhetorical education.[19]

Imitation was the way that boys become men who could speak and act aptly to any occasion. And the gender of these pronouns is historically accurate and critically significant: Grammar schools were for boys only in this period, and boys trained in the classical tradition absorbed the strongly yet strangely gendered vocabulary of imitation. Children resemble their fathers, not their mothers; but they also sought through developing their *ingenium* to give birth to new texts. Eve, the recreatress of an Ovidian episode, is in this respect the offspring of the curious gendered relationships which underlay discussions of *imitatio*. Grown men told young boys to give birth to new works from their digestion of old works.

The young Milton spent almost all day almost every day in his youth doing exercises in classical literature.[20] He was weaned on the nightmare of early modern schoolboys, which was an exercise known as 'double translation', advocated by Ascham and still recommended by Hoole in the 1650s: a pupil would be given a passage of Cicero and asked to translate it. Then the Latin would be taken away and he would have to translate the translation back into good Ciceronian Latin.[21] This exercise was designed to encourage both understanding and practical skill in rhetoric, and for some Ciceronians at least was supposed to generate eloquent and virtuous citizens. With those exercises went repeated inculcation in the theory and practice of imitation.

---

19. Charles Hoole, *A New Discovery of the Old Art of Teaching Schoole* (London, 1659), pp. 68–9.
20. Donald Lemen Clark, *John Milton at St Paul's School: A Study of Ancient Rhetoric in English Renaissance Education* (New York, 1948), pp. 152–84.
21. Hoole, *Teaching Schoole*, p. 122: 'Yet I would advise him to translate some little Books of himself; first out of Latine into English, and then out of English into Latine.' See Clark, *Milton at St Paul's*, p. 172; cf. Roger Ascham, *English Works*, ed. William Aldis Wright (Cambridge, 1904), p. 239.

The sheer persistence within the educational system of the traditional vocabulary for describing *imitatio* is remarkable. A good illustration of this is Thomas Farnaby's *Index Rhetoricus* of 1625, a text to which I shall return. This was an abbreviated manual of rhetoric for students which was reprinted thirteen times in England before 1700.[22] Farnaby was himself a highly successful school-teacher, and his *Index* was read by thousands of schoolboy readers, probably including Milton, in the course of the century.[23] It contains a masterly brief digest of Seneca's, Quintilian's, Sturm's, and Horace's views on *imitatio*, which rehearses the entire panoply of metaphorical language— of digestion, birth, exercise of the body and mind—compressed into a few digestible pages.[24] This was the diet of all seventeenth-century schoolboys.

However, by the mid-seventeenth century anyone who regarded themselves as fashionable in their thinking about education would have regarded the rhetorical training advocated by Farnaby as venerable but old-fashioned. The idea that you should imitate a classical original until you 'grow very he, or so like him as the copy may be mistaken for the principal'[25] (in Ben Jonson's memorable formulation) did not go away, but it became overlayered by other intellectual concerns. Two of these in particular had a strong influence on Milton. The first was Ramism. As we saw in Chapter 6, Ramus did not value the practice of imitating ancient texts as a means of developing a rhetorical style. For a hard-line Ramist an initial *analysis* of a text would show how its parts were connected; analysis then might or might not be followed with *genesis*, or an attempt to replicate the structure of the original work. Imitation would be motivated by an intention to replicate the excellence of the original rather than any specific features of its language or style.[26] Milton was influenced by Ramus's logic to the extent that his own

22. R. W. Serjeantson, 'Thomas Farnaby (1575?–12 June 1647)', in Edward A. Malone, ed., *British Rhetoricians and Logicians, 1500–1660: First Series* (Detroit and London, 2001), 108–16.
23. See Clark, *Milton at St Paul's*, pp. 149–51. In 1693 Locke mocked 'a learned Country Schoolmaster (who has all the Tropes and Figures in *Farnaby's Rhetorick* at his Fingers ends)', John Locke, *Some Thoughts Concerning Education*, ed. Jean S. Yolton and John W. Yolton (Oxford, 1989), p. 243.
24. Thomas Farnaby, *Index rhetoricus, scholis & institutioni tenerioris Aetatis accommodatus* (London, 1625), pp. 32–7.
25. Ben Jonson, *The Cambridge Edition of the Works of Ben Jonson*, ed. David M. Bevington, Martin Butler, and Ian Donaldson, 7 vols. (Cambridge, 2012), 7.583.
26. Clark, *Milton at St Paul's*, p. 153 cites the Ramistic Charles Butler's *Oratoriae Libri duo* (1629), epilogus: 'Exercise consists in Genesis and Analysis. It is Genesis when we compose our own orations according to the precepts of Art and in imitation of the Orators. It is Analysis when we take apart [*resolvimus*] the orations of others, observing in them what rules of Art are followed and what virtues of the authors are worthy of imitation. It is imitation when we copy the method [*rationem*] of speaking of another. There are two rules in Imitation: that we should imitate those who are excellent and those qualities in them which are excellent.'

Art of Logic substantially derived from Ramus's *Dialecticae libri duo* as well as from George Downame's and other commentaries on that work, and there is little doubt that the wider traditions of Ramism coloured his thinking about imitation.[27]

The other movement that had a surprisingly strong influence on Milton's thinking about *imitatio* was that of the group of educational reformers who were friends and correspondents of Samuel Hartlib.[28] The influence is surprising because writers associated with the Hartlib circle have notably little to say about the imitation of authors. Their encyclopaedic reforming schemes for new methods of learning and teaching tended to begin with practical experience, and much of their energy was concentrated on developing an understanding of the world that could enable their pupils to act directly upon it. As a result practical guides to agriculture and astronomy—Varro, Columella, Aratus—tended to feature in their writings more prominently than Cicero or Quintilian. Samuel Hartlib's *The Reformed Commonwealth of the Bees* (1655) is indicative of the interests of his wider circle, many members of which contributed letters and thoughts to this volume about agricultural reform. It begins with a quotation from Varro 'Concerning the profit of bees', and proceeds to try and work out in present-day English money exactly how much profit the Roman author made from beekeeping.[29] There is nary a buzz from the creatively imitating bees of the Senecan tradition. Members of the Hartlib circle had a profound respect for God and his works, but that was frequently articulated through negative statements about acts of imitation in general: so Hartlib's translation of his master Comenius's *Reformation of Schools* (1642) emphasizes that God is not an imitator: 'God imitates none but himself, because he neither can, nor will do otherwise: he cannot, because he can behold nothing but himself in his infinite eternity: whence then should he borrow either the beginning, or rule of his works?'[30]

---

27. See *CPW*, 8.144–205, and the careful distinctions made between Milton and Ramus in Phillip J. Donnelly, *Milton's Scriptural Reasoning: Narrative and Protestant Toleration* (Cambridge, 2009), pp. 39–48.
28. See the summary in Barbara Kiefer Lewalski, *The Life of John Milton: A Critical Biography* (Oxford, 2003), pp. 172–5.
29. Samuel Hartlib, *The Reformed Common-wealth of Bees* (London, 1655), pp. 1–2.
30. Johann Amos Comenius and Samuel Hartlib, *A Reformation of Schooles Designed in Two Excellent Treatises* (London, 1642), p. 37.

Milton was an admirer, though not in a simple way a follower, of Samuel Hartlib. Hartlib himself described Milton by 1643 as 'a great traveller and full of projects and inventions'.[31] Milton's treatise *Of Education* (1644) was dedicated to Hartlib, and was clearly influenced by his thinking, although the precise relationship is a matter of some disagreement.[32] The practical bias of the Hartlib circle is immediately apparent in the reading recommended in *Of Education*. Milton foregrounds texts which offer practical instruction: Cato the Censor's *De Re Rustica* alongside Columella's and Varro's works on agriculture in particular serve the purpose of 'inciting and inabling them hereafter to improve the tillage of their country' (*CPW*, 2.388–9). When Milton's charges are ready for poetry they might read Lucretius, Manilius 'and the rural part of Virgil' (*CPW*, 2.396) rather than the *Aeneid*. Texts that tell their readers how to do things are commended before texts which enact a style, such as Cicero's epistles, or Virgil's *Aeneid*, or Ovid's *Metamorphoses*. Although *Of Education* attempts to weld a Hartlibian practicality onto the rhetorical tradition, it does not talk about imitation at all—or rather (with remarkable consistency) restricts uses of that noun and its related verb to the ethical emulation of God or other admirable figures. It finally allows that England when perfected by Milton's educational system will prompt other nations to 'imitate us' (*CPW*, 2.414).[33]

Human beliefs are made up of sedimentary layers of practice and opinions. Even the most zealous revolutionary remains embedded in the attitudes that they acquired at school and in their home. *Of Education* gives repeated signs

---

31. Hartlib Papers, 30/4/89A.
32. For the view that *Of Education* differs significantly from Comenius, see *CPW*, 2.186; Charles Webster, ed., *Samuel Hartlib and the Advancement of Learning* (Cambridge, 1970), p. 43 insists 'there was no basic antagonism between the Hartlib circle and Milton'. Julian Koslow, '"Not a Bow for Every Man to Shoot": Milton's *Of Education*, between Hartlib and Humanism', *Milton Studies* 47 (2008), 24–53 argues that the treatise is not a compromise between humanism and Comenianism; it is anti-humanist in its content, yet the rhetorically powerful figure of the teacher suggests Milton's continuing affection for a humanistic legacy. Timothy Raylor, 'Milton, the Hartlib Circle, and the Education of the Aristocracy', in Nicholas McDowell and Nigel Smith, eds., *The Oxford Handbook of Milton* (Oxford, 2012), 382–406 argues that Milton was designing a reformed version of the French academy and was in the mainstream of Hartlibian reformers in the 1640s. For a detailed attempt to relate the reading recommended in *Of Education* to Milton's poetry, see Richard J. DuRocher, *Milton Among the Romans: The Pedagogy and Influence of Milton's Latin Curriculum* (Pittsburgh, 2001).
33. *CPW*, 2.366: 'The end then of learning is to repair the ruins of our best parents by regaining to know God aright, and out of that knowledge to love him, to imitate him, to be like him, as we may the neerest by possessing our souls of true vertue, which being united to the heavenly grace of faith makes up the highest perfection.'

that Milton never entirely lost touch with his early education at St Paul's, which was still effectively a sixteenth-century humanistic training.[34] The metaphorical structures and priorities of the *Institutio Oratoria* (the first two books of which Milton commends to his pupils, *CPW*, 2.384) in particular remained a deep part of Milton's thinking about how and why people learned. There is a very oblique allusion to Quintilian in a passage in *Of Education* in which Milton discusses what we now call revision, as in overlooking what one has previously been taught in preparation for an examination:

> In which methodicall course it is so suppos'd they must proceed by the steddy pace of learning onward, as at convenient times for memories sake to retire back into the middle ward, and sometimes into the rear of what they have been taught, untill they have confirm'd, and solidly united the whole body of their perfected knowledge, like the last embattelling of a Romane legion.
>
> (*CPW*, 2.406–7)

'Methodicall course' nods to the Ramistic emphasis on 'method' in all aspects of learning. But the comparison of revision to the formation of a tightly formed legion of knowledge points towards Milton's larger aim in *Of Education*. Milton insists that his kind of education will equip his citizens for peace or war.[35] But because reading books has no evident or necessary connection with an ability to fight he has to suggest that reading and writing have military teeth through metaphor. These metaphors, and indeed this whole passage, are based on a distant memory of a passage from Quintilian which displays his characteristic military-industrial metaphors for describing the art of rhetoric; and it is a passage in which Quintilian discusses revision in a rather narrower sense:

> To do this with due care, we shall repeatedly have to go over what we wrote last. Apart from the fact that better connections are made in this way between what has gone before and what follows, the warmth of our thought, which has cooled down in the time spent writing, recovers strength and gathers fresh impetus, as it were, from going over the ground again. We see this happening in jumping competitions, where the competitors start their attempt a long way back, and run up to the area in which the jump is to be made. In javelin-throwing, likewise, we draw back our arms, and when we are about to shoot an arrow, we pull the bow-string back.

34. Clark, *Milton at St Paul's*, ch. 7. Barbara Kiefer Lewalski, 'Milton and the Hartlib Circle: Educational Projects and Epic *Paideia*', in Diana Benet and Michael Lieb, eds., *Literary Milton: Text, Pretext, Context* (Pittsburgh, 1994), 202–19.

35. Martin Dzelzainis, 'Milton and the Limits of Ciceronian Rhetoric', in Neil Rhodes, ed., *English Renaissance Prose: History, Language, and Politics* (Tempe, Ariz., 1997), 203–26 (pp. 209–10) sets *Of Education* in the context of Parliamentarian military defeats, 1643–4.

Quae quidem ut diligentius exsequamur, repetenda saepius erunt scriptorum proxima. Nam praeter id quod sic melius iunguntur prioribus sequentia, calor quoque ille cogitationis, qui scribendi mora refrixit, recipit ex integro vires, et velut repetito spatio sumit impetum; quod in certamine saliendi fieri videmus, ut conatum longius petant, et ad illud, quo contenditur, spatium cursu ferantur; utque in iaculando bracchia reducimus et expulsuri tela neruos retro tendimus. (*Institutio*, 10.3.6)[36]

The resemblance lies more in metaphoric structures than in exact verbal allusion. That makes it more rather than less significant, since it testifies to the very deep penetration of Quintilianic thinking into Milton's beliefs about education. Although the imitative arts advocated in the rhetorical tradition are not an explicit part of Milton's argument in *Of Education*, that tradition is smuggled back into the treatise in the form of metaphor. A student should recoil, regroup, revise ready to fight the wars of truth.

The second moment when the ghost of Quintilian walks across Milton's metaphorical language in *Of Education* occurs when he is discussing higher or later studies, in which tragedies and epic poems could play a part, and which leads on to the moment when his pupils can study 'simple, sensuous and passionate' poetry. It is here that the rhetorical tradition really sings through the treatise:

> When all these employments are well conquer'd, then will the choise Histories, *heroic poems*, and *Attic* tragedies of statliest, and most regal argument, with all the famous Politicall orations offer themselves; which if they were not only read; but some of them got by memory, and solemnly pronounc't with right accent, and grace, as might be taught, would endue them even with the spirit, and vigor of *Demosthenes* or *Cicero*, *Euripides*, or *Sophocles*. (*CPW*, 2.400–1)

The key terms here are 'spirit and vigor'. They are the direct equivalents of that central term used by Quintilian when he is describing what his young orators should take from Cicero or Demosthenes: repeatedly Quintilian says that what really matters in an orator is his *vis*—power, force, energy, spirit, vigour. Demosthenes has *vis* and sinew (*nervis*), as does Caesar (*Institutio*, 10.2.24). Like Quintilian before him, Milton is establishing the social value and military muscle of his educational system by using metaphors of force.

But this passage shares another feature with Quintilian. It is conceptually opaque. That is, there is no explanation of *how* someone who reads, remembers, and pronounces the speeches of Demosthenes will be 'endued' with

---

36. Text and translations from Quintilian, *The Orator's Education*, ed. Donald A. Russell, 5 vols. (Cambridge, Mass., and London, 2001).

the 'spirit and vigor' of those classical orators. This is a residue of the most striking feature of classical writing on *imitatio*: it is metaphorically rich in direct proportion to its conceptual thinness. Most of the positive comparisons for imitation (resemble your original as a child resembles his father rather than as a portrait resembles a sitter; absorb your texts as the bees gather nectar and turn it into honey; digest your reading into your own substance, blend your reading into a single harmony like a choir, don't just follow in the footsteps, bring forth a new birth) are associated with the corporeal and forceful and living—digestion, birth, the production of honey. But that key question, '*how* do you endue yourself with the spirit and vigour of Demosthenes?' remains unanswered. And that unanswered question remains with Milton even in his tentative experiment in Hartlibian educational reform in the 1640s. Can simply reading Demosthenes or Cicero aloud *really* transmit their 'spirit' and 'vigour' to a pupil? *Of Education* suggests that Milton was powerfully influenced by two aspects of classical writing on imitation: he was highly responsive to its metaphors, but also was heir to its central conceptual problem. How does a new writer generate a bodily replica of the force and spirit of an ancient orator?

That question takes us to a text which played a crucial role in the reception of Quintilian in the seventeenth century, and which happened to have been written by a friend of Milton. This was Francis Junius the younger's *De Pictura Veterum* ('The Painting of the Ancients'), which was published in an English version in 1638.[37] Junius's treatise was about painting, but it includes a discussion of imitation which is explicitly indebted to Quintilian, and which cites Book 10 chapter two of the *Institutio* (the chapter on *imitatio*) frequently and directly. Junius brought out very clearly the potential conflicts within Quintilian's treatment of the topic. He gave extremely strong emphasis to all of Quintilian's negative remarks about 'mere imitation' or 'apish imitation'. Disparaging imitation was not in itself unusual or new: the phrase 'apish imitation' is quite frequent in anti-Catholic polemic from the 1560s onwards (Catholic priests are accused of apishly replicating the rituals of worship rather than inwardly grasping them), and satirists of the 1590s bandied accusations of 'servile imitation' around with some freedom.[38] But

---

37. Franciscus Junius, *The Painting of the Ancients*, trans. Richard Hodgkinson (London, 1638). For the friendship, see William Riley Parker, *Milton: A Biography*, ed. Gordon Campbell (Oxford, 1996), p. 250.

38. Théodore de Bèze, *A Confession of Fayth Made by Common Consent of Divers Reformed Churches*, trans. John Old (London, 1568), sig. D3r: the errors of Catholic theology arise from 'their blinde zeale and apishe imitation of others'. For 'servile imitation', see Thomas Nashe, *Works*,

Junius draws particular attention to the dangers of what he terms 'the slavish custom of imitation' (p. 30), and is (according to the database of TCP/EEBO at least) the first English writer to use the phrase 'mere imitator' (p. 29). By the 1650s negative usages of 'imitator' and related verbs in literary contexts were common: William Davenant objected that 'whilst we imitate others, wee can no more excell them, then he that sailes by others Mapps can make a new discovery'.[39] But Junius brought that unease with *imitatio* into his reading of Quintilian.

As well as emphasizing the dangers of imitation Junius also insists—and again his emphasis is unusually strong—that an imitator should grasp the *spirit* embodied in a work of art: 'As many then as desire to expresse the principall vertues of the best and most approved Artificers, must not content themselves with a slender and superficiall viewing of the workes they meane to imitate, but they are to take them in their hands againe and againe, never leaving till they have perfectly apprehended the force of Art that is in them, and also thoroughly acquainted themselves with that spirit the Artificers felt whilest they were busie about these workes' (p. 33). Furthermore Junius also restates and amplifies Quintilian's emphasis on the inimitability of such *vis* or animating spirit: 'such things as doe deserve to be most highly esteemed in an Artificer, are almost inimitable; his wit, namely, his Invention, his unstrained facilitie of working, and whatsoever cannot be taught us by the rules of Art' (p. 34). What Junius did was in effect draw attention to the deep conceptual split within Quintilian's thinking about *imitatio*. Acquisition of a skill went along with an appreciation that the skill which was sought was in fact inimitably particular to the original author.

This gives a key context for Milton's uneasy attitude towards *imitatio* in general, and to his treatment of Quintilian's thought and metaphors in *Of Education* in particular: an *unholy* conception of 'spirit' was emerging in seventeenth-century responses to Quintilian. Milton was extremely good at representing himself as a singular figure of virtue, but he was also highly responsive to developments in the history of scholarship. And as a result he was not so much the creator of shifts in attitudes towards imitation in the later seventeenth century as the product of a series of minor transformations in the use of the word and of the practice in that period, which he brilliantly aids and exploits.

ed. R. B. McKerrow and F. P. Wilson, 4 vols. (Oxford, 1958), 1.246; *Scourge of Villainy*, 9.23 in John Marston, *The Poems*, ed. A. Davenport (Liverpool, 1961).

39. William Davenant and Thomas Hobbes, *A Discourse upon Gondibert* (Paris, 1650), p. 13.

As we have seen, *imitatio* has never been fully separable from allusion: commentaries on Latin poetry had almost from the very beginning noted resemblances between Virgil and Homer, and had cited parallel passages which enabled comparisons between the two writers, and which were frequently referred to as imitations. Macrobius's comparison of Homer with Virgil was of course the *locus classicus* for identifying these directly allusive forms of imitation. The word *imitatio*, however, was given a strong nudge towards the sense 'a local and identifiable allusion to an earlier work which invites comparison with that earlier text' by developments in the way classical texts were edited and presented to their readers in the first half of the seventeenth century. Milton also responded to these developments, which were the culmination of earlier tendencies rather than radical departures, but they had a deep impact on classicizing poets later in the century.

So the massive three-volume folio edition of Virgil's *Aeneid* by the Spanish Jesuit Juan Luis de La Cerda which appeared in 1642 not only records extensive parallels from Homer (and indeed from imitators of Virgil such as Statius) but often marks these by a marginal note to his commentary labelled 'Imitatio'. This made the incorporation of textual materials from another writer instantly visible to a reader of this edition. But La Cerda also brought critical comparison between Homer and Virgil into the substance of his commentary. He had evidently been influenced by the lengthy comparison of the two authors, to the detriment of Homer, in the *Poetices* (5.2) of Julius Caesar Scaliger (1561), since La Cerda repeatedly declares, in marginal notes which provide a very visible cue to readers, that here 'Virgil overgoes Homer' ('Homerum superat Virgilius').

These features of the layout of classical editions brought to the fore not only the long-standing association between *imitatio* and local allusion but also that between imitation and emulation—what Longinus terms *zēlōsis*—or a desire to conquer and overgo a previous text whilst alluding to it. Editions such as La Cerda's made reading classical literature increasingly a comparative exercise, in which one passage would be read in conjunction with another, which was either supplied by the memory of the reader or which was quoted by a commentator. This brought not just comparison but also comparative evaluation right into the process of reading classical literature, and it embodied those activities in the very form in which classical texts were read.

The commentary tradition fostered a culture of reading which made overt markers of supremacy—signs of conquering, of exceeding, or of transcending the imitated text—part of the experience of classical literature.

This was not driven by beliefs about the inferiority of pagan culture to Christian, but by the detailed local comparison of the merits of one author with another. The Holy Spirit may or may not have murmured in Milton's ear that he should seek to transcend the *Odyssey* or the *Aeneid*. But if it did so the Holy Spirit was simply amplifying what the secular print culture of Milton's time was telling him to do. And of course that Spirit shared a name with the elusive and inimitable 'spirit' of an earlier author which Milton's friend Francis Junius had insisted the imitator should seek to imitate.

By the later seventeenth century there had been further developments in the way the word 'imitation' was used in the vernacular, which provide a further context for Milton's activity as an imitating author. They also had such a strong influence on future ways of imitating both classical and vernacular authors that in describing them I will extend the narrative beyond the lifetime of Milton. This will show the dominant direction of travel in thinking about *imitatio* in seventeenth-century England.

By the time Milton published *Paradise Lost* relatively free adaptations of classical originals might be called 'imitations'.[40] This usage again had deep roots, and brought with it some measure of lexical and conceptual unease. Abraham Cowley's *Poems* (1656) included translations which were described as 'in imitation of Horace his ode' and 'in imitation of Martial his epigram'. In his preface to his translations and adaptations of Pindar, Cowley acknowledged that his work (as what would now be called a 'free' translator) occupied a lexical gap between translation and imitation. He said: 'I am not so much enamoured of the Name Translator, as not to wish rather to be Something Better, though it want yet a Name'.[41] 'Imitator' was an awkward term in the 1650s.

As *Paradise Lost* was coming off the press in late 1667 the vocabulary used to describe poems which imitated classical texts was becoming clearer than it had been a decade before. Two of the earliest poems to refer to themselves as '*An* Imitation' (rather than as poems written '*in* imitation' of a classical author) appeared in print just at this point. John Denham's 'Occasional imitation of a Game of Chess', which was a parody of William Davenant's

40. Harold F. Brooks, 'The "Imitation" in English Poetry, Especially in Formal Satire, before the Age of Pope', *The Review of English Studies* OS 25 (1949), 124–40. For readings of Milton in relation to Restoration conventions, see Blair Hoxby and Ann Baynes Coiro, eds., *Milton in the Long Restoration* (Oxford, 2016).
41. Abraham Cowley, *Poems: i. Miscellanies. ii. The Mistress. iii. Pindarique Odes. iv. Davideis* (London, 1656), pp. 20–1, and sig. Aaa2v.

Gondibert, appeared in Denham's *Poems and Translations* of 1668.[42] 'The Earl
of Roscommon to Orinda: an imitation of HORACE', was appended to
Katherine Philips's *Poems* (1667).[43]

Those two poems nicely illustrate the surprising co-dependency of two
quite different ways of using the word 'imitation' in literary contexts by the
end of the seventeenth century. 'An Imitation of [a classical author]' could
be an adaptive imitation or a kind of translation that overtly substituted
English customs and interests for their Roman equivalents, or a poem, as
Samuel Johnson was to put it, 'in which the ancients are familiarised
by adapting their sentiments to modern topicks, by making Horace say
of Shakespeare what he originally said of Ennius'.[44] 'An Imitation of
[an English author]', on the other hand, could be an exercise in stylistic
mimicry—either with or without satirical intent—which testified to the
author's ability to recognize the stylistic mannerisms of the imitated text.
Poems called 'Imitations' of vernacular authors might draw on the distinctive vocabulary or rhyme-scheme of a well-known writer in deliberately
incongruous ways, as Denham did with the unfortunate Davenant.

Milton himself, whose style was even more overtly imitable than that of
Ben Jonson, was by the first years of the next century to suffer this form of
imitation. John Philips's *The Splendid Shilling: A Poem in Imitation of Milton*
(first pirated in 1701, but written some time before) entertainingly transforms Milton's Sin and Death into a dun and a catchpoll who pursue the
poet for a debt.[45] Philips's work was itself parodied in *Cerealia: An Imitation
of Milton* (1706)—which was formerly ascribed to Philips but was in fact
written by one of Milton's future biographers Elijah Fenton.[46] This is a
Miltonizing encomium of beer, the gems in which include 'Delicious
Tipple! that in heav'nly Veins | Assimilated, vig'rous ICHOR bred'.[47]

42. John Denham, *Poems and Translations: with The Sophy* (London, 1668), pp. 126–7.
43. For mutual imitations of Cowley and Katherine Philips, see Elizabeth Scott-Baumann, *Forms
    of Engagement: Women, Poetry, and Culture 1640–1680* (Oxford, 2013), pp. 81–112.
44. Johnson, *Lives*, 4.45.
45. John Philips, *The Splendid Shilling. A Poem, in Imitation of Milton. By the Author of Bleinheim*
    (London, 1705), p. 5: 'So horrible he seems! his faded brow | Entrench'd with many a Frown,
    and Conic beard...'. For early eighteenth-century imitations of Milton's style, see also Paul Davis,
    'Addison's Forgotten Poetic Response to Paradise Lost: "Milton's Stile Imitated, in a Translation
    of a Story out of the Third Aeneid" (1704): An Edited Text, with Annotation and Commentary',
    Milton Quarterly 49 (2015), 243–74. See also Anthony Welch, 'Paradise Lost and English Mock
    Heroic', in Hoxby and Baynes Coiro, eds., *Milton in the Long Restoration*, pp. 465–82.
46. See Juna Christian Pellicer, 'Cerealia (1706): Elijah Fenton's Burlesque of Milton and Spenser
    in Critique of John Philips', *Notes and Queries* 50 (2003), 197–201, and Poole, *Making of Paradise
    Lost*, p. 291.
47. Elijah Fenton, *Cerealia: an Imitation of Milton* (London, 1706), p. 4.

Fenton's 'Life' of Milton prefixed to his 1725 edition of *Paradise Lost* remarks that 'no One of our *English* Poets hath excited so many Admirers to imitate his Manner, yet I think never any was known to aspire to emulation'.[48] Imitating an author's 'manner', and oneself having a 'manner' that could be imitated, was becoming central to authorship; and Milton himself deliberately cultivated such an imitable manner.

These two kinds of poem called 'Imitations'—the adaptation of a classical text to contemporary mores on the one hand, and the pastiche of a vernacular author on the other—were in principle distinguishable, but there was much by-play between them. Charles Cotton's *Scarronides* (1664) had burlesqued Virgil's *Aeneid*. 'Imitations' of classical texts in the adaptive sense were akin to parodies in that they deliberately played off their readers' knowledge of the text which was being transformed.[49] But these two forms of imitation, just becoming overtly formulated in Milton's writing life-time, were of immense historical significance. Indeed, if we gaze ahead of Milton to the time of Alexander Pope's *Dunciad* (which was published in revised versions from 1728–43), the distinction between implicitly parodic 'imitations' of vernacular texts on the one hand and adaptive 'imitations' of classical poems on the other had hardened into a convention clear enough to be itself the subject of parody. In the sections of the notes to the *Dunciad* headed 'Imitations' (the layout of the poem imitates that of a classical text) the word 'parody' is used only of lines which echo vernacular authors, while 'imitations' of classical texts are simply marked by quoting the originals. So the start of Book 2 of the *Dunciad in Four Books*, 'High on a gorgeous seat, that far out-shone | Henley's gilt tub, or Flecknoe's Irish throne' is described as a 'Parody of Milton, book 2'.[50]

But for Pope a distinction between concepts was always a pretext for confusing them, and he regularly played with hybrid forms which at once were 'imitations' of classical authors and of the styles of his contemporaries. So in his *Imitations of Horace* in the 1730s Pope, being Pope, even presented

48. John Milton, *Paradise Lost, a Poem. To which is prefix'd an account of his life [by E. Fenton]* (London, 1725), p. xxii.

49. For parody as imitation 'with critical distance', see Linda Hutcheon, *A Theory of Parody: The Teachings of Twentieth Century Art Forms* (New York and London, 1985), p. 36.

50. Alexander Pope, *The Dunciad: in Four Books*, ed. Valerie Rumbold (Harlow, 2009), p. 147; cf. p. 240, recording a parody of Denham, and the preliminary advertisement to the *Variorum Dunciad*: 'The *Imitations* of the Ancients are added, to gratify those who either never read, or may have forgotten them; together with some of the Parodies, and Allusions to the most excellent of the Moderns', Alexander Pope, *The Dunciad: with Notes, Variorum and the Prolegomena of Scriblerus* (London, 1729), p. 4.

one of his 'imitations' (of Horace's *Sermones*, 2.1) anonymously to the world as having been 'Imitated in the Manner of Mr Pope', thus imitating himself as imitator, and another as 'Imitated in the Manner of Dr Swift'.[51] And, moreover, in his notes to the imitation of his own style of imitating, Pope imitated the splenetic style of the classical scholar Richard Bentley by supplying an annotation on the word 'imitated' which runs 'Why imitated? Why not translated? *Odi Imitatores* ["I hate imitators"—alluding to Horace, *Epistles*, 1.19.19].'[52] In imitating in this way Pope was himself imitated by Isaac Hawkins Browne, whose popular *A Pipe of Tobacco in Imitation of Six Several Authors* of 1734 described the joys of smoking in the various styles of Ambrose Philips, James Thomson, Edward Young, Pope himself, Colley Cibber, and Swift. Browne had a positively Popean ear for the characteristic features of Pope's style in particular: 'Blest Leaf! Whose aromatic Gales dispense | To Templers Modesty, to Parsons Sense: | So raptur'd Priests, at Dodona's Shrine | Drank Inspiration of the Steam divine.'[53] That 'imitation' captured Pope's 'manner' so completely that there was no need for Browne to identify who he was parodying.

All that fun lay in the future. The crucial point about this larger narrative so far as Milton is concerned is that *Paradise Lost* was composed in the period when these distinctions and creative indistinctions were being formed, and the word 'imitation' was one of shifting sense in that period. The conventions for writing adaptive 'imitations' of classical works in this sense developed steadily after Cowley's and Katherine Philips's experiments in the 1650s and 1660s.[54] John Oldham in 1681 put Horace in 'modern dress' by 'making him speak, as if he were living, and writing now'. Oldham made 'use of English names of Men, Places, and Customs . . . which I conceiv'd would give a kind of new Air to the poem, and render it more agreeable to the relish of the present age'.[55] And that meant that what were termed 'imitations' of classical texts moved closer and closer to what we would now call translations

51. On Pope's response to the tradition, see Frank Stack, *Pope and Horace: Studies in Imitation* (Cambridge, 1985), pp. 18–24. The 1734 edition of *Sober Advice from Horace to the Young Gentleman about Town . . . Imitated in the Manner of Mr Pope* was published anonymously.
52. Alexander Pope, *Imitations of Horace*, ed. John Butt (London and New Haven, 1953), p. 74.
53. Isaac Hawkins Browne, *A Pipe of Tobacco in Imitation of Six Several Authors* (London, 1736), p. 19.
54. Howard D. Weinbrot, *The Formal Strain: Studies in Augustan Imitation and Satire* (Chicago, Ill., 1969), p. 16: 'On the one side we see the pure translator and the Imitator who is generally faithful to his author's sense and meaning, but modernizes allusions, places, and names. On the other side we see the "independent" Imitator who, depending on his aims, may either parallel or differ from an acknowledged model which he subordinates to a new poetic intention.'
55. John Oldham, *Poems*, ed. Harold Brooks and Raman Selden (Oxford, 1987), p. 87. See Paul Hammond, *John Oldham and the Renewal of Classical Culture* (Cambridge, 1983).

or adaptations. Indeed in later seventeenth-century England the most sophisticated accounts of what I have called adaptive imitation, where a poem is 'translated' into the cultural terms of a new age, tended to occur in programmatic statements about the nature of translation rather than of imitation. Those statements usually came from English royalist writers who had direct knowledge of French translation theory.[56] So Sir John Denham's *Destruction of Troy* (1656) is prefixed by a note that declares: 'if Virgil must needs speak English, it were fit he should speak not only as a man of this nation, but as a man of this age'.[57] John Dryden elaborated this conception in his prefatory matter to his translation of the *Aeneid* at the very end of the century: 'I have endeavour'd to make *Virgil* speak such *English* as he wou'd himself have spoken, if he had been born in *England*, and in this present Age.'[58]

This view of imitation as writing 'as if' Virgil or Horace were a modern has deep roots which extend, like so much new thinking about *imitatio*, to the Ciceronian debates of the sixteenth century, and particularly to Erasmus's insistence in *Ciceronianus* that speech be adapted to the decorum of new times. By the early seventeenth century Bartholomaeus Keckerman could present the practice of adapting texts to new times in this way as simply one of several methods by which an imitator might conceal a debt to an original.[59] That marvellous trouble-maker and fertile transformer of the language of imitation Alexander Pope duly satirized this form of culturally adaptive imitation in *Peri Bathous: Martinus Scriblerus his Treatise of the Art of Sinking in Poetry* of 1728 when he wrote 'Therefore, when we sit down to write, let us bring some great author to our mind, and ask ourselves this question; How would Sir Richard [Blackmore, whom Pope despised] have said this.'[60]

It is tempting to see these developments in neoclassicism and, in Pope's case, of the arts of teasing in poetry, as being entirely alien to Milton. But

56. T. R. Steiner, *English Translation Theory 1650–1800* (Assen, 1975), pp. 12–25; Matthew Reynolds, *The Poetry of Translation: From Chaucer and Petrarch to Homer and Logue* (Oxford, 2011), pp. 121–6.

57. John Denham, *The Destruction of Troy: an Essay upon the Second Book of Virgils Aeneis. Written in the year, 1636* (London, 1656), sig. A3r–v.

58. John Dryden, *The Works*, ed. Edward Niles Hooker, H. T. Swedenberg, and Vinton A. Dearing, 20 vols. (Berkeley, 1956–2000), 5.330–1. On the evolution of Dryden's theory of translation, see David Hopkins, *Conversing with Antiquity: English Poets and the Classics, from Shakespeare to Pope* (Oxford, 2010), pp. 113–29, and Stuart Gillespie, *English Translation and Classical Reception: Towards a New Literary History* (Oxford, 2011).

59. Bartholomaeus Keckermannus, *Systema Rhetoricae* (Hanover, 1608), p. 909. On Milton's knowledge of Keckermann's logic, see Donnelly, *Milton's Scriptural Reasoning*, p. 40.

60. Alexander Pope, *The Prose Works*, ed. Rosemary Cowler, 2 vols. (Oxford, 1936–86), 2.203.

they were not *entirely* alien to his practice. He worked alongside, partly
with, partly against the grain of, this wider body of conventions. He worked,
indeed, while those conventions were being forged around him. That was
why he imitated classical writers in a way that established such a distinctively
'Miltonic' lexis: an imitating author sought to become an object of
imitation, with a recognizable and imitable style. And there are several points
of convergence between Milton's spiritual and intellectual concerns and
the emerging neoclassical conventions which surrounded him. Later
seventeenth-century discussions of translation as imitation often adopted a
language of volatility, in which it is said that the aim of the imitator or translator is to capture a fleeting essence or 'spirit' of the original. This chimes
with the vocabulary and concerns of Francis Junius's discussion of imitation
in *De Pictura Veterum*, in which the 'air' or spirit of a text is the object of
imitation: 'The Spirit of an Author may be tranfus'd, and yet not lost', as
Dryden put it.[61] The *vis* and *ingenium* of an earlier author consequently
became equated with a ghostly spirit or soul, which the imitator might
transfuse into his own spirit and into the customary language of his age.

This spirit was of course not holy, let alone the Holy Spirit, but it was a
spirit; and the relation between an imitator or translator and an earlier poet
could be endued with quasi-spiritual overtones. As the Earl of Roscommon
put it in his description of the relationship between an ideal translator and
the original in *An Essay on Translated Verse* (1685) 'Your thoughts, your Words,
your Stiles, your Souls agree'.[62] Roscommon ended his *Essay on Translated
Verse* with a triumphant claim of mastery over classical antiquity: 'Why
should not We their ancient Rites restore, | And be what Rome or Athens
were Before?' He then went on to quote a long passage from Milton's
description of the war in heaven to illustrate the way that an ancient spirit
can be reborn. Milton would probably have been appalled to be cited in
this way—although, as Roscommon's willingness to quote *Paradise Lost* with
approval indicates, this predominantly royalist tradition of theory and practice was not simply antipathetical towards the republican Milton. Capturing
the 'spirit' of an author, mastering classical culture so as to take ownership
of its authority—those aims were not un-Miltonic.

Setting Milton alongside these shifts in the practice of imitation, however,
does serve to highlight a striking fact that does set him apart from Denham
or Cowley or their heirs. Milton—the most completely and complexly

classical poet in English—never *called* any poem of his an 'imitation' of a classical text. This may simply have been because the convention of naming poems in that way seems to have emerged after he had lost his sight. But it is something that he could very readily have done, since the *practice* of adaptive imitation had been thriving from a decade or so before Milton was born. It was already implicit in the generic imitations of classical epigrammatists and satirists by Ben Jonson (and indeed those of his friend and rival John Marston, and in the satires of Marston's rival Joseph Hall). Ben Jonson's 'Speech According to Horace' (where 'according to' means something like 'in harmony with', perhaps in a gesture towards Seneca's suggestion that the imitator's voice can blend with that of his original like voices in a choir) was an adaptive imitation of this kind.

Milton not only avoided the name of 'An Imitation of [Horace]' but also the practice which preceded the name. He never wrote any direct imitation of a classical text which overtly sought to adapt that work to the customs and manners of his times. He was willing to follow Ben Jonson in producing a perfect 'formal' translation which sought to replicate the tenses, stanza structures, and vocabulary of an original: he did this notably in his version of Horace Odes 1.5, which is described as having been 'Rendered almost word for word without rhyme according to the Latin measure, as near as the language will permit'.[63] He was also a master of generic transposition across time and space: he could refashion classical pastoral elegy into 'Lycidas', with its rich evocations of the British landscape, and of course could reimagine epic in a form to suit Christian belief, and include in it the archetypically modern inventions of gunpowder and the telescope. But he was not willing to follow Jonson in writing poems which overtly substituted English customs and settings for ancient equivalents.

There were some obvious reasons for this. More or less from its origins in England the genre of imitation as cultural adaptation had clear political affiliations: it was favoured by royalist poets such as John Denham. But Milton's resistance to this form of poetic activity lay one step deeper than politics. The first sentence of *The Tenure of Kings and Magistrates* (1649) indicates why Milton was likely to be hostile to adaptive imitation: 'If Men within themselves would be govern'd by reason, and not generally give up their understanding to a double tyrannie, of custome from without, and blind affections within, they would discerne better what it is to favour and

63. John Milton, *Complete Shorter Poems*, ed. John Carey (London, 1997), p. 100.

uphold the Tyrant of a Nation' (*CPW*, 3.190). Custom, tyranny, and the passions were for Milton an unholy trinity. To adapt a classical text as Cowley advocated in his preface to his translations of Pindar in 1656 was therefore potentially anathema to Milton. Cowley said 'We must consider in Pindar the great difference of time betwixt his age and ours, which changes, as in Pictures, at least the Colours of Poetry, the no less difference betwixt the Religions and Customs of our Countreys, and a thousand particularities of places, persons, and manners, which do but confusedly appear to our eyes at so great a distance.'[64] Imitating so as to acknowledge 'the great difference of time' went along with a reification and an idealization of the 'customs' of both the present and the past, and a consequent subordination of poetry to custom.

Milton, by contrast, was keen to present himself as responding to ancient writing in a way that more or less reversed the subservience to custom implicit in producing 'imitations' in the later seventeenth-century sense. The key piece of evidence here is the note on 'The Verse' appended to the 1674 edition of *Paradise Lost*, which declares: 'The measure is English heroic verse without rhyme, as that of Homer in Greek, and of Virgil in Latin; rhyme being no necessary adjunct or true ornament of poem or good verse, in longer works especially, but the invention of a barbarous age, to set off wretched matter and lame metre.' That programmatic passage suggests that following ancient example could be a means of escaping from the corrupt conventions of the present, rather than an opportunity to reconstruct those conventions through their present equivalents. We can see in Milton, indeed, two kinds of imitation practised by Ben Jonson splitting apart with an audible snap: imitation of an ancient metrical form might be a means of resisting the corruptions of the times; but adaptive imitation, which adapted ancient customs to modern equivalents, was potentially a means of succumbing to the barbarism of the present.

That might help to explain Milton's reluctance to engage in a specific form of imitation which was particular to his age. But it does not quite get within the extremely equivocal attitude towards the larger tradition of *imitatio* that is displayed in the Sin and Death episodes in *Paradise Lost*. To achieve a richer understanding of this we need to venture a little further into cultural history.

Although adaptive imitation had a strongly royalist flavour by 1660, there was no intrinsic association between *imitatio* as described in the rhetorical tradition and any particular political or cultural allegiance. Indeed the imitation

---

64. Cowley, *Poems*, sig. Aaa2.

of those heroes of liberty Cicero and Demosthenes could appeal to the most zealous of republicans, since they spoke for freedom against tyranny; moreover Longinus's zealous form of emulous *imitatio* had acquired strong republican associations in seventeenth-century Britain.[65] But it is not hard to find signs of a gradual association between the more traditional forms of rhetorical education and what Milton might be expected to regard as the forces of darkness.

It is notable that the great digester of imitation theory for English school-boys Thomas Farnaby, whose frequently printed *Index Rhetoricus* contained a compendium of lore about *imitatio*, had spent part of the 1590s in a Catholic College in Spain, and was in the 1640s a fervent supporter of the King. Farnaby edited texts—Juvenal and Persius—which were perfect for adaptive imita-tion, and the products of his school included Sir Richard Fanshawe, the pronounced royalist and translator of Horace. Not only that, but the verso of the title page to editions of Farnaby's *Index Rhetoricus* after 1633 bore the royal privilege which conferred on its author the exclusive right to the copy of that volume.[66] Imitation: was it becoming at once a kingly art and a mark of slavish dependency on custom? Milton's strong association of Satan with imitation, and of Sin and Death, the brood of Satan, with distorted versions of the language of imitation, was a direct response to all these currents within seventeenth-century attitudes towards the activity of imitating ancient writing. The venal Mammon claims 'cannot we his light | Imitate when we please?' (*PL*, 2.269–70). He does so in hell. Satan sits 'High on a throne of royal state' (*PL*, 2.1) in the 'God-like imitated state' (*PL*, 2.511) which Pope was to imitate in *The Dunciad*. He does so in hell. God, how-ever, does not imitate. Cutting human and diabolic acts of imitation down to size was one of Milton's more overt aims in *Paradise Lost*—in an almost literal sense, as the next section will suggest.

Modelling the ancients

In cutting imitation down to size Milton had what might appear to be a surprising ally. In Thomas Farnaby's *Index Rhetoricus*, buried among the digests of Senecan injunctions to digest one's reading, and among the paraphrases of familiar passages from Horace, Quintilian, and Sturm, were

65. Quentin Skinner, *Reason and Rhetoric in the Philosophy of Hobbes* (Cambridge, 1996), esp. pp. 426–37; David Norbrook, *Writing the English Republic: Poetry, Rhetoric and Politics, 1627–1660* (Cambridge, 1999), pp. 212–21.
66. Serjeantson, 'Thomas Farnaby', p. 112.

some striking introductory remarks about *imitatio*. Farnaby declares 'What else are the works of the finest artificers, what else are Ideas conceived in the mind, than prototypical examples, original models or moulds, which skill might imitate, which art expresses or stamps out?' ('Quid enim aliud sunt opera summorum artificum? quid aliud Ideae mente conceptae? quam exempla quaedam prototypa, originales quidam moduli; quae imitetur solertia, quos ars exprimit').[67] The notion that an imitator imitates 'ideas' or forms had spread outwards from the early Ciceronian debates to become more or less a commonplace by the end of the sixteenth century. Underlying Farnaby's concern with 'prototypa' is probably Longinus's defence of imitation as being 'no theft; it is rather like the reproduction (*diatyposis*) of good character by sculptures or other works of art' (*Sublime*, 13.4). The imitator imitated the *tupos* or stamp of a prior text.

But what Farnaby brought into the mainstream of discussion about *imitatio* is that word 'modulus', or 'model'. Farnaby was well known to Milton's teachers the Gills (Alexander Gill the younger was an usher at Farnaby's school), and also to Ben Jonson, who wrote dedicatory poems for two of his editions of classical texts. The claim that an imitator imitates what we call a 'model' is today so embedded in critical discourse that even the most acute critics make the claim with hardly a second (or, indeed, perhaps, even a first) thought about the history of the word. Donald Russell's excellent Loeb classical library translation of Quintilian repeatedly uses the word 'model', as classicists routinely do today, to translate 'that which is imitated' or to replace the word *exemplum* in the original.[68] This is a convenient shorthand; but the familiarity of the word 'model' in literary contexts today has obscured its complex history, in which Milton played a major part. What is at stake in regarding a prior text as a 'model', and how did people come to use that word of an imitated text? Answering those questions will cast a great deal of light on the way attitudes towards *imitatio* developed in England, and in particular on Milton's attitudes towards the texts which he imitated; and doing so also might serve as a reminder never to use the word unreflectively.

The word 'model' entered the English language via mathematics. *OED* (as well as the growing but by no means complete database of digital texts

---

67. Farnaby, *Index*, p. 32.
68. e.g. *Institutio*, 10.1.112, where Cicero as the *exemplum* is translated by 'model', and 10.1.8: 'And we shall achieve this by reading and hearing the best models' ('Id autem consequemur optima legendo atque audiendo'), literally 'best things'. Various forms of 'model' occur 67 times in the 61 pages of Gian Biagio Conte, *Stealing the Club from Hercules: On Imitation in Latin Poetry* (Berlin and Boston, 2017).

included in TCP/EEBO) cites John Dee's preface to an English translation of Euclid's *Geometry* as the first usage. Dee declares that mathematics is useful because it enables the construction of scale replicas: 'Thus, of a Manneken, (as the Dutch Painters terme it) in the same Symmetrie, may a Giant be made: and that, with any gesture, by the Manneken vsed: and contrarywise. Now, may you, of any Mould, or Modell of a Ship, make one, of the same Mould (in any assigned proportion) bigger or lesser.'[69] The word took a hold in the English language in the late sixteenth century chiefly through translations from French, such as Joshua Sylvester's version of Du Bartas. Sylvester suggests that a Christian 'model' can outdo its pagan derivatives when he writes of Eden: 'Ye Pagan Poets…from henceforth still be dumb | Your fabled praises of Elisium, | Which by this goodly modell [i.e. paradise] you have wrought.'[70] Sylvester's Du Bartas was (as we now say) one of Milton's own 'models' for poetry about the creation, so the notion that a model could be 'a morally superior object of subsequent inferior imitation' was entirely within Milton's ken.

The word had been used in poetic contexts since the late sixteenth century. Sir Philip Sidney's admirer William Scott in his recently discovered treatise of poetics called 'The Model of Poesy' of 1599 used the term to mean something like 'the underlying principles', presumably by analogy with a mathematical formula or set of geometric ratios which could enable the replication of an ideal type in a wide range of different scales and styles.[71] There are also strong architectural associations to the word in Scott, which become common in technical manuals about architecture from the later seventeenth century, in which 'model' is used both of a plan and of a unit of scale, or 'a measure that is made use of to regulate all the proportion of the fabric'.[72] So an illustrated plan in the much-reprinted 1663 English translation of Palladio's *First Book of Architecture* says 'From the middle of one column unto the middle of the other is 15 models', or units of scale.[73]

69. Euclid and John Dee, *The Elements of Geometrie of the Most Auncient Philosopher Euclide of Megara* (London, 1570), sig. c3v.

70. Guillaume de Salluste Du Bartas, *Du Bartas His Deuine Weekes and Workes Translated*, trans. Joshua Sylvester (London, 1611), p. 217.

71. William Scott, *The Model of Poesy*, ed. Gavin Alexander (Cambridge, 2013), p. lxvi–lxx; and for the logical foundations of Scott's treatise, see Michael Hetherington, ' "An Instrument of Reason": William Scott's Logical Poetics', *The Review of English Studies* 67 (2016), 448–67.

72. M. Vitruvius Pollio and Claude Perrault, *An Abridgment of the Architecture of Vitruvius* (London, 1692), sig. O4v.

73. Andrea Palladio, *The First Book of Architecture*, trans. Godfrey Richards (London, 1663), illustration on p. 43.

The wide dissemination of Farnaby's *Index* doubtless contributed to the spread of the word 'model' as a term for a text from which an imitated work derives, and by the later seventeenth century that usage was well established. John Oldham described Ben Jonson in 1678 as the architect of the stage: 'All the fair Model and the workmanship was thine.'[74] And when John Dryden declared of Oldham that 'For sure our Souls were near ally'd; and thine | Cast in the same Poetick mould with mine' he was well aware that 'mould' and 'model' were cognate, and deliberately pressed the two concepts together in order to suggest that the two poets not only shared principles but were identical, like two products of the same mould.[75]

By the end of the seventeenth century, again particularly among English critics influenced by French writing, a 'model' was akin to a structural support for a later text: W. J.'s preface to his 1695 translation of Le Bossu's treatise on the epic addresses the comparison between Homer and Virgil by saying 'if any one thinks the Latin Poet to be best, 'tis because he had so excellent a Model to imitate'.[76] In Henry Felton's *Dissertation on Reading the Classics*, written in 1709 but much reprinted, a literary 'model' is explicitly akin to an architectural template. Felton declares that Virgil 'built his *Aeneid* upon the Model of the *Iliad*, and the *Odysseïs*', and is quite sure that authors should imitate the 'plan' or architectural design of their originals. As he put it, tragedians 'have most excelled, when they formed their Plays on the Grecian Plan, or built them, at least, after the ancient Models'.[77]

That history of the word 'model' is significant for three reasons. The first is that it implicitly associates imitation not simply with replication or transposition of texts from one author to another, but with proportion and design. Hence it not only allows for the possibility of formal imitation, such as the structural imitation of a metrical or stanzaic form, or imitations which follow not the plots but the structural principles which underpin the structure of a classical play, for instance, but also encourages *scalar* replication. An imitation might be a larger version of its 'model', or it could be a tiny miniaturized work which preserves the internal proportions of the earlier text. That association between imitation and miniaturization, as we shall see in a moment, was vital to Milton's poetics.

74. Oldham, *Poems*, p. 194.   75. Dryden, *The Works*, 2.175.
76. René Le Bossu, *Monsieur Bossu's Treatise of the Epick Poem*, trans. W. J. (London, 1695), sig. a6v.
77. Henry Felton, *A Dissertation on Reading the Classics, and Forming a Just Style. Written in the year 1709* (London, 1715), pp. 24, 265.

The second reason that the history of the word 'model' matters is it provided a natural extension of the sixteenth-century tendency to associate *imitatio* with patterns, or replicable formulae, for composing works, rather than with specific verbal collocations or allusions. It therefore had the potential to separate imitation (regarded as a replication of the proportions but not the language of a prior text) from plagiarism, or exact verbal repetition. In this respect scalar imitation acted as an alternative to 'adaptive' imitation: where adaptive imitation avoided any accusation of servile word-for-word replication by substituting modern 'dress' or 'customs' for ancient ones, scalar imitation took from its original a form or a plan, but not a language.

But the third and most significant reason why we should attend to how the word 'model' came to be used of a prior text from which a later text derives is that Milton assisted the emergence of this usage. He anticipates this sense of the noun 'model' when he uses the verb in his preface to *Samson Agonistes*: 'In the modelling therefore of this poem, with good reason, the ancients and Italians are rather followed, as of much more authority and fame.'[78] His tragedy is 'modelled' after the ancients in that it adopts their formal features. And although Milton does not use the word 'model' very often, when he does so it is always significant. He writes of God laughing at scientists who 'come to model heaven' (*PL*, 8.79)—presumably either in mathematical formulae or through miniature physical replicas. A 'model' in Milton's vocabulary tends to be a retrospective attempt to understand the incomprehensible or to contain the unrepresentable. As a result models are often for him potentially risible, things that are unable to equal divine majesty. When Satan sees the gates of heaven they are described as

> inimitable on earth
> By model, or by shading pencil drawn.
> The stairs were such as whereon Jacob saw
> Angels ascending and descending, bands
> Of guardians bright, when he from Esau fled
> To Padan-Aram in the field of Luz,
> Dreaming by night under the open sky,
> And waking cried, *This is the gate of heaven*.   (*PL*, 3.508–15)

'Model' here may mean a plan on paper (which was a common sense in this period) or a physically scaled down replica; but either way it is linked with

---

78. Milton, *Complete Shorter Poems*, p. 356.

an attempt at earthly imitation of a heavenly truth, of a thing 'inimitable on earth'. The model for Milton is tiny, earth-bound, and its inadequacy is a testament to the inimitability of heaven.

This leads us back to one of the commonplaces in discussions of Milton's relationship to classical literature. It is often observed that allusions to epic conventions in *Paradise Lost*—similes in particular—can bring with them shifts of scale and perspective. The classic example of this is the comparison of Satan's shield to the moon seen through Galileo's telescope:[79]

> his ponderous shield
> Ethereal temper, massy, large, and round,
> Behind him cast; the broad circumference
> Hung on his shoulders like the moon, whose orb
> Through optic glass the Tuscan Artist views
> At evening from the top of Fesole,
> Or in Valdarno, to descry new lands,
> Rivers or mountains in her spotty globe.
> His spear, to equal which the tallest Pine
> Hewn on Norwegian hills, to be the mast
> Of some great ammiral, were but a wand,
> He walked with to support uneasy steps
> Over the burning marl...   (*PL*, 1.284–96)

Satan's shield is an imitation of the shield of Achilles in the *Iliad* and the shield of Aeneas in the *Aeneid*, which themselves are emblems of the way in which an artist can miniaturize and enclose civilizations within the bounds of art. But where those shields in classical epic offer visions of life or of empire, Milton gives us a close-up of the moon, the most shifting and unreliable of heavenly bodies. That creates dazzling uncertainties about who is looking from where and how big what is looked at actually might be. Richard Bentley declared 'The Moon, as she appears to the naked Eye, is too small a Comparison. As it's *magnified* by the Telescope, is the fittest one possible. But this *Magnifying* the Author quite omits here', and proposed that Milton's lines should be emended to 'like the moon, whose Orb ENLARG'D | Thro Optic glass'.[80] Bentley, as so often, sees the point by missing it: massy, large and round as it is, the shield is from an earthly perspective tiny, an orb in the

---

79. On the shifts of scale and perspective here, see Geoffrey H. Hartman, *Beyond Formalism; Literary Essays, 1958–1970* (New Haven, 1970), pp. 118–22. On Milton and optics, see Jane Partner, *Poetry and Vision in Early Modern England* (Basingstoke, 2018), pp. 213–58.

80. John Milton, *Milton's Paradise Lost*, ed. Richard Bentley (London, 1732), pp. 14–15.

sky; then we have our noses pressed up to it, hunting with Galileo for signs of life on its surface.

There are of course plenty of comparisons of great things with small in classical similes, and these often invite their readers to look at a 'heroic' event from a new perspective, but none of these unsettles our sense of what is big and what is small as this simile does.[81] Critics have often related this to Milton's attitudes to his classical predecessors, taking a cue from Harold Bloom's claim that Milton's 'backward glance to Satanic origins reveals the full truth of which Homer, Virgil, Tasso give only incomplete reflections'.[82] These passages which shift scale, make big things look small and small things look big are, the story goes, Milton's bold and confident way of suggesting that his Christian epic presents vast archetypes of events of which classical epics are a mere imitation.[83] He operates on a cosmic scale which makes his predecessors look tiny and belated.

That triumphalist and agonistic view of Milton has been very influential. But it brings in aggression and dominance where the issue is actually scale and relative proportion. And relationships of scale between a 'model' and the product of a model are intrinsically two-way. Milton could regard the texts he imitated as 'models', and consequently the creation of a new text might transform a prior text into a 'model'. This could be taken in two distinct ways. The prior 'models' might be regarded as archetypes, great originals, moulds (a term which as we have seen is cognate with 'models'), or 'forms' from which the new text is produced, and which might indeed be so vast that they are actually inimitable. But once a prior text is regarded as a 'model' in a scalar sense, then the relationship of scale between the imitand and the imitator could also be reversed. A classical text which is a 'model' for a subsequent work might be regarded as a tiny structure which illustrates not the size but merely the proportions and structure of a major work which is constructed after its example and design.

This makes the act of imitation a kind of double-ended telescope, which might enlarge or diminish the work which was the 'model' of the new text;

81. See the classic article, John S. Coolidge, 'Great Things and Small: The Virgilian Progression', *Comparative Literature* 17 (1965), 1–23, which argues (p. 18) that for Milton 'the great things of the pagan epic are to the terms of the Christian epic as the small things of the *Eclogues* and *Georgics* were to the *Aeneid*'.
82. Harold Bloom, *A Map of Misreading* (New York and Oxford, 1975), p. 135.
83. e.g. Martindale, *Transformation*, p. 9: 'Milton thus cleverly overgoes his predecessors, showing that their "great things" are trivialities in comparison with the subject-matter of his epics.' See Stephen B. Dobranski, 'Pondering Satan's Shield in Milton's *Paradise Lost*', *English Literary Renaissance* 35 (2005), 490–506.

and hence it makes *imitatio* intrinsically prone to use the effects of deliberate disproportion and amplification which were later to become characteristic features of the mock heroic. Massive warriors might become, as they do in Alexander Pope's *Rape of the Lock*, tiny sylphs. Big Homeric warriors might be enlarged, as they are in Milton's war in heaven, into massive angelic and cosmic warriors who heave mountains through the sky and whose battles rend the cosmos, whose amplification of heroic actions might make the actions of their literary archetypes seem tiny or their own actions absurdly amplified.

In this respect making an earlier text into a 'model' can make physical one of the methods for concealing an act of imitation which were advocated by German Protestant rhetoricians: Keckermann, for instance, argued that an imitator could perform *dilatio* on a prior text, and expand it, or subject it to *brevitas*, or deliberate shortening.[84] Turning a prior text into a model can *simultaneously* dilate and abbreviate: a predecessor's work can be presented as a tiny encapsulation of the great subsequent work which it has enabled, or it can be presented as so vast that it is only by grasping its proportions and diminishing its scale that an imitator can reproduce it. This duplicity of the model enables past writing to be regarded not as a crippling burden or the work of a giant race on whose shoulders the authors of the present perch awkwardly, but as an enabling miniature, a set of quasi-mathematical formulae on which greater works can in future be built. And the making of that new work on the 'model' of the old might also be regarded as labour which makes its predecessors seem tiny, so it might bring a kind of scalar triumph with it.

In regarding what we call 'sources' as 'models' in this scalar sense Milton was alive to the wider cultural history of the term. The word 'model' had by the Restoration acquired a great deal of uneasy power. Cromwell's 'new model army' was a zealous refashioning of the Parliamentarian forces. Programmes of political or ecclesiastical reform were frequently presented during the civil war as presenting 'models', or templates for reform. This was particularly the case with works written by members of the Hartlib circle, such as John Dury's *A Model of Church Government* (1647), which sought to establish foundations for concord within the Church.

The conceptual foundations of those Hartlibian 'models' were often architectural. When Jeremy Collier translated Johann Comenius's *Diatyposis* in 1651 and dedicated it to Samuel Hartlib, he gave it the title *A patterne of*

---

84. Keckermannus, *Systema Rhetoricae*, p. 909.

universall knowledge, in a plaine and true draught: or A diatyposis, or model. Collier began 'We consulting about. . . the structure of the Temple of Wisdom, to the honour of God Almighty, the common use of mankinde, and prae-ludium of the life to come, it's meet we imitate the skill of wise Architects, who use not to attempt the rearing of any great worke without a foregoing delineation therof. . . For having erected the proportion or Idea of a future worke, we may readily perceive whether the fulnesse of the whole, the Symmetry of the parts, and the comelinesse in each regard sufficiently agree.'[85] The model there becomes an intellectual encapsulation of a grand scheme, the realization of which can transform its readers and revolutionize learning.

Both Comenius and Hartlib frequently use the metaphor of a 'Temple' to describe that ideal scheme of learning. This was partly because the rebuild-ing of the Temple at Jerusalem was one of the preconditions of bringing about the millennium and the return of the Messiah; but it was also because the Temple of Solomon was the clearest biblical instance of a structure described through numerical proportions: chapter 40 of the book of Ezekiel describes the Temple as so many cubits by so many cubits.[86] There was some uncertainty about what the modern equivalent of a 'cubit' might be, but Ezekiel gave clear guidance about the *ratios* between the different elements of the Temple. This great archetype of religious worship was therefore a scal-able model of uncertain size. And that religious 'model' without doubt gave an additional dimension to Milton's thinking about the literary 'models' which underlay his writing.

The new model commonwealths imagined by reformers during the civil war were matched in miniature after the Restoration by a rather different kind of new model navy: Samuel Pepys, the naval administrator and diarist, eagerly collected model ships.[87] For Pepys (as indeed in John Dee's very

85. Joannes Amos Comenius, *A Patterne of Universall Knowledge, in a Plaine and True Draught: or A Diatyposis, or Model of the Eminently Learned, and Pious Promoter of Science in Generall*, trans. Jeremy Collier (London, 1651), sig. A5r.
86. See, e.g., Hartlib's translation of Comenius and Hartlib, *Reformation of Schooles*, pp. 71–4. For the Messianic associations of the Temple, see Mark Greengrass, Michael Leslie, and Timothy Raylor, eds., *Samuel Hartlib and Universal Reformation: Studies in Intellectual Communication* (Cambridge, 1994), pp. 120–2.
87. On Saturday 5 October 1661 Pepys was lent a model of the *Royal James* by his patron the Earl of Sandwich. On 30 July 1662 he noted that models were learning aids: 'Cooper came to me and begun his lecture upon the body of a ship, which my having of a modell in the office is of great use to me, and very pleasant and useful it is', *The Diary of Samuel Pepys: A New and Complete Transcription*, ed. Robert Latham and William Matthews, 11 vols. (London, 1970), 3.149. On Tuesday 12 August 1662 Anthony Deane the shipbuilder 'promises me also a modell of a ship, which will please me exceedingly, for I do want one of my own', and on Monday 29

early use of the word 'model in English) a model is a miniature version of a grand project, a tiny thing on which the imagination can erect vastness. A model ship enables its owner simultaneously to relish the minute artistry of the craftsman who made the model and to imagine or reproduce a full-scale equivalent, with which the English could defeat the Dutch navy or augment trade. And this casts more than a faint sidelight on Milton's comparison of Satan's shield to the moon. The heroic spear of Satan makes the 'mast | On some great ammiral' seem 'but a wand' (*PL* 1.293–4). Satan is so huge that he makes our vast ships seem like mere model-sized versions, with wands for masts. But the comparison could diminish him too: is he hobbling on a staff, using a tiny wand as a walking stick?

The wider cultural associations of 'models' in Restoration England indicate that to declare heaven or its architectural features 'inimitable by model' in the late 1660s has a characteristically Miltonic edge of cultural asperity: it conveys a 'pah' to collectors of model ships like Pepys. It also may convey contempt for the neoclassical architects who regularly used models to test the viability of their designs. When Lord General Fairfax was presented with a model of the new Appleton house, as he apparently was, he could marvel at the way in which it went beyond the lineaments of the old nunnery on which the present house was based.[88] The fashion for architectural model-making received a massive stimulus after the Great Fire of London in 1666, where the process of imagining new model cities or churches or cathedrals emerging out of the flames of London was an essential part of transforming razure and defeat into new building and renewal. English *imperium* could be reborn from the flames with the help of new model cities—literally small scale models.

The model was therefore in the 1660s an embodiment of modernizing energies, which in a Restoration context might also be classicizing energies,

September 1662 the promise was fulfilled: 'Mr. Deane, of Woolwich, hath sent me the modell he had promised me; but it so far exceeds my expectations, that I am sorry almost he should make such a present to no greater a person; but I am exceeding glad of it, and shall study to do him a courtesy', Pepys, *Diary*, 2.163, 208. Models were objects of great value: the shipbuilder Peter Pett was accused of failing to save the King's ships and of rescuing his own models instead: 'He said he used never a boat till they were all gone but one; and that was to carry away things of great value, and these were his models of ships; which, when the Council, some of them, had said they wished that the Dutch had had them instead of the King's ships, he answered, he did believe the Dutch would have made more advantage of the models than of the ships, and that the King had had greater loss thereby; this they all laughed at', Wednesday 19 June 1667, Pepys, *Diary*, 8.279. They were wrong to laugh: models of ships were akin to blueprints of secret weapons. See also E. Keble Chatterton, *Ship-models* (London, 1923), pp. 14–15.

88. Nicholas Cooper, *Houses of the Gentry 1480–1680* (New Haven and London, 1999), p. 39.

which might in turn also suggest the erasure of earlier gothic models of piety. The new model London emerging from the flames of the 1660s was classical.[89] It was exciting, but when *Paradise Lost* was first published in 1667 was still tiny, in embryo. Christopher Wren, arch-rebuilder, has left the most grandiose architectural model from the period in the Great Model of St Paul's Cathedral, which was finished by a team of joiners in 1674 (in time for the second edition of *Paradise Lost* but too late to have directly influenced Milton), and which was so big that in February of that year Robert Hooke described himself as 'At Paules with Sr ch. Wren. Saw module and walkd through it'.[90]

The seventeenth-century vogue for architectural models takes us directly back to Milton's hell. In particular it takes us to the devils' construction of Pandemonium in Book 2, which is 'Built like a temple' (*PL*, 1.713). This is a vast grandiose palace of gold, created by the Miltonic predecessor of injection moulding. Under the orders of Mammon, the architect, the devils

> formed within the ground
> A various mould, and from the boiling cells
> By strange conveyance filled each hollow nook,
> As in an organ from one blast of wind
> To many a row of pipes the sound-board breathes.　　　(*PL*, 1.705–9)

A 'mould' derives, like 'model', from late Latin 'modulus'. It can mean a model or plan for a building as well as a template into which liquid material is poured. The New Model Temple of Pandemonium has been related to dozens of sources: it is sometimes seen as a parody of the Pantheon or the Temple of Jerusalem, while the council scene that it is built to house has been seen as parody or imitation of similar scenes in Virgil, Homer, Lucan, or even Trissino.[91]

---

89. A proclamation of 17 September 1666 announced 'we shal cause a Plot or Model to be made for the whole building through those ruined places, which being well examined by all those people who have most concernment as well as experience, We make no question but all men will be pleased with it', *His majestie's declaration to his city of London, upon occasion of the late calamity by the lamentable fire* (London, 1666), pp. 8–9.

90. Kerry Downes, *The Architecture of Wren* (Reading, 1988), p. 68. Wren provided a model of a chapel for Emmanuel College, Cambridge, in 1667 (p. 45) and advocated the building of a model of St Paul's as early as 1666 (p. 48). On the reconstruction, see Leo Hollis, *The Phoenix: St Paul's Cathedral and the Men who Made Modern London* (London, 2008), esp. pp. 178–83. On the history of architectural models, see Tessa Morrison, *Isaac Newton and the Temple of Solomon: An Analysis of the Description and Drawings and a Reconstructed Model* (Jefferson, NC, 2016), pp. 39–52.

91. DuRocher, *Milton among the Romans*, ch. 3 explores its debts to Vitruvius; William McClung, 'The Architecture of Pandemonium', *Milton Quarterly* 15 (1981), 109–12, assesses relationships to St Peter's suggested by R. W. Smith, 'The Source of Milton's Pandemonium', *Modern Philology* 39 (1931), 187–98. Gordon Campbell and Thomas N. Corns, *John Milton: Life, Work,*

The most likely physical model for the building of Pandemonium is St Peter's Basilica in Rome, for which Michelangelo made an elaborate model, which is itself a grandiose structure standing seventeen feet high. It survives and is displayed within the Basilica itself. That means St Peter's to the tourist, in the seventeenth century as today, is both a vast, awe-inspiring, classical achievement, and a tiny model of itself. So within (as Milton would see it) a vast temple of papistical decadence, the very house of Satan's deputy on earth, the Pope, was a tiny replica of the same palace of sin. Vasari relates that Michelangelo 'headed to Saint Peter's to see the wooden model San Gallo had executed and the building itself in order to examine it'. He found it unsatisfactory, and set about making a model of his own design, which took him fifteen days: 'Finally the model Michelangelo had executed which reduced Saint Peter's to a smaller size but also greater grandeur was approved by the pope'.[92]

It is likely that Milton saw—and at that stage of course he could see— that model of the basilica of St Peter's, which at once reduced it to 'a smaller size but also greater grandeur', during the two months he spent in Rome in October and November 1638. And that combination of the huge and the tiny, which bewilders our sense of scale, is a highly suggestive parallel to the palace created by his devils. For Pandemonium is at once vastly grand and so tiny that the devils have to shrink themselves to the size of bees in order to get into it.[93] Again Richard Bentley's bewilderment can illuminate Milton's aim here: Bentley objects to the comparison of the 'spacious hall' of Pandemonium to 'a covered field, where champions bold | Wont ride in armed, and at the soldan's chair | Defied the best of paynim chivalry' (PL, 1.763–5), and declares the lines spurious with 'The immense Hall of Pandemonium compar'd to a Saracen's Tent; a first rate Man of War to a Skuller'.[94]

and Thought (Oxford, 2008), p. 410 rightly express scepticism about the precise architectural details Smith alleged to be shared between St Peter's and Pandemonium. Quint, Inside Paradise Lost, p. 24 notes the belief that St Peter's was the true version of Solomon's Temple.

92. Giorgio Vasari, The Lives of the Artists, trans. Julia Conaway Bondanella and Peter E. Bondanella (Oxford, 1991), pp. 466–7. Michelangelo also used clay or wax models as prototypes for both paintings and sculptures, a large collection of which were preserved in the cabinet of Paul von Praun (1548–1616), whose collection at Nuremberg was open for viewing by visitors until the early eighteenth century. See Paul James LeBrooy, Michelangelo Models Formerly in the Paul von Praun Collection (Vancouver, 1972).

93. On the shrinking devils and Milton's understanding of proportion, see Quint, Inside Paradise Lost, pp. 24–9, 187–8.

94. Milton, ed. Bentley, Milton's Paradise Lost, p. 34.

The framing conceit of Pandemonium is to use the model of the model to suggest that there is a scalar wonder, but finally something diminutive, about imitation. A golden temple of uncertain scale, an imitation of heaven, of St Peter's, which was itself an imitation of the Temple of Solomon, in which the devils can walk, as Wren and Hooke were to do in the new model St Paul's, Pandemonium is a model which has at once the power that comes from being a prototype of a greater structure and the tiny lameness of an attempt to 'model heaven', to replicate something which is 'inimitable by model'. But because hell is the realm of the model it has an energy and a growing potential which Milton is unable to hold in check. Hell has a vast, flaming sublimity; but it also has a self-containing miniaturism. And that is why readers of the poem have so often, rightly, been unsure quite how to take it: how big is it? And is it archetypical and prototypical or secondary?

Those questions feed into one of Milton's most visible local imitations of Virgil in his hell: the simile which compares the devils who enter the new model Temple of Pandemonium to bees. This passage directly invites comparison with Virgil and Homer, and encourages the kind of evaluative and comparative response to that intertextual relationship which was fostered by seventeenth-century commentaries on classical texts:

> As bees
> In spring time, when the Sun with Taurus rides,
> Pour forth their populous youth about the hive
> In clusters; they among fresh dews and flowers
> Fly to and fro, or on the smoothed plank,
> The suburb of their straw-built citadel,
> New rubbed with balm, expatiate and confer
> Their State affairs.   (*PL*, 1.768–75)

Bee similes can just innocently be bee similes. But Seneca in his 84th Epistle famously compared the act of imitation to the activity of bees, who cull honey from a number of sources and then combine them together. That adds metapoetic overtones to the simple buzzing of a bee.[95] Through bee similes the imitator can be thinking about his own art and his own world, envisioning his own work as a small effort by a labourer within a greater cultural whole, or metaphorically representing the labour of culling a whole field of texts into a single savour.

95. *Epistles*, 84.5–7. On the history of the simile, see Jürgen v. Stackelberg, 'Das Bienengleichnis: Ein Beitrag zur Geschichte der literarischen *Imitatio*', *Romanische Forschungen* 68 (1956), 271–93.

But Milton's devil-bees are pointedly doing no such thing. They are emphatically *not* making honey. They 'fly to and fro'. They buzz about 'state affairs'. They are London bees, urban burblers, who buzz around their straw-built model city talking about not much, having first put on their hair oil ('New rubbed with balm'). Compare (and early modern readers were trained by the classical editions they read to compare) Virgil's proverbially busy bees, the Carthaginians who are actually building their city—a passage which Seneca quoted in his 84th Epistle and which he thereby welded inseparably into the language of imitation:

> qualis apes aestate nova per florea rura
> exercet sub sole labor, cum gentis adultos
> educunt fetus, aut cum liquentia mella
> stipant et dulci distendunt nectare cellas,
> aut onera accipiunt venientum, aut agmine facto
> ignavum fucos pecus a praesepibus arcent;
> fervet opus redolentque thymo fragrantia mella.   (*Aen.*, 1.430–6)

> Such is their Toyl, and such their buisy Pains,
> As exercise the Bees in flow'ry Plains;
> When Winter past, and Summer scarce begun,
> Invites them forth to labour in the Sun:
> Some lead their Youth abroad, while some condense
> Their liquid Store, and some in Cells dispence.
> Some at the Gate stand ready to receive
> The Golden Burthen, and their Friends relieve.
> All, with united Force, combine to drive
> The lazy Drones from the laborious Hive;
> With Envy stung, they view each others Deeds;
> The fragrant Work with Diligence proceeds.   (trans. Dryden, 1.598–609)[96]

Driven by '*labor*', gathering nectar; these bees are consciously imitating Homer's bees in the *Iliad* (2.87–90), and they are pointedly busier about their children and about their food than their Homeric originals. Dryden, well aware of the association between bees and acts of imitation, even gives to their activity a savour of emulation by adding the phrase 'With Envy stung'.

This particular simile was a *locus classicus* for the comparison of Homer with Virgil: when Macrobius directly compared the two bee similes in the *Saturnalia* he declared that 'Vergil's imitations sometimes have more substance than the originals' and noted that he 'portrays the duties which [the

---

96. Dryden, *The Works*, 5.362–3.

bees'] nature has taught them to perform'.[97] Renaissance commentators regularly noted how much busier and more creative Virgil's bees were than Homer's. Jean de Sponde, or Spondanus, the editor of the text of Homer which Milton is most likely to have used, specifically notes the builderly zeal ('aedificantium diligentiam') of Virgil's bees, which he contrasts with the simple multiplicity of their Homeric prototypes.[98] Meanwhile La Cerda's notes on Virgil (which Milton may well have consulted) record how the bees are the perfect vehicle by which to evoke the zeal of the Carthaginians for their republic.[99] The passage is also a *locus classicus* for bringing effects of scale into the act of imitating: Virgil's imitation of Homer's bees makes the Carthaginians as they build their city instantly both admirable and tiny as they seek, in effect, to model Rome. In making his devil-bees honeyless replicants of their earlier 'models' Milton knew just what he was doing. In hell imitation has become its own end. The creation of a model, an imitation of heaven, has taken over the imitative process and has destroyed its sweetness.

And here again Milton was thinking about the world around him at the same time as his classical 'models': William Mew, one of Samuel Hartlib's correspondents whose views are recorded in the *Commonwealth of the Bees*, had made a model of a new kind of ultra-efficient transparent beehive. This was subsequently to inspire Wren and the experimentalist John Wilkins to develop new model hives to increase the production of English honey.[100] Milton's urban drones occupy a traditional inefficient straw hive. With the manufacture of the model temple of Pandemonium comes a downscaling of activity, a loss of honey, a loss of bodily presence, of activity and weight, a transformation of the model empire of the Carthaginians into a 'straw-built

97. Ambrosius Aurelius Theodosius Macrobius, *The Saturnalia*, trans. Percival Vaughan Davies (New York and London, 1969), p. 322 [5.11]. 'si tamen me consulas, non negabo non numquam Vergilium in transferendo densius excoluisse'. Cf. the comparison of the two similes, also in Virgil's favour, in Julius Caesar Scaliger, *Poetices libri septem = Sieben Bücher über die Dichtkunst*, ed. Luc Deitz, Manfred Fuhrmann, and Gregor Vogt-Spira, 6 vols. (Stuttgart, 1994–8), 4.182–4 (5.3.230b).

98. Homer, *Homeri quæ extant omnia*, ed. Jean de Sponde (Basel, 1606), p. 31.

99. Virgil, *Aeneidos. . . Argumentis, Explicationibus et Notis Illustrata*, ed. Juan Luis La Cerda (Cologne, 1642), 1.83: 'A most apt comparison. For who when describing the building of a city, the industriousness of the Carthaginians, their social bonds, laws, and magistracy, could bring any better comparison to mind than the universal republic of the bees?' ('Prudentissima comparatio. Nam, qui urbis novae aedificationem describit, Poenorum sedulitatem, iura, leges, magistratus, quid potuit illustrius afferre, quam apum Rempublicam universam?') For Milton's use of La Cerda, see Martindale, *Transformation*, p. 3.

100. Hartlib, *Common-wealth of Bees*, p. 47.

citadel', a transformation of the Temple, or St Peter's, or St Paul's, into a gilded replicette.

The arguments presented so far in this chapter run in parallel to many of the traditional stories about Milton and imitation. To the traditional story that Milton makes the texts he imitates seem tiny because he is Christian and they are pagan I have suggested that it is more helpful to regard him as a Restoration man who regarded his classical predecessors in a literal sense as 'models'; and the various attitudes to models in this period—ideal templates of a Hartlibian kind, or miniature replicas of neoclassical and imperial aspirations—help to explain why Milton's classical 'models' often appear at once tiny and powerful. To the traditional story that says Milton is a poet anxious that his own creativity might be only a Satanic imitation of God's creativity I have added the thought that much of the language through which that anxiety is articulated can be traced back to the metaphors used to describe *imitatio* in the classical tradition, to the ways in which those metaphors were unstitched and reassembled in the seventeenth century, and to the particular character of Milton's own relationship to that educational tradition. Thinking about Milton's attitudes towards imitation in this broad and largely secular way can explain, as the traditional narratives may fail to do, why it was John Milton rather than any other Christian poet who wrote as John Milton did; why, that is, it was someone trained at St Paul's school, who became a friend of Francis Junius and who was influenced by Hartlib in the 1640s, and who lived through various attempts to 'remodel' England and London, who worried so fruitfully about how creative artists might imitate the works of God.

Paradise Regained: the Temple as template

But religion does play a foundational part in Milton's poetics of imitation. It acts as a massive amplification device for the scalar effects which follow from regarding earlier texts as 'models'. What can be extraordinary—and this is particularly true of Milton's later writing—is the violence, and sometimes the relentlessness, with which he allows these scalar effects to operate. So in the fourth book of *Paradise Regained*, published in 1671 along with *Samson Agonistes*, Satan attempts a last wave of temptations of Jesus in the wilderness. Milton introduces his renewed efforts by a rare triple-decker simile:

But as a man who had been matchless held
In cunning, over-reached where least he thought,
To salve his credit, and for very spite
Still will be tempting him who foils him still,
And never cease, though to his shame the more;
Or as a swarm of flies in vintage-time,
About the wine-press where sweet must is poured,
Beat off, returns as oft with humming sound;
Or surging waves against a solid rock,
Though all to shivers dashed, the assault renew,
Vain battery, and in froth or bubbles end;
So Satan, whom repulse upon repulse
Met ever; and to shameful silence brought,
Yet gives not o'er though desperate of success,
And his vain importunity pursues.   (*PR*, 4.10–24)

The first part of the simile almost breaks the primary rule of a simile, that there should be some element of unlikeness in the comparison. Satan *is* someone held to be matchless in cunning, who tries again when rebuffed. But that simile is designed to hint at a comparison between Satan and the ever-cunning, all-enduring Odysseus. That turns an apparent non-comparison into an implicit comparison between the action of Milton's brief epic and the moral heroism of Homer's diffuse epic. The flies around the wine also do not simply diminish Satan in scale, but hint at an allusive method that goes beyond that of the simile: Christ is frequently compared in the emblematic tradition to a wine-press, and wine—well, a sacramental transcendence of the methods of the simile cannot be far away.

The final strand in the comparison is rather more orthodox and perhaps also rather more complex in the way it establishes a dialogue with pagan writing. The comparison to waves breaking against rocks is a well-established one for repeated military encounters (*Iliad*, 15.618–22), but the comparison is usually focalized on the rocks—the warrior who withstands the waves—rather than on the vanity of the waves. So Virgil compares Latinus to an unmoved cliff when he is urged to fight in *Aeneid* 7:

ille velut pelagi rupes immota resistit,
ut pelagi rupes magno veniente fragore,
quae sese, multis circum latrantibus undis,
mole tenet; scopuli nequiquam et spumea circum
saxa fremunt laterique inlisa refunditur alga.   (*Aen.*, 7.586–90)

He, like an unmoved ocean-cliff, resists; like an ocean-cliff, which, when a
great crash comes, stands steadfast in its bulk amid many howling waves; in
vain the crags and foaming rocks roar about, and the seaweed, dashed upon its
sides, is whirled back.

This simile was presented in La Cerda's edition of 1642 as representing the
constantia of Latinus. La Cerda, as was his wont, notes what he terms the
'imitatio' of Homer (*Iliad*, 15.618–22 and 17.725–59), and declares, in one of
his favoured phrases, that it is another place in which 'Homerum superat
Virgilius',Virgil overgoes Homer.[101]

Milton responds to that eristic and ethical reading. To the rock-solid
repetition of Virgil's 'ocean-cliff' (*pelagi rupes . . . pelagi rupes*) Milton responds
with an uncertainty about the substance of the thing which assails the rock:
it is 'froth *or* bubbles', a tiny shower of doubtful nothingness. And he brings
to the whole simile a shift in scale and perspective which focuses not on the
rock, but on the vain efforts of the waves. There is an energy of classical
reminiscence flickering through the whole sequence: the faintly implied
comparison between Satan and the wily Odysseus in the first leg of the simile might call to mind the destructive power of waves, which can shipwreck
a classical hero; the *Aeneid* allusion might bring to mind the wider context
of Virgil's simile, in which the constancy of Latinus is followed abruptly by
his crumpling confession that 'Alas, we are shipwrecked by fate' (*frangimur
heu! fatis*), after which he drops the reins of rule. By shifting perspective to
the waves and away from the rocks Milton leaves Satan's adversary Jesus
undescribed, unmoved, a blank force of total constancy who reverses the
perspectives of the classical world.

In the episodes that immediately follow this trio of similes the shift of
perspective which they imply becomes literal. Satan shows Jesus the empire
of Rome as though in a map or a model, or as though viewed through a
panoptic telescope:

> an imperial city stood
> With towers and temples proudly elevate
> On seven small hills, with palaces adorned,
> Porches and theatres, baths, aqueducts,
> Statues and trophies, and triumphal arcs,
> Gardens and groves presented to his eyes
> Above the height of mountains interposed.

101. Virgil, ed. La Cerda, *Aeneidos*, 3.98.

By what strange parallax or optic skill
Of vision multiplied through air, or glass
Of telescope, were curious to inquire.   (*PR*, 4.33–42)

The imperial city of Rome is thus reduced to a model of which the very intricacy trivializes the contents. We see not just one grand theatre, which might be an object of awe, but many theatres; we see not just one triumphal arch but so many that the individual triumphs seem not to matter any more. This is Rome at once scaled up and diminished: the price of looking at the vast totality of Rome through a telescope is to diminish it to the scale of a model.

There is a qualitative difference between Milton's biblically inspired and his secularly inspired writing. By using the word 'qualitative' here I am not simply suggesting that when Milton imitates the Bible he is less good than when he imitates Homer. What tends to happen when Milton imitates biblical material is a powerful kind of negation that readers tend to experience as a kind of flatness or lack. The principal thing that disappears is the metaphorical energy that Milton derived from classical imitation theory— energy which as we have seen ramifies in *Paradise Lost* outwards from the metaphorical to the metapoetic and out from that towards the interpersonal and the theological. The passage from *Paradise Lost* which describes the gates of heaven and declares them to be inimitable by model indicates the nature of the poetic problem: Milton's assertion that the real thing is inimitable by model prompts sustained allusion to biblical prototypes. But those allusions do not in turn prompt metaphorical activity. They lead into a simple truth, which is sublime in its simplicity but which declares its simplicity simply by using the verb to be: this *is* the gate of heaven, and everything else, every metaphorical vehicle, every other gate, no matter how splendid, is *not* as large or impressive the gate of heaven.

This might be the root cause why Blake made his famous complaint that Milton wrote in fetters when he wrote about divine matters. Biblical truths just are; they do not grow, superfoetate, acquire unsteadying layers of meta-phorical power, or turn to *simulacra* as we watch. Indeed they can appear to be a template which underlies a grandiose classical vision and cuts it down to size: what if the story of Sin and Death were just, as St James has it 'Then when lust hath conceived, it bringeth forth sin: and sin, when it is finished, bringeth forth death'? The archetype can function as a little mocking voice within the upscaled imitation of it. But it also has the potential to make the upscaled imitation of it appear merely to be inflated and aggrandized.

That inner voice of mockery is central to *Paradise Lost* by virtue of being almost always there, but quietly so. In *Paradise Regained* it is everywhere, and is often plain and loud. This is one reason for the disappointment that any reader who is willing to be honest about it feels when reading that poem. But there is gain as well as loss, as the extraordinary moment in *Paradise Regained* when Satan tempts Jesus in the wilderness by offering him classical wisdom indicates:

> To whom our Saviour sagely thus replied.
> Think not but that I know these things, or think
> I know them not; not therefore am I short
> Of knowing what I ought: he who receives
> Light from above, from the fountain of light,
> No other doctrine needs, though granted true;
> But these are false, or little else but dreams,
> Conjectures, fancies, built on nothing firm.   (*PR*, 4.285–92)

There is a lot to smile about here—the tangles of nots and disavowals, the self-arresting internal rhymes of 'short' and 'ought' which suggest that small knowledge is dutiful knowledge. It *is* writing in fetters. It is indeed trying to sound like writing in fetters by drawing itself up 'short' where it 'ought', as though deliberately chaining itself within what Milton himself called 'the troublesome and modern bondage of rhyme'.

The conceptual problem with that passage, though, lies in the simple verb 'know'. Classical knowledge is here presented as a class of information. It could, indeed, be part of the practical assemblage of data advocated by a confirmed Hartlibian educationalist.[102] Jesus presents engagement with classical philosophy and literature as a matter of doing the knowledge, an act of due diligence, and a mastery of content. It is not a process that requires you to learn how to resemble your sources as a child resembles a father, or which requires you to buzz like a bee gathering honey from a variety of sources, or to labour acquiring the skill of an ancient orator. It is much simpler to drink light from above. Knowing the truth involves a *kenōsis*—an emptying out of the self—because it is so simple: the *imitatio Christi* is ethical emulation, which requires the imitator to drink in a truth rather than reconstruct a text, or reanimate the spirit that produced that text.

To say that *Paradise Regained* is dull because it lacks the fraught engagement with the classical of *Paradise Lost* would not be much of a claim. *Paradise*

---

102. See Lewalski, 'Hartlib Circle'.

Regained does lose that metaphorical cloud of glory that can surround Milton's directly classical imitations in *Paradise Lost*. But some of its strange way of being powerful derives from Milton's continuing interest in models, in how a person or a text can be a scaled-down prototype of another person or text, and how diminution in scale may be accompanied by an enlargement in significance—as though once you have prototype or the mathematical ratio of a thing you can remake it in any size you like.

There was a strong tradition of holy model-making in the later seventeenth century, and travellers to the Holy Land in the mid-century would often bring home models of its architectural monuments. John Tradescant's 1656 catalogue of his cabinet/museum recorded 'modells of the Sepulcher at Jerusalem; one in wood: the other in plaster'.[103] One of the favourite subjects for model-building was the Temple of Solomon.[104] The Jesuit Juan Bautista Villalpando had produced sumptuous scale drawings of the Temple as early as the first decade of the seventeenth century, which provided both elevations and ground plans for the building. Villalpando derived his drawings from the ratios of scale recorded in the visions of Ezekiel, and he regarded the Temple as the archetype of all the classical orders.[105] His lavish illustrations of the Temple were a Jesuit Pandemonium as prototype, a temple which included all subsequent forms of architecture within itself, but which also proclaimed its decadence through its very lavishness.

The most famous 'model' of Solomon's Temple was rather less elaborate. It was made in the 1640s by Jacob Jehudah Leon, a Dutch Rabbi, who took the name 'Templo' after the fame of his model spread.[106] His work enjoyed great popularity among classical architects during the Restoration, and was brought to England in the mid-1670s. Robert Hooke's diary records in 1674 'With Sr Chr. Wren. Long discourse with him about the module of the temple at Jerusalem'.[107]

103. O. R. Impey and Arthur MacGregor, *The Origins of Museums: The Cabinet of Curiosities in Sixteenth- and Seventeenth-Century Europe* (Oxford, 1985), p. 40.

104. J. A. Bennett and Scott Mandelbrote, *The Garden, the Ark, the Tower, the Temple: Biblical Metaphors of Knowledge in Early Modern Europe* (Oxford, 1998), pp. 135–56. On Milton and Leon, see Jeffrey S. Shoulson, *Milton and the Rabbis: Hebraism, Hellenism and Christianity* (New York and Chichester, 2001), pp. 72–6.

105. Jeronimo Prado and Juan Bautista Villalpando, *In Ezechielem explanationes et apparatus vrbis, ac Templi Hierosolymitani*, 3 vols. (Rome, 1605), 2.88 ff.

106. Jacob Judah Aryeh Leon Templo, *Portraict du Temple de Salomon* (Amsterdam, 1643). The fullest account of Leon's Temple and its influence is Adri Offenberg, 'Dirk van Santen and the Keur Bible: New Insights into Jacob Judah (Arye) Leon Templo's Model Temple', *Studia Rosenthalia* 37 (2004), 401–22.

107. Lydia M. Soo, *Wren's "Tracts" on Architecture and Other Writings* (Cambridge, 1998), p. 123.

This particular imitation of antiquity—in which a biblical building, the fount and foundation of all religion, became literally a model—had also, however, been popular with Hartlibian reformers in the 1640s. John Dury wrote to Samuel Hartlib on 31 August 1646 about Leon's model of the Temple that 'amongst all the Rarities & Antiquities which are to bee taken notice of there is none to bee compared thereunto'.[108] That is an arresting comment: Dury suggests that a model can be a modern wonder which is actually preferable to the works of antiquity, a tiny reconstruction of ancient biblical truths which testify to the ingenuity and power of the present.

In the later 1650s in England several writers expressed a wish not only to create a model of the Temple but to do so in as pure and unornamented form as possible, so that it might be regarded, not as the elaborate architectural monument so lavishly imagined by the Jesuit Villalpando, but as a proto-Protestant place of worship. The non-conformist Samuel Lee produced a chaste ground-plan and description of the Temple, in which he averred 'that there was never such a Temple extant, as is described by Villalpandus', and argued that the Temple was both much smaller and far less architecturally elaborate than the Jesuit had claimed.[109] Radical Englishmen tended to make a bolder claim, that 'it is a most high contempt of God to revive it [Levitical forms of worship, but by extension the Temple itself] by imitation from mans brain'.[110]

This fascination with the model Temple feeds into the visionary moment at the climax of *Paradise Regained*, when Jesus is raised up and taken to the top, not of Solomon's, but of Herod's rebuilt Temple:

> So saying he [Satan] caught him [Jesus] up, and without wing
> Of hippogrif bore through the air sublime
> Over the wilderness and o'er the plain;
> Till underneath them fair Jerusalem,
> The holy city lifted high her towers,
> And higher yet the glorious Temple reared
> Her pile, far off appearing like a mount

---

108. Hartlib Papers, 3/3/33B.
109. Samuel Lee, *Orbis Miraculum; or, The Temple of Solomon Pourtrayed by Scripture-light* (London, 1659), sig. A2v. After a lengthy discussion of how to convert cubits into English feet he concludes (p. 19) 'the judicious Reader may imagine its length, according to his own most exact conception, and so conceive the House as large and magnificent as he please'.
110. Anon., *An Endevour after the Reconcilement of that Long Debated and Much Lamented Difference between the Godly Presbyterians, and [the godly] Independents, about Church-Government* (London, 1648), pp. 26–7.

> Of alabaster, topped with golden spires:
> There on the highest pinnacle he set
> The Son of God...   (*PR*, 4.541–50)

Josephus's descriptions of Jerusalem underlie Milton's piece of scalar wonder: he says of the Temple of Herod that 'to approaching strangers it appeared from a distance like a snow-clad mountain; for all that was not over-laid with gold was of purest white'.[111] These words were echoed in Leon Templo's description of his model of the Temple in the 1640s, and in the absence of a hippogriff they were the best way for the blind Milton to have imagined this vision of a miniature Temple viewed from above.[112]

In *The Reason of Church Government* Milton had resisted interpreting the visions of Ezekiel as providing a literal model for the reconstruction of the Temple. Although he confessed that God 'gave to David for Solomon not only a pattern and modell of the Temple, but a direction for the courses of the Priests and the Levites' he went on to deny that the vision of Ezekiel should be 'patch'd afterwards, and varnish't over with the devices and imbellishings of mans imagination' (*CPW*, 1.756–7). God rather 'cast his line and level upon the soule of man which is his rationall temple'. God's simple architecture of the soul—his model and pattern of ideal religion—should be left as an abstraction, subsisting in its pure mathematical form.

That tallies with the insistence of Milton's Jesus in *Paradise Regained* that simple Hebrew truths underpin classical learning and literature, and that imitation contaminates the purity of those truths: 'Greece from us these arts derived; | Ill imitated' (*PR*, 4.338–9). The underpinning truth deriving from a biblical model can make the wisdom deriving from classical philosophy appear to be mere *simulacra*, nothing more than dreams: 'Who therefore seeks in these | True wisdom, finds her not, or by delusion | Far worse, her false resemblance only meets, | An empty cloud' (*PR*, 4.318–21). In the description of Herod's temple in *Paradise Regained* all of these conflicting pressures create an extraordinary vision of flight and aspiration: the spires seem almost to be surging above those who surge above them, vast and tiny

---

111. Flavius Josephus, *The Jewish War*, trans. H. St J. Thackeray, 3 vols. (Cambridge, Mass., 1997), 3.71 (5.5.6).
112. Compare the description in Jacob Judah Aryeh Leon Templo, *A Relation of the Most Memorable Thinges in the Tabernacle of Moses, and the Temple of Salomon, According to Text of Scripture* (Amsterdam, 1675), pp. 16–17: 'the mount or hill whereon the Temple stood...did afarre of seeme to bee a snowy hil, and the glittering gould be[t]weene, did shine and reflect as the dazeling Sun'.

at once, the very model of a model, as Milton takes us high, higher, highest, even as presumably Satan and Jesus are soaring *down* from above. That passage leads on to the great final scene of *Paradise Regained*, where Jesus is perched on the temple roof like a neoclassical statue on the pediment of St Paul's, both superhumanly agile and as frail as a miniature manikin. A man, just resisting temptation, balancing, anticlimactically, becomes the model of human virtue, both a template for a human temple of virtue and a humanly inimitable wonder.

William Blake stated in the preface to *Milton: A Poem in Two Books* (1804–8) that 'The Stolen and Perverted Writings of Homer & Ovid, of Plato & Cicero, which all Men ought to contemn, are set up by artifice against the sublime of the Bible ... We do not want either Greek or Roman Models if we are but just & true to our own Imaginations, those worlds of Eternity in which we shall live for ever in Jesus our Lord.'[113] This is clearly a statement from another age than Milton's, but is not from another world. Milton would not have talked of 'our own imaginations' as a source of truth, and might have choked at the description of Homer or Ovid's work as 'Stolen and Perverted'. But in saying that 'Greek or Roman Models' should be set aside in order to acquire a better template of truth Blake was talking a language that Milton would have understood, since it was one which he played a part in creating. Milton is too often regarded as simply ending the era of imitation, or as standing heroically alone as the creative demiurge who inspired romantic poetry. It is better to regard him as standing above and looking down on his times as though they were a model: all man, like Jesus on the Temple roof, he was balanced perilously between worlds.

113. William Blake, *Complete Writings*, ed. Geoffrey Keynes (London and New York, 1957), p. 480.

9

Imitation in the Age
of Literary Property

Pope to Wordsworth

In Book 10 of the *Aeneid* Juno creates a *simulacrum* of Virgil's Aeneas with which she seeks to distract Turnus from pursuing Virgil's hero. As Chapter 3 showed, that *simulacrum* was both an imitation of Homer and intimately related to the metaphors used to describe *imitatio* in the Latin rhetorical tradition. Inevitably that episode was much imitated, and, like so many topoi from classical epic it reappears in a metamorphosed form in Alexander Pope's *Dunciad*. The goddess Dullness invites authors and stationers to pursue a phantasm of a plagiaristic poet:

> A Poet's form she plac'd before their eyes,
> And bade the nimblest racer seize the prize;
> No meagre, muse-rid mope, adust and thin,
> In a dun night-gown of his own loose skin;
> But such a bulk as no twelve bards could raise,
> Twelve starv'ling bards of these degen'rate days.
> All as a partridge plump, full-fed, and fair,
> She form'd this image of well-body'd air;
> With pert flat eyes she window'd well its head;
> A brain of feathers, and a heart of lead;
> And empty words she gave, and sounding strain,
> But senseless, lifeless! idol void and vain!
> Never was dash'd out, at one lucky hit,
> A fool, so just a copy of a wit.   (*Dunciad in Four Books*, 2.35–48)[1]

---

1. Quotations from Alexander Pope, *The Dunciad: in Four Books*, ed. Valerie Rumbold (Harlow, 2009).

In the section of notes on this passage headed 'Imitations' Pope records:

> This is what Juno does to deceive Turnus, Aen. x. 'Tum Dea nube cava, tenuem *sine viribus umbram* / In faciem Aeneae (visu mirabile monstrum!) / Dardanis ornat telis, clypeumque jubasque / Divini assimilat capitis.../ Dat *inania verba*, / Dat *sine mente sonum.*' ['Then the goddess out of hollow mist fashions a thin, strengthless phantom in the likeness of Aeneas, a monstrous marvel to behold, decks it with Dardan weapons, and counterfeits the shield and plumes on his godlike head, gives it unreal words, gives it a voice without thought.'] The reader will observe how exactly some of these verses suit with their allegorical application here to a Plagiary: There seems to me a great propriety in this Episode, where such an one is imagined by a phantom that deludes the grasp of the expecting Bookseller.   (p. 151)

Pope was exceptionally acute in observing the unruly confluences of ideas which run through the history of imitation, and which were creating turbulence in the literary world around him. Even the layout of *The Dunciad* is a virtuoso piece of imitative art: it mimics the *mise en page* of Claude Brossette's 1716 edition of Boileau's works (a copy of which Pope owned), which itself imitated in the vernacular the tendency in editions of classical texts to separate allusions from other kinds of commentary under the separate heading of 'imitatio'.[2] The spoof preface to *The Dunciad*, 'Martinus Scriblerus of the POEM', which appears in editions from 1729 onwards, describes the whole poem as an imitation of the lost *Margites* of Homer: 'Now, forasmuch as our poet had translated those two famous works of Homer which are yet left, he did conceive it in some sort his duty to imitate that also which was lost.'[3] The aim of imitating a lost work—an ambition which had animated Petrarch's attempt to imitate the lost *Annales* of Ennius in the *Africa*—here provides a spoof scholarly genealogy for the comic epic, and makes it, as a genre founded on a text which is not there, a literary kind in which the pursuit of a poet who is a figure of airy nothing is a particularly appropriate activity.

Pope's Scriblerus (drawing on the theory of Le Bossu) goes on to insist that the hero of an epic poem ought to be no more than a 'phantom': 'A *Person* must next be fixed upon to support this Action. This *Phantom* in the poet's mind must have a *Name*: He finds it to be— —; and he becomes of course the Hero of the poem.'[4] That transformation of a blank space or a

2. J. McLaverty, *Pope, Print, and Meaning* (Oxford, 2001), pp. 87–90.
3. Pope, *The Dunciad: in Four Books*, p. 70.
4. Pope, *The Dunciad: in Four Books*, p. 72. On Pope and Le Bossu, see Frederick M. Keener, 'Pope, *The Dunciad*, Virgil, and the New Historicism of Le Bossu', *Eighteenth Century Life* 15 (1991),

phantom into a hero is a deep-level parody of the notion that a poet imitates not the concrete particulars of an earlier text but instead imitates an idea abstracted from a model, or from previous instances of a generic series. The hybrid poet whom the Grub Street publishers pursue in imitation of Turnus's pursuit of the imitation Aeneas is at once plump as a partridge and thin as air; and his dubious ontological status shows that Pope recognized the long-standing tendency for writers on imitation to suggest that imitative texts have the potential to be either re-embodiments of or spectral images of their originals. A plagiarist is both at once: he is stuffed full of other people's words while at the same time completely lacking substance of his own.

The episode of the phantom poet illustrates that by the 1730s the divide between imitation and plagiarism was narrower than it had ever been. The link had always been there: discussions of *imitatio* at least from Macrobius onwards were frequently accompanied by anxious attempts to distinguish it from theft. But eighteenth-century thinking about *imitatio* was also deeply influenced by the increasingly commercialized market for printed texts. Publishers and poets alike were dependent upon preserving the right to publish and to benefit financially from the writings of both the past and present, and these material concerns had an influence on both the theory and practice of imitation. Both became intimately connected with arguments about literary property. Mark Rose suggested in 1988 that 'the romantic elaboration of such notions as originality, organic form, and the work of art as the expression of the unique personality of the artist was in a sense the necessary completion of the legal and economic transformation that occurred during the copyright struggle.'[5] I shall suggest in this chapter that although legal and economic struggles over copyright did indeed have a great influence on how poets thought about their own creative powers and their relations to their predecessors in this period, nonetheless those material concerns were deeply connected to the much longer narrative of arguments about the nature of authorship and literary imitation. That wider context is vital to understanding the relationship between English romantic poetry and both its vernacular and classical predecessors; and exploring it will

35–57 and McLaverty, *Pope, Print, and Meaning*, pp. 99–105. Cf. Homer 'has given the Name of Achilles to a valiant and angry Phantom; that of Agamemnon to his General', René Le Bossu, *Monsieur Bossu's Treatise of the Epick Poem*, trans. W. J. (London, 1695), p. 19.

5. Mark Rose, 'The Author as Proprietor: Donaldson v. Becket and the Genealogy of Modern Authorship', *Representations* 23 (1988), 51–85, p. 76. The thesis is developed in the same author's *Authors and Owners: The Invention of Copyright* (Cambridge, Mass., and London, 1993).

create a pathway from Pope's imitation of Virgil in his plagiaristic poet in the 1730s to William Wordsworth's imitations of Milton in the early nineteenth century.

Literary property

One component in the prehistory of the concept of literary property lay, as Kathy Eden has eloquently shown, in the use by Roman rhetoricians of the term 'proprietas' to describe a style that was appropriate to personal and intimate exchanges. The word 'proprietas' could also be used in legal discourse of what we now call property. Behind the rhetorical use of the term lay Aristotle's conception of a style which he termed *oikeia*, domestic or intimate (*Rhetoric*, 3.7.4), but which also might be one's own just as much as one's house is one's own, and might have its own 'furniture' and riches.[6]

By the end of the seventeenth century the metaphorically rich but conceptually fuzzy body of thinking about imitation came up against a rather different conception of property, which had a major influence on attitudes towards both imitation and specifically literary property in the century to come. This was the theory of property set out in John Locke's *Two Treatises of Government* (1690). Locke was not himself particularly interested in imitation: in *Some Thoughts Concerning Education* (1693) he allowed that pupils should be 'made not only to Translate, but have set before them as Patterns for their daily imitation' what he terms 'ancient Classick Authors', but he expresses contempt for those teachers of rhetoric who take their understanding of figures and tropes from that key text for the popular dissemination of classical theories of *imitatio*, Thomas Farnaby's *Index Rhetoricus*.[7] Nor did *Two Treatises of Government* explicitly address proprietorial rights over words or texts, since in them Locke's principal concern was with material property. However, responses simple and complex to Locke's complex understanding of material and real property had a profound and long-running influence on literary history. The key reasons for Locke's influence in this area were that his particular arguments about property could be readily adapted to

---

6. See Hall Björnstad and Kathy Eden, eds., *Borrowed Feathers: Plagiarism and the Limits of Imitation in Early Modern Europe* (Oslo, 2008) and Kathy Eden, *The Renaissance Rediscovery of Intimacy* (Chicago, Ill., 2012), esp. pp. 11–48.
7. John Locke, *Some Thoughts Concerning Education*, ed. Jean S. Yolton and John W. Yolton (Oxford, 1989), pp. 242–3.

immaterial goods. And, partly because they did not quite add up, they became helpful for theorists who sought to explain how an author might own and take the benefit from an apparently unownable common good such as words. A brief outline of Locke's theory is therefore necessary.

Locke begins by imagining a man in the state of nature, who gathers acorns or apples in order to support life, and argues that common goods become the property of the person who labours to appropriate them: 'No Body can deny but the nourishment is his. I ask then, When did they begin to be his? When he digested? Or when he eat?...And 'tis plain, if the first gathering made them not his, nothing else could. That *labour* put a distinction between them and common.'[8] It is notable that Locke initially places eating and digestion—those familiar metaphors for imitative assimilation—among the very first things we might assume would confer ownership. He then goes on to argue that property is a right gained as a result of mixing one's labour with a material thing.

But the apparently simple claim that a person has a right to the fruits of his own labour when he gathers hitherto common goods is complicated by the fact that Locke was concerned to justify the ownership not only of food and artefacts but also of land. This means that he adds a public benefit argument to his labour-based theory of property. As he continues: 'We see in *Commons*, which remain so by Compact, that 'tis the taking any part of what is common, and removing it out of the state Nature leaves it in, which *begins the property*; without which the Common is of no use.' He goes on to argue that a person who appropriates common land by working upon it generates a public benefit in the form of increased productivity, and so enables land originally given to all by God to support growing human needs: 'he who appropriates land to himself by his labour, does not lessen, but increase the common stock of mankind' (p. 312; 2.37).

Locke uses this argument to justify the appropriation of land from native peoples in America, where the weaknesses as well as the historical and racial bias of his arguments become particularly apparent.[9] Common land which is in the state of nature is unproductive and so may be appropriated. Locke

---

8. John Locke, *Two Treatises on Government*, ed. Peter Laslett (Cambridge, 1960), p. 306 (2.28). For a sophisticated account of Locke's arguments, see Jeremy Waldron, *The Right to Private Property* (Oxford, 1988), pp. 137–252; my crude discussion is intended to show only how Locke's thinking fed into arguments about imitation.

9. See James Tully, *An Approach to Political Philosophy: Locke in Contexts* (Cambridge, 1993), pp. 137–76; cf. Jeremy Waldron, *God, Locke, and Equality: Christian Foundations of John Locke's Political Thought* (Cambridge, 2002), pp. 165–7.

believed that the aboriginal peoples in America were in a state of nature; hence a colonist may appropriate land there, work on it, and increase production of sugar or cotton: 'let any one consider, what the difference is between an Acre of Land planted with Tobacco or Sugar, sown with Wheat or Barley, and an Acre of the same Land lying in common, without any Husbandry upon it, and he will find, that the improvement of *labour makes* the far greater part of the *value*' (p. 314; 2.40).

As a result of his concern with colonial expansion and the enrichment of European society Locke's view of property—to present a contentious and complex matter very crudely—pulls in two different directions. One aspect is the belief that labour creates a right of ownership, which we might call a possessive individualist model of property: I whittle a stick into a tool and it becomes mine by virtue of my labour. The other might be called a Whig colonialist model of property: I occupy a piece of untilled common land and increase its utility for mankind in general by cultivation, and thus establish my proprietary right over it.

If these principles were transposed to the world of texts the conflicts between them would become more or less irreconcilable, and their implications for the history of imitation profound. The possessive individualist strand might lead to the conclusion that an author labours on the 'common' matter of language to produce a new text, and therefore an author should have a right to ownership over the result of that labour (though at what level—the phrase, the sentence, a distinct sequence of ideas, or only the exact words of the entire text—is a moot point). This might bring as a corollary the notion that literary imitation was a species of appropriation.

The strand in Locke's thought concerned with maximizing public utility from common goods through labour, however, sets up a counter-argument to this proprietorial model: labouring on and acquiring property rights in a common good can lead to the expansion of trade or knowledge, or to the increased productivity of the land. Hence it might be argued that acts of literary labour should be rewarded for their enhancement of a common store of learning; and since that public utility depends upon their being used and shared, imitators who absorb and transform the works of prior authors—which might be regarded as a common store awaiting enrichment by its later cultivation—are further enhancing the common good; and their works, as part of a common store, should in turn be freely available for transformation by the labour of others.

These are extrapolations from Locke's theory rather than principles he articulates. But in 1695 the Licensing Act lapsed, and with it the comfortable arrangement whereby the Stationers' Company oversaw the rights of individual stationers to publish particular works of which they owned (as they called it) the 'copy', or what would now be called the copyright. The act had in effect though not always in practice protected printers' monopolies over the production of texts by authors both ancient and modern. Locke was involved in the long series of discussions which preceded and followed the lapsing of the act. In those arguments he expressed a particular concern for the free availability of what he termed 'Classic Authors': he declared 'That any person or company should have patents for the sole printing of Ancient authors is very unreasonable and injurious to learning.' But he also proposed that stationers who bought copies from living authors should have their right to reprint protected for 'suppose 50 or 70 years' after the death of the author or the first printing of the book.[10]

The distinction Locke makes between 'Classic' and modern authors indirectly replicates the divergent strands in his thought about real property. The protection of living authors' rights honours what I have termed the possessive individualist current in his thinking, since it rewards the labour of modern authors and their stationers with a limited period of protection. The free availability of 'Classic' authors, on the other hand, honours the Whig colonialist model of property, because it ensures that the common store of ancient texts is freely available for all to read and to use for the profit of mankind.

After a series of legislative hiccups these discussions ultimately led to the 1710 act of Queen Anne, commonly called the first Copyright Act.[11] This, like most subsequent legislation on literary property in Britain, sought to balance the competing pressures towards private ownership of the right to copy on the one hand and public benefit on the other. The act of Anne for the first time in any nation allowed authors a limited right (initially for fourteen years) to profit from the publication of their works, after which it would become common property. Previously an author sold the manuscript 'copy' to a printer and had effectively no further proprietary right to it,

10. John Locke, *The Correspondence*, ed. Esmond Samuel De Beer, 8 vols. (Oxford, 1976), 5.791; Ronan Deazley, *On the Origin of the Right to Copy: Charting the Movement of Copyright Law in Eighteenth-Century Britain (1695–1775)* (Oxford, 2004), pp. 1–10.
11. John Feather, *Publishing, Piracy and Politics: An Historical Study of Copyright in Britain* (London, 1994), pp. 37–63 gives a clear account. For Locke's interventions in the debate that led to the first copyright act of 1710, see Feather, *Copyright*, p. 50.

unless they could secure a specific royal privilege to print their work—as, for example, Thomas Farnaby had done with his frequently reprinted *Index Rhetoricus*. These provisions were intended not to protect the rights of authors but rather to secure a return for publishers. As Adrian Johns and others have shown, the 1710 Act and the arguments about its meaning which rumbled on throughout the century were driven by a structural problem in the market for printed books in a United Kingdom.[12] London stationers bought and sold what they called 'copies', the rights to print particular works. These were expensive assets from which they hoped to make a large profit and which they hoped to transfer to their heirs. Scottish and Irish printers, however, pirated these works, and produced cheaper editions which were then sold in London. These undercut the products of the London book-trade. The London publishers wished to establish that an author had a perpetual right to enjoy the financial benefits of his labour in order to be able to claim to have bought that permanent literary property from the author.

It is hard to overstate the conceptual confusions to which the 1710 Act gave rise, or the impact of combining those confusions with the long-standing intellectual confusions about the status and value of *imitatio*. Could an author be said to have established ownership over a particular concatenation of ideas and words by exerting labour on the common goods of earlier literature? Could others then legitimately take a reward for reproducing the same words in the same order? And how is the concept of private literary property reconcilable with the public benefit that accrues from the free exchange of ideas? And on what foundation was the common good of 'Classic' authors to be distinguished from the protected property of the moderns? And could the category of 'Classic' authors include venerable works in the vernacular as well as Latin and Greek texts?

This set of questions interacted with the already muddled tradition of thinking about literary imitation in several ways. The distinction between 'Classic' and modern authors is indirectly apparent in many imitative texts. As Chapter 8 showed, in the notes to the *Dunciad* Pope refers to his overt allusions to classical authors such as Virgil as 'imitations'; but when he alludes to or transforms *vernacular* texts in ways that most readers would notice he tends to call such moments 'parodies'. He was happy to display his

---

12. Adrian Johns, *Piracy: The Intellectual Property Wars from Gutenberg to Gates* (Chicago, Ill., and London, 2009), pp. 109–78.

debts to the common storehouse of ancient writers, but drew attention to his transformative artistry when he imitated works in his own tongue.

Editions of and critical arguments about the works of John Milton followed rather similar lines. Through the 1740s readers who had recently enjoyed Pope's 'Imitations of Horace' (1733–8) were tracking and recording Milton's imitations of the ancients. And 'Milton's imitations' (in the plural) was the phrase that tended to be used. These were on the whole what would now be called 'allusions', short passages in *Paradise Lost* which displayed close analogies to classical texts. Identifying these and comparing them with their originals became a fashionable pleasure, and the isolation of such parallel passages necessarily raised questions about the propriety of one author taking words or ideas from another. In 1741 appeared the anonymous *Essay upon Milton's Imitations of the Ancients*, which is ascribed in a copy in the Bodleian Library to an otherwise unknown C. Falconer.[13] This *Essay* was a defence of Milton and of imitation generally. Literary imitation according to Falconer was a source of readerly pleasure. If an author imitated an imitation of another imitation then the pleasure simply multiplies:

> when one good Poet imitates another, we have a double Pleasure; the first proceeding from comparing the Description with its Object; and the second, from comparing the one Description with the other from which it was imitated.

This means that for Falconer the more imitations there are the better:

> when a Poet imitates a Description from another Poet, which very Description had been imitated from a Third, our Pleasure is still the greater; therefore in this Respect, the Imitations in Milton are beyond those in Virgil because he has imitated some Places of Virgil which are Imitations of Homer.[14]

Imitation is for Falconer not a pedagogical process, a matter of acquiring a habit or of digesting earlier words into a new substance, or of generating a text which resembles its *exemplum* as a child resembles its father. A reader spots a parallel, compares it with its original, and enjoys the relationship.

13. [C. Falconer], *An Essay upon Milton's Imitations of the Ancients, in his Paradise Lost: With Some Observations on the Paradise Regain'd* (London, 1741). The ascription to Falconer is in Bodleian Library, Oxford, shelfmark Vet. A4 e.1700(1). Library catalogues frequently ascribe this work to William Lauder, but its sympathetic account of imitation and of Milton marks it as surely the work of another author.

14. Falconer, *Milton's Imitations of the Ancients*, p. 4. Cf. the concept of a 'window reference' in Richard F. Thomas, 'Virgil's Georgics and the Art of Reference', *Harvard Studies in Classical Philology* 90 (1986), 171–98.

These are the pleasures of a cultivated man of letters who has access to an annotated text of an author, and who can therefore see how one passage relates to equivalents in earlier authors. To call this a consumerist idea of imitation would be excessively negative; but it is a view of imitation as offering pleasures to the observer rather than a view of imitation which grows from the practices of an author. It was these pleasures which the variorum edition of *Paradise Lost* by Thomas Newton (1749) sought to augment, by listing Milton's 'imitations and allusions to other authors, whether sacred or profane, ancient or modern'.[15] The identification of 'imitations' became a pursuit for the literary gentleman, and indeed a foundational skill in the emergent practice of literary criticism.

At exactly the same time as Thomas Newton was labouring to list Milton's imitations of the ancients in his edition, a Scottish schoolmaster called William Lauder was pursuing a different course.[16] He sought to display Milton's literary thefts. Lauder was a Jacobite during the unrest of the 1740s. He had a particular political motive for wanting to make Milton look like a thief, since by the 1740s Milton had been in effect canonized as the giant original of the English Whig poetic tradition. In *The Gentleman's Magazine* of 1747 Lauder published a string of letters which detected Milton's supposed plagiarisms.

Lauder claimed that Milton had taken much of *Paradise Lost* from the *Adamus Exsul* of Hugo Grotius, as well as from other Neo-Latin poems by Andrew Ramsay, Caspar Staphorstius (the author of *Carmen epinicium ac protrepticum de bello Britannico*, 1655), and others. Lauder gathered his evidence together in 1749 as *An Essay on Milton's Use and Imitation of the Moderns, in his Paradise Lost*. This appeared with a Preface by Samuel Johnson, who was no admirer of Milton's politics or of the Whig cause. Lauder presented Milton as a sort of Satanic thief, who 'shines, indeed, but with a borrowed lustre, a surreptitious majesty'.[17] Lauder concludes that 'he is not the original author of any one single thought in *Paradise Lost*, but has only digested into order the thoughts of others, and cloathed them in an elegant English dress'

---

15. John Milton, *Paradise Lost: a Poem in Twelve Books*, ed. Thomas Newton, 2 vols. (London, 1749), sig. a4v. Newton notes the imitation of Ovid's Narcissus in Eve's story of her creation 'as the reader may easily observe by comparing both together', p. 264.

16. See Paul Baines, *The House of Forgery in Eighteenth-Century Britain* (Aldershot, 1999), pp. 81–102, and Nick Groom, 'Forgery, Plagiarism, Imitation, Pegleggery', in Paulina Kewes, ed., *Plagiarism in Early Modern England* (Basingstoke, 2003), 74–89.

17. William Lauder, *An Essay on Milton's Use and Imitation of the Moderns, in his Paradise Lost* (London, 1750), p. 115.

(p. 155). Milton 'digests' his texts, so far as Lauder is concerned, only in the sense of creating abbreviated epitomes of them. He is not like Seneca's description of the imitative bees, who 'digerunt', assimilate or digest what they gather into a savour of their own. He is a thievish compiler.

Lauder accused Milton of stealing from Neo-Latin and near-contemporary poetry. That Lauder made this particular accusation is highly significant, since the allegation hit exactly the cross-over point between 'ancient' or 'Classic' authors—the rights over whom according to Locke should be freely available for the common good—and modern authors, who might enjoy a proprietorial right over their the products of their labour. It also had deep roots in the earlier history of thinking about literary appropriation. In Latin literature charges of literary theft tended to cluster in particular genres (especially Roman comedy, satirical poetry, and epigrams), and were generally restricted to particular types of textual exchange.[18] Augustan authors who imitated *their* ancients—whether these were Greek authors or the earlier Roman poets who had become part of a Latin literary canon such as Lucretius or Ennius—were (with the notable exception of arguments in later antiquity about Virgil's relation to Homer) usually praised for doing so, especially if they were the first to compose in a particular genre in Latin or were the first to imitate a text which had been hitherto unknown in Rome. The general body of earlier writing could be regarded as a common store of property, which as early as the 79th Epistle of Seneca the younger was referred to as 'publica', public property.[19] But trespassing on texts composed in the same language by contemporaries might attract charges of theft. When Terence imitated plays by Menander he does not appear to have been accused of appropriation until he imitated works which had already been imitated in Latin by his contemporaries (the prologue to *Eunuchus*, which plays on the word *fur*, thief, provides a particularly clear case). Martial used the word 'plagiarius' (kidnapper) to describe not someone who imitated a Greek, but a contemporary who had stolen Martial's own very words (1.52.9).

---

18. See Scott McGill, *Plagiarism in Latin Literature* (Cambridge, 2012); Björnstad and Eden, eds., *Borrowed Feathers*; Bertrand A. Goldgar, 'Imitation and Plagiarism: The Lauder Affair and its Critical Aftermath', *Studies in the Literary Imagination* 34 (2001), 1–16; Kewes, ed., *Plagiarism in Early Modern England*.

19. 'He who writes last has the best of the bargain; he finds already at hand words which, when marshalled in a different way, show a new face. And he is not pilfering them, as if they belonged to someone else, when he uses them, for they are common property (*sunt enim publica*)', Seneca, *Epistles*, 79.6; cf. Seneca's insistence that some maxims of the Epicureans are 'public', *Epistulae Morales*, 21.9; 33.2.

Lauder, though, extends the range of plagiarism by accusing Milton, who of course wrote in English, of stealing from recent Neo-Latin poetry. Neo-Latin epics were in a different language from *Paradise Lost*, but were roughly contemporary with Milton, so to use them as a source might be regarded as stealing from a 'modern' rather than imitating an ancient. Lauder's other reason for grounding his attack on Milton on this particular battlefield was that he was confident that no one apart from him would have read any of the Neo-Latin poems which he adduced as evidence of Milton's theft.

Sadly for Lauder, he was wrong about this. And sadly too when Lauder argued that Milton was a plagiarist he had spiced up the evidence for his case. Among the Latin passages from Grotius and others that Lauder cited in order to allege that Milton was plagiarist he inserted several extracts which were in fact taken from William Hog's 1690 Latin translation of *Paradise Lost*. Unsurprisingly these Latin translations of *Paradise Lost* closely resembled passages from *Paradise Lost*. Lauder's opponents had a field-day with a forger who was claiming someone else was a plagiarist.

Under the patronage of the Earl of Bath, who was, not coincidentally, also the patron of Thomas Newton's edition of *Paradise Lost*, the counter-charge against Lauder was led by John Douglas.[20] Douglas argued, with Longinus, that 'Imitation and Emulation of the former great Writers and Poets' was 'one of the Ways that leads to the Sublime',[21] so Milton would not have committed a crime even if he *had* imitated these poems. He also adapts and develops the concept that an earlier author might provide a quasi-architectural 'model' for an imitator, and does so to Milton's advantage: 'An architect who does nothing but copy a Plan of an Edifice out of Palladio gives no Proof of his Skill; but if he has united the Beauties of many Palaces erected by other Masters, so as that they shou'd all have a Place in One; in this Case we cannot refuse owning him as a skilful Architect, because his connecting together Beauties originally detached from each other, and his working them up into a One uniform Design, is Proof of his Capacity' (p. 13). Creating an architectural 'Design' or model distinguishes an imitating author from a plagiarist. But not only was Milton remaking his 'models' into a new design: he was also in many cases not actually imitating his alleged models at all because they were in fact Latin translations of Milton's own works.

---

20. See Michael J. Marcuse, '"The Scourge of Impostors, the Terror of Quacks": John Douglas and the Exposé of William Lauder', *Huntington Library Quarterly* 42 (1979), 231–61. Newton's dedication records that the Earl of Bath paid for the engravings to his 1749 edition of *Paradise Lost*.
21. John Douglas, *Milton Vindicated from the Charge of Plagiarism* (London, 1751), p. 8.

Since Lauder had falsified the evidence there were absolutely no grounds for the charges, and the alleged crime was not in fact a crime anyway. Lauder was annihilated, and was compelled by Samuel Johnson to print a confession of his falsifications.

The Lauder affair spawned some delicious incidental by-products, including the youthful Robert Lloyd's anonymously published poem *The Progress of Envy: A Poem in Imitation of Spenser Occasioned by Lauder's Attack on the Character of Milton* (1751). This was also dedicated to the Earl of Bath, who is described (hyperbolically) as 'Patron of Milton and his Vindicators'. Lloyd's poem related (in modified Spenserian stanzas and in imitation of Spenser's style) how Envy roused Malice from his lair to invade Parnassus and kill Milton. Finally and fortunately, however, 'The stricken Bard fresh vital heat renews' as a result of the hero Douglas's interventions, and 'ENVY and LAUDER die.'[22] After this early exercise in imitating Spenser Lloyd was to go on to become a member of the Nonsense Club, a group of writers from Westminster School that specialized in burlesque, whose output included parodies of Thomas Gray's Odes.[23]

But the Lauder affair also had more serious longer-term consequences. It explicitly brought a language of propriety and property into the traditional language for talking about imitation, and pushed discussion of *imitatio* in slightly new directions. It blurred the divide between borrowing from the ancients and stealing from the moderns. Samuel Johnson was more than a little embarrassed by his connections with Lauder and by his own part in the affair.[24] Shortly after this quarrel had subsided Johnson wrote two pieces for the *Rambler* in 1751 on the subject of *imitatio*. Neither article mentions Lauder. Both, however, make slight but significant changes to the traditional body of metaphors for describing imitation. Johnson regards imitative poets as persistent pluckers of the common store of nature: 'There are other flowers of fiction so widely scattered and so easily cropped, that it is scarcely

22. Robert Lloyd, *The Progress of Envy: A Poem in Imitation of Spenser Occasioned by Lauder's Attack on the Character of Milton* (London, 1751), p. 16.
23. See Lance Bertelsen, *The Nonsense Club: Literature and Popular Culture, 1749–1764* (Oxford, 1986).
24. James L. Clifford, 'Johnson and Lauder', *Philological Quarterly* 54 (1975), 342–56 gives a detailed account, but rather understates the longer-term influence of the affair on Johnson. Patricia Phillips, *The Adventurous Muse: Theories of Originality in English Poetics, 1650–1760* (Uppsala and Stockholm, 1984), pp. 133–8 associates the *Rambler* with a general tendency in journal publications of the mid-century to downplay the value of imitation, as part of their mission to inform and entertain a less classically aware readership. For the impact of the Lauder affair on Johnson and on the general tendency to disparage imitation in the second half of the eighteenth century, see Richard Terry, '"In Pleasing Memory of All He Stole": Plagiarism and Literary Detraction, 1747–1785', in Kewes, ed., *Plagiarism in Early Modern England*, 181–200.

just to tax the use of them as an act by which any particular writer is despoiled of his garland; for they may be said to have been planted by the antients in the open road of poetry for the accommodation of their successors, and to be the right of every one that has art to pluck them without injuring their colours or their fragrance.'[25]

Johnson's vocabulary here—'Despoil' and 'tax'—indicates that ownership of the flowers of fancy is at least an issue, even if those flowers lie 'in the open road of poetry'. Johnson goes on to develop the metaphor of the free path over the land of the ancients: 'an inferior genius may without any imputation of servility pursue the path of the antients, provided he declines to tread in their footsteps.'[26] Johnson's account of imitation presents no new theory or distinct departure from earlier thinking, but he gently brings out the proprietorial fringes of the traditional language—follow the path of an earlier author rather than trudging in his footsteps, and as you do so attend with care to the flowers that can be plucked from the verges of his way. This positions the act of literary imitation within a landscape of natural commodities which are ready for use, but which might prompt questions about property and propriety if they were culled with excessive vigour.

These slight adjustments to the language of imitation were Johnson's guilty responses to the Lauder affair. But in making them he may well also have been influenced by another work which appeared after and responded to Lauder's accusations and the consequent debates. Henry Fielding's *Tom Jones* was published in 1749, right at the height of arguments about Milton's imitations and literary property. Fielding also allows the arguments about literary property to seep into the metaphoric language he uses to describe acts of imitation, and in particular to suffuse his magnificent description of imitation of the ancients as a matter of sharing the common goods of the natural world. Fielding also makes hay (as it were) with Locke's arguments about the way labour can confer ownership over common goods:

> The Antients may be considered as a rich Common, where every Person who hath the smallest Tenement in Parnassus hath a free Right to fatten his Muse. Or, to place it in a clearer Light, we Moderns are to the Antients what the Poor are to the Rich. By the Poor here I mean, that larger and venerable Body which, in *English*, we call the Mob. Now, whoever hath had the Honour to be admitted to any Degree of Intimacy with this Mob, must well know that it is

25. Samuel Johnson, *The Yale Edition of the Works, Volumes 3–5: The Rambler*, ed. W. J. Bate and Albrecht B. Strauss, 3 vols. (New Haven, 1969), 4.398.
26. Johnson, *The Rambler*, 4.401.

one of their established Maxims, to plunder and pillage their rich Neighbours without any Reluctance...In like Manner are the Ancients, such as Homer, Virgil, Horace, Cicero, and the rest, to be esteemed among us Writers, as so many wealthy Squires, from whom we, the Poor of Parnassus, claim an immemorial Custom of taking whatever we can come at.This liberty I demand, and this I am as ready to allow again to my poor Neighbours in their turn. All I profess, and all I require from my brethren, is to maintain the same strict Honesty among ourselves, which the Mob shew to one another.To steal from one another, is indeed highly criminal and indecent.[27]

The debates about Milton's alleged plagiarism in the later 1740s underlie Fielding's comic but nonetheless radical transformation of some of the established metaphors used to describe imitation.The paradox of regarding the ancients as a common good from which we can freely steal is marked by that wonderfully subversive suggestion that like all good radicals in a mob we should steal the squire's corn because it is common property, and in any case he has too much of everything so can spare a little for the poor. Fielding also suggests that the mob of moderns should only steal from the rich (i.e. the ancients) and spare each other.

The passage jocularly transforms Locke's belief that common land needs to be owned and worked and shared in order to bring human benefit. Fielding caps that with a delicious hidden pun on the word 'mob', which was a recent abbreviation of the Latin *mobile vulgus*. Writers in the *vulgar* tongue are implicitly represented as a thieving mob, who should at least display the basic honour among thieves of not stealing from fellow writers in the vernacular.That picks out and develops the chief issue in the Lauder affair, which was Milton's alleged theft from modern rather than ancient authors. The arguments about literary property in the 1740s encourage Fielding to imagine writers as working on a common estate, where the free use of ancient riches is separated, by a distinction so fine that it has no conceptual force at all, from theft from the moderns.

The first pamphlet to include the phrase 'Literary Property' in its title was by William Warburton, who had compiled alongside Pope some of the commentary and ancillary materials to *The Dunciad in Four Books*. Warburton's pamphlet appeared in 1747, three years after the death of Pope and two years before *Tom Jones*.That date is significant.Warburton was probably inspired to write on this subject by the fact that he was Pope's

---

27. Henry Fielding, *The History of Tom Jones, a Foundling*, ed. Martin C. Battestin and Fredson Bowers, 2 vols. (Oxford, 1974), p. 620.

literary executor and wanted to keep his friend's literary estate intact, and by
the fact that his own edition of Shakespeare (of which the copyright was
assigned to the publishing firm of the Tonsons) had just appeared. He had a
material interest in literary property, and his work on the subject was exactly
contemporaneous with Lauder's first allegations about Milton in *The
Gentleman's Magazine*.

Warburton's way of arguing in favour of literary property at first glance
might seem odd. His chief endeavour was to make a distinction between
texts and machines. So, a person who bought a watch could take it apart,
copy it, and make what Warburton calls an 'imitation' of it, which he could
then sell. He could do so legally unless the watch he was copying was protected by a specific patent. The reason this was acceptable, Warburton argued,
was that the craftsman–copyist used real skill in making his copy. A person
who simply copied out a *text* verbatim, however, was quite different. He
used only a mechanical skill: 'He who makes an utensil, in imitation of
another he sees made, must necessarily work with the same ideas the
original operator had, and so fitly acquires a property in the work of his
own hands. But the most learned book in the world may be copied by one
who hath no ideas at all. What pretence, then, hath such a one to property,
in a work of the *mind*, who hath employed, in copying it, only the labour of
the *hand*.'[28]

Warburton set the tone for debates through the 1760s and 1770s which
attempted to define literary property. These debates tended to equate imitations with exact replicas (which might be either replicas of a mechanical
invention or unlicensed reprints of texts over which other publishers
enjoyed rights). They also unleashed the full chaotic consequences of Locke's
theory of property when it migrated to the literary sphere. On the one
hand words and ideas were common to all, and an author who recombines
those common goods into newly productive forms is performing a public
benefit; but on the other hand human beings are entitled to own the products
of their labour. So what was the status of common ideas, words, and experiences, after they had been subjected to an author's labour? Should someone
who wrote a text be regarded as having a greater claim to ownership over
it than the printer who performs the mechanical labour of reproducing it,
and on what grounds?

---

28. [William Warburton], *A Letter from an Author to a Member of Parliament, Concerning Literary
Property* (London, 1747), p. 409.

These arguments about literary property rapidly fed back into discussion about literary imitation. Richard Hurd was a protégé of William Warburton. In 1751 Hurd appended an essay on imitation to his edition of Horace. This argued that 'The objects of imitation, like the materials of human knowledge, are a common stock, which experience furnishes to all men.'[29] Hence, Hurd argues, descriptions derived from nature might legitimately resemble each other. We should suspect plagiarism, however, not when two writers describe a sunset in roughly similar terms, but only when one writer uses exactly the same words as another: 'An identity of phrase or diction, is a much surer note of plagiarism' (p. 183).

That formulation of what literary property might be was immensely influential, although it appeared in a work of literary criticism. It fed into the most influential legal definition of literary property in the eighteenth century, that by William Blackstone in his *Commentaries on the Laws of England*, who famously defined literary property as 'the same conceptions, cloathed in the same words'.[30] The arguments about literary ownership also fed back into literary criticism to the detriment of imitating authors. Another Fellow of Blackstone's college (All Souls College, Oxford), was Edward Young. His *Conjectures on Original Composition* (1759) stated that the works of a writer who 'reverences himself' and avoids imitation 'will stand distinguished; his the sole Property of them; which Property alone can confer the noble title of an *Author*'.[31]

By the 1760s it became very common indeed to argue that classical literature belonged to a special category of literary property. Classical literature was (as Fielding had humorously indicated in *Tom Jones*) equivalent to the common goods of the earth which were necessary to sustain life, and over which it was wrong to claim ownership. Often this view was presented more or less explicitly in language drawn from theories of natural law. The anonymous author of the 1762 tract *An Enquiry into the Nature and Origin of Literary Property* asked: 'To whom then do the Copies [by which he means the right to print] of antient Authors appertain?' The author goes on to argue that 'the Copies of antient Authors (and all Copies are of the same Nature) are no more susceptible of Property than the Elements of

---

29. Richard Hurd, *Q. Horatii Flacci Epistola ad Augustum, with an English Commentary and Notes. To which is Added, A Discourse Concerning Poetical Imitation, by the Author of the Commentary on the Epistle to the Pisos* (London, 1751), p. 158.
30. William Blackstone, *Commentaries on the Laws of England*, 2 vols. (Oxford, 1766), 2.406.
31. Edward Young, *Conjectures on Original Composition: In a Letter to the Author of Sir Charles Grandison* (London, 1759), p. 54.

Air and Water, which are for the common Benefit of Mankind.' The author continues: 'One might as well pretend to exclude all others from the Benefit of a refreshing Breeze, or the View of a beautiful Prospect: Because we first felt the one, or saw the other.'[32] The classics were a part of nature. They were the elements in which we all live and which sustain life. No one can claim possession of those common elements without depriving his fellow beings of life.

The author of *An Enquiry* does not imagine those 'copies' being absorbed into the copious proprietorial body of the imitator or reader: they remain part of the ambient environment, elements which must remain free so as to enable their enjoyment by all. The water that we drink, the food that we gather from the pasture of the ancients, become ours as we absorb them; but the breeze, a prospect, a landscape, are necessarily common to all since they are not consumed when they are enjoyed. And here Fielding's pun on 'common'—meaning both the *communia* which support life and the village common, a specific piece of sustaining land set aside for the use of all—has surely left its mark on arguments about literary property. That metaphor is widening its scope to enable an argument that the entire landscape, both the literal landscape which poets imitate and the poems which they imitate too, is akin to the free goods of the mind. And further still behind that we can detect the distant but clear influence of Justinian's *Institutes*, in which there is at the very start of the second book a discussion of 'communia', or goods which are according to the law of nature common to all—goods which include air, flowing water, and the sea.[33]

These rights-based contributions to the debates about literary property probably had a wider cultural influence than the technical arguments in the courts about the foundations of copyright in the English common and statute law, although the latter have tended to dominate discussions of the origins of literary property. Through the mid-eighteenth century there were extensive debates in the courts about what the Copyright Act of 1710 really meant. Did it create a new right of literary ownership, or did it limit

---

32. Anon., *An Enquiry into the Nature and Origin of Literary Property* (London, 1762), p. 6. On the attribution of this pamphlet to Arthur Murphy, see Donald W. Nichol, 'Warburton (not!) on Copyright: Clearing up the Misattribution of *An Enquiry into the Nature and Origin of Literary Property* (1762)', *Journal for Eighteenth-Century Studies* 19 (1996), 171–82.

33. 'By the law of nature these things are common to mankind—the air, running water, the sea, and consequently the shores of the sea' ('Et quidem naturali jure communia sunt omnium haec: aer, acqua profluens, et mare et per hoc litera maris'), Justinian, *The Institutes of Justinian with English Translation and Notes*, ed. Thomas Collett Sandars (London, 1874), p. 89.

a pre-existing right under common or natural law which granted a person permanent ownership over the fruits of their literary labours?[34] If the latter case were proven, then stationers could crack open the champagne, since it would mean that they, their heirs and assigns, could acquire the right to print Shakespeare's works or Milton's *Paradise Lost* in perpetuity, and live comfortably on the proceeds.

The legal arguments rumbled on through the courts until the much misinterpreted case of *Donaldson v. Beckett* in 1774, which decided by a narrow margin there was not a common law perpetual right of literary property. There was also a series of parallel cases in the Scottish courts (notably *Hinton v. Donaldson* in 1773) on which Samuel Johnson's biographer James Boswell was to report, coincidentally while the great doctor was visiting him in Edinburgh.[35] These debates repeatedly touched on arguments about imitation, and they also repeatedly borrowed both argument and image from those literary disputes.

During the legal battle between Donaldson and Beckett, and away from the centre of the legal arguments about literary property in London, however, there developed a distinct body of radical thought which argued for a perpetual authorial copyright. The first significant contributor to this tradition was Catharine Macaulay in her *Modest Plea for the Property of Copyright* of 1774. Macaulay was a supporter of Wilkes, and was a known republican. She also worshipped Milton as an exemplary republican citizen. Writing from Bath and in confessed partial ignorance of the legal arguments being rehearsed in *Donaldson v. Beckett*, Macaulay proceeded largely from first principles. She argued from the law of nature that where labour has been exerted on common goods then the person performing the labour was entitled to own the fruits of his or her activity: 'It is the opinion of the noble Lord, that if there is any thing in the world common to all mankind, science and learning are in their nature *publici juris*; and they ought to be as free and general as air and water...But sure if there is any thing which an individual can properly call his own, it is, acquired science, and those high gifts of

---

34. See notably Mark Rose, *Authors and Owners*, and Martha Woodmansee, 'The Genius and the Copyright: Economic and Legal Conditions of the Emergence of the "Author"', *Eighteenth-Century Studies* 17 (1984), 425–48. The prehistory of these arguments in the case of *Pope v. Curl* has been explored in relation to the emergence of professionalized authorship in Brean S. Hammond, *Professional Imaginative Writing in England, 1670–1740: 'Hackney for Bread'* (Oxford, 1997).

35. James Boswell, *The Decision of the Court of Session upon the Question of Literary Property* (Edinburgh, 1774).

genius and judgment, with which the Almighty has in a peculiar manner distinguished some of his creatures.'[36]

Macaulay repeatedly refers to the products of literary labour as 'fruits', and in doing so she is not casually deploying an organic metaphor for the activities of the mind. She has a notion of the author as an active agrarian producer: 'There are some low-minded geniusses, who will be apt to think they may, with as little degradation to character, traffic with a bookseller for the purchase of their mental harvest, as opulant landholders may traffic with monopolizers in grain and cattle for the sale of the more substantial product of their lands' (pp. 14–15). This passage clearly registers the influence both of Locke and, perhaps, of Fielding's jocular response to the Lauder affair, with its common pastures and mean-spirited landlords. But Macaulay has a political purpose in reserving the 'mental harvest' of authors to the authors themselves. Fielding is being brought firmly back within the Lockean tradition, which insisted that labour conveyed the right of ownership. The engrossers of the common good, the booksellers, enslave the gullible author and deprive men of the fruits of the land. Macaulay caps her argument by insisting that only perpetual copyright can save authors from servility to patrons.

William Enfield's *Observations on Literary Property*, also of 1774, is often neglected in discussions of the arguments over copyright, but it made a significant contribution. Enfield was a Unitarian minister, who in 1774 was the master of *belles lettres* at the dissenting academy at Warrington. This was one of a number of northern academies which were established to give a university education to those Dissenters who could not attend Oxford or Cambridge as a result of their religious beliefs.[37] As a teacher of rhetoric and the author of a popular anthology of literary texts called *The Speaker* (1774), Enfield was well aware both of the rhetorical tradition and of the value of selectively imitating literary texts. In his *Observations on Literary Property*, however, Enfield couched his arguments in favour of perpetual literary property almost exclusively in the terms of the natural law tradition. His *Observations* begin with an epigraph drawn from the theorist

36. Catharine Macaulay, *A Modest Plea for the Property of Copyright* (Bath, 1774), pp. 28–9. On Macaulay's relationship to Enlightenment historiography, see Karen O'Brien, *Women and Enlightenment in Eighteenth-Century Britain* (Cambridge, 2009), pp. 152–72.
37. On Warrington Academy, see P. O'Brien, *Warrington Academy, 1757–86: Its Predecessors and Successors* (Wigan, 1989). David L. Wykes, 'The Contribution of the Dissenting Academy to the Emergence of Rational Dissent', in Knud Haakonssen, ed., *Enlightenment and Religion: Rational Dissent in Eighteenth-Century Britain* (Cambridge, 1996), 99–138.

of natural law Samuel von Pufendorf. But Enfield goes further than Macaulay in insisting that 'Labour has a kind of creating power, bringing into existence something of real value, which had before no being, and consequently no owner; the property of which must therefore reside in the person who gave it existence.'[38]

Enfield explicitly puts natural law theory to the service of a theory of literary creativity. A series of ideas is the most distinctive property that a person can possess: 'surely nothing more peculiarly belongs to a man than his own ideas . . . the train of thoughts and sentiments which a man forms in his mind, though compounded of ideas which might have before existed in other minds, and expressed in words which have before been used, is nevertheless truly and properly his own' (p. 19). The notion of 'proprietas', a personal style analogous to household effects, is here at once extended and narrowed from its roots within the rhetorical tradition and is reconstituted within the traditions of Lockean epistemology and political thought. The train of thoughts and sentiments which a man forms in his mind is not a style (a disposition to order words in a particular way), but a specific sequence of words that is 'proper' to a person. That series of words is the creative product both of a distinctive character and of labour.

The labour of ploughing and cultivating and growing of seeds, which Quintilian had used as metaphors to describe the training of an orator, is cross-fertilized in Enfield's treatise with the natural law tradition: 'And it is not more evident, that the corn which the husbandman gathers into his barn is the fruit of his labour in manuring the ground, sowing the seed, and gathering in the harvest; than that a train of ideas and words, not to be found in any other work, hath been the result of genius and understanding industriously employed to produce this effect' (p. 20). A genius labours to create, and should own those creations. Authorial and agrarian labour are here identified in a manner that transforms the grand estate imagined by Fielding into a respectable semi-detached villa: 'No man, therefore, can have a better right to the house which he has built on his own ground and with materials which he has purchased or collected from his estate, than an author has to the productions of his genius and industry' (p. 21). For Enfield every author is his own landlord, tenant farmer, architect, and builder.

Enfield, as well as imagining in very physical form what we still call 'a literary estate', also imagines footpaths and rights of way across it. And, as in

38. William Enfield, *Observations on Literary Property* (London, 1774), p. 17.

Johnson's response to the Lauder case, treading in the path of another person may bring with it a violation of his proprietorial rights. To suppose that an author sells the right to his labour along with a copy of a book, Enfield argues, is as absurd as to claim that 'the owner of an estate, by granting his neighbour a path through his grounds, gives him the property of all the produce of the field' (pp. 27–8). That image implies an imitator might have a right to follow the direction laid down by an earlier work, but has no right to appropriate its exact words.

There is one additional strand running through the legal and philosophical arguments about literary property which had a major consequence for the history of *imitatio*. In these debates epic poetry was often treated as a special case. Epic was special either as a result of its antiquity or because the cultural majesty it afforded its author was so great that it dwarfed mere questions about literary property and financial rewards.[39] It was a genre of such prestige that even modern examples of it might be regarded as 'Classics', and therefore as a common good. Lord Camden notoriously claimed in the case of *Donaldson v. Beckett* that 'When the booksellers offered Milton five pounds for his Paradise Lost, he did not reject it and commit his poem to the flames, nor did he accept the miserable pittance as the reward of his labours; he knew that the real price of his work was immortality, and that posterity would pay it.'[40]

Refuting this claim that the true reward of literary activity was intangible fame became one of the familiar topoi of arguments about literary property in the following years: Robert Southey among others quoted and attacked Camden at length.[41] As the category of 'the classics' became extended to include major vernacular works, so the greatest of all English 'classics', *Paradise Lost*, became the central field of dispute. Indeed this whole series

39. Lord Auchinleck argued against a common law right of ownership over literary works because 'anciently very valuable performances were preserved only by the memory. It is said Homer was so, and Ossian. When that was the case, what privilege could the author have? The poem of Chevy-chace, so much celebrated, and upon which we have a criticism by Mr. Addison, was, in my remembrance, repeated by every body. Was there a copy of this little heroic poem? What privilege could the author have in it, after he had let one man get it by heart?', Boswell, *Literary Property*, p. 5. Lord Gardenstone presented the alternative view, that theft from a classic is a Promethean crime: 'Who steals from common authors, steals trash; but he who steals from a Spencer, a Shakespeare, or a Milton, steals the fire of heaven, and the most previous gifts of nature. So we must have new statutes to regulate those literary felonies', Boswell, *Literary Property*, p. 26.
40. Anon., 'Donaldson v. Beckett', *Hansard*, 1st ser., 17 (1774), 953–1003.
41. Robert Southey, 'An Inquiry into the Copyright Act', *Quarterly Review* 21 (1819), 196–213 (p. 211).

of interconnected legal and literary quarrels positioned Milton by the last quarter of the eighteenth century right at the tangled epicentre of the cultural history of imitation and of literary property.[42]

Milton became a very special case: he was an original author who was also, according to Lauder at least, a plagiarist, but whose epic, being an epic, belonged to the special category of literary works which are akin to the natural world in being a common resource. The belief that his writings were a common good was invisibly reinforced by the growing influence of Milton's distinctive style and vocabulary over the normal language of English poetry throughout the eighteenth century. As an English vernacular 'classic' he was as free as the breeze, or as Alexander Donaldson, the pirate printer who provoked the test case of *Donaldson v. Beckett*, had insisted (misquoting and incidentally also plagiarizing the author of *An Enquiry into the Nature and Origin of Literary Property*) 'copies are no more susceptible of property after publication than the elements of air and water, a refreshing breeze, or a beautiful prospect, which are for the common benefit of mankind'.[43] Yet for Catharine Macaulay and for those who defended literary property as a natural right to the enjoyment of the fruits of one's labours the fact that this hero of republican letters had signed away his rights to *Paradise Lost* for an initial fee of £5 to enable booksellers to become rich while his descendants were living in poverty was one of the major arguments in favour of a perpetual authorial copyright. She argued that if literary property stood on the same footing on which it was supposed to stand 'before the fatal decision against it in the House of Lords' Milton could have commanded a fee that

---

42. Examples from the printing history of *Paradise Lost* run through the legal argument in *Donaldson v. Beckett*. Milton's sale of the 'copy' of *Paradise Lost* for three payments of £5 was used by the London booksellers as an argument for literary property. Donaldson argued this was specious: 'Milton indeed sold his Paradise Lost to a London bookseller for fifteen pounds, from which purchase they draw an inference of perpetual monopoly to the trade in London, and it matters not whether there are now any descendents from that bookseller who paid Milton fifteen pounds; he that possessed that shop, or the nearest bookseller to the spot of ground where this shop stood, is now the proprietor of Milton's works, and he retails this illustrious author amongst his brethren at many hundreds of pounds', Alexander Donaldson, *Some Thoughts on the State of Literary Property* (London, 1764), p. 18. Edmund Thurlow referred back to a Chancery case concerning the Tonsons' ownership of the copy of *Paradise Lost*: 'In the case of Newton's Milton, the court of chancery decreed generally; they did not, as had been observed on the other side, divide the author's text from the commentator's notes' (970). See R. Deazley, 'Commentary on Milton's Contract 1667', in L. Bently and M. Kretschmer, eds., *Primary Sources on Copyright (1450–1900)* (http://www.copyrighthistory.org, 2008), and Deazley, *Origin*, pp. 133–7.

43. Donaldson, *Some Thoughts*, p. 21. Cf. n. 32 above.

would have made 'a decent provision for his posterity'.[44] The same point
was echoed in the legal arguments in the case of *Donaldson v. Beckett*: 'It may
be presumed, Milton could not wish, that *Paradise Lost*, which was sold for
5 l. and two further sums of 5 l. to be paid conditionally, should continue a
SPLENDID FORTUNE in the Hands of a BOOKSELLER, and his
GRAND-DAUGHTER be obliged to beg a *Charity-Play* at Drury Lane
Theatre, 1752.'[45]

   Paradise Lost was not only at the centre of arguments about who owned
and had rights over a literary text in the second half of the eighteenth
century. It was itself a hot commercial property. The great family firm of
publishers the Tonsons laboured in the courts to ensure that they enjoyed
the exclusive right to print *Paradise Lost*, from which, through regularly
commissioning new annotated editions such as Thomas Newton's, they
commanded substantial returns. Those proprietorial battles were registered
very clearly within the editions which they published: Thomas Newton, as
well as drawing attention in his annotations to Milton's 'imitations' from the
ancients, related in his introduction the transmission of the right to print
Paradise Lost from the stationer to whom Milton had originally sold the
copy all the way down to his own publishers, J. and R. Tonson.[46] The question of who owned Milton, and who could benefit from his greatest
creation, was central to arguments about imitation and literary property in
the eighteenth century.

The path to Wordsworth

These arguments about literary property might be expected to influence
poetic practice in the later eighteenth century in two main ways. First of all
they would both reinforce and complicate Milton's central position in the
canon of English poetry. They encouraged people to think of *Paradise Lost*
simultaneously as a classic work common to all and as a piece of intellectual
property with heirs and owners. And if one were to look for the cultural
rather than psychological origins of Harold Bloom's notion of the anxiety

44. Macaulay, *Copyright*, pp. 24–5.
45. Alexander Donaldson, *The Cases of the Appellants [A. and J. Donaldson] and Respondents in the
    Cause of Literary Property* (London, 1774), p. 10.
46. Newton records the transfer up to the older Tonson, whose 'family have enjoyed the right of
    copy ever since', Milton, ed. Newton, *Paradise Lost*, p. xxxix.

of influence—in which Milton plays such a central part in the imaginary genealogy of romanticism—it is in this legal and literary uncertainty surrounding the status of Milton that one would discover them. *Paradise Lost* was a massive poem which was either the property of everyman or stamped with the seal of its author. Or both.

These arguments about literary property might also be expected to have influenced the way in which vernacular texts were imitated, as well, perhaps, as the way in which those archetypical 'common goods' of landscape and breeze were thought about and represented. Those who resisted the notion of a perpetual or extended right of literary property would present classic works of the human mind as common goods which could not or should not be owned, and which were akin to a breeze, a prospect, a sunset. Those who defended the principle of literary property, on the other hand, might compare literary productions to a house or an estate over which a person might enjoy full proprietorial rights. Between these two zones—the fully proprietorial image of an estate on the one hand, and the notion that literature, like the breeze, was a common good on the other—lay a median zone, which is best imagined through William Enfield's and indeed through Samuel Johnson's metaphor of the path or right of way, which enabled free passage over a terrain, rather than ownership of it.

That image already had great literary authority: Lucretius had described beating a path over trackless wastes in pursuit of Epicurus in *De Rerum Natura*, and Milton had imitated that pursuit in the bridge built across Chaos by Sin and Death as they hungrily follow in Satan's footsteps towards the fallen earth. A landscape criss-crossed by roads across which the original genius must track a zig-zagged course is even a feature of Edward Young's *Conjectures on Original Composition*, in which a true genius is described as 'crossing all publick roads into fresh untrodden ground' (p. 55). The image of the path implied that an imitator could follow a predecessor without slavishly replicating an earlier text, and might wander off from the public road into a landscape of the fancy which lay beyond its borders.

But that image also suggested that an author might freely pass over a domain owned by another person and yet not trespass on that person's rights of ownership, just as a pedestrian might pass over an estate owned by another person along a public right of way. That meant the metaphor of imitation as following a path acquired enormous explanatory power by the later eighteenth century: it could be used to articulate a relationship with prior texts which simultaneously treated them as a free public benefit akin to a right of way, whilst acknowledging that those pathways traversed land which was under private ownership. It also provided a ready and easy way to indicate that a poet was exercising the freedom of the imagination: a poet might wander off in pursuit of a fancy of his own, leaving behind the paths and regulated by-ways which ran across the landscape.

The potential of that metaphor is most clearly realized in the poetry of William Wordsworth, a poet famous both for having drawn deeply and repeatedly on the works of John Milton, and for his representations of land-scapes, of free creative breezes, and of paths and public roads. Wordsworth was also no stranger to the classical tradition. The half-title page of the 1802 edition of the *Lyrical Ballads*, which includes the famous definition of poetry as 'the spontaneous overflow of powerful feelings', has an epigraph from Quintilian's chapter on improvisation (*Institutio*, 10.7): 'It is the heart and the power of the mind that make us eloquent. This is why even the unskilled, so long as they are stirred by some emotion, are not short of words' ('Pectus enim id est quod disertos facit, & vis mentis; ideoque imperitis quoquo, si modo sint aliquo affectu concitati, verba non desunt').[47] The quotation is drawn from Quintilian's discussion of the acquired skill of extempore speech, a skill which can be learnt by habitual exercise (10.7.15). That Wordsworth should have cited it to legitimate his poetry of 'a man speaking to men', which aims 'to imitate, and, as far as possible, to adopt the very language of men', and which seeks to avoid received 'poetic diction', is less surprising than it might appear.[48] As we saw in Chapter 8, Francis Junius in 1628 had pressed Quintilian's arguments about *imitatio* in two potentially conflicting directions: on the one hand he emphasized how Quintilian dis-paraged slavish imitation, while on the other he brought to the fore the rhetorician's interest in the inimitable power of each author's own *vis* and *ingenium*—the *vis mentis* which Quintilian says, in the passage quoted by Wordsworth, is necessary for the successful improviser.

An admiration for the inimitable creative genius of a poet was always nestling within the rhetorical tradition, and James Beattie (whose poem *The Minstrel* Wordsworth greatly admired) cites Quintilian 10.3 in support of the notion that the habits of speaking correctly and elegantly 'are most effectually acquired by the frequent use of the pen, not in extracting com-mon places from books, but in giving permanence and regularity to our

47. William Wordsworth and Samuel Taylor Coleridge, *Lyrical Ballads: with Pastoral and Other Poems, in Two Volumes*, 2 vols. (London, 1802), pp. l and lxv.
48. Wordsworth and Coleridge, *Lyrical Ballads*, p. xviii.

own thoughts expressed in our own words'.[49] *Exercitatio* to achieve fluency remained an ideal right to the end of the eighteenth century, though that fluency is a product of reiterations of 'our own' rather than another's thoughts and words. And if Wordsworth had discussed literary imitation with Coleridge he would not have been treated to a simple diatribe about its limitations. Coleridge in his notes to Aphorism 8 in *Aids to Reflection* suggests that imitation is a mode of practical understanding: 'In ATTENTION, we keep the mind *passive*: In THOUGHT we rouse it into activity. In the former, we submit to an impression—we keep the mind steady in order to *receive* the stamp. In the latter, we seek to *imitate* the artist, while we ourselves make a copy or duplicate of his work.'[50] In the notebook entry which became 'On Poesy or Art' Coleridge also echoed the concern of generations of theorists, including Quintilian, with the relationship between likeness and difference in the act of imitating: 'philosophically we understand that in all Imitation two elements must exist, and not only exist, but must be perceived as existing—Likeness and unlikeness, or Sameness and Difference'.[51]

At Hawkshead grammar school Wordsworth read swathes of classical literature, and was taught by people who had an active knowledge of the rhetorical tradition.[52] In the 1780s he wrote imitations of Virgil's *Georgics*; in 1795 he collaborated over an imitation of Juvenal's Satire 8 in imitation of Samuel Johnson's topical imitations of Satires 3 and 10, while in 1823 he translated parts of the *Aeneid*.[53] He was at times a conscious imitator of Pope, and, like Pope, was highly responsive to the series of intensive debates about imitation which ran through the eighteenth century.[54]

And a faint ghost not just of Pope but of Pope's plagiaristic phantom poet in *The Dunciad* passes over one of Wordsworth's earliest poems, *The Vale of Esthwaite*, first drafted in 1787, which is a fairly typical young Wordsworthian hybrid of bits of James Thomson's *Seasons* flavoured with fragments of

49. James Beattie, *Essays: on Poetry and Music, as They Affect the Mind; on Laughter, and Ludicrous Composition; on the Usefulness of Classical Learning* (London, 1779), pp. 517–18.
50. Samuel Taylor Coleridge, *Aids to Reflection*, ed. John B. Beer (London and Princeton, 1993), p. 14.
51. Samuel Taylor Coleridge, *The Notebooks*, ed. Kathleen Coburn, 9 vols. (London, 2002), 3.4397.
52. See Richard W. Clancey, *Wordsworth's Classical Undersong: Education, Rhetoric, and Poetic Truth* (Basingstoke, 2000).
53. William Wordsworth, *Early Poems and Fragments, 1785–1797*, eds. Carol Landon and Jared R. Curtis (Ithaca, NY, and London, 1997), pp. 615–46; 786–825. On Wordsworth's Juvenal, see Stuart Gillespie, *English Translation and Classical Reception: Towards a New Literary History* (Oxford, 2011), pp. 123–49.
54. Howard Erskine-Hill, 'The Satirical Game at Cards in Pope and Wordsworth', *The Yearbook of English Studies* 14 (1984), 183–95.

Thomas Gray's 'Elegy' and Milton's 'Il Penseroso', with added doses of gothic Spenserian horror to thicken the brew. The poet flees from one Gothic encounter to meet 'a tall thin Spectre', who is akin not just to Pope's plagiaristic poet in *The Dunciad* but to the larger tradition of simulacral imitations of which he is a part:

> Like two wan wither'd leaves his eyes
> Black were his bones seen through his skin
> As the pale moonbeam wan and thin
> Which through a chink of rock we view
> On a lone sable blasted yew
> And on his feeble arm he bore
> What seem'd the poet's harp of yore
> He wav'd his hand and would have spoke
> But from his trembling shadow broke
> Faint murmuring sad and hollow moans
> As if the wind sigh'd through his bones.[55]

The young Wordsworth borrows greedily from Spenser's many descriptions of attenuated and ghostly forms—there are ghosts of Spenser's Maleger and Malbecco here—and more than a trace of James Beattie's *The Minstrel* looms in the background; but the poet-ghost-plagiarist of Pope's *Dunciad* (along with Pope's notes on the hollow noises it makes) also animates this Wordsworthian gothic bard, who is himself so suffused in the common matter of earlier English poets that the only sound he can emit is not words, but that archetype of common property, wind.

Young Wordsworth met that spectre while following his own fancy through a landscape. That is an early sign of how significant it was for Wordsworth to think of himself weaving his way along or across a path, either led by fancy or by the footprints of others. His mature representations of poetic activity repeatedly involve a poet wandering down a road or public way, at the end of which they encounter visions and episodes which are, with surprising frequency, Miltonic in their origins.

This is particularly apparent in poems associated with Wordsworth's projected philosophical epic on the mind of man which was to have been called *The Recluse*. Sometimes the paths are literal ('I love a public road', *The Prelude*, 1805, 12.142),[56] but they may also be literary: in *The Prelude* the poet

---

55. Wordsworth, *Early Poems and Fragments, 1785–1797*, pp. 440–2.
56. Quotations from William Wordsworth, *The Prelude, 1799, 1805, 1850: Authoritative Texts, Context and Reception, Recent Critical Essays*, ed. Jonathan Wordsworth, M. H. Abrams, and Stephen Gill (New York, 1979).

is followed by a dog 'Obsequious to my steps' (1805, 4.98) while 'in the public roads at eventide | I sauntered, like a river murmuring | And talking to itself', producing poems which respond to the common and visible goods around him. Later on, walking along the 'public way' the poet follows 'the road's wat'ry surface' (1805, 4.371) which seems like 'another stream', as the work of man dissolves into the work of nature in a gentle reminiscence of the moment Milton's Eve perceives herself reflected in the pool in *Paradise Lost*. But in this apparently aimless movement along a path he suddenly encounters a dispossessed figure who has distinctly Miltonic lineaments, as though the literal act of following the common way leads inevitably towards *Paradise Lost*:

> While thus I wandered, step by step led on,
> It chanced a sudden turning of the road
> Presented to my view an uncouth shape,
> So near that, slipping back into the shade
> Of a thick hawthorn, I could mark him well,
> Myself unseen. He was of stature tall,
> A foot above man's common measure tall,
> Stiff in his form, and upright, lank and lean—
> A man more meagre, as it seemed to me,
> Was never seen abroad by night or day.
> His arms were long, and bare his hands; his mouth
> Shewed ghastly in the moonlight; from behind,
> A milestone propped him, and his figure seemed
> Half sitting, and half standing. I could mark
> That he was clad in military garb,
> Though faded yet entire.   (1805, 4.400–15)

The 'uncouth shape' of the discharged soldier is a Wordsworthian rewriting of his own earlier poet-ghost in *The Vale of Esthwaite*; but it is also an imitation of that great simulacral figure of Death from *Paradise Lost*, whose 'shape, | If shape it might be called that shape had none | Distinguishable in member, joint, or limb, | Or substance might be called that shadow seemed'.[57] Milton's description of Death had been regarded as 'full of sublime ideas' by generations of literary critics from Addison to Burke.[58] Here the universal monarch is deliberately rendered common. Gone is Death's dart, and the 'likeness of kingly crown' (*PL*, 2.673) on his head is replaced by faded uniform.

---

57. *PL*, 2.666–9. Quotations from John Milton, *Paradise Lost*, ed. Alastair Fowler (London and New York, 1998). For the genesis and significance of the episode, see Jonathan Wordsworth, *William Wordsworth: The Borders of Vision* (Oxford, 1982), p. 13.

58. Milton, ed. Newton, *Paradise Lost*, p. 127, citing Addison.

Milton's language is so much a 'common' resource that even this skeletal
figure,'A foot above man's *common* measure tall', suggests at once the sublime
singularity of Milton's Death and a common soldier, whose experiences
might stand for that of many others in a similar state. That figure is encountered on a 'public road', a space across which anyone may travel at will.

Wordsworth's soldier is propped up by a milestone. This might seem like
a trivial piece of realism that serves to anchor this rewriting of Milton's
sublime imagining to a particular place and time. But the presence of the
milestone has some significance, since it implies that the road on which
the encounter with the Miltonic discharged solder takes place is a Turnpike
Road, and therefore maintained at the cost and to the benefit of a specific
Turnpike Trust. The Trusts were from 1766 required to fund the erection of
milestones at regular intervals along their toll-roads. Turnpike Trusts (dozens
of which sprang up across the United Kingdom in the last third of the
eighteenth century) did not own the land over which the road passed, but
they did invest significant sums in its improvement so that they could charge
a fee to all wheeled vehicles that passed along it.[59]

Roads also—and again this gives additional richness to the metaphor of
following the path laid down by another writer—raised complex questions
about who could benefit from the natural resources around and below
them. Under the terms of the Highways Act of 1773 (13 Geo 3 c78) those
who owned land onto which roads were widened retained the rights to
the timber that grew on the land and over the minerals beneath it.[60] The
metaphor of a common road was also by the late eighteenth century deeply
embedded in legal writing about literary property. So William Blackstone
declared in his influential discussion of copyright that anonymous publication

59. Geoffrey Norman Wright, *Turnpike Roads* (Princes Risborough, 1992), p. 31, and J. V. Beckett,
   Coal and Tobacco: The Lowthers and the Economic Development of West Cumberland, 1660–1760
   (Cambridge, 1981), pp. 172–7. The twenty-foot width of a Turnpike Road was for the
   Wordsworths a natural unit by which to estimate distance, as in Dorothy Wordsworth's famous
   journal entry about daffodils on 15 April 1802: 'as we went along there were more and yet
   more; and at last, under the boughs of the trees, we saw that there was a long belt of them
   along the shore, about the breadth of a country turnpike road', *Journals of Dorothy Wordsworth*,
   ed. Ernest De Sélincourt, 2 vols. (London, 1941), 1.131. 'The turnpike system introduced a
   means of privatising a public resource, "the common highway". Turnpike trustees were, in
   effect, agents managing a public right of passage, with powers to improve it, but no powers to
   assume legal ownership of the land within the highway', Wright, *Turnpike Roads*, p. 24.
   Pedestrians did not pay a toll. On the significance of Turnpikes and ways in Wordsworth, see
   Alan Liu, *Wordsworth: The Sense of History* (Stanford, 1989), pp. 98–100.
60. Anon., *Abstracts of Two Acts of Parliament, Passed in the Thirteenth Year of the Reign of his Present
   Majesty King George the Third* (London, 1773), p. 9.

was akin to a pure act of public benefit, like the 'building of a church, or the laying out of a new highway'.[61]

A Turnpike Road, however, did not simply exist for public benefit. It made money for its investors, and those who passed along it in a wheeled vehicle had to pay to do so. In the sonnet 'London, 1802' Wordsworth says of Milton 'So didst thou travel on life's common way'. Milton was not an easy or an entirely comfortable influence for Wordsworth, and could draw his writing towards abstraction and litotes. But that influence was by no means simply oppressive, since for Wordsworth Milton was both a literary character with his own proprietorial figures of style and turns of phrase and also, potentially, a free and common good, a poet over whose works one could wander at will. And that combination of a private resource and a public good points towards the deep structural kinship between legislation about literary property and about public thoroughfares in the later eighteenth century. Both sought to reconcile public benefit with private ownership.

A right of way was just that, a right to pass over a piece of land rather than to take possession of it. Rights over and ownership of Turnpike Roads in particular had deep analogies to beliefs about the ownership of 'classic' texts in this period. Both were public goods which could be privately owned, and both might be exploited for the benefit of both their owners and of a wider public. And that mingling of the public and the proprietorial is something which Wordsworth can seldom eradicate either from his representations of paths or from his imitations of Milton. Sometimes, indeed, following a Miltonic path can be represented as a material constraint imposed upon the free movement of the imagination across the landscape. The strongest example of this occurs in Book 5 of *The Prelude* when Wordsworth complains about modern educators. This passage distinctly follows a path laid down more than a century before by John Milton:

> These mighty workmen of our later age,
> Who with a broad highway have overbridged
> The froward chaos of futurity,
> Tamed to their bidding—they who have the art
> To manage books, and things, and make them work
> Gently on infant minds as does the sun
> Upon a flower—the tutors of our youth,
> The guides, the wardens of our faculties
> And stewards of our labour, watchful men

61. Blackstone, *Commentaries*, 2.406.

And skilful in the usury of time,
Sages, who in their prescience would controul
All accidents, and to the very road
Which they have fashioned would confine us down
Like engines—when will they be taught,
That in the unreasoning progress of the world
A wiser spirit is at work for us,
A better eye than theirs, most prodigal
Of blessings, and most studious of our good,
Even in what seem our most unfruitful hours?   (1805, 5.370–88)

This passage is unmistakably based on the moment in Book 2 of *Paradise Lost* when Sin and Death follow Satan to earth, and beat a pathway across Chaos to enable 'spirits perverse' to pass over it:

Sin and Death amain
Following his track, such was the will of heaven
Paved after him a broad and beaten way
Over the dark abyss, whose boiling gulf
Tamely endured a bridge of wondrous length
From hell continued reaching the utmost orb
Of this frail world...   (*PL*, 2.1024–30)

In *Paradise Lost* it seems as though the feet of Sin and Death pack down Chaos into substrate, and 'pave' it simply by passing heavily and frequently across it. Their route to earth is a physical image of the well-trodden pathway followed by an imitator, which becomes a primrose path to the everlasting bonfire. It is here as though Milton is transforming Lucretius's description of how he followed the path set down by Epicurus (*DRN*, 3.1–13) into a vision of enslavement and damnation: the path most followed becomes a road to hell. Wordsworth, however, makes his road explicitly the product of labour. His 'Sages' become 'mighty workmen' who build roads and then force people to follow the route they have created, from which all deviation is prohibited.

There are many reasons why Wordsworth should have transformed this particular passage from *Paradise Lost* in this way. One was that the episode of building the road to hell in *Paradise Lost* raised questions about propriety in various senses of the word. The bridge across Chaos was often regarded by Milton's editors as only dubiously Miltonic: Richard Bentley argued it was an interpolation, and even the sober Thomas Newton recorded doubts about the propriety of positioning it at the end of Book 2, and declared it dangerously without precedent in the epic tradition.[62] It was at once Milton at his most original, and so un-Miltonic that (according to Bentley at least) it might not have been written by Milton at all. The passage about the road to hell therefore raised questions about Milton's judgement and even about his authorship which prompt Wordsworth to turn it into a passage about those who seek to constrain and control a free path over the landscape.

Wordsworth may have turned Milton's diabolical road-making into a metaphor for despotic educators for more narrowly material reasons too. The Lowther family, for whom Wordsworth's father worked as an agent ('stewards of our labour' indeed), had played a major part in establishing Turnpike Trusts in Cumbria in order to enable the transport of coal.[63] Those Trusts did not encourage free and easy poetical peregrinations across the English countryside, since the boundaries of Turnpike Roads were tightly regulated in order to prevent travellers evading tolls or weigh-stations by deviating from them.[64] Wordsworth is not here presenting Milton as himself a tyrannical and possessive author, who builds a road along which he constrains others to follow; he is rather taking the common matter of Milton's chaos and working on it so as to suggest that modern educators (and modern road-builders and enclosers) restrict the routes along which the imagination may travel.

Johnson's discussions of imitation in the *Rambler* (a journal whose title so genially suggests a free movement across the land), in which the imitator may follow a path but not promiscuously strip the flowers from its margins, remained very visible in the literary landscape in the early nineteenth century. They were quoted in *The Gentleman's Magazine* in the context of arguments about Byron's alleged plagiarisms in 1816.[65] For Wordsworth the footsteps of a predecessor could be a 'public road' along which the imagination freely wanders, or it could be a narrowly proprietorial way which constrains the direction of travel even as it enables it to happen. And that uneasy concern with the ways in which writers drive roads across terrain trodden by others

---

62. 'Let the lines themselves be approv'd; yet it must be allow'd, it is wrong conduct and want of oeconomy for the whole poem. And we cannot recollect a parallel instance in Homer or Virgil, or any authorized poet', Milton, ed. Newton, *Paradise Lost*, p. 158.
63. Laurence Albert Williams, *Road Transport in Cumbria in the Nineteenth Century* (London, 1975), pp. 29, 85.
64. Anon., *Two Acts*, p. 52.
65. *The Gentleman's Magazine* (March 1818), 390–1. See Tilar J. Mazzeo, *Plagiarism and Literary Property in the Romantic Period* (Philadelphia, 2007), p. 89.

runs through his discussion of the creative power of a genius in his *Essay, Supplementary to the Preface* of 1815:

> The predecessors of an original Genius of a high order will have smoothed the way for all that he has in common with them;—and much he will have in common; but for what is peculiarly his own, he will be called upon to clear and often to shape his own road.[66]

That passage is partly about creating a receptive audience. But its language— of road-building and of what writers share in 'common'—indicates how deeply Wordsworth's imaginary landscape was suffused by the terminology used in discussions about imitation and literary property. The landscape of *The Prelude* itself also is shaped in part by debates over what it meant to own texts, or pathways across a wider literary landscape, and by the wider foundations of those debates in earlier discussions of *imitatio*. The common goods of the earth and the proprietary mingle in the fashioning of a new path through land which belongs to another, and which has already been trodden by another foot.

Wordsworth's deep association between Milton and literary property, and between literary property and paths, runs through other poems conceived as part of *The Recluse*, which was supposed to be his great transformative imitation of *Paradise Lost*. 'Home At Grasmere' was inspired by the Wordsworths' return to Grasmere in the winter of 1799. It was begun in early 1800, shortly after they had secured the lease of Dove Cottage, was revised and extended in 1806, and its final section was published as 'The Prospectus' to *The Recluse* along with *The Excursion* in 1814.[67] It is therefore one of the main surviving sections of the poem in which Wordsworth aspired to follow Milton down an epic path.

'Home at Grasmere' begins with a description of the common goods of nature as seen through the eyes of a young poet. The schoolboy Wordsworth stops 'Once on the brow of yonder Hill' on Loughrigg:

> Who could look
> And not feel motions there? I thought of clouds
> That sail on winds; of breezes that delight
> To play on water...

---

66. *The Prose Works of William Wordsworth*, ed. W. J. B. Owen and Jane Worthington Smyser, 3 vols. (Oxford, 1974), 3.80.

67. William Wordsworth, *Home at Grasmere: Part First, Book First of 'The Recluse'*, ed. Beth Darlington (Ithaca, NY, and Hassocks, 1977), pp. 10–22.

Of Sunbeams, Shadows, Butterflies, and Birds,
Angels, and winged Creatures that are Lords
Without restraint of all which they behold.
I sate, and stirred in Spirit as I looked,
I seemed to feel such liberty was mine...   (24–35)[68]

This boy ranges pathlessly through the landscape, and can 'flit from field to rock, from rock to field' while enjoying the free benefits of nature. This is, however, not simply a landscape full of common goods. The possessive 'such liberty was *mine*' anticipates the voice of the mature poet whose acquisition of Dove Cottage in Grasmere (which was, incidentally, situated directly beside a major Turnpike Road) provided the immediate pretext for the poem. Wordsworth retrospectively finds in the landscape a kind of personal estate, which draws a convenient veil over the fact that he did not own but was simply renting Dove Cottage for £8 a year.[69] This right of occupancy, however, brought with it a sense of permanent ownership over the landscape: 'And now 'tis *mine* for life: dear Vale, | One of thy lowly dwellings is *my* home!' and 'This solitude is *mine*... The unappropriated bliss hath found | An owner, and that owner I am he' (83–6). The previously unowned paradise acquires distinct flavours of the proprietorial: it becomes a *proprium*, a piece of personal property.[70]

Those marks of individual ownership are again complicated, however, by an under-presence of allusions to *Paradise Lost*, many of which are sinister. 'Lords | Without restraint' (32–3) echoes Eve's hungry consumption of the apple in *Paradise Lost* ('Greedily she engorged without restraint, | And knew not eating death', *PL*, 9.791–2). Wordsworth's apostrophe to the place which has become his own, 'Embrace me then, ye Hills, and close me in' (129), uncomfortably echoes that of Adam after the Fall: 'cover me ye pines, | Ye cedars, with innumerable boughs | Hide me, where I may never see them more' (*PL*, 9.1088–90).[71] In 'Home at Grasmere' a common stream or breeze is first experienced by a boy who follows his own path through the landscape; it then comes to be 'owned' by virtue of having been experienced in a way distinctive to this particular child; metaphorical ownership is then enjoyed more literally through the tenure of property. But its echoes of

---

68. Quotations from the transcription of MS B in Wordsworth, *Home at Grasmere*.
69. Stephen Gill, *William Wordsworth: A Life* (Oxford, 1989), p. 169.
70. For Wordsworth's habitual association between literary property and a manor or estate, see Mazzeo, *Plagiarism and Literary Property*, pp. 146–73.
71. Cf. the claim in Geoffrey H. Hartman, *Wordsworth's Poetry, 1787–1814* (New Haven, 1964), p. 172: 'His muse riots; his creative energies almost evoke the terrestrial paradise.'

Milton counterpoint that story, suggesting that claims to ownership over common goods—Milton, the landscape, the breeze—may bring with them a kind of fall. Milton, we might remember, describes wedded love as 'sole propriety [i.e. property], | In Paradise of all things common else' (*PL*, 4.751–2). 'Home at Grasmere' seems dangerously to compromise the commonality of natural goods by declaring the poet's ownership of them.

In 'The Prospectus' to *The Recluse* (as lines 959–1048 of 'Home at Grasmere' were presented when published in 1814), Wordsworth sets out the programme for his epic poem on the mind of man. Its subject-matter positions the proposed poem exactly on the intersection between universal, common experience and personal ownership. The mind of man is common to all; but (like death) is something which each person can only ever experience for himself. Wordsworth's journey towards that common subject-matter is, perhaps inevitably, described through the most overt imitation of Milton in his mature *oeuvre*. To journey into the mind of man does not entail simply following a well-worn path or travelling down a public road. It requires a bold leap across the elemental richness of material chaos. The 'Prospectus' begins with a direct quotation of Milton's appeal to 'fit audience find though few', and continues:

> thus prayed the Bard,
> Holiest of Men. Urania, I shall need
> Thy guidance, or a greater Muse, if such
> Descend to earth or dwell in highest heaven!
> For I must tread on shadowy ground, must sink
> Deep, and, aloft ascending, breathe in worlds
> To which the Heaven of heavens is but a veil.
> All strength, all terror, single or in bands,
> That ever was put forth in personal forms—
> Jehovah, with his thunder, and the quire
> Of shouting angels and the empyreal throne—
> I pass them unalarmed. The darkest Pit
> Of the profoundest Hell, chaos, night,
> Nor aught of [blinder] vacancy scooped out
> By help of dreams can breed such fear and awe
> As fall upon us often when we look
> Into our minds, into the mind of Man,
> My haunt and the main region of my song.   (973–90)

That final shimmy of pronouns, which range from the collective '*our* minds' to the general 'mind of Man' and thence to the emphatically possessive

'*My* haunt', takes 'The Prospectus' back towards the uneasy fusion of common and proprietorial experience of the landscape which had been displayed at the opening of 'Home at Grasmere'. Young Wordsworth witnessed common things and ranged without a path; older Wordsworth aspired to own them. Future Wordsworth is then imagined seeking a sublime space which goes beyond the path set out by *Paradise Lost* into what is at once the commonest and the most individual domain of all—the mind of man. He aspires to achieve that end by following a fragmented version of the pathway across Chaos initially taken by Milton's Satan, and then paved into a common way by Sin and Death.

But in the 'Prospectus' to 'The Recluse' all traces of a pathway have been obliterated. There is no beaten path, no Turnpike, no milestone, no workman to pave it over. It is a journey through sublime vacancy, across unowned and uncreated space or 'shadowy ground'. An imitator's following of a predecessor's path has become a great leap into a void. With so little common ground beneath his feet it is not surprising that Wordsworth did not manage to complete this proposed great work. Following a prior path can be constraining, and it can risk trespassing on another's work; but without any path at all the very ground beneath one's feet can vanish. That is in part why 'Home at Grasmere' puts such emphasis on the reassuring fact of being at home within a landscape that is a habitual companion. The domestic estate provides an anchor for his solitary journey across the void.

Late in life Wordsworth was much concerned with the legal aspects of intellectual property. The proposal in 1808 to extend copyright to twenty-eight years after an author's death attracted his attention.[72] From 1838 onwards he engaged in extensive lobbying (as well as the composition of two poems, 'A Plea for Authors' and 'A Poet to his Grandchild') to assist the passage of what was to become the Copyright Act of 1842.[73] In a letter to Edward Quillinan in March 1840 he declared that the bookseller Thomas Tegg 'has the impudence to affirm, that another *Paradise Lost*, or a poem as good, would at once produce £10,000 from Mr Murray and others ... *Paradise*

---

72. *The Letters of William and Dorothy Wordsworth*, ed. Ernest De Sélincourt, Mary Trevelyan Moorman, Chester L. Shaver, and Alan G. Hill, 8 vols. (Oxford, 1967–88), 2.1.266: 'I am told that it is proposed to extend the right from 14 years, as it now stands, after the decease of authors, till 28, this I think is far too short a period ... The law as it now stands merely consults the interests of the useful drudges in Literature ... while men of real power, who go before their age, are deprived of all hope of their families being benefited by their exertions.'

73. Wordsworth, *Letters*, 6.3.536–46.

Lost is indeed bought because people for their own credit must now have it. But how few, how very few, read it...But even were it true that substantial work would at once secure a wide circulation, justice would still be violated, by withholding from the Descendants or Heirs of a great Author the further advantage he is strongly entitled to.'[74]

This concern with copyright legislation has sometimes been presented as a manifestation of the later Wordsworth's conservatism, or as the commercial concomitant of a romantic poet's sense of his proprietorship over the creative productions of his own genius.[75] The history of arguments about intellectual property which I have presented here suggests a slightly different interpretation. Wordsworth's concern for intellectual property in the 1830s was a continuation of earlier arguments about literary property which had been woven into the texture of his verse, into his ways of imitating Milton, and into his representations of the landscape.[76] His position on this subject would not have appeared to him as simply conservative. Even in the 1840s Wordsworth was talking about literary property in terms which had much in common with those used by the republican Catharine Macaulay and by the northern Dissenting tradition as represented by William Enfield's *Observations on Literary Property* in the 1770s.[77] Wordsworth shows just Macaulay's concern for the persistence of an authorial estate, and uses exactly the same example to argue for a perpetual copyright—the

---

74. Wordsworth, *Letters* 7.43. Cf. his letter to Richard Sharp, on 27 September 1808, *Letters*, 1.266.
75. Susan Eilenberg, 'Wordsworth and the Reform of Copyright', *ELH* 56 (1989), 351–74 notes Wordsworth's attitude to his poems 'sometimes resembled that of a landowner towards his lands. A powerful sense of literary territoriality is apparent not only in his fierce resentment of plagiarisms committed against his own and his friends' literary property but also, in a different mode, in the strong identification of poetry with place.' Richard G. Swartz, 'Wordsworth, Copyright, and the Commodities of Genius', *Modern Philology* 89 (1992), 482–509 at 506 states that 'Romantic literary culture depended upon the belief that there is an essential identity between the maker and the work.' The careful factual account of Wordsworth's activities in Catherine Seville, *Literary Copyright Reform in Early Victorian England: The Framing of the 1842 Copyright Act* (Cambridge, 1999), pp. 159–75 may underestimate Wordsworth's financial motives for supporting the act of 1842: in 1835 his writings had generated income of £200 a year, while by 1838 they were bringing approximately £500. See Mary Trevelyan Moorman, *William Wordsworth: A Biography*, 2 vols. (Oxford, 1957), 2.552.
76. Wordsworth was familiar with Fielding from his boyhood (see Duncan Wu, *Wordsworth's Reading, 1770–1799* (Cambridge, 1993), pp. 58–9 and 115); but there is no evidence that he read *The Rambler* before 1815, see Duncan Wu, *Wordsworth's Reading, 1800–1815* (Cambridge, 1995), p. 121.
77. Wu, *Wordsworth's Reading, 1800–1815*, pp. 85–6 notes that Dorothy met Enfield in 1788 and that she and William read his popular miscellany of extracts from the English poets *The Speaker*. The long, favourable review of Enfield's work in *The Monthly Review* 51 (1774) disseminated his thinking.

poverty of Milton's biological heirs.[78] He was effectively rehearsing the non-metropolitan, non-conformist, and (in its day) radical thinking about intellectual property which had grown up in parallel to the debates in the courts about intellectual property in the later eighteenth century.

However, by the late 1830s the political scene had moved on. The newer generation of Radical MPs were in general hostile to attempts to extend authorial copyright for an additional period after an author's death. They regarded copyright in general as a quasi-monopolistic practice which restricted the free dissemination of knowledge, and which was analogous to stamp and paper duties in being effectively a tax on learning.[79] For them, as for our contemporary advocates of what are still referred to as 'creative commons' (ideas on which all can freely graze), freedom was the freedom to replicate without redress. Wordsworth's position on copyright by the late 1830s consequently had come to appear conservative, but its roots lay in radical, non-conformist thinking of the 1760s and 1770s.

There is a pleasing irony to this turn of events. One of Wordsworth's aims in lobbying for an extension of copyright was to ensure that his family would benefit from the posthumous publication of that richly Miltonic work which he had derived from his own experiences in the late eighteenth century: *The Prelude, or the Growth of a Poet's Mind*, which remained unpublished at Wordsworth's death. That poem—with its representations of prospects and breezes which were at once common to all and uniquely inspiring to Wordsworth, with its sublime landscapes criss-crossed by paths which twisted and turned towards and away from the common store of literary goods presented in *Paradise Lost*—was itself in part the product of mid-eighteenth-century arguments about imitation and literary property.

78. This had become a commonplace: Robert Southey in 'An Inquiry into the Copyright Act' presents as an argument for perpetual copyright the fact that 'The last descendants of Milton died in poverty' (p. 212).
79. Seville, *Copyright Reform*, pp. 46–8. Wordsworth records a conversation with Sir Robert Peel in which Peel 'dwelt in general terms upon the evils of monopoly and in the particular he deprecated the mischief which might arise from confining the circulation of improved processes in Science', Wordsworth, *Letters*, 7.4.300.

10

The Promethean Moment

Mary Shelley and Milton's Monstrous Progeny

One of the deepest indirect influences on thinking about imitation after the seventeenth century was a text which has almost nothing at all to say about literature: Descartes's *Discourse on Method* of 1637. Descartes is often positioned at or over the threshold of modernity because of his insistence that mind and matter are separate, and that knowledge must first be grounded in the introspection of an agent into his own processes of thinking. Whether or not these claims make him midwife to the birth of modern consciousness is a moot point. But some of the less central claims and themes of the *Discourse* did have a significant long-term effect on attitudes towards and practices of imitation. The 1649 English translation of the *Discourse* shares the concern for 'models' in the architectural and mathematical senses that emerged so strongly in later seventeenth-century discussions of *imitatio*. Descartes is keen to insist that his independent, foundationalist mode of thinking is grounded in mathematical rigour, but that it is not a 'model' to be imitated by everyone: he declares that 'But though I present you here with a Modell of my work, because it hath sufficiently pleased me; I would not therefore counsell any one to imitate it.'[1]

The most influential aspect of the *Discourse* on literary history, however, was not this incidental overlap of vocabulary, but a famous passage in which Descartes made a comparison between human beings and automata or animals

---

1. René Descartes, *A Discourse of a Method, for the Well-Guiding of Reason, and the Discovery of Truth in the Sciences*, trans. John Holden (London, 1649), p. 24. References in square brackets are to the first French edition, René Descartes, *Discours de la methode pour bien conduire sa raison* (Leiden, 1637).

(which he regarded as no more than highly sophisticated automata) in order to support his claim that human beings were not simply material things:[2]

> if there were such Machines which had organs, and the exterior figure of an Ape, or of any other unreasonable creature, we should finde no means of knowing them not to be altogether of the same nature as those Animals: whereas, if there were any which resembled our bodies, and imitated ['imitatassent' (1637), p. 56] our actions as much as morally it were possible, we should always have two most certain ways to know, that for all that they were not reall men: The first of which is, that they could never have the use of speech, nor of other signes in framing it, as we have, to declare our thoughts to others: for we may well conceive, that a Machine may be so made, that it may utter words, and even some proper to the corporal actions, which may cause some change in its organs; as if we touch it in some part, and it should ask what we would say; or so as it might cry out that one hurts it, and the like: but not that they can diversifie them to answer sensibly to all what shall be spoken in its presence, as the dullest men may do. And the second is, That although they did divers things aswel, or perhaps better, then any of us, they must infallibly fail in some others, whereby we might discover that they act not with knowledge, but onely by the disposition of their organs: for whereas Reason is an universal instrument which may serve in all kinde of encounters, these organs have need of some particular disposition for every particular action: whence it is, that its morally impossible for one Machine to have severall organs enough to make it move in all the occurrences of this life, in the same manner as our Reason makes us move.   (pp. 91–2)

An automaton might adequately replicate the outer actions of a human being, but it would lack two defining features of humanity. The first is the power to produce speech which is apt to any occasion, and therefore provides evidence of rationality. The second is related to the first in that Reason is 'an universal instrument' which enables man not simply to perform one task, like a machine, but to respond to 'all the occurrences of this life'. Reason is for Descartes therefore something akin to an aptness engine, which enables people to respond to unpredictable circumstances. He goes on to say that 'Pyes [Magpies] and Parrots can utter words even as we can, and yet cannot speak like us; that is to say, with evidence that they think what they say' (p. 93). Hence mankind cannot be imitated by a mechanism, or by an animal that lacks reason, and hence there must be a non-material

---

2. For Descartes's early experiences of automata at Fontainebleau or Saint-Germain-en-Laye, see John W. Yolton, *Thinking Matter: Materialism in Eighteenth-Century Britain* (Oxford, 1984), pp. 29–30.

power of reason superadded to the corporeal mechanisms of the human body in order to explain the distinction between human beings and animals or automata.

Descartes's discussion of automata had two major consequences for the history of *imitatio*. It potentially added to the growing penumbra of negative associations that clung to the concept, since it implied that a perfect imitator of another person was not simply a parrot or a magpie but actually something inhuman or akin to an automaton, which replicated its original as though a series of wheels and intricate escarpments rotated within his or her hands and head. A 'mechanical' imitator might lack the ability rationally to adapt to all circumstances which was a defining characteristic of humanity.

But Descartes also nudged thinking about imitation in quite different and potentially more positive directions. Because he argued that imitation of *speech* was beyond even the most sophisticated automaton, the concept of an automaton that could talk (or indeed an animal that could not just echo words but use language in the manner of a rational creature) acquired exceptional conceptual power. Not only would it miraculously transgress the divide between the human and the non-human; it would also have the potential to destabilize the mind/body dualism which Descartes was attempting to establish.

This made automata and talking animals fraught with philosophical significance for future thinkers who were less sure than Descartes that man was a hybrid of matter and spirit. John Locke in particular resisted this aspect of Descartes's thought. Rather than insisting that spirit was entirely distinct from matter, Locke allowed that God could endow matter with sentience and rationality. As a result he was willing to accept that in principle an animal could use language like a human being.[3] In a section of his extremely influential chapter on personal identity in the *Essay Concerning Human Understanding* (2.27.8) Locke relates a passage from the memoirs of Sir William Temple, which (with careful insistence that it simply reports the words of a witness) records an encounter with a remarkable talking parrot. That parrot could respond appropriately to questions (in Brazilian, translated variously into Dutch and French) with an apparently human intelligence. So when someone pointed at the prince of Nassau, and asked the parrot 'what he thought that Man was' it replied 'Some General or other'.[4]

3. Yolton, *Thinking Matter*, p. 35.
4. John Locke, *An Essay Concerning Human Understanding*, ed. P. H. Nidditch (Oxford, 1975), p. 333.

The talking parrot therefore cut across Descartes's rigid division between the 'mechanical' imitation of utterances by an animal or an automaton on the one hand and the rationality of human beings on the other. It supported Locke's argument that the defining characteristic of a person must be material continuity and a particular shape as well as rationality. But it also allowed that even a non-human imitator of human speech could display the human characteristics of using language aptly and rationally.

Descartes's arguments about the distinction between human beings and automata not only gave enormous conceptual power to articulate parrots. They also gave uncanny strength to a particular kind of imitator. What if an artist or an engineer was able to create a machine that could convincingly imitate human speech, and which might appear to think and reason? Such a creation would not simply threaten Descartes's binary distinction between mind and matter, but its inventor might legitimately claim to possess a creative power analogous to that of God, who could endow a purely material entity with reason. A person who created a mechanical imitation of a human being which appeared to think might be regarded as a kind of new Prometheus, who possessed a secret skill of bringing life to matter.

Imitating humans

Automata of course had a rich history well before Descartes: Homer's Hephaistos is at work creating a team of twenty robotic tripods which would come and go at his command in the *Iliad* (18.373–420). Mechanical marvels which appeared to live and so threatened the distinction between art and nature were staples of fiction from the middle ages onwards.[5] But Descartes gave a huge stimulus to the makers of these marvels—indeed he did so to such an extent that by the eighteenth century the myth had arisen that Descartes himself had constructed a mechanical model of his illegitimate daughter, and that he travelled with this mechanical human in a trunk. The

5. For a general history of automata, see Minsoo Kang, *Sublime Dreams of Living Machines: The Automaton in the European Imagination* (Cambridge, Mass., and London, 2011). For medieval automata, see Elly Rachel Truitt, *Medieval Robots: Mechanism, Magic, Nature, and Art* (Philadelphia, 2015); for the early modern period, see Wendy Beth Hyman, *The Automaton in English Renaissance Literature* (Farnham, 2011), the suggestive study by George L. Hersey, *Falling in Love with Statues: Artificial Humans from Pygmalion to the Present* (Chicago, Ill., and London, 2009), and Jonathan Sawday, *Engines of the Imagination: Renaissance Culture and the Rise of the Machine* (London, 2007), pp. 185–206.

daughter was called Francine, and, so the myth had it, was perhaps even named after the Francini brothers, who had constructed elaborate automata in Saint-Germain-en-Laye.[6] Was it possible to create machines that imitated life and speech so convincingly that they appeared to think or reason, or even to be substitute daughters?

By the 1780s a citizen strolling around London with time and five shillings to spare might have chosen to spend an afternoon in the company of a group of automata created by the ingenious inventors and clockmakers Pierre and Henri-Louis Jaquet-Droz, which were prodigiously realistic imitations of human beings. The fourth of these clockwork miracles was

> A figure representing a child of two years of age, seated on a stool, and writing at a desk. This figure dips its pen in the ink, shakes out what is superfluous, and writes distinctly and correctly whatever the company think proper to dictate, without any person's touching it. It places the initial letters with propriety, and leaves a suitable space between the words as it writes. When it has finished a line it passes on to the next, always observing the proper distance between the lines: while it writes, its eyes are fixed on its work, but as soon as it has finished a letter or a word, it casts a look at the copy, seeming to imitate it.[7]

Imitated life: what could it do but imitate texts? The great technical achievements of Jaquet-Droz built on the most notorious eighteenth-century automaton, which was a mechanical duck constructed by Jacques Vaucanson in 1738. This roboduck was designed to eat grain, digest it, and defecate. It was so lifelike that Vaucanson was compared by Voltaire to Prometheus, the bringer of fire and life, although its digestive processes fell a little short of the biological reality.[8] Those technical marvels in turn both built on and encouraged philosophical work by followers and critics of Descartes. Julien de La Mettrie's *L'Homme Machine* (translated in 1748 as *Man a Machine*) developed Descartes's account of automata in deliberately counter-Cartesian

---

6. See Stephen Gaukroger, *Descartes: An Intellectual Biography* (Oxford, 1995), pp. 1–2; and for a detailed account of Descartes's views on automata, pp. 276–90.
7. Henri-Louis Jaquet-Droz, *A Description of Several Pieces of mechanism . . . And which are now to be seen at the Great Room, no. 6, in King-Street, Covent-Garden* (London, 1780).
8. Jacques de Vaucanson, *An Account of the Mechanism of an Automaton . . . playing on the German Flute*, trans. John Theophilus Desaguliers (London, 1742), pp. 21–2: 'The Matter digested in the Stomach is conducted by Pipes, (as in an Animal by the Guts) quite to the Anus, where there is a Sphincter that lets it out. I don't pretend to give this as a perfect Digestion, capable of producing Blood and nutritive Particles for the support of the Animal. I hope no body will be so unkind as to upbraid me with pretending to any such Thing. I only pretend to imitate the Mechanism of that Action . . .'. See Christian Bailly and Sharon Bailly, *Automata: The Golden Age, 1848–1914* (London, 1987), p. 14. For Vaucanson's life and work, see André Doyon and Lucien Liaigre, *Jacques Vaucanson, mécanicien de génie* (Paris, 1966).

directions. La Mettrie adopted a hard-line mechanistic view of life as simply 'organized matter', akin to a finely tuned mechanical apparatus, and argued that not only animals but also human beings were mechanisms of this kind. Our reflexes automatically train us to imitate:

> We learn insensibly, from those we live with, their gestures, accents, &c., just as the eye-lid falls at the threatening of a blow, or as the body imitates mechanically and involuntarily all the postures and movements of a good pantomime.[9]

This emphasis on the mechanical foundations of human behaviour removed Descartes's distinction between men and animals, and hence La Mettrie could argue against Descartes that even animals might be trained to imitate human beings, and learn to speak:

> Why then should the education of baboons and monkeys be impossible? Why might they not at length, by dint of care, imitate, after the example of the deaf, the motions necessary for articulation? ... Mr Lock who certainly was never suspected of credulity, made no difficulty in believing the history Sir William Temple gives us in his memoirs, of a parrot that answered pertinently to every thing it was asked, and learnt like us to hold a conversation.[10]

La Mettrie was familiar not only with Locke's thinking about animated matter, but also with Vaucanson's marvellous automata, and goes so far as to imagine the creation of an automaton that talked—the creator of which would be a Prometheus, a god who could take the clay of matter and turn it into life:

> Since it required more art in Vaucanson to frame his mechanical musician, than in making his duck, sure then it must require still a greater degree of skill to form a speaking machine, which, perhaps, may not be altogether impossible, if we suppose a new Prometheus to start up, and put his hands to the work.   (pp. 61–2)

By the end of the eighteenth century mechanized models of human beings were not only philosophical reminders that mind and matter might be one substance, but also became fairground attractions. When William Wordsworth describes his residence in London in around 1791 in Book 7 of the 1805

---

9. Julien Offray de La Mettrie, *Man a Machine, Translated from the French of the Marquiss d'Argens* (London, 1749), p. 17. For the philosophical background and the French text, see Julien Offray de La Mettrie, *L'homme machine: A Study in the Origins of an Idea*, ed. Aram Vartanian (Princeton, 1960). For discussion of the relationship between Vaucanson and La Mettrie, see Catherine Liu, *Copying Machines: Taking Notes for the Automaton* (Minneapolis and London, 2000), pp. 76–105.

10. La Mettrie, *Man a Machine*, p. 21.

Prelude he represents the city as a place of imitated, rather than real, life. It is full of monstrous dreams and 'chattering monkeys' (1805, 7.668), of 'imitations fondly made in plain | Confession of man's weakness and his loves' (1805, 7.254–5). London is also full of models which, like the visions of the Temple in Milton's *Paradise Regained*, represent 'By scale exact, in model, wood or clay...St Peter's Church; or, more aspiring aim, | In microscopic vision Rome itself' (1805, 7.266–73). Wordsworth's description of this urban world of mimicry is distinctively Miltonic. Bartholomew Fair in particular is presented as a version of pandemonium: 'What a hell | For eyes and ears, what anarchy and din | Barbarian and infernal—'tis a dream, | Monstrous in colour, motion, shape, sight, sound' (1805, 7.659–62). It is also a place in which automata writhe and wriggle in Promethean mimicry of man:

> The bust that speaks and moves its goggling eyes,
> The waxwork, clockwork, all the marvellous craft
> Of modern Merlins, wild beasts, puppet-shows,
> All out-o'-th'-way, far-fetched, perverted things,
> All freaks of Nature, all Promethean thoughts
> Of man—his dulness, madness, and their feats
> All jumbled up together to make up
> This parliament of monsters.   (1805, 7.685–92)

This is a rewrite of Milton's hell as an urban world of automata. But this 'parliament of monsters' also imitates that other great imitative poet, Ben Jonson. Any description of Bartholomew Fair almost necessarily carried Jonsonian resonances because of his play of that name, but Wordsworth's tableau of automatic replicants of human beings also directly imitates a passage in Ben Jonson's poem the 'Execration upon Vulcan' (*Underwood* 43) which attacks the fantastical imaginings of romances:

> the whole sum
> Of errant knighthood, with their dames and dwarves,
>   The charmèd boats and their enchanted wharves,
> The Tristrams, Lanc'lots, Turpins, and the peers;
>   All the mad Rolands and sweet Oliveers
> To Merlin's marvels' and his cabal's loss,
>   With the chimera of the Rosy-cross,
> Their seals, their characters, hermetic rings,
>   Their gem of riches, and bright stone that brings
> Invisibility, and strength, and tongues...   (66–75)[11]

---

11. Text from Ben Jonson, *The Cambridge Edition of the Works of Ben Jonson*, ed. David M. Bevington, Martin Butler, and Ian Donaldson, 7 vols. (Cambridge, 2012).

Wordsworth's echoes of Jonson go beyond the references to Merlin and the marvellous into syntax and structure: 'And the peers' has a close metrical resemblance to Wordsworth's 'and their feats'. Wordsworth was reading Jonson's poems in February 1802 (from volume 4 of Anderson's *British Poets*)[12] just a few months before his visit in September 1802 to the real life Bartholomew Fair. That reading feeds back into the account of his experiences in London in the 1790s.[13] It created a curious fusion: the automotive, La Mettrie-style, mechanized imitations of life at the fair are described in words which imitate Jonson's contemptuous descriptions of romances.

This does not reflect a negative view of Jonson, or simply align him with the robotic mimicry of life, since Wordsworth admired his verse: a laurelled portrait of Ben still hangs in Rydal Mount.[14] Rather the London passage of *The Prelude* implicitly aligns the city as satirized by Jonson with the world of inorganic replication, of automata, and of soulless mechanical imitation of the human heart. This replica world was an enemy of the world of nature. That opposition is a distant descendent of Descartes's thinking: mind, life, and nature are ontologically distinct from their mechanized replicas in the city.

It is, however, highly suggestive that even as Wordsworth decries the artificial modelling of human behaviour in Bartholomew Fair he also represents it as a product of the 'Promethean thoughts | Of man'. In the romantic imagination the imitation of life by mechanical means occupied a strangely paradoxical zone. It reduced man to merely external behaviours, to the jolts and galvanic movements of the limbs, and thus implicitly reduced humanity to the status of a mere mechanism. But at the same time the artistry of the person who could imitate life so as to recreate it in this way was akin to that of Prometheus, the bringer of life. Automata therefore simultaneously made humans appear to be merely material things and akin to the gods.

This paradox made automata objects of a kind of double fear, at once of the maker and the thing. It was the principal reason why, by the second decade of nineteenth century, elaborately constructed artificial mechanisms which imitated not just prior texts but life itself became staples of gothic

12. Duncan Wu, *Wordsworth's Reading, 1800–1815* (Cambridge, 1995), pp. 121–2; Anne Barton, 'The Road from Penshurst: Wordsworth, Ben Jonson and Coleridge in 1802', *Essays in Criticism* 37 (1987), 209–33.

13. Ian Donaldson, *Ben Jonson: A Life* (Oxford, 2011), p. 194. Although Donaldson here discusses Wordsworth's description of Bartholomew Fair he does not connect it with the 'Execration'.

14. Barton, 'Road from Penshurst', p. 223.

horror fiction. The most famous example of such an ingenious human replicant was of course the beautiful clockwork woman Olympia in E. T. A. Hoffman's tale 'The Sandman' (which was written in 1815), who enchants the deranged hero Nathaniel. 'The Sandman' is presented as the primary instance of the uncanny in Sigmund Freud's 1919 essay on the subject; and Freud's essay begins by citing Ernst Jentsch's claim that 'one of the most successful devices for easily creating uncanny effects is to leave the reader in uncertainty whether a particular figure in the story is a human being or an automaton.'[15] Freud himself rapidly dismisses this claim, and locates the uncanny instead in the return of varieties of the repressed.

But Jentsch's claim does display historical acuity. 'The Sandman' is steeped in late eighteenth-century concerns about 'living imitations' of human beings, and the uncanny power possessed by those who create them. The hero Nathaniel relates his childish horror of the Sandman, who puts sand in the eyes of a sleepy child, and then comes to identify that figure with the sinister lawyer Coppelius, in whose presence his father dies while experimenting with alchemy. The hero is then given a telescope by a barometer seller called Coppola (whom he again identifies with the Sandman and the lawyer Coppelius), through which he views the beautiful daughter of his professor of physics, Olympia, with whom he falls in love. She turns out to be an automaton, whose language is limited to a repeated 'Ah—Ah'.[16]

The whole tale of the Sandman shows the fictional potential of the language traditionally used to describe imitation when it fused together with late eighteenth-century interests in automata. The hybrid being who creates the illusion of mechanical life, the Sandman/Coppelius/Coppola, is described as 'hideous spectral monster', while Clara, Nathaniel's human beloved, declares that he does not exist, but is no more than a 'phantom of ourselves'. The *simulacrum* becomes both the maker of artificial life and an external embodiment of our own fears. Meanwhile the Sandman reduces the living Nathaniel himself to a mechanical body (in a dream vision he 'screwed off my hands and feet' as though he were a machine (p. 144)). Nathaniel writes a poem about the Sandman which the living Clara urges him to destroy, at which he calls his living lover 'Thou inanimate, accursed

15. Sigmund Freud, *The Standard Edition of the Complete Psychological Works of Sigmund Freud*, ed. James Strachey and Anna Freud, 24 vols. (London, 2001), 17.227. On Hoffman's automata stories and their precursors, see Kang, *Automaton*, pp. 185–222.

16. Quotations from the earliest English translation in John Oxenford and C. A. Feiling, *Tales from the German: Comprising Specimens from the Most Celebrated Authors* (London, 1844), pp. 140–65.

automaton' (p. 154). 'The Sandman', which Freud saw as an uncanny fable about the repressed fear of castration, is rather more overtly a tale generated by post-Cartesian fears about the mechanization of life. The imitator becomes simultaneously the sinister double of the divine, the creator of artificial life, and also a force that reduces actual living beings to mechanized processes.

There is, however, something uncanny in the Freudian sense about this, because tales about the creation and destruction of automata feed off two deep human fears. One is the simple fear that human agents might themselves be no more than mechanical entities, who are entirely replicable through behavioural simulation, and whose bodies could be disassembled into material pieces. The other is the fear that a creator who could make such a being transgressed a boundary between the human and the divine. A simulated human being therefore embodies two taboos at once: it kills off the notion of a divine creator of the human soul and then revives that creator in human form. The fears arising from this are products of a widening division between the two aspects of literary imitation which in the entire history of thinking about the concept have never quite been resolved. An imitator might be a mechanical Cicero, assembling words in accordance with a prior pattern, or an imitator might be a great re-maker, whose talent can generate organic life, sinews and strength, from the materials of prior artists. Material and intellectual developments had the potential to probe these stress lines within the concept of imitation, and enable imitating authors to make from them fictions of uncanny power. Mary Shelley was to do just that.

Mary Shelley

In the interval between the writing of 'The Sandman' and its publication in 1817 there occurred a famous social gathering of the second generation of English romantic poets. In June 1816 Percy Bysshe Shelley, his new wife Mary Wollstonecraft, and Lord Byron whiled away an evening at the Villa Diodati near Geneva.[17] They read German ghost stories in French

---

17. On the composition, see Mary Wollstonecraft Shelley, *Frankenstein; or, The Modern Prometheus*, ed. Michael Kennedy Joseph (Oxford, 1969), pp. 224–7. Mary Shelley's journal from the period does not survive, and only resumes in July 1816. See Mary Wollstonecraft Shelley, *The Journals, 1814–1844*, ed. Paula R. Feldman and Diana Scott-Kilvert, 2 vols. (Oxford, 1987), 1.103–9. The account of the ghost stories related in August 1816 by 'Monk' Lewis, in Shelley, ed. Feldman and Scott-Kilvert, *The Journals, 1814–1844*, 1.126–9, may give a flavour of the evening.

translations, and decided to write their own versions of these widely imitated texts, out of a 'playful desire of imitation', as Percy Bysshe Shelley put it in 1817.[18] Mary Shelley in the Preface to the 1831 edition of *Frankenstein* describes herself attempting to create a tale in response to this imitation game. Wracking her brains for a story she found, if not nothing then an interior parallel to the Chaos of Milton's universe: 'Invention, it must be humbly admitted, does not consist in creating out of void, but out of chaos; the materials must, in the first place, be afforded: it can give form to dark, shapeless substances, but cannot bring into being the substance itself.'[19]

Some of those chaotic and overtly Miltonic dark 'materials'—matter from which the artist must generate life—were provided by a collection of French translations of German gothic tales called *Fantasmagoriana*, the English version of which begins by noting the 'multitude of contemptible imitations' of Mrs Radcliffe.[20] Other elements of what was to become *Frankenstein* grew from a thunderstorm on 13th June, and from group discussions about the very principles of life, and perhaps of the power of galvanism, on the 15th.[21] After these conversations Mary Shelley described herself having a dream in which she says she saw the ghostly origins of what became her most original and lasting creation: Frankenstein's monster: 'I saw the hideous phantasm of a man stretched out, and then, on the working of some powerful engine, show signs of life, and stir with an uneasy, half vital motion' (p. 441). That passage, like the whole novel, absorbs and reanimates the centuries-long arguments about what constitutes a 'living' imitation of a past text or of a human being.

That vision of a creature struggling between matter and life was coloured by Mary Shelley's own experience of giving birth to a child that died.[22] But it is also drenched in Milton. Mary Shelley is presenting herself as a new Eve, who dreams a dream which chaotically recombines memories of her last evening's talk, but which supplements those conversations (as Adam puts

18. Shelley, ed. Joseph, *Frankenstein*, p. 14.
19. Mary Wollstonecraft Shelley, *Frankenstein: or the Modern Prometheus: the Original Two-Volume Novel of 1816–1817 from the Bodleian Library manuscripts*, ed. Charles E. Robinson (Oxford, 2008), p. 440. Quotations are from this edition.
20. Sarah Elizabeth Utterson, *Tales of the Dead. Principally Translated from the French* (London, 1813), sig. a1.
21. John William Polidori, *The Diary of Dr John William Polidori, 1816: Relating to Byron, Shelley, etc*, ed. William Michael Rossetti (London, 1911), pp. 123–4.
22. Cf. the touching journal entry 19 March 1815, Shelley, *The Journals, 1814–1844*, 1.70: 'Dream that my little baby came to life again—that it had only been cold & that we rubbed it by the fire & it lived—I al awake & find no baby—I think about the little thing all day—not in good spirits.'

it when he describes the dream with which Satan inspires Eve in *Paradise Lost*) 'with addition strange' (*PL*, 5.226). This dream generates the materials from which a monstrous living 'phantasm' is created, a vision which resembles the sublime figure of Milton's Death, and which has a shadowy affinity with that earlier revenant, Virgil's ghost of Hector.[23] Frankenstein's monster unites the two aspects of imitation that so frequently occur in opposition to one another in this history: it is presented as a dream phantasm which is no more than an assemblage of matter and past experiences, but it is also presented as miraculous piece of mimicry which replicates the power of the creator by imitating life itself. It is the singular and inhumanly destructive production of a genius who can make matter into life, but it is also the uncanny destroyer of life.

The fact that *Frankenstein* was subtitled *The New Prometheus* is significant. Part of the monster's shadowy origins lie with the early makers of automata: like Vaucanson, the maker of mechanical flute-players and of mechanical defecating ducks, and like the puppets and automata described by Wordsworth, Frankenstein's monster is a product of Promethean creativity.[24]

However, Mary Shelley's monster is not a mechanical replicant of a human being like Olympia in 'The Sandman'. He augments the uncanniness of a material replicant by being a biological assemblage of parts gathered from the dead. The mechanical skill of early eighteenth-century makers of automata is replaced by what would now be called biological engineering, or what Mary Shelley herself calls chemistry. In the monster Promethean creative skill converges with grave-robbing and necromancy. And those themes are highlighted by Mary Shelley's self-conscious display of the acts of literary imitation from which the novel derives. The monster says that

23. Burton R. Pollin, 'Philosophical and Literary Sources of *Frankenstein*', *Comparative Literature Studies* 17 (1965), 97–108, pp. 104–5 summarizes the debts to *Paradise Lost*, without noting the extensive allusions to Eve, as does Brian Wilson Aldiss, *Billion Year Spree: The History of Science Fiction* (London, 1973), p. 27. Chris Baldick, *In Frankenstein's Shadow: Myth, Monstrosity, and Nineteenth-Century Writing* (Oxford, 1987), p. 40, notes but does not comment on what he calls 'the travesty of Eve's similar revelation in Book IV'.

24. Jon Turney, *Frankenstein's Footsteps: Science, Genetics and Popular Culture* (New Haven and London, 1998), p. 16. Cf. Samuel Holmes Vasbinder, *Scientific Attitudes in Mary Shelley's Frankenstein* (Ann Arbor, Mich., 1984), p. 49: 'the artificial man in *Frankenstein* is a markedly different creature from the automaton. Mary Shelley's being moves with ease and grace without a trace of clockwork action.' There is no clear evidence that Shelley read La Mettrie, but for parallels between the two writers, see Seamus Deane, *The French Revolution and Enlightenment in England, 1789–1832* (Cambridge, Mass., and London, 1988), p. 97. For the influence of other works of materialist philosophy, including Condillac's *Treatise on the Sensations* and David Hartley's *Observations on Man*, see Vasbinder, *Scientific Attitudes*, pp. 39–45.

when he first learnt to read he worked his way through three books:
Plutarch's *Lives*, Goethe's *The Sorrows of Werther*, and *Paradise Lost*. He explicitly
compares his experiences to those of Milton's Adam, who 'was allowed to
converse and acquire knowledge from beings of a superior nature' but 'considered Satan as my fitter mate' (p. 155).

The deepest origins of the monster, however—that male creation by a
fictional male scientist in a fiction created by a female author—lie with
Milton's 'mother of human race', Eve. Mary Shelley's description of the
monster's first moments of self-consciousness is a deliberate rewriting of Eve's
awakening into life. The monster hides in a hovel and observes the lives of
the residents in a pastoral cottage. From these humble folk this inhuman
creation acquires by imitation, like Locke's parrot, not just the ability to
repeat words but to use speech like a rational agent. Language acquisition is
rapidly followed by self-consciousness. He sees himself reflected in a 'transparent pool':

> I had admired the perfect forms of my cottagers—their grace, beauty, and
> delicate complexions: but how was I terrified, when I viewed myself in a
> transparent pool! At first I started back, unable to believe that it was indeed
> I who was reflected in the mirror; and when I became fully convinced that
> I was in reality the monster that I am, I was filled with the bitterest sensations
> of despondence and mortification.   (p. 139)

The echo of Eve echoing Ovid's Narcissus is unmissable: 'I started back'
quotes from Milton's imitation of Ovid's Narcissus ('I started back, | It
started back', *PL*, 4.462–3). Equally unmissable is the departure from the
source: the episode pointedly does not conclude as Milton does with
'pleased I soon returned'.[25] Mary Shelley without doubt recognized Milton's
overt allusion to Ovid's Narcissus in his description of Eve's creation: she
was reading Ovid through the spring of 1815, and Thomas Newton had
recorded that Milton 'expressly imitated' what he terms 'the famous story of
Narcissus in Ovid' in his 1749 edition of *Paradise Lost*.[26] Mary Jacobus has

25. Mary 'Read a little Ovid' on 23 April 1815 (Shelley, *The Journals, 1814–1844*, 1.76), and had been
    reading passages from the *Metamorphoses* (in Latin, *The Journals*, 1.89) throughout the middle
    of that month. She interwove this with reading Spenser, while her husband was reading
    Ariosto, and she also records *Paradise Lost* among her reading during the same period, as well
    as Humphrey Davy's *Elements of Chemical Philosophy* (1.96).

26. John Milton, *Paradise Lost: a Poem in Twelve Books*, ed. Thomas Newton, 2 vols. (London, 1749),
    1.264. Percy Shelley gave Mary the 1747 Dublin edition of *Paradise Lost* in 1814 or 1815 (which
    contains only notes on textual matters by John Hawkey), and regularly read to her from the
    poem. See Frederick L. Jones, 'Shelley and Milton', *Studies in Philology* 49 (1952), 488–519.
    There is no certainty about which other editions of Milton Shelley may have possessed: see

said that 'the most striking absence in *Frankenstein*, after all, is Eve's'.[27] The plot does indeed turn on Frankenstein's refusal to provide the monster with a bride and therewith the potential to reproduce itself. But although Milton's Eve may not be a literal presence in the work, she is an overwhelmingly strong influence on its poetics. The preface represents Mary Shelley's dreams and imagination as working with the sinister transformative power of Eve, and the monster's first moment of self-awareness is the mirror image of Eve's self-attraction towards her own image in the pool.

And that indicates the radicalism of *Frankenstein*. It is creating original life out of a feminized version of imitation theory. Erasmus had urged the imitator to bring forth a new birth when imitating. Generations of men trained in the arts of imitation were encouraged to model their activity as imitators on the power of the female body to give birth to a new child, which differed from but resembled its parents. Mary Shelley in effect makes Milton's Eve the origin both of her own act of invention and of the moment when her creation becomes self-aware. She produces a feminized version of Descartes's cogito: the monster sees what he is at the moment he most closely imitates Milton's Eve. He thinks, and he is; and at that moment he both learns to speak and imitates Eve.

The awakening of the monster through this imitation of Eve owes much to what might be called an affective turn in writing about imitation in the later eighteenth century—in which Milton's Eve played a significant part. In particular it recalls a notable passage in Edward Young's *Conjectures on Original Composition* (1759). Young, who was no friend to imitators, laments that Nature 'brings us into the world all Originals: No two faces, no two minds, are just alike; but all bear Nature's evident mark of Separation on them. Born Originals, how comes it to pass that we die Copies?' The reason, he declares, is 'that Ape imitation'.[28] He then goes on to ask a key question. How does a poet *know* when he has produced an 'original' rather than a copy? Young's answer to this question is striking. He compares the moment when a writer recognizes his own genius to the episode in which Eve sees herself reflected in the lake: 'During his happy confusion, it may be said to

Jean de Palacio, 'Shelley's Library Catalogue', *Revue de Littérature Comparée* 36 (1962), 270–6. Pollin, 'Philosophical and Literary Sources of *Frankenstein*', pp. 102–3 discusses the influence of Ovid's Pygmalion and Prometheus on Mary Shelley.

27. Mary Jacobus, 'Is there a Woman in this Text?', *New Literary History* 14 (1982), 117–41 (p. 130).
28. Edward Young, *Conjectures on Original Composition: In a Letter to the Author of Sir Charles Grandison* (London, 1759), p. 42.

him as to Eve at the Lake, "What there thou seest, fair creature is thyself". Genius, in this view, is like a dear friend in our company under disguise; who while we are lamenting his absence, drops his mask, striking us at once with equal surprize and joy."[29]

Young was more than moderately audacious in making this comparison: he knew very well that the lines in which Milton described Eve's first moments were an exact metaphrase from Ovid, and yet he quotes them at the moment he describes the self-recognition of an original, creative genius. The maker creates and then recognizes his own replicant in his Genius, and that replicant becomes the object of an emotional reaction. It may be a friend or—as it was to become in *Frankenstein*—a fiend. Young also more than once associates the creation of life with the power of Prometheus. Where Addison's *Cato* is like a cold statue, Shakespeare or Otway, he argues, 'would have outdone Prometheus' (p. 93) if they had addressed the same subject. A genius creates, Prometheus-like, his own living image, a secret friend and double of himself.

In making this argument Young himself developed a longer-term set of shifts in thinking about imitation. Richard Hurd's 1751 *Discourse Concerning Poetical Imitation* had argued that authors can resemble each other and even fall in love one with another: 'similarity of genius, alone, will almost necessarily determine a writer to the love and studious emulation of some other. For, though it is with the minds, as the faces of men, that no two are exactly and in every feature alike; yet the general cast of their genius, as well as the air and turn of the countenance, will frequently be very *similar* in different persons. When two such spirits approach, they run together with eagerness and rapidity: the instinctive bias of the mind towards *imitation* being now quickened by *passion*.'[30] That description of the relationship between an imitator and an *exemplum* amplifies the Earl of Roscommon's injunction to translators in 1684, to 'chuse an *Author* as you chuse a *Friend*. | United by this Sympathetick Bond, | You grow Familiar, Intimate and Fond'.[31]

Hurd suggested that an imitator could legitimately display a loving resemblance to an original which was based on a natural affinity between the two authors, but the vocabulary in which he makes that claim is particularly

29. Young, *Original Composition*, p. 51.
30. Richard Hurd, *Q. Horatii Flacci Epistola ad Augustum, with an English Commentary and Notes. To which is Added, A Discourse Concerning Poetical Imitation, by the Author of the Commentary on the Epistle to the Pisos* (London, 1751), p. 196.
31. Wentworth Dillon, Earl of Roscommon, *An Essay on Translated Verse* (London, 1684), p. 7.

rich: 'the air and turn of the countenance' is an evocation of the elusive spirit, the *quidditas*, of a person that inheres in transient gesture and idiosyncratic expressions, and which is distinctive to an individual. Imitation is therefore presented as a version of falling in love with your own image and likeness, to which you will never have a *perfect* resemblance, because each person has their own 'air' or distinctive mode of being. Like Eve by the pool, an imitator can fall in love with his double; but the imitator will always differ from the work with which she falls in love or in which she recognizes herself. From this it was a short but significant step to Young's claim that the original artist produces and recognizes a work which is his genius, his *own* image and likeness, at once like and not like its creator, 'a dear friend in our company under disguise'. The creation of genius consequently becomes a creature with a potentially frightening autonomy.

Frankenstein's monster becomes Frankenstein's double, the shadowy enemy and Promethean creation of his genius that always walks beside him; and the monster's own frustrated desire for a friend and likeness in a female monster with whom he might bring forth more imitated men turns into a violent desire to destroy his maker. Traces of that violent transformation of the imitative arts can also be found in Young, who argued that an excessive admiration for the ancients was potentially a source of crushing fear: 'Too formidable an Idea of their Superiority, like a Spectre, would fright us out of a proper use of our Wittes; and dwarf our Understanding, by making a Giant of theirs' (p. 25). That sentence has been seen as evidence for the growing sense of the 'burden of the past' in later eighteenth-century writing.[32] But it also potentially implies that imitation could create a double bind of fear: looking back to the past makes ancient texts become terrifying in their inimitable and gigantic scale; but creating something new from these giants of the past might generate something in the present which shared their monstrous vastness.

Frankenstein is unclassical in its intellectual origins to the point of deliberately drawing attention to the fact—perhaps in order to distinguish it from the overtly Greek-based transformation of Prometheus in the *Prometheus Unbound* by Mary Shelley's husband. The scientific discoveries of the hero are associated with Eastern rather than Western science, perhaps as a result of the emphasis placed by Humphry Davy on the Arabic origins of chemistry in his *Elements of Chemical Philosophy*, which the Shelleys were

32. Walter Jackson Bate, *The Burden of the Past and the English Poet* (London, 1971), pp. 55–6.

reading at this time, and the monster learns to speak at the same time as Safie, the daughter of a Turkish merchant, rather than through, say, overhearing Latin lessons at a grammar school.[33] But in 1815 Mary Shelley, herself working through Ovid in Latin, was surrounded by the classical world: in July 1816 her husband was reading Lucretius and Pliny's letters, and by August had moved on to Tacitus as well, of course, as *Paradise Lost*, which he read aloud to his wife on several evenings in November 1816.[34] The giant figure of Frankenstein's monster is not overtly an imitation of the ancients, but he is a monster who recalls in living form the gigantic work of Milton. He is a shadow who follows his creator, turning the creative output of the imitator of God into a source of terror and destruction, and transforming the love a genius might feel for his creations into fear.

The conceptual shape of *Frankenstein* displays a further debt to the classical rhetorical tradition. For Quintilian the *vis*, the original spark, the *ingenium* of an author is inimitable, and cannot be encapsulated in rules or methods. It is only visible in exemplary form, which may be not only unique but also in practice inimitable. The parallel mystery in *Frankenstein* is the secret of the monster's vitality, which remains a dark mystery—indeed something akin to a jealously guarded piece of intellectual property. The monster's two creators, both Mary Shelley and Victor Frankenstein, do not wish to reveal the processes of his creation. This is presented as a moral matter by Frankenstein, since he does not want to allow others to imitate his terrible fate. But it was obviously convenient for Mary Shelley, since it freed her from providing the full experimental recipe for the creation of new life, which might, shall we say, have been a trifle hard for her to do. Whatever its origins, however, that withholding of the central scientific mystery of the novel has the effect of transforming the inimitable Promethean ingenuity that creates a living being from the fragments of earlier writers into a scientific miracle over which its author wishes to retain control, and which no other person will be able to imitate.

And that emphasis on the singularity and inimitability of the monster is lightly echoed in the imagery of the novel. The monster is a creation of such striking novelty that no one can tread in his footsteps. When it is first glimpsed across the ice 'it was impossible to follow his track' (p. 52), and the narrator Walton seeks in the extreme north to 'tread a land never before

33. Humphry Davy, *Elements of Chemical Philosophy. Part 1. Vol. 1* (London, 1812), p. 17: 'The speculative ideas of the Arabians were more or less adopted by their European disciples.'
34. Shelley, *The Journals, 1814–1844*, 1.121, 130, 146–7.

imprinted by the foot of man' (p. 45). *Frankenstein* leads us back to that realm of trackless wastes over which that great innovator Lucretius had sought to plot a path, and into which Wordsworth had attempted to soar in *The Recluse*. Frankenstein's monster grows from eighteenth-century debates about mechanical life and from later eighteenth-century imitation theory; and those elements, hybridized with eighteenth-century arguments about literary property, combine together in the fashionable shape of highly imitable German gothic tales.[35]

From monsters to clones

Mary Shelley's creation had, as we now say, 'a life of its own' in the monster's afterlife and imitations in film and in fiction.[36] Those imitations cast a long oblique light on the way in which the history of thinking about imitation has influenced present-day concerns. If we, like Frankenstein's monster spying on his cottagers, peer through the window of an average living-room in the age of the DVD we might see a scene of family contentment. The dog is on the sofa. The children are swearing. They stroke the dog and munch popcorn in order to avoid reading the following words on the screen:

> This copyrighted work has been licensed for private use only and any other use of the whole or any part of the material (including adapting, copying, issuing copies, unauthorised lending, public performance, broadcasting or making the same available to or via the internet or wireless technology or authorising any of the foregoing) is strictly prohibited.

These forbidding words appear every time a DVD of the TV series *Battlestar Galactica* is played. The subject-matter of *Battlestar Galactica* is ultra-neoclassical. It begins with the destruction of an empire, from which a remnant of humanity flees in search of a new home planet. Our heroes are guided to a new planet by hints and warnings from ambiguous gods. Those on the

---

35. For the irony that the work was rarely reprinted in the mid-nineteenth century because its copyright was owned by the publisher Richard Bentley, who was not interested in exploiting it for a popular market, see William St. Clair, *The Reading Nation in the Romantic Period* (Cambridge, 2004), pp. 357–73.

36. Albert J. Lavalley, 'The Stage and Film Children of *Frankenstein*: A Survey', in George Levine and U. C. Knoepflmacher, eds., *The Endurance of Frankenstein* (Berkeley, Los Angeles, and London, 1979), 243–89, and Andrew Smith, *The Cambridge Companion to Frankenstein* (Cambridge, 2016), pp. 175–255.

space-ship are the Aeneases of the future, seeking a new empire without end somewhere on a new planet.

They are also on the run from their enemies, the Cylons. These are second-generation robots, machine-made *simulacra* of human beings, who have flesh and blood and emotions. There are only twelve types of these fleshly Cylons, but there are many instances of each type. When an individual Cylon is killed, however, the experiences of that particular instance of the type are downloaded into a new identical body. This means that as each example of each Cylon lives its life (repeatedly), and is repeatedly reborn in a new version of the same body, he or she accumulates memories and experiences. As a result each individual instance of each type increasingly diverges in experience and attitudes from the other physically identical members of their type. Some of the Cylons are under deep cover on board the battlestar itself. These imitations of humans are perfect: they behave like humans and believe themselves to be humans.[37] They have all the experiences we think of as uniquely human: they feel pain, have consciousness, fall in love. The Cylons, allegories as they are of ethnic minorities and reds under the bed, are variously called by humans 'machines' and 'toasters'. It is said that their emotions and experiences are just programming. But as some of the people who thought they were humans discover that they in fact are Cylon sleepers, the boundary between the replicant and the human becomes confused. The reds, the robots, the replicants, could be sitting beside you on the sofa. They could even be you. We might all be perfect, artificial humans, copied exactly from nature, but mechanically assembled, each believing ourselves to be a person with their own unique life story.

The plot of the replicant that thinks of itself is human, and in which humans and replicants are all but indistinguishable, has become the counter-Cartesian cliché of science fiction. Indeed *Battlestar Galactica*, a remake of an earlier TV series, is itself a kind of replicant of the conventions of clone and android fiction, a set of conventions which go back at least to *Frankenstein*, in which mechanically engineered replicants of human beings pose questions about the nature of humanity, and embody the fear that the

---

37. Cf. 'By the late twentieth century, our time, a mythic time, we are all chimeras, theorized and fabricated hybrids of machine and organism; in short we are cyborgs. The cyborg is our ontology; it gives us our politics. The cyborg is a condensed image of both imagination and material reality', Donna Haraway, 'A Manifesto for Cyborgs', in Linda J. Nicholson, ed., *Feminism/Postmodernism* (New York and London, 1990), 190–233 (p. 191). On clones in allusive fictions, see Sarah Annes Brown, *A Familiar Compound Ghost: Allusion and the Uncanny* (Manchester, 2012), pp. 70–2.

human power of artificial creation is potentially self-destructive, that a talion or punishment lies in wait for those who seek to replicate the skill of their own maker.[38]

But *Battlestar Galactica* is also itself a clever thinking machine. The way in which the Cylon-copies become 'unique' and almost indistinguishable from humans illustrates a very deep feature of our culture, which is a legacy from late romantic responses to the history of imitation. The uncertainty about how an imitation is to be distinguished from its copy has led to the ever-increasing valuation of aspects of human beings which are or ought to be 'inimitable'—which might be external qualities, such as the 'air' or distinctive character of their countenance, or internal ones, such as memories, desires, loves, and creative impulses.

Indeed the rise in the value attached to these 'inimitable' aspects of human beings is so closely connected to the rise of technologies of reproduction that this connection might even be formulated in the form of a crude law, which we might call the Law of Replicants. This states that value attached to unique and supposedly inimitable human attributes like consciousness, creativity, and imagination is directly proportional to the ease with which it is possible to create exact copies in any medium. The law might be regarded as the flip-side of Walter Benjamin's claim that the age of mechanical reproduction dissolves the aura which surrounds the work of art: the possibility of bio-mechanical reproduction of human beings generates an intense and anxious valuation of things in the mind which are not replicable.[39]

As possibilities for digital, physical, biological, and mechanical replication multiply, so human beings increasingly desire to believe that they are, as creative or experiential agents, inimitable. The ability to copy and paste a text with a couple of clicks is accompanied by growing sanctions against plagiarism and rewards for 'independence of mind' and 'creativity'. Those legal and cultural sanctions have psychological equivalents in the beliefs that only human beings can fall in love, have consciousness, have a creative imagination or desires. That insistence on the uniqueness of interior experience can also have a religious dimension: as one writer on cloning has put it 'If a clone is created, how could its soul be different from the soul of the person who is cloned?'[40] The things about us that are not replicable are

---

38. See Robert Plank, 'The Golem and the Robot', *Literature and Psychology* 15 (1965), 12–27.
39. Walter Benjamin, *Illuminations*, ed. Hannah Arendt (London, 1970), p. 220.
40. Gina Bari Kolata, *Clone: The Road to Dolly, and the Path Ahead* (London, 1997), p. 7. Wendy Doniger, 'Sex and the Mythological Clone', in Martha Craven Nussbaum and Cass R. Sunstein,

the features which separate us from the idols of the marketplace, the infinitely replicable objects which factories, Microsoft, Apple, and biotech companies sell to us—and which they sell to us in ways that attempt to ensure we can only buy one, and not replicate it.

The ability to create copies of human beings in biological as well as mechanical form both amplifies the valuation of the 'unique' and generates increasingly unsustainable distinctions between the unique biological form of a person and the copies which are physically indistinguishable from that person. There is a strong analogy here to the role played by technologies of print in the Ciceronian controversies in early modernity: a desire to replicate the inimitable *vis* and *ingenium* of an earlier orator grows in proportion to the ease with which his words can be codified and manipulated and repeated.

A crude version of this law operates in many fictions and fantasies and even beliefs about clones. The leader of a sect known as the Raëlists, Claude Vorilhon, otherwise known as Raël, believes that he was abducted by aliens called the Elohim and cloned: 'I saw the Elohim insert a cell taken from my forehead into a huge aquarium-like machine... and then watched a perfect copy of myself grow in just a few seconds.'[41] This experience, which he swears is his own, but which sounds suspiciously like a bad memory of a left-over episode of the *X-Files*, has made Raël a firm advocate of human cloning. He believes we should make clones of ourselves—or at least of nice rich people—and then download our consciousness into these clones. He is a little vague about how this will be done, perhaps because he wishes to keep his patent methods for perfectly reproducing consciousness itself a secret.

Raël's revelatory tract, called *Yes to Human Cloning*, has a preface by his psychoneuroimmunologist (a professional group which is perhaps only to be found in California) Dr Marcus Wenner. Dr Wenner assures us that in the future we will be able to 'grow wings just for the beauty of it' and 'Since computers will take care of all our basic needs, the least replaceable human characteristics of love, imagination and consciousness will become the most

eds., *Clones and Clones: Facts and Fantasies about Human Cloning* (New York and London, 1997), 114–38 gives a wide-ranging survey of writing about clones and doubles. Joan Haran, Jenny Kitzinger, Maureen McNeil, and Kate O'Riordan, *Human Cloning in the Media: From Science Fiction to Science Practice* (London, 2008) surveys anxieties about the topic in a range of media. Genevieve Liveley, 'Science Fictions and Cyber Myths: or, Do Cyborgs Dream of Dolly the Sheep?', in Vanda Zajko and Miriam Leonard, eds., *Laughing With Medusa* (Oxford, 2006), 275–94 discusses classical predecessors of automata and cyborgs.

41. Claude Vorilhon [a.k.a. Raël], *Yes to Human Cloning* (London, Sydney, and Los Angeles, 2001), p. 26.

precious commodities and the order of the day' (p. 25). It is hard to imagine a clearer instantiation of the rule that the valuation of human consciousness as a unique phenomenon is directly proportional to the ease with which it is thought to be possible to generate copies: consciousness, love, and imagination become items of high price on a menu, 'the order of the day' in an environment in which bodies can be reduplicated. It is these inimitable qualities which will be downloaded into clones of our bodies by Raël's organization Clonaid, and allowed to live for ever in endlessly replicated and renewed bodies. Clonaid offers a future with wings, and with regular consciousness downloads one need never get old.

The belief that the precious singularity that is our consciousness needs simply to be re-embodied in order to live for ever is among the grubbier relics of Cartesian dualism. But that belief is also historically entangled with the longer history related in this book. The human clone hits a raw nerve in the history of thinking about imitation because it renders unstable the claim that an imitator resembles the imitated author as a child resembles its parent. The promise of biological differentiation implicit in the metaphor of parentage collapses back into identity, and the clone is at once child and the shadowy semblance or *simulacrum* of its original; meanwhile the inimitable qualities of the original, its singular being, its *vis* and *ingenium*, its inner consciousness or the ghost in its shell, become the *je ne sais quoi*, the undefinable uniqueness, the unreproducible treasure that is separable from its bodily form. And that treasure of uniqueness becomes more valued the more it is threatened by its replicas.

One of the more immediate sources of Raëlism was David Rorvik's *In His Image: The Cloning of a Man* (1978), which purported to relate a true story of how a rich person called Max paid biologists to have himself cloned. The book resulted in newspaper headlines which declared human cloning had happened, and was followed by angry denials from scientists that human cloning was possible, and even a hearing in Congress.[42] *In His Image* is mostly written in the flat style appropriate to paid reportage; but its larger historical significance lies in the artistry with which Rorvik repeatedly entangled a scientific fable about cloning with larger concerns about reproduction and imitation.

So the surrogate mother of Max2 becomes obsessed with Max, whose clone she is carrying. She draws a picture of him. It is unlikely that Rorvik

---

42. Kolata, *Clone*, pp. 80–90.

was directly aware of Dionysius of Halicarnassus or of the traditional associations of imitation with both physical replication and pictorial representation, but Max 'would often sneak glances, he told me, at a painting of him she was working on—and continued to work on for some months. Her changing conception of him, he felt, was reflected in the painting; it seemed to be undergoing constant metamorphosis. After she finds out that the child she was carrying would be his heir, he claimed, her portrayal of him became both "more handsome" and "a bit more sinister".'[43] The evident artifice in this relationship between art and life (faint shadows of Dorian Gray colour the scientific experiment) should have made it obvious that this novel was a work of fiction: the mother of a clone is an artist whose 'conception' (at once biological and artistic) grows with her foetus. The imitator, the mother who draws the father of her child, brings forth at once a pictorial representation and a biological reproduction, a biological reproduction which resembles its original even more closely than a child resembles its father or a portrait its sitter.

Max is also haunted by doubles. He has both a living clone and a *simulacrum* in the mind: 'when he was very young he had persistent dreams in which his phantom playmate looked exactly like himself' (pp. 69–70). The twin concerns of duplication through birth and replication through art, those shadowy legacies of Plato's *Republic*, become ever more entangled as a result of developments within the biological sciences.

The possibility of replicating human beings exactly has prompted a desperate desire to believe that there is in fact something unreproducible in each of us. It becomes almost irresistible to believe that one is beyond imitation when one is aware that there are so many means of reproducing our lives and our texts that one is clearly *not* beyond imitation. This complex has given rise to a particular form of postmodern pessimism in which the infinite reproducibility of texts and of persons provokes a nostalgic reaction for the pre-postmodern era (whenever that was) in which Selves had Others and parents against which to define themselves, and in which life was not just a pale imitation of the models of it that we see in the movies.

What we might term the clone nexus—in which the possibility of exact replication ad infinitum of a model leads to the valuation of the *exemplum* as a precious and unique archetype even as it is absorbed into a multiplicity of its own *simulacra*—is a deep structural feature of postmodernism. Jean

43. David M. Rorvik, *In his Image: The Cloning of a Man* (London, 1978), p. 68.

Baudrillard is the shrewdest exponent and anatomist of this viewpoint. He regards cloning as an extension of the prostheses of civilization into the very structures of the cell and of personal identity. The infinite mechanical reproducibility of people generates a kind of hell—not a Sartrean hell of other people, but a hell of universal sameness, in which all people become replications of other people, and in which science and technology create endless reduplications of sameness with no identifying difference. That multiplication of sameness becomes destructive: 'By becoming transparent in its genetic, biological and cybernetic being, the body even develops an allergy to its own shadow. Otherness denied becomes a spectre and returns in the form of a self-destructive process. This, too, is the transparency of Evil.'[44]

As in *Frankenstein*, Baudrillard's *simulacrum* returns as a destructive force which exerts punishment for the arts of scientific replication. And for Baudrillard the world of postmodernity is one big *simulacrum*, in which 'A whole generation of films is emerging that will be to those one knew what the android is to man: marvellous artefacts, without weakness, pleasing simulacra that lack only the imaginary, and the hallucination inherent to cinema.'[45] Baudrillard's cultural criticism here is hard to distinguish from the remarks of a grumpy old man in the back row of *Blade Runner 2049* who complains that it is not as good as the original which it imitates. Clone fictions do not simply display a usurpation of the real by its simulacral resemblance, or mark the decline of culture into a shower of alluring semblances, but something very different: they show that experientially distinctive concepts such as imagination and creativity are increasingly imbued with disproportionate value as a result of the reproducibility of their outer bodily semblances. The multiplication of visually or biologically or cinematically indistinguishable doubles produces a yearning for the 'original' and the authentic. The 'real' in this sense is not the antithesis of the replicable but a function of its replicability.

It was characteristic of the postmodern moment to attach great weight to scientific discoveries, the multiplication of media, and industrial transformations, and to present these material changes as permeating and radically transforming attitudes towards the ego. Indeed it may be a characteristic shared by most ages that construct themselves *as* ages to exaggerate the differences between their own condition and that of the past, and perhaps

44. Jean Baudrillard, *The Transparency of Evil: Essays on Extreme Phenomena*, trans. James Benedict (London, 1993), p. 139.
45. Jean Baudrillard, *Simulacra and Simulation*, trans. Sheila Faria Glaser (Ann Arbor, Mich., 1994), p. 45.

thereby to occlude the historical origins of their own thinking. What creative genius of singularity would not wish to occlude the forces by which she was made? The possibility of a mind becoming a machine and vice versa, or of a test-tube substituting for the dances of seduction and reproduction, come to be seen as the key determinants of thought about personal identity. Technological forces distinctive to the modern world make us (we want to believe) unlike any previous generation in losing all sense of the other and all sense of being able to distinguish ourselves from the prostheses and technologies which could (who knows) have made us. Cloning becomes a metaphor for a horror of undifferentiated existence in which all are one, seamlessly connected to the technologies which enable the infinite reduplication of human beings who are identical.

This is a powerful mythology. But it is a mythology. It brings with it the easy consolation of apparent uniqueness: we postmoderns are entirely unique in being infinitely replicable, in being people into whom industrial and digital processes can bury themselves as though they are part of ourselves, as extensions or prostheses or replications of mind. The technological developments in the twentieth century are indeed innovations. But the discourses with which we describe these technologies are ancient. A central reason why these technological developments appear so sinister is because they interact with a much deeper fault-line within the ways in which human identity and difference have been talked about in the West.

When someone imitates another person, what occurs? If the beneficent version of that process is represented as a quasi-genetic relationship between imitator and *exemplum*, in which the former recreates the latter in a new shape but with a family resemblance, and the maleficent version of it is a spectral resemblance that is the same as an archetype but lacks its bodily presence, then cloning and digital replication almost necessarily generate anxiety. Those material practices set a larger vocabulary for self-constitution at war with itself. The language used in the literary tradition to describe the imitation of authors is among the discursive constitution of postmodern pessimism, just as much as the possibility of cloning and the prostheticization of the human intellect are among its material foundations. Baudrillard could not have written about biotechnology and digital technologies in the terms which he uses if it had not been for Quintilian, for Plato, and for the larger history of *imitatio*. Anxiety that our whole world is a *simulacrum* is a consequence of the way that the language of imitation has spun outwards and away from the larger classical tradition.

But that anxiety is not therefore trivial. It has the potential for great literary power because it cuts so deep into inherited conceptions of personal identity, of artistic skill, of how human beings replicate, and of creativity. Kazuo Ishiguro's *Never Let Me Go* (2005) is a novel about a group of children who are apparently in an orphanage. They are gradually revealed to be clones. They have been reproduced in order to provide organs which could prolong the lives of the wider population of 'real' people—which is one of the long-standing fears about the potential abuse of cloning.[46] Ishiguro never uses the word 'imitation' in the novel, but *Never Let Me Go* is a species of imitation, which follows at a distance those unfollowable footprints of Frankenstein's monster.[47]

Ishiguro marks that imitation—as imitating authors often do—by an allusion. Frankenstein's monster learns to speak from a family who live in a cottage. In *Never Let Me Go*, the cloned organ-donors move from school to 'the Cottages' in the later part of their lives. Here they watch and learn from the 'veterans', slightly older clones, who have been out in the world for some time. The new arrivals start to copy the behaviour of the veterans. The imitators begin to notice in turn that 'so many of their mannerisms were copied from the television'.[48] 'I began to notice all kinds of other things the veteran couples had taken from TV programmes: the way they gestured to each other, sat together on sofas, even the way they argued and stormed out of rooms' (p. 110). There is a Baudrillardian pessimism in the air here: how deep does cloning go? Are our behaviours as well as our genes purely a matter of social replication?

The child clones do not know whose genetic material was used to make them, but inevitably they call the people from whom they were 'copied' their 'models'.[49] Ishiguro plays on that complex word in various ways. The narrator Kathy at one point flips rapidly through a collection of pornographic magazines in search of her 'model', since she is convinced that she is so subject to sexual urges that she must take her genesis from a 'model' in

46. George Johnson, 'Soul Searching', in Nussbaum and Sunstein, eds., *Clones and Clones*, 67–70, p. 69: 'Nightmare of the week goes to those who imagine docile flocks of enslaved clones raised for body parts. But the most fundamental fear is that the soul will be taken by this penetrating new photography called cloning.'

47. See Aldiss, *Billion Year Spree*, pp. 7–39 for the now traditional positioning of *Frankenstein* at the origins of science fiction.

48. Kazuo Ishiguro, *Never Let Me Go* (London, 2005), p. 110.

49. 'I don't see how it matters. Even if you found your possible, the actual model they got you from. Even then, I don't see what difference it makes to anything', Ishiguro, *Never Let Me Go*, p. 151.

this sense (pp. 122–5). This play on the word 'model' has become a recurrent trope in clone fictions: in the film *The Island* (2005) the 'original' of the clone played by Scarlett Johansson is also a 'model' in the photographic sense, whom the clone first sees on an advertising hoarding, in images apparently of herself which are multiplied around her like visual *simulacra*, just as she reproduces her biological 'model' in physical form. *The Island*, indeed, stands in relation to *Never Let Me Go* as private medicine does to the National Health Service, since in it the rich pay to have themselves cloned so they can have a store of their own organs in case they become ill. In *Never Let Me Go*, on the other hand, the organs of the clones are implicitly common property which can be used to cure any 'real' human who is in need.

But it is here that Ishiguro plays a clever trick with the conceptual nexus which had grown up around cloning and inimitability in the twentieth century. The clones believe that if they can persuade the authorities that they have whatever it is that makes 'real' and distinctive human beings they will be saved from having their organs harvested. Might they possess something akin to Edward Young's conception of genius, which will turn them from mere reflections of their 'model' into living alternatives to it? At their school they are encouraged to draw pictures. The best, the most distinctive, are taken off for a gallery. Can the clones create? Love? Can they do all the singular and inimitable things which make people more than bodies? The law of replicants is absolutely at the heart of this novel, which casts a dark and sardonic light on myths about human creativity: in an environment in which exact copies of the human are infinitely producible, the distinctive and supposedly inimitable human capacity to create new life from a 'model' becomes of infinite value: that ability is what might carry replicants over the arbitrary boundary between the human and the merely material resource, and save their lives.

Never Let Me Go suggests that the 'distinctive' human abilities to love and to create are illusions, and illusions moreover which are designed to keep the world as it is. One of the main clone characters, Tommy, has failed to draw pictures in his youth. Near the end of his life-term, as his organs are about to be harvested and he is about to be killed, he starts drawing strange animals. Later still, he believes that his pictures could be used to show that he has a soul, and so save him. So he tries even harder to produce original works. These later pictures represent weird versions of frogs. Kath, the narrator, says 'It came to me that Tommy's drawings weren't as fresh now. Okay, in many ways these frogs were a lot like what I'd seen back at the Cottages.

But something was definitely gone, and they looked laboured, almost like they'd been copied' (p. 221).

It had to be frogs rather than anything else that Tommy the clone draws in these efforts to prove that he is a creative artist. The first organism to have been cloned in 1952 was a tadpole, and the earliest experiments in cloning were conducted on amphibians—which resulted in some strange doubled versions of tadpoles.[50] Weird pictures of frogs, the most clonable creature, and pictures that themselves look like copies, are all the poor clone can produce as a testament to his soul. The replica human believes himself to be creating; but all he is doing is replicating the origin of his origins, the cloning of frogs. *Brekekex koax koax*, over and over again—in exactly the same voice, a chorus of clones, drawing pictures of mutant frogs. Oh brave new world that has the same people in it over and over again—and in which the myth that what distinguishes the human from the non-human is an ability to create enables us to kill others in order to prolong our own singular lives.

Imitation is one of the great migrant concepts in Western literature, and in clone fiction it migrates and mutates from classics to clastics—a word which according to the *OED* entered the English language in the late nineteenth century to describe '(Of a model) Composed of a number of separable pieces; pertaining to such a model'. The word derives from *klan*, to break up, and has the same root as the Greek word klōn, which means 'twig', and which is the origin of the English word 'clone'. It is possible for life to be disassembled into its constituent organs, and then reassembled, like Frankenstein's monster, or for it to be replicated from DNA taken out of the nucleus of frog cells to create a perfect copy of an earlier life form. The confused arguments over imitation in the classical tradition—how do you distinguish a 'living' imitation from a mere *simulacrum*?—have migrated away from the classical tradition, but mutant remnants of them surround our lives and shape our understanding of ourselves. Present-day Anglo-American culture values myths of individuality and uniqueness to the point at which

50. Robert Briggs and Thomas J. King, 'Transplantation of Living Nuclei from Blastula Cells into Enucleated Frogs' Eggs', *Proceedings of the National Academy of Science* 38 (1952), 455–63. The method is anticipated in Hans Spemann, *Embryonic Development and Induction* (New Haven and London, 1938). In 1958 John Gurdon reported that he had cloned frogs (South African clawed frogs, rather than *Rana pipiens*) from fully differentiated nuclei: see J. B. Gurdon, T. R. Elsdale, and M. Fischberg, 'Sexually Mature Individuals of Xenopus Laevis from the Transplantation of Single Somatic Nuclei', *Nature* 182 (1958), 64–5. For earlier experiments on parthenogenesis of sea urchins and later frogs, by Jacques Loeb, see Turney, *Frankenstein's Footsteps*, pp. 67–72 and Jacques Loeb, 'Further Experiments on the Sex of Parthenogenetic Frogs', *Proceedings of the National Academy of Sciences* 4 (1918), 60–2.

it is impossible for any human being to realize those ideals. It looks to 'models' as models of unattainable beauty to which we might aspire, but whose singular beauty makes them singularly wealthy and singularly inimitable, and potentially a source of despair to those who seek to imitate them through their bodies, their clothes, or their behaviour.

There is of course a strong counter-current of resistance to these tendencies within contemporary culture, but these can be seen as the product of the same cultural configuration. We are urged to copy more, to make heroes of those who resist the commercial pressures from which the concept of intellectual property has arisen, and to rejoice in the creativity that can result from apparently 'uncreative' acts like that of pasting text into new contexts.[51] These tendencies within the present world are amplified versions of two conflicting currents within earlier thinking about *imitatio*. The fear of the *simulacrum* is opposed to the desire for a 'living' recreation of an original, which will reanimate its *vis* and *ingenium*, its life and creative power. Do we rejoice in replicants and reproducibility, or glorify the unique model of creative agency? Do we glorify the digibot or the genius, or do we attempt to argue that the master of copying is in fact the real genius?

One way of breaking the potentially sterile deadlock between arguments about the relationship between copying and creativity is to recall a third component in early thinking about *imitatio*, which has gradually faded from view in the course of its long history. Imitation has, largely as a result of the cultural and literary history described in this book, come to be associated chiefly with sinister forms of replication, with ghosts, *simulacra*, and clones, as well as with a gallery of more or less undesirable textual practices ranging from quotation and allusion to textual appropriation. These do not have simply negative consequences: textual sampling and creative quotation can become the grounds of new forms of creativity, and regarding an earlier text as a ghostly presence can grant both it and the new text an uncanny power.[52] But what has tended to be marginalized in the more recent history of imitation is the aspect of it which was most central to the rhetorical tradition. That is the view that the imitator learns from an *exemplum* a practice rather than a series of texts or a sequence of words, and that the end of imitation

---

51. Marjorie Perloff, *Unoriginal Genius: Poetry by Other Means in the New Century* (Chicago, Ill., and London, 2010); Marcus Boon, *In Praise of Copying* (Cambridge, Mass., 2010); Adrian Johns, *Piracy: The Intellectual Property Wars from Gutenberg to Gates* (Chicago and London, 2009); Kenneth Goldsmith, *Uncreative Writing: Managing Language in the Digital Age* (New York, 2011).
52. See Brown, *Allusion and the Uncanny*.

is the acquisition of a habituated skill, rather than a specific set of actions or phrases. We might return to that key sentence of Quintilian about that subject with fresh eyes:

> But these rules of style, while part of the student's theoretical knowledge, are not in themselves sufficient to give him oratorical power (*vim*). In addition he will require that assured facility which the Greeks call *hexis*.
>
> Sed haec eloquendi praecepta, sicut cogitationi sunt necessaria, ita non satis ad vim dicendi valent, nisi illis firma quaedam facilitas, quae apud Graecos ἕξις nomitatur, accesserit.   (*Institutio*, 10.1.1)

Quintilian's reliance on Greek here, as we saw in the Introduction, is deeply significant. It has always been hard to find words to describe how someone imitates a practice in order to acquire a habituated articulacy. As a result the concept that imitation is an aspect of practical wisdom, a habituated ability to do, has successively been overlayered by the metaphorical language which was often used in the Latin tradition to articulate it—the opposition between an imitation with its own bodily substance as against the shadowy semblance, of replicant or textual thief as against the eclectic and assimilative bee. We have seen that language acquire an uncanny vitality in the history of imitation since *Frankenstein*, as it has seeped outwards into the ways in which biological and technological replication are written and thought about. This is among the most profound long-term intellectual consequences of the poverty of Latin as a language for philosophical reflection: that simple Greek word *hexis*, habituated practice, is most readily grasped through a metaphorical elaboration of it, and that metaphorical elaboration then has the potential to radiate outwards and mutate into new forms.

As this book has argued, *imitatio* is a moving target. But imitating authors do not inherit a set of social or textual markers of resemblance to a prior authority. The imitated author or authors do not lay down a template for future writing, but provide a 'model' which can be rescaled and adapted in ways that are apt to different circumstances. They might supply an 'idea' of style, or a set of ways of writing or of structuring writing. Imitation may issue in performances which are so completely fluent that they do not appear to be imitated at all, like those of Castiglione's courtier, or in performances so different in their detail from their origins that they seem to bear only a distant genealogical relationship to those *exempla*. That is what happens when a skill and a practice, rather than just a set of actions, is transmitted from one agent to another.

The notion that *imitatio* chiefly inheres in learning practices from prior examples could be formulated in the form of four propositions which are easy to state but very hard to believe equally and at the same time. The propositions are these: (1) Human beings resemble and learn from other human beings; (2) Human beings become distinctive by learning from other human beings; (3) What human beings learn from each other may be an ability to perform an act which does not resemble any act performed by the *exemplum*; (4) Imitating earlier authors can in these respects resemble imitating other human beings.

These propositions sound very simple, but they suggest that most of what we think we know about imitation we do not in fact know. Authors acquire neither preformed identities nor sections of text from what they read and imitate. Rather they acquire a complex blend of words, habits, forms, figures of speech, and ways of proceeding. This does not make the act of imitating simple, or simply a cold matter of acquiring a set of techniques. Learning from another author, like learning from another person, is partly an evaluative activity: it might entail making judgements about the work of earlier authors, and about which aspects of them are good and which are bad. And, as what I have termed the late eighteenth-century 'affective turn' in the history of this rich and various concept illustrates, that can generate complexes of emotion in relation to prior examples—of admiration turning into a desire to be like someone, or of a growing aversion to a person or a text one has considered masterly and in whom one comes to see weaknesses. It can even mean that the imitator engages in a dialectical revulsion from the object of imitation and creates a vengeful replicant of the imitand, which might, either in actuality or desire, destroy or overturn or transform the thing imitated. The imitator can share the powerful hostility of the destructive parodist or the disillusioned pupil, or alternatively experience the abjection of a lover who fails to see the evident faults in the loved object. The imitator can also become a narcissist, whose self-identification with the object of imitation enables love for the *exemplum* to be carried over into the imitator's own creations, like a new Pygmalion. The desire to imitate might derive from a sense of endangered awe at a cultural authority that threatens the imitator, or even the autonomy of the imitator's nation, and might prompt her to produce a rebellious double of that authority which might destroy it. Imitation can also lead to the complex of affects, of aspiration and envy and desire, that come from being drawn to someone who is capable of something of which one wants oneself to be capable. An imitator may be amazed by the skill manifested by an earlier work, and then painstakingly analyse and seek to replicate the skill that made that object of amazement, and this might lead either to a recognition that the imitating author can do it a newer and a better way or a recognition that he cannot. Imitation is a practice surrounded with both opportunities and hazards.

But the wider consequence of recognizing that imitation is principally a matter of acquiring a set of habituated ways of doing—a practice or a *hexis*—and that this is something all language users necessarily do whether they want to or not, is to accept that we are partly other people, and we are also partly what we have read. Accepting that does not entail any loss of autonomy or the unfreedom which has been a repeated source of anxiety throughout the wider history of thinking and writing about *imitatio*. Human beings are skilful and self-conscious learners who continually adapt the practices they have learnt from others to new uses. The imitating author, indeed, may radically misunderstand the object of imitation, and remake a version of it on the basis of that mistake. Or a new cultural context may make old words seem to mean something new, and so even a devoted imitator may, like Don Quixote, find that an attempt at exact imitation produces an entirely new kind of text. Indeed such misunderstandings and mutations of sense—of individual words, of concepts, and of entire texts—are what have given the concept of imitation such a rich history. Given that times and conventions, languages and customs, genes and genres, change through the generations, someone who imitates a previous person's linguistic behaviour will necessarily and involuntarily differ from that person, and will display a complex of relationships to that previous person which will be both distinctive to those individuals and inseparable from the wider conventions and traditions within which they operate.

Recognizing that the pressures which have built up in later modernity not to be a clone or a copy but to be an 'original' are products of a longer history might remind us that those pressures can be resisted. Between the sharp opposition of 'originality' and 'replication' is a huge zone, occupied by the acquisition of practices, of learning skills, and the wider, wilder and more emotionally turbulent uplands of influence. That strange definition of *imitatio* in the *Ad Herennium*, 1.2.3, which we encountered in Chapter 2, may appear gnomically evasive, but it does convey a large truth in little: 'Imitation is that by which we are impelled, in accordance with a careful method, to flourish in speaking by being like others.' That statement implies that imitation is an urge which results in a fusion of emotion and practice—a desire to be like—in which emotion and practice are constantly feeding each other. Following that urge offers the prospect of flourishing: new thoughts, new worlds, new texts could be produced by the labour of understanding and mastering the practices of earlier examples, because the practices manifested in those ancient examples are not rules or finite injunctions, but ways of doing things which could be extrapolated into ways of doing new things. *Imitatio* produces transformation rather than replication, and it always leaves open the question 'what will happen next?'

Posthuman Postscript

Poems more Durable than Brass

Consider the following poem:

Brass
Gathering brass
A soul of
    grips
An agent
An intention

J. H. Prynne

The contemporary poet J. H. Prynne has been described as 'the ultimate poet of anti-pathos', and 'Brass' seems well-suited to that description.[1] It is gnomic, and evades the monumental even as it evokes it. The title suggests literary permanence through an apparent allusion to Horace's claim that his poems are 'more durable than brass' (*Odes*, 3.30.1), but the poem itself scrupulously avoids claims to immortality, and does not offer any overt verbal reference to Horace. It contains a single sparing but exacting verb ('grips') which relates awkwardly to its apparent (abbreviated) subject 'A soul of' (A soul of brass?); and that verb (which could also be a noun) puts a tourniquet of matter around the abstractions 'agent' and 'intention'.

The poem is in fact an imitation, but it is not an imitation even at several removes of Horace. It was first published in 2008 in *Issue 1*, a PDF journal with the impossibly odd number of 3,785 pages, which was compiled by a

1. David Wheatley, https://www.theguardian.com/books/2015/may/08/poems-jh-prynne-review. Accessed February 2018.

literary collective called Forgodot.[2] It turns out that 'Brass', like all the poems in *Issue 1*, was created not by J. H. Prynne but by a computer programme named 'Erica T. Carter', which 'assembles word associations from a dictionary database and then uses probability models to construct syntactic phrases that it assembles into discrete utterances'.[3] These verbal assemblages were then supplied with ascriptions to one or other of 3,164 living poets.

Not all of the poets who were thus gifted electronically generated contributions to their *oeuvre* were unequivocally pleased, and some of them threatened legal action (the Forgodot.com website has since retreated, perhaps defensively, into Japanese). 'Erica T. Carter's' imitation of a 'Prynne' poem is, however, by no means uninteresting. It is extraordinary that 30 per cent of the words in a poem which purports to have been generated mechanically are abstract nouns connected to the deliberative and creative origins of poetry as it is traditionally imagined: 'soul', 'agent', 'intention'. Those words also make the poem unlike what a competent reader might describe as 'Prynnean', since Prynne's verse is programmatically sparing of soul, intention, and agency. Were it a Prynne, such clear echoes of old mythologies of literary creation would have been more thoroughly ironized. But I may say that simply because I know it was not written by J. H. Prynne.

'Brass', or Erica's Prynne, if we can call it that, leads off into a broad field of twentieth- and twenty-first-century technologically extended versions of verbal imitation, most of which use forms of probability modelling to create texts which appear to resemble works produced by direct human intentional action. These forms of imitation go on every day in our pockets. The predictive text engine on a smartphone can anticipate with uncanny skill the next word which its operator will suggest, and Google can often tell us what we will want to type or see next. As a result one can now, day to day, experience oneself as an imitable pattern of verbal predilections. If I start to type the title word of Edna T. Carter's poem 'Brass' into my smartphone I am relieved to discover that 'Brass' is its second choice after 'bra' (don't ask). If I then follow each of my phone's first word-choices after this initial choice of the word 'brass' for ten successive words, to see if I can remake the

2. The text of *Issue 1* is at http://www.ubu.com/ubu/unpub/Unpub_040_Issue1.pdf (accessed February 2018). 'Brass' appears on p. 1662. The volume was edited by Jim Carpenter and Stephen McLaughlin, to whom I am grateful for permission to quote.

3. Craig Douglas Dworkin and Kenneth Goldsmith, eds., *Against Expression: An Anthology of Conceptual Writing* (Evanston, Ill., 2011), p. 414.

Prynne-algorithm-generated poem, I then get an imitation Prynne poem transformed by some kind of Burrowish stylistic process into:

> Brass upholstery
> cleaning
> up the good work
> and the other

I am not unduly alarmed about the moral nature of my algorithm: an obsession with cleaning and virtue and the other—it clearly has me worked out. If I follow the second choices proposed by my phone I turn from hygienic househusband into brassnecked Robodon, and deny all responsibility for anything:

> Brass body is
> not
> responsible to get
> your email

However, I imagine I am not alone in laughing at my smartphone for being not always so smart, or in trying to outsmart it by typing a word which is *not* the one it has suggested, because (I flatter myself) my muse is a Pegasus and that horse can *fly* beyond the hoof prints of predictability; but even as I do so I have a sinking certainty that my phone does know something about my style and more about the clichés which dominate most of my life than it should. I also can imagine that the next generation of artificial intelligence might be able to learn that its operator is perversely resistant to the mannerisms of her own style, and adjust accordingly, and so predict the word I would have written in order to circumvent the cliché it would otherwise have suggested.

There is a venerable history behind these mechanical imitations of human composition. An early glimpse of that history can be seen in England during those critical years in the later seventeenth century when so much changed in thinking about imitation. In 1677 John Peter published a volume called *Artificial Versifying*, which provided a list of tables from the use of which 'any one of the meanest Capacity, that only knows the A.B.C. and can count 9. (though he understands not one word of Latin, or what a Verse is) may be immediately taught how to Compose Hundreds of Hexameter Verses'.[4] By selecting numbers from the tables provided by Peter, and then

---

4. John Peter, *Artificial Versifying or, The School-boy's Recreation* (London, 1677), sig. B3.

recording the words which corresponded to those numbers, even the least poetically-minded schoolboy could create correct Latin hexameters.

In the 1840s the paper tables of Peter's practical guide took on mechanical form when John Clark of Bridgwater (a relative of the founder of Clark's shoes, which gives a nice mechanical twist to the idea of the imitator following in another's footsteps) built what he proudly called 'The Eureka Machine'. This handsome automaton was displayed in the Egyptian Hall in Piccadilly in 1845 for those who were willing to pay a shilling to see it. It used a system of cogs and levers to produce Latin hexameter lines, while (apparently) playing 'God Save the Queen' at the same time.[5] The application of artisanal skill mechanically to replicate the elite arts of Latin verse composition had an implicit social agenda, since The Eureka Machine made the arcana of classical imitation available to the mass consumers of spectacle.

But Clark's machine had limitations. It was designed only to produce verses which followed the bare rules of metrical correctness, and did not aspire to follow in the footprints of individual authors. However, once Charles Babbage had in 1837 invented his prototypical computer called the Analytical Engine (for which Ada Lovelace, Byron's daughter, conceived a couple of years before *Frankenstein*, compiled what is often said to be the first computer program) the automated imitation of a specific human poet became at least a distant possibility.[6] Could *imitatio* be reduced to a sophisticated algorithm, in which an elaborate calculation based on the frequency and proximity of words in an earlier writer's work would become the 'model' or 'formula', the little mould, the shaping principle, or what Giovanni Pico called the 'last' or foot shape, of a subsequent poem? And could such a composition be distinguished from one written by a human being?

The creation of a poetry machine, like that of the automata and replicants discussed in Chapter 10, was not simply a technical challenge. It was potentially the clearest means to refute Descartes's claim that a soul lurked ghostlike within the machine of the human body. If a machine could write a poem that appeared to derive from emotions and thoughts it might simultaneously prove that machines could think and that human consciousness was reducible to physical or electrical phenomena. For this reason

---

5. Jason Hall, 'Popular Prosody: Spectacle and the Politics of Victorian Versification', *Nineteenth-Century Literature* 62 (2007), 222–9. The restored machine can be seen at the Alfred Gillett Trust in Street, Somerset.

6. Pamela McCorduck, *Machines Who Think: A Personal Inquiry into the History and Prospects of Artificial Intelligence* (San Francisco, 1979), p. 26.

computer-generated poems became a recurrent theme in discussions of artificial intelligence by the middle of the twentieth century. In a lecture of 1949 the neuroscientist Geoffrey Jefferson declared that 'Not until a machine can write a sonnet or compose a concerto because of thoughts and emotions felt, and not by the chance fall of symbols, could we agree that machine equals brain.'[7] Partly in response to this claim Alan Turing wrote his famous article of 1950, 'Computing Machinery and Intelligence'.[8] This described what Turing called 'the imitation game', in which a human being tries to determine if a respondent whose body is not visible was a human or a machine.

Turing's article was published in the journal *Mind*, which was edited by Gilbert Ryle, whose *The Concept of Mind* (1949) was at the forefront of a strong mid-century revolt against Cartesian dualism. Ryle had resisted what he termed 'the official doctrine' that a distinct thing called 'mind' inhabited the human body, and that its operations were not observable by external witnesses. This he termed the doctrine of 'the ghost in the machine', or the belief that mind was a separate thing from its embodiment.[9] If Descartes were right and there were a non-corporeal entity within the body which was only accessible through introspection, Ryle argued, a person 'could never tell the difference between a man and a Robot' apart from the 'doubtful exception of himself' (p. 21). Ryle supposed we could infer mind and its dispositions from a person's actions, and hence (presumably) that it would be possible to distinguish a human from a robot by inferences from its behaviour. Turing, who had a far deeper understanding of mathematical and mechanical forms of intelligence than Ryle, was not so sure.

His article built on Ryle's anti-Cartesianism. It considered the ways in which a range of logical and other rules, combined with a set of educational processes, could create a computational machine that would avoid all the foreseeable objections to the claim that it was capable of thought. His article was epoch-marking in the history of fiction, since it opened up the world of *Blade Runner, Battlestar Galactica, Ex Machina*, and a myriad of films and novels which anxiously explore the porous boundary between human beings and androids. But Turing was very much a man of his age in using poetry—a mode of language in which there are rules, but in which there

7. Geoffrey Jefferson, 'The Mind of Mechanical Man', *British Medical Journal* 1 (1949), 1105–10 (p. 1106).
8. A. M. Turing, 'Computing Machinery and Intelligence', *Mind* 59 (1950), 433–60.
9. Gilbert Ryle, *The Concept of Mind* (London, 1949), pp. 11–24.

are also large spaces for the uncodifiable operations of human taste and judgement—as the key testing-ground for success in the imitation game. In formulating the 'Turing Test' of machine intelligence Turing imagined a dialogue or *viva* between an Interrogator and a Witness, who is a sonnet-writing machine gifted with the ability to sound human:

> *INTERROGATOR*: In the first line of your sonnet which reads 'Shall I compare thee to a summer's day,' would not 'a spring day' do as well or better?
>
> *WITNESS*: It wouldn't scan.
>
> *INTERROGATOR*: How about 'a winter's day'? That would scan all right.
>
> *WITNESS*: Yes, but nobody wants to be compared to a winter's day.
>
> *INTERROGATOR*: Would you say Mr Pickwick reminded you of Christmas?
>
> *WITNESS*: In a way.
>
> *INTERROGATOR*: Yet Christmas is a winter's day, and I do not think Mr Pickwick would mind the comparison.
>
> *WITNESS*: I don't think you're serious. By a winter's day one means a typical winter's day, rather than a special one like Christmas.[10]

The test is designed to assess the Witness's ability to develop extra-logical cultural associations without producing any solecisms, and Turing's Witness speaks in the way he imagines a computer would speak if that computer were to strike an interlocutor as human. Turing evidently associated knowledge of literary texts—of principles of metrical regularity, of the works of Shakespeare and of Dickens—with achieving the appearance of being human. Amusingly enough, however, he seems not to have noticed that the Witness fails the Turing test with its very first response, since he does not demur when he is addressed as though he were the author of Shakespeare's Sonnet 18 ('*your* sonnet'?). Any educated Westerner in 1950 would surely have responded to that question with 'you mean *Shakespeare's* sonnet?' It is as though Turing wants his ultimate computing machine to be a Shakespeare engine, capable not just of sustaining a human conversation, but of becoming the author himself.

After Turing a number of theorists of artificial intelligence articulated the processes and risks associated with artificial intelligence through literary examples. Among those examples the work of that great imitative poet John Milton loomed large. When O. G. Selfridge made one of the early break-throughs in pattern-recognition programming in 1958 he did so by creating

---

10. Turing, 'Computing Machinery and Intelligence', p. 446.

a hierarchical model of sub-programs called 'demons'. These were arranged in a sequence which would enable each 'demon' to 'shout' at the one immediately above it in the hierarchy when it noted what might be a pattern in the part of an image which was its particular responsibility. This hierarchy Selfridge named 'Pandemonium', after the palace of the devils in *Paradise Lost*, which as Chapter 8 showed, was the product of Milton's own thinking about models and imitations of God's creation.[11]

In Norbert Wiener's *God and Golem, Inc.* of 1964 Milton's *Paradise Lost* is presented as a paradigm of the relationship between a creator and an intelligent machine which was capable of independent learning. The intelligent replicant of the creator (Satan) tries to defeat the creator through following rules and examples which had been made by his creator. Wiener saw this fable as encapsulating the risk endemic to cybernetic systems (in which artificial intelligence feeds the outputs of its behaviour back into its inputs), which might become fatal to mankind if the creators of those cybernetic systems put them in charge of decisions about making war and peace. In the aftermath of the Cuban missile crisis Wiener imagined nuclear catastrophe resulting from such delegation of human decision-making to artificial intelligence.[12] A poem establishes a model of rebellion by the imitator against his creator which is then replicated by a machine that learns from itself and so destroys us all. *Paradise Lost* becomes a fable not just about creation of Frankenstein's monster, but about the creation of intelligent systems capable of ending the world of the human.

These are not just signs that early theorists of AI had read their Milton, or that *Paradise Lost* has a natural affinity with science fiction writing. Rather they indicate how powerful the analogies are between the processes of machine-learning and acts of literary imitation. Those analogies are present both at a mythical and a practical level. An imitator of a prior creative agent is an inherently threatening thing, a being or a child who can usurp the functions and skills of its maker, grasp what that maker can offer, and then, potentially, overturn him. But at a practical level an imitator has deep structural

---

11. O. G. Selfridge, 'Pandemonium: A Paradigm for Learning', in *Mechanisation of Thought Processes: Proceedings of a Symposium held at the National Physical Laboratory on 24th, 25th, 26th and 27th November 1958* (London, 1959), 513–26.

12. Norbert Wiener, *God and Golem, Inc.: A Comment on Certain Points where Cybernetics Impinges on Religion* (London, 1964), pp. 24–5: God 'is actually engaged in a conflict with his creature, in which he may very well lose the game…In constructing machines with which he plays games, the inventor has arrogated to himself the function of a limited creator, whatever the nature of the game-playing machines that learn by experience.'

analogies with the self-learning systems of artificial intelligence. An imitator operates within a feedback loop which is akin to that of a learning machine: imitators extrapolate a set of rules from a set of prior instances and use those rules as a means of generating new instances which can then be added to and which can modify the prior series. Self-learning strategies of a similar kind have led most recently to the creation of a machine that can be programmed with the rules of Go, be allowed to play against itself for a few days, and then create a whole set of hitherto unimagined strategies which enable it to defeat the best living human players.[13] This was achieved without providing the machine with any prior instances of successful strategies for victory, or examples of prior games between humans. Could a machine do the same thing with poetry, and replicate the activities of a human imitator—or even be Shakespeare?

The answer to that question at the moment, and at least for several decades to come, is no—partly because contemporary work on AI has moved its focus towards more serious matters, such as gaming the stock-exchange, and away from the alluring post-Cartesian ideal of a machine that might replicate human consciousness. But we can learn a great deal about literary imitation by thinking in the abstract about why it would be so difficult for a machine to succeed as a poet. One simple reason is the poverty of the methods which are presently used to produce poems like Erica T. Carter's 'Brass'. On the whole these are produced by 'formulae' based on Markov chains or on Bayesian probability analysis of datasets of poems—techniques which have also been used to produce the computer-generated *Harry Potter and the Portrait of What Looked Like a Large Pile of Ash*, which lives up to the lack of promise of its title.[14] The aim of such programs is to determine the probability that particular words will appear in particular contexts within an existing corpus, and to use those probabilities to create new contributions to that corpus which share its central characteristics.

Some poems produced by probability modelling of this kind have passed a modest version of the Turing test by persuading their readers that they were written by a human being. The website 'bot or not' (http://www.botpoet.com) generates most of its poems from a range of computer programs ('That Can Be My Next Tweet' mines Twitter for poems; 'Janus Node' can 'morph your texts using Markov chaining'). Visitors to the site

13. On the development of AlphaGo by the Google owned subsidiary deepmind, see D. Silver, 'Mastering the Game of Go without Human Knowledge', *Nature* 550 (2017), 354–9.
14. See http://botnik.org/content/harry-potter.html (accessed February 2018).

are presented with a random sample, which is either a robopoem or a work by Emily Dickinson or Gertrude Stein or William Blake, and have to guess if the poem in front of them was written by a human being or not. Success rates in making the distinction wobble around the 50 per cent mark, although it is reassuring that William Blake's 'The Fly' presently tops the leader-board of poems believed to be by human beings (80 per cent of users—presumably human users, rather than bots—think a human wrote it).

'Bot or not' is, however, extremely limited in the kinds of poem it can produce. It generates free verse. That means it can exploit the majority of its users' uncertainty about the distinction between the humanly produced and the randomly associative in contemporary poetry. It would be a more impressive achievement if a computer were to produce rhymed stanzas in entirely orthodox grammar which persuaded their readers that these were the work of a human—or indeed if it were to produce a convincingly 'Shakespearean' sonnet. There are online sonnet generators, but these, even when primed with a user-selected set of nouns, verbs, and adjectives to produce a sonnet of a particular kind, fail to produce even a minimally regular pentameter line, and appear to know nothing of the finer points of feminine rhymes and elision.[15] Acquiring those skills is of course not in theory beyond the wit of bots, but they have some way to go.

The larger problem facing machine-generated poetry is that a literary imitation is not simply a predictable output from the input of previous poems, and, when imitation is performed by human beings, it is not consciously based on an assessment of word frequencies. Imitation can occur at many different levels (beyond the base level of acquiring linguistic competence), and an imitator can imitate at one or more of these levels at any one time. A poet might imitate Ben Jonson by drinking plenty of Canary wine, by setting scenes of a play in St Paul's, by giving particular stress to monosyllabic terms for virtue, by using the word 'stand' with a peculiar emphasis, by adopting his stanzaic forms, or by emulating his practice of adapting an ancient author to the customs of the present. Imitation also frequently shades off into the 'inspired by' model, in which a single striking feature of an earlier work prompts a later writer to do something which is similar to that work in respect solely of that feature. If a set of highly skilled programmers were funded to work on a program called The Poet, the aim of which would be to produce poems indistinguishable in quality but distinct in content from a common benchmark of poetic quality such as the poems included in the *Oxford Book of English Verse*, it is likely that even the smartest and best legion of literary nerds would be stumped by the challenge of replicating the multi-levelled nature of literary imitation.

The core reason that the methods of present-day AI are unlikely to succeed in making The Poet work is that poetry is not like Go or chess. It has many conventions, but these do not apply in all circumstances, and all of its conventions are flexible. As a result the criteria of success for a poem are to a significant degree non-codifiable. Furthermore they change so much through time and space that many poems generally agreed to be outstanding are often not recognized as such in their own time. A machine can learn to win at chess or at Go or at gaming the stock-exchange because it is presented with the end in view as well as the rules of the game, and can extrapolate strategies from past games in order to refine its ability to achieve the end. That makes it relatively easy to feed an evaluation of outcomes back into the performance of the activity. A given move in a chess program can be assessed in relation to the probability of its achieving the desired outcome of check-mate.

In more complex environments where the criteria of success are less obvious than they are in a game, such as machine translation, theorists of AI have tended to incorporate 'valuation stages' into the process by which a machine refines its activities, and this might take the form of feedback from a human agent. In the 1960s Norbert Wiener presented a scenario (curiously akin to the early modern practice of 'double translation' by which students would learn Latin by translating a Latin text into English and then translating it back into Latin) in which a machine translated Danish into English, and then another translated the English back into Danish.[16] A human agent would then assess the success of the re-translation and feed back into the process an evaluative element which might subsequently refine its outcomes. Even this kind of beneficial feedback, however, requires the overall end of the process to be clear: in the case of machine translation, for instance, the end is to produce text which a native speaker would not regard as gibberish or as grammatically defective. The case of poetic composition is far more complex. Do poems aim to delight? To instruct? To outrage? To rhyme? To do to Horace what Horace did to Alcaeus? To mimic the deconstruction of consciousness? To perform a radical transformation of

16. Wiener, *God and Golem*, p. 82.

the conventions of the genre of epigram? To take your breath away? These possible goals are not only multiple but in many cases incommensurable.

This is why The Poet, which could electronically produce the best poems, irrespective of their genre or period or individual characteristics, is unlikely to be either a theoretical or a practical possibility. There are simply too many criteria for success in poetic composition. But we *might* imagine a series of programs which evolved by recursive processes into a series of distinct poets, each of which fed differing criteria of success back into the processes of composition. Fed with one, or with a dozen, distinct but not logically incompatible criteria of success, plus a thousand or a million instances of poems agreed to be successful according to those criteria, a machine might be able to imitate, then to evaluate the imitation, and then to feed its own evaluations back into the process of producing further poems. And before long one might have an *oeuvre* of something that looked like a particular kind of poet.

In this hypothetical canon of botpoetry we might well imagine that the work of each of these poet programs would become so involved in its own peculiar criteria of success that its productions rapidly became unintelligible to most human readers. That might be (from the perspective of the machine) what made those poems excellent; but if the criteria of success were self-created by the machine through multiple iterations of an evaluation loop we would never be able to know whether this was so or not, because even if we could understand the words from which the computer's poems were composed, the principles on which it was evaluating them might rapidly become so distinctive to that program that human readers would be unable to determine what they were. If a lion could speak, we would not understand it; and if a computer could write poems according to its own standards of success human readers would find in them either nothing, or dark shadows of a poetic tradition which we only dimly recognized.

A further conceptual problem facing the construction of The Poet is more challenging, but also more helpful for thinking about what poetic imitation is as a practice. This might be called the variable rule problem. When a person learns to be a poet they are, inter alia, extrapolating rules and conventions which they can follow from a series of interconnected instances. Some of those rules are low-order and readily replicable ('Sonnets usually contain fourteen lines and rhyme either ababcdcdefefgg or abbaabbacdecde, but the following substitutions are allowed...'). Some are rules with codifiable exceptions ('Sonnets can have twelve lines, sometimes'). Some are author-specific preferences ('Spenser is fond of prefixing past participles with "y-"'). Human poets, however, often engage in situationally appropriate rule-breaking, and these acts of situationally appropriate rule-breaking are often the most visible and emulable features of their verse from the perspective of an imitator. They are what make a poet appear 'original' or distinctive. A reversed first foot at the start of the second quatrain of a sonnet, for instance, might strike a reader as particularly 'Shakespearean'; a broken line distantly alluding to Dante might seem peculiarly 'Eliotean'. When a poet imitates an earlier poet they might just adopt vocabulary and metrical structures from that poet. But they might also imitate what that poet is doing with a prior system of conventions. Indeed they might even extrapolate from a transgression of an implied rule at one level of an earlier author's practice the transgression of a different kind of rule at a different level.

The example of Milton is again helpful here. His willingness to take the conventions of epic and bring into them conventions from other modes and genres—to describe domestic scenes in heroic terms, or to inflate the military encounters of classical epic into implausibly vast battles between the angels—is in multiple ways exemplary of the imitative process. It illustrates the flexibility of conventions in general, and shows that an imitator can follow one convention whilst deliberately breaking another. This is the aspect of Milton's practice that enabled Wordsworth and Blake and Mary Shelley to take *Paradise Lost* as an instance of the larger value of generic transformation and of transgression more generally, either against political conventions, or poetic conventions, or both. *Imitatio* does not mean just following a rule or an example; it can also mean following an example in breaking a rule. What we call human creativity is probably in large measure the product of this (potentially anarchic) aspect of imitation: it is a manifestation of an ability to infer a rule or the transgression of a rule from a practice and then port either the rule or the practice or the transgression of the rule to a new sphere. The Poet program would therefore need to have what we might call a perversity engine built into it.[17] That is, it would have to be

---

17. Cf. Gian Biagio Conte, *The Rhetoric of Imitation: Genre and Poetic Memory in Virgil and Other Latin Poets*, trans. Charles Segal (Ithaca, NY, and London, 1986), p. 142 on the 'epic code': 'This term refers not to features that allow us, through concrete induction, to see each text as governed by the rules of a specific literary genre but to a much more general system, whose potential may be implemented in new ways without causing the reader to doubt that the work is an epic poem even if this or that rule traditionally imposed by the system has been broken'; and p. 150: the code is 'a progressively extendable combinatorial capability'. Gian Biagio Conte, *Stealing the Club from Hercules: On Imitation in Latin Poetry* (Berlin and Boston, 2017), p. 32 invokes Chomsky's notion of competence to describe the grasping of an imitative system: 'the act of imitation is the outcome of a generative competence which starts from the models but then disassembles and reassembles them.'

able not just to follow an example but to extrapolate from it occasions on which it might be right *not* to follow the example, or to follow it in an entirely unpredictable way.

A simplified example might clarify this point. A poet writes a poem which follows the conventions of epic except for the fact that everyone in it is very small. This radically changes the effect of 'epic' despite appearing to follow the conventions of the form, since beefy heroes acquire squeaky voices. Now suppose that by analogy with the activity of the author of a mock or miniaturized epic a hypothetical lyric poet decided to write a love poem written from a gnat to a bumblebee. In the process the imitative author creates a mock love lyric by analogy with the mock epic; and the principal thing imitated is not the original poem but its implied 'new' rule that conventions about size and scale can be broken.

When a poet writes there is whirl of rules, and of transpositions of rules, and of ingrained conventional proprieties, and probably too an element of stubborn resistance to all regulation; a poet learns from her predecessor by imitating both the rule and prior patterns of transgression of rules. An AI Poet-program might from time to time recombine words according to a probabilistic model that would generate a persuasively poem-like, or even a persuasively Wordsworthian or Gertrude Stein-like construct; but to write in a way that had an impact on the wider tradition of Western poetry it would have to display an ability to learn both from the rule-following and from the rule-breaking of prior examples. This ability to produce codified transgression is central to the history and to the practice of imitation, and it is the central reason why imitation is not alien to but intrinsic to human creativity. Human beings learn practices from others, but they also learn from others how to depart from earlier practices.

Nonetheless, one of the most enduring fantasies of modernity (and it is an enticing fantasy because it also has the potential to become a nightmare) is that art can or should either itself become, or at least make use of, a form of mechanical reproduction. Sol LeWitt in his influential 'Paragraphs on Conceptual Art', written in 1967 during the most intensive period of research into artificial intelligence, declared that 'When an artist uses a conceptual form of art, it means that all of the planning and decisions are made beforehand and the execution is a perfunctory affair. The idea becomes a machine that makes the art.'[18] LeWitt has been followed by a whole

18. Sol LeWitt, 'Paragraphs on Conceptual Art', *Artforum* 5 (1967), 79–83.

generation of conceptual writers who seek to strip away the myth of the unique and inimitable genius from the process of artistic creation, and who advocate what has been called 'uncreative writing'.[19] This might consist of copying texts from one situation to another, or it might lead artists to generate Warholesque factory duplicates of their creations.

Behind these projects often lies Walter Benjamin's belief that the age of mechanical reproduction has stripped away the aura of cult and singularity from the work of art.[20] Benjamin's fascination with the infinitely replicable, democratized work of art also frequently now feeds into the belief that unrestrained acts of copying and duplication can free the present-day artist from the pernicious legacy of romantic ideas of creativity, and its dark double, copyright law.[21] From the widest historical perspective there is nothing radically new about connecting artistic creation with the technologies of material reproduction, or in seeing art as the product of an impersonal 'idea' rather than of a particular individual's skill. When Plato talked of an imitation bearing the 'tupos' or stamp of its archetype (see Chapter 1) he drew on the language of reproductive technologies to illuminate fictional representation. When Greek and Roman rhetoricians talk of 'characters' of style they used a metaphor from the impression left on a coin, where the resemblance between two 'characters' guarantees their validity. Conceptual art systematically foregrounds those metaphors and seeks to literalize them.

But it is curious how often the language of singularity and of biological reproduction slips back unawares into the vocabulary even of highly self-aware writers who are attempting to remove the ghost of emotions or human genius from the machinery of art. Kenneth Goldsmith, the doyen of 'uncreative writing', for instance, describes how a work of art can be produced through the direct copying of data. He takes a text which he holds on his hard drive (in 'the safe stasis of my local ecology') and duplicates it onto a server: 'Now let's say I take that same transcript and upload a copy of it to a publicly accessible server where it can be downloaded, while keeping a copy on my PC. I have identical text in two places, operating in two

19. See Marjorie Perloff, *Unoriginal Genius: Poetry by Other Means in the New Century* (Chicago, Ill., and London, 2010) and Kenneth Goldsmith, *Uncreative Writing: Managing Language in the Digital Age* (New York, 2011).

20. Walter Benjamin, *Illuminations*, ed. Hannah Arendt (London, 1970), p. 220.

21. Adrian Johns, *Piracy: The Intellectual Property Wars from Gutenberg to Gates* (Chicago, Ill., and London, 2009); Marcus Boon, *In Praise of Copying* (Cambridge, Mass., 2010).

distinct ecosystems, like twins, one who spends his life close to home and the other who adventures out into the world; each textual life is marked accordingly.'[22] The twin—a genetic replica which is also non-identical, a clone which can develop through a separate history despite being genetically identical to its sister—is an alluring metaphor still for describing something which is the same and not the same, a bit-identical replica which nonetheless has its own singular identity; and the biological metaphor (in what sense is a person's hard drive an 'ecosystem'?) forces that non-identity onto bit-identical similarity. Even a copy is never the same as that which is copied.

The biological metaphors used by early theorists of *imitatio*—that the imitator resembles the *exemplum* as a child resembles its parent, that texts are 'digested' into the body of the imitator—have proved extremely durable. There appears to be a deep human desire to believe that even a copy is a distinct entity in a quasi-biological sense, and is never *exactly* the same as an original. And curiously even some of the most technically skilled mathematicians who have written about AI have suggested that there is something special about the biological form of human beings which resists replication through digital methods. John Von Neumann saw the human brain as massively more powerful than the computing machines available in his lifetime. He described 'chromosomes and their constituent genes' as 'memory elements which by their state affect, and to a certain extent determine, the functioning of the entire system', which were infinitely more effective than electronic forms of memory. Von Neumann also argued that the language of mathematics itself was structurally distinct from the primary language of the central nervous system.[23] More controversially, Roger Penrose and his collaborators have argued that quantum effects occur within the human brain that make it intrinsically unreplicable by binary systems.[24] These claims indicate that belief in the inherent unreplicability of biological processes persists in mutated form even in mathematical discussions of how to replicate aspects of human cognition. The descendant of the rhetoricians' concept of human *ingenium*, the inimitable *vis*, appears to have migrated into a cellular or even a quantum level.

---

22. Goldsmith, *Uncreative Writing*, p. 32.
23. John Von Neumann, *The Computer and the Brain* (New Haven and London, 1979), pp. 65, 82.
24. See Roger Penrose, *Shadows of the Mind: A Search for the Missing Science of Consciousness* (Oxford, 1994) and Roger Penrose, *The Emperor's New Mind: Concerning Computers, Minds and the Laws of Physics* (London, 1990).

The myth of biological difference—the belief that even the production of identical copies in the human world always issues in difference—is so pervasive that it might even be thought of as a truth rather than a myth. When people make replicas *something*, even if it is only the setting in which those copies are perceived, or the environments occupied by genetically identical clones, is always different. Transformation is a necessary consequence of replication, even if that replication consists of the exact copying of a text into a new setting. The machine of life is a machine that changes things as it reproduces them.

To illustrate this strange but reassuring truth we might finally consider a piece of contemporary conceptual poetry which is also a meditation on the nature of imitation and cultural transmission. This is the Canadian poet Christian Bök's project called *The Xenotext* (2015). Bök began with a radical aim: to embed a poem within the genetic code of the extremely durable bacterium *Deinococcus radiodurans*, which, as its name suggests, could even survive a nuclear holocaust. The poem encoded in this way would become the biological equivalent of a poem more durable than brass, since when the DNA of the original bacterium divided in order to reproduce itself the archetype poem was supposed to produce another poem. The source poem Bök calls 'Orpheus' and the partner poem that divides off from it is called 'Eurydice'. As he has put it: 'I am, in effect, engineering a life-form so that it becomes not only a durable archive for storing a poem, but also an operant machine for writing a poem—one that can persist on the planet until the sun itself explodes.'[25]

The experiment has not yet fully succeeded, but it is not purely science fiction. It grew from the successful attempt by a group of geneticists to encode a line from Virgil's *Georgics* into the DNA of thale cress (*Arabidopsis thaliana*—the first plant to have had its entire genome sequenced, and which, no doubt coincidentally, shares its name with that of Thalia, the Muse of Comedy and Pastoral).[26] The particular line embedded in this way was from Virgil's *Georgics*: 'Nec vero terrae ferre omnes omnia possunt', 'Nor can all of the earth bring forth all fruit alike' (*Georgics*, 2.109).

---

25. https://www.poetryfoundation.org/harriet/2011/04/the-xenotext-works (accessed February 2018).

26. Sylvestre Marillonnet, Victor Klimuk, and Yuri Gleba, 'Encoding Technical Information in GM Organisms', *Nature Biotechnology* 21 (2003), 224–6. The code uses sequences of the four amino acids in DNA (adenine (A), thymine (T), guanine (G), and cytosine (C)) to indicate letters of the alphabet, with one or more of the 64 available triplet codons denoting alphanumeric characters.

Whoever chose that line to imprint in a plant had a good eye: it positions within the very mechanism of biological replication a line that insists on the variation of all living things across space. Not only that, but Virgil's line was imitated from a passage in Lucretius's *De Rerum Natura*, in which Lucretius counterfactually describes what the world would be like if everything had been created from nothing, and as a result any form of life could derive from any other: 'Nor would the same fruits stay constant to the trees, but all would change: all trees would be able to bear all kinds of fruit' ('nec fructus idem arboribus constare solerent, | sed mutarentur, ferre omnes omnia possent', *DRN*, 1.165–6).

The original experiment to embed a line of Virgil in thale cress by Marillonnet and partners was, however, not simply a sportive literary venture. It was a late and potentially sinister outcrop of the historical entanglement between imitation and notions of intellectual property, since it was designed to prove that a stable marker of origin or authorship could be encoded within a genetically modified crop, and hence a biotech company could indelibly insert their signature of ownership into the products of their laboratories. Bök's experiment in *The Xenotext* was designed to unsettle this project of copyrighting (un)natural forms. He sought to embed a poem in the *radiodurans* bacterium which did not simply produce an exact copy of itself, but which would generate a new poem each time its DNA divided. That biological imitation of the creative process should continue to reproduce itself, given the exceptional durability of the *radiodurans* bacterium, for eternity.

Bök's posthuman venture revives and transforms one of the oldest analogies for the process of imitating a poem. Imitators no longer resemble their *exempla* as children resemble their parents. Instead poems are independently generated from the processes of genetic reproduction, processes which simultaneously ensure continuity and difference within the evolving work. Other relics of the longer history of *imitatio* run through Bök's *Xenotext* too. It begins by welcoming its 'wraith and reader', the ghost reader of the future, who is led through a series of apocalyptic visions and an anagrammatical rewriting of Keats's poem 'When I have fears that I may cease to be'. The *simulacrum*, that double of the biologically vital 'living' imitation whom we have encountered so often in this study, becomes the reader, who might be able to remember and reassemble the archetypes of the texts which she reads. Bök goes on to provide a transformation or translation or imitation of the fourth book of Virgil's *Georgics*. That is a particularly appropriate text to imitate: not only was the *Georgics* the source of the line of verse that was successfully embedded in the genetic code of thale cress, but its fourth book is about our old friends (and recurrent metaphors for imitation) the bees, whose present-day dip in population as a result of the use of neonicoto-noids is one of the shadows of apocalypse hanging over Bök's work.

Bök refashions *Georgics* 4 into a sequence of fifty quasi-sonnets of fourteen lines, which take us through the death of the bees, through Virgil's story of Orpheus and Eurydice, and on to the rebirth of the bees from the decom-position of cattle:

> Writhing in the innards of these cattle
> there swells a gale of bees, overboiling
> in a cloud, uprising through the rent ribs
> to assemble themselves, like an apple
> clinging upon the bough in the treetops.[27]

This powerful image of biological regeneration is followed by reports of a series of experiments which seek to embed poems within genetic structures, and to extract acrostic poems from sequences of nucleic acids. *The Xenotext* concludes with 'Alpha Helix', a kind of hymn to the double helix and its reduplication throughout the world around us, and to its capacity to con-tinue in the posthuman world:

> Whatever lives must also write. It must strive to leave its gorgeous mark upon the eclogues and the georgics already written for us by some ancestral word-smith. It must realign each ribbon of atoms into a string of words, typing out each random letter in a stock quote, spooling by us on a banner at the bourse. It is alive because it can rebuild itself from any line of text.   (p. 140)

That combination of digital replication ('a banner at the bourse') and biological replication ('alive because it can build itself') is a response to the longer history of *imitatio*, in which the fear of exact replication is repeatedly offset by the delight that arises as each new response to an earlier text necessarily departs from its predecessor. As Virgil put it, 'Nec vero terrae ferre omnes omnia possunt', not all soils can produce the same fruit; or as Quintilian put it in his chapter on *imitatio*: 'Total similarity is so difficult to achieve that even Nature herself has failed to prevent things which

---

27. Christian Bök, *The Xenotext, Book I* (Toronto, 2015), p. 73. I am grateful to Professor Bök for permitting me to quote from the poem.

seem to match and resemble each other most closely from being always distinguishable in *some* respect' ('tantam enim difficultatem habet similitudo, ut ne ipsa quidem natura in hoc ita evaluerit, ut non res quae simillimae, quaeque pares maxime videantur, utique discrimine aliquo discernantur', *Institutio*, 10.2.10). Imitation, that great cultural mutant and agent of mutation, will no doubt prove to be both more mutable and more durable than brass.

Bibliography

PRIMARY WORKS

Alighieri, Dante, *The Divine Comedy*, ed. C. S. Singleton, 3 vols. (Princeton, 1982)

Anon., *An Endevour after the Reconcilement of that Long Debated and Much Lamented Difference between the Godly Presbyterians, and [the godly] Independents, about Church-Government* (London, 1648)

Anon., *His majestie's declaration to his city of London, upon occasion of the late calamity by the lamentable fire* (London, 1666)

Anon., *An Enquiry into the Nature and Origin of Literary Property* (London, 1762)

Anon., *Abstracts of Two Acts of Parliament, Passed in the Thirteenth Year of the Reign of his Present Majesty King George the Third* (London, 1773)

Anon., 'Donaldson v. Beckett', *Hansard*, 1st ser., 17 (1774), 953–1003

Aristophanes, *Aristophanes*, trans. J. Henderson, 5 vols. (Cambridge, Mass., and London, 1998)

Aristophanes, *Thesmophoriazusae*, ed. C. Austin and S. D. Olson (Oxford, 2004)

Aristotle, *The Nicomachean Ethics*, trans. H. Rackham (London and New York, 1926)

Aristotle, Longinus, and Demetrius, *Aristotle Poetics; Longinus On The Sublime; Demetrius On Style*, trans. S. Halliwell, D. A. Russell, W. H. Fyfe, and D. Innes (Cambridge, Mass., and London, 1995)

Ascham, Roger, *Familiarium epistolarum libri tres*, ed. E. Grant (London, 1576)

Ascham, Roger, *English Works*, ed. W. A. Wright (Cambridge, 1904)

Ascham, Roger, *Letters of Roger Ascham*, ed. A. Vos (New York, 1989)

Bacon, Sir Francis, *Works*, ed. J. Spedding, R. L. Ellis, and D. D. Heath, 14 vols. (London, 1857–74)

Beattie, James, *Essays: on Poetry and Music, as They Affect the Mind; on Laughter, and Ludicrous Composition; on the Usefulness of Classical Learning* (London, 1779)

Blackstone, William, *Commentaries on the Laws of England*, 2 vols. (Oxford, 1766)

Blake, William, *Complete Writings*, ed. G. Keynes (London and New York, 1957)

Bök, Christian, *The Xenotext, Book I* (Toronto, 2015)

Borges, Jorge Luis, *Ficciones* (London, 1993)

Boswell, James, *The Decision of the Court of Session upon the Question of Literary Property* (Edinburgh, 1774)

Bracciolini, Poggio, *Poggiana, ou la vie, le caractere, les sentences, et les bons mots de Pogge florentin, avec son Histoire de la republique de Florence*, ed. J. Lenfant, 2 vols. (Amsterdam, 1720)

Bracciolini, Poggio and Niccoli, Niccolò, *Two Renaissance Book Hunters; the Letters of Poggius Bracciolini to Nicolaus de Niccolis*, ed. P. W. G. Gordan (New York, 1974)

Browne, Isaac Hawkins, *A Pipe of Tobacco in Imitation of Six Several Authors* (London, 1736)

Buchler, Johann and Pontanus, Jacob, *Sacrarum profanarumq[ue] phrasium poeticarum thesaurus* (London, 1624)

Calcagnini, Celio, *De imitatione eruditorum quorundam libelli...puta, Caeli Calcagnini...super imitatione commentatio* (Strasbourg, 1535)

Callimachus, *Aetia, Iambi, Lyric Poems*, trans. C. A. Trypanis (Cambridge, Mass., and London, 1958)

Callimachus and Lycophron, *Hymns and Epigrams*, trans. A. W. Mair and G. R. Mair (Cambridge, Mass., and London, 1955)

Carson, Anne, *Nox* (New York, 2010)

Castiglione, Baldassarre, *The Courtyer of Count Baldessar Castilio*, trans. T. Hoby (London, 1561)

Castiglione, Baldassarre, *Il cortegiano, con una scelta delle opere minori*, ed. B. Maier (Turin, 1955)

Cervantes Saavedra, Miguel de, *The Ingenious Hidalgo Don Quixote de la Mancha*, trans. J. Rutherford (London, 2000)

Chaucer, Geoffrey, *The Riverside Chaucer*, ed. L. D. Benson and F. N. Robinson (Boston, 1987)

Cicero, Marcus Tullius, *Marci Tullii Ciceronis De oratore libri tres. Eiusdem de perfecto oratore ad M. Brutum liber*, ed. P. Melanchthon (London, 1573)

Cicero, Marcus Tullius, *De Oratore*, trans. E. W. Sutton and H. Rackham (Cambridge, Mass., and London, 1942)

Cicero, Marcus Tullius, *De Inventione; de Optimo Genera Oratorum; Topica*, trans. H. M. Hubbell (Cambridge, Mass., 1949)

Cicero, Marcus Tullius, *Brutus; Orator*, trans. G. L. Hendrickson and H. M. Hubbell (Cambridge, Mass., and London, 1952)

[Cicero], *Rhetorica ad Herennium*, ed. Harry Caplan (Cambridge, Mass., and London, 1954)

Coleridge, Samuel Taylor, *Aids to Reflection*, ed. J. B. Beer (London and Princeton, 1993)

Coleridge, Samuel Taylor, *The Notebooks*, ed. K. Coburn, 9 vols. (London, 2002)

Comenius, Joannes Amos, *A Patterne of Universall Knowledge, in a Plaine and True Draught: or A Diatyposis, or Model of the Eminently Learned, and Pious Promoter of Science in Generall*, trans. J. Collier (London, 1651)

Comenius, Johann Amos and Hartlib, Samuel, *A Reformation of Schooles Designed in Two Excellent Treatises* (London, 1642)

Cowley, Abraham, *Poems: i. Miscellanies. ii. The Mistress. iii. Pindarique Odes. iv. Davideis* (London, 1656)

Davenant, William and Hobbes, Thomas, *A Discourse upon Gondibert* (Paris, 1650)

Davies, John, *The Poems*, ed. R. Krueger (Oxford, 1975)

Davy, Humphry, *Elements of Chemical Philosophy. Part 1. Vol. 1* (London, 1812)

de Bèze, Théodore, *A Confession of Fayth Made by Common Consent of Divers Reformed Churches*, trans. John Old (London, 1568)

de Nolhac, Pierre, *Pétrarque et l'humanisme: d'après un essai de restitution de sa bibliothèque* (Paris, 1892)

DellaNeva, JoAnn, ed., *Ciceronian Controversies* (Cambridge, Mass., and London, 2007)

Demetrius, *Demetrius on Style: The Greek Text of Demetrius De Elocutione*, ed. W. R. Roberts (Cambridge, 1902)

Denham, John, *The Destruction of Troy: an Essay upon the Second Book of Virgils Aeneis. Written in the year, 1636* (London, 1656)

Denham, John, *Poems and Translations: with The Sophy* (London, 1668)

Descartes, René, *Discours de la methode pour bien conduire sa raison* (Leiden, 1637)

Descartes, René, *A Discourse of a Method, for the Well-Guiding of Reason, and the Discovery of Truth in the Sciences*, trans. J. Holden (London, 1649)

Dionysius of Halicarnassus, *On Literary Composition: being the Greek Text of the De Compositione Verborum*, ed. W. R. Roberts (London, 1910)

Dionysius of Halicarnassus, *The Critical Essays*, trans. S. Usher, 2 vols. (Cambridge, Mass., and London, 1974)

Dionysius of Halicarnassus, *Opuscules Rhétoriques*, ed. G. Aujac, 5 vols. (Paris, 1992)

Donaldson, Alexander, *Some Thoughts on the State of Literary Property* (London, 1764)

Donaldson, Alexander, *The Cases of the Appellants [A. and J. Donaldson] and Respondents in the Cause of Literary Property* (London, 1774)

Douglas, John, *Milton Vindicated from the Charge of Plagiarism* (London, 1751)

Dryden, John, *The Works*, ed. E. N. Hooker, H. T. Swedenberg, and V. A. Dearing, 20 vols. (Berkeley, 1956–2000)

Du Bartas, Guillaume de Salluste, *Du Bartas His Deuine Weekes and Workes Translated*, trans. J. Sylvester (London, 1611)

Duppa, Brian, *Ionsonus virbius: or, The memorie of Ben: Iohnson revived by the friends of the Muses* (London, 1638)

Eliot, T. S., *The Poems*, ed. C. Ricks and J. McCue, 2 vols. (London, 2015)

Enfield, William, *Observations on Literary Property* (London, 1774)

Ennius, Quintus, *The Annals of Q. Ennius*, ed. O. Skutsch (Oxford, 1985)

Erasmus, Desiderius, *De recta Latini Graecaeque sermonis pronuntiatione dialogus. Eiusdem dialogus cui titulus, Ciceronianus, siue, De optimo genere dicendi* (Basel, 1528)

Erasmus, Desiderius, *Opera omnia Desiderii Erasmi*, ed. J. H. Waszink, L. E. Halkin, C. Reedijk, and C. M. Bruehl, 30 vols. (Amsterdam, 1969–)

Erasmus, Desiderius, *The Correspondence of Erasmus*, ed. R. A. B. Mynors, D. F. S. Thomson, W. K. Ferguson, A. Dalzell, C. Fantazzi, and J. M. Estes, 17 vols. (Toronto and London, 1974)

Erasmus, Desiderius, *Collected Works of Erasmus. Vol. 28, Literary and Educational Writings 6: Ciceronianus*, ed. A. H. T. Levi (Toronto, 1986)

Euclid and Dee, John, *The Elements of Geometrie of the Most Auncient Philosopher Euclide of Megara* (London, 1570)

Euripides, *Helen*, ed. W. Allan (Cambridge, 2008)

[Falconer, C.], *An Essay upon Milton's Imitations of the Ancients, in his Paradise Lost: With Some Observations on the Paradise Regain'd* (London, 1741)

Farnaby, Thomas, *Index rhetoricus, scholis & institutioni tenerioris Aetatis accommodatus* (London, 1625)

Fausto, Sebastiano, *Dialogo del Fausto da Longiano del modo de lo tradurre d'una in altra lingua segondo le regole mostrate da Cicerone* (Venice, 1556)

Felton, Henry, *A Dissertation on Reading the Classics, and Forming a Just Style. Written in the year 1709* (London, 1715)

Fenton, Elijah, *Cerealia: an Imitation of Milton* (London, 1706)

Fielding, Henry, *The History of Tom Jones, a Foundling*, ed. M. C. Battestin and F. Bowers, 2 vols. (Oxford, 1974)

Fletcher, Giles and Fletcher, Phineas, *Poetical Works*, ed. F. S. Boas, 2 vols. (Cambridge, 1908)

Freud, Sigmund, *The Standard Edition of the Complete Psychological Works of Sigmund Freud*, ed. J. Strachey and A. Freud, 24 vols. (London, 2001)

Gellius, Aulus, *The Attic Nights of Aulus Gellius*, trans. J. C. Rolfe, 3 vols. (London and New York, 1927)

Giraldi, Giambattista Cinzio, *Discorsi intorno al comporre de i romanzi, delle comedie, e delle tragedie, e di altre maniere di poesie* (Venice, 1554)

Giraldi, Giambattista Cinzio, *Giraldi Cinthio on Romances: Being a Translation of the Discorso intorno al comporre dei romanzi*, ed. H. L. Snuggs (Lexington, 1968)

Hall, Joseph, *The Poems*, ed. A. Davenport (Liverpool, 1969)

Hartlib, Samuel, *The Reformed Common-wealth of Bees* (London, 1655)

Harvey, Gabriel, *Gabrielis Harveij Ciceronianus, vel Oratio post reditum* (London, 1577)

Harvey, Gabriel, *Pierces Supererogation, or a New Prayse of the Old Asse* (London, 1593)

Hermogenes, *Hermogenis . . . de dicendi generibus siue formis orationum libri ii, Lat. donati et scholis explicati atque illustr. a J. Sturmio*, ed. J. Sturm and J. Kocìn (Strasburg, 1571)

Herrick, Robert, *The Complete Poetry*, ed. T. Cain and R. Connolly, 2 vols. (Oxford, 2013)

Heubeck, Alfred, West, Stephanie, Hainsworth, J. B., Russo, Joseph A., and Fernández-Galiano, Manuel, eds., *A Commentary on Homer's Odyssey*, 3 vols. (Oxford, 1988)

Homer, *Homeri quæ extant omnia*, ed. Jean de Sponde (Basel, 1606)

Homer, *The Iliad*, trans. P. Green (Oakland, Calif., 2015)

Hoole, Charles, *A New Discovery of the Old Art of Teaching Schoole* (London, 1659)

Horace, *Q. Horatius Flaccus, ex fide atque auctoritate decem librorum manuscriptorum, Opera*, ed. D. Lambin (Venice, 1566)

Horace, *Horace: The Epistles, Translated into English Verse with Brief Comment*, trans. C. Macleod (Rome, 1986)

Humphrey, Laurence, *Interpretatio Linguarum* (Basel, 1559)

Hurd, Richard, *Q. Horatii Flacci Epistola ad Augustum, with an English Commentary and Notes. To which is Added, A Discourse Concerning Poetical Imitation, by the Author of the Commentary on the Epistle to the Pisos* (London, 1751)

Ishiguro, Kazuo, *Never Let Me Go* (London, 2005)

Isocrates, *Isocrates*, trans. G. Norlin and L. Van Hook, 3 vols. (London and New York, 1928)

Jaquet-Droz, Henri-Louis, *A Description of Several Pieces of mechanism . . . And which are now to be seen at the Great Room, no. 6, in King-Street, Covent-Garden* (London, 1780)

Jerome, Saint, *Liber de optimo genere interpretandi (Epistula 57)*, ed. G. J. M. Bartelink (Leiden, 1980)

Johnson, Samuel, *The Yale Edition of the Works, Volumes 3–5: The Rambler*, ed. W. J. Bate and A. B. Strauss (New Haven, 1969)

Johnson, Samuel, *The Lives of the Most Eminent English Poets; With Critical Observations on their Works*, ed. R. Lonsdale, 4 vols. (Oxford, 2006)

Jonson, Ben, *The Cambridge Edition of the Works of Ben Jonson*, ed. D. M. Bevington, M. Butler, and I. Donaldson, 7 vols. (Cambridge, 2012)

Josephus, Flavius, *The Jewish War*, trans. H. St J. Thackeray, 3 vols. (Cambridge, Mass., 1997)

Junius, Franciscus, *The Painting of the Ancients*, trans. R. Hodgkinson (London, 1638)

Justinian, *The Institutes of Justinian with English Translation and Notes*, ed. T. C. Sandars (London, 1874)

Keckermannus, Bartholomaeus, *Systema Rhetoricae* (Hanover, 1608)

La Mettrie, Julien Offray de, *Man a Machine, Translated from the French of the Marquiss d'Argens* (London, 1749)

La Mettrie, Julien Offray de, *L'homme machine: A Study in the Origins of an Idea*, ed. A. Vartanian (Princeton, 1960)

Lauder, William, *An Essay on Milton's Use and Imitation of the Moderns, in his Paradise Lost* (London, 1750)

Le Bossu, René, *Monsieur Bossu's Treatise of the Epick Poem*, trans. W. J. (London, 1695)

Lee, Samuel, *Orbis Miraculum; or, The Temple of Solomon Pourtrayed by Scripture-light* (London, 1659)

Lipsius, Justus, *Iusti Lipsii epistolarum selectarum centuria quarta (quinta) miscellanea postuma* (Antwerp, 1613)

Lipsius, Justus, *Principles of Letter-Writing: A Bilingual Text of Justi Lipsii Epistolica Institutio*, ed. R. V. Young and M. T. Hester (Carbondale, Ill., 1996)

Lloyd, Robert, *The Progress of Envy: A Poem in Imitation of Spenser Occasioned by Lauder's Attack on the Character of Milton* (London, 1751)

Locke, John, *Two Treatises on Government*, ed. P. Laslett (Cambridge, 1960)

Locke, John, *An Essay Concerning Human Understanding*, ed. P. H. Nidditch (Oxford, 1975)

Locke, John, *The Correspondence*, ed. E. S. De Beer, 8 vols. (Oxford, 1976)

Locke, John, *Some Thoughts Concerning Education*, ed. J. S. Yolton and J. W. Yolton (Oxford, 1989)

Longinus, *Peri Hypsous, or, Dionysius Longinus on the Height of Eloquence*, trans. J. Hall (London, 1652)

Longinus, *On the Sublime*, ed. D. A. Russell (Oxford, 1964)

Lucretius Carus, Titus, *Titi Lucreti Cari de rerum natura libri sex.*, ed. C. Bailey, 3 vols. (Oxford, 1947)

Lyly, John, *Euphues: The Anatomy of Wit and Euphues and His England*, ed. L. Scragg (Manchester, 2003)

Macaulay, Catharine, *A Modest Plea for the Property of Copyright* (Bath, 1774)

Macrobius, Ambrosius Aurelius Theodosius, *The Saturnalia*, trans. P. V. Davies (New York and London, 1969)

Macrobius, Ambrosius Aurelius Theodosius, *Saturnalia*, trans. R. A. Kaster, 3 vols. (Cambridge, Mass., and London, 2011)

Marston, John, *The Poems*, ed. A. Davenport (Liverpool, 1961)

Martial, *Epigrams*, trans. D. R. Shackleton Bailey, 3 vols. (Cambridge, Mass., and London, 1993)

Marvell, Andrew, *The Poems*, ed. Nigel Smith (London, 2003)

Melanchthon, Philipp, *Erotemata dialectices* (Wittenberg, 1593)

Melanchthon, Philipp, *Philippi Melanthonis Opera quae supersunt omnia*, ed. K. G. Bretschneider, H. E. Bindseil, and C. A. Schwetschke und Sohn, 28 vols. (Halle, 1834)

Meres, Francis, *Palladis Tamia* (London, 1598)

Milton, John, *Paradise Lost, a Poem. To which is prefix'd an account of his life [by E. Fenton]*, ed. E. Fenton (London, 1725)

Milton, John, *Milton's Paradise Lost*, ed. R. Bentley (London, 1732)

Milton, John, *Paradise Lost: a Poem in Twelve Books*, ed. T. Newton, 2 vols. (London, 1749)

Milton, John, *Complete Shorter Poems*, ed. J. Carey (London, 1997)

Milton, John, *Paradise Lost*, ed. A. Fowler (London and New York, 1998)

Nashe, Thomas, *Works*, ed. R. B. McKerrow and F. P. Wilson, 4 vols. (Oxford, 1958)

Nizolius, Marius, *Observationum in M. T. Ciceronem prima [et secunda] pars* (Prato, 1535)

Nizolius, Marius, *Nizolius, sive Thesaurus Ciceronianus, nunc iterum, C.S. Curionis labore auctior* (Basel, 1559)

Oldham, John, *Poems*, ed. H. Brooks and R. Selden (Oxford, 1987)

Omphalius, Jacobus, *De elocutionis imitatione ac apparatu liber vnus* (Basel, 1537)

Ovid, *Metamorphoses*, trans. F. J. Miller and G. P. Goold, 2 vols. (Cambridge, Mass., and London, 1977)

Oxenford, John and Feiling, C. A., *Tales from the German: Comprising Specimens from the Most Celebrated Authors* (London, 1844)

Palladio, Andrea, *The First Book of Architecture*, trans. G. Richards (London, 1663)

Pepys, Samuel, *The Diary of Samuel Pepys: A New and Complete Transcription*, ed. R. Latham and W. Matthews, 11 vols. (London, 1970)

Peter, John, *Artificial Versifying or, The School-boy's Recreation* (London, 1677)

Petrarca, Francesco, *L'Africa*, ed. N. Festa (Firenze, 1926)

Petrarca, Francesco, *Le familiari*, ed. V. Rossi and U. Bosco, 4 vols. (Firenze, 1933)

Petrarca, Francesco, *Letters on Familiar Matters: Rerum familiarium libri*, trans. A. S. Bernardo, 3 vols. (Baltimore and London, 1975–85)

Petrarca, Francesco, *Petrarch's Africa*, trans. T. G. Bergin and A. S. Wilson (New Haven, 1977)

Philips, John, *The Splendid Shilling. A Poem, in Imitation of Milton. By the Author of Bleinheim* (London, 1705)

Pico della Mirandola, Giovanni Francesco, *Io. Francisci Pici Mirandulae domini . . . Physici libri duo, i. De appetitu primae materiae . . . ii. De elementis. Et Rhetorici duo, De imitatione, ad Petrum Bembum. P. Bembi de imitatione liber unus* (Basel, 1518)

Plato, *Theaetetus; Sophist*, trans. H. N. Fowler (London, 1921)

Plato, *The Republic*, trans. P. Shorey, 2 vols. (Cambridge, Mass., 1930)

Plutarch, *Plutarch's Lives*, trans. B. Perrin, 11 vols. (Cambridge, Mass., and London, 1914–26)

Plutarch, *Plutarch's Moralia*, trans. F. C. Babbit, 16 vols. (Cambridge, Mass., 1927–69)

Polidori, John William, *The Diary of Dr John William Polidori, 1816: Relating to Byron, Shelley, etc*, ed. W. M. Rossetti (London, 1911)

Pontanus, Jacobus, *Jacobi Pontani . . . poeticarum institutionum libri iii* (Ingolstadt, 1600)

Pope, Alexander, *The Dunciad: with Notes, Variorum and the Prolegomena of Scriblerus* (London, 1729)

Pope, Alexander, *The Prose Works*, ed. R. Cowler, 2 vols. (Oxford, 1936–86)

Pope, Alexander, *Imitations of Horace*, ed. J. Butt (London and New Haven, 1953)

Pope, Alexander, *The Poems: A One-Volume Edition of the Twickenham Text with Selected Annotations*, ed. J. Butt (London, 1963)

Pope, Alexander, *The Dunciad: in Four Books*, ed. V. Rumbold (Harlow, 2009)

Prado, Jeronimo and Villalpando, Juan Bautista, *In Ezechielem explanationes et apparatus vrbis, ac Templi Hierosolymitani*, 3 vols. (Rome, 1605)

Quintilian, *M. Fabii Quintiliani Institutionis Oratoriae liber I*, ed. F. H. Colson (Cambridge, 1924)

Quintilian, *The Orator's Education*, trans. D. A. Russell, 5 vols. (Cambridge, Mass., and London, 2001)

Quintilian, *Institutio Oratoria. Book 2*, ed. Tobias Reinhardt and Michael Winterbottom (Oxford, 2006)

Ramus, Petrus, *Ciceronianus* (Paris, 1557)

Ramus, Petrus, *P. Rami Scholae In Tres Primas Liberales* (Frankfurt, 1581)

Ramus, Petrus, *Arguments in Rhetoric against Quintilian: Translation and Text of Peter Ramus's Rhetoricae Distinctiones in Quintilianum (1549)*, ed. J. J. Murphy and C. E. Newlands (DeKalb, Ill., 1986)

Randolph, Thomas, *Poems; With the Muses Looking-Glasse* (London, 1638)

Reich, Stephan, ed., *In M. Fabij Quintiliani Institutionum librum decimum, doctissimorum virorum annotationes, nempe P. Melanthonis . . . in ordinem digestæ & æd. per M. Riccium* (Leipzig, 1570)

Richardson, Jonathan, *Explanatory Notes and Remarks on Milton's Paradise Lost* (London, 1734)

Richardson, N. J., ed., *Three Homeric Hymns: To Apollo, Hermes, and Aphrodite, hymns 3, 4, and 5* (Cambridge, 2010)

Rorvik, David M., *In his Image: The Cloning of a Man* (London, 1978)

Roscommon, Wentworth Dillon Earl of, *An Essay on Translated Verse* (London, 1684)

Ryle, Gilbert, *The Concept of Mind* (London, 1949)

Salutati, Coluccio, *Epistolario di Coluccio Salutati*, ed. F. Novati, 4 vols. (Rome, 1891)

Scaliger, Joseph, *Autobiography of Joseph Scaliger: with Autobiographical Selections from his Letters, his Testament and the Funeral Orations by Daniel Heinsius and Dominicus Baudius*, ed. George W. Robinson (Cambridge, 1927)

Scaliger, Joseph Juste and Daillé, Jean, *Scaligerana* (Cologne, 1667)

Scaliger, Julius Caesar, *Poetices libri septem = Sieben Bücher über die Dichtkunst*, ed. L. Deitz, M. Fuhrmann, and G. Vogt-Spira, 6 vols. (Stuttgart, 1994–8)

Scott, William, *The Model of Poesy*, ed. G. Alexander (Cambridge, 2013)

Seneca, Lucius Annaeus, *L. Annaei Senecae ad Lucilium epistulae morales*, ed. A. Beltrami, 2 vols. (Rome, 1949)

Seneca, Lucius Annaeus (the elder), *Declamations*, trans. M. Winterbottom (Cambridge, Mass., and London, 1974)

Servius, Maurus, *Servii Grammatici qui feruntur in Vergilii Carmina Commentarii*, ed. G. Thilo and H. Hagen, 2 vols. (Leipzig, 1878–83)

Shelley, Mary Wollstonecraft, *Frankenstein; or, The Modern Prometheus*, ed. M. K. Joseph (Oxford, 1969)

Shelley, Mary Wollstonecraft, *The Journals, 1814–1844*, ed. P. R. Feldman and D. Scott-Kilvert, 2 vols. (Oxford, 1987)

Shelley, Mary Wollstonecraft, *Frankenstein: or the Modern Prometheus: the Original Two-Volume Novel of 1816–1817 from the Bodleian Library manuscripts*, ed. C. E. Robinson (Oxford, 2008)

Sidney, Sir Philip, *An Apology for Poetry or the Defence of Poesy*, ed. G. Shepherd (Manchester, 1973)

Soranus, *Soranus' Gynecology*, trans. O. Temkin (Baltimore, 1956)

Southey, Robert, 'An Inquiry into the Copyright Act', *Quarterly Review* 21 (1819), 196–213

Spenser, Edmund, *The Faerie Queene*, ed. A. C. Hamilton, H. Yamashita, and T. Suzuki, 2nd edn (Harlow, 2001)

Stesichorus, *The Poems*, ed. M. Davies and P. Finglass (Cambridge, 2014)

Sturm, Johannes, *Ad Werteros Fratres, Nobilitas literata* (Strasburg, 1556)

Sturm, Johannes, *A Ritch Storehouse or Treasure for Nobilitye and Gentlemen*, trans. T. Browne (London, 1570)

Sturm, Johannes, *Hermogenis ... de dicendi generibus siue formis orationum libri ii, Lat. donati et scholis explicati atque illustr. a J. Sturmio* (Strasburg, 1571)

Sturm, Johannes, *De Imitatione Oratoria Libri Tres* (Strasburg, 1574)

Sturm, Johannes, *Johann Sturm on Education: The Reformation and Humanist Learning*, ed. L. W. Spitz and B. S. Tinsley (St. Louis, Mo., 1995)

Tacitus, Cornelius, *Agricola; Germania; Dialogus*, trans. W. Peterson, M. Hutton, R. M. Ogilvie, E. H. Warmington, and M. Winterbottom (Cambridge, Mass., and London, 1970)

Tasso, Torquato, *Gerusalemme liberata*, ed. L. Caretti (Turin, 1980)

Tasso, Torquato, *Godfrey of Bulloigne: A Critical Edition of Edward Fairfax's Translation of Tasso's Gerusalemme liberata*, ed. K. M. Lea and T. M. Gang (Oxford, 1981)

Templo, Jacob Judah Aryeh Leon, *Portraict du Temple de Salomon* (Amsterdam, 1643)

Templo, Jacob Judah Aryeh Leon, *A Relation of the Most Memorable Thinges in the Tabernacle of Moses, and the Temple of Salomon, According to Text of Scripture* (Amsterdam, 1675)

Theophrastus, *Characters*, trans. I. C. Cunningham, A. D. Knox, and J. S. Rusten (Cambridge, Mass., and London, 1993)

Utterson, Sarah Elizabeth, *Tales of the Dead. Principally Translated from the French* (London, 1813)

Vasari, Giorgio, *The Lives of the Artists*, trans. J. C. Bondanella and P. E. Bondanella (Oxford, 1991)

Vaucanson, Jacques de, *An Account of the Mechanism of an Automaton . . . playing on the German Flute*, trans. J. T. Desaguliers (London, 1742)

Veronese, Guarino, *Epistolario di Guarino Veronese*, ed. R. Sabbadini, 3 vols. (Turin, 1959)

Virgil, *Aeneidos . . . Argumentis, Explicationibus et Notis Illustrata*, ed. J. L. La Cerda (Cologne, 1642)

Virgil, *Virgil*, trans. H. R. Fairclough, 2 vols. (Cambridge, Mass., and London, 1978)

Virgil, *P. Vergili Maronis Aeneidos, liber secundus*, ed. R. G. Austin (Oxford, 1980)

Virgil, *Georgics*, ed. R. F. Thomas, 2 vols. (Cambridge, 1988)

Virgil, *Georgics*, ed. R. A. B. Mynors (Oxford, 1990)

Virgil, *Aeneid 10: With Introduction, Translation and Commentary*, ed. S. J. Harrison (Oxford, 1991)

Virgil, *Aeneid. Book XII*, ed. R. J. Tarrant (Cambridge, 2012)

Virgil and Petrarca, Francesco, *Francisci Petrarcae Vergilianus codex: ad Publii Vergilii Maronis diem natalem bis millesimum celebrandum quam simillime expressus atque in lucem editus*, ed. G. Galbiati (Mediolani, 1930)

Vitruvius, M. Pollio and Perrault, Claude, *An Abridgment of the Architecture of Vitruvius* (London, 1692)

Vives, Juan Luis, *Io. Lodouici Viuis . . . opera* ed. H. Coccius (Basel, 1555)

Vives, Juan Luis, *Vives: On Education: a Translation of the De Tradendis Disciplinis*, trans. F. Watson (Cambridge, 1913)

Vorilhon, Claude [a.k.a. Raël], *Yes to Human Cloning* (London, Sydney, and Los Angeles, 2001)

[Warburton, William], *A Letter from an Author to a Member of Parliament, Concerning Literary Property* (London, 1747)

Weever, John, *Epigrammes in the Oldest Cut, and Newest Fashion* (London, 1599)

West, M. L., ed., *Iambi et Elegi Graeci ante Alexandrum Cantati*, 2 vols. (Oxford, 1989)

West, M. L., ed., *Greek Lyric Poetry* (Oxford, 1993)

West, M. L., ed., *Homeric Hymns, Homeric Apocrypha, Lives of Homer* (Cambridge, Mass., and London, 2003)

Wordsworth, Dorothy, *Journals of Dorothy Wordsworth*, ed. E. De Sélincourt, 2 vols. (London, 1941)

Wordsworth, William, *The Prose Works of William Wordsworth*, ed. W. J. B. Owen and J. W. Smyser, 3 vols. (Oxford, 1974)

Wordsworth, William, *Home at Grasmere: Part First, Book First of 'The Recluse'*, ed. B. Darlington (Ithaca, NY, and Hassocks, 1977)

Wordsworth, William, *The Prelude, 1799, 1805, 1850: Authoritative Texts, Context and Reception, Recent Critical Essays*, ed. J. Wordsworth, M. H. Abrams, and S. Gill (New York, 1979)

Wordsworth, William, *Early Poems and Fragments, 1785–1797*, ed. C. Landon and J. R. Curtis (Ithaca, NY, and London, 1997)

Wordsworth, William and Coleridge, Samuel Taylor, *Lyrical Ballads: with Pastoral and Other Poems, in Two Volumes*, 2 vols. (London, 1802)

Wordsworth, William and Wordsworth, Dorothy, *The Letters of William and Dorothy Wordsworth*, ed. E. De Sélincourt, M. T. Moorman, C. L. Shaver, and A. G. Hill, 8 vols. (Oxford, 1967–88)

Young, Edward, *Conjectures on Original Composition: In a Letter to the Author of Sir Charles Grandison* (London, 1759)

SECONDARY WORKS

Abrams, M. H., *The Mirror and the Lamp: Romantic Theory and the Critical Tradition* (New York and London, 1958)

Ahern, John, 'Good-Bye Bologna: Johannnes Andreae and *Familiares* IV 15 and 16', in T. Barolini and H. W. Storey, eds., *Petrarch and the Textual Origins of Interpretation* (Leiden and Boston, 2007), pp. 185–204

Aldiss, Brian Wilson, *Billion Year Spree: The History of Science Fiction* (London, 1973)

Alighieri, Pietro, *Comentum super poema Comedie Dantis*, ed. M. Chiamenti (Tempe, Ariz., 2002)

Allen, Kenneth P., 'Cervantes' "Galatea" and the "Discorso intorno al comporre dei Romanzi" of Giraldi Cinthio', *Revista Hispánica Moderna* 39 (1976), 52–68

Arbib, Michael A., *From Action to Language: The Mirror Neuron System* (Cambridge, 2006)

Arbib, Michael A., *How the Brain got Language: The Mirror System Hypothesis* (Oxford, 2012)

Armstrong, David, *Vergil, Philodemus, and the Augustans* (Austin, 2004)

Auerbach, Erich, *Mimesis: The Representation of Reality in Western Literature* (Princeton, 1953)

Auerbach, Erich, *Scenes from the Drama of European Literature*, trans. P. Valesio (Manchester, 1984)

Bailly, Christian and Bailly, Sharon, *Automata: The Golden Age, 1848–1914* (London, 1987)

Baines, Paul, *The House of Forgery in Eighteenth-Century Britain* (Aldershot, 1999)

Baldick, Chris, *In Frankenstein's Shadow: Myth, Monstrosity, and Nineteenth-Century Writing* (Oxford, 1987)

Baranski, Zygmunt G. and Cachey, T. J., *Petrarch and Dante: Anti-Dantism, Metaphysics, Tradition* (Notre Dame, Ind., 2009)

Barchiesi, Alessandro, *La traccia del modello: effetti omerici nella narrazione virgiliana* (Pisa, 1984)

Barchiesi, Alessandro, *Homeric Effects in Vergil's Narrative*, trans. I. Marchesi and M. Fox (Princeton, 2015)

Bardel, Ruth, 'Eidola in Epic, Tragedy, and Vase Painting', in N. K. Rutter and B. A. Sparkes, eds., *Word and Image in Ancient Greece* (Edinburgh, 2000), pp. 140–60

Barkan, Leonard, *Unearthing the Past: Archaeology and Aesthetics in the Making of Renaissance Culture* (New Haven and London, 1999)

Barney, Rachel, 'The Carpenter and the Good', in D. Cairns, F.-G. Herrmann, and T. Penner, eds., *Pursuing the Good: Ethics and Metaphysics in Plato's 'Republic'* (Edinburgh, 2007), pp. 293–319

Barton, Anne, 'The Road from Penshurst: Wordsworth, Ben Jonson and Coleridge in 1802', *Essays in Criticism* 37 (1987), 209–33

Baswell, Christopher, *Virgil in Medieval England: Figuring the Aeneid from the Twelfth Century to Chaucer* (Cambridge, 1995)

Bataillon, Marcel, *Érasme et l'Espagne: recherches sur l'histoire spirituelle du XVIe siècle* (Paris, 1937)

Bate, Walter Jackson, *The Burden of the Past and the English Poet* (London, 1971)

Baudrillard, Jean, *The Transparency of Evil: Essays on Extreme Phenomena*, trans. J. Benedict (London, 1993)

Baudrillard, Jean, *Simulacra and Simulation*, trans. S. F. Glaser (Ann Arbor, Mich., 1994)

Beal, Peter, 'Notions in Garrison: The Seventeenth-Century Commonplace Book', in W. S. Hill, ed., *New Ways of Looking at Old Texts* (Binghampton, NY, 1993), pp. 131–47

Beckett, J. V., *Coal and Tobacco: The Lowthers and the Economic Development of West Cumberland, 1660–1760* (Cambridge, 1981)

Bednarz, James P., *Shakespeare and the Poets' War* (New York, 2001)

Benjamin, Walter, *Illuminations*, ed. H. Arendt (London, 1970)

Bennett, J. A. and Mandelbrote, Scott, *The Garden, the Ark, the Tower, the Temple: Biblical Metaphors of Knowledge in Early Modern Europe* (Oxford, 1998)

Bernardo, Aldo S., 'Petrarch's Attitude toward Dante', *PMLA* 70 (1955), 488–517

Bernardo, Aldo S., *Petrarch, Scipio and the 'Africa': The Birth of Humanism's Dream* (Westport, Conn., 1978)

Bertelsen, Lance, *The Nonsense Club: Literature and Popular Culture, 1749–1764* (Oxford, 1986)

Bhabha, Homi K., *The Location of Culture* (London, 1994)

Binns, J. W., 'Ciceronianism in Sixteenth Century England: The Latin Debate', *Lias* 7 (1980), 199–203

Björnstad, Hall and Eden, Kathy, eds., *Borrowed Feathers: Plagiarism and the Limits of Imitation in Early Modern Europe* (Oslo, 2008)

Blair, Ann, 'Textbooks and Methods of Note-Taking in Early Modern Europe', in E. Campi, S. De Angelis, A.-S. Goeing, and A. Grafton, eds., *Scholarly Knowledge: Textbooks in Early Modern Europe* (Geneva, 2008), pp. 39–73

Blank, D., 'Philodemus on the Technicity of Rhetoric', in D. Obbink, ed., *Philodemus and Poetry* (Oxford, 1995), pp. 178–88

Blank, Paula, 'Jonson's Family Values', in A. Boesky and M. T. Crane, eds., *Form and Reform in Renaissance England: Essays in Honor of Barbara Kiefer Lewalski* (Newark and London, 2000), pp. 127–49

Blessington, Francis C., *Paradise Lost and the Classical Epic* (Boston, 1979)

Bloom, Harold, *The Anxiety of Influence: A Theory of Poetry* (Oxford and New York, 1973)

Bloom, Harold, *A Map of Misreading* (Oxford and New York, 1975)

Boehrer, Bruce Thomas, *The Fury of Men's Gullets: Ben Jonson and the Digestive Canal* (Philadelphia, 1997)

Bonner, Stanley F., *The Literary Treatises of Dionysius of Halicarnassus: A Study in the Development of Critical Method* (Cambridge, 1939)

Bonner, Stanley F., *Education in Ancient Rome: From the Elder Cato to the Younger Pliny* (London, 1977)

Boon, Marcus, *In Praise of Copying* (Cambridge, Mass., 2010)

Boskoff, Priscilla S., 'Quintilian in the Late Middle Ages', *Speculum: A Journal of Medieval Studies* 27 (1952), 71–8

Braden, Gordon, *The Classics and English Renaissance Poetry: Three Case Studies* (New Haven, 1978)

Brammall, Sheldon, *The English Aeneid: Translations of Virgil, 1555–1646* (Edinburgh, 2015)

Brayman Hackel, Heidi, *Reading Material in Early Modern England: Print, Gender, and Literacy* (Cambridge, 2005)

Briggs, Robert and King, Thomas J., 'Transplantation of Living Nuclei from Blastula Cells into Enucleated Frogs' Eggs', *Proceedings of the National Academy of Sciences* 38 (1952), 455–63

Briggs, W. W., 'Eurydice, Venus and Creusa: A Note on Structure in Virgil', *Vergilius* 25 (1979), 43–4

Brooks, Harold F., 'The "Imitation" in English Poetry, Especially in Formal Satire, before the Age of Pope', *The Review of English Studies* OS 25 (1949), 124–40

Brown, Robert D., 'Lucretius and Callimachus', *Illinois Classical Studies* 7 (1982), 77–97

Brown, Sarah Annes, *A Familiar Compound Ghost: Allusion and the Uncanny* (Manchester, 2012)

Brownlee, Kevin, 'Power Plays: Petrarch's Genealogical Strategies', *Journal of Medieval and Renaissance Studies* 35 (2005), 467–88

Bruère, Richard T., 'Lucan and Petrarch's *Africa*', *Classical Philology* 56 (1961), 83–99

Burke, Peter, *The Fortunes of the Courtier: The European Reception of Castiglione's Cortegiano* (Cambridge, 1995)

Burnyeat, M. F., 'Aristotle on Learning to be Good', in A. O. Rorty, ed., *Essays on Aristotle's Ethics* (Los Angeles, 1980), pp. 69–92

Burnyeat, M. F., 'Culture and Society in Plato's *Republic*', *Tanner Lectures in Human Values* 20 (1999), 215–324

Burnyeat, M. F., *The Theaetetus of Plato*, trans. M. J. Levett (Indianapolis and Cambridge, 1990)

Burrow, Colin, *Epic Romance: Homer to Milton* (Oxford, 1993)

Burrow, Colin, ' "Full of the Maker's Guile": Ovid on Imitating and on the Imitation of Ovid', in P. Hardie, ed., *Ovidian Transformations: Essays on Ovid's Metamorphoses and its Reception* (Cambridge, 1999), pp. 271–87

Burrow, Colin, *Shakespeare and Classical Antiquity* (Oxford, 2013)

Burrow, Colin, 'Shakespeare's Authorities', in K. Halsey and A. Vine, eds., *Shakespeare and Authority: Citations, Conceptions and Constructions* (London, 2018), pp. 31–53

Burrow, Colin and Beadle, Richard, eds., *English Manuscript Studies 1100–1700 16: Manuscript Miscellanies 1450–1700* (London, 2011)

Burrow, J. A., *Ricardian Poetry: Chaucer, Gower, Langland and the Gawain Poet* (London, 1971)

Butler, Martin, 'The Dates of Three Poems by Ben Jonson', *Huntington Library Quarterly* 55 (1992), 279–94

Campbell, Gordon and Corns, Thomas N., *John Milton: Life, Work, and Thought* (Oxford, 2008)

Cave, Terence, *The Cornucopian Text: Problems of Writing in the French Renaissance* (Oxford, 1979)

Chartier, Roger, *Inscription and Erasure: Literature and Written Culture from the Eleventh to the Eighteenth Century* (Philadelphia, 2007)

Chatterton, E. Keble, *Ship-models* (London, 1923)

Cheney, Patrick, Copeland, Rita, Hardie, Philip, Hopkins, David, Martindale, Charles, Vance, Norman, and Wallace, Jennifer, eds., *The Oxford History of Classical Reception in English Literature*, 5 vols. (Oxford, 2012–)

Clancey, Richard W., *Wordsworth's Classical Undersong: Education, Rhetoric, and Poetic Truth* (Basingstoke, 2000)

Clare, Janet, *Shakespeare's Stage Traffic: Imitation, Borrowing and Competition in Renaissance Theatre* (Cambridge, 2014)

Clark, Donald Lemen, 'The Requirements of a Poet: A Note on the Sources of Ben Jonson's "Timber", Paragraph 130', *Modern Philology* 16 (1918), 413–29

Clark, Donald Lemen, *John Milton at St Paul's School: A Study of Ancient Rhetoric in English Renaissance Education* (New York, 1948)

Clark, James G., Coulson, Frank Thomas, and McKinley, Kathryn L., eds., *Ovid in the Middle Ages* (Cambridge, 2011)

Clarke, Michael, *Flesh and Spirit in the Songs of Homer: A Study of Words and Myths* (Oxford, 1999)

Classen, Carl Joachim, 'Cicero inter Germanos Redivivus, II', *Humanistica Lovaniensia* 39 (1990), 157–76

Classen, Carl Joachim, 'Quintilian and the Revival of Learning in Italy', *Humanistica Lovaniensia* 43 (1994), 77–98

Classen, Carl Joachim, *Antike Rhetorik im Zeitalter des Humanismus* (Munich, 2003)

Clay, Diskin, *Paradosis and Survival: Three Chapters in the History of Epicurean Philosophy* (Ann Arbor, Mich., 1998)

Clifford, James L., 'Johnson and Lauder', *Philological Quarterly* 54 (1975), 342–56

Colvin, Stephen C., *Dialect in Aristophanes: and The Politics of Language in Ancient Greek Literature* (Oxford, 1999)

Connors, Catherine, 'Field and Forum: Culture and Agriculture in Roman Rhetoric', in William J. Dominik, ed., *Roman Eloquence: Rhetoric in Society and Literature* (London, 1997), pp. 71–89

Conte, Gian Biagio, *The Rhetoric of Imitation: Genre and Poetic Memory in Virgil and Other Latin Poets*, trans. C. Segal (Ithaca, NY, and London, 1986)

Conte, Gian Biagio, *The Poetry of Pathos: Studies in Virgilian Epic* (Oxford, 2007)

Conte, Gian Biagio, *Stealing the Club from Hercules: On Imitation in Latin Poetry* (Berlin and Boston, 2017)

Coolidge, John S., 'Great Things and Small: The Virgilian Progression', *Comparative Literature* 17 (1965), 1–23

Cooper, Helen, 'Choosing Poetic Fathers: The English Problem', in L. Erne and G. Bolens, eds., *Medieval and Early Modern Authorship* (Tübingen, 2011), pp. 29–50

Cooper, Nicholas, *Houses of the Gentry 1480–1680* (New Haven and London, 1999)

Copeland, Rita, *Rhetoric, Hermeneutics and Translation in the Middle Ages: Academic Traditions and Vernacular Texts* (Cambridge, 1991)

Copeland, Rita, ed., *The Oxford History of Classical Reception in English Literature. Volume 1, 800–1558* (Oxford, 2016)

Coulter, Cornelia C., 'Boccaccio's Knowledge of Quintilian', *Speculum: A Journal of Medieval Studies* 33 (1958), 490–6

Crane, Mary Thomas, *Framing Authority: Sayings, Self, and Society in Sixteenth Century England* (Princeton, 1993)

Croll, Morris W., *Style, Rhetoric, and Rhythm: Essays*, ed. J. M. Patrick (Princeton, 1966)

Cummings, Brian and Simpson, James, eds., *Cultural Reformations: Medieval and Renaissance in Literary History* (Oxford, 2010)

Cummings, Robert, 'Liberty and History in Jonson's *Invitation to Supper*', *Studies in English Literature, 1500–1900* 40 (2000), 103–22

D'Ascia, Luca, *Erasmo e l'umanesimo romano* (Firenze, 1991)

David, Jean-Michel, *Le patronat judiciaire au dernier siècle de la République romaine* (Rome, 1992)

Davis, Paul, 'Addison's Forgotten Poetic Response to *Paradise Lost*: "Milton's Stile Imitated, in a Translation of a Story out of the Third Aeneid" (1704): An Edited Text, with Annotation and Commentary', *Milton Quarterly* 49 (2015), 243–74

Deane, Seamus, *The French Revolution and Enlightenment in England, 1789–1832* (Cambridge, Mass., and London, 1988)

Deazley, R., 'Commentary on Milton's Contract 1667', in L. Bently and M. Kretschmer, eds., *Primary Sources on Copyright (1450–1900)* (http://www.copyrighthistory.org, accessed February 2018)

Deazley, Ronan, *On the Origin of the Right to Copy: Charting the Movement of Copyright Law in Eighteenth-Century Britain (1695–1775)* (Oxford, 2004)

Derrida, Jacques, *Dissemination*, trans. B. Johnson (London, 1981)

Diels, Hermann, *Doxographi Graeci* (Berlin, 1965)

Dionisotti, Carlo, *Gli umanisti e il volgare fra Quattro e Cinquecento* (Florence, 1968)

Dobranski, Stephen B., 'Pondering Satan's Shield in Milton's *Paradise Lost*', *English Literary Renaissance* 35 (2005), 490–506

Dominik, William J., ed., *Roman Eloquence: Rhetoric in Society and Literature* (London, 1997)

Dominik, William J. and Hall, Jon, eds., *A Companion to Roman Rhetoric* (Malden, Mass., and Oxford, 2007)

Donaldson, Ian, *Jonson's Magic Houses* (Oxford, 1997)

Donaldson, Ian, '"The Fripperie of Wit": Jonson and Plagiarism', in P. Kewes, ed., *Plagiarism in Early Modern Europe* (Basingstoke, 2003), pp. 119–33

Donaldson, Ian, 'Talking with Ghosts: Ben Jonson and the English Civil War', *Ben Jonson Journal* 17 (2010), 1–18

Donaldson, Ian, *Ben Jonson: A Life* (Oxford, 2011)

Doniger, Wendy, 'Sex and the Mythological Clone', in M. C. Nussbaum and C. R. Sunstein, eds., *Clones and Clones: Facts and Fantasies about Human Cloning* (New York and London, 1997), pp. 114–38

Doniger, Wendy and Spinner, Gregory, 'Misconceptions: Female Imaginations and Male Fantasies in Parental Imprinting', *Daedalus* 127 (1998), 97–129

Donnelly, Phillip J., *Milton's Scriptural Reasoning: Narrative and Protestant Toleration* (Cambridge, 2009)

Downes, Kerry, *The Architecture of Wren* (Reading, 1988)

Doyon, André and Liaigre, Lucien, *Jacques Vaucanson, mécanicien de génie* (Paris, 1966)

DuRocher, Richard J., *Milton and Ovid* (Ithaca, NY, 1985)

DuRocher, Richard J., *Milton Among the Romans: The Pedagogy and Influence of Milton's Latin Curriculum* (Pittsburgh, 2001)

Dworkin, Craig Douglas and Goldsmith, Kenneth, eds., *Against Expression: An Anthology of Conceptual Writing* (Evanston, Ill., 2011)

Dyson, Julia T., 'Dido the Epicurean', *Classical Antiquity* 15 (1996), 203–21

Dzelzainis, Martin, 'Milton and the Limits of Ciceronian Rhetoric', in N. Rhodes, ed., *English Renaissance Prose: History, Language, and Politics* (Tempe, Ariz., 1997), pp. 203–26

Eden, Kathy, *Hermeneutics and the Rhetorical Tradition: Chapters in the Ancient Legacy and its Humanist Reception* (New Haven and London, 1997)

Eden, Kathy, *Friends Hold all Things in Common: Tradition, Intellectual Property, and the Adages of Erasmus* (New Haven and London, 2001)

Eden, Kathy, 'Literary Property and the Question of Style', in H. Björnstad and K. Eden, eds., *Borrowed Feathers: Plagiarism and the Limits of Imitation in Early Modern Europe* (Oslo, 2008), pp. 21–38

Eden, Kathy, 'Cicero Redivivus and the Historicizing of Renaissance Style', *Nottingham Medieval Studies* 56 (2012), 143–69

Eden, Kathy, *The Renaissance Rediscovery of Intimacy* (Chicago, Ill., 2012)

Edmunds, Lowell, 'The Latin Invitation-Poem: What Is It? Where Did It Come From?', *The American Journal of Philology* 103 (1982), 184–8

Edwards, Catharine, 'Self-Scrutiny and Self-Transformation in Seneca's Letters', in John G. Fitch, ed., *Seneca* (Oxford, 2008), pp. 84–101

Eilenberg, Susan, 'Wordsworth and the Reform of Copyright', *ELH* 56 (1989), 351–74

Eisner, Martin, 'In the Labyrinth of the Library: Petrarch's Cicero, Dante's Virgil, and the Historiography of the Renaissance', *Renaissance Quarterly* 67 (2014), 755–90

Else, Gerald F., 'Imitation in the Fifth Century', *Classical Philology* 53 (1958), 73–90

Erskine-Hill, Howard, 'The Satirical Game at Cards in Pope and Wordsworth', *The Yearbook of English Studies* 14 (1984), 183–95

Espie, Jeff, 'Literary Paternity and Narrative Revival: Chaucer's Soul(s) from Spenser to Dryden', *Modern Philology* 114 (2016), 39–58

Fallon, Stephen M., *Milton's Peculiar Grace: Self-Representation and Authority* (Ithaca, NY, and London, 2007)

Fanon, Frantz, *The Wretched of the Earth*, trans. C. Farrington (Harmondsworth, 1967)

Fantham, E., 'Imitation and Evolution: The Discussion of Rhetorical Imitation in *De Oratore* 2, 87–97', *Classical Philology* 73 (1978), 1–16

Fantham, Elaine, *Comparative Studies in Republican Latin Imagery* (Toronto, 1972)

Fantham, Elaine, 'Imitation and Decline: Rhetorical Theory and Practice in the First Century after Christ', *Classical Philology* 73 (1978), 102–16

Fantham, Elaine, 'On the Use of Genus-Terminology in Cicero's Rhetorical Works', *Hermes* 107 (1979), 441–59

Fantham, Elaine, 'The Concept of Nature and Human Nature in Quintilian's Psychology and Theory of Instruction', *Rhetorica* 13 (1995), 125–36

Fantham, Elaine, *The Roman World of Cicero's De Oratore* (Oxford, 2004)

Feather, John, *Publishing, Piracy and Politics: An Historical Study of Copyright in Britain* (London, 1994)

Feeney, D. C., 'Horace and the Greek Lyric Poets', in N. Rudd, ed., *Horace 2000: A Celebration. Essays for the Bimillennium* (London, 1993), pp. 41–63

Feingold, Mordechai, 'English Ramism: A Reinterpretation', in Mordechai Feingold, Joseph S. Freedman, and Wolfgang Rother, eds., *The Influence of Petrus Ramus: Studies in Sixteenth and Seventeenth Century Philosophy and Science* (Basel, 2001), pp. 127–76

Feingold, Mordechai, Freedman, Joseph S., and Rother, Wolfgang, eds., *The Influence of Petrus Ramus: Studies in Sixteenth and Seventeenth Century Philosophy and Science* (Basel, 2001)

Fera, Vincenzo, *La revisione petrarchesca dell'Africa* (Messina, 1984)

Fichter, Andrew, *Poets Historical: Dynastic Epic in the Renaissance* (New Haven, 1982)

Figueira, Thomas J. and Nagy, Gregory, eds., *Theognis of Megara: Poetry and the Polis* (Baltimore, 1985)

Fish, Stanley, 'Author-Readers: Jonson's Community of the Same', *Representations* 7 (1984), 26–58

Fitch, John G., ed., *Seneca* (Oxford, 2008)

Fitzgerald, William, *Martial: The World of the Epigram* (Chicago, Ill., and London, 2007)

Fitzgerald, William and Gowers, Emily, eds., *Ennius Perennis: The Annals and Beyond* (Cambridge, 2007)

Forcione, Alban 'Cervantes, Tasso, and the Romanzi Polemic', *Revue de Littérature Comparée* 44 (1970), 433–43

Ford, Andrew Laughlin, *The Origins of Criticism: Literary Culture and Poetic Theory in Classical Greece* (Princeton, 2002)

Foster, Jonathan, 'Petrarch's *Africa*: Ennian and Vergilian Influences', *Papers of the Liverpool Latin Seminar* 2 (1979), 277–98

Foucault, Michel, *Language, Counter-Memory, Practice: Selected Essays and Interviews*, trans. D. F. Bouchard and S. Simon (Ithaca, NY, 1977)

Fowler, Don, 'The Didactic Plot', in M. Depew and D. Obbink, eds., *Matrices of Genre: Authors, Canons, and Society* (Cambridge, Mass., and London, 2000), pp. 205–19

Gale, Monica, *Myth and Poetry in Lucretius* (Cambridge, 1994)

Gale, Monica, 'Poetry and the Backward Glance in Virgil's "Georgics" and "Aeneid"', *Transactions of the American Philological Association* 133 (2003), 323–52

Galligan, Francesca, 'Poets and Heroes in Petrarch's *Africa*', in M. L. McLaughlin, L. Panizza, and P. Hainsworth, eds., *Petrarch in Britain: Interpreters, Imitators, and Translators over 700 Years* (Oxford, 2007), pp. 85–93

Galloway, Andrew, 'Ovid in Chaucer and Gower', in J. F. Miller and C. E. Newlands, eds., *A Handbook to the Reception of Ovid* (Chichester, 2014), pp. 187–201

Gaukroger, Stephen, *Descartes: An Intellectual Biography* (Oxford, 1995)

Genette, Gérard, *Palimpsests: Literature in the Second Degree*, trans. C. Newman and C. Doubinsky (Lincoln, Neb., 1997)

Giamatti, A. Bartlett, *Exile and Change in Renaissance Literature* (New Haven and London, 1984)

Gill, Stephen, *William Wordsworth: A Life* (Oxford, 1989)

Gillespie, Stuart, 'Literary Afterlives: Metempsychosis from Ennius to Jorge Luis Borges', in P. Hardie and H. Moore, eds., *Classical Literary Careers and Their Reception* (Cambridge, 2010), pp. 209–25

Gillespie, Stuart, *English Translation and Classical Reception: Towards a New Literary History* (Oxford, 2011)

Girard, René, *Deceit, Desire, and the Novel: Self and Other in Literary Structure*, trans. Y. Freccero (Baltimore, 1976)

Goldgar, Bertrand A., 'Imitation and Plagiarism: The Lauder Affair and its Critical Aftermath', *Studies in the Literary Imagination* 34 (2001), 1–16

Goldman, Alvin I., 'Imitation, Mind Reading, and Simulation', in S. L. Hurley and Nick Chater, eds., *Perspectives on Imitation: From Neuroscience to Social Science*, 2 vols. (Cambridge, Mass., and London, 2005), 2.79–93

Goldschmidt, Nora, 'Absent Presence: Pater Ennius in Renaissance Europe', *Classical Receptions Journal* 4 (2012), 1–19

Goldschmidt, Nora, *Shaggy Crowns: Ennius' Annales and Virgil's Aeneid* (Oxford, 2013)

Goldsmith, Kenneth, *Uncreative Writing: Managing Language in the Digital Age* (New York, 2011)

Gould, John, *The Development of Plato's Ethics* (Cambridge, 1955)

Gransden, K. W., *Virgil's Iliad: An Essay on Epic Narrative* (Cambridge, 1984)

Green, Lawrence D. and Murphy, James Jerome, *Renaissance Rhetoric Short-Title Catalogue 1460–1700* (Aldershot, 2006)

Green, Mandy, *Milton's Ovidian Eve* (Farnham, 2009)

Greenblatt, Stephen, *The Swerve: How the World Became Modern* (New York, 2011)

Greene, Thomas M., 'Ben Jonson and the Centered Self', *Studies in English Literature* 10 (1970), 325–48

Greene, Thomas M., *The Light in Troy: Imitation and Discovery in Renaissance Poetry* (New Haven and London, 1982)

Greengrass, Mark, Leslie, Michael, and Raylor, Timothy, eds., *Samuel Hartlib and Universal Reformation: Studies in Intellectual Communication* (Cambridge, 1994)

Gregerson, Linda, *The Reformation of the Subject: Spenser, Milton, and the English Protestant Epic* (Cambridge, 1995)

Grillo, Luca, 'Leaving Troy and Creusa: Reflections on Aeneas' Flight', *The Classical Journal* 106 (2010), 43–68

Groom, Nick, *The Forger's Shadow: How Forgery Changed the Course of Literature* (London, 2002)

Groom, Nick, 'Forgery, Plagiarism, Imitation, Pegleggery', in P. Kewes, ed., *Plagiarism in Early Modern England* (Basingstoke, 2003), pp. 74–89

Grube, G. M. A., 'Theophrastus as a Literary Critic', *Transactions of the American Philological Association* 83 (1952), 172–83

Guest, Clare Lapraik, *The Understanding of Ornament in the Italian Renaissance* (Boston, 2016)

Gurdon J. B., Elsdale, T. R., and Fischberg, M., 'Sexually Mature Individuals of Xenopus Laevis from the Transplantation of Single Somatic Nuclei', *Nature* 182 (1958), 64–5

Haakonssen, Knud, ed., *Enlightenment and Religion: Rational Dissent in Eighteenth-Century Britain* (Cambridge, 1996)

Habinek, Thomas N., *The Politics of Latin Literature: Writing, Identity, and Empire in Ancient Rome* (Princeton, 1998)

Habinek, Thomas N., *Ancient Rhetoric and Oratory* (Malden, Mass., and Oxford, 2004)

Hall, Jason, 'Popular Prosody: Spectacle and the Politics of Victorian Versification', *Nineteenth-Century Literature* 62 (2007), 222–9

Halliwell, Stephen, *The Aesthetics of Mimesis: Ancient Texts and Modern Problems* (Princeton, 2002)

Hammond, Brean S., *Professional Imaginative Writing in England, 1670–1740: 'Hackney for Bread'* (Oxford, 1997)

Hammond, Paul, *John Oldham and the Renewal of Classical Culture* (Cambridge, 1983)

Hammond, Paul, *Dryden and the Traces of Classical Rome* (Oxford, 1999)

Hampton, Timothy, *Writing from History: The Rhetoric of Exemplarity in Renaissance Literature* (Ithaca, NY, 1990)

Haran, Joan, Kitzinger, Jenny, McNeil, Maureen, and O'Riordan, Kate, eds., *Human Cloning in the Media: From Science Fiction to Science Practice* (London, 2008)

Haraway, Donna, 'A Manifesto for Cyborgs', in L. J. Nicholson, ed., *Feminism/Postmodernism* (New York and London, 1990), pp. 190–233

Hardie, Philip R., *Virgil's Aeneid: Cosmos and Imperium* (Oxford, 1986)

Hardie, Philip, 'After Rome: Renaissance Epic', in A. J. Boyle, ed., *Roman Epic* (London and New York, 1993), pp. 294–313

Hardie, Philip, *The Epic Successors of Virgil: A Study in the Dynamics of a Tradition* (Cambridge, 1993)

Hardie, Philip R., *Virgil* (Oxford, 1998)

Hardie, Philip R., *Ovid's Poetics of Illusion* (Cambridge, 2002)

Hardie, Philip R., *Lucretian Receptions: History, the Sublime, Knowledge* (Cambridge, 2009)

Hardie, W. R., 'The Dream of Ennius', *The Classical Quarterly* 7 (1913), 188–95

Harrison, Stephen, 'Ennius and the Prologue to Lucretius *DRN* 1 (1.1–148)', *Leeds International Classical Studies* 1 (2002), 1–13

Harrison, Stephen, 'Epicurean Subversion? Lucretius's First Proem and Contemporary Roman Culture', in David Norbrook, Stephen Harrison, and Philip Hardie, eds., *Lucretius and the Early Modern* (Oxford, 2015), pp. 29–43

Harrison, Stephen, 'Vergil's Metapoetic Katabasis: The Underworld of *Aeneid* 6 and the History of Epic', in H.-C. Günther, ed., *Virgilian Studies: A Miscellany Dedicated to the Memory of Mario Geymonat* (Nordhausen, 2015), pp. 169–94

Harsting, Pernille, 'Quintilian, Imitation and "Anxiety of Influence"', in T. Albaladejo Mayordomo, E. Del Río, and J. A. Caballero López, eds., *Quintiliano: historia y actualidad de la retórica* (Logroño [Spain], 1998), pp. 1325–36

Hartman, Geoffrey H., *Wordsworth's Poetry, 1787–1814* (New Haven, 1964)

Hartman, Geoffrey H., *Beyond Formalism: Literary Essays, 1958–1970* (New Haven, 1970)

Heath, Malcolm, 'Dionysius of Halicarnassus On Imitation', *Hermes* 117 (1989), 370–3

Heinze, Richard, *Virgil's Epic Technique*, trans. D. Harvey, H. Harvey, and F. Robertson (London, 1993)

Hersey, George L., *Falling in Love with Statues: Artificial Humans from Pygmalion to the Present* (Chicago, Ill., and London, 2009)

Hetherington, Michael, '"An Instrument of Reason": William Scott's Logical Poetics', *The Review of English Studies* 67 (2016), 448–67

Heurgon, J., 'Un exemple peu connu de la *retractatio* Virgilienne', *Revue des études latines* 9 (1931), 258–68

Heyes, Cecilia, *Cognitive Gadgets: The Cultural Evolution of Thinking* (Cambridge, Mass., and London, 2018)

Heyes, Celia and Bird, Geoffrey, 'Correspondence Problem and Mechanisms— Imitation: Thoughts about Theories', in Chrystopher L. Nehaniv and Kerstin Dautenhahn, eds., *Imitation and Social Learning in Robots, Humans and Animals: Behavioural, Social and Communicative Dimensions* (Cambridge, 2007), pp. 23–34

Hinds, Stephen, *Allusion and Intertext: Dynamics of Appropriation in Roman Poetry* (Cambridge, 1998)

Hinds, Stephen, 'Petrarch, Cicero, Virgil: Virtual Community in Familiares 24, 4', *Materiali e discussioni per l'analisi dei testi classici* 52 (2004), 157–75

Holford-Strevens, Leofranc, *Aulus Gellius: An Antonine Scholar and his Achievement* (Oxford, 2003)

Hollis, Leo, *The Phoenix: St Paul's Cathedral and the Men who Made Modern London* (London, 2008)

Hopkins, David, 'Milton's Sin and Shakespeare's *Richard III*', *Notes and Queries* 29 (1982), 502–3

Hopkins, David, *Conversing with Antiquity: English Poets and the Classics, from Shakespeare to Pope* (Oxford, 2010)

Hoven, René, Grailet, Laurent, Maas, Coen, and Renard-Jadoul, Karin, *Lexique de la prose latine de la Renaissance* (Leiden and Boston, 2006)

Hoxby, Blair and Baynes Coiro, Ann, eds., *Milton in the Long Restoration* (Oxford, 2016)

Huet, Marie-Hélène, 'Monstrous Imagination: Progeny as Art in French Classicism', *Critical Inquiry* 17 (1991), 718–27

Hurley, S. L. and Chater, Nick, eds., *Perspectives on Imitation: From Neuroscience to Social Science*, 2 vols. (Cambridge, Mass., and London, 2005)

Hutcheon, Linda, *A Theory of Parody: The Teachings of Twentieth Century Art Forms* (New York and London, 1985)

Hutson, Lorna, 'Liking Men: Ben Jonson's Closet Opened', *ELH* 71 (2004), 1065–96

Hyman, Wendy Beth, *The Automaton in English Renaissance Literature* (Farnham, 2011)

Iacoboni, Marco, Kaplan, Jonas, and Wilson, Stephen, 'A Neural Architecture for Imitation and Intentional Relations', in Chrystopher L. Nehaniv and Kerstin Dautenhahn, eds., *Imitation and Social Learning in Robots, Humans and Animals: Behavioural, Social and Communicative Dimensions* (Cambridge, 2007), pp. 71–87

Impey, O. R. and MacGregor, Arthur, *The Origins of Museums: The Cabinet of Curiosities in Sixteenth- and Seventeenth-Century Europe* (Oxford, 1985)

Innes, Doreen C., 'Theophrastus and the Theory of Style', in W. W. Fortenbaugh, ed., *Theophrastus of Eresus: On his Life and Work* (New Brunswick, NJ, 1985), pp. 251–67

Jacobus, Mary, 'Is there a Woman in this Text?', *New Literary History* 14 (1982), 117–41

Jaeger, C. Stephen, *Enchantment: On Charisma and the Sublime in the Arts of the West* (Philadelphia, 2012)

Janaway, Christopher, *Images of Excellence: Plato's Critique of the Arts* (Oxford, 1995)

Janko, Richard, *Homer, Hesiod, and the Hymns: Diachronic Development in Epic Diction* (Cambridge, 1982)

Jardine, Lisa, *Erasmus, Man of Letters: The Construction of Charisma in Print* (Princeton, 1993)

Javitch, Daniel, *Proclaiming a Classic: The Canonization of Orlando Furioso* (Princeton, 1991)

Jefferson, Geoffrey, 'The Mind of Mechanical Man', *British Medical Journal* 1 (1949), 1105–10

Johns, Adrian, *Piracy: The Intellectual Property Wars from Gutenberg to Gates* (Chicago, Ill., and London, 2009)

Johnson, George, 'Soul Searching', in M. C. Nussbaum and C. R. Sunstein, eds., *Clones and Clones: Facts and Fantasies about Human Cloning* (London and New York, 1997), pp. 67–70

Jones, Frederick L., 'Shelley and Milton', *Studies in Philology* 49 (1952), 488–519

Kahn, Victoria, 'Allegory and the Sublime in *Paradise Lost*', in A. Patterson, ed., *John Milton* (London, 1992), pp. 185–201

Kallendorf, Craig, *In Praise of Aeneas: Virgil and Epideictic Rhetoric in the Early Italian Renaissance* (Hanover, 1989)

Kallendorf, Craig, *The Other Virgil: 'Pessimistic' Readings of the Aeneid in Early Modern Culture* (Oxford, 2007)

Kang, Minsoo, *Sublime Dreams of Living Machines: The Automaton in the European Imagination* (Cambridge, Mass., and London, 2011)

Keener, Frederick M., 'Pope, *The Dunciad*, Virgil, and the New Historicism of Le Bossu', *Eighteenth Century Life* 15 (1991), 35–57

Kennedy, George A., 'Theophrastus and Stylistic Distinctions', *Harvard Studies in Classical Philology* 62 (1957), 93–104

Kennedy, George A., *The Art of Persuasion in Greece* (Princeton, 1963)

Kennedy, George A., *A New History of Classical Rhetoric* (Princeton, 1994)

Kerrigan, John, *Shakespeare's Originality* (Oxford, 2018)

Kesson, Andy, *John Lyly and Early Modern Authorship* (Manchester, 2014)

Kewes, Paulina, ed., *Plagiarism in Early Modern England* (Basingstoke, 2003)

Kilgour, Maggie, ' "Thy perfect image viewing": Poetic Creation and Ovid's Narcissus in *Paradise Lost*', *Studies in Philology* 102 (2005), 307–39

Kilgour, Maggie, *Milton and the Metamorphosis of Ovid* (Oxford, 2012)

Kirby, John T., 'Ciceronian Rhetoric: Theory and Practice', in William J. Dominik, ed., *Roman Eloquence: Rhetoric in Society and Literature* (London, 1997), pp. 10–26

Kolata, Gina Bari, *Clone: The Road to Dolly, and the Path Ahead* (London, 1997)

Koslow, Julian, ' "Not a Bow for Every Man to Shoot": Milton's *Of Education*, between Hartlib and Humanism', *Milton Studies* 47 (2008), 24–53

Kronenberg, Leah 'Mezentius the Epicurean', *Transactions of the American Philological Association* 135 (2005), 403–31

Kusukawa, Sachiko, *The Transformation of Natural Philosophy: The Case of Philip Melanchthon* (Cambridge, 1995)

Kyriakou, Poulheria, 'Aeneas' Dream of Hector', *Hermes* 127 (1999), 317–27

Laird, Andrew, 'Re-inventing Virgil's Wheel: The Poet and his Work from Dante to Petrarch', in P. Hardie and H. Moore, eds., *Classical Literary Careers and their Reception* (Cambridge, 2010), pp. 138–59

Lanham, Richard A., *The Motives of Eloquence: Literary Rhetoric in the Renaissance* (Eugene, Oreg., 1976)

Lanzillotta, M. Accame, 'Le postille del Petrarca a Quintiliano (Cod. Parigino lat. 7720)', *Quaderni Petrarcheschi* 5 (1988), 1–201

Lausberg, Heinrich, Orton, David E., and Anderson, R. Dean, *Handbook of Literary Rhetoric: A Foundation for Literary Study* (Leiden, 1998)

Lavalley, Albert J., 'The Stage and Film Children of *Frankenstein*: A Survey', in G. Levine and U. C. Knoepflmacher, eds., *The Endurance of Frankenstein* (Berkeley, Los Angeles, and London, 1979), pp. 243–89

LeBrooy, Paul James, *Michelangelo Models Formerly in the Paul von Praun Collection* (Vancouver, 1972)

Leigh, Matthew, 'Petrarch's Lucan and the *Africa*', in S. J. Heyworth, P. G. Fowler, S. J. Harrison, and D. Fowler, eds., *Classical Constructions: Papers in Memory of Don Fowler, Classicist and Epicurean* (Oxford, 2007), pp. 242–57

Lewalski Barbara Kiefer, 'Milton and the Hartlib Circle: Educational Projects and Epic *Paideia*', in D. Benet and M. Lieb, eds., *Literary Milton: Text, Pretext, Context* (Pittsburgh, 1994), pp. 202–19

Lewalski, Barbara Kiefer, *The Life of John Milton: A Critical Biography* (Oxford, 2003)

Lewis, C. S., *English Literature in the Sixteenth Century, Excluding Drama* (Oxford, 1954)

LeWitt, Sol, 'Paragraphs on Conceptual Art', *Artforum* 5 (1967), 79–83

Liu, Alan, *Wordsworth: The Sense of History* (Stanford, 1989)

Liu, Catherine, *Copying Machines: Taking Notes for the Automaton* (Minneapolis and London, 2000)

Lively, Genevieve, 'Science Fictions and Cyber Myths: or, Do Cyborgs Dream of Dolly the Sheep?', in V. Zajko and M. Leonard, eds., *Laughing With Medusa* (Oxford, 2006), pp. 275–94

Lockwood, Thornton C., 'Habituation, Habit, and Character in Aristotle's *Nicomachean Ethics*', in T. Sparrow and A. Hutchinson, eds., *A History of Habit: From Aristotle to Bourdieu* (Plymouth, 2013), pp. 19–36

Loeb, Jacques, 'Further Experiments on the Sex of Parthenogenetic Frogs', *Proceedings of the National Academy of Sciences* 4 (1918), 60–2

Loewenstein, Joseph, 'The Jonsonian Corpulence; Or, The Poet as Mouthpiece', *ELH* 53 (1986), 491–518

Loewenstein, Joseph, *Ben Jonson and Possessive Authorship* (Cambridge, 2002)

Looney, Dennis, *Compromising the Classics: Romance Epic Narrative in the Italian Renaissance* (Detroit, 1996)

Lynch, Jack, 'William Henry Ireland's Authentic Forgeries', *The Princeton University Library Chronicle* 66 (2004), 79–96

Lyne, Raphael, *Memory and Intertextuality in Renaissance Literature* (Cambridge, 2016)

McClung, William, 'The Architecture of Pandemonium', *Milton Quarterly* 15 (1981), 109–12

McCorduck, Pamela, *Machines Who Think: A Personal Inquiry into the History and Prospects of Artificial Intelligence* (San Francisco, 1979)

MacDowell, Douglas M., *Aristophanes and Athens: An Introduction to the Plays* (Oxford, 1995)

McElduff, Siobhán, *Roman Theories of Translation: Surpassing the Source* (New York, 2013)

MacFaul, Tom, *Poetry and Paternity in Renaissance England: Sidney, Spenser, Shakespeare, Donne and Jonson* (Cambridge, 2010)

McGill, Scott, *Plagiarism in Latin Literature* (Cambridge, 2012)

McKeon, Richard, 'Literary Criticism and the Concept of Imitation in Antiquity', *Modern Philology* 34 (1936), 1–35

McKitterick, David, *A History of Cambridge University Press*, 3 vols. (Cambridge, 1992)

McLaughlin, Martin L., *Literary Imitation in the Italian Renaissance* (Oxford, 1995)

McLaverty, J., *Pope, Print, and Meaning* (Oxford, 2001)

McNelis, Charles, 'Grammarians and Rhetoricians', in W. Dominik and J. Hall, eds., *A Companion to Roman Rhetoric* (Oxford, 2007), pp. 285–96

McPherson, David, 'Ben Jonson Meets Daniel Heinsius, 1613', *English Language Notes* 14 (1976), 105–9

Mack, Peter, *Renaissance Argument: Valla and Agricola in the Traditions of Rhetoric and Dialectic* (Leiden, 1993)

Mack, Peter, *Elizabethan Rhetoric: Theory and Practice* (Cambridge, 2002)

Mack, Peter, 'Vives's *De Ratione Dicendi*: Structure, Innovations, Problems', *Rhetorica* 23 (2005), 65–92

Mack, Peter, *A History of Renaissance Rhetoric, 1380–1620* (Oxford, 2011)

Maguire, Laurie E. and Smith, Emma, 'What is a Source? Or, How Shakespeare Read his Marlowe', *Shakespeare Survey* 68 (2015), 15–31

Mann, Nicholas, *Petrarch Manuscripts in the British Isles* (Padua, 1975)

Marcuse, Michael J., ' "The Scourge of Impostors, the Terror of Quacks": John Douglas and the Exposé of William Lauder', *Huntington Library Quarterly* 42 (1979), 231–61

Marillonnet, Sylvestre, Klimuk, Victor, and Gleba, Yuri, 'Encoding Technical Information in GM Organisms', *Nature Biotechnology* 21 (2003), 224–6

Martindale, Charles, *John Milton and the Transformation of Ancient Epic* (London, 1986)

Maus, Katherine Eisaman, 'A Womb of His Own: Male Renaissance Poets in the Female Body', in J. G. Turner, ed., *Sexuality and Gender in Early Modern Europe: Institutions, Texts, Images* (Cambridge, 1993), pp. 266–88

Mazzeo, Tilar J., *Plagiarism and Literary Property in the Romantic Period* (Philadelphia, 2007)

Mellinghoff-Bourgerie, Viviane, *Les incertitudes de Virgile: contributions épicuriennes à la théologie de l'Enéide* (Bruxelles, 1990)

Miller, Andrew M., *From Delos to Delphi: A Literary Study of the Homeric Hymn to Apollo* (Leiden, 1986)

Monfasani, John, 'The Ciceronian Controversy', in G. P. Norton, ed., *The Cambridge History of Literary Criticism, Volume 3: The Renaissance* (Cambridge, 1999), pp. 395–401

Monk, Samuel Holt, 'A Grace Beyond the Reach of Art', *Journal of the History of Ideas* 5 (1944), 131–50

Moorman, Mary Trevelyan, *William Wordsworth: A Biography*, 2 vols. (Oxford, 1957)

Morgan, Teresa, *Literate Education in the Hellenistic and Roman Worlds* (Cambridge, 1998)

Morrison, Tessa, *Isaac Newton and the Temple of Solomon: An Analysis of the Description and Drawings and a Reconstructed Model* (Jefferson, NC, 2016)

Moss, Anne, *Printed Commonplace-Books and the Structuring of Renaissance Thought* (Oxford, 1996)

Most, Glenn, 'Il poeta nell'Ade: catabasi epica e teoria dell'epos tra Omero e Virgilio', *Studi italiani di filologia classica* 10 (1992), 1014–26

Motta, Uberto, 'La "questione della lingua" nel primo libro del *Cortegiano*: dalla seconda alla terza redazione', *Aevum* 72 (1998), 693–732

Moul, Victoria, *Jonson, Horace and the Classical Tradition* (Cambridge, 2010)

Murphy, James J., *Rhetoric in the Middle Ages: A History of Rhetorical Theory from Saint Augustine to the Renaissance* (Berkeley and London, 1974)

Murphy, James J., 'The Key Role of Habit in Roman Rhetoric and Education, as Described by Quintilian', in T. Albaladejo Mayordomo, E. Del Río, and J. A. Caballero López, eds., *Quintiliano: historia y actualidad de la retórica* (Logroño [Spain], 1998), pp. 141–50

Nagy, Gregory, 'Early Greek Views of Poets and Poetry', in G. A. Kennedy, ed., *The Cambridge History of Literary Criticism 1: Classical Criticism* (Cambridge, 1989), pp. 1–77

Nehamas, Alexander, *Virtues of Authenticity: Essays on Plato and Socrates* (Princeton, 1999)

Nehaniv, Christopher L. and Dautenhahn, Kerstin, eds., *Imitation and Social Learning in Robots, Humans and Animals: Behavioural, Social and Communicative Dimensions* (Cambridge, 2007)

Newton, Richard C., 'Jonson and the (Re-)Invention of the Book', in C. J. Summers and T. L. Pebworth, eds., *Classic and Cavalier: Essays on Jonson and the Sons of Ben* (Pittsburgh, 1982), pp. 31–55

Nichol, Donald W., 'Warburton (not!) on Copyright: Clearing up the Misattribution of *An Enquiry into the Nature and Origin of Literary Property* (1762)', *Journal for Eighteenth-Century Studies* 19 (1996), 171–82

Norbrook, David, *Writing the English Republic: Poetry, Rhetoric and Politics, 1627–1660* (Cambridge, 1999)

Norbrook, David, Harrison, Stephen, and Hardie, Philip R., eds., *Lucretius and the Early Modern* (Oxford, 2015)

Norton, Glyn P., *The Ideology and Language of Translation in Renaissance France and their Humanist Antecedents* (Geneva, 1984)

O'Brien, Karen, *Women and Enlightenment in Eighteenth-Century Britain* (Cambridge, 2009)

O'Brien, P., *Warrington Academy, 1757–86: Its Predecessors and Successors* (Wigan, 1989)

Offenberg, Adri, 'Dirk van Santen and the Keur Bible: New Insights into Jacob Judah (Arye) Leon Templo's Model Temple', *Studia Rosenthalia* 37 (2004), 401–22

Ong, Walter J., *Ramus, Method, and the Decay of Dialogue* (Cambridge, Mass., and London, 1983)

Orgel, Stephen, 'The Renaissance Artist as Plagiarist', *ELH* 48 (1981), 476–95

Orgel, Stephen, *The Reader in the Book: A Study of Spaces and Traces* (Oxford, 2015)

Palacio, Jean de, 'Shelley's Library Catalogue', *Revue de Littérature Comparée* 36 (1962), 270–6

Panofsky, Erwin, *Idea: A Concept in Art Theory*, trans. J. J. S. Peake (New York, 1975)

Parker, Patricia A., *Inescapable Romance: Studies in the Poetics of a Mode* (Princeton, 1979)

Parker, Patricia, 'Virile Style', in L. Fradenburg and C. Freccero, eds., *Premodern Sexualities* (London, 1996), pp. 199–222

Parker, William Riley, *Milton: A Biography*, ed. G. Campbell (Oxford, 1996)

Partner, Jane, *Poetry and Vision in Early Modern England* (Basingstoke, 2018)

Partridge, Edward, 'Jonson's Epigrammes: The Named and the Nameless', *Studies in the Literary Imagination* 6 (1973), 153–98

Passannante, Gerard Paul, *The Lucretian Renaissance: Philology and the Afterlife of Tradition* (Chicago, Ill., and London, 2011)

Patterson, Annabel M., *Hermogenes and the Renaissance: Seven Ideas of Style* (Princeton, 1970)

Patterson, Annabel M., *Censorship and Interpretation: The Conditions of Writing and Reading in Early Modern England* (Madison, Wis., 1984)

Patterson, Annabel M., *Reading Between the Lines* (Madison, Wis., 1993)

Pellicer, Juna Christian, '*Cerealia* (1706): Elijah Fenton's Burlesque of Milton and Spenser in Critique of John Philips', *Notes and Queries* 50 (2003), 197–201

Penrose, Roger, *The Emperor's New Mind: Concerning Computers, Minds and the Laws of Physics* (London, 1990)

Penrose, Roger, *Shadows of the Mind: A Search for the Missing Science of Consciousness* (Oxford, 1994)

Pepperberg, Irene M., *The Alex Studies: Cognitive and Communicative Abilities of Grey Parrots* (Cambridge, Mass., and London, 1999)

Perloff, Marjorie, *Unoriginal Genius: Poetry by Other Means in the New Century* (Chicago, Ill., and London, 2010)

Peterson, Richard S., *Imitation and Praise in the Poems of Ben Jonson* (New Haven, 1981)

Phillips, Patricia, *The Adventurous Muse: Theories of Originality in English Poetics, 1650–1760* (Uppsala and Stockholm, 1984)

Pigman, G. W., 'Imitation and the Renaissance Sense of the Past: The Reception of Erasmus' *Ciceronianus*', *The Journal of Medieval and Renaissance Studies* 9 (1979), 155–77

Pigman, G. W., 'Versions of Imitation in the Renaissance', *Renaissance Quarterly* 33 (1980), 1–32

Pigman, G. W., 'Barzizza's Treatise on Imitation', *Bibliothèque d'Humanisme et Renaissance* 44 (1982), 341–52

Pigman, G. W., III, *Grief and the English Renaissance Elegy* (Cambridge, 1985)

Plank, Robert, 'The Golem and the Robot', *Literature and Psychology* 15 (1965), 12–27

Pollin, Burton R., 'Philosophical and Literary Sources of *Frankenstein*', *Comparative Literature Studies* 17 (1965), 97–108

Poole, William, *Milton and the Making of Paradise Lost* (Cambridge, Mass., and London, 2017)

Pugliese, Olga, Lorenzo Bartoli, Filomena Calabrese, Adriana Grimaldi, Ian Martin, Laura Prelipcean, and Antonio Ricci, eds., 'The Early Extant Manuscripts of Baldassar Castiglione's *Il libro del cortegiano*', <https://www.researchgate.net/publication/277867222_The_Early_Extant_Manuscripts_of_Baldassar_Castiglione%27s_Il_libro_del_cortegiano_transcriptions>; accessed February 2018

Pugliese, Olga Zorzi, *Castiglione's The Book of the Courtier (Il libro del cortegiano): A Classic in the Making* (Naples, 2008)

Quilligan, Maureen, *Milton's Spenser: The Politics of Reading* (Ithaca, 1983)

Quint, David, *Origin and Originality in Renaissance Literature: Versions of the Source* (New Haven, 1983)

Quint, David, *Inside Paradise Lost: Reading the Designs of Milton's Epic* (Princeton, 2014)

Raven, James, Small, Helen, and Tadmor, Naomi, eds., *The Practice and Representation of Reading in England* (Cambridge, 1996)

Raylor, Timothy, 'Newcastle's Ghosts: Robert Payne, Ben Jonson, and the "Cavendish Circle"', in C. J. Summers and T. L. Pebworth, eds., *Literary Circles and Cultural Communities in Renaissance England* (Columbia and London, 2000), pp. 92–114

Raylor, Timothy, 'Milton, the Hartlib Circle, and the Education of the Aristocracy', in N. McDowell and N. Smith, eds., *The Oxford Handbook of Milton* (Oxford, 2012), pp. 382–406

Reeve, M. D., 'Conceptions', *Proceedings of the Cambridge Philological Society* 215 (1989), 81–112

Reynolds, Matthew, *The Poetry of Translation: From Chaucer and Petrarch to Homer and Logue* (Oxford, 2011)

Richards, Jennifer, 'Assumed Simplicity and the Critique of Nobility: Or, How Castiglione Read Cicero', *Renaissance Quarterly* 54 (2001), 460–86

Richardson, Brian, *Print Culture in Renaissance Italy: The Editor and the Vernacular Text, 1470–1600* (Cambridge, 1994)

Ricks, Christopher, *Allusion to the Poets* (Oxford, 2002)

Rico, Francisco 'Petrarca e il medioevo', in Accademia dei Lincei, ed., *La cultura letteraria italiana e l'identità europea: sotto l'alto patronato del Presidente della Repubblica (Roma, 6–8 aprile 2000)* (Rome, 2001), pp. 39–56

Robertson, Ritchie, *Mock-Epic Poetry from Pope to Heine* (Oxford, 2009)

Rolland, E., *De l'influence de Sénèque le père et des rhéteurs sur Sénèque le philosophe* (Gand, 1906)

Rose, Mark, 'The Author as Proprietor: Donaldson v. Becket and the Genealogy of Modern Authorship', *Representations* 23 (1988), 51–85

Rose, Mark, *Authors and Owners: The Invention of Copyright* (Cambridge, Mass., and London, 1993)

Ross, David O., *Backgrounds to Augustan Poetry: Gallus, Elegy, and Rome* (Cambridge, 1975)

Rowe, George E., *Distinguishing Jonson: Imitation, Rivalry, and the Direction of a Dramatic Career* (Lincoln, Neb., 1988)

Rummel, Erika, *Erasmus as a Translator of the Classics* (Toronto, 1985)

Russell, D. A., 'De Imitatione', in D. West and T. Woodman, eds., *Creative Imitation and Latin Literature* (Cambridge, 1979), pp. 1–16

Russell, D. A., *Greek Declamation* (Cambridge, 1983)

Russell, D. A., 'Rhetoric and Criticism', in A. Laird, ed., *Oxford Readings in Ancient Literary Criticism* (Oxford, 2006), pp. 267–83

Rutherford, Ian, *Canons of Style in the Antonine Age: Idea-Theory in its Literary Context* (Oxford, 1998)

Ryan, Lawrence V., *Roger Ascham* (Stanford and London, 1963)

Sabbadini, Remigio, *Le scoperte dei codici latini e greci ne'secoli XIV e XV*, 2 vols. (Firenze, 1905)

Saccone, Eduardo, 'Grazia, Sprezzatura, Affettazione in the *Courtier*', in R. W. Hanning and D. Rosand, eds., *Castiglione: The Ideal and the Real in Renaissance Culture* (New Haven, 1983), pp. 45–67

Savage, John J., 'Quintilian and Lucretius', *The Classical Weekly* 46 (1952), 37

Sawday, Jonathan, *Engines of the Imagination: Renaissance Culture and the Rise of the Machine* (London, 2007)

Schiesaro, Alessandro, 'Lucrezio, Cicerone, l'oratoria', *Materiali e discussioni per l'analisi dei testi classici* 19 (1987), 29–61

Schiesaro, Alessandro, *Simulacrum et imago: gli argomenti analogici nel De rerum natura* (Pisa, 1990)

Schmidt, Charles Guillaume A., *La vie et les travaux de Jean Sturm* (Strasbourg, 1855)

Scholar, Richard, *The Je-Ne-Sais-Quoi in Early Modern Europe: Encounters with a Certain Something* (Oxford, 2005)

Scott, Izora, *Controversies over the Imitation of Cicero* (New York, 1910)

Scott-Baumann, Elizabeth, *Forms of Engagement: Women, Poetry, and Culture 1640–1680* (Oxford, 2013)

Scott-Warren, Jason, 'Commonplacing and Originality: Reading Francis Meres', *The Review of English Studies* 68 (2017), 902–23

Seagraves, Richard, *The Influence of Vergil on Petrarch's 'Africa'* (Ann Arbor, Mich., 1977)

Sedley, D. N., *Lucretius and the Transformation of Greek Wisdom* (Cambridge, 1998)

Selfridge, O. G., 'Pandemonium: A Paradigm for Learning', in *Mechanisation of Thought Processes: Proceedings of a Symposium held at the National Physical Laboratory on 24th, 25th, 26th and 27th November 1958* (London, 1959), pp. 513–26

Serjeantson, R. W., 'Thomas Farnaby (1575?–12 June 1647)', in E. A. Malone, ed., *British Rhetoricians and Logicians, 1500–1660: First Series* (Detroit and London, 2001), pp. 108–16

Seville, Catherine, *Literary Copyright Reform in Early Victorian England: The Framing of the 1842 Copyright Act* (Cambridge, 1999)

Sherman, William H., *Used Books: Marking Readers in Renaissance England* (Philadelphia, 2008)

Shifflett, Andrew Eric, *Stoicism, Politics, and Literature in the Age of Milton: War and Peace Reconciled* (Cambridge, 1998)

Shoulson, Jeffrey S., *Milton and the Rabbis: Hebraism, Hellenism and Christianity* (New York and Chichester, 2001)

Silk, M. S., *Aristophanes and the Definition of Comedy* (Oxford, 2000)

Silver, D., 'Mastering the Game of Go without Human Knowledge', *Nature* 550 (2017), 354–9

Simpson, James, *Reform and Cultural Revolution* (Oxford, 2002)

Simpson, James, 'Subjects of Triumph and Literary History: Dido and Petrarch in Petrarch's *Africa* and *Trionfi*', *Journal of Medieval and Early Modern Studies* 35 (2005), 489–508

Skinner, Quentin, *Reason and Rhetoric in the Philosophy of Hobbes* (Cambridge, 1996)

Smith, Andrew, ed., *The Cambridge Companion to Frankenstein* (Cambridge, 2016)

Smith, R. W., 'The Source of Milton's Pandemonium', *Modern Philology* 39 (1931), 187–98

Soo, Lydia M., *Wren's "Tracts" on Architecture and Other Writings* (Cambridge, 1998)

Spemann, Hans, *Embryonic Development and Induction* (New Haven and London, 1938)

St. Clair, William, *The Reading Nation in the Romantic Period* (Cambridge, 2004)

Stack, Frank, *Pope and Horace: Studies in Imitation* (Cambridge, 1985)

Stackelberg, Jürgen v., 'Das Bienengleichnis: Ein Beitrag zur Geschichte der literarischen *Imitatio*', *Romanische Forschungen* 68 (1956), 271–93

Steiner, Hans-Rudolf, *Der Traum in der Aeneis* (Bern, 1952)

Steiner, T. R., *English Translation Theory 1650–1800* (Assen, 1975)

Stillman, Robert E., *Philip Sidney and the Poetics of Renaissance Cosmopolitanism* (Aldershot, 2008)

Stover, Justin A., 'Space as Paratext: Scribal Practice in the Medieval Edition of Ammianus Marcellinus', in M. J. Teeuwen and I. Van Renswoude, eds., *The Annotated Book in the Early Middle Ages: Practices of Reading and Writing* (Turnhout, 2017), pp. 305–21

Summers, Claude J. and Pebworth, Ted Larry, eds., *Classic and Cavalier: Essays on Jonson and the Sons of Ben* (Pittsburgh, 1982)

Swartz, Richard G., 'Wordsworth, Copyright, and the Commodities of Genius', *Modern Philology* 89 (1992), 482–509

Tate, J., '"Imitation" in Plato's *Republic*', *Classical Quarterly* 22 (1928), 16–23

Tate, J., 'Plato and "Imitation"', *Classical Quarterly* 26 (1932), 161–9

Terry, Richard, '"In Pleasing Memory of All He Stole": Plagiarism and Literary Detraction, 1747–1785', in P. Kewes, ed., *Plagiarism in Early Modern England* (Basingstoke, 2003), pp. 181–200

Thill, André, *'Alter ab illo': recherches sur l'imitation dans la poésie personnelle à l'époque augustéenne* (Lille, 1976)

Thomas, Richard F., 'Virgil's Georgics and the Art of Reference', *Harvard Studies in Classical Philology* 90 (1986), 171–98

Thomas, Richard F., 'The Isolation of Turnus', in H.-P. Stahl, ed., *Vergil's Aeneid: Augustan Epic and Political Context* (London, 1998), pp. 271–302

Thury, Eva M., 'Lucretius' Poem as a Simulacrum of the Rerum Natura', *The American Journal of Philology* 108 (1987), 270–94

Too, Yun Lee, *The Idea of Ancient Literary Criticism* (Oxford, 1998)

Trimpi, Wesley, *Ben Jonson's Poems: A Study of the Plain Style* (Stanford, 1962)

Trousdale, Marion, 'Recurrence and Renaissance: Rhetorical Imitation in Ascham and Sturm', *English Literary Renaissance* 6 (1976), 156–79

Truitt, Elly Rachel, *Medieval Robots: Mechanism, Magic, Nature, and Art* (Philadelphia, 2015)

Tully, James, *An Approach to Political Philosophy: Locke in Contexts* (Cambridge, 1993)

Turing, A. M., 'Computing Machinery and Intelligence', *Mind* 59 (1950), 433–60

Turney, Jon, *Frankenstein's Footsteps: Science, Genetics and Popular Culture* (New Haven and London, 1998)

van Nortwick, Thomas, 'Aeneas, Turnus, and Achilles', *Transactions of the American Philological Association* 110 (1980), 303–14

Vasbinder, Samuel Holmes, *Scientific Attitudes in Mary Shelley's Frankenstein* (Ann Arbor, Mich., 1984)

Velli, Giuseppe, 'Il Dante di Francesco Petrarca', *Studi petrarcheschi* NS 2 (1985), 185–99

Vickers, Brian, *Francis Bacon and Renaissance Prose* (Cambridge, 1968)

Vickers, Brian, 'Epideictic and Epic in the Renaissance', *New Literary History* 14 (1983), 497–537

Vickers, Brian, *In Defence of Rhetoric* (Oxford, 1988)

Vickers, Brian, 'The Myth of Francis Bacon's "Anti-Humanism"', in J. Kraye and M. W. F. Stone, eds., *Humanism and Early Modern Philosophy* (London and New York, 2000), pp. 135–58

Vine, Angus, 'Commercial Commonplacing: Francis Bacon, the Waste-Book, and the Ledger', *English Manuscript Studies* 16 (2011), 197–218

Volk, Katharina, *The Poetics of Latin Didactic: Lucretius, Vergil, Ovid, Manilius* (Oxford, 2002)

Von Neumann, John, *The Computer and the Brain* (New Haven and London, 1979)

Vos, Alvin, '"Good Matter and Good Utterance": The Character of English Ciceronianism', *Studies in English Literature 1500–1900* 19 (1979), 3–18

Waldron, Jeremy, *The Right to Private Property* (Oxford, 1988)

Waldron, Jeremy, *God, Locke, and Equality: Christian Foundations of John Locke's Political Thought* (Cambridge, 2002)

Walsh, G. B., 'Sublime Method: Longinus on Language and Imitation', *Classical Antiquity* 7 (1988), 252–69

Wareh, Tarik, *The Theory and Practice of Life: Isocrates and the Philosophers* (Boston and London, 2012)

Waszink, J. H., *Biene und Honig als Symbol des Dichters und der Dichtung in der griechisch-römischen Antike* (Opladen, 1974)

Watkins, John, *The Specter of Dido: Spenser and Virgilian Epic* (New Haven, 1995)

Weaire, Gavin, 'The Relationship between Dionysius of Halicarnassus' *De imitatione* and *Epistula ad Pompeium*', *Classical Philology* 97 (2002), 351–9

Webster, Charles ed., *Samuel Hartlib and the Advancement of Learning* (Cambridge, 1970)

Weinberg, Bernard, *A History of Literary Criticism in the Italian Renaissance*, 2 vols. (Chicago, Ill., 1961)

Weinbrot, Howard D., *The Formal Strain: Studies in Augustan Imitation and Satire* (Chicago, Ill., 1969)

Welch, Anthony, 'Paradise Lost and English Mock Heroic', in Blair Hoxby and Ann Baynes Coiro, eds., *Milton in the Long Restoration* (Oxford, 2016), pp. 465–82

West, M. L., *The Making of the Odyssey* (Oxford, 2014)

West, David Alexander and Woodman, A. J., *Creative Imitation and Latin Literature* (Cambridge, 1979)

Whipple, T. K., *Martial and the English Epigram from Sir Thomas Wyatt to Ben Jonson* (Berkeley, 1925)

White, Harold Ogden, *Plagiarism and Imitation during the English Renaissance: A Study in Critical Distinctions* (Cambridge, 1935)

Whitmarsh, Tim, *Greek Literature and the Roman Empire: The Politics of Imitation* (Oxford, 2001)

Wiener, Norbert, *God and Golem, Inc.: A Comment on Certain Points where Cybernetics Impinges on Religion* (London, 1964)

Williams, Laurence Albert, *Road Transport in Cumbria in the Nineteenth Century* (London, 1975)

Wilson, Emily, '*Quantum Mutatus ab Illo*: Moments of Change and Recognition in Tasso and Milton', in M. Clarke, B. Currie, and R. O. A. M. Lyne, eds., *Epic Interactions: Perspectives on Homer, Virgil, and the Epic Tradition* (Oxford, 2006), pp. 273–99

Wilson-Okamura, David Scott, *Spenser's International Style* (Cambridge, 2013)

Winterbottom, Michael, 'Quintilian the Moralist', in T. Albaladejo Mayordomo, E. Del Río, and J. A. Caballero López, eds., *Quintiliano: historia y actualidad de la retórica* (Logroño [Spain], 1998), pp. 317–34

Witt, Ronald G., *In the Footsteps of the Ancients: The Origins of Humanism from Lovato to Bruni* (Leiden, 2000)

Wittkower, Rudolph, 'Genius: Individualism in Art and Artists', in P. P. Wiener, ed., *Dictionary of the History of Ideas: Studies of Selected Pivotal Ideas*, 5 vols. (New York, 1973), 2.297–312

Woodbury, Leonard, 'Helen and the Palinode', *Phoenix* 21 (1967), 157–76

Woodmansee, Martha, 'The Genius and the Copyright: Economic and Legal Conditions of the Emergence of the "Author"', *Eighteenth-Century Studies* 17 (1984), 425–48

Woods, Marjorie Curry, *Weeping for Dido: The Classics in the Medieval Classroom* (Princeton, 2018)

Wordsworth, Jonathan, *William Wordsworth: The Borders of Vision* (Oxford, 1982)

Wright, Geoffrey Norman, *Turnpike Roads* (Princes Risborough, 1992)

Wu, Duncan, *Wordsworth's Reading, 1770–1799* (Cambridge, 1993)

Wu, Duncan, *Wordsworth's Reading, 1800–1815* (Cambridge, 1995)

Wykes, David L., 'The Contribution of the Dissenting Academy to the Emergence of Rational Dissent', in Knud Haakonssen, ed., *Enlightenment and Religion: Rational Dissent in Eighteenth-Century Britain* (Cambridge, 1996), pp. 99–138

Yolton, John W., *Thinking Matter: Materialism in Eighteenth-Century Britain* (Oxford, 1984)

Index